MW01713876

Chromebook for Seniors

2021 Edition

Kevin Wilson

Elluminet Press
www.elluminetpress.com

Chromebook for Seniors: 2021 Edition

Publisher: Elluminet Press
Director: Kevin Wilson
Lead Editor: Steven Ashmore
Technical Reviewer: Mike Taylor, Robert Ashcroft
Copy Editors: Joanne Taylor, James Marsh
Proof Reader: Mike Taylor
Indexer: James Marsh
Cover Designer: Kevin Wilson

eBook versions and licenses are also available for most titles. Any source code or other supplementary materials referenced by the author in this text is available to readers at `www.elluminetpress.com/resources`

For detailed information about how to locate your book's resources, go to `www.elluminetpress.com/resources`

Table of Contents

About the Author

With over 20 years' experience in the computer industry, Kevin Wilson has made a career out of technology and showing others how to use it. After earning a master's degree in computer science, software engineering, and multimedia systems, Kevin has held various positions in the IT industry including graphic & web design, programming, building & managing corporate networks, and IT support.

He serves as senior writer and director at Elluminet Press Ltd, he periodically teaches computer science at college, and works as an IT trainer in England while researching for his PhD. His books have become a valuable resource among the students in England, South Africa, Canada, and in the United States.

Kevin's motto is clear: "If you can't explain something simply, then you haven't understood it well enough." To that end, he has created the Exploring Tech Computing series, in which he breaks down complex technological subjects into smaller, easy-to-follow steps that students and ordinary computer users can put into practice.

Acknowledgements

Thanks to all the staff at Luminescent Media & Elluminet Press for their passion, dedication and hard work in the preparation and production of this book.

To all my friends and family for their continued support and encouragement in all my writing projects.

To all my colleagues, students and testers who took the time to test procedures and offer feedback on the book

Finally thanks to you the reader for choosing this book. I hope it helps you to use your Chromebook with greater understanding.

Have fun!

1 What is a ChromeBook?

A ChromeBook is a laptop or tablet that runs an operating system called Chrome OS and uses Google's Chrome Web Browser to run web apps. On later ChromeBook devices, you can also run Android and Linux apps.

ChromeBooks are designed to be used online, meaning you must be connected to the internet all the time whether you are at home, the office, in school, college, the library, or generally out and about. Without an internet connection, your ChromeBook can still function but will be limited at best.

It's worth noting what a ChromeBook can do and what it can't do. ChromeBooks are great for online collaboration - creating and sharing documents, spreadsheets and presentations. Using the web, checking your email/social media, posting photographs and videos. Video chatting with friends as well as streaming music, TV programmes and films directly to your ChromeBook.

A ChromeBook on the other hand would be a bad choice if you needed a laptop/device to edit video, make music, manipulate photographs, or anything that requires a lot of data storage and processing speed. ChromeBooks are not designed for this.

ChromeBooks look very similar to traditional style windows or mac laptops. The main difference is ChromeBooks are a lot more light weight, usually smaller, have less built in storage space and have no DVD/CD drives.

Let's take a closer look. Along the sides of your chromebook you'll find some ports. Not all manufacturers put the same ports on their devices or put them in the same place however, you'll find the most common ones on all devices.

Your power port is either along the side or the rear panel. This is usually a standard power connector or on some models a USB-C port.

or

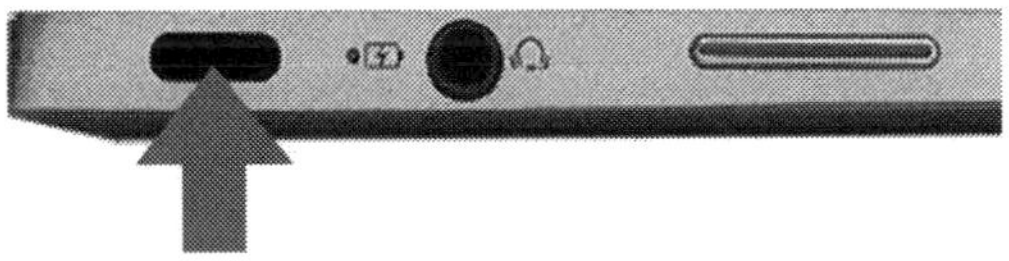

Along the side you'll find your USB ports. How many you have will depend on the model but you'll usually find at least two. You'll find USB 2 or USB 3 ports.

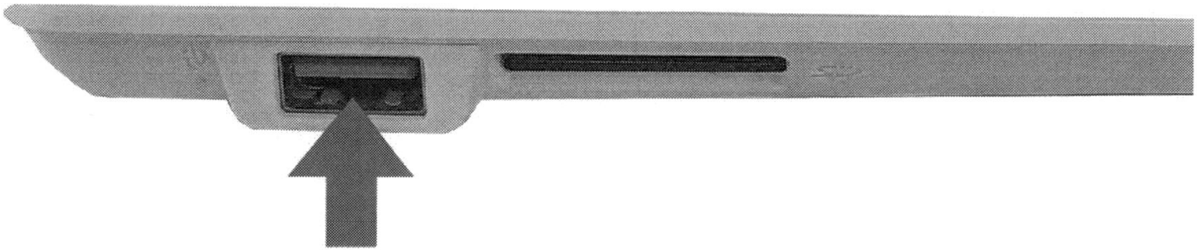

On some of the newer models, you'll find USB C ports.

One some models, you'll also find an HDMI port either on the rear or along the side.

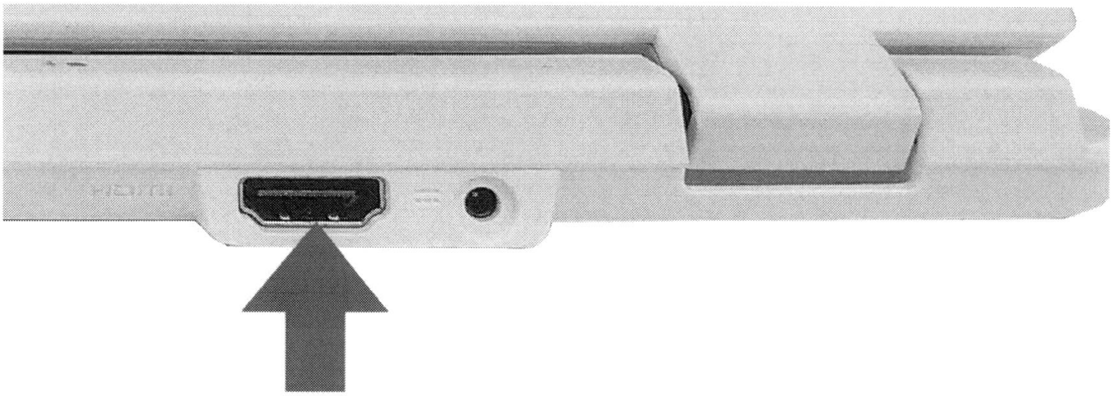

Also included is a 1/8th inch (3.5mm) headphone jack and will usually be located along the side.

You can plug in headphones or speakers.

Some models include a built in card reader for SD cards. You'll either find a full size SD card reader:

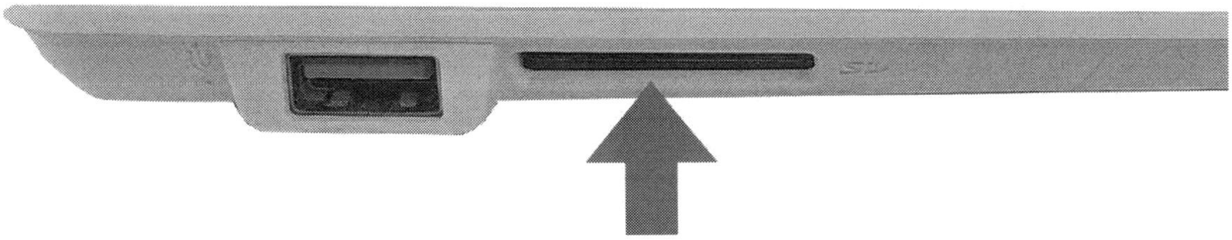

Or a microSD card reader:

SD Cards can be full sized card or Micro.

Standard SD Micro SD

You can get an SD Card adapter if your SD card reader does not read Micro SD cards.

SD Card Adapter

New style ChromeBooks also feature touch screens, with some being hybrid devices that you can use in the form of a laptop or a tablet.

With these types of devices, you can fold the screen all the way back tucking the keyboard behind the device turning it into a tablet.

Other ChromeBooks come in tablet form, called ChromeBook Tablets such as the Google Pixel Slate.

With these devices, you can use a touchscreen, a pen on some models, and add detachable keyboards.

ChromeBooks run Chrome OS which is a fast, stripped down operating system meaning many of the non-web features have been removed, such as bulk storage for software applications, user's data, and various device drivers you'd find on traditional operating systems such as Windows 10 and MacOS.

Because of this, Chrome OS will run on a more modest hardware specification, eg: 2GB of RAM, 1.6 GHz processor, and a 32GB solid state drive to store Chrome OS itself plus any locally stored files or apps for offline use. This makes ChromeBooks more light weight, and cheaper to buy.

At its core, Chome OS is a linux based operating system and will run on hardware with either intel/amd x86/64 or ARM processors.

You don't install software on a ChromeBook in the traditional sense. Instead, you run apps over the internet. These are called web apps or hosted apps, and they run within the Chrome Web Browser. Some apps are self contained which are not confined to the Chrome Browser. These are called packaged apps and install themselves onto your ChromeBook, so they are available offline if needed and have access to local storage.

You can use GMail for your email, files app to access your files on Google Drive or local storage, and apps for entertainment.

You'll find countless apps for your ChromeBook in the Chrome Web Store.

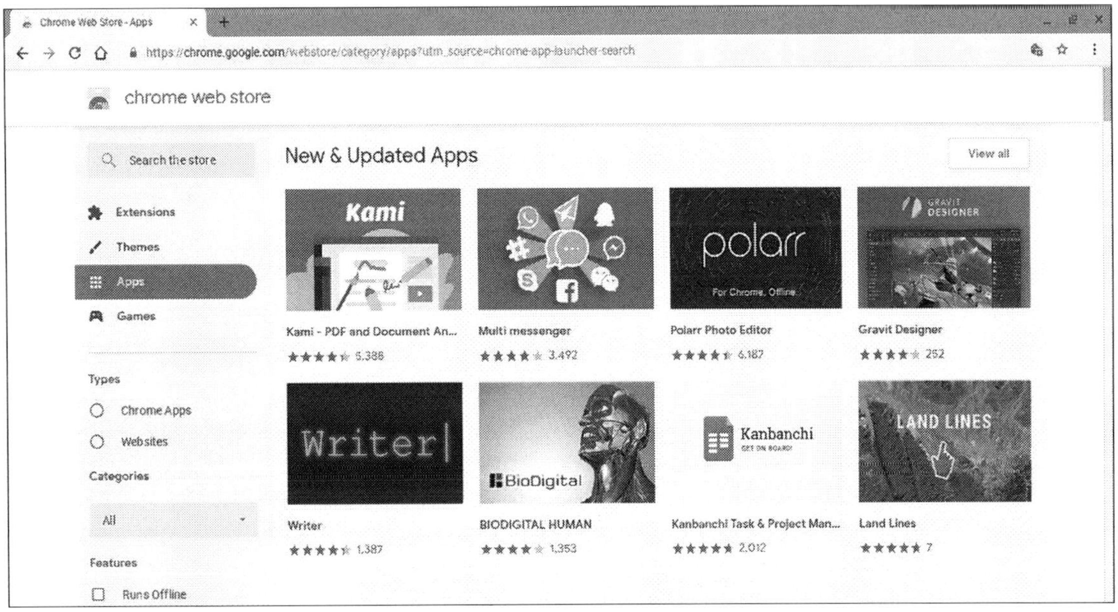

Popular web apps include Google Docs word processor, Google Sheets spreadsheet, and Google Slides presentation.

You can write and edit documents using Google Docs, analyse numbers with Google Sheets SpreadSheet, and create presentations using Google Slides. These work in a similar fashion to Microsoft Office.

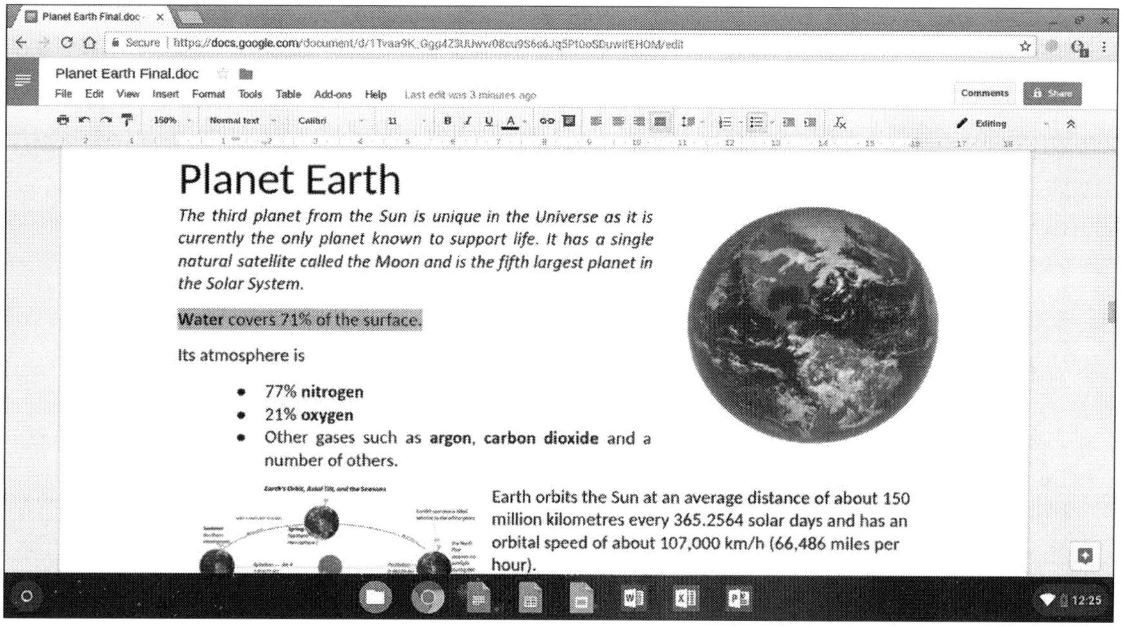

A ChromeBook is known as a 'cloud device', meaning all your files, photographs and work are stored in the cloud, and you edit your files online. All your files are stored on Google Drive.

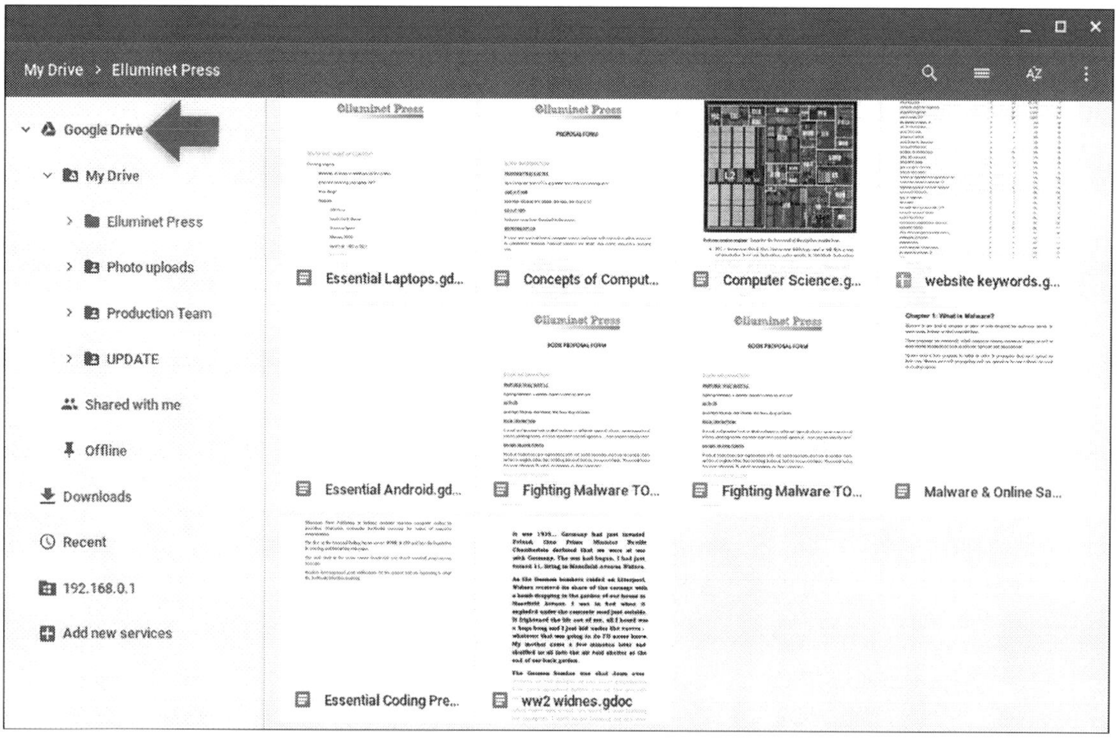

This is called cloud computing and allows on-demand access to a pool of computing resources such as apps, file storage, email, social media and other services not stored locally on your device.

In the illustration below, the lightning bolts represent a WiFi or cellular internet connection, and the cloud represents the cloud platform, where all your email, photos, music, documents and apps are stored.

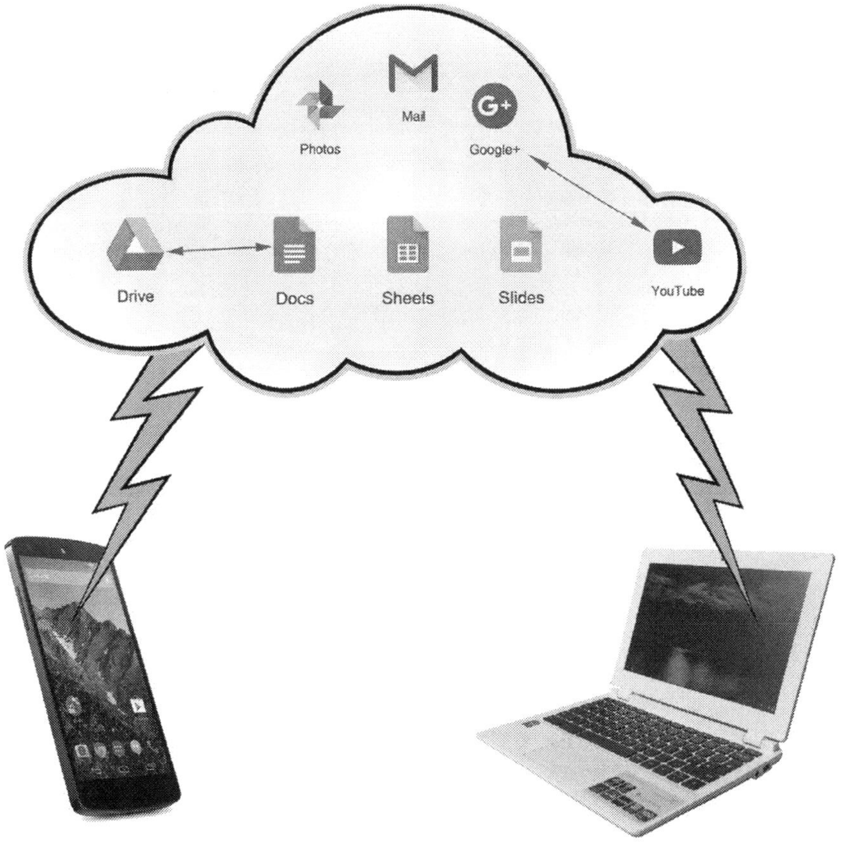

The cloud platform is hosted on a large server farm like the one pictured below and is managed by the cloud service.

This means you can access your email, photos or do your work anywhere with an internet connection.

2 Setting up your ChromeBook

ChromeBooks are very easy to set up. They come pre-installed with Chrome OS. All you need to do is go through the initial setup, sign in with your Google Account and you're pretty much ready to go.

In this chapter, we'll take a look at getting your ChromeBook set up.

We'll go through the initial setup when you turn your ChromeBook on for the first time. As well as personalisation, transferring your files from an old computer, setting up a printer, and connecting bluetooth devices.

For this chapter, take a look at the video resources section. Open your browser and navigate to the following website

`videos.tips/using-chromebook`

Creating a Google Account

If you use Gmail you will already have a Google Account. If this is the case, you don't need to create a new Google Account so you can skip this step.

If you don't have one, you can create one online before you start, if you have another computer by opening your web browser and browsing to the following page

`accounts.google.com/signup`

Fill in your name in the first two fields, then under 'username', type in the name you want to appear in your email address. This can be a nickname or your full name. The name must be unique, so if someone else has already taken the name, you'll need to choose a new one or add a couple of numbers. Google will tell you if the username you entered has already been used.

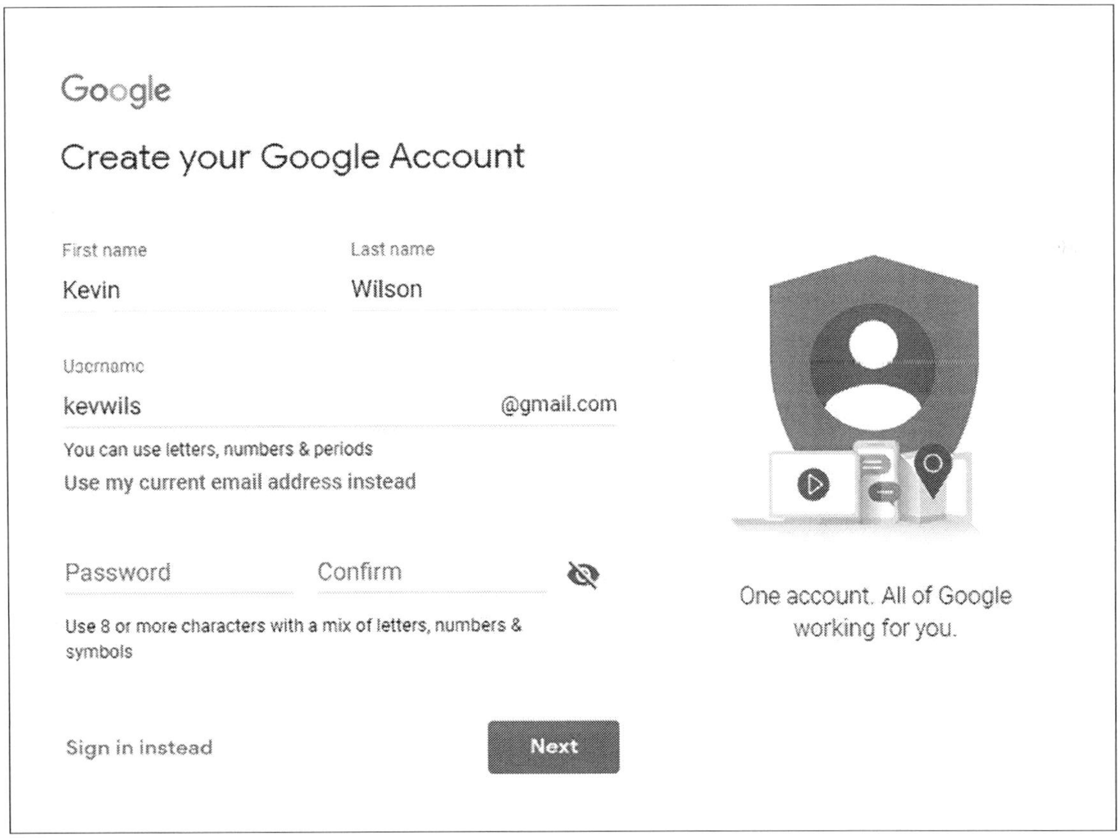

Enter the password you want to use in the 'password' field, then type it again to confirm it in the 'confirm' field.

Click 'next'.

Initial Setup

When you first turn on your ChromeBook, you'll come to the welcome screen. From here, select your language and your keyboard layout specific to your country.

Once you have done that, select a network. This is usually your wifi network if you have one at home. This can also be a hotspot in a coffee shop, library, airport, office, school/college and so on.

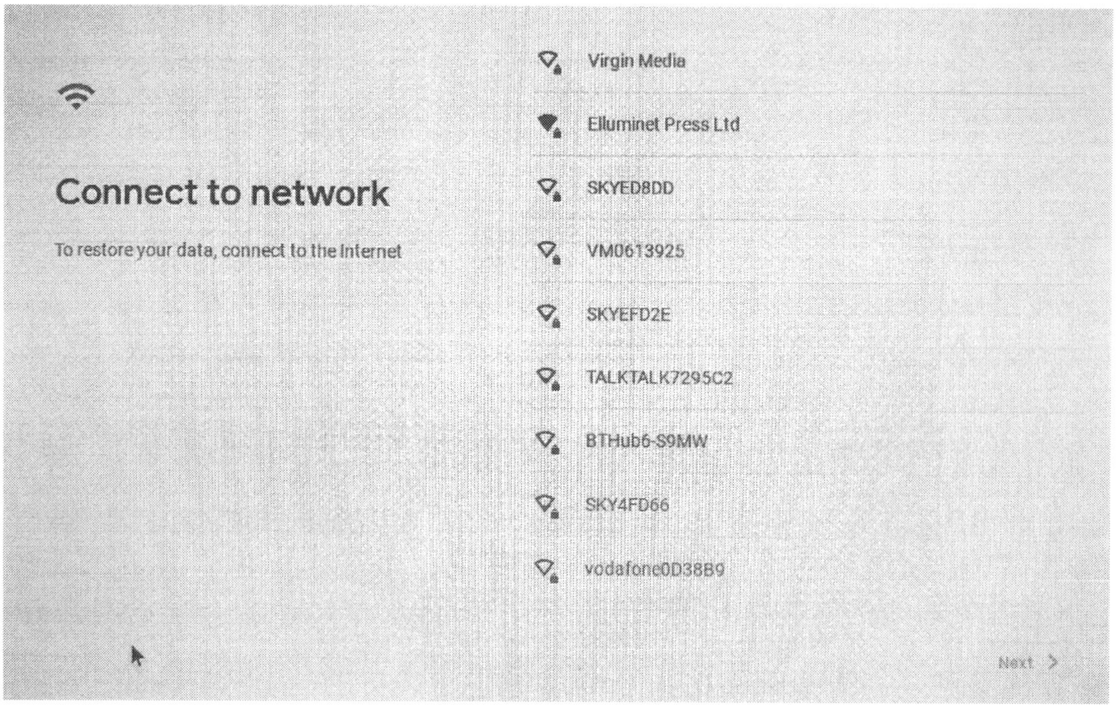

Enter your wifi password or key and click 'connect'. Your wifi network name and password/key is usually printed on the back of your router .

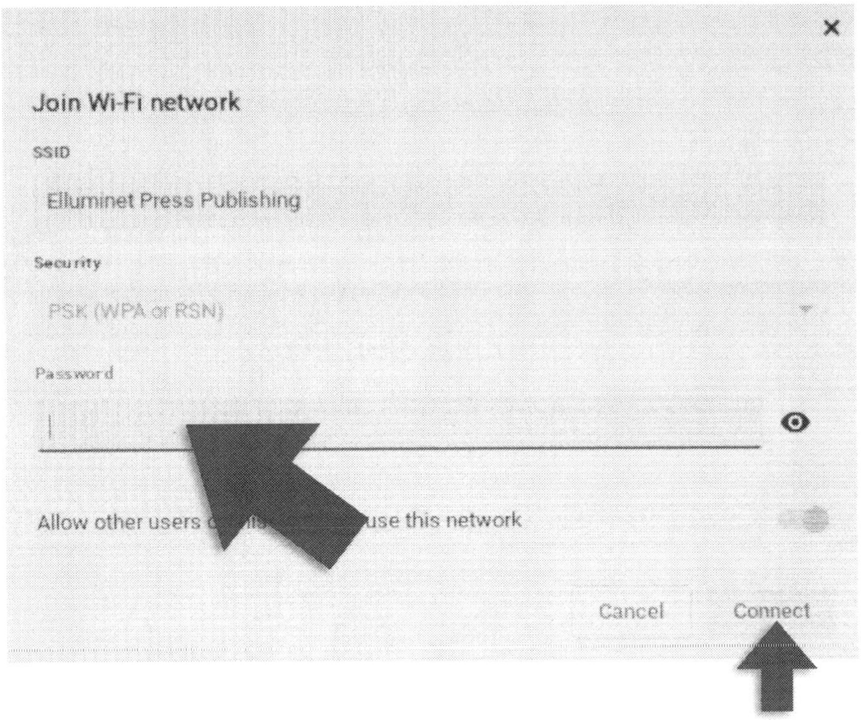

If you do not have access to WiFi, you can buy a USB adapter or modem for your internet connection type. The one pictured below is for an ethernet cable and can be used with most cable modems.

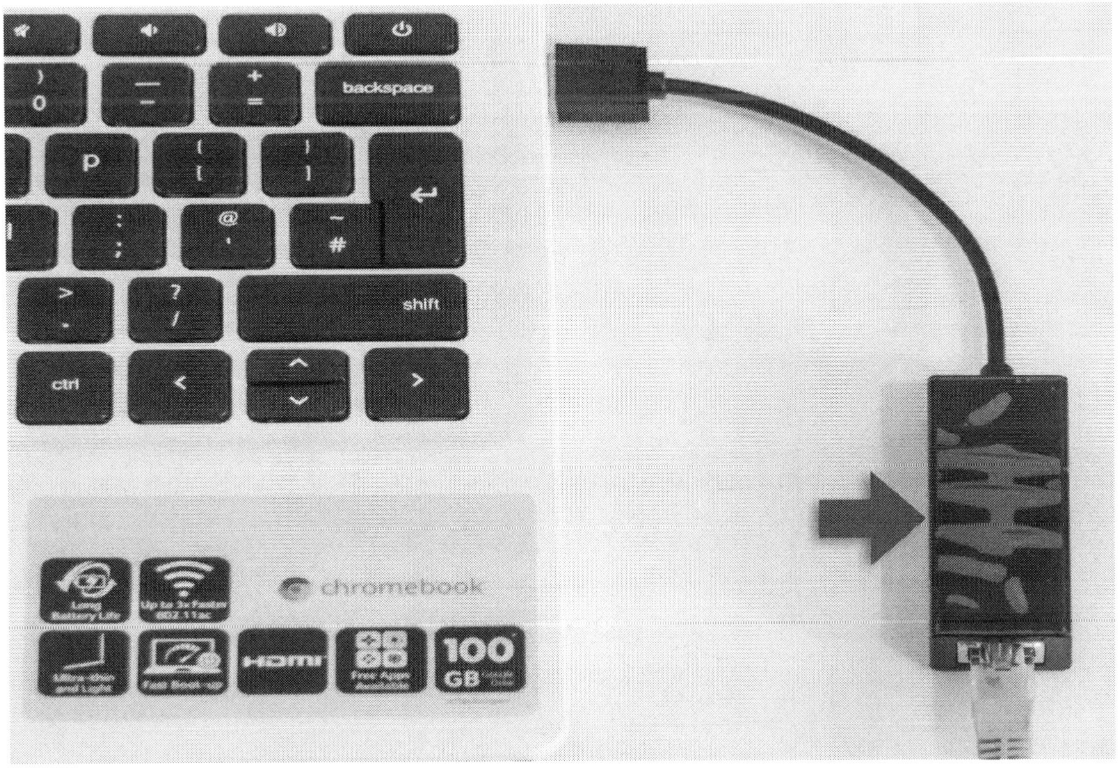

Select which person you want to set up your Chromebook for. Select 'you' if it's for yourself or another adult. Select 'a child' if you want to create a child account so you can monitor your child's activity.

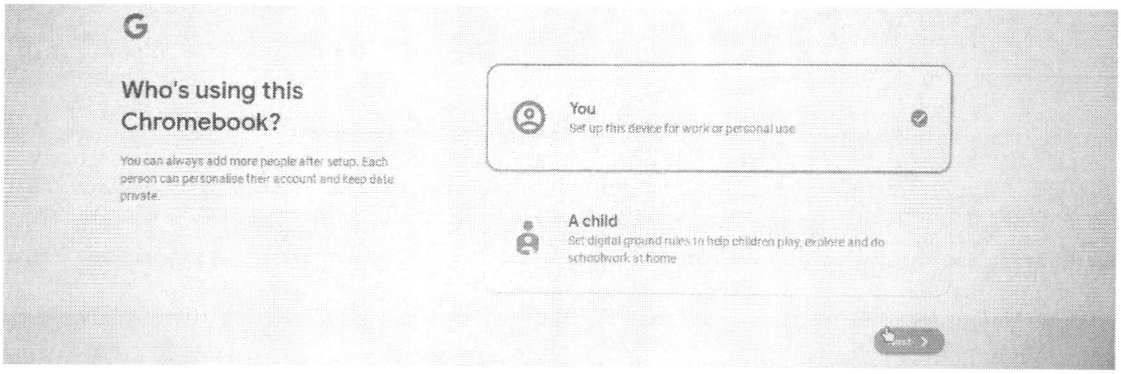

On the 'terms and conditions' page, turn off the 'optional. Help make Chrome OS better by automatically sending diagnostic and usage data to Google'. Then click 'accept and continue'.

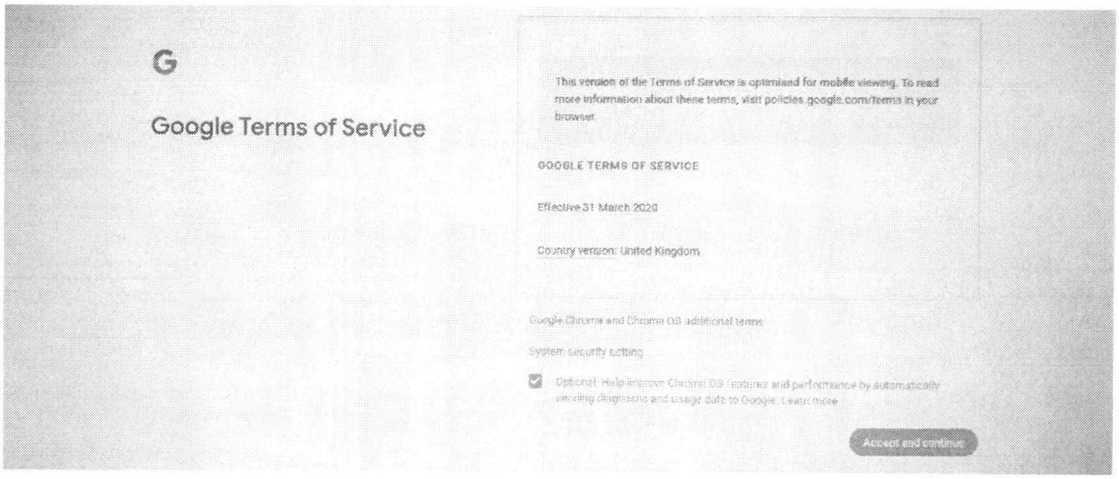

Next, enter your Google Account username and password. If you have a Gmail account, then you will have a Google Account. Just enter these details and click 'next'.

If you don't have one, click 'more options', then 'create new account' and enter your details as prompted.

Accept the terms of service. On the last screen click 'accept and continue'.

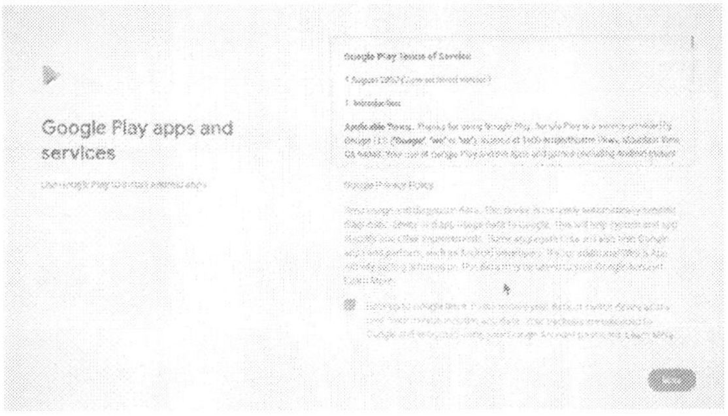

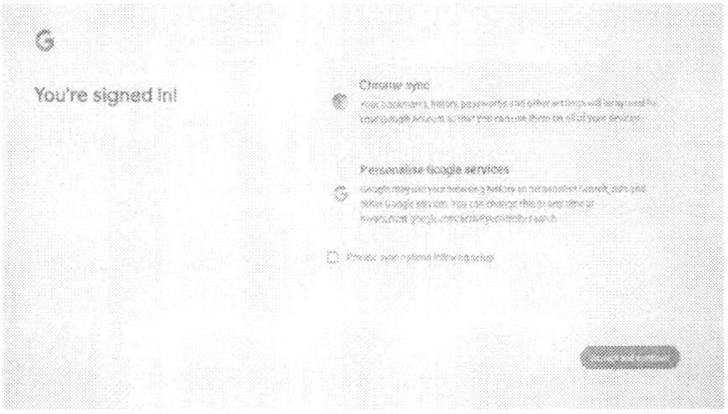

Click 'get started'. Set up Google Assistant, click 'I agree'.

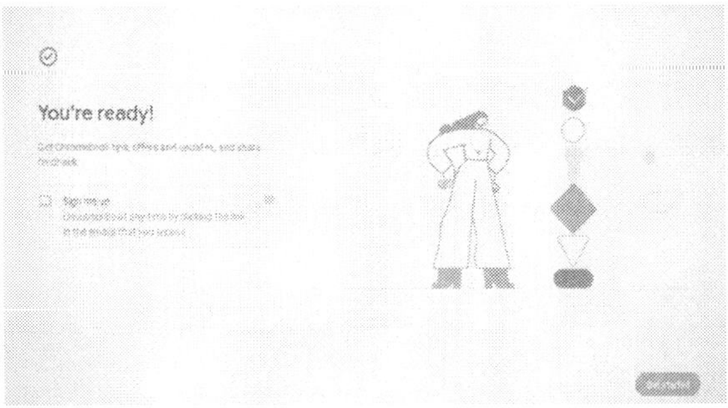

Once the setup is complete, you'll find yourself on the main desktop.

Take a look at "Desktop and the App Shelf" on page 89 for more details on getting around the desktop.

Personalise your ChromeBook

You can personalise your ChromeBook in a few ways - the most obvious one being your desktop picture or wallpaper.

Desktop Wallpaper

Right click on your desktop. To do this, tap with two fingers on the touchpad.

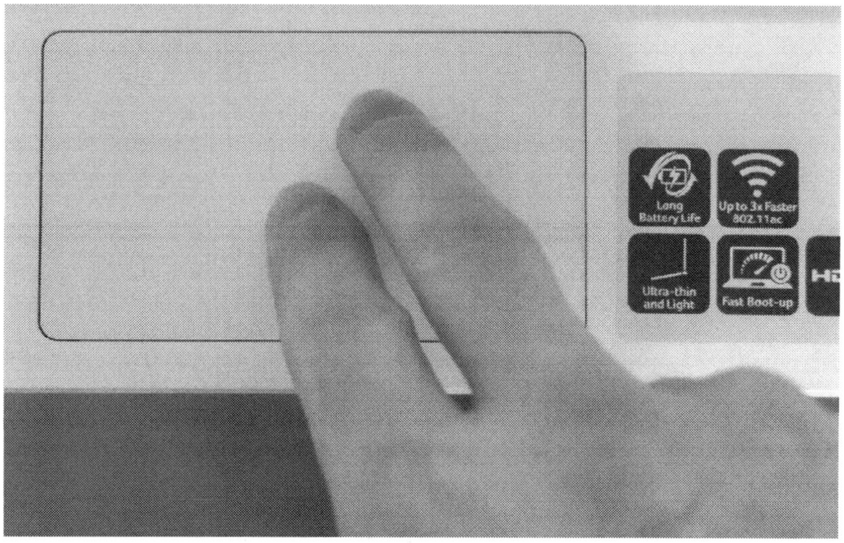

From the popup menu, select 'set wallpaper'.

You'll see some categories along the left hand side of the window, select one.

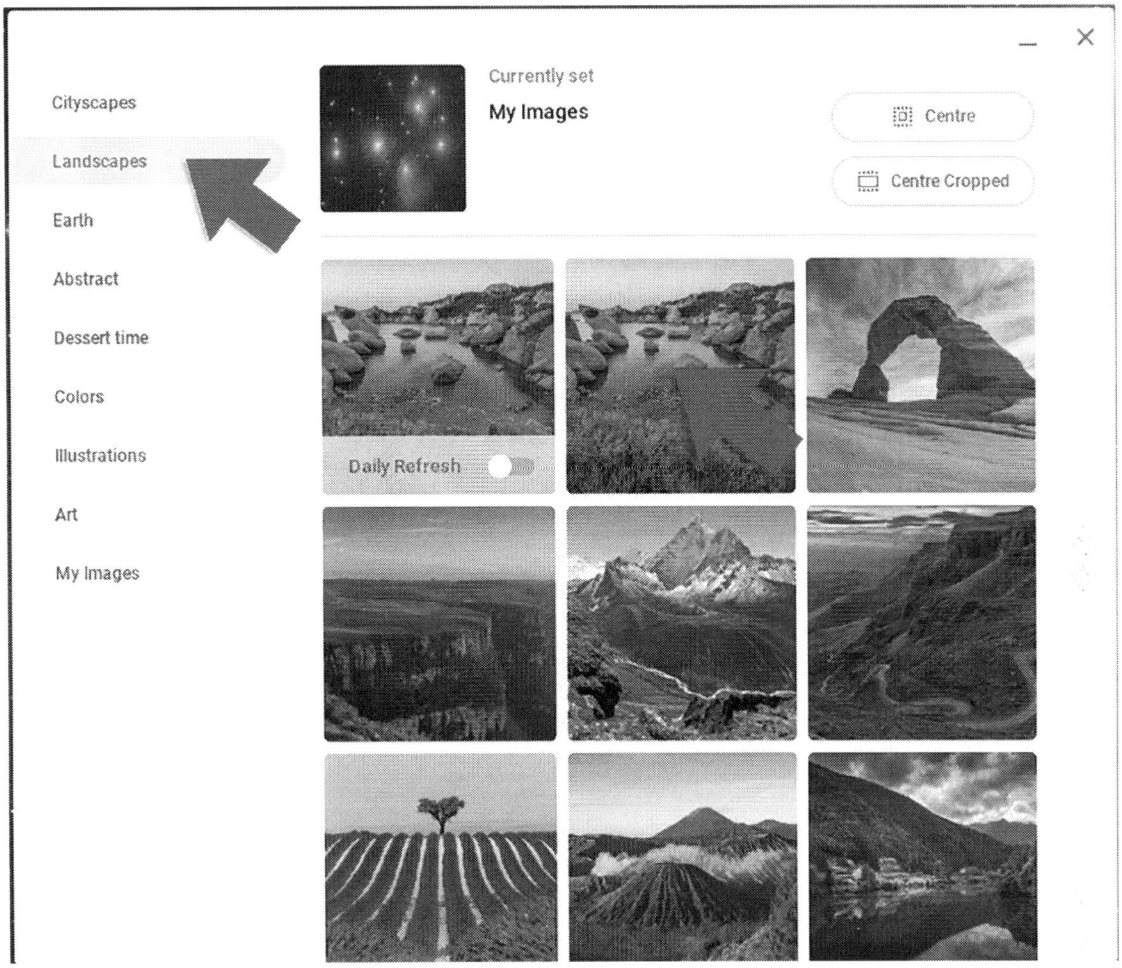

Scroll down the thumbnail previews of all the wallpapers and click on one you like.

Using your Own Photos

If you want to add your own image, open Google Drive in your file explorer.

You'll find your file explorer on the shelf along the bottom of the screen. If it isn't there, you'll find the icon on your launcher on the far left hand side.

Browse through your photos - you'll find your photos in 'My Files' or 'Google Drive'.

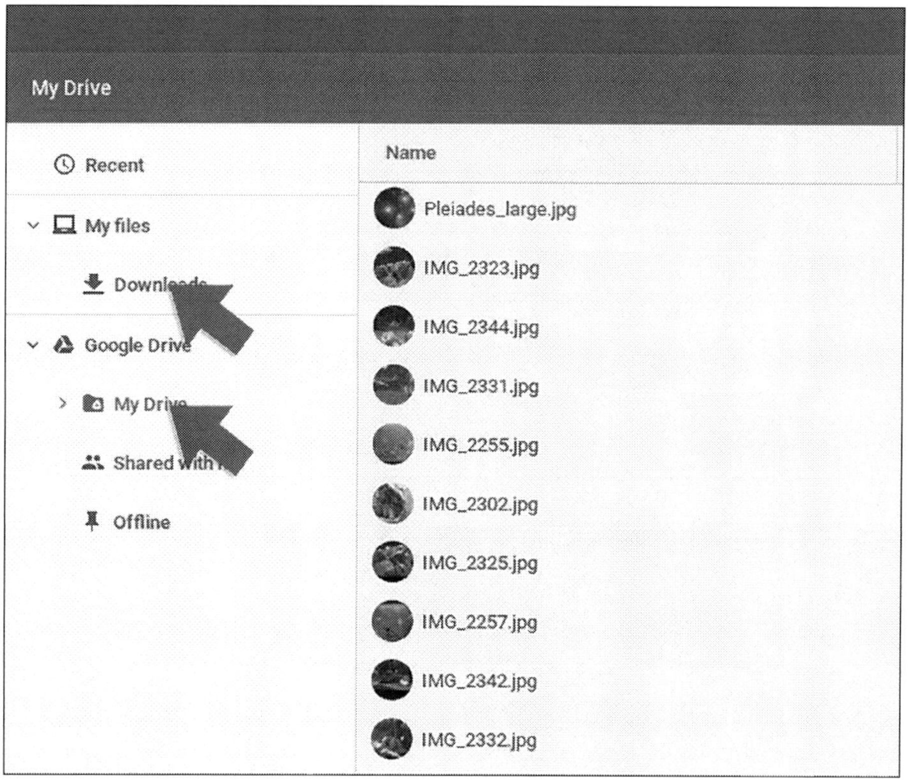

Right click on the one you want to use (to right click, tap on the image with two fingers on the touch pad).

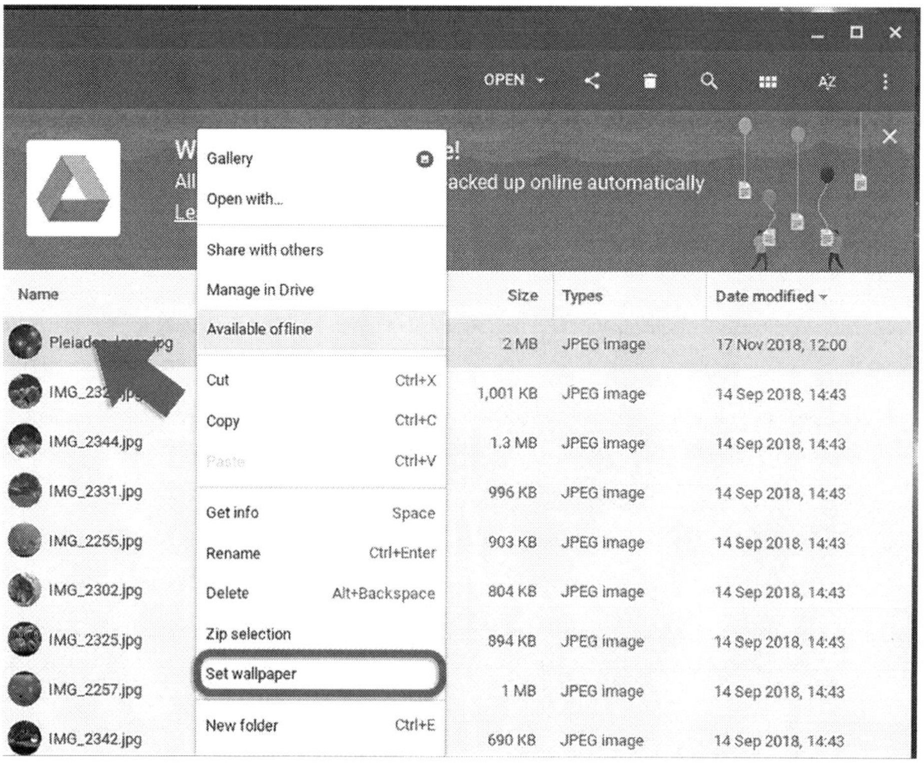

If the photo you want isn't there, it might be on Google Photos. To open Google Photos, click the launcher on the far left hand side of the screen.

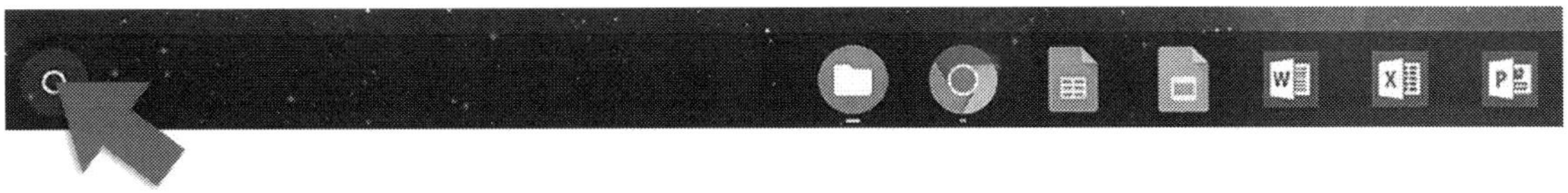

Open the launcher to full screen

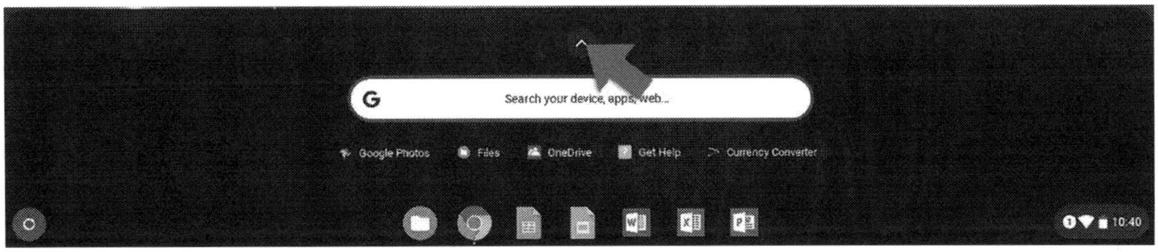

Click on the Photos app.

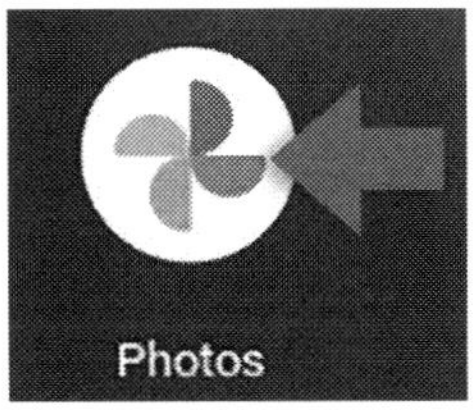

Browse through your photos. Click on the photo you want to use.

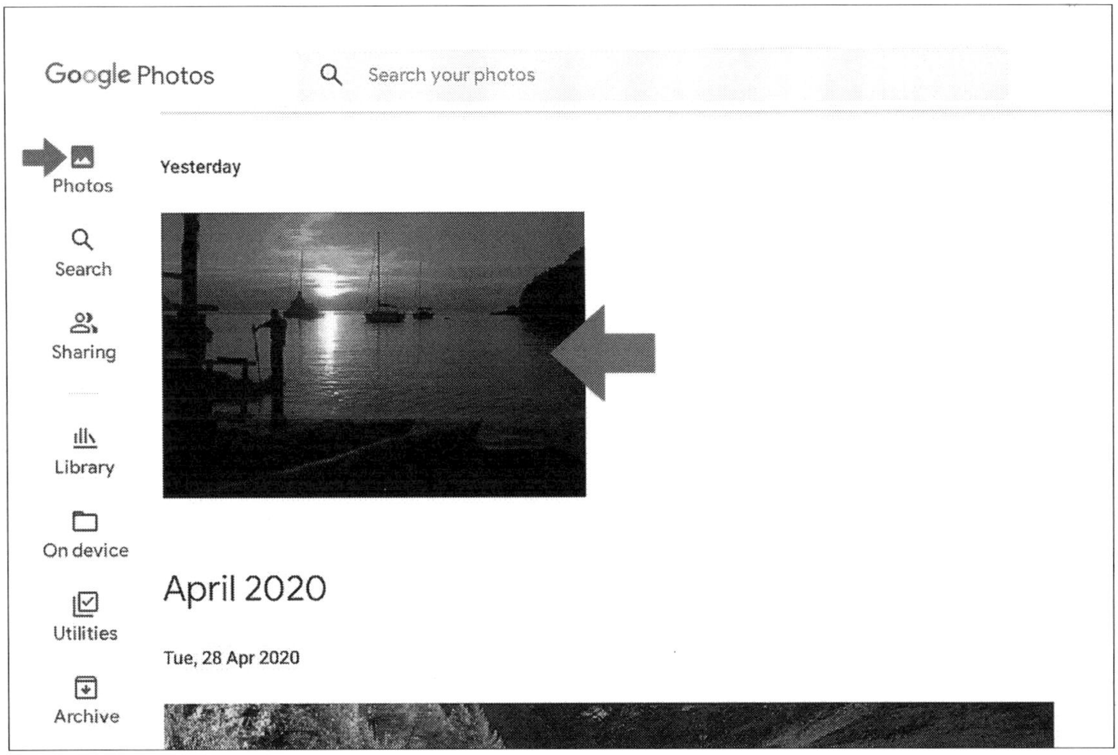

Click the three dots icon on the top right, then from the drop down menu, select 'download'.

Open your file explorer from the shelf along the bottom of the screen.

Go to 'my files', then select 'downloads'. Right click on the photo you just downloaded. From the popup menu, select 'set as wallpaper'.

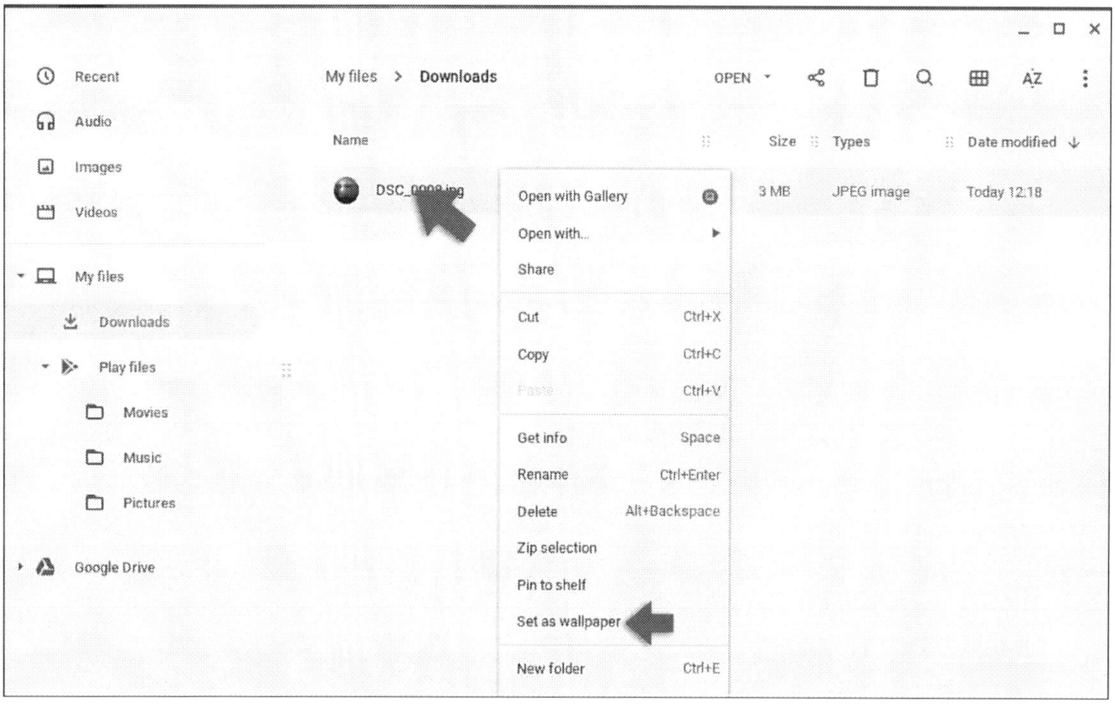

Account Image

Click the clock on the bottom right to open the system tray, then click the 'settings' icon.

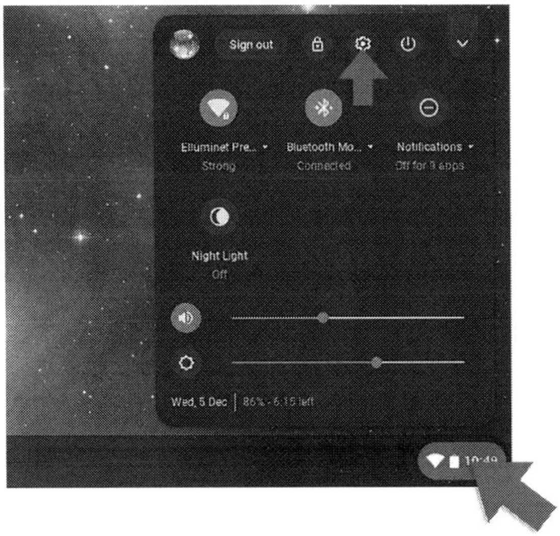

Select 'Personalisation' from the list on the left hand side, then click 'change device account image'.

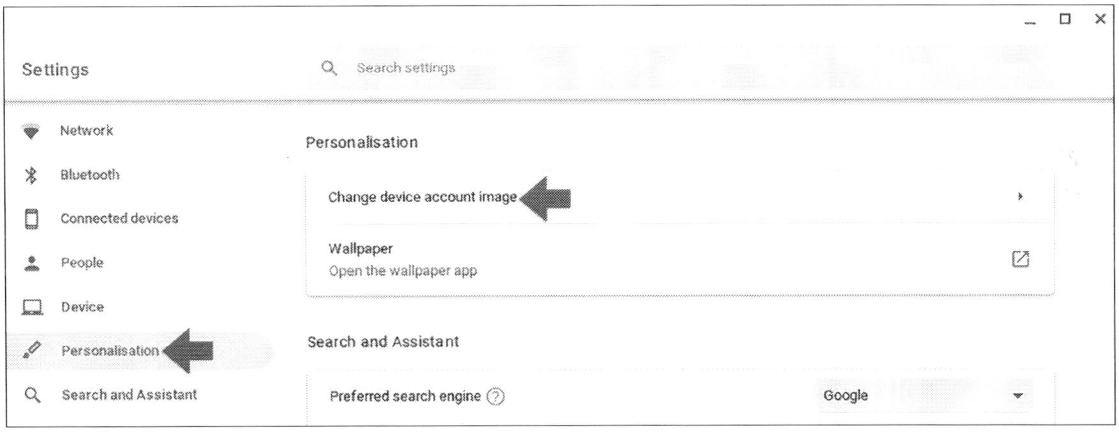

Select an image from the library.

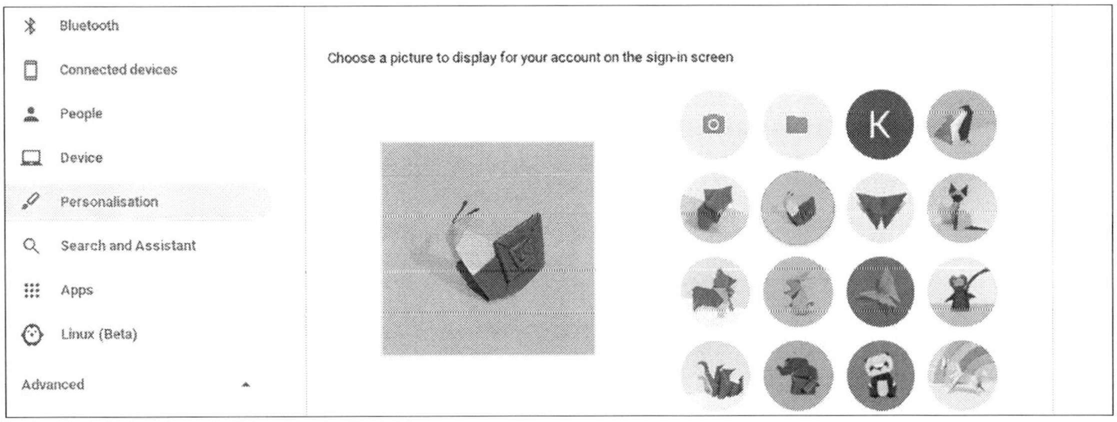

You can also take a selfie of yourself using the webcam.

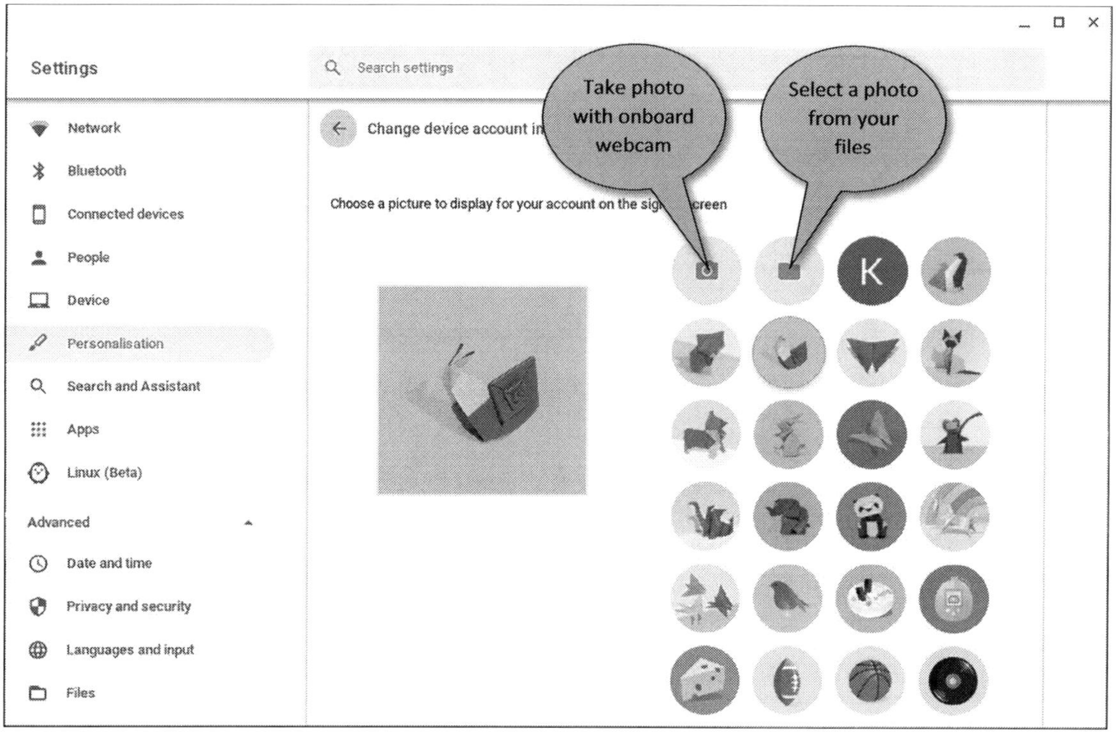

To do this, select the camera icon and then take photo.

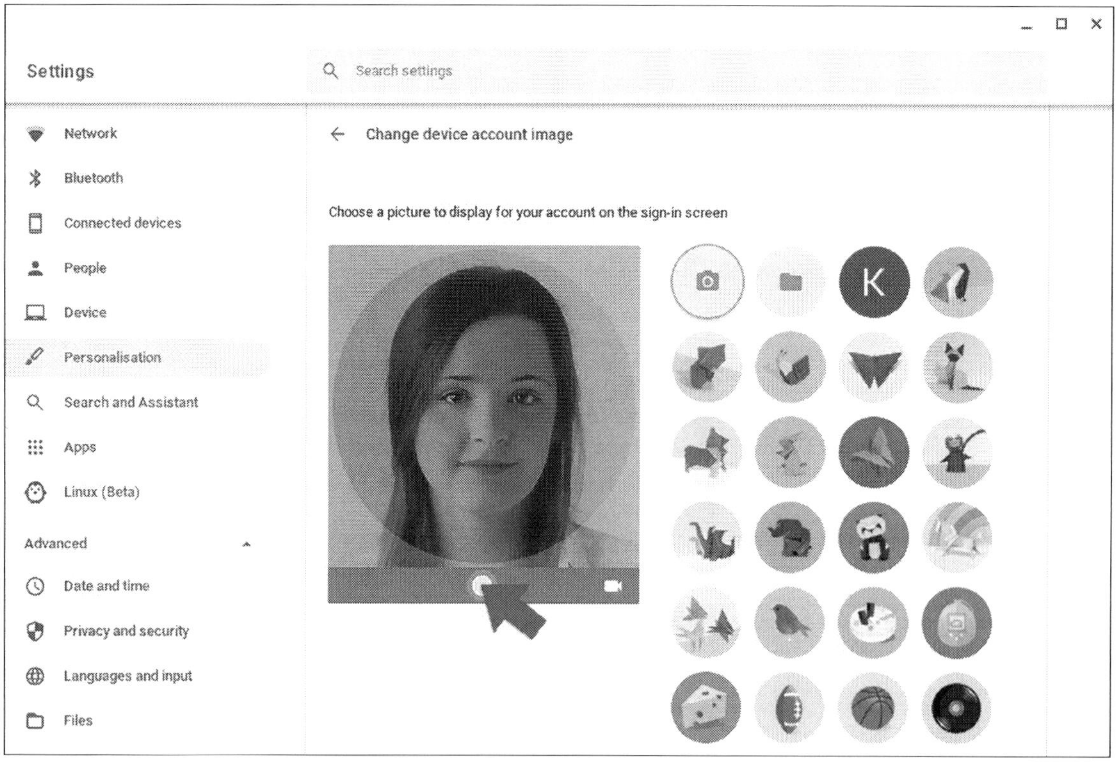

To upload your own photo, select the 'file' icon then choose one from your files on Google Drive.

Sync & Google Services

Your Chromebook synchronises data between your machine and the cloud. This keeps your data consistent between all your devices. You can control what data is synchronised.

Click the clock on the bottom right to open the system tray, then click the 'settings' icon.

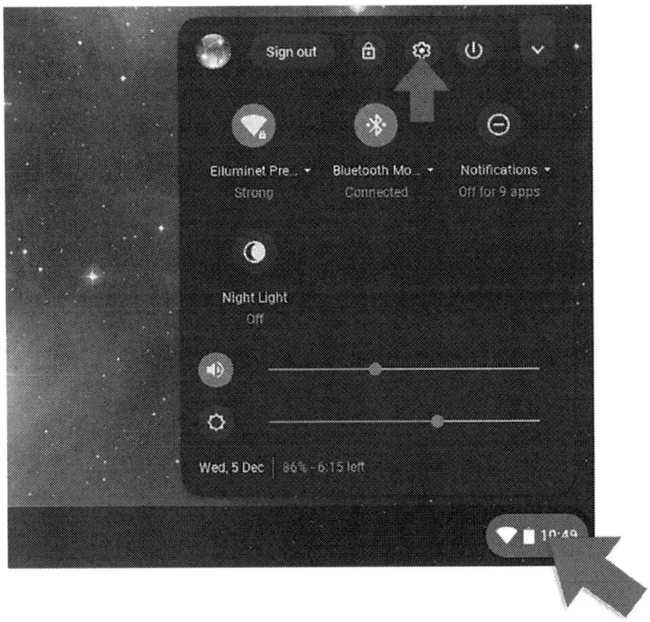

In the 'people' section, select 'sync and google services'.

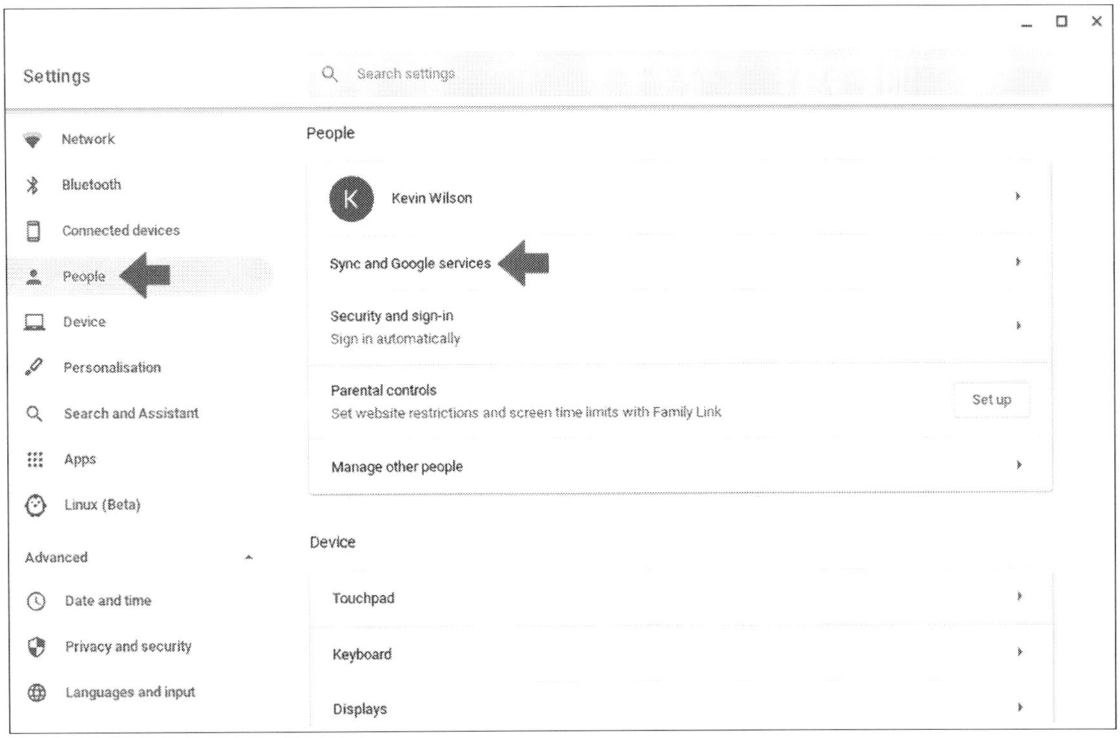

Under the 'sync' section, select 'manage sync'.

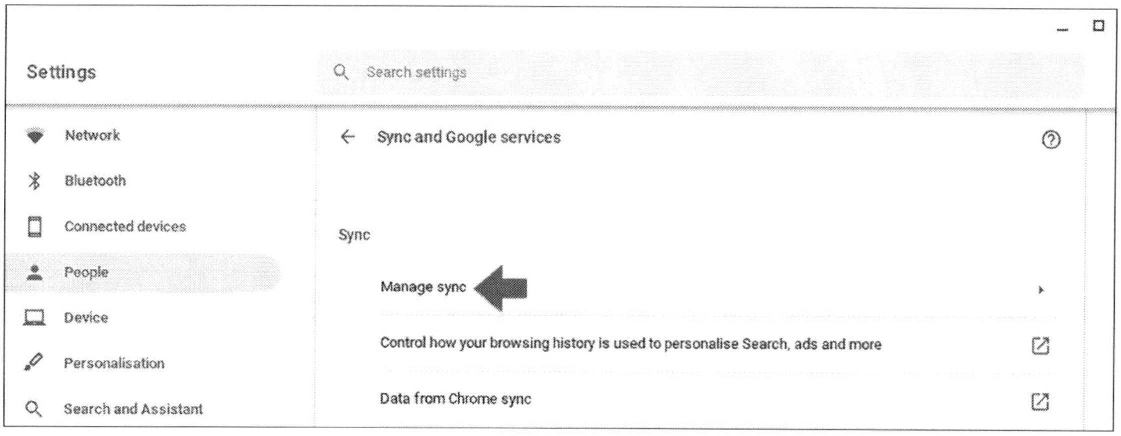

Choose what you want to sync. To sync everything, turn on 'sync everything'.

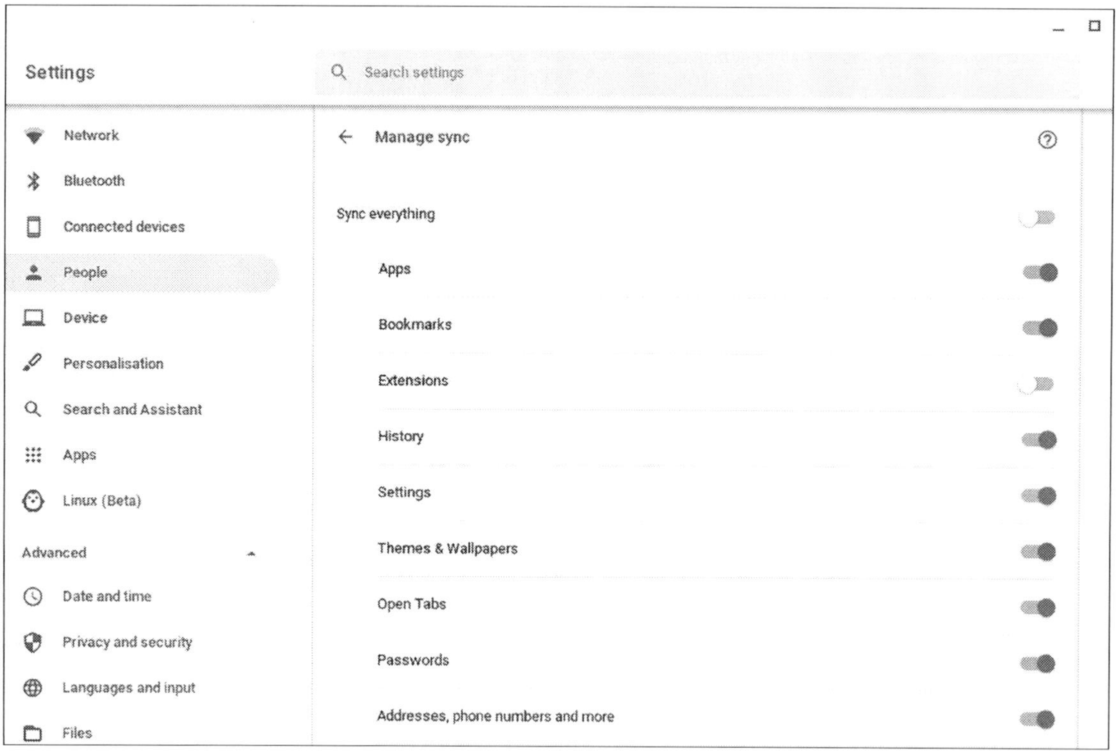

If you only want to sync certain things such as bookmarks, history or passwords, turn off 'sync everything'.

Then turn off all the items you don't want to sync, leaving the ones you do.

Transferring your Files to ChromeBook

There are various ways to transfer your files over to your ChromeBook.

Using Google Drive

You can upload files to Google Drive directly from your old computer or device.

Note with Google Drive you get 15GB free. If you need any more, you'll need to pay a subscription fee.

On your old computer, open your web browser and navigate to

`drive.google.com`

Sign in with your Google Account, then from the Google Drive home page, click 'my drive' on the left hand side of your browser window.

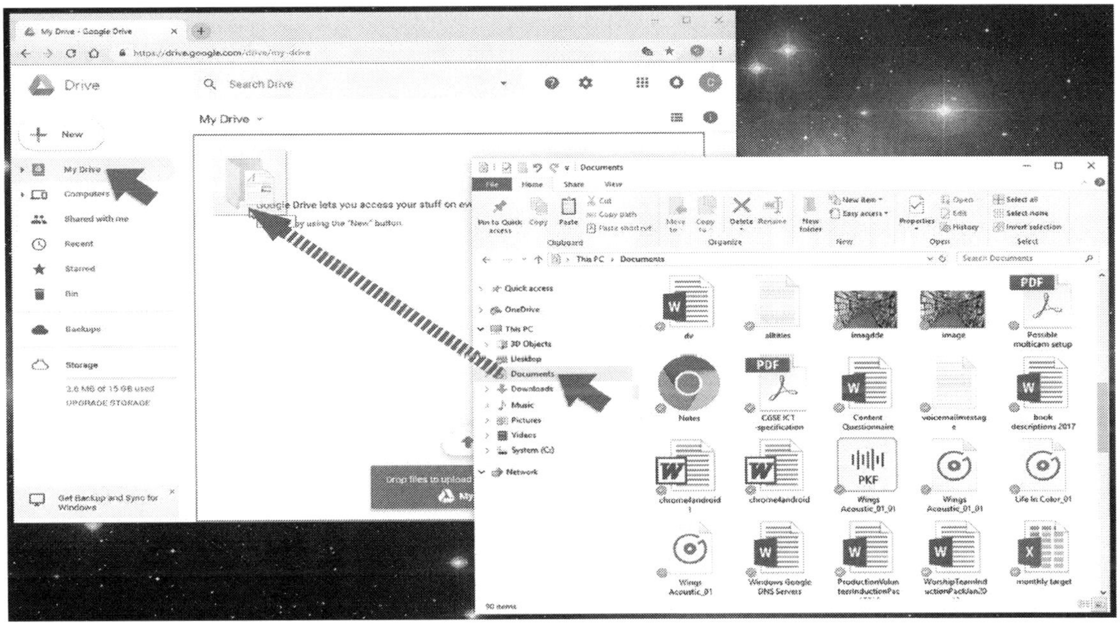

Now open file explorer and navigate to where your files are saved. This is usually under the 'this pc' section on the left hand side.

Click 'documents', then drag the folder over to the Google Drive home page, as shown above. It helps to position your windows side by side.

Do the same for any other folders such as 'pictures', 'music', and 'videos'. Allow the files to upload - it could take a while depending on the speed of your internet connection. Keep in mind that you can only upload 15GB of data. If you need more space you'll need to pay a subscription fee.

Using an External Drive

You can use a flash drive or external hard drive that has enough space to store your data.

Plug the external drive or flash drive into a USB port on your old computer. Then open up file explorer. Your external drive will show up as a USB Drive.

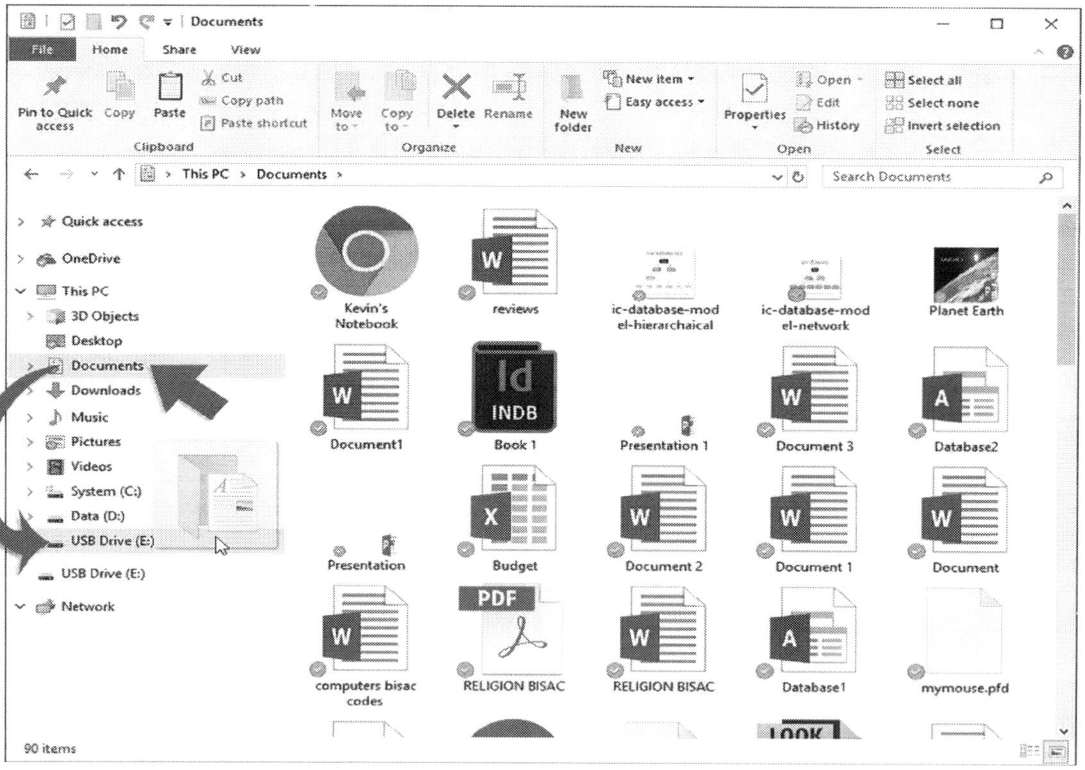

Navigate to where your files are saved. This is usually under the 'this pc' section on the left hand side.

Click 'documents', then drag the folder over to the USB Drive, as shown above. Do the same for any other folders such as 'pictures', 'music', and 'videos'.

Once the files have finished copying, remove the drive from your old computer and plug it into a USB port on your ChromeBook.

Now, on your ChromeBook, open 'files' from the app shelf. You'll also find it on your launcher.

Select your USB drive from the panel on the left hand side of the window.

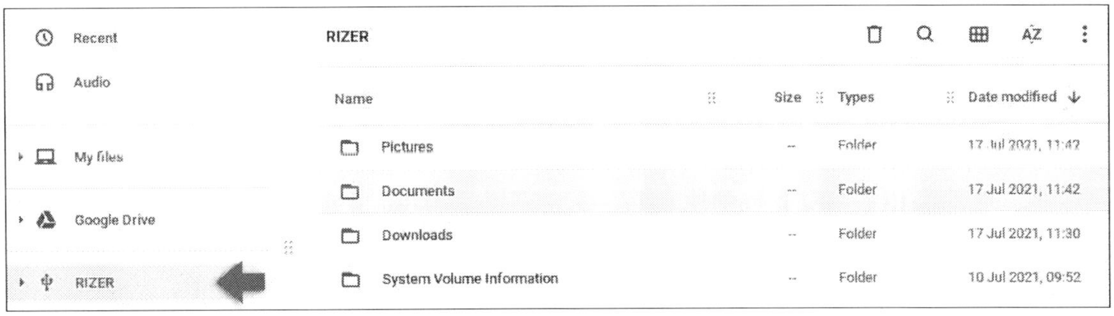

Open Google Drive. Click and drag the 'documents' folder from the USB drive to 'my drive'. Do the same with the rest of the folders you copied from your old device.

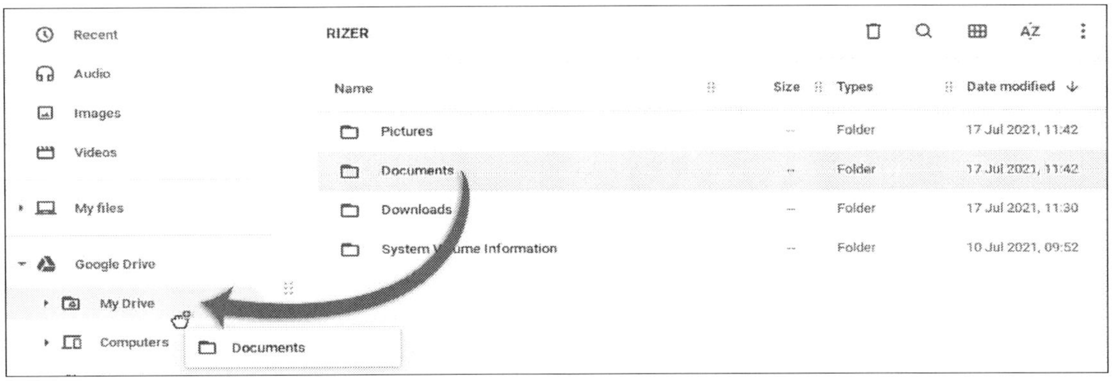

Setting up Printers

If you have a fairly modern printer - such as a wireless printer or cloud ready printer, you can usually add it with no problem. Traditional and older printers can still be used but are a bit more temperamental to add and some are just not supported.

Cloud Enabled Wireless Printers

Your printer needs to support Google Cloud Print - you can check this in the documentation that came with your printer.

Turn on your printer and make sure it's connected to your WiFi.

On your ChromeBook, click the clock on the bottom right to open the system tray, then click the 'settings' icon.

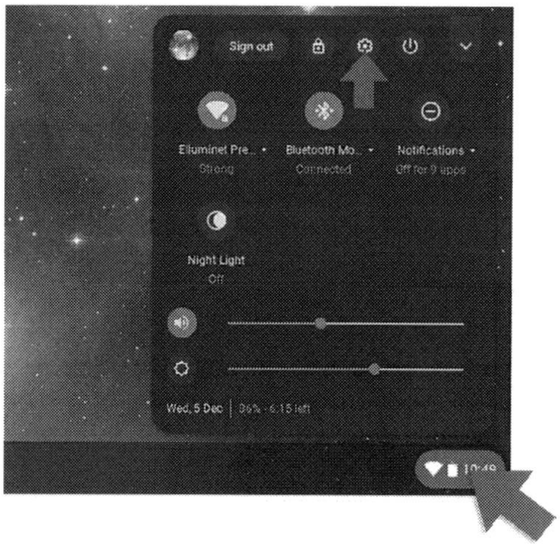

Scroll down to the bottom of the page and click 'advanced' to reveal the advanced settings, then select 'printing'

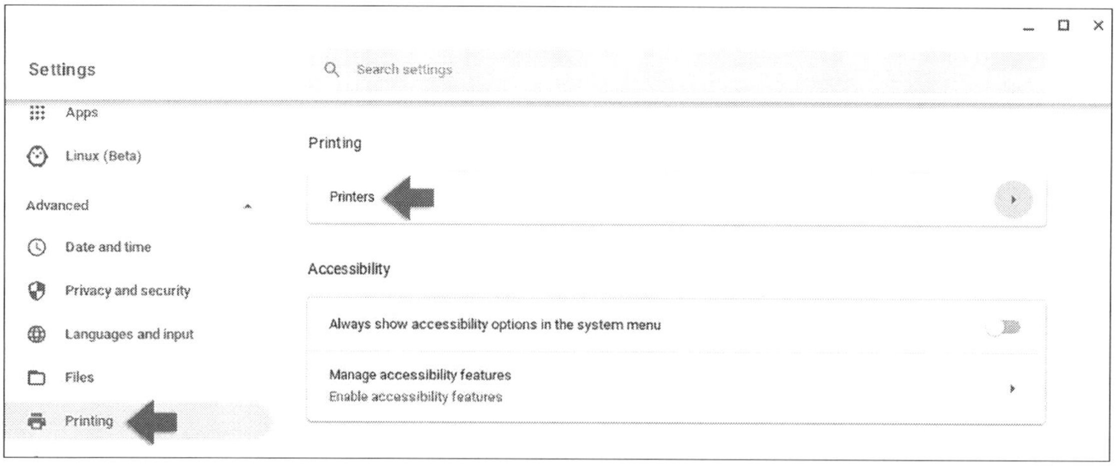

Click 'printers'.

Your chromebook will detect any cloud ready printers and list them on this page. Sometimes it takes a while for them to show up. When your printer pops up on the list, click 'save'.

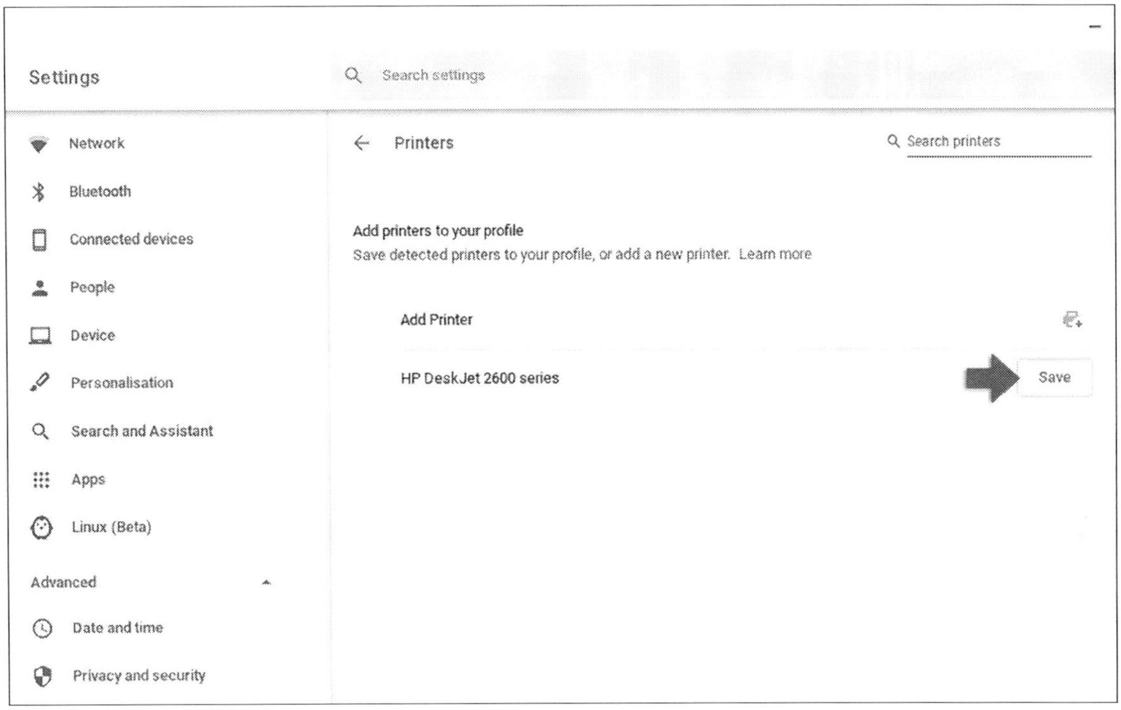

Your cloud printer will be listed below.

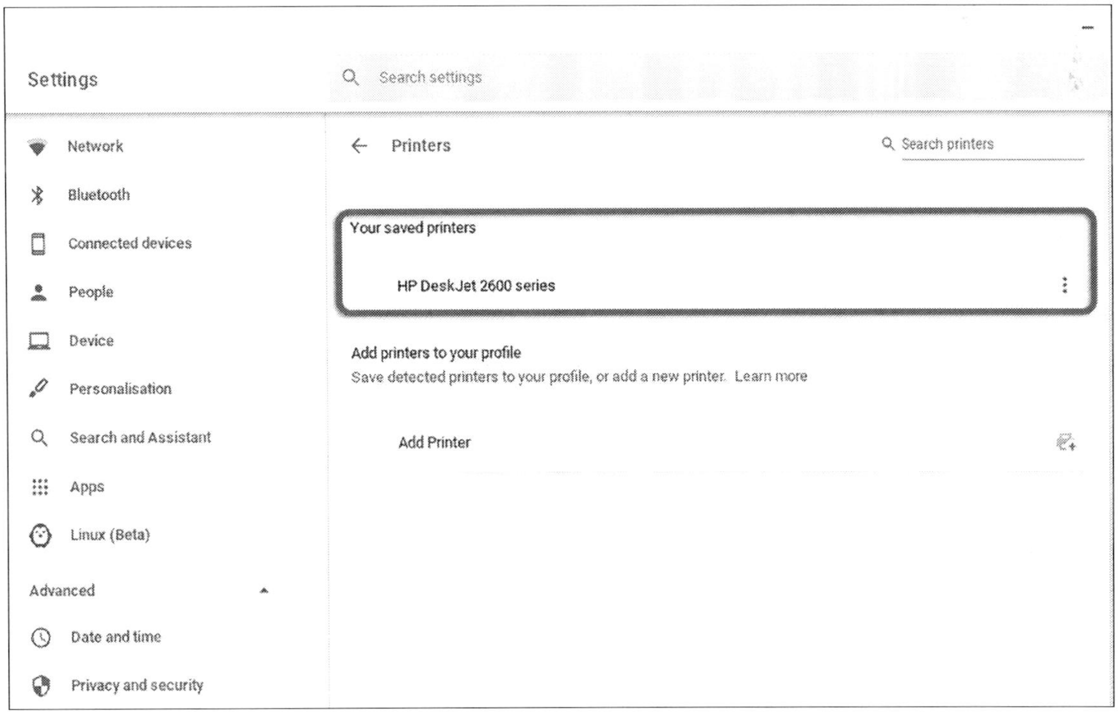

That's all you need to do. You'll be able to select this printer when printing from an app on your chromebook.

Traditional Printers

If your printer is a bit older and isn't cloud enabled, you can plug it into your ChromeBook using a USB cable. This is the simplest way to connect an older printer.

First, plug your printer into your ChromeBook using a USB cable.

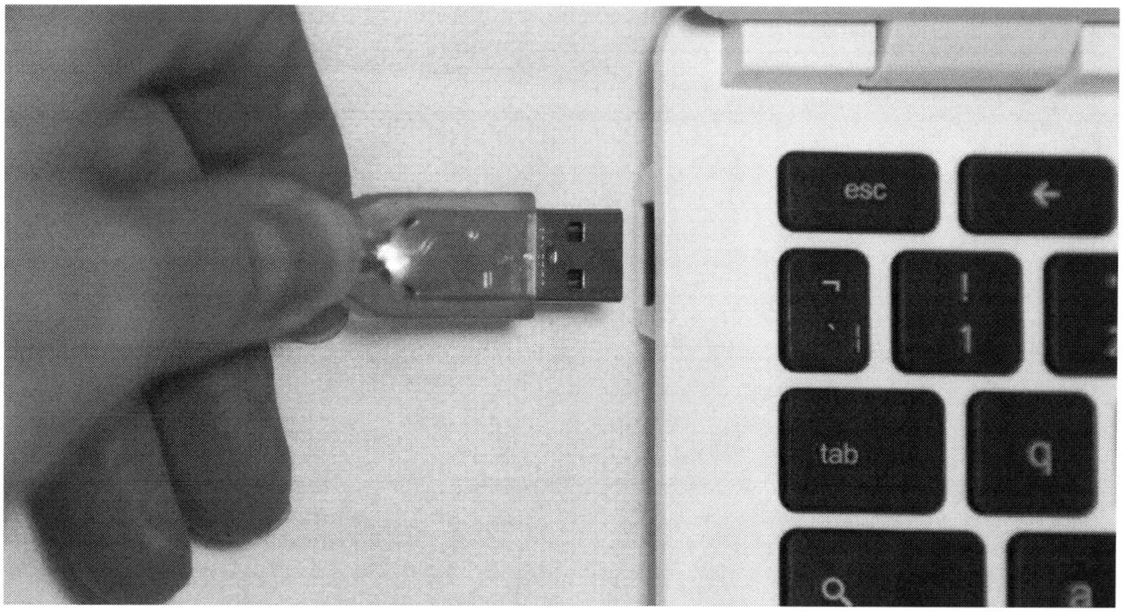

On your ChromeBook, click the clock on the bottom right of your screen to open the system tray.

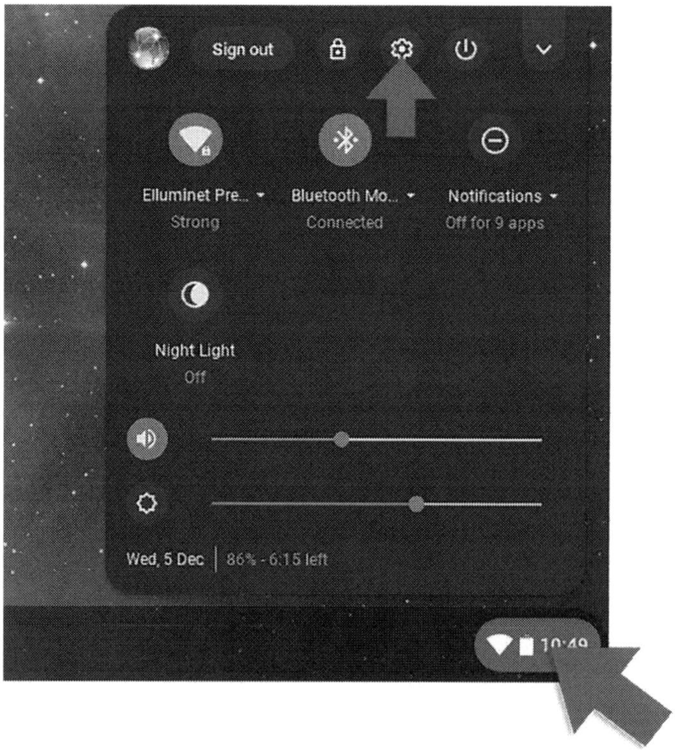

Scroll down to the bottom of the page and click 'advanced' to reveal the advanced settings, then select 'printing'. Click 'printers'.

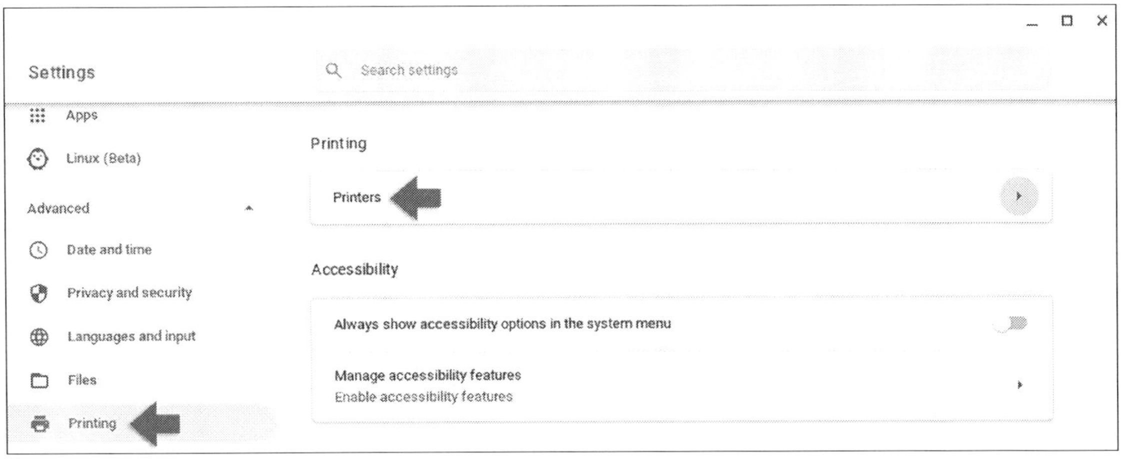

Your printer should show up in the list. Click 'set up'.

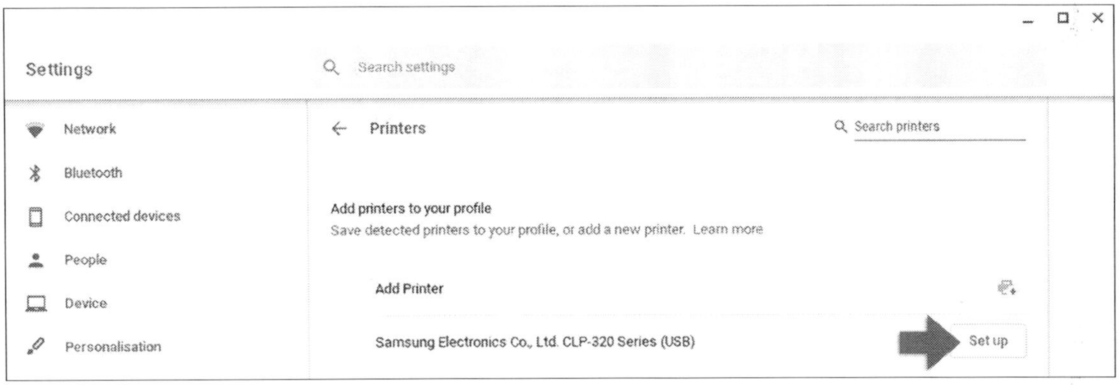

In the setup screen select manufacturer, and model.

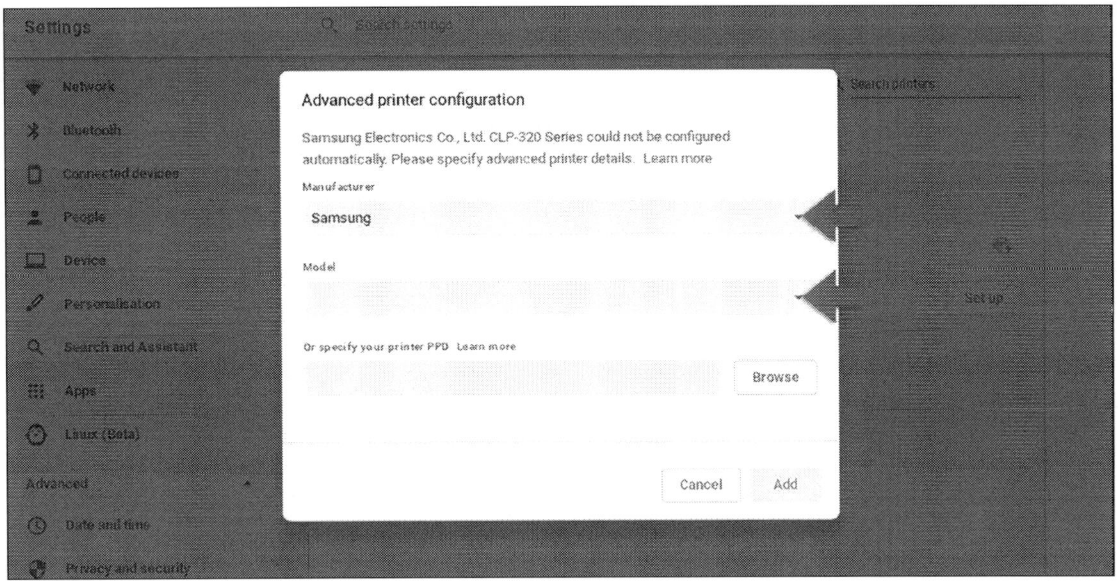

Click 'add'.

Adding Bluetooth Devices

You can add bluetooth mice, headphones, keyboards to your ChromeBook. This process is called pairing.

To add a bluetooth device, you need to put the device into pairing mode. To do this, press the pairing button on the bottom of the device - you might need to read the device's instructions on how to do this.

In this example, I'm going to add a bluetooth mouse. First power the mouse on and press the pairing button underneath. The light will begin to flash.

On your ChromeBook, click on the clock on the bottom right to open the system tray.

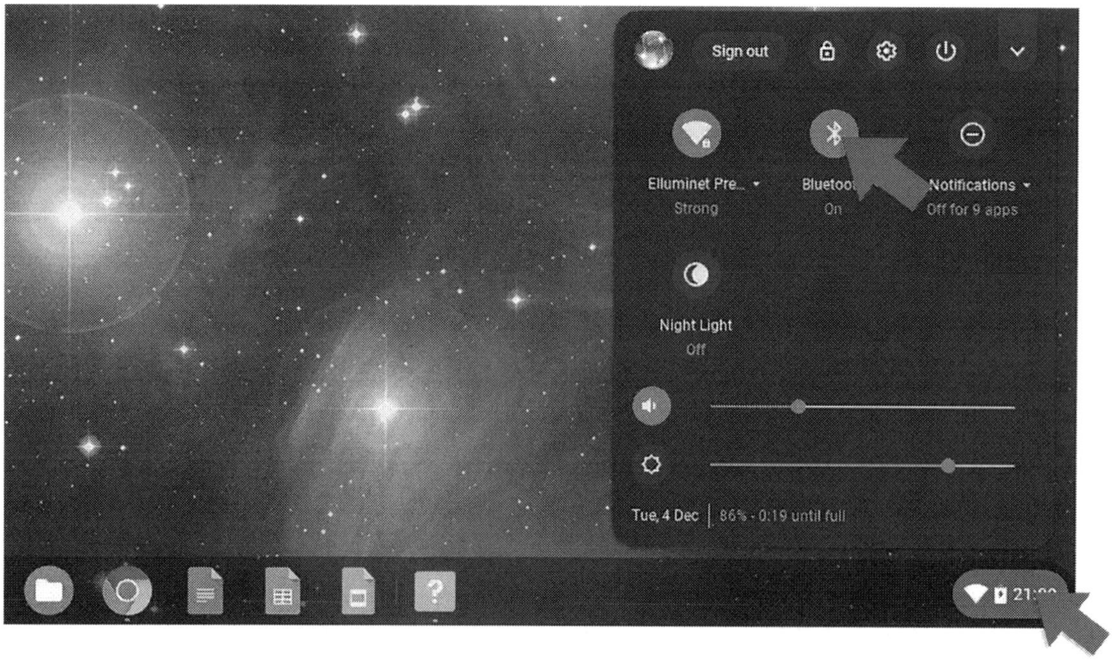

Select the bluetooth icon and turn it on if it isn't already.

Allow your ChromeBook to scan for nearby devices, this will take a minute or two. Once a device has been found, it will appear in the list.

Click on the device in the list to connect it.

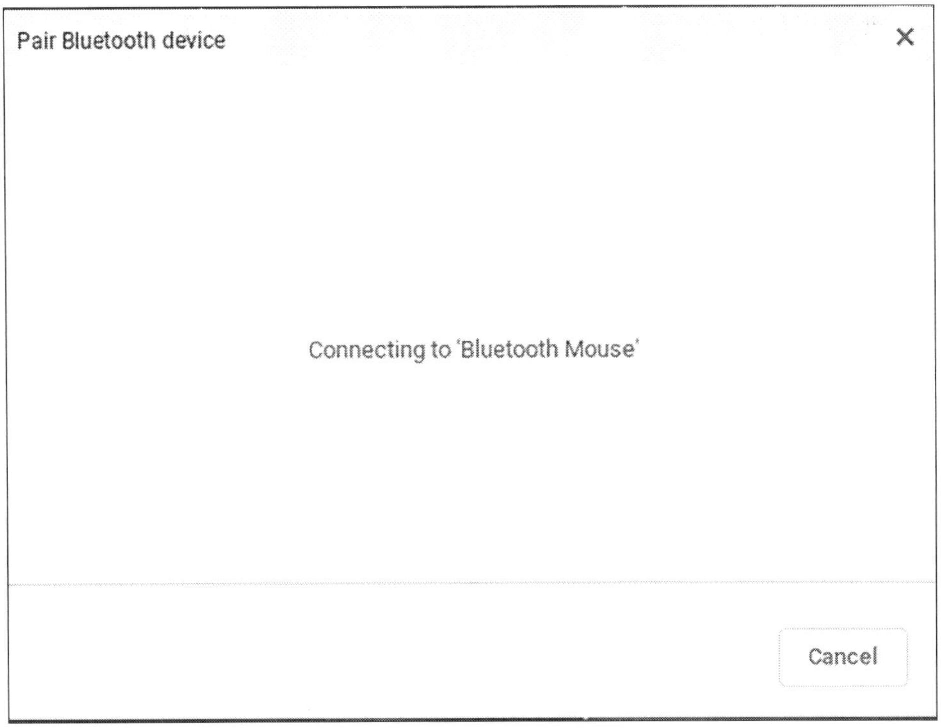

Once your ChromeBook has made a connection, you can use your device as normal.

Connect your Phone

You can connect an android phone to your Chromebook. You'll need a new Chromebook with ChromeOS 71 or later and an Android phone with Android 8.1 or later. You'll also need to be signed in with the same Google Account on all devices.

To set this up, on your Chromebook, click the clock on the bottom right to open the system tray, then click the 'settings' icon.

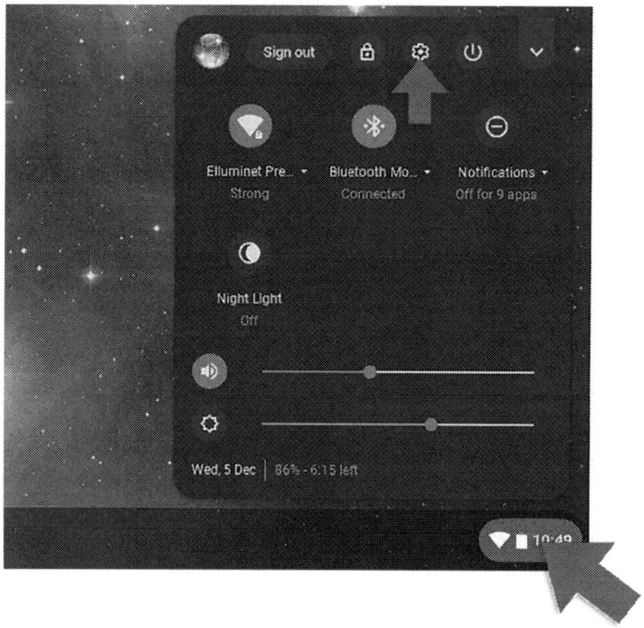

Select 'connected devices' from the list on the left hand side. Under the 'Android phone' section select 'set up'.

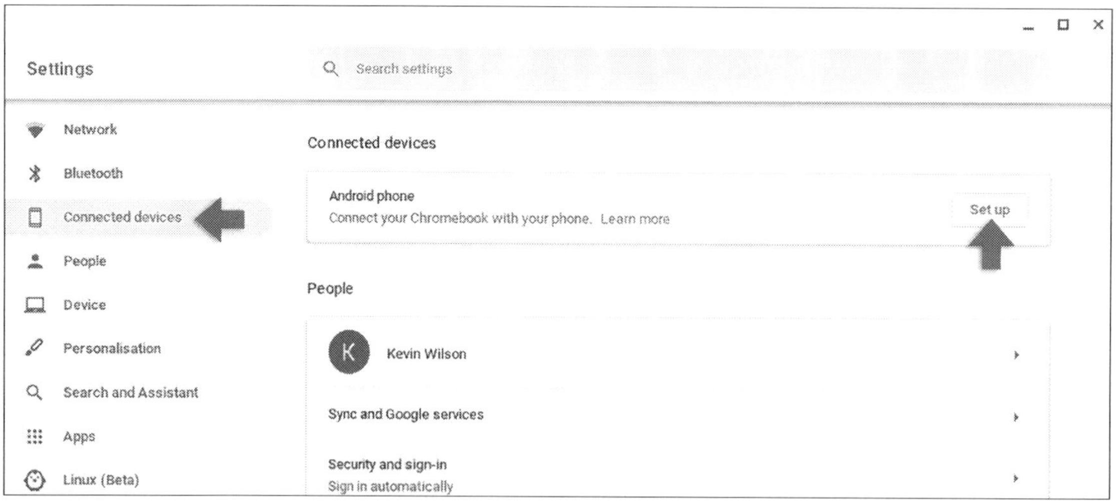

Any detected phones that are eligible will be listed here. If not make sure your phone and chromebook are signed in with the same Google Account.

On the 'connect your phone' screen, select 'accept' on the bottom right. Enter your Google Account password, click 'done'. Click 'done' on the following screen.

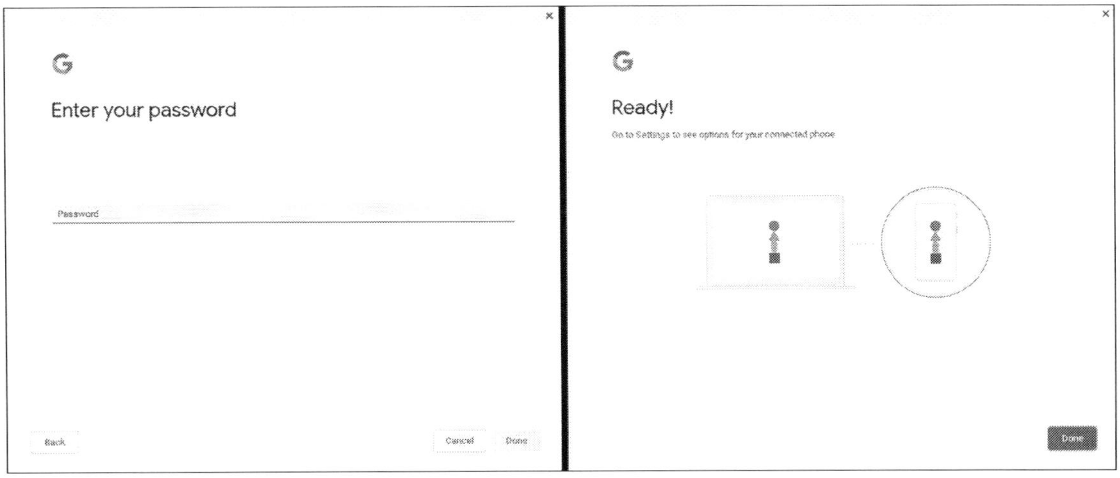

On your Chromebook, under 'connected devices', you'll see your phone listed. Click on your device to select features you want to turn on.

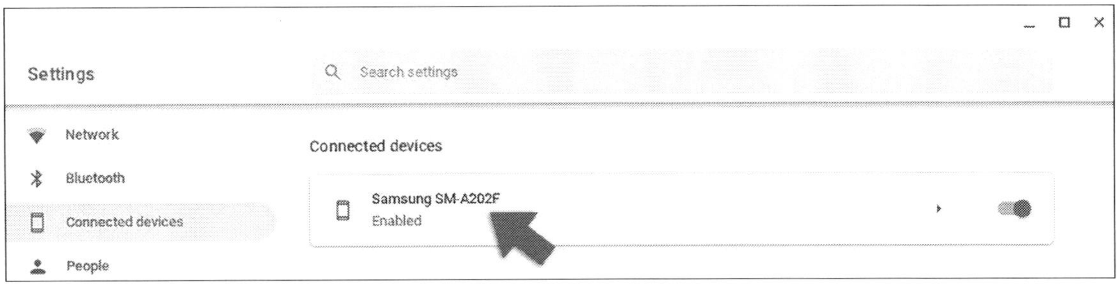

Here, you can turn on 'smart lock' - this unlocks your chromebook when you're phone is in range. Instant tethering allows you to select your phone's mobile data to get on the internet if wifi isn't available.

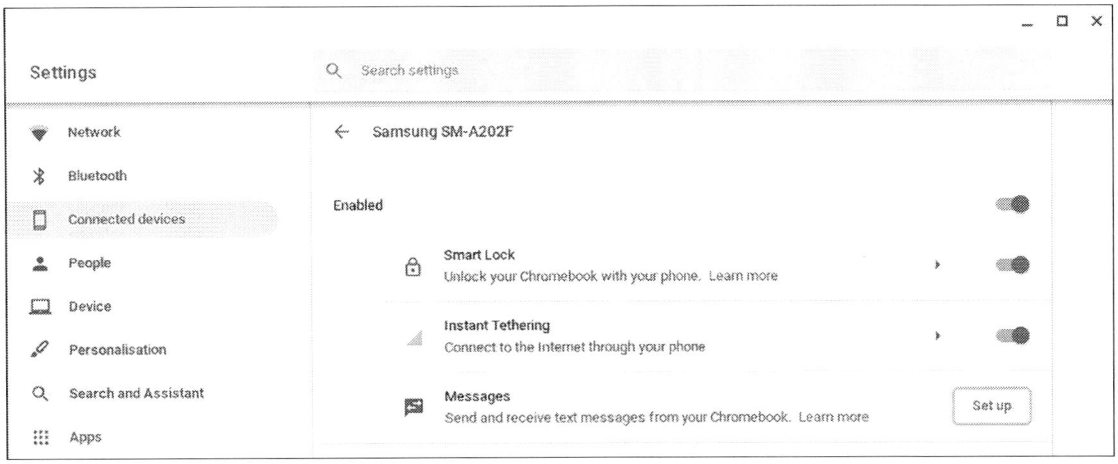

To send and receive texts on your chromebook, select 'setup' next to 'messages'.

Now, on your phone, open the google messages app and select the three dots icon on the top right. From the drop down menu select ‘messages for web’.

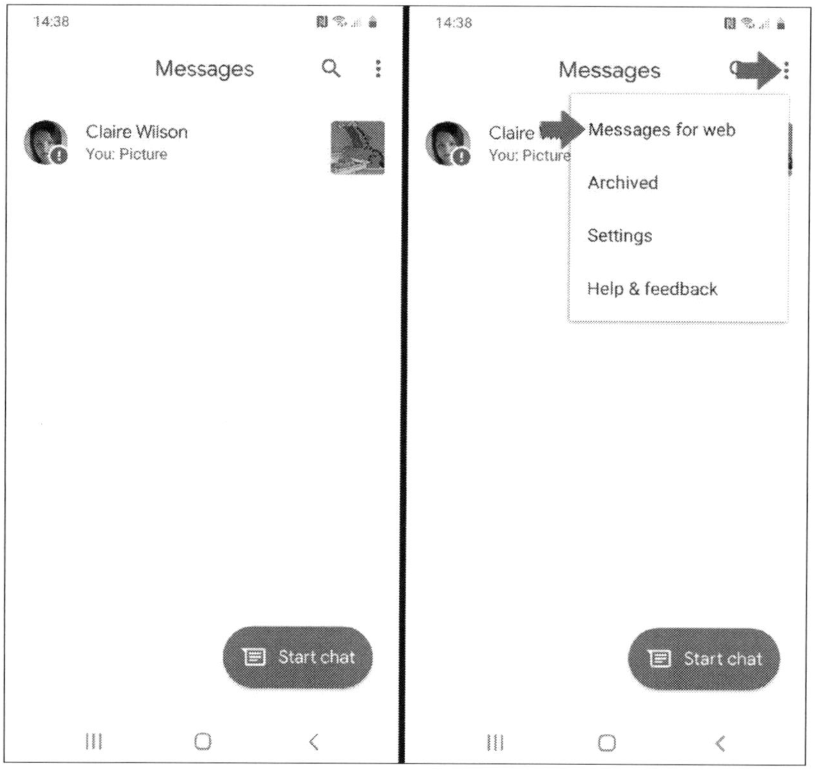

Select ‘QR code Scanner’.

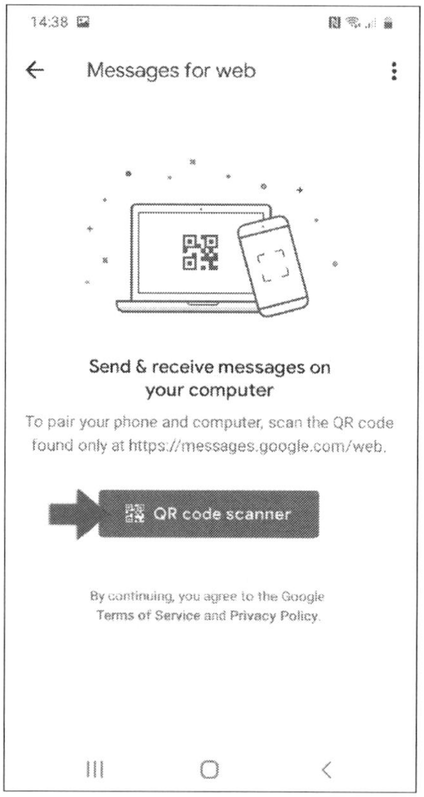

Scan the code on your chromebook's screen with your phone.

Now you'll be able to read your text messages and respond from your chromebook. Just start the messages app on your chromebook

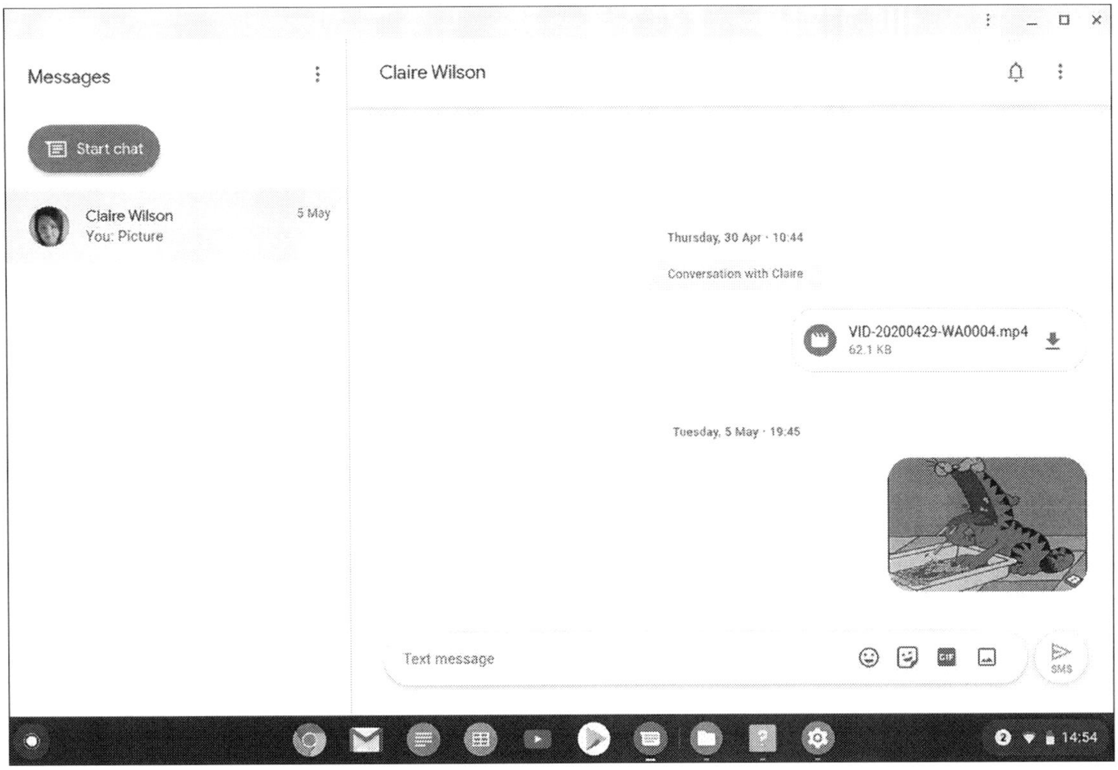

Connect to WiFi

To connect to a WiFi network, click the clock on the bottom right of the screen, then select the WiFi icon.

Select the network you want to connect to...

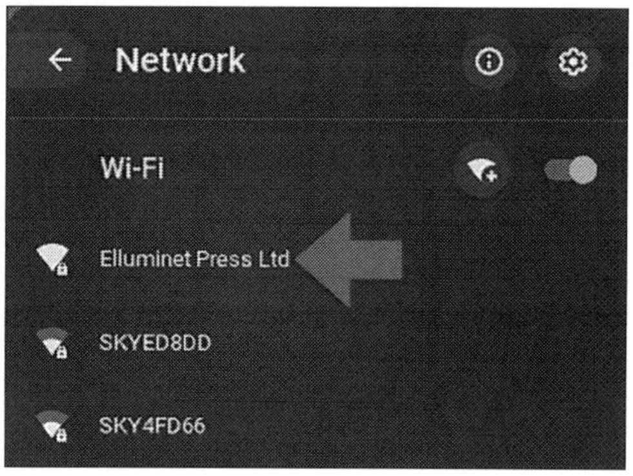

Enter the WiFi passcode in the 'password' field.

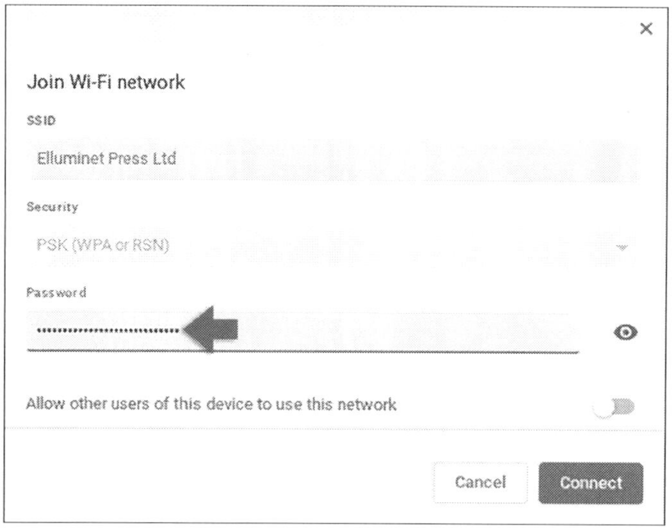

Click 'connect'.

Managing Users

You can add multiple users to your ChromeBook. This is useful if more than one person uses your ChromeBook and need access to their own email, apps, and files.

You can add two types of users to your ChromeBook. The first is a guest. This allows any user to get onto your ChromeBook without having to sign in with a Google Account. Guest users do not have access to the Google Play store, Web store or a email, they can pretty much just browse the internet.

The other type, is a user with a Google Account. This is the recommended way to use your ChromeBook.

Adding a User

On the login screen click 'add person' on the bottom left of the screen.

Select the account type you want to add. Select 'you' if you're adding your own account, or for someone else. If you're setting up the Chromebook for a child where you can monitor their activity select 'a child'. Click 'next'.

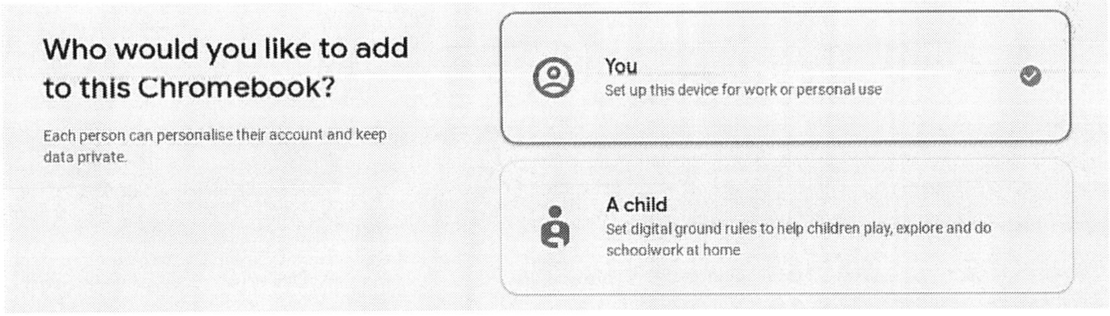

Enter the Google Account email address and password of the account you want to add. Click 'next'.

If they haven't got an account, click 'create account' then fill in the details.

Click ‘accept & continue’, click ‘more’ on the ‘terms & services’ screen, then click ‘accept’.

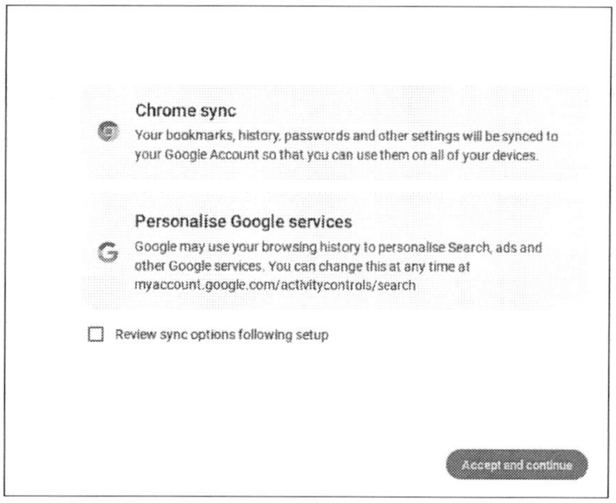

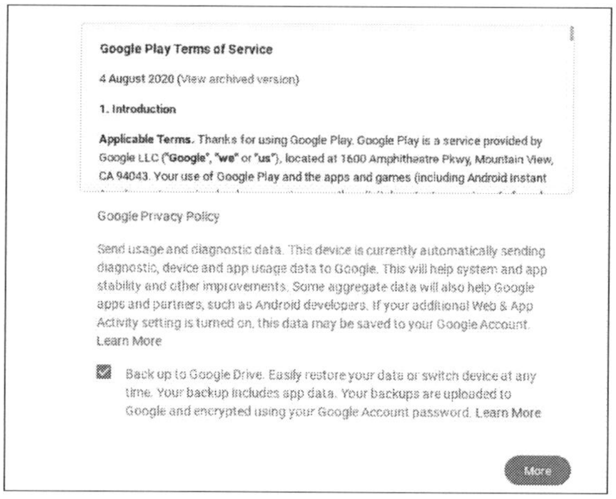

Click ‘I agree’ on the ‘google assistant’ screen and follow the instructions. Click ‘done’.

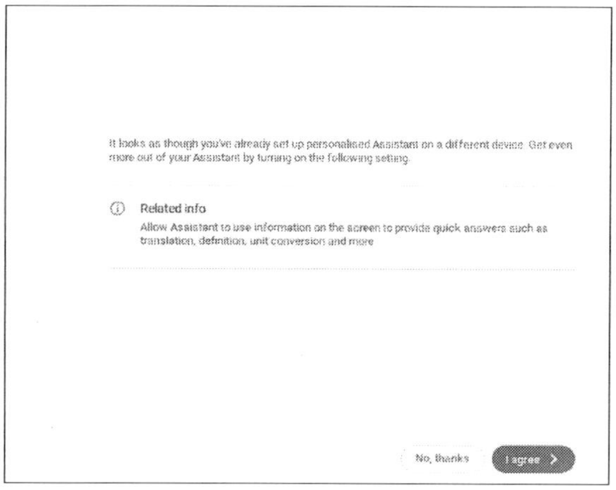

Now this person will be able to select their name from the login screen and use their own account.

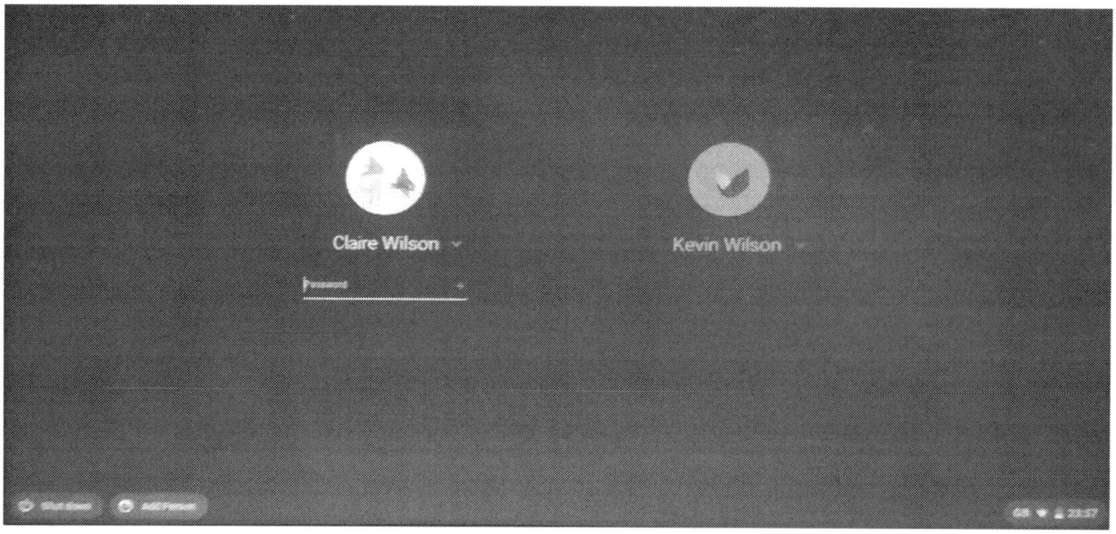

Deleting Users

On the login screen, select the small arrow next to the profile you want to remove.

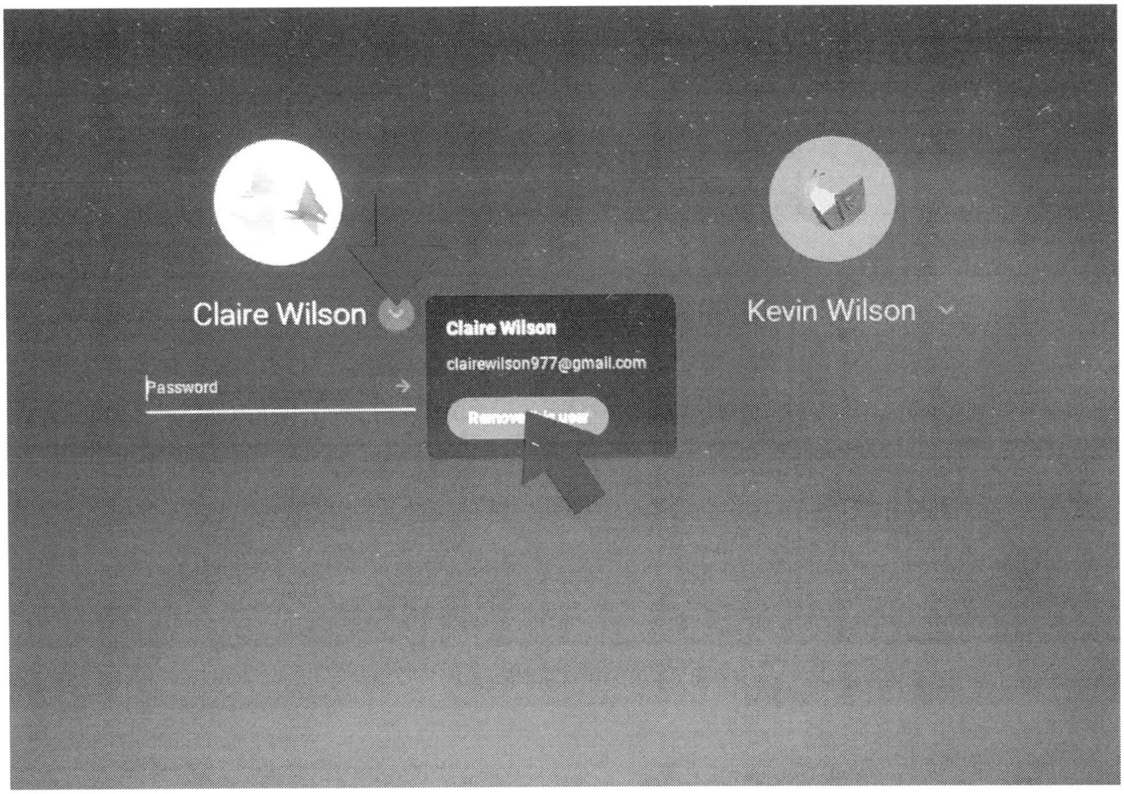

Select 'remove this user' from the popup menu. In the confirmation box that appears, select 'remove this user'.

This will completely remove the user from your chromebook.

Parental Controls

You can set up 'child accounts' on your chromebook. This allows you to impose limitations on apps and services they can access as well as monitor web activity.

You will be able to manage which websites your children can visit and block most sexually explicit and violent sites.

You can set Chrome to block most sexually explicit and violent sites.

Add a Child Account

First you'll need to add a new user - see 'adding a user' on page 51.

Set up Parental Controls

Sign into your chromebook with your child's account. Click the clock on the bottom right to open the system tray, then click the 'settings' icon.

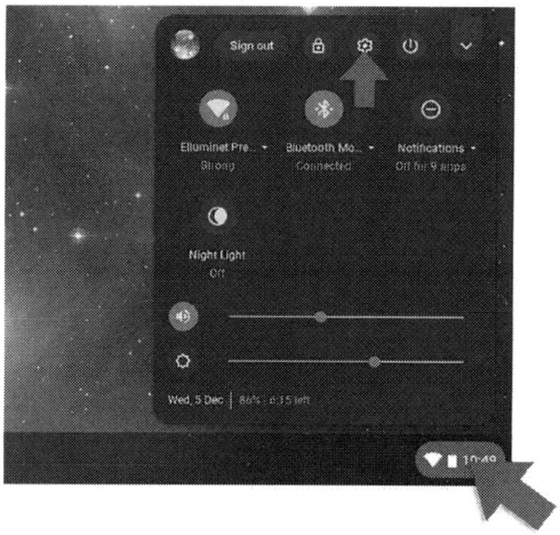

Select 'people' from the list on the left hand side, then click 'setup' next to 'parental controls'.

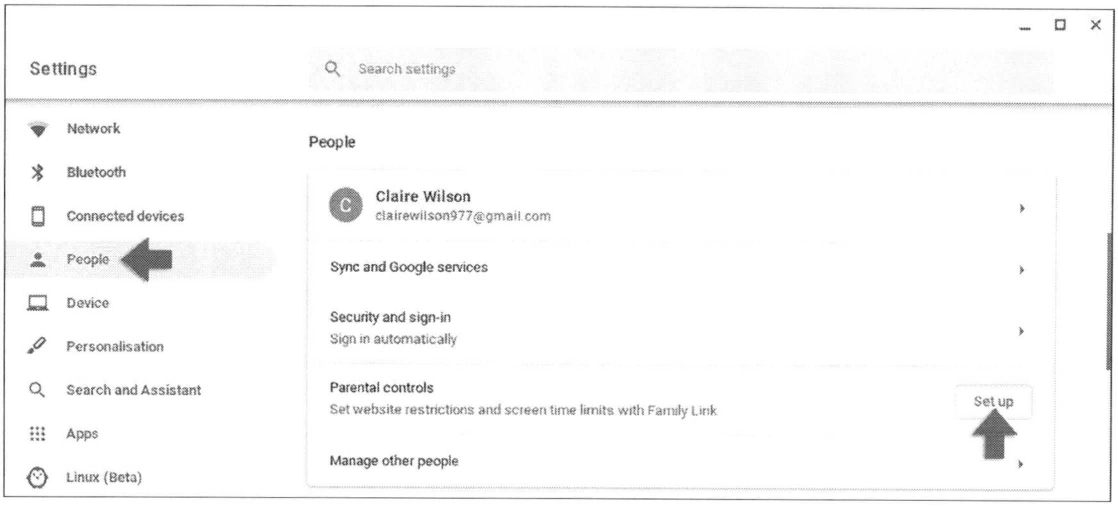

Select 'getting started'.

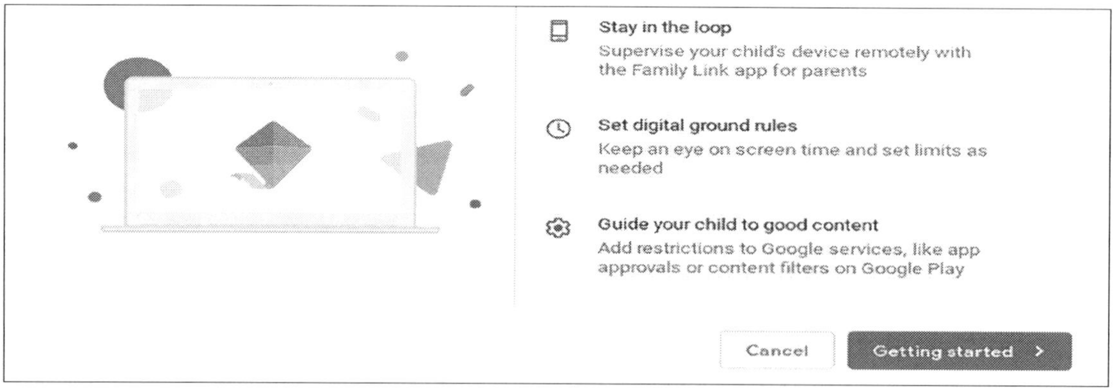

Click 'next' on the 'how to set up parental controls' screen. Then select 'yes' on the supervisor screen.

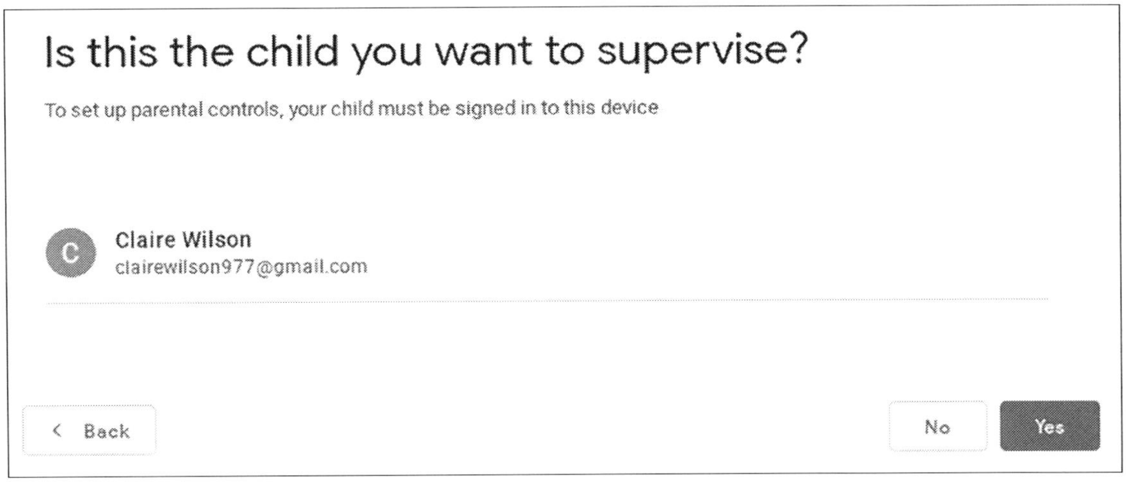

Click 'next'.

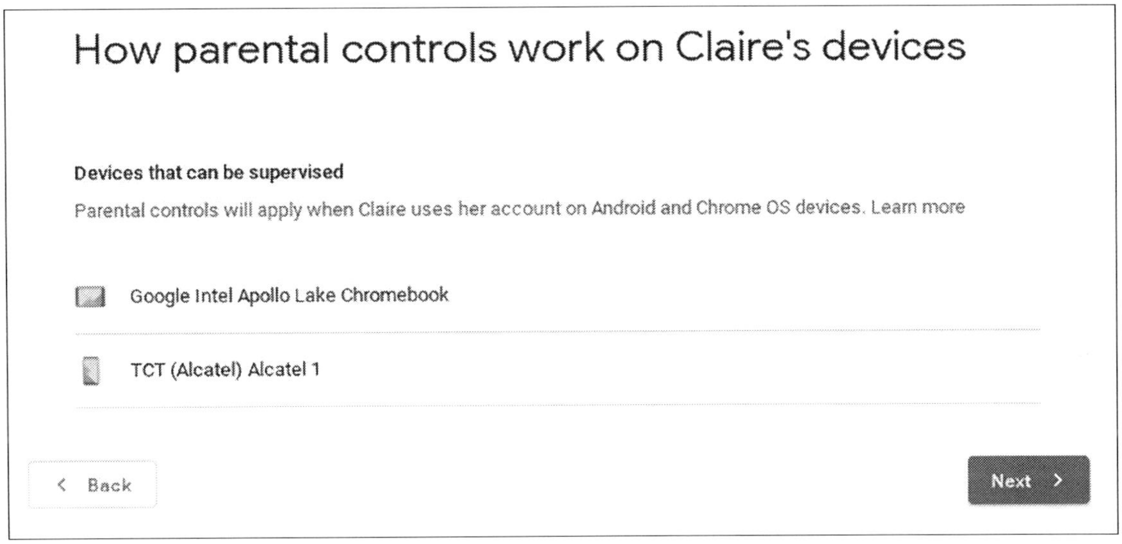

Now, sign in with your own Google account email and password.

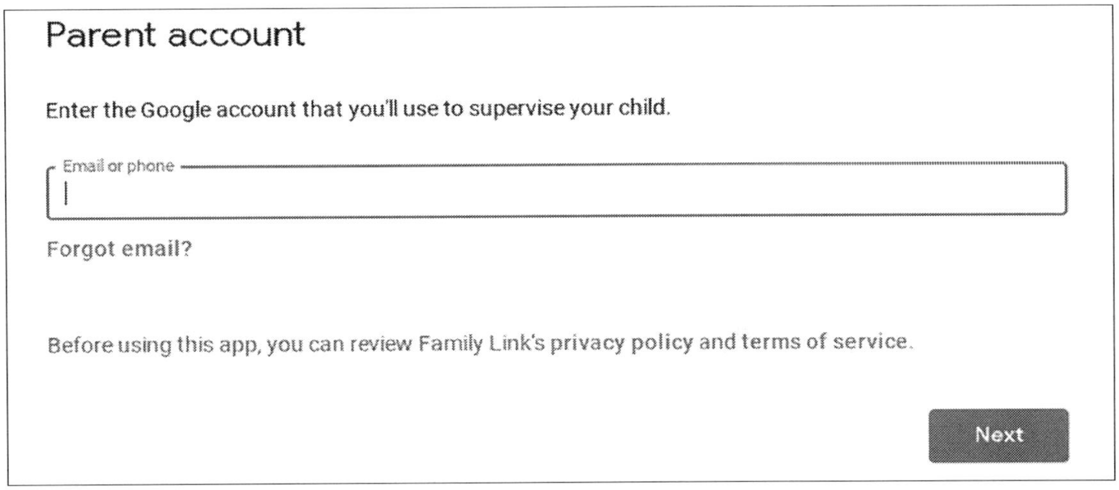

Scroll down to the bottom of the 'about supervision' page, enter the password for your child's account then click 'agree'.

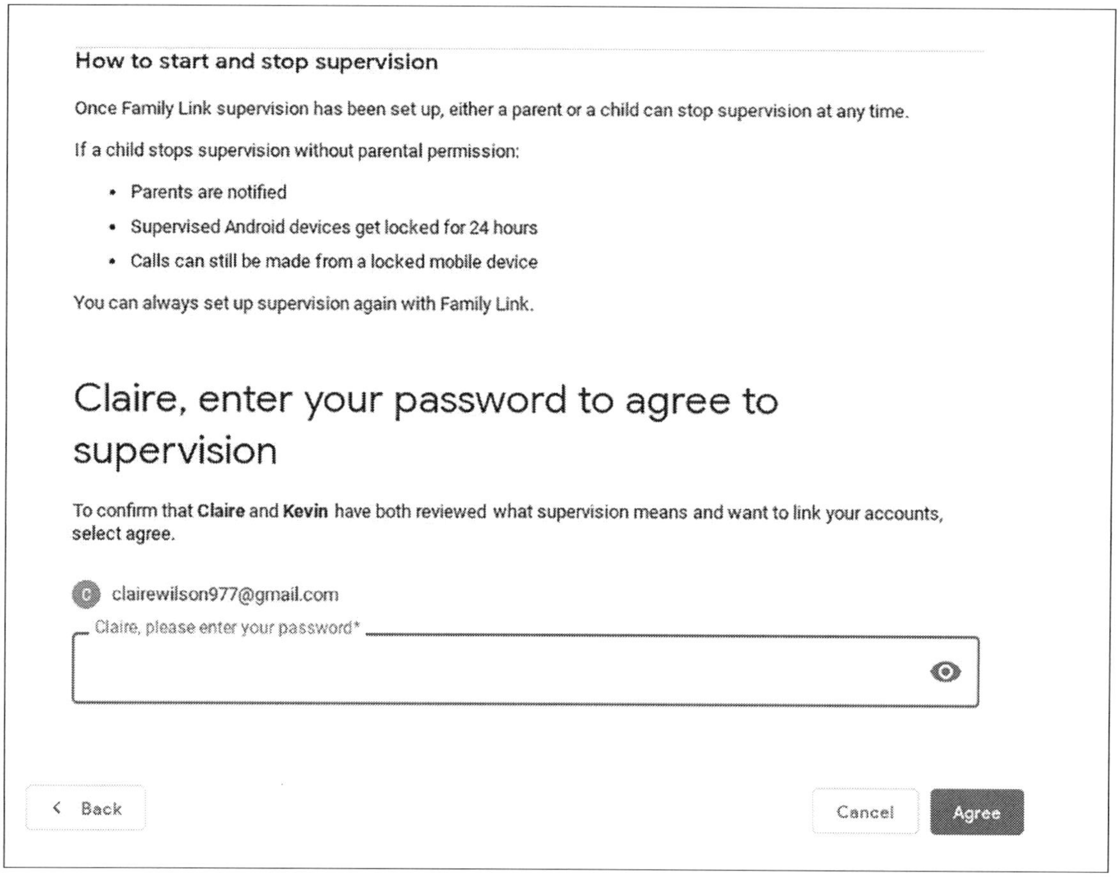

Your accounts will now be linked. Click 'next' on the confirmation screen.

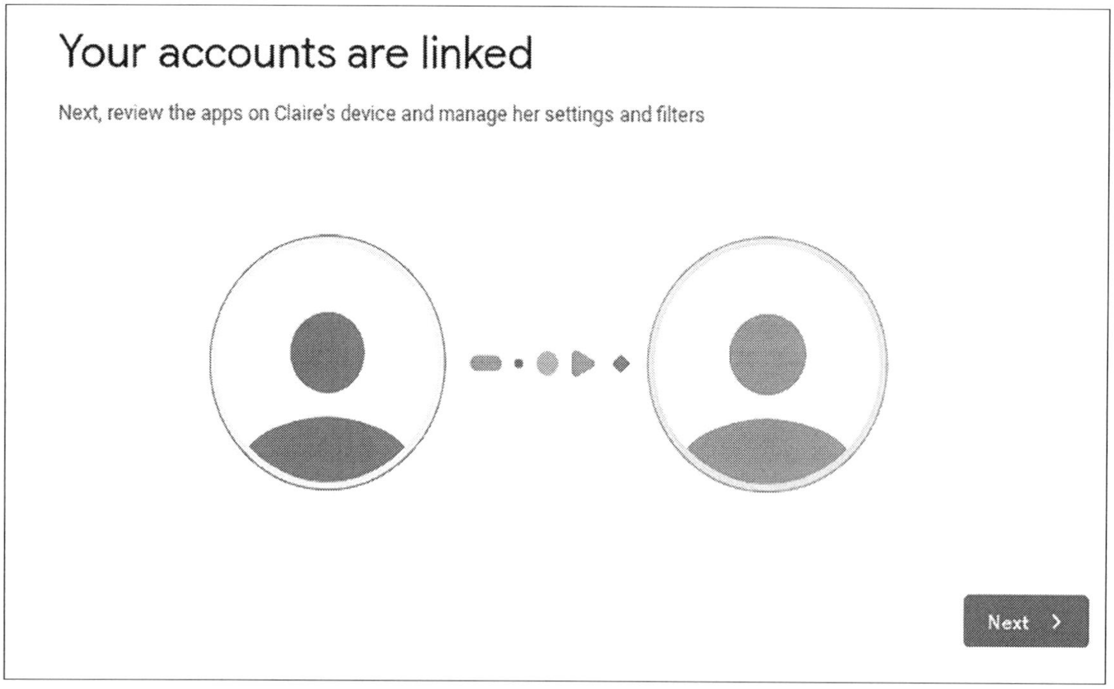

Now review the apps, un-select any apps you don't want your child to use. Scroll to the bottom and click 'next'.

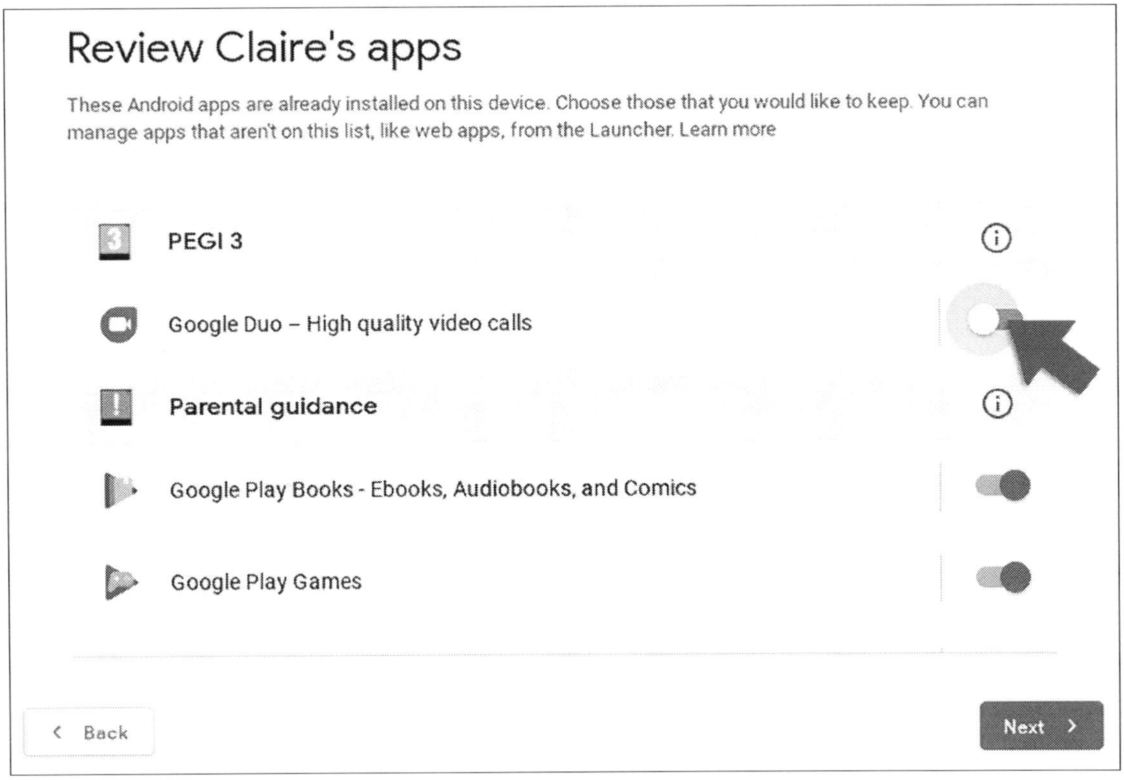

Scroll through the filters, click each one to review the settings. Most of these you can leave on the default settings. Click 'next'.

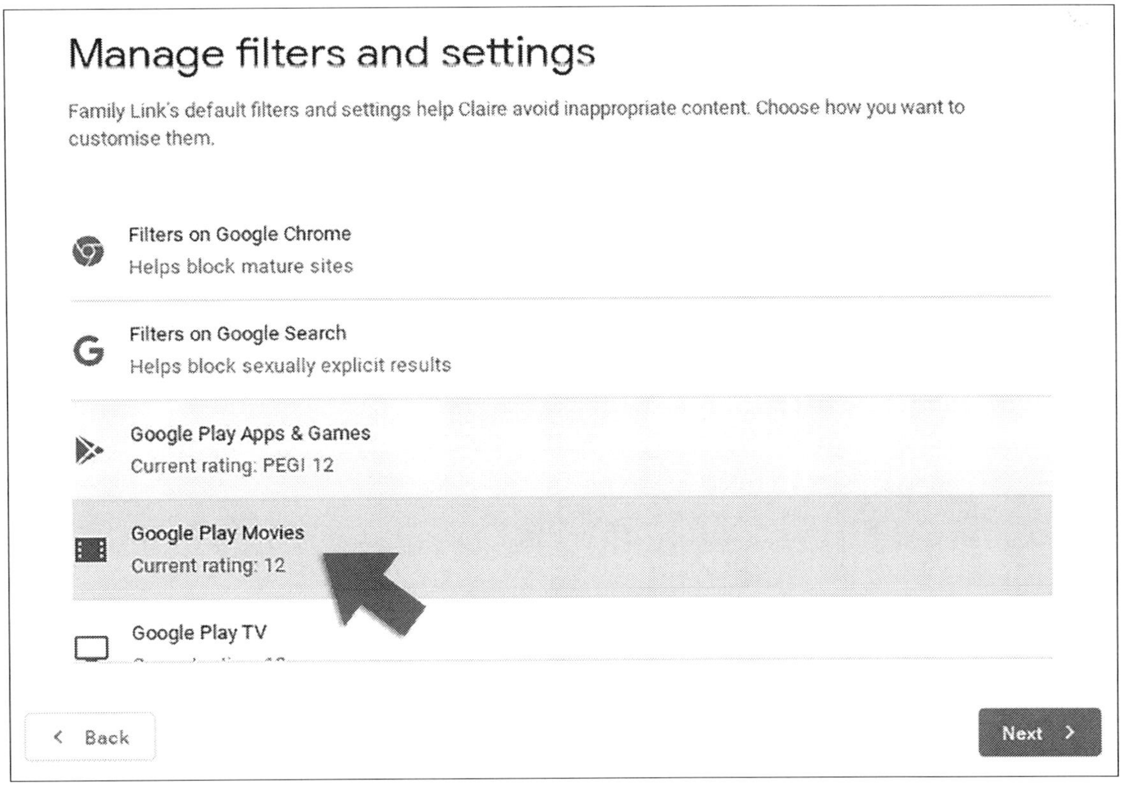

Click 'next' on the 'supervise from personal device' screen. Then select the devices you want to install 'family link' on. This allows you to monitor what your child is doing from your other devices such as your phone. Select them all then click 'install'.

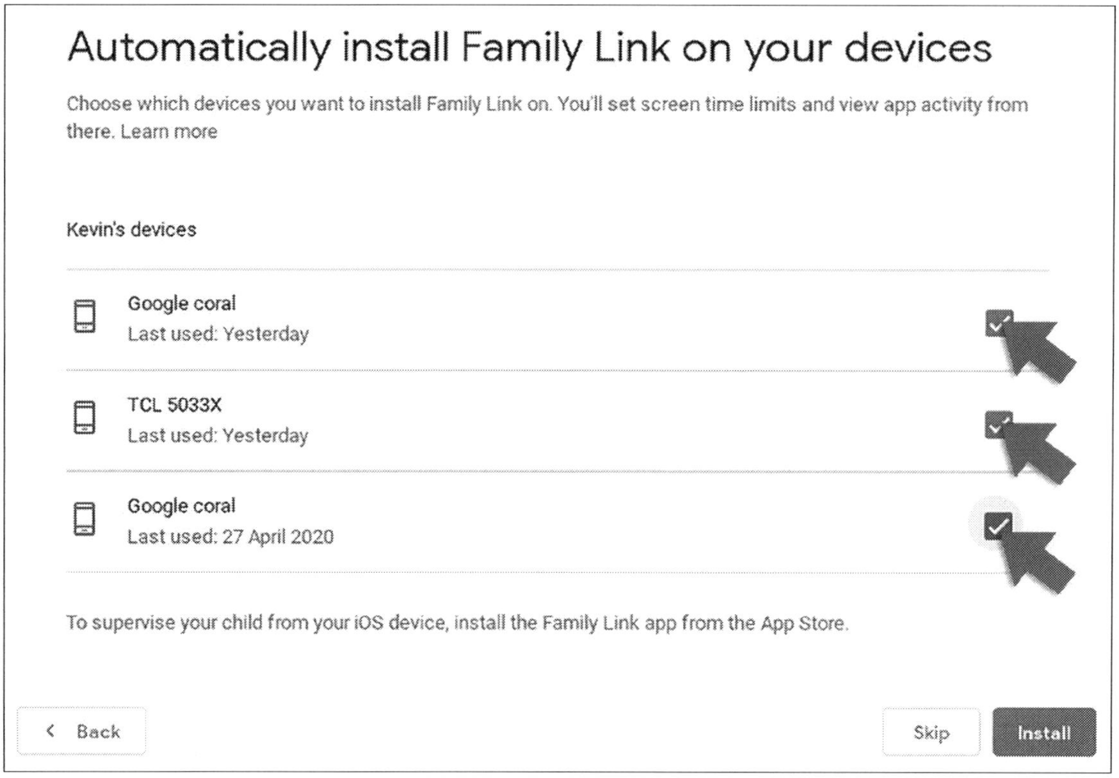

Click 'next'

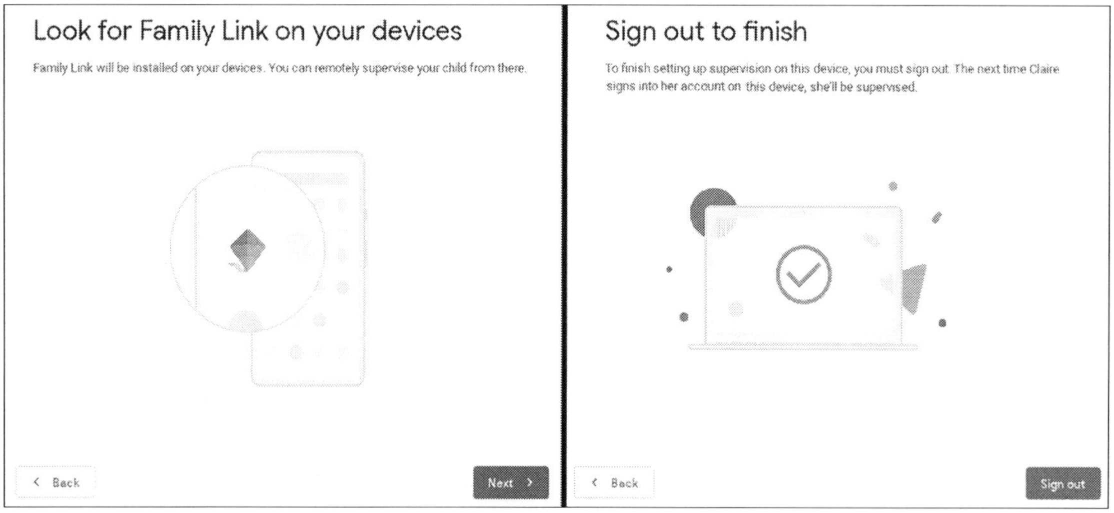

Click 'sign out'.

When you sign into your device, the 'family link' app will be installed automatically. You'll find the app on your launcher. If not, go to the google play store and search for and install 'family link'.

Monitoring Child Accounts with Family Link

Once you have set up your child account and enabled parental controls as discussed in the previous section, you can use family link to monitor your child's online activity. To do this, make sure you're signed in with your own account - not a child's account, then click the circle icon on the bottom left of your screen to open app launcher.

Click the arrow on the top middle of the launcher to open it up.

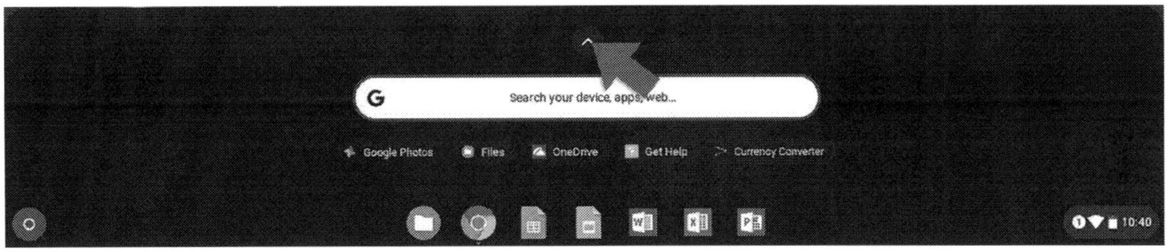

Click the 'family link' icon.

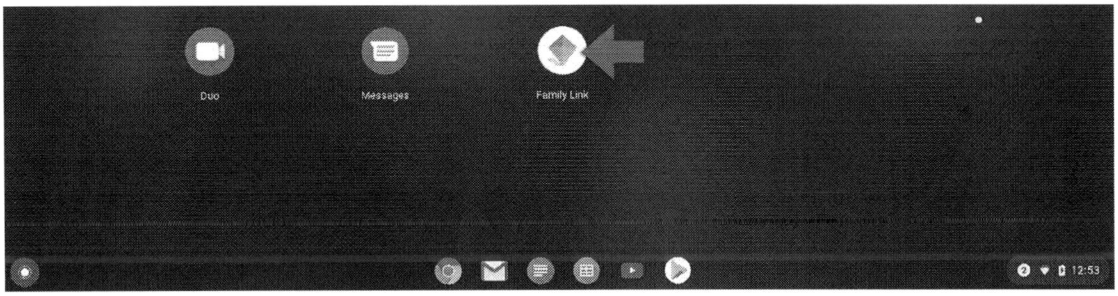

Click the blue arrow to scroll through the intro... click 'get started'.

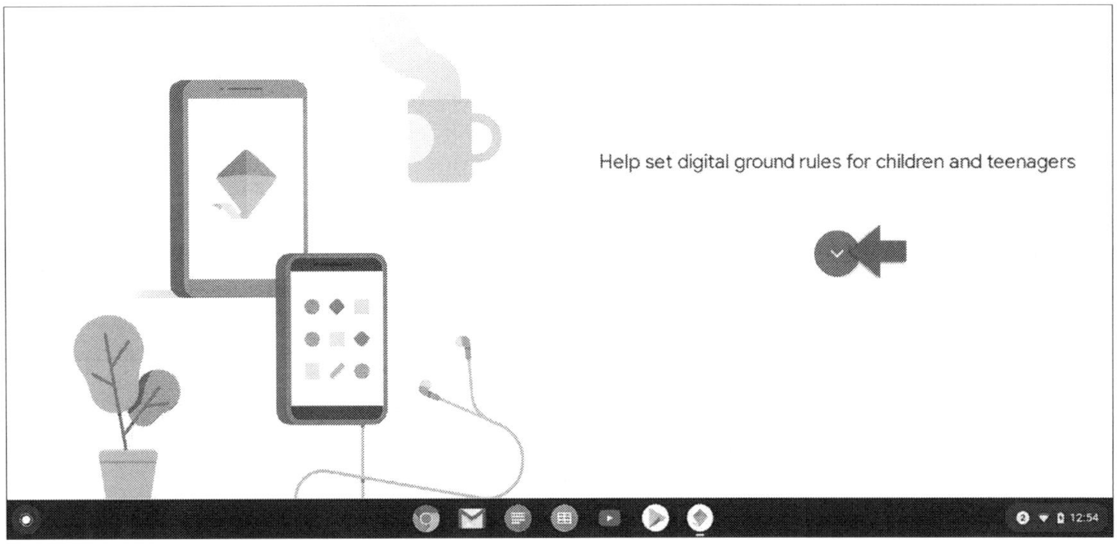

Allow or Block Apps

Open family link and select your child's account. Scroll down to the 'apps installed' section, then click 'more'.

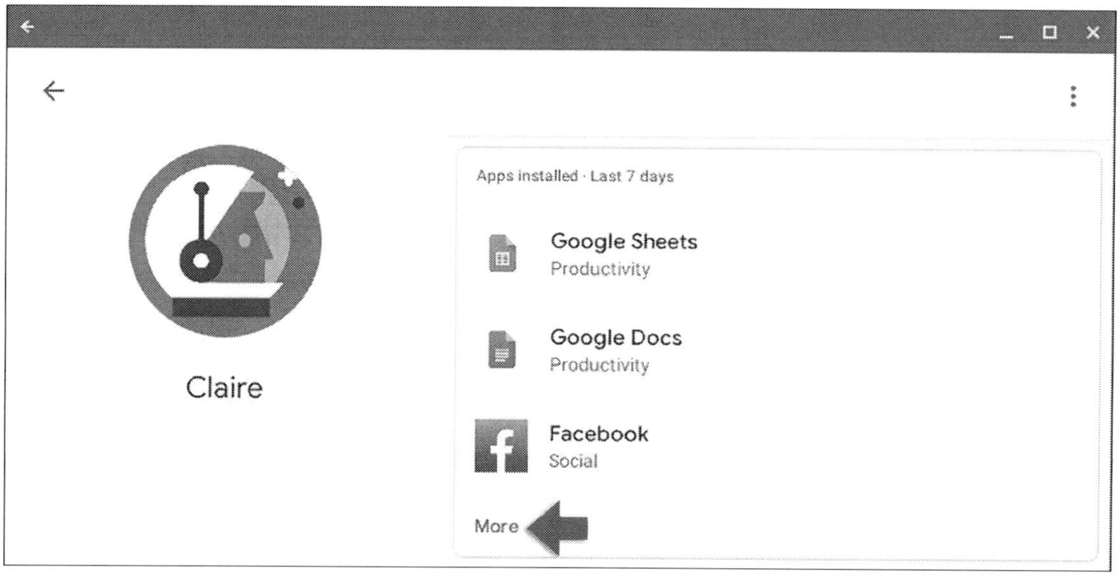

Select the 'limits' tab, then tap the block/allow icon next to the app you want to allow or block.

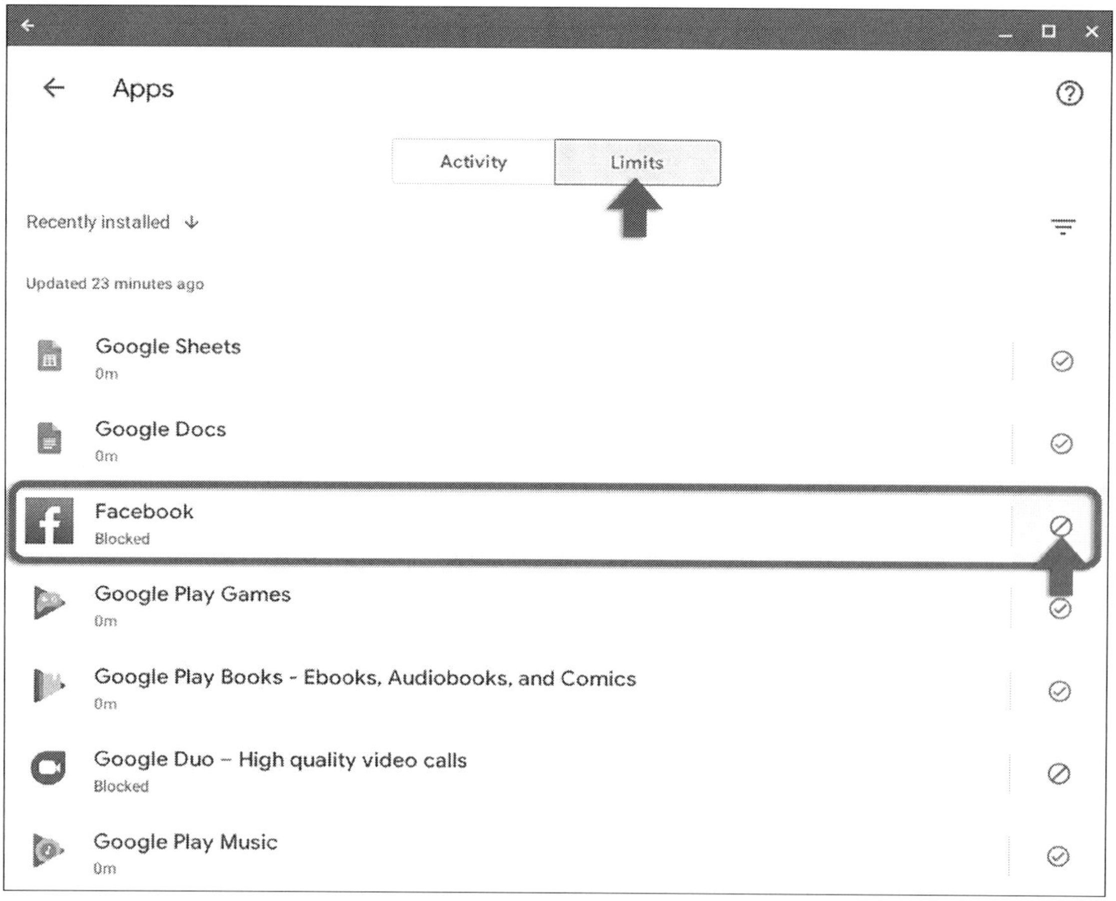

Manage Web Browsing

Open family link and select your child's account. Click manage settings, then select 'filters on Google Chrome'.

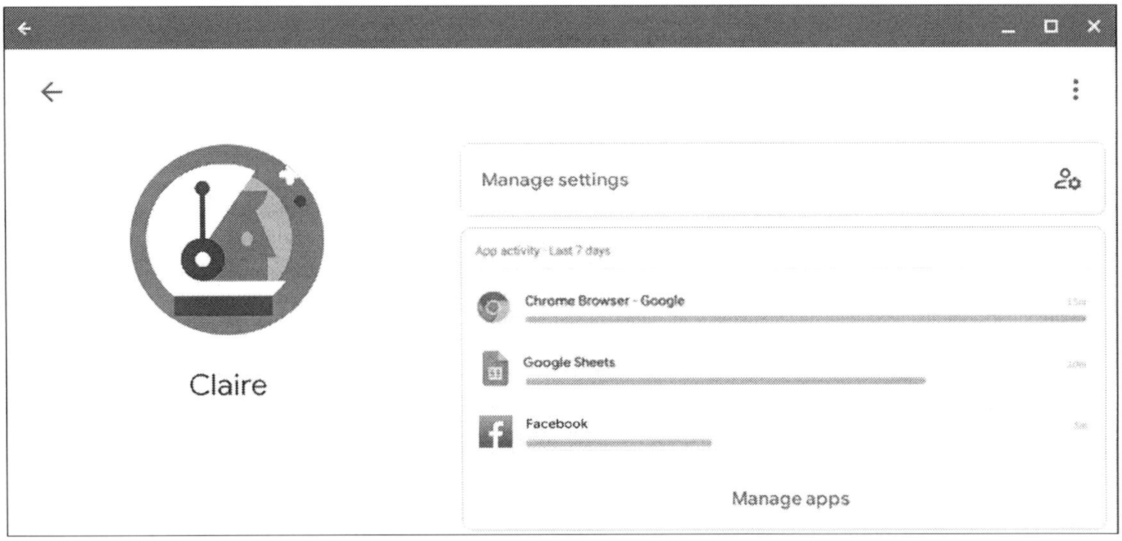

Choose the setting that's right for your family: allow all sites, try to block mature sites, or only allow certain sites.

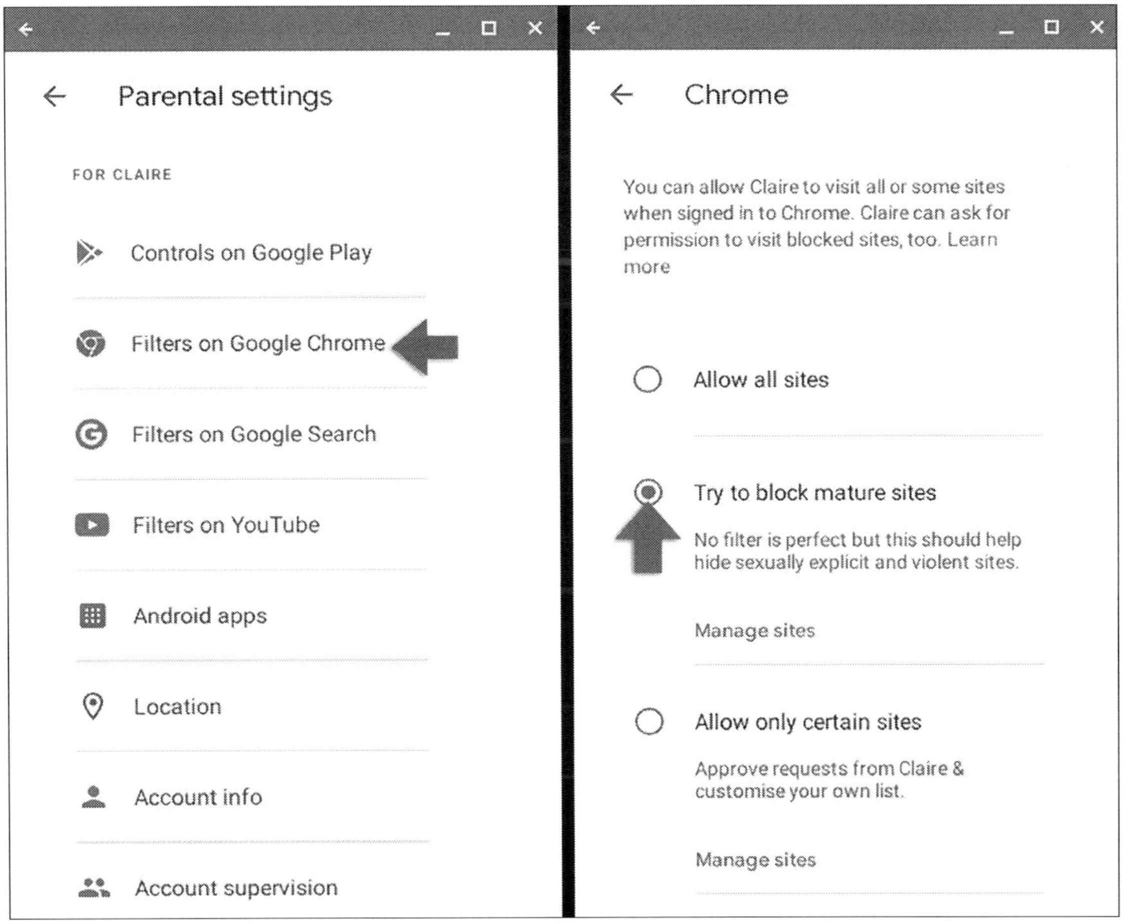

To allow or block a website, click 'manage settings'. On the 'manage sites' pop up dialog select whether you want to block or approve a website. Eg select 'blocked' to block a website.

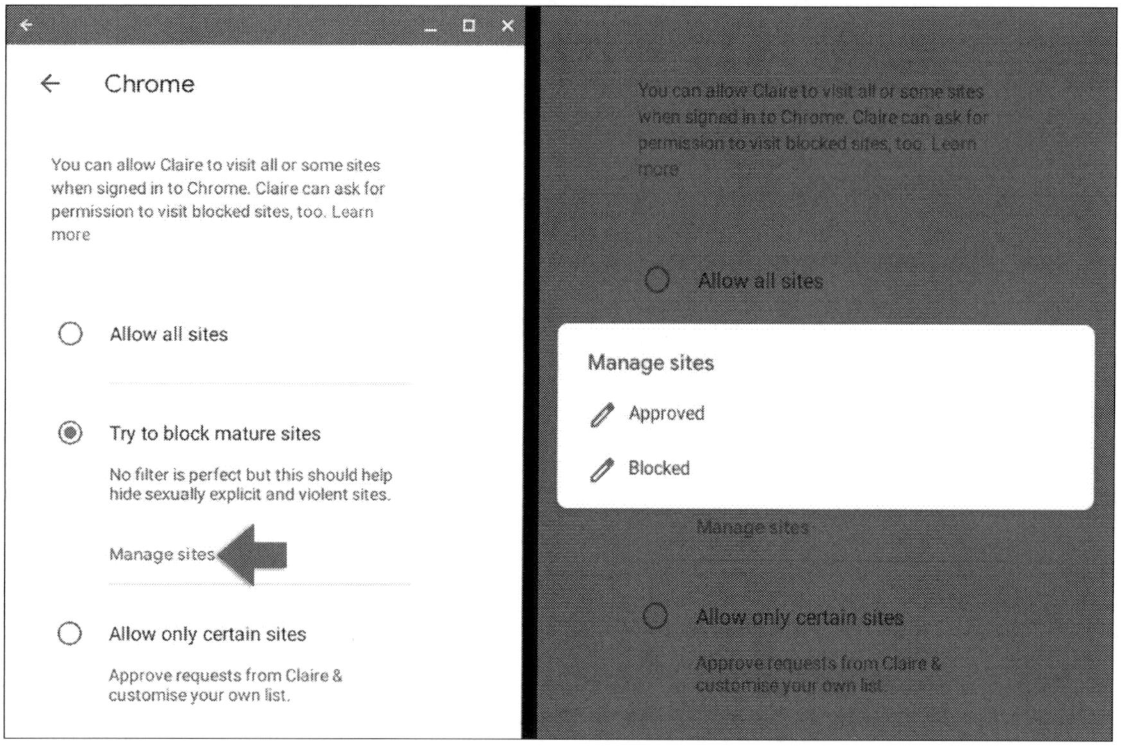

Click 'add a website', then type in the website address or domain. Eg bigfishgames.com

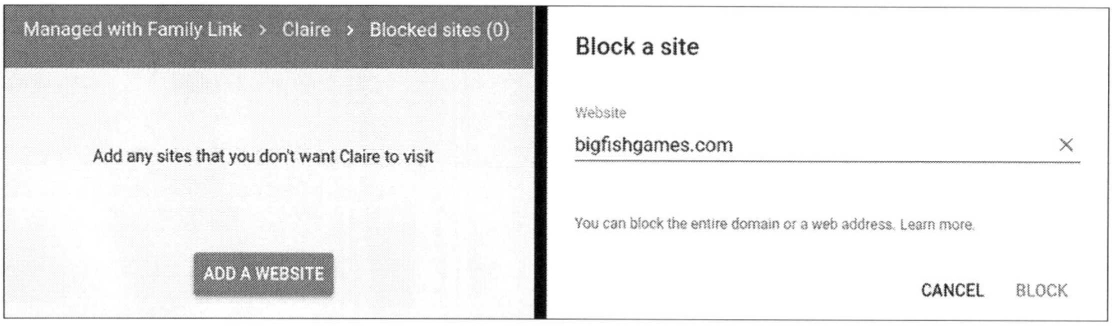

Click 'block'. (or 'allow' if you're approving a website).

To release the website click the small x on the right.

Configuring Other Settings

To change settings on your Chromebook, click the clock on the bottom right to open the system tray, then click the 'settings' icon.

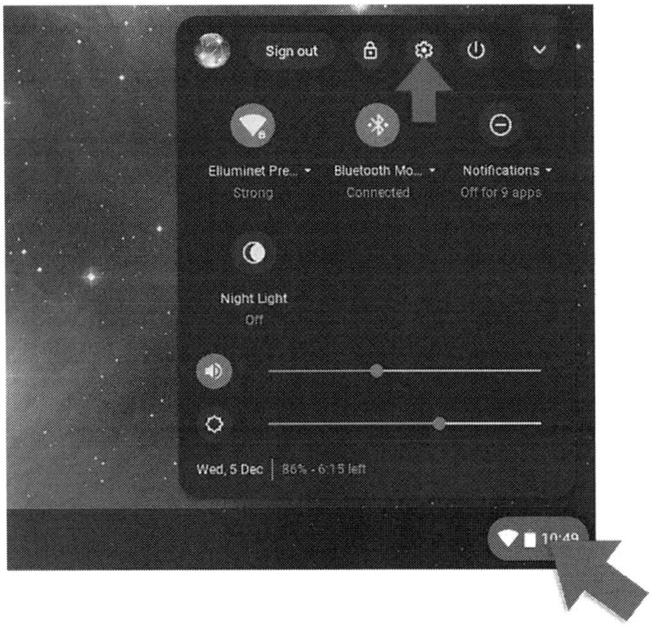

From here, you can configure settings. Settings are divided into categories which you'll find listed down the left hand side of the window. Select one of these to jump to the settings.

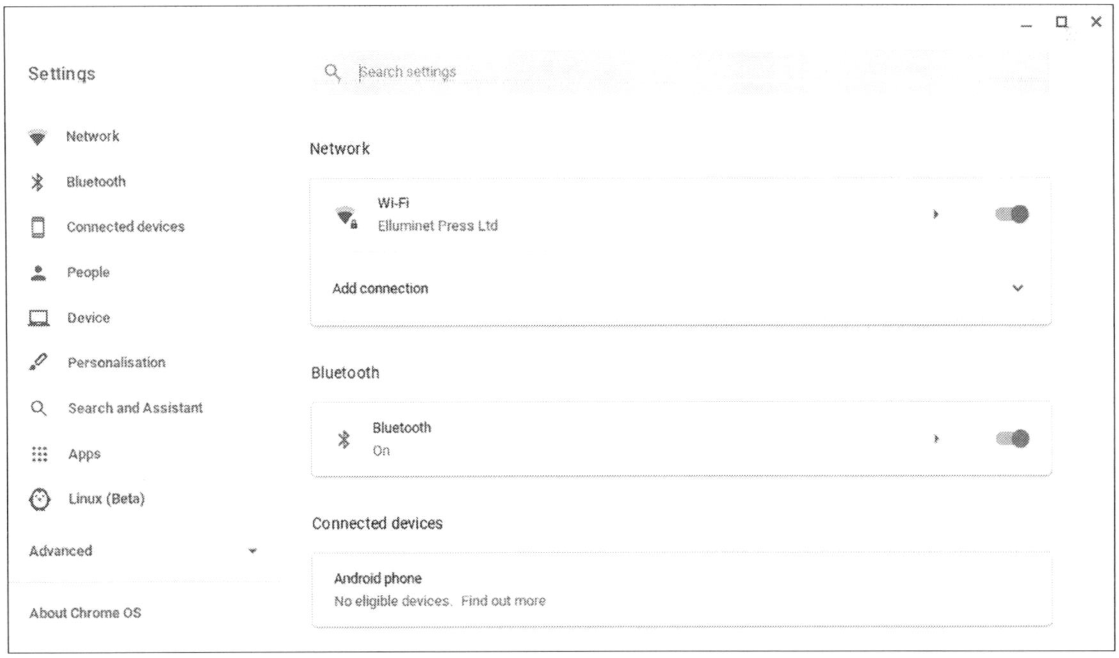

You can also search for a setting. To do this, type the name of the setting into the 'search settings' field on the top of the screen.

Mouse & Touchpad

To configure your mouse and touchpad settings, select 'device' from the list on the left hand side of the settings window.

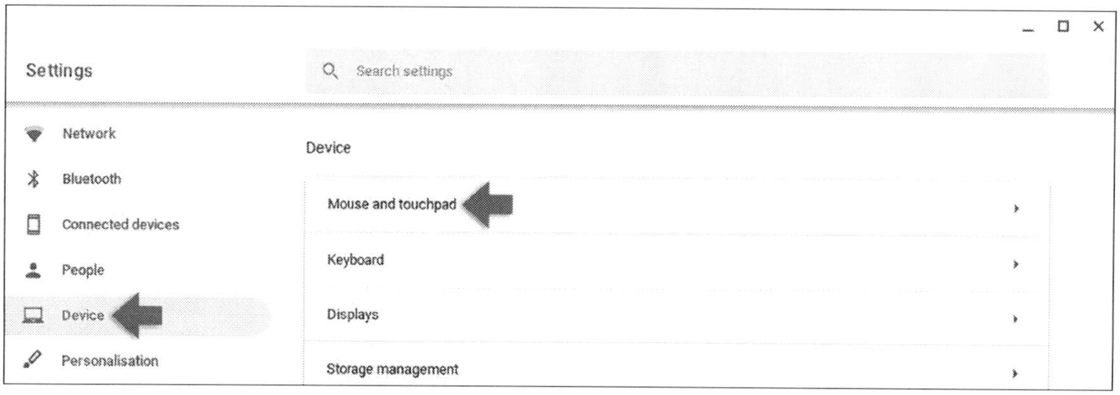

If you have a mouse connected, you can swap the mouse buttons - useful if you're left handed. You can also reverse the scrolling. Enable mouse acceleration makes it easier to control the mouse pointer, so the mouse pointer moves faster when you move the mouse faster and slower when you move the mouse slowly. Mouse speed allows you to increase the mouse pointer speed and sensitivity.

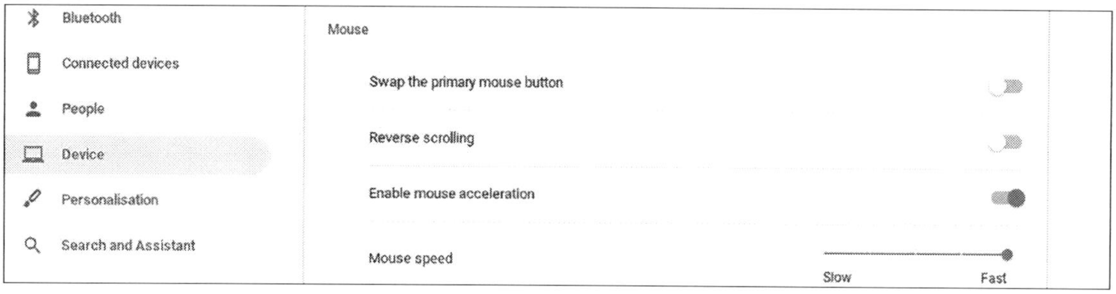

Similarly on the touchpad settings.

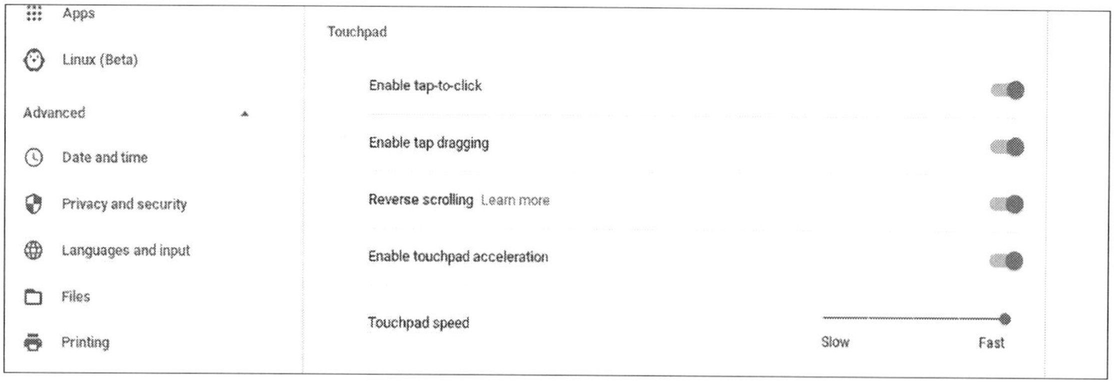

Tap click allows you to tap on an icon instead of having to press the touchpad or touchpad button. Tap dragging allows you to tap and hold on an object and drag it to another position on the screen.

Internal Display Settings

Select 'devices' from the list on the left hand side of the settings window, then select 'displays'.

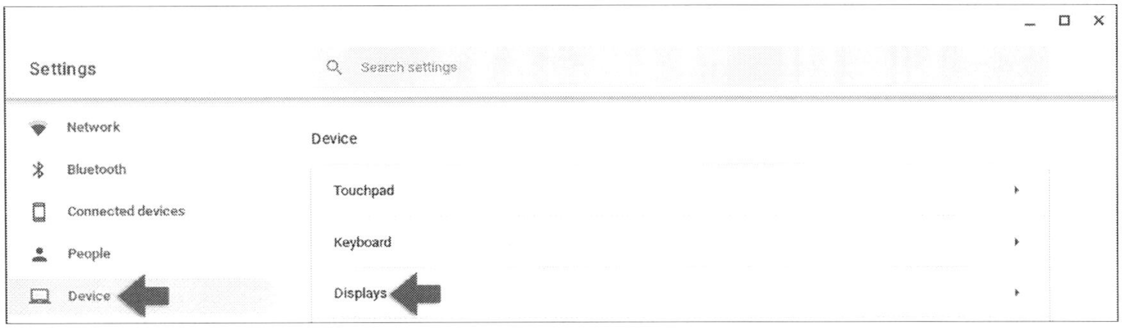

To adjust your chromebook screen, select 'internal display'.

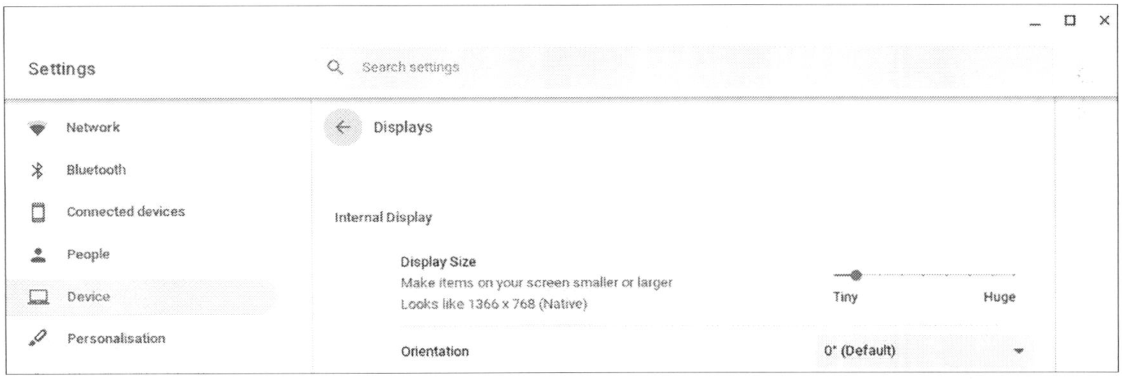

Use the 'display size' slider to make items on your screen smaller or larger. Use the 'orientation' drop down menu to rotate your screen. You can also toggle between the rotations by pressing ctrl, shift and refresh on your keyboard.

You can also turn on the night light. This reduces the amount of blue light coming from your screen. Click the slider switch next to 'night light' to enable/disable.

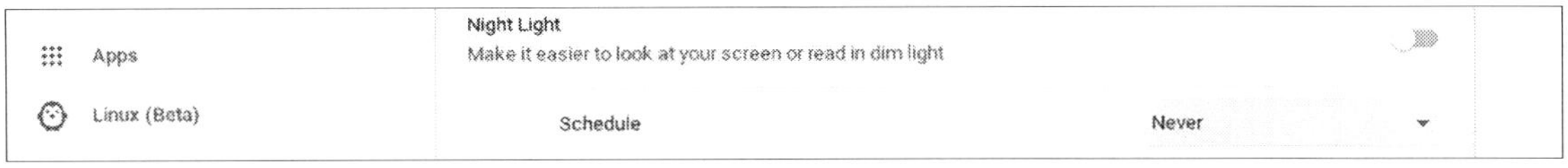

You can also schedule this, click the drop down menu next to 'schedule'. Select 'sunset to sunrise' to automatically turn it on at night. Click 'customise' to select a time to turn it on and a time to turn it off.

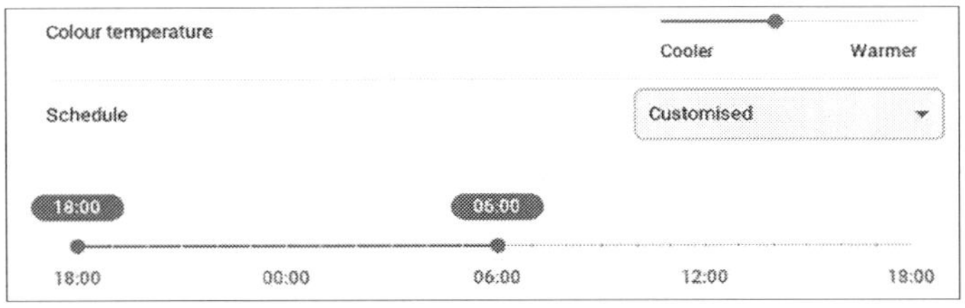

External Display Settings

An external display could be a TV, monitor, or projector. Your Chromebook usually does a good job at detecting the correct resolution for a display. To configure an external screen, open your settings.

Select 'devices' from the list on the left hand side, then select 'displays'.

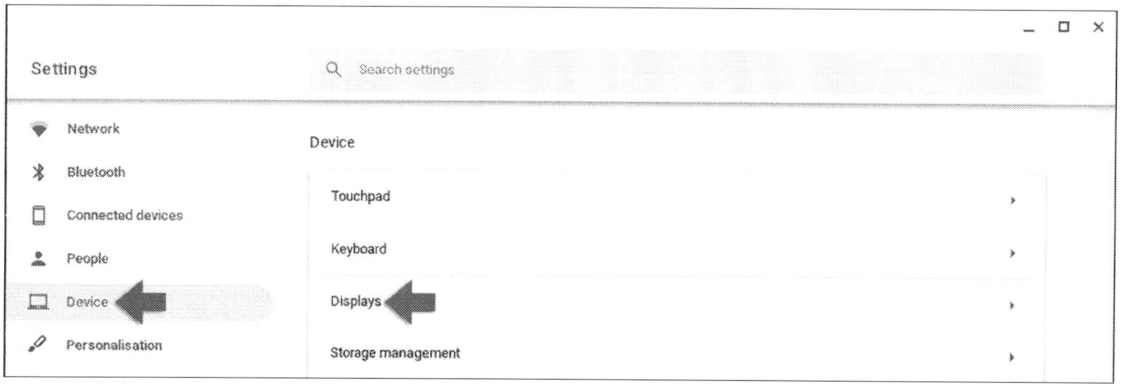

Under the 'arrangement' section, arrange the displays so the external screen extends the left or right side of your internal display.

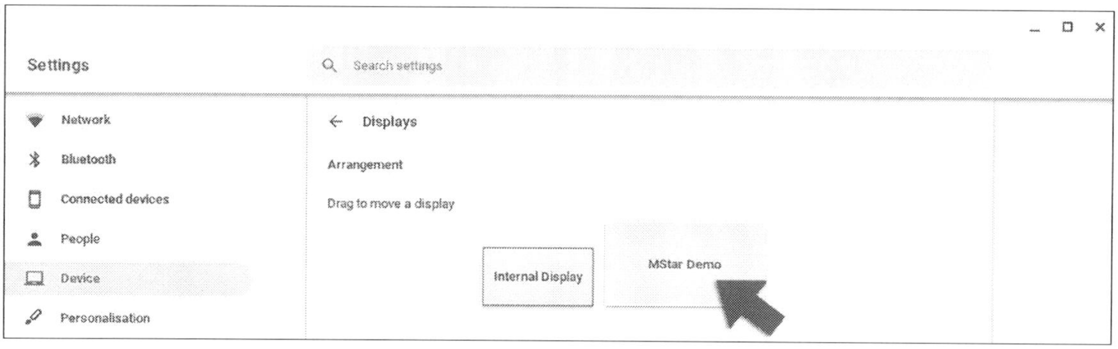

It's best to mirror your setup. If your external screen is on the right of your chromebook, move the rectangle to the right of the 'internal display' as shown below.

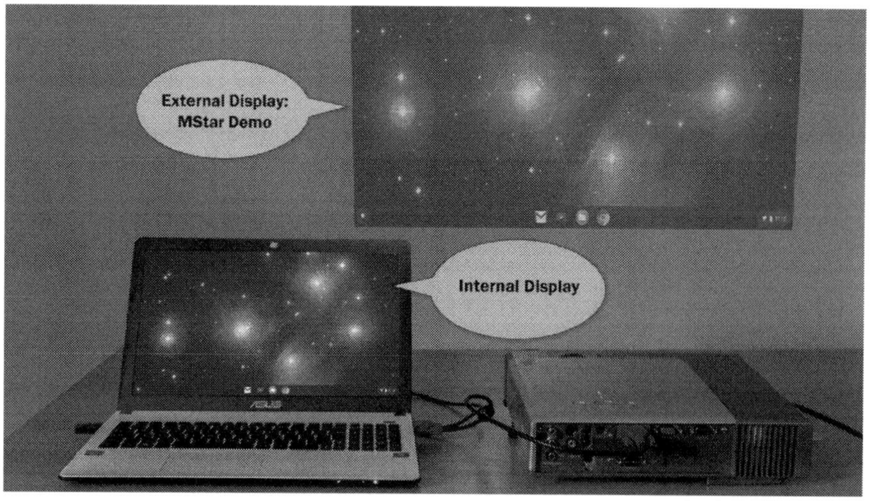

To adjust an external screen, select the screen name.

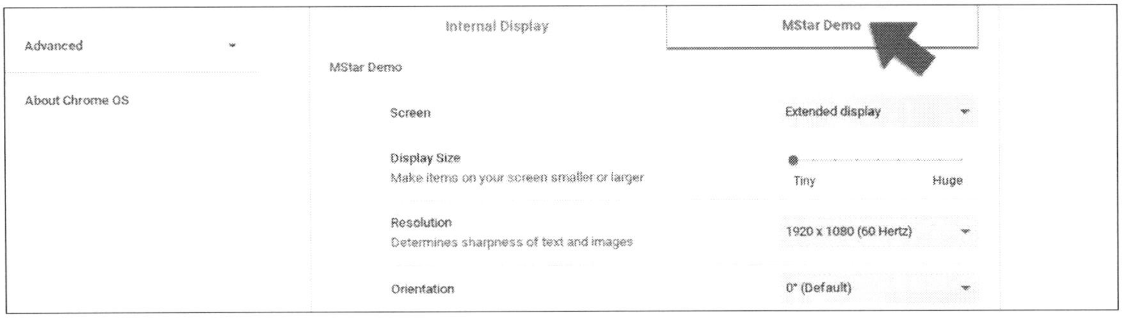

Use the 'screen' drop down to extend the display - make the external screen an extension of the internal display. Change the drop down to 'mirror internal display' if you want both screens to project the same image.

Use the 'display size' slider to make items on your screen smaller or larger.

Use the 'resolution' drop down to change the external screen's resolution (eg 1920x1080 is HD).

Use the 'orientation' drop down menu to rotate your screen. You can also toggle between the rotations by pressing ctrl, shift and refresh on your keyboard.

Time Zone

The time zone on your chromebook usually sets itself according to your location. If you need to change it, you'll find the option in the settings. Click 'advanced' on the left hand side, then click 'date and time'.

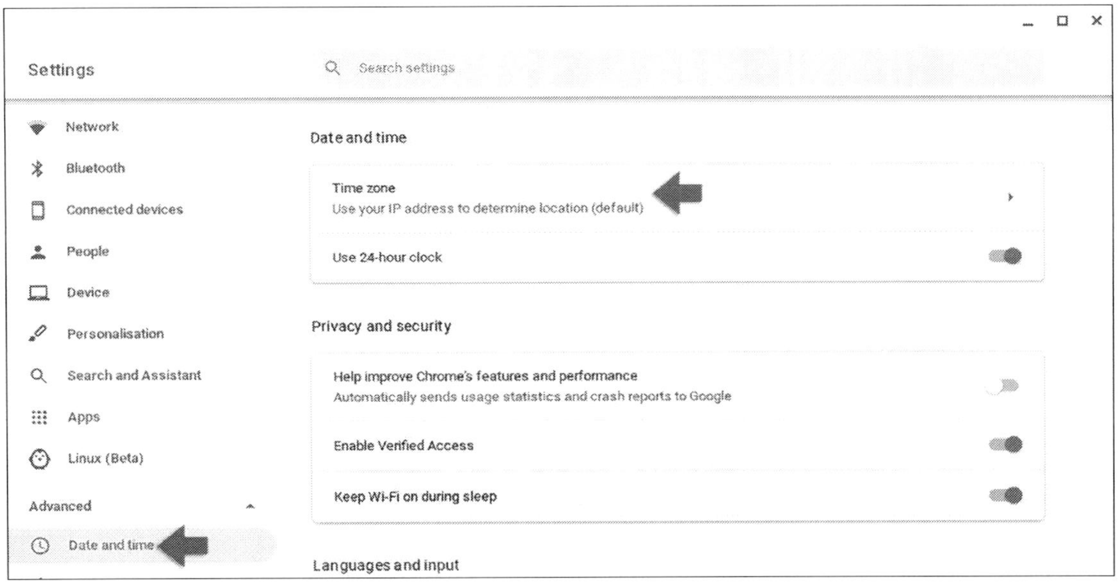

Select 'choose from list', select a time zone from the drop down menu.

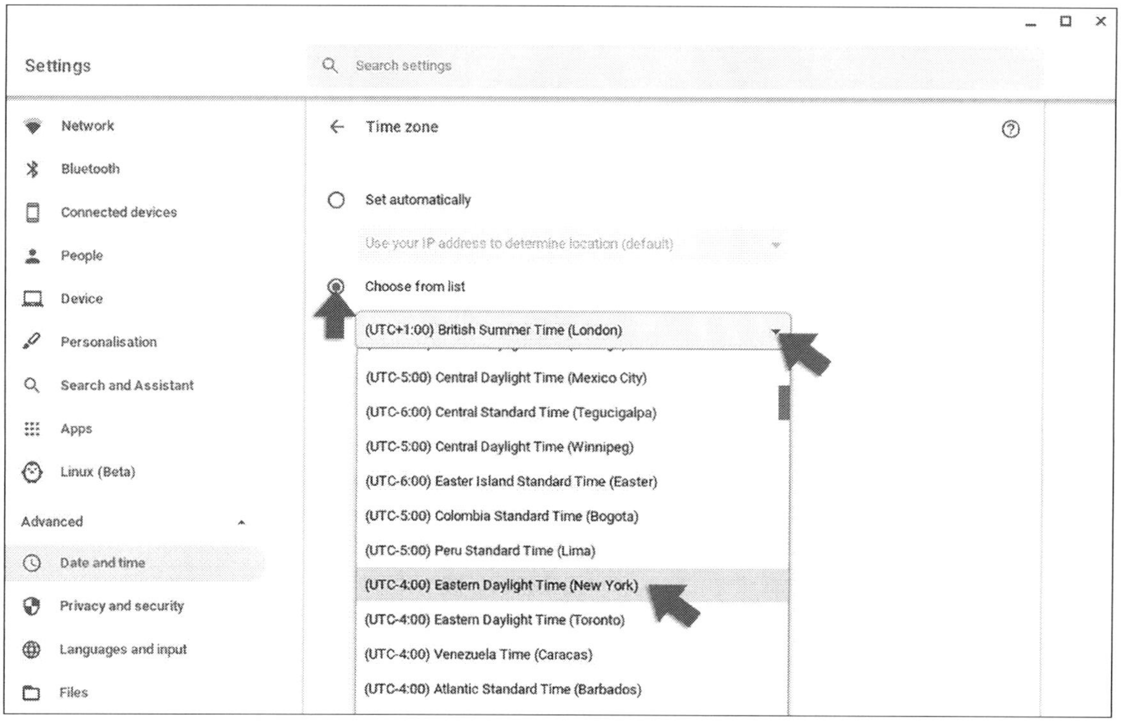

Change Language

You can change the display language from the settings. To do this open the settings window and select 'advanced', then click 'languages and input'.

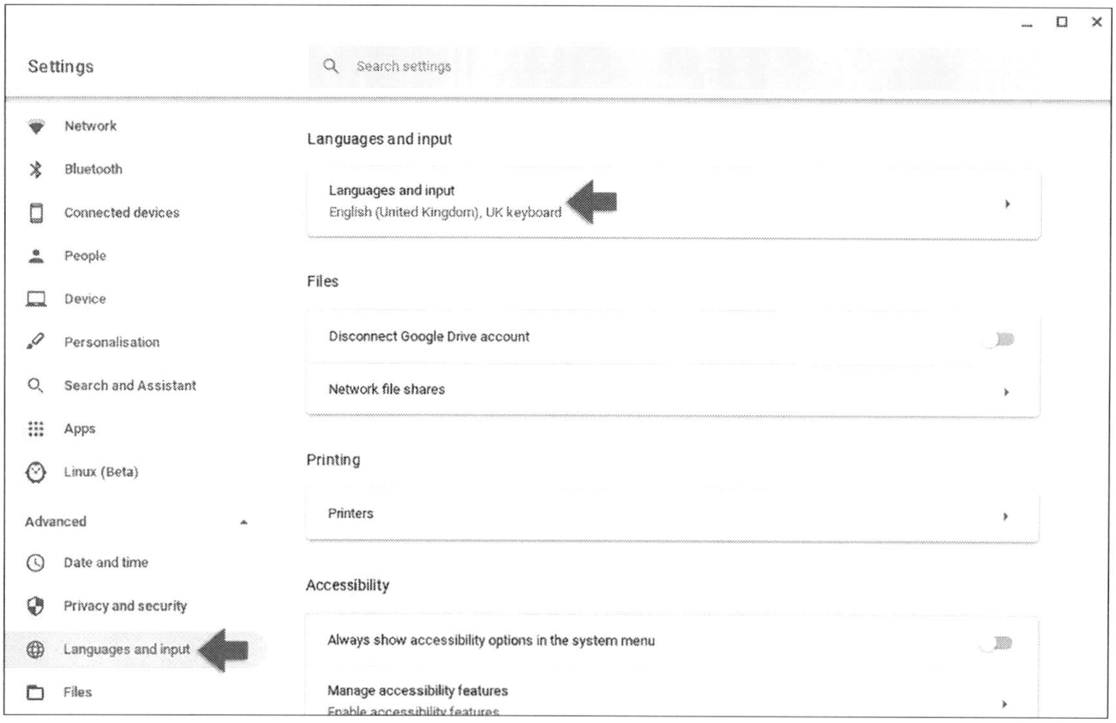

Click 'add languages' and select the language you want from the list.

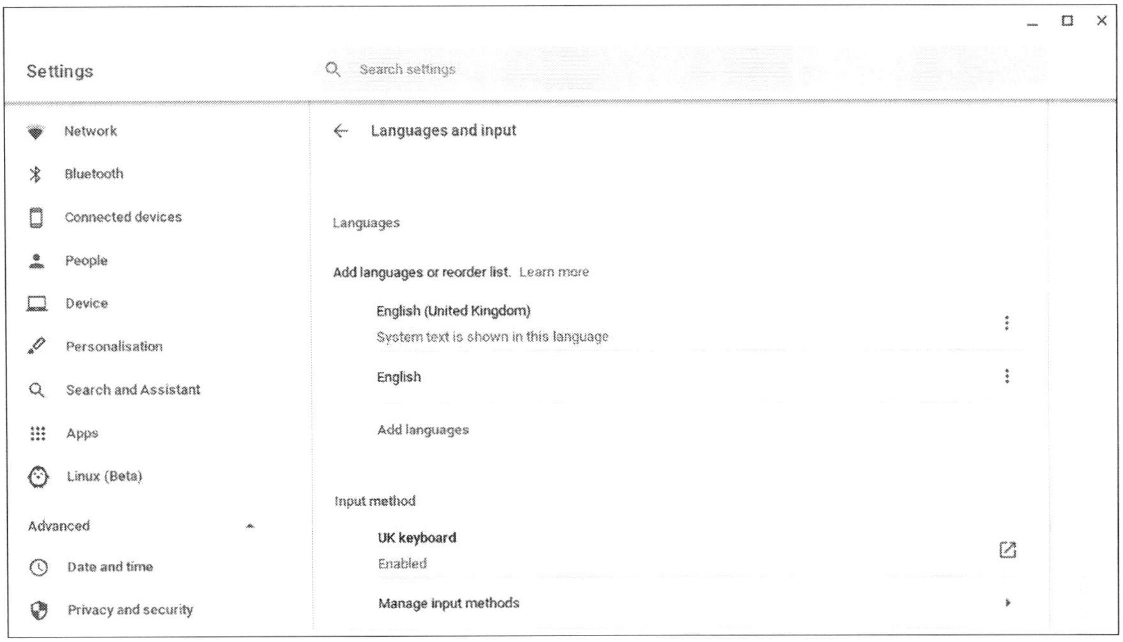

Click the three dots icon next to the language you just added. From the drop down menu select 'show system text in this language'.

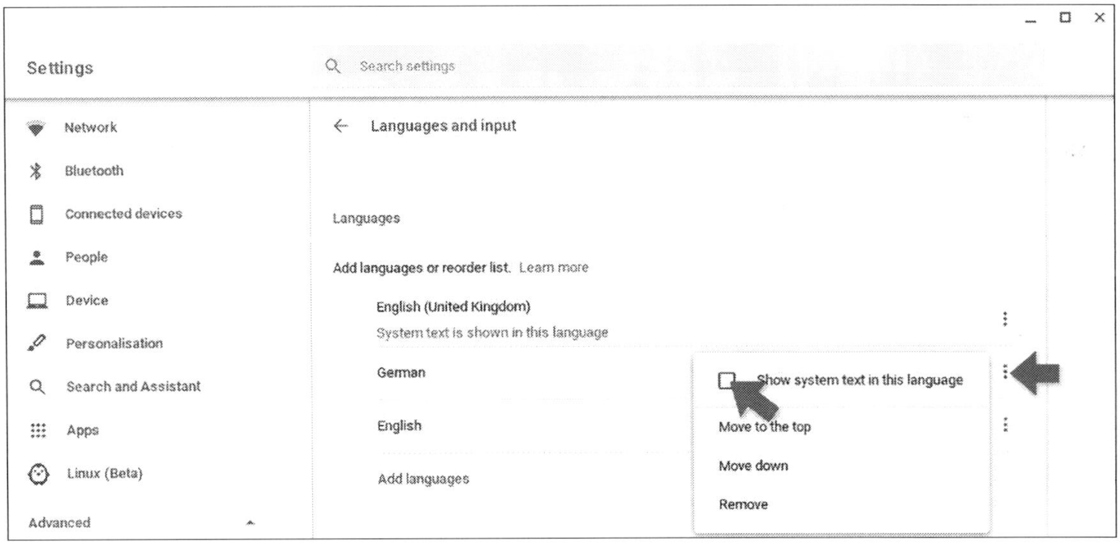

Then click 'restart now'.

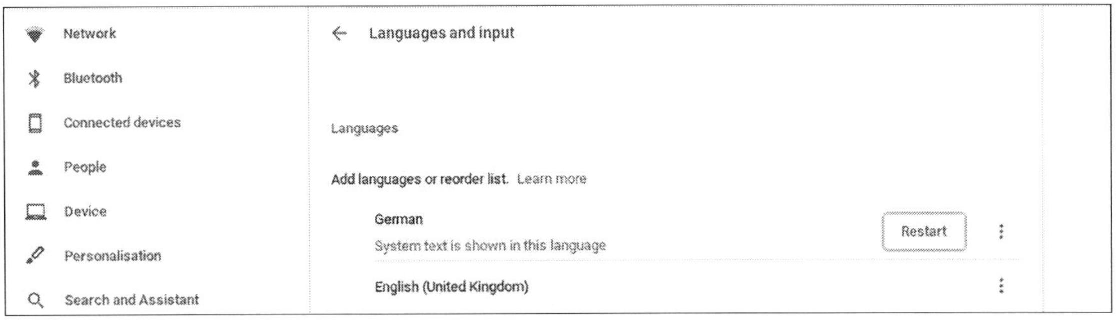

Keyboard Layout

You can change the keyboard layout from the settings. To do this open the settings window and select 'advanced', then click 'languages and input'.

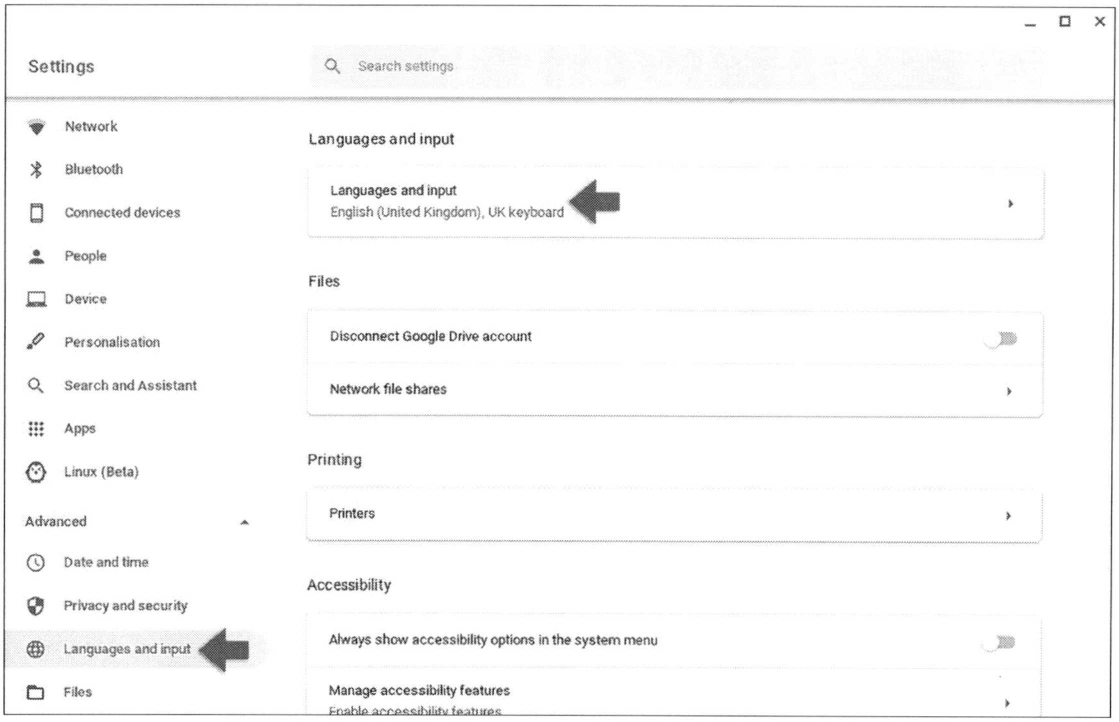

From the 'input method' section, click 'manage input methods'.

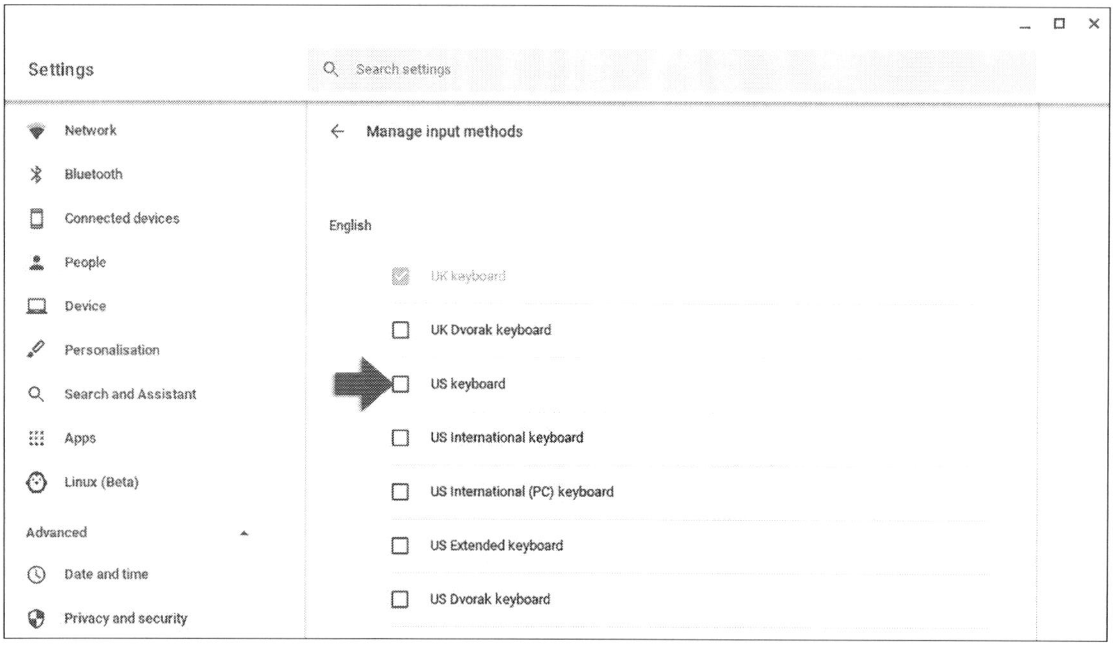

Select a keyboard layout. If your keyboard isn't listed, make sure you've added the corresponding language in the previous section.

Keyboard Settings

You can change the keyboard settings such as auto-correct, and edit dictionary entries. To do this open the settings window and select 'advanced', then click 'languages and input'.

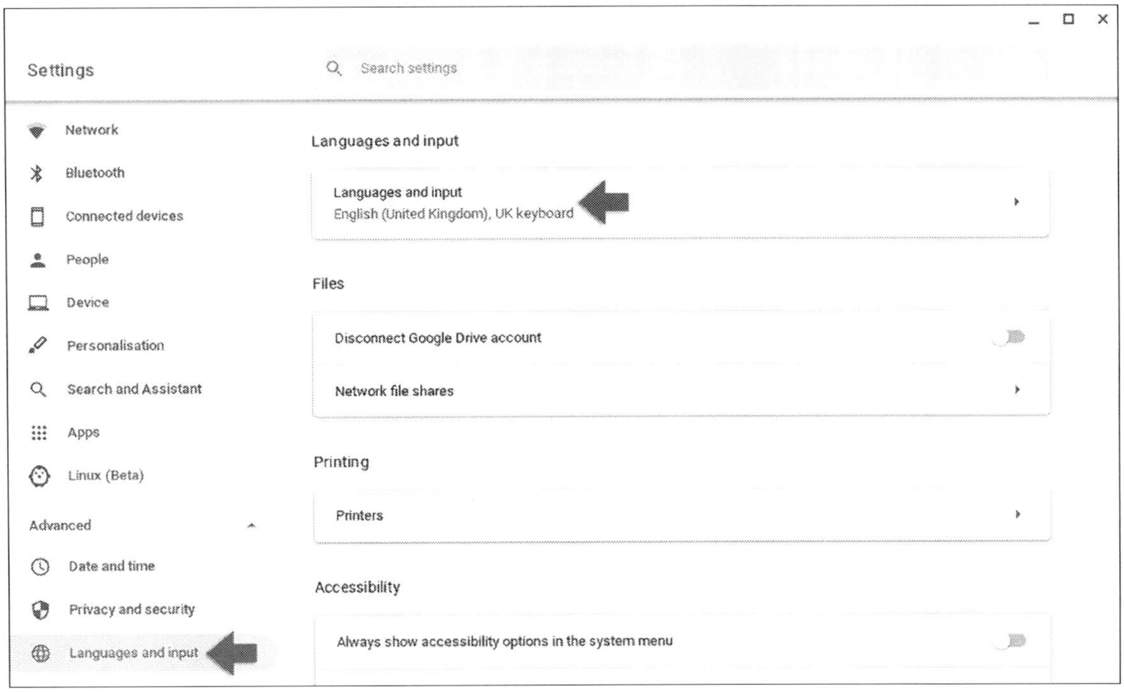

Click the icon next to your keyboard under the 'input method' section

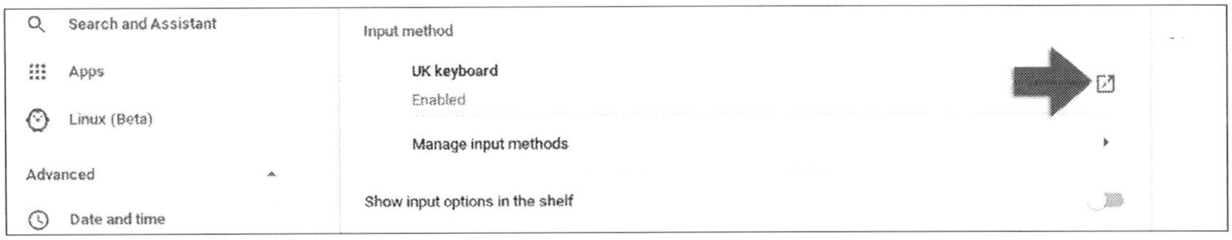

Here, you can enable/disable auto correct. Select 'edit dictionary entries' to add/remove dictionary term.

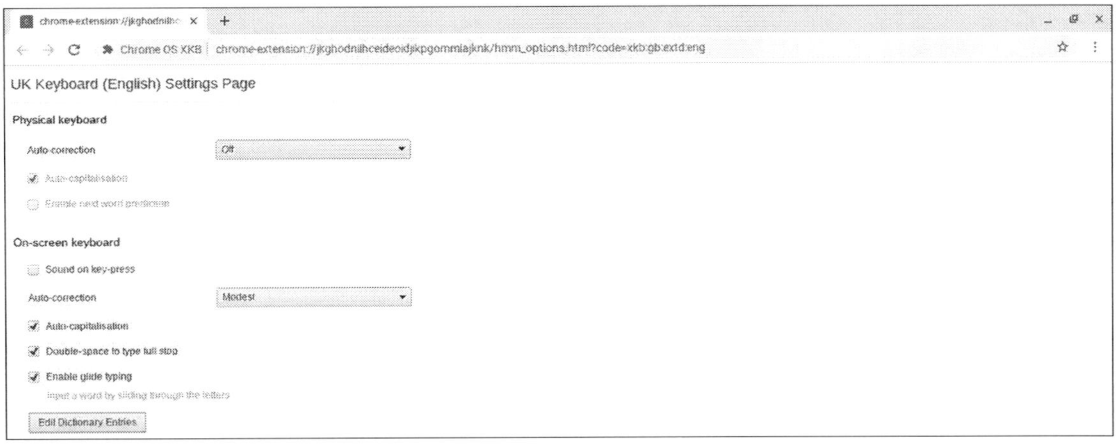

Network Settings

Once you are connected to a WiFi network, you can change settings such as DNS servers, assign static IP addresses, connect to proxy servers and VPNs. To do this click the clock on the bottom right to open the system tray, then click the 'settings' icon.

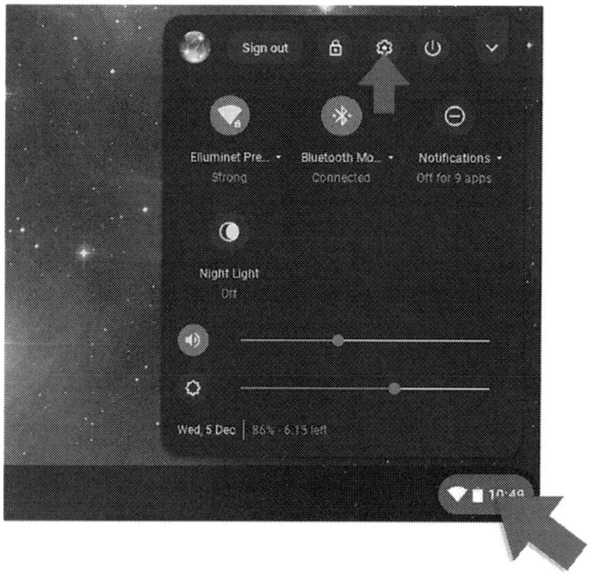

From the settings window, select 'network', then select your WiFi network.

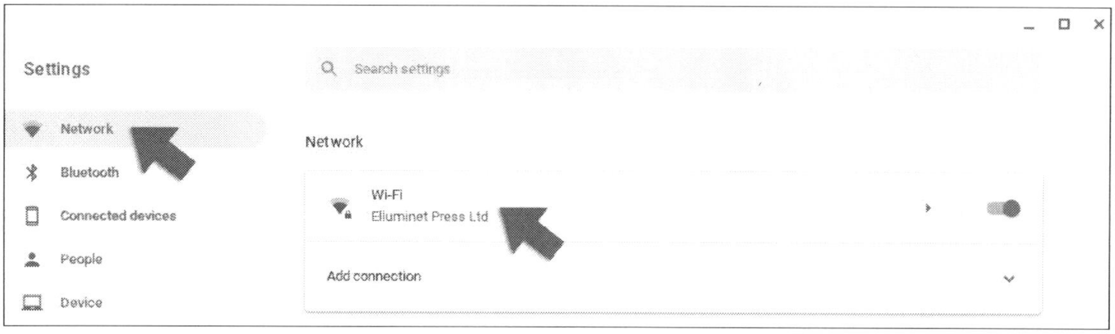

Select your network from the list

To set a static IP address or change the DNS servers, click 'network'.

From here click the switch next to 'configure IP address automatically'. This will allow you to enter an IP address, subnet mask, and gateway/ router IP into the fields.

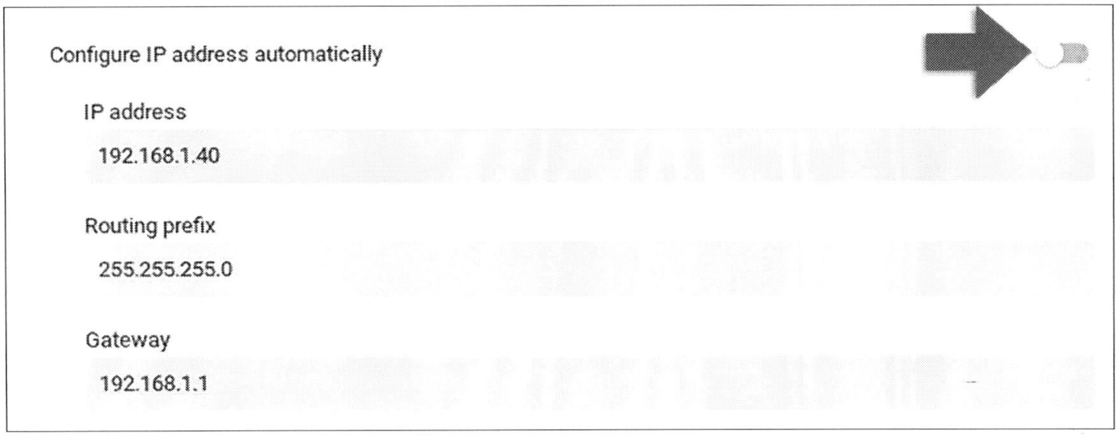

To change the DNS servers, scroll down to 'name servers' and select 'custom name servers'.

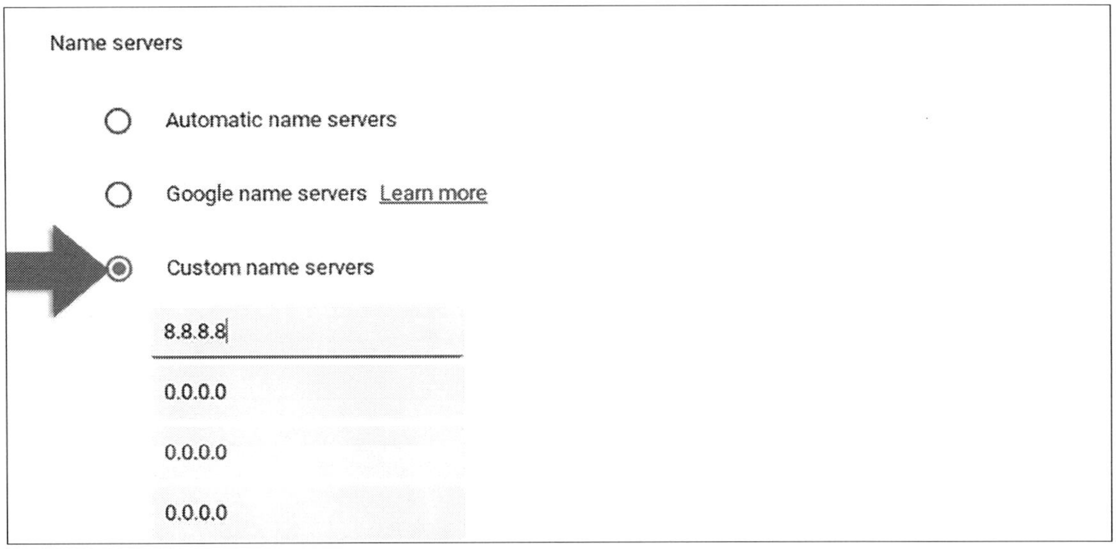

Enter the IP addresses of the DNS servers in the fields.

Power Options

There is no power saving mode in the traditional sense on a Chromebook. If you close the lid Chromebook, it will go into sleep mode. If your chromebook is idle for 6 minutes, it will automatically sleep.

To adjust the options, open the settings

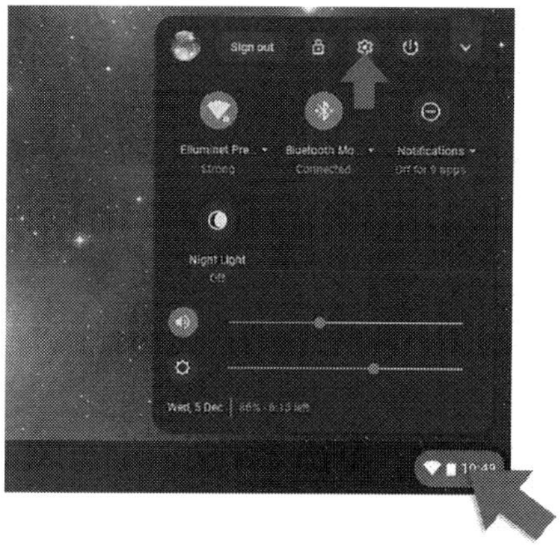

On the left, select 'device', then click 'power'.

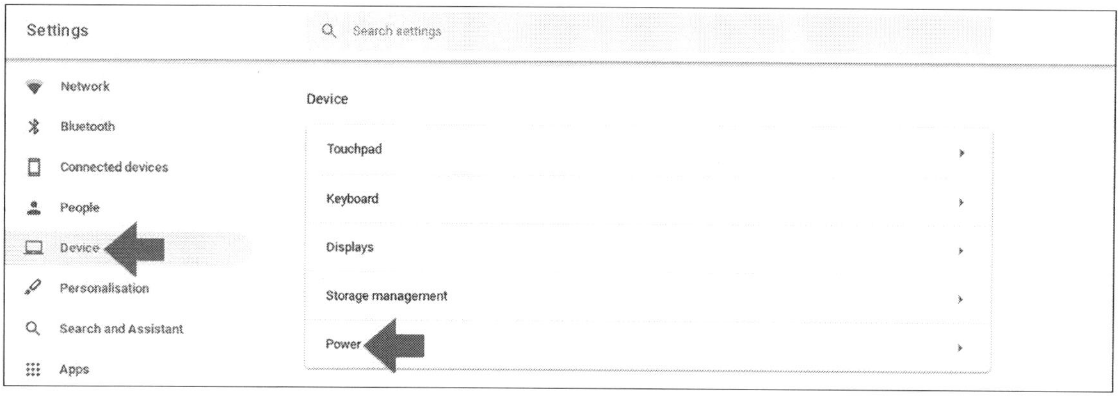

At the bottom, you can select what you want your chromebook to do while you aren't using it (idle). Click in the drop down boxes to change the settings.

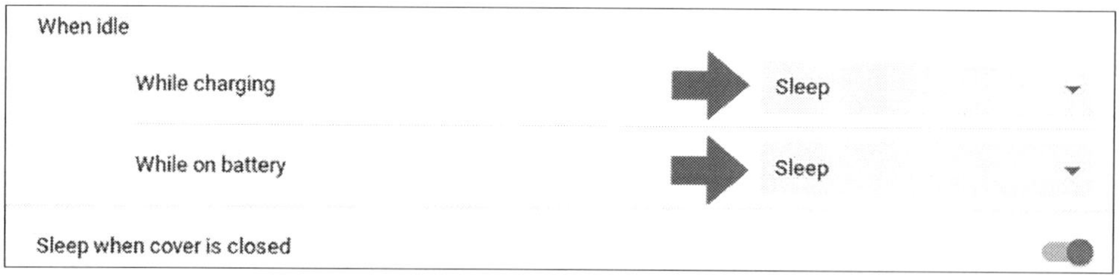

Sleep powers your chromebook down to minimum power saving, 'turn off display' just turns off the screen but leaves your chromebook running, 'keep display on' leaves your chromebook running with the display on all the time.

Integrate DropBox

If you have a DropBox account, you can integrate the service into the Files app on your Chromebook.

To do this, open the Files app, click the three-dot icon in its top-right corner, then select 'Add new service'.

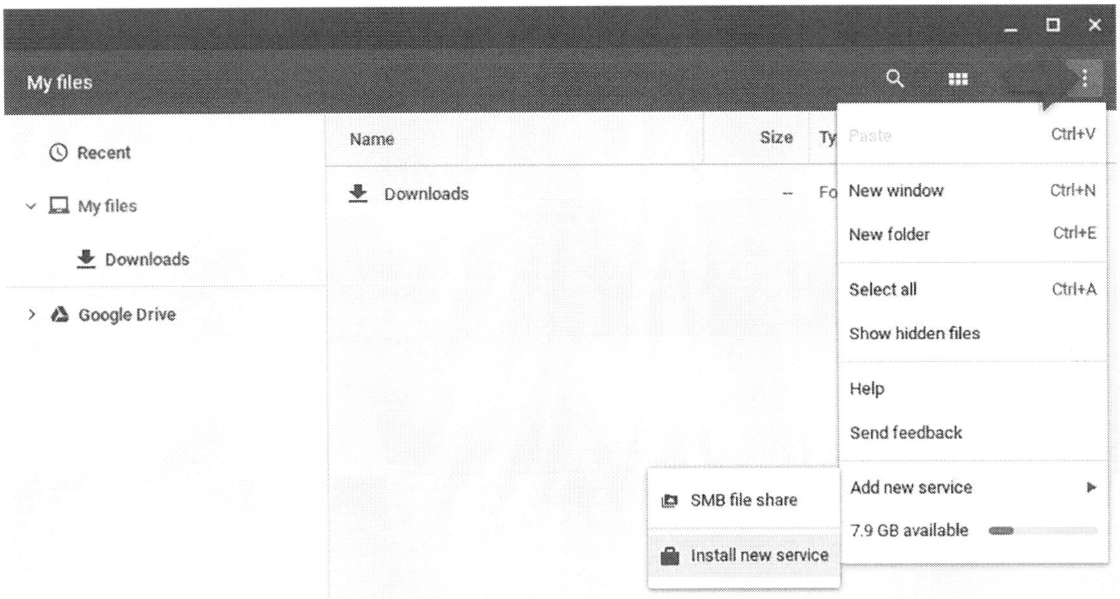

Select 'install' next to the DropBox service.

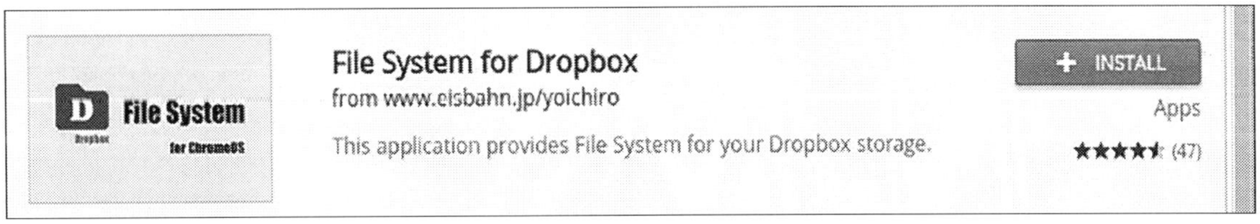

Click 'mount your DropBox', then sign in with your DropBox username and password

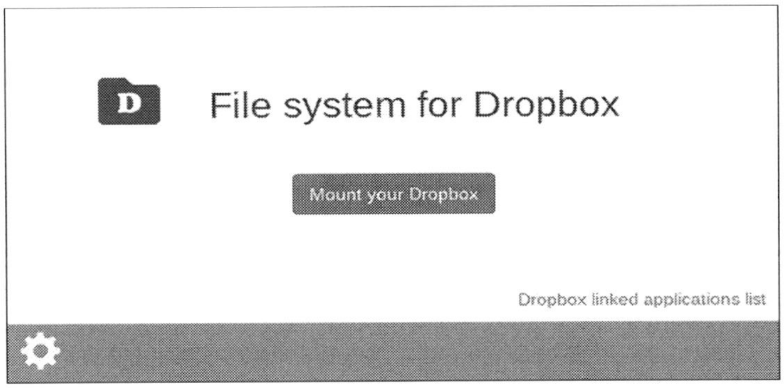

You'll find your DropBox listed down the left hand side of your Files app.

Integrate OneDrive

If you have a OneDrive account, you can integrate the service into the Files app on your Chromebook. To do this, open the Files app, click the three-dot icon in its top-right corner, then select 'Add new service'.

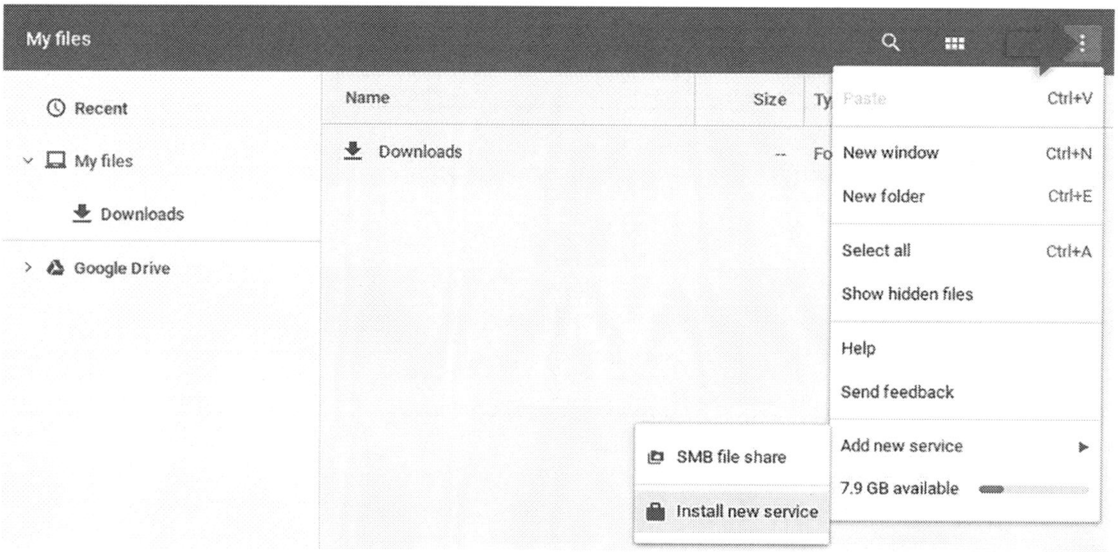

Select 'install' next to the OneDrive service.

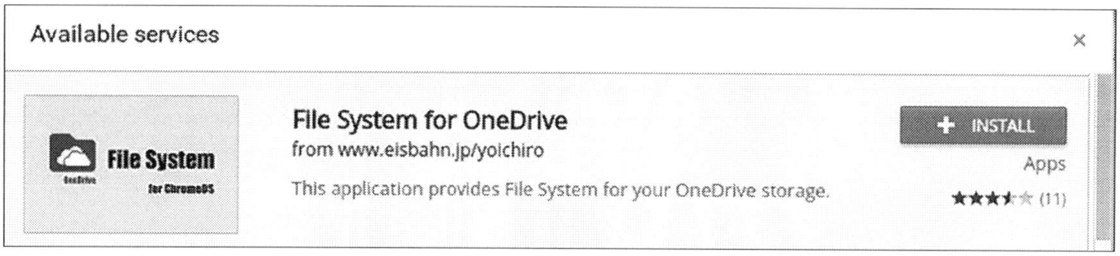

Click 'mount', then sign in with your Microsoft Account username and password

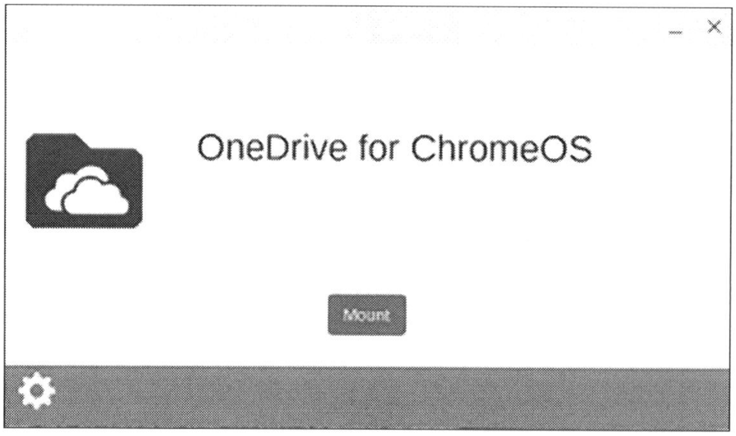

You'll find your OneDrive listed down the left hand side of your Files app.

Remote Desktop

You can access another computer remotely such as your Windows PC, or Mac from your Chromebook. First you need to set it up.

Setup

On the machine you want to access remotely (eg your Windows PC), open the Google Chrome Browser, navigate to the following website:

`remotedesktop.google.com`

Scroll down the page, click 'get started'. Sign in with your Google Account.

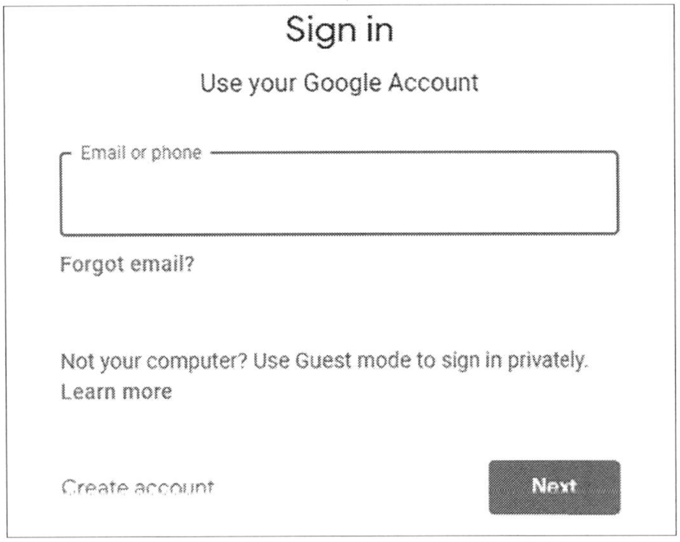

Click the blue download icon to install the remote desktop chrome extension.

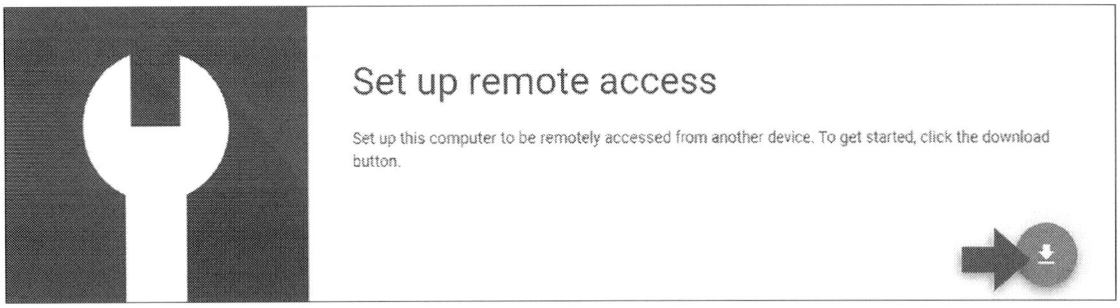

Click 'add to chrome', and accept any confirmation prompts.

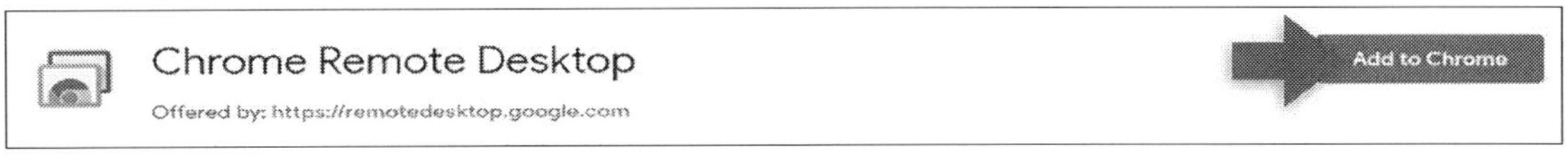

Click ‘accept and install’.

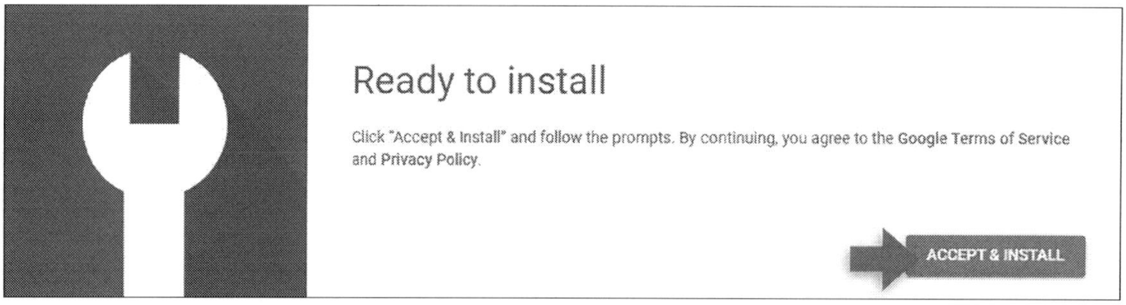

Type in a name for your computer, then click ‘next’.

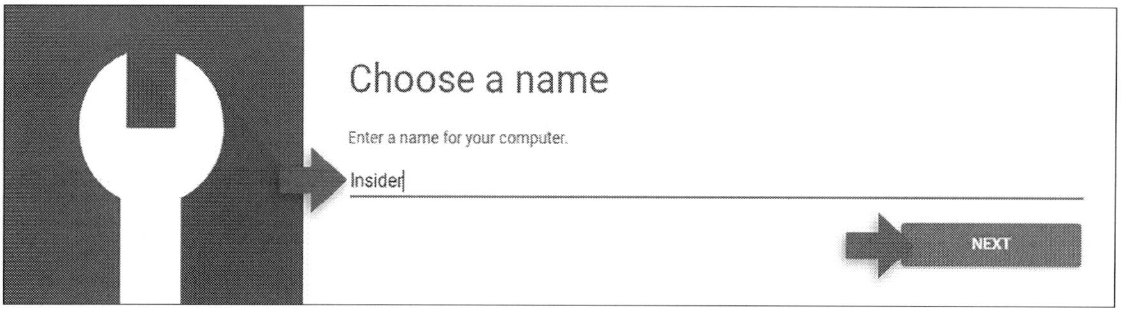

Enter a PIN code to secure your PC. Click ‘start’.

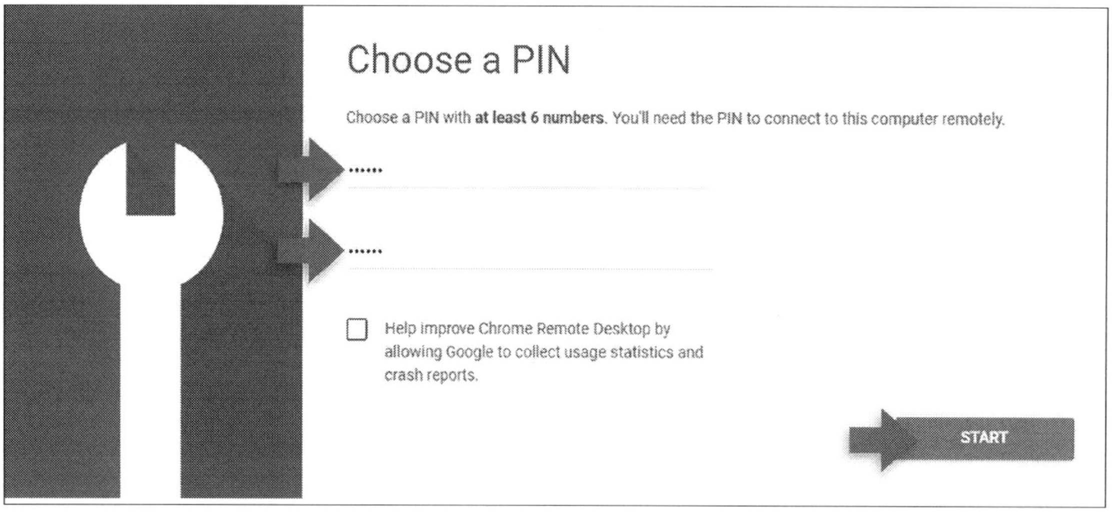

Connecting

Note the machine you’re connecting to will need to remain on for this to work.

On your Chromebook, open the Chrome browser, then navigate to the following website and sign in:

`remotedesktop.google.com`

At the top of the page, you'll see your computers that have chrome remote desktop enabled. Click on the one you want to use.

Enter the PIN code you created earlier.

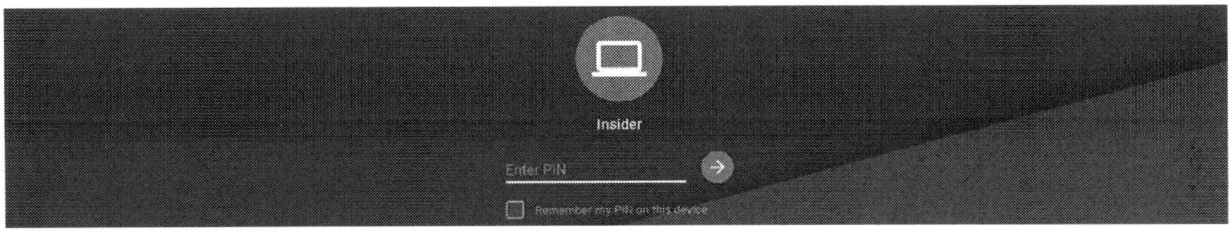

Now you can use your PC on your Chromebook.

3 Getting around ChromeBook

ChromeBooks are very easy to navigate. If you're familiar with browsing the web, you'll be able to use your ChromeBook with little difficulty.

In this chapter, we'll take a look at navigation around the interface, as well as touch gestures you can use on your touch pad to perform certain tasks with a tap or swipe.

Learn to find your way around the app shelf, desktop, app launcher, and the system tray.

First thing you'll need to do, if you haven't already done so, is sign in with your Google Account email and password.

Take a look at the video demos. Open your web browser and navigate to the following website

`videos.tips/chromebook-nav`

Power Up & Power Down

To power up your ChromeBook, press the power key on the top right hand side of the keyboard. The Chrome logo will appear on the screen while the system starts.

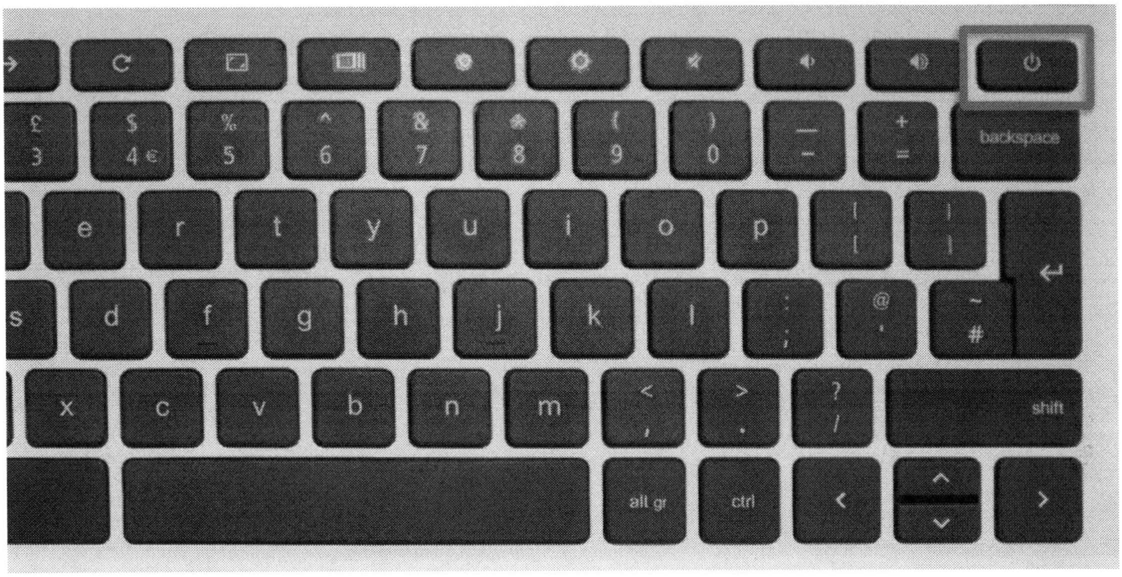

To shut down your ChromeBook, hold the power button for 1 second, you'll see three options pop up onto the screen.

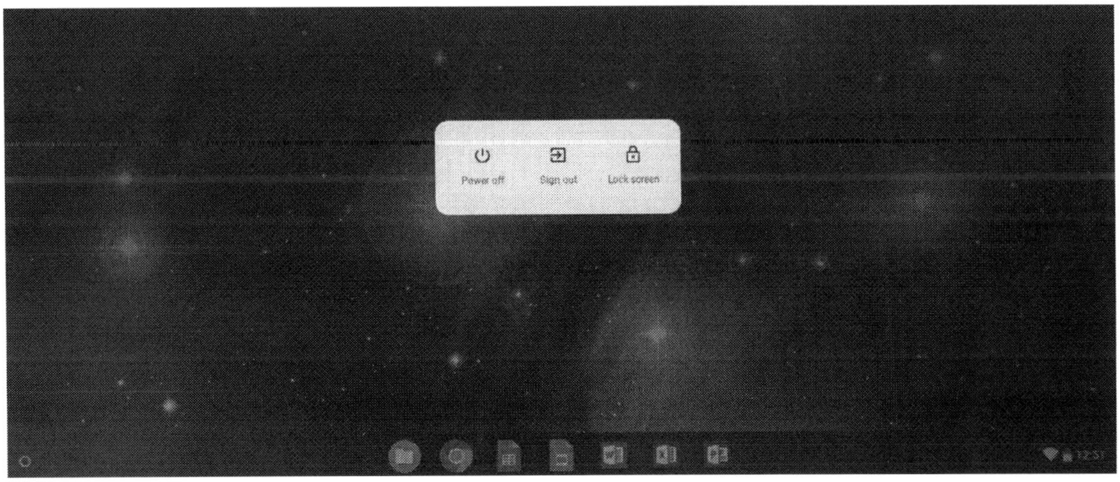

Click 'power off' to shut down your ChromeBook. Click 'sign out' to sign out of your account and return to the login screen. Click 'lock screen' to lock your screen - useful if you are working on something and need to quickly lock your screen if you need to leave your ChromeBook for a few minutes without having to sign out completely.

If your ChromeBook has frozen or crashed, hold the power key until the screen goes blank. Wait a few seconds, then press the power key again to start up your ChromeBook

The Login Screen

The login screen, sometimes called the lock screen, is the first screen you'll see when you turn on your ChromeBook. Along the bar at the bottom, you'll see a few icons. From here, you can shut your ChromeBook down, allow someone to browse as a guest (without a Google Account) and add a new user with a Google Account to your ChromeBook.

On the bottom right of the screen, you'll see your wifi settings, battery and the clock. Click on this to reveal the options menu, where you can change wifi network, accessibility, volume and brightness controls.

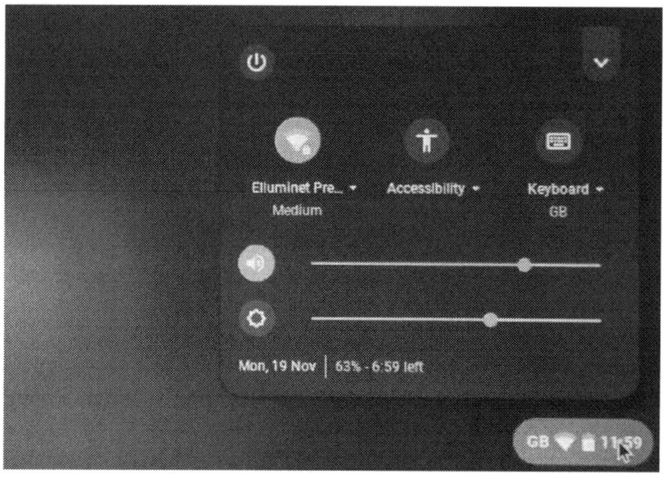

In the centre of the screen, you'll see your user account you registered when you set up your ChromeBook. Enter your password to log in.

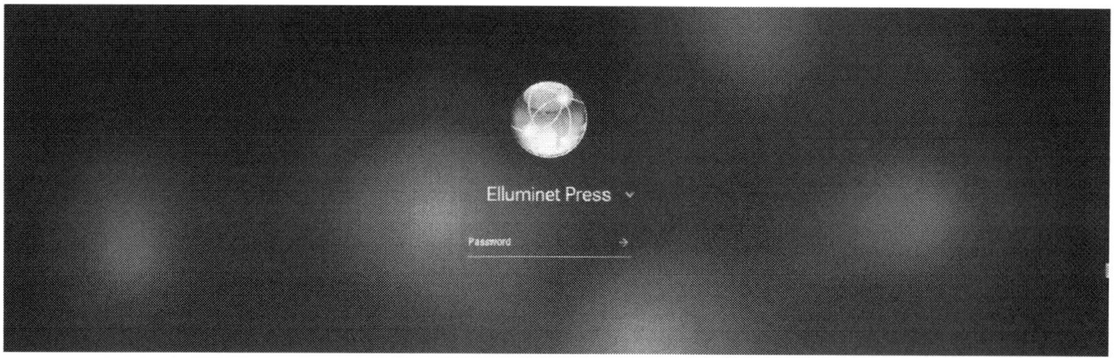

Once your ChromeBook is set up, you will need to log in with your Google Account, so on the login screen, enter your password.

Before we go any further, lets take a look at some navigation features we can use to get around the user interface of your ChromeBook.

The Touch Pad

If you have used a laptop before, then you'll be familiar with the touch pad or track pad.

You can use your fingers to move your pointer around the screen using what are called gestures.

One Finger Tap

This is like your left mouse button and can be used to select objects such as icons or text fields on the screen. Just tap your finger on the pad.

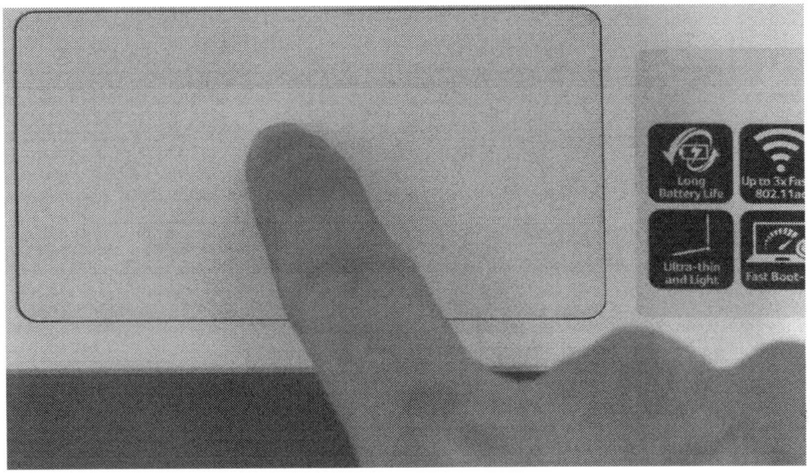

Two Finger Tap

This is like the right mouse button and can be used to right click on objects such as icons to reveal a context menu of options. Just tap both fingers on the pad at the same time.

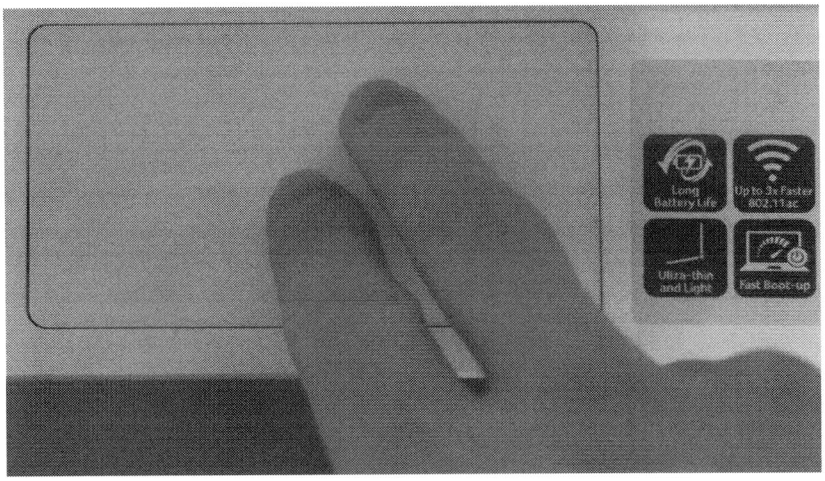

One Finger Click and Drag

Position your pointer on to an object such as window title bar, or image on your screen, then press your finger on the touch pad until you hear a click, then without releasing your finger, drag across the track pad to move the object.

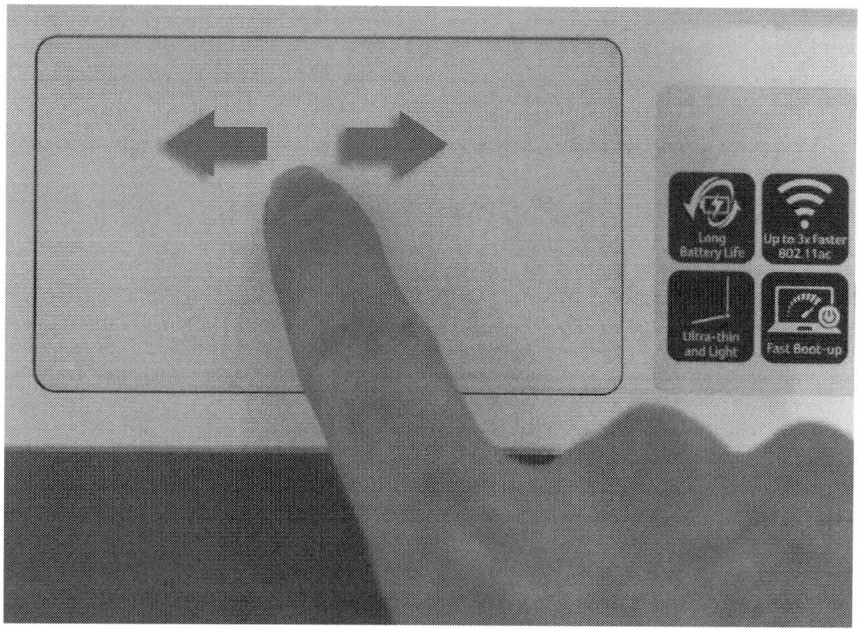

Two Finger Scroll

You can use two fingers on the track pad to scroll up and down windows, web pages, maps and so on.

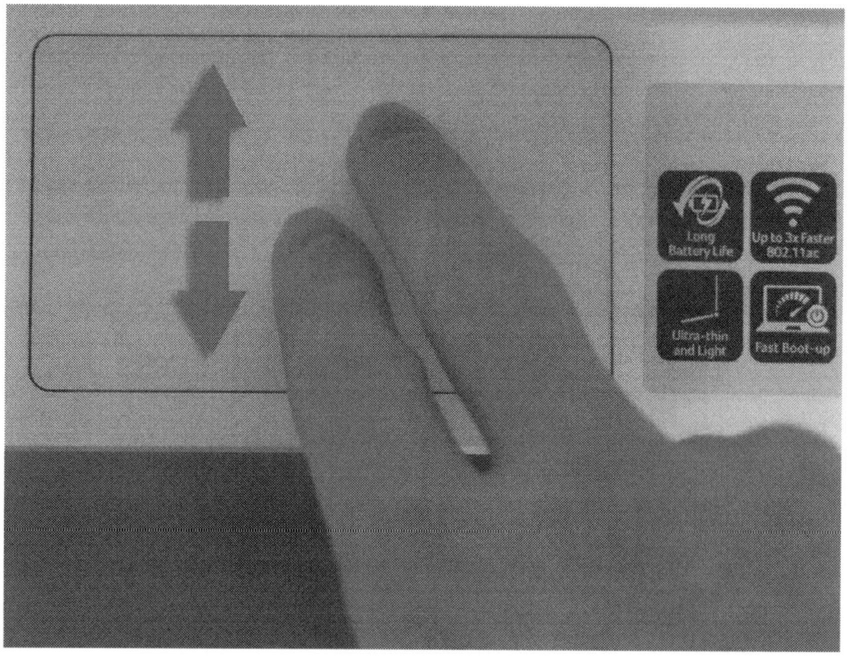

Two Finger Swipe

While you are browsing the web, you can go back to a previous page by swiping your two fingers to the left on the track pad and advance forward a page you have visited by swiping to the right.

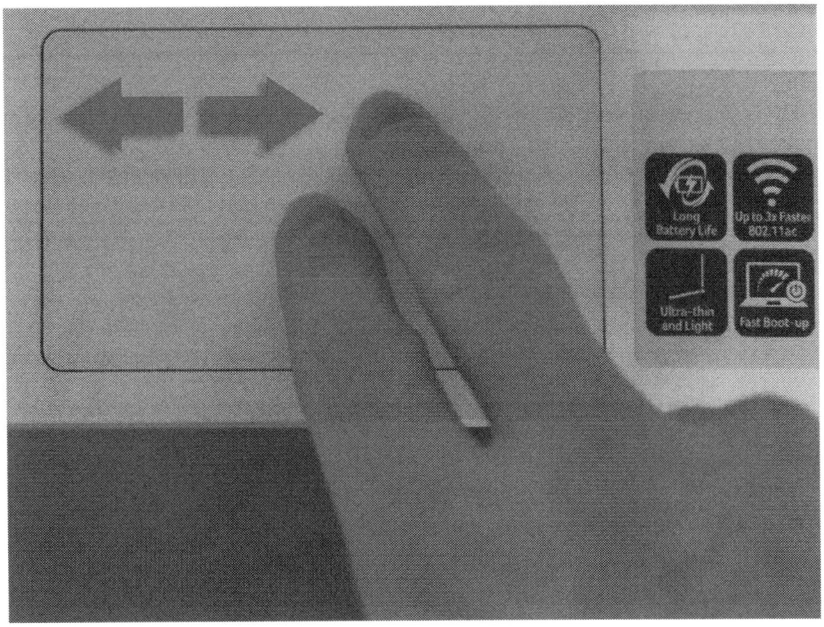

Three Finger Swipe

You can quickly display all your open apps by swiping your three fingers downwards on the track pad.

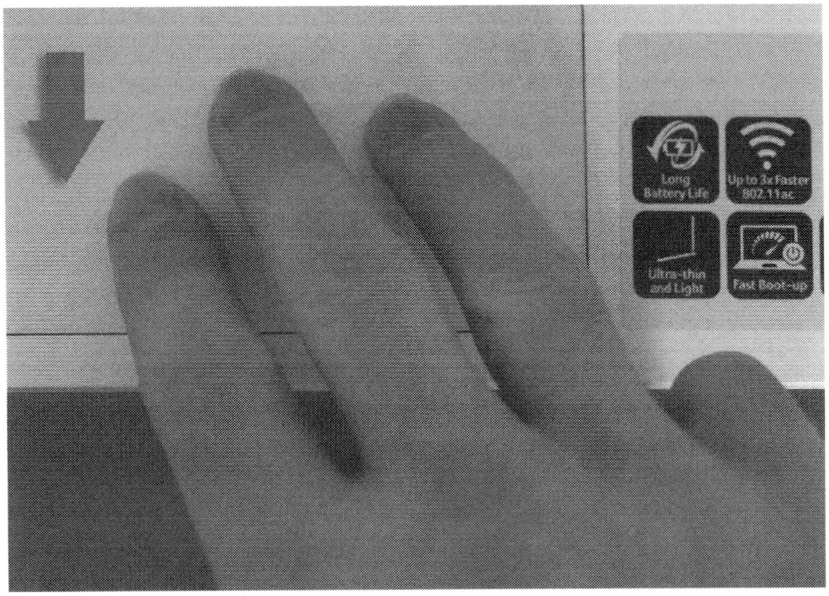

You'll see any open apps show up as thumbnail previews. You can click on these to open them or close them down.

The Keyboard

Here is a typical ChromeBook keyboard. It looks like a conventional keyboard you'll find on any computer, but it's worth noting the keys along the top.

Along the top of your keyboard, you'll see some special keys. These help when using the Chrome web browser.

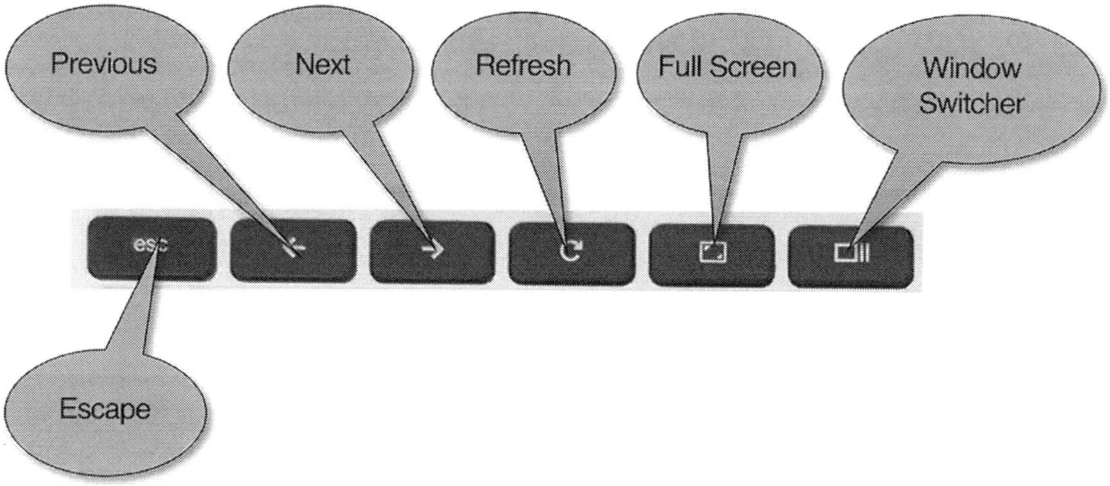

Towards the right hand side of the row, you'll see some keys that allow you to change the brightness of the screen and adjust audio volume.

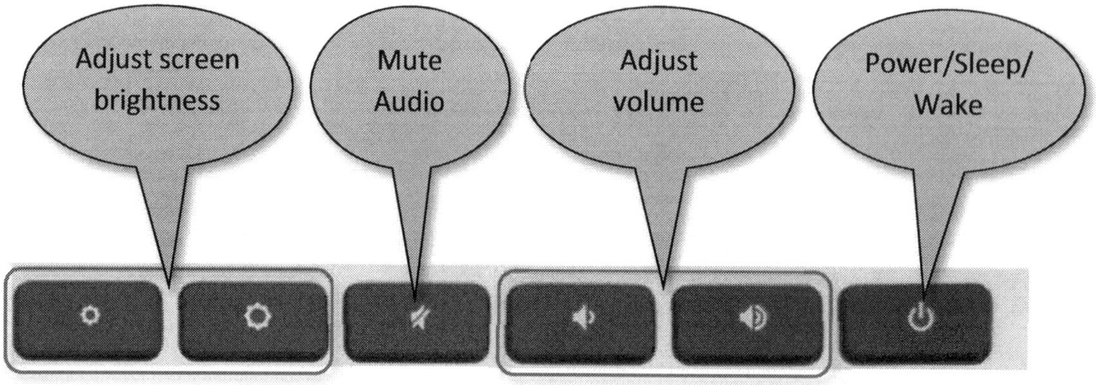

Onscreen Keyboard Help

Your chromebook contains a help screen that shows you all the keyboard shortcuts available. Press **ctrl alt ?** to reveal the help screen.

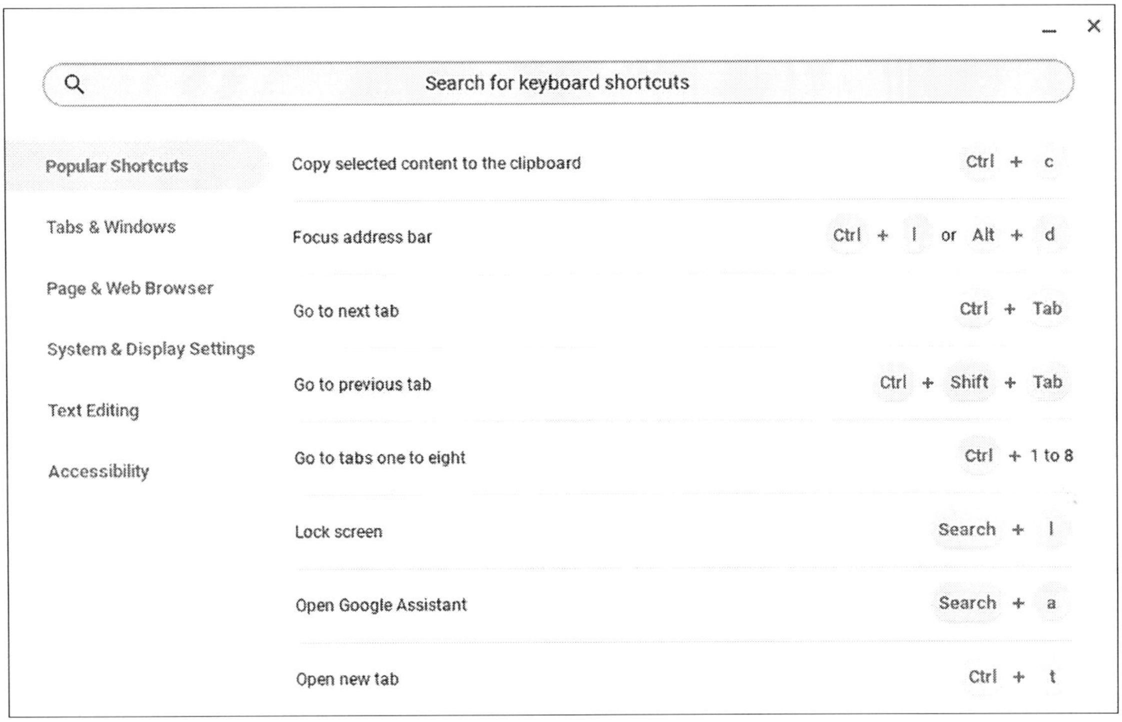

Scroll through the keyboard shortcuts. You can also browse through the categories on the left hand side.

Or you can search for keyboard shortcuts using the search field on the top of the screen.

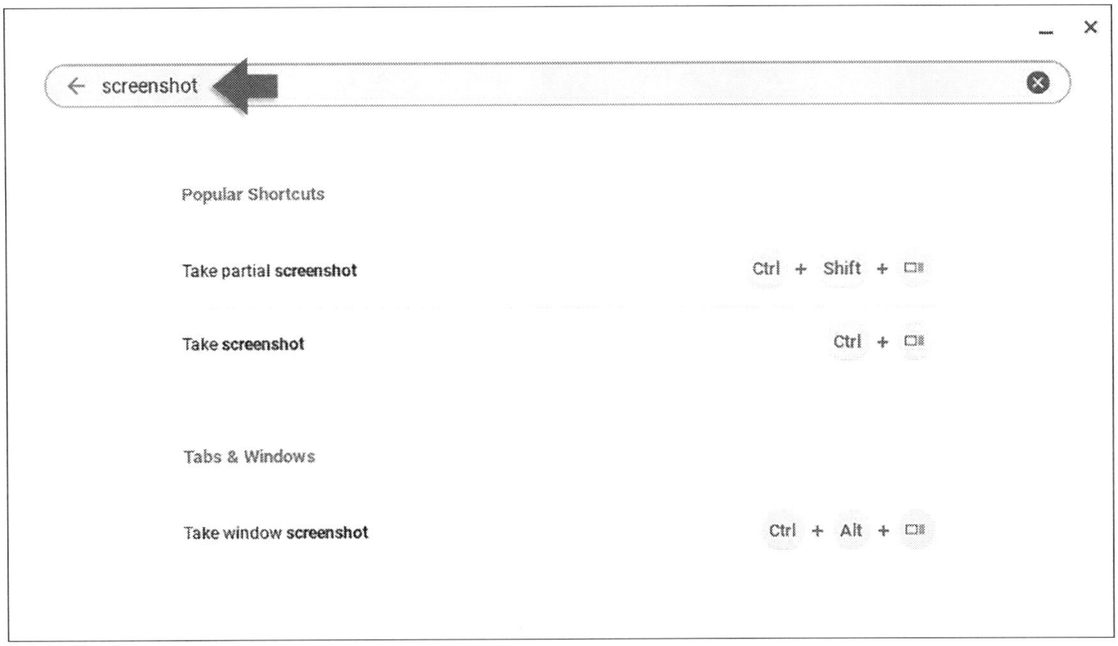

ChromeBook Task Manager

Hold down the **search** key, then tap **escape**. The search key looks like a small magnifying glass, you'll find it on the left hand side of your keyboard. On the old ChromeBooks press shift-escape.

You'll see a window pop up with a list of tasks (apps) that are currently running, as well as how much memory and cpu time they're using.

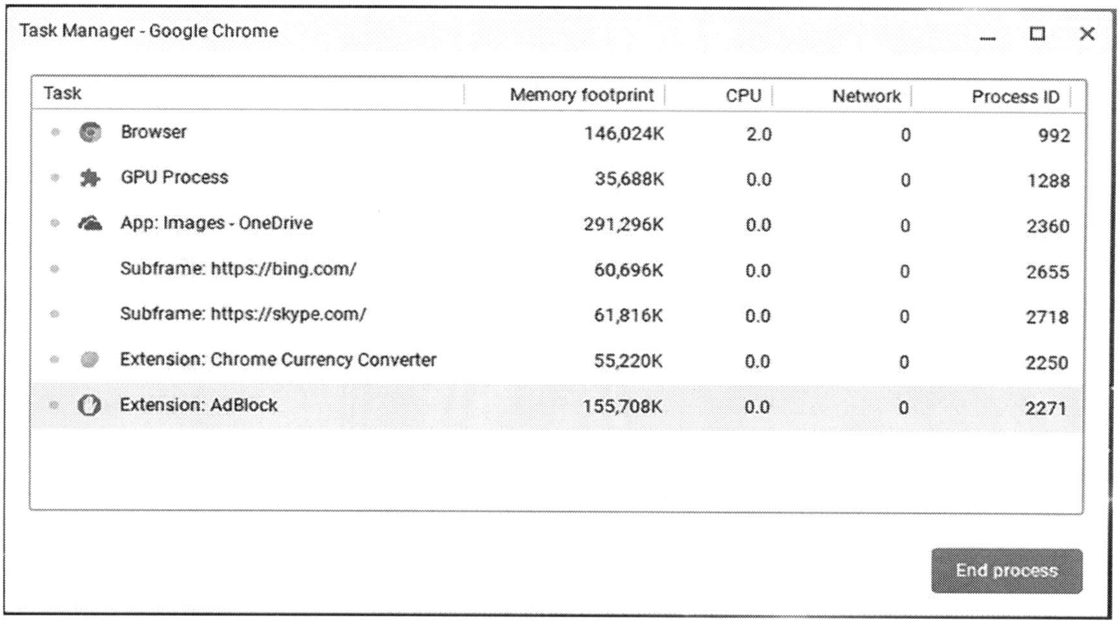

Task Manager - Google Chrome

Task	Memory footprint	CPU	Network	Process ID
Browser	146,024K	2.0	0	992
GPU Process	35,688K	0.0	0	1288
App: Images - OneDrive	291,296K	0.0	0	2360
Subframe: https://bing.com/	60,696K	0.0	0	2655
Subframe: https://skype.com/	61,816K	0.0	0	2718
Extension: Chrome Currency Converter	55,220K	0.0	0	2250
Extension: AdBlock	155,708K	0.0	0	2271

End process

The task manager is useful if an app is not responding or has crashed.

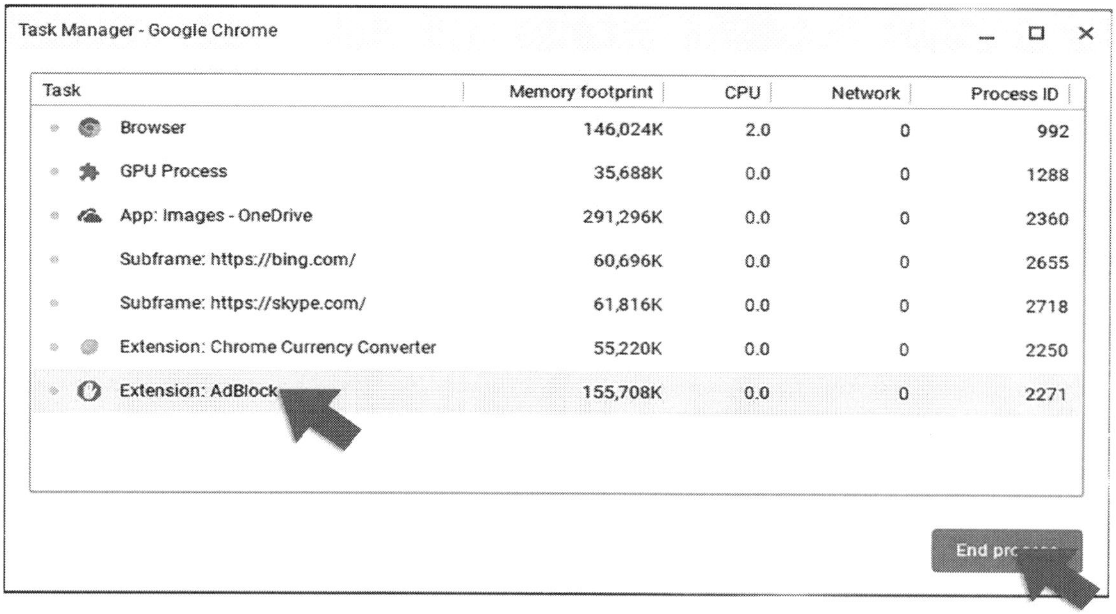

Task Manager - Google Chrome

Task	Memory footprint	CPU	Network	Process ID
Browser	146,024K	2.0	0	992
GPU Process	35,688K	0.0	0	1288
App: Images - OneDrive	291,296K	0.0	0	2360
Subframe: https://bing.com/	60,696K	0.0	0	2655
Subframe: https://skype.com/	61,816K	0.0	0	2718
Extension: Chrome Currency Converter	55,220K	0.0	0	2250
Extension: AdBlock	155,708K	0.0	0	2271

Just click on the task (app) in the list, then click 'end process'. The non-responsive app is usually labelled 'not responding'.

Desktop and the App Shelf

The desktop looks similar to a lot of operating systems out there, you have a background image or wallpaper and along the bottom you have what Google calls the App Shelf. This is very much like the task bar found in Windows 10 or the App Dock found on a Mac.

On the left hand side of the app shelf you have what looks like a magnifying glass icon. This is your App Launcher and allows you to open any app that has been added to your ChromeBook, as well as searching the web.

The next icon along is the Google Chrome web browser. This works just like any web browser you would find on a PC or Mac and allows you to search the web, use web apps, and use the internet how you would on any other computer.

The space on the app shelf after the Google Chrome icon can be for pinning any other app for quick access. For example, you could add, Google Photos, Gmail, Google Drive, word processing apps and so on.

On the right hand side of the app shelf you will find a few small icons.

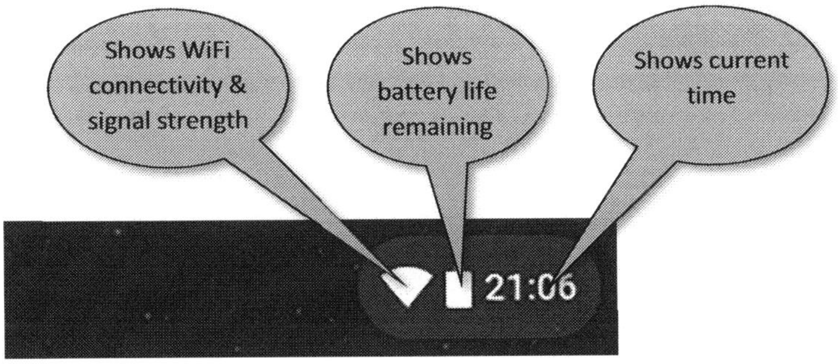

The first one along shows notifications such as new emails or system messages, reminders and so on. The next one across shows WiFi or ethernet connectivity. Next you have an icon for battery level, and the clock. Click on the icon to reveal the system tray.

System Tray

The system tray contains all your controls to connect to a WiFi network, pair a bluetooth device such as a mouse, change audio volume, screen brightness, sign in & out, shut down ChromeBook, as well as access the system settings, and display notification messages.

To reveal the system tray, click on the clock status icon on the bottom right of your screen.

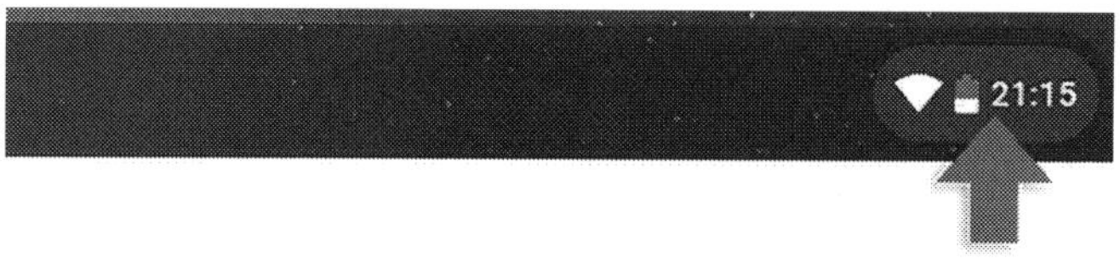

Along the top of the system tray, you'll see all the system notifications. Click on them to view details, or click 'clear all' to clear them.

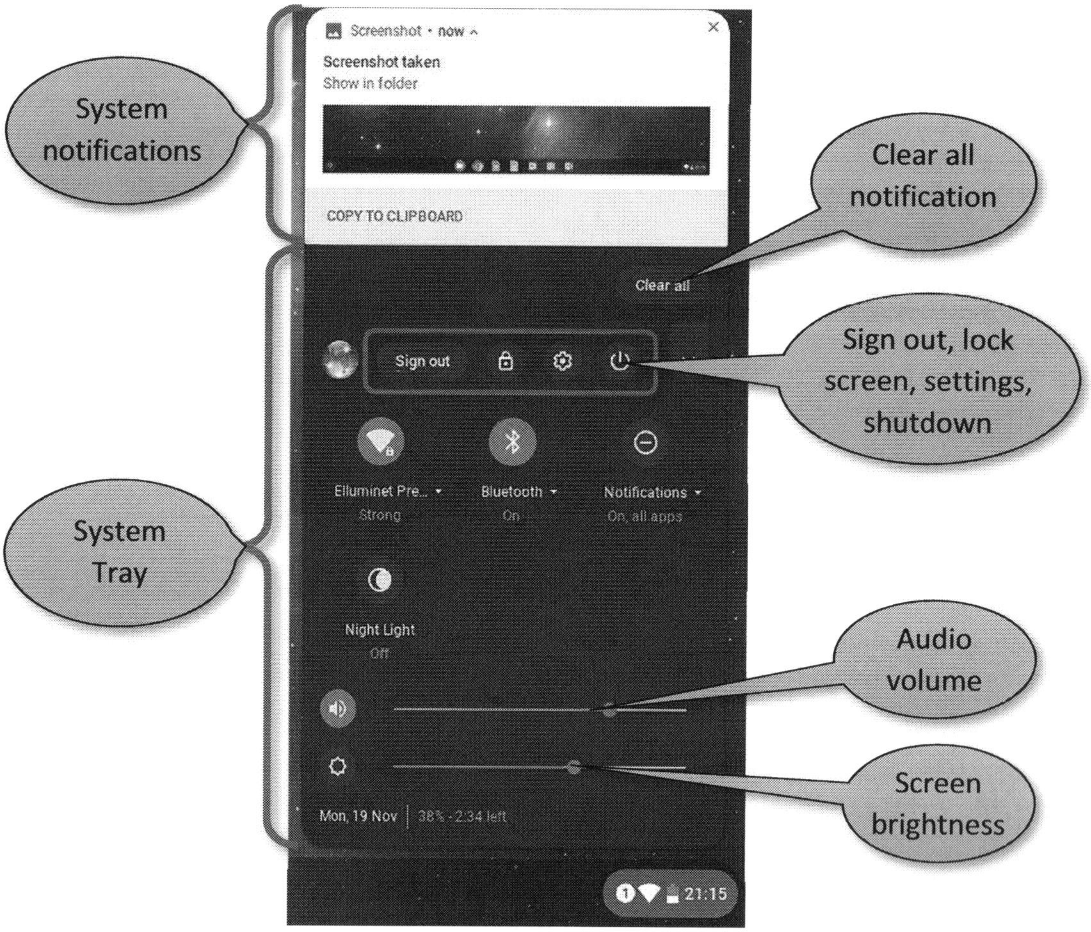

Underneath you'll see your system controls. Here you can sign out, lock your screen or shut down your ChromeBook, as well as connect to WiFi networks, bluetooth devices, control the brightness and volume and access system settings.

Notifications

Notifications appear on the right side of the screen, and on the top of the system tray.

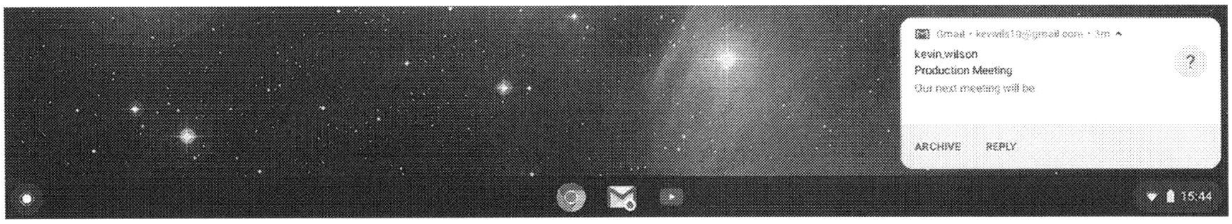

You can adjust which apps show notifications, or silence notifications from the system tray. To do this, click the clock on the bottom right of your screen, then click 'notifications'.

From here, you can select which apps to allow:

Remove the tick on the app to exclude.

Turn on 'do not disturb' to mute all notifications from all apps.

Pinned Files & Holding Space

You can pin files such as documents or pictures to the app shelf from the files app. You'll also see screenshots, screen captures, and files you've downloaded.

You'll find the holding space on the bottom right of your screen. Click on this icon to open it up

Files that have been pinned to your shelf will show up on the bottom right of your screen.

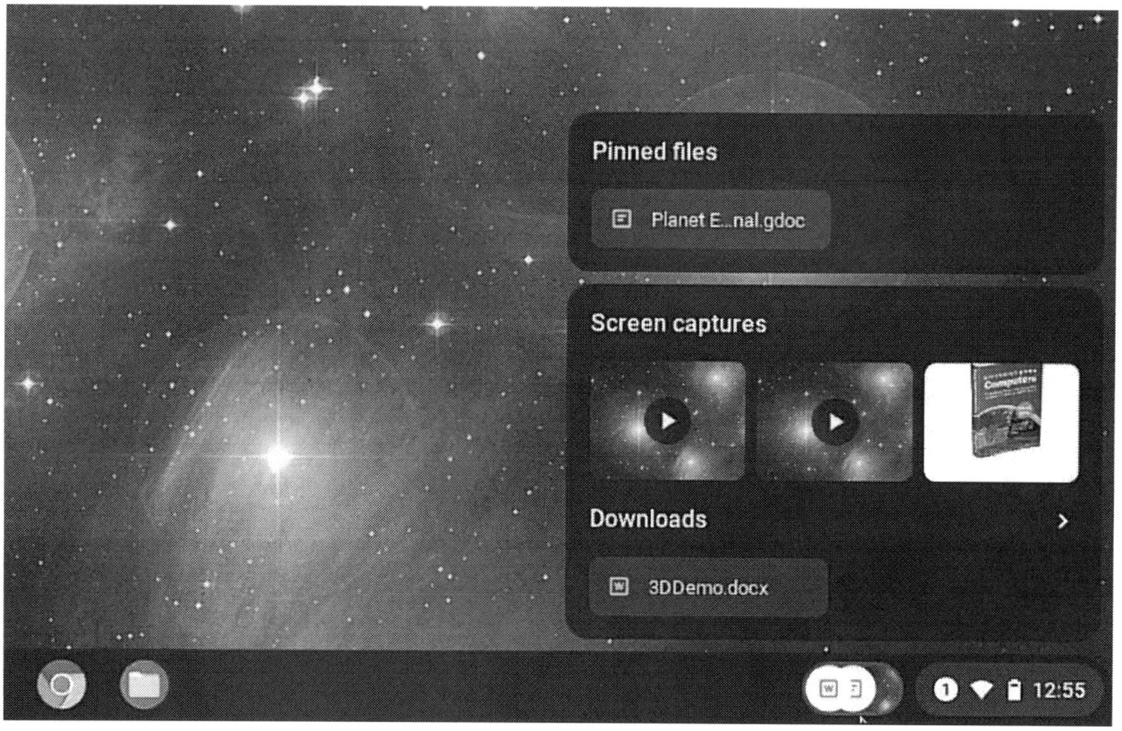

To pin a file to the holding space, right click on the file icon in the files app, select 'pin to shelf'

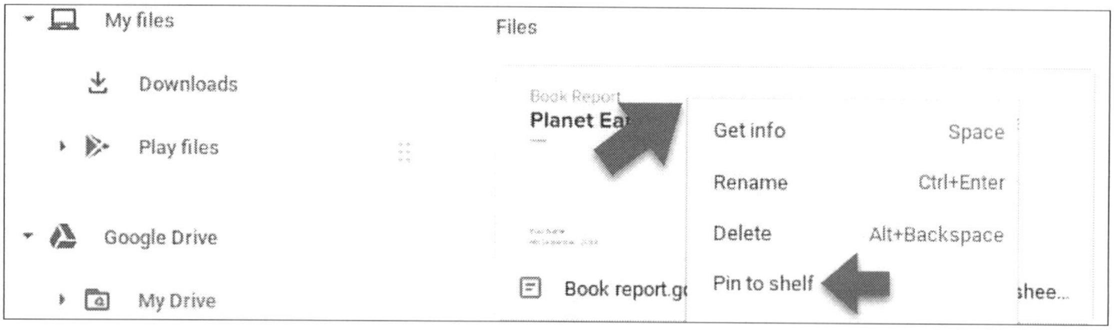

App Launcher

The App Launcher is very much like your start menu in Windows and is where you will find all the apps that have been installed on your ChromeBook.

Opening

To reveal the App Launcher, click the circle icon on the bottom left of your screen.

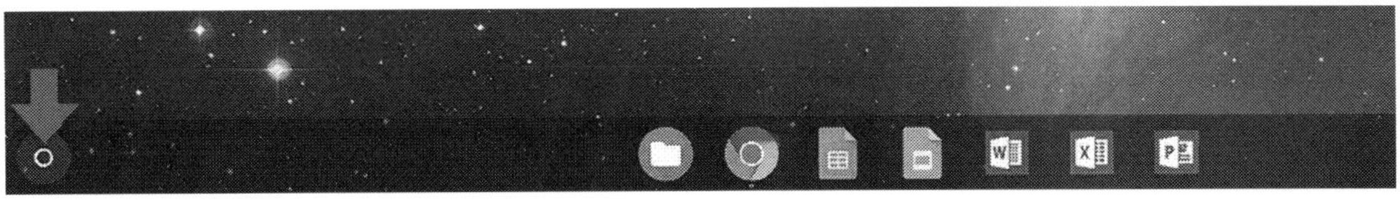

Click the arrow on the top middle of the launcher to open it up.

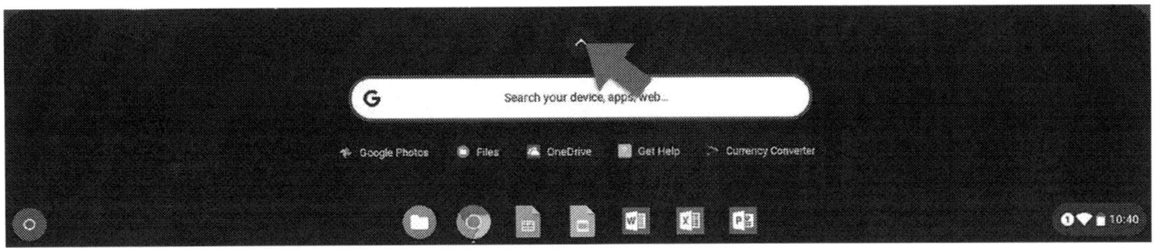

From here, you can search the web by entering a web site address or some keywords as you would normally do when using Google Search.

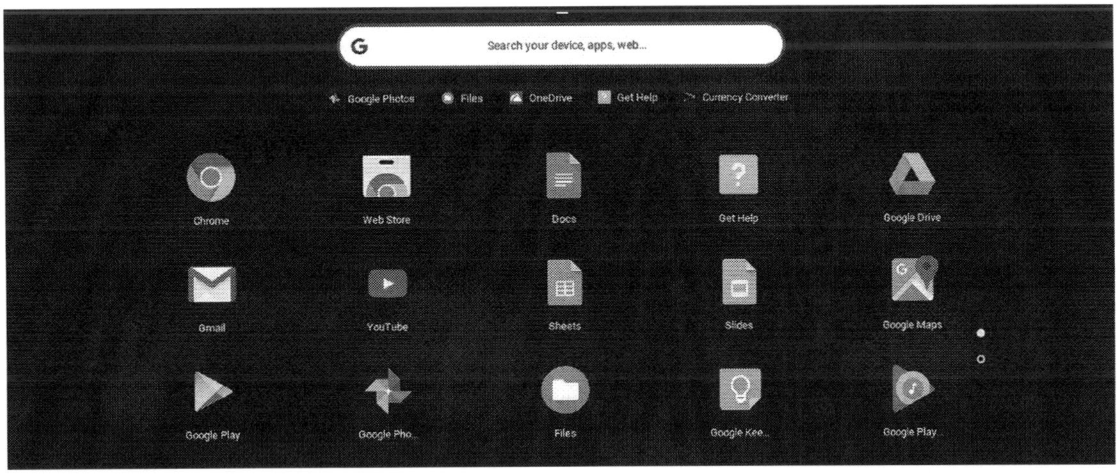

Below this, you'll see icons representing the apps installed on your ChromeBook.

Scroll up and down to see apps on the additional pages if required.

Click on an icon to start the app.

Anatomy

Lets take a closer look at the launcher. Here, below you can see the main sections.

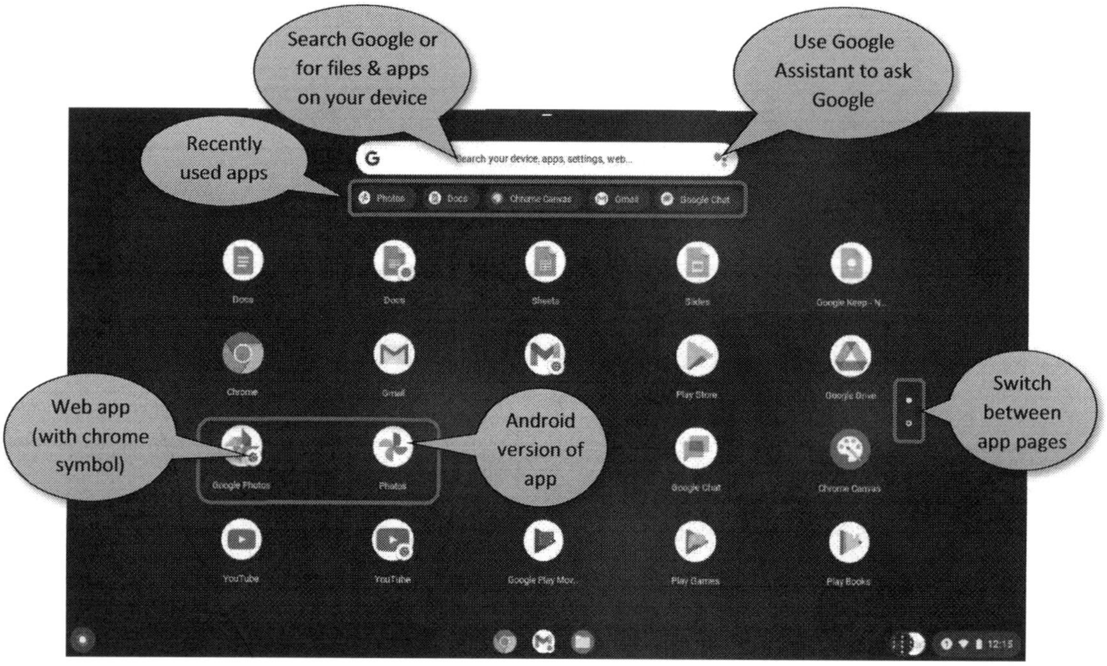

Along the top, you'll see a search bar. Here, you can use Google to search the web. You can also search for apps, files, documents, or photos on your Chromebook.

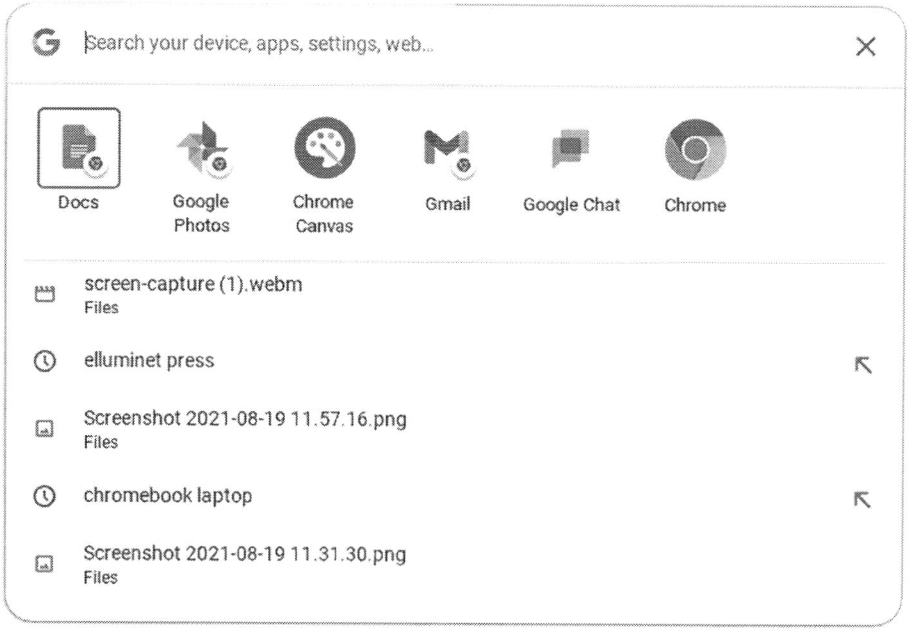

When you start typing a keyword into the search field, you'll see some suggested apps, and a list of previous searches and files.

App Types

When you open the app launcher in full, notice there are different types of apps. This will explain why you might see two different icons for the same app. Here in the app launcher, you can see two icons for docs, gmail, and google photos.

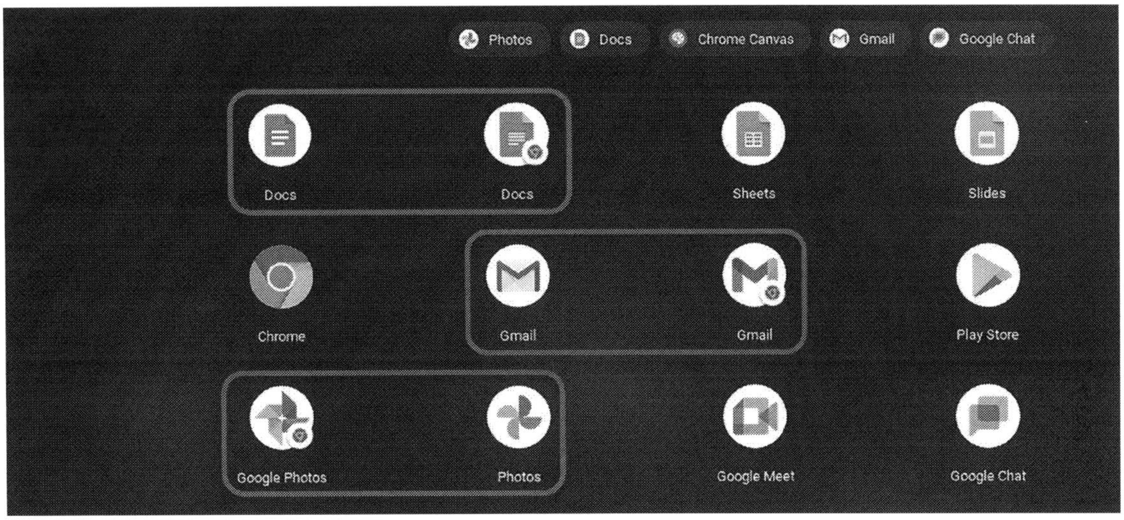

The app with the small chrome icon on the bottom right, is a chrome app, and will open in Google Chrome. The icon without the small chrome icon is usually an android app that will run in its own window.

Here, we can see the chrome version of Google Photos on the left, and the android app version on the right.

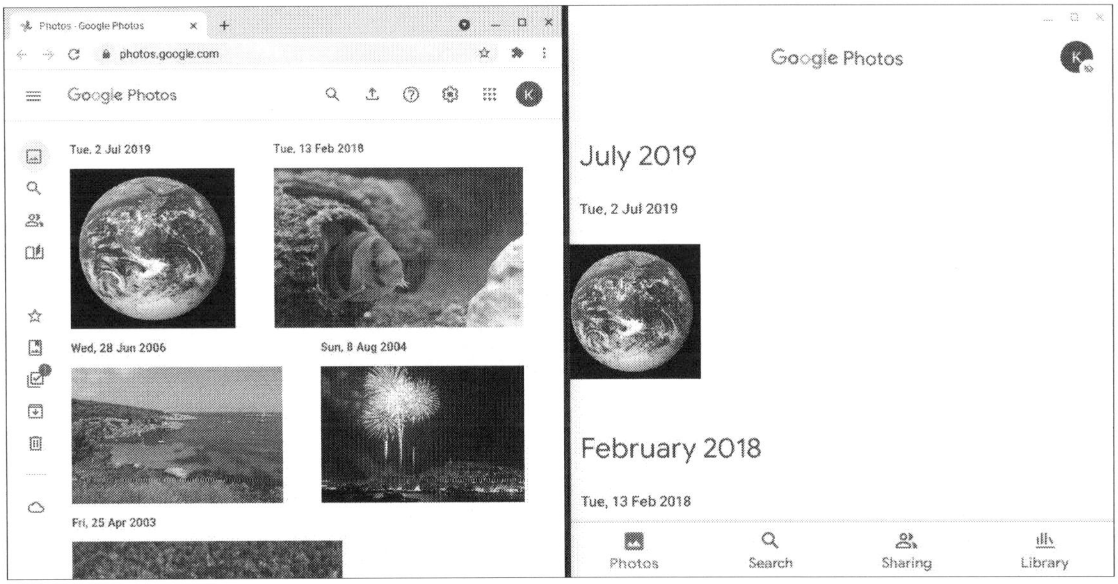

Create App Folders

You can group your apps into folders on your app launcher. The idea is to group apps that are of the same type. For example, you can group all your productivity apps together, eg Docs, Sheets, Slides.

To do this, just click and drag an icon on top of another.

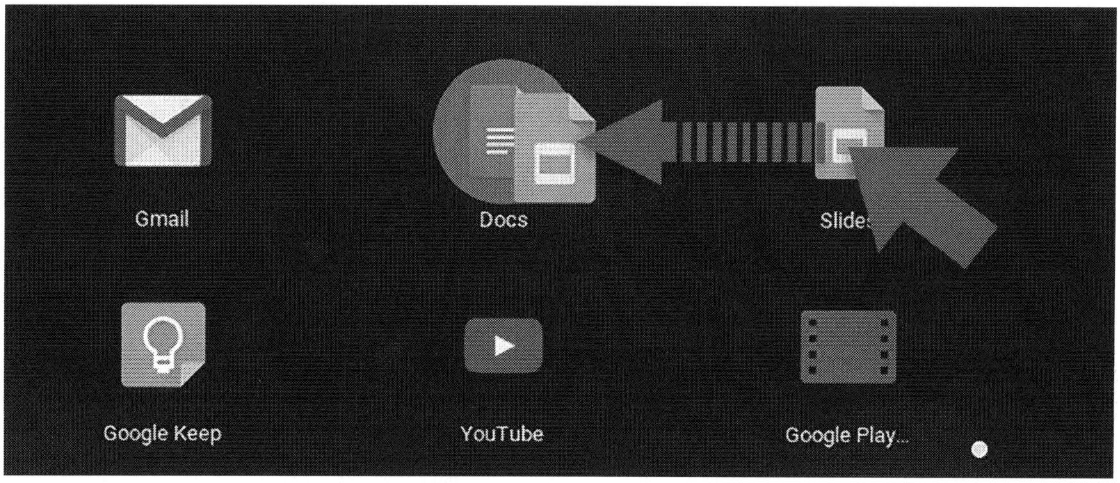

Click on the new folder to open it up.

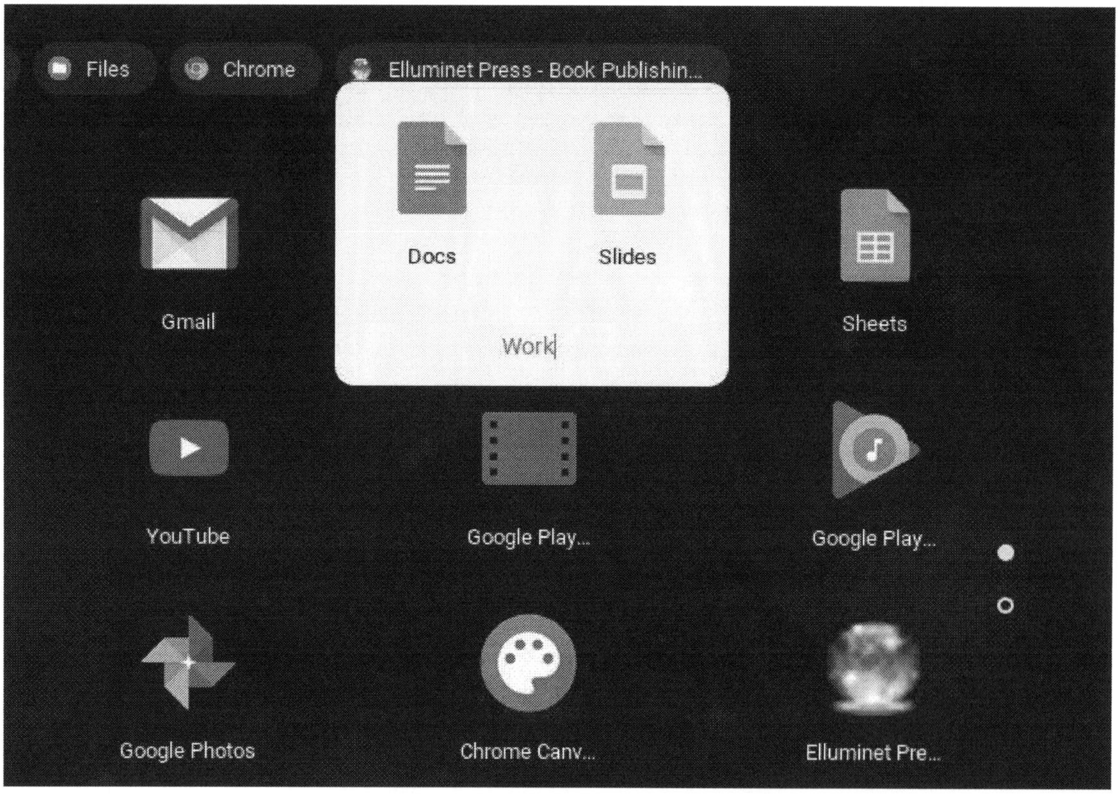

Click on the 'untitled' name at the bottom of the folder and type in something more meaningful.

Pin Apps to your App Shelf

The app shelf is similar to the task bar in Windows 10 and you can pin app icons to this shelf for quick access. So you can add all your most used apps to this shelf and click them when you need them.

To do this, open up your App Launcher and click the arrow at the top to reveal all the apps.

From this window, right click on the app icon you want to pin to your shelf.

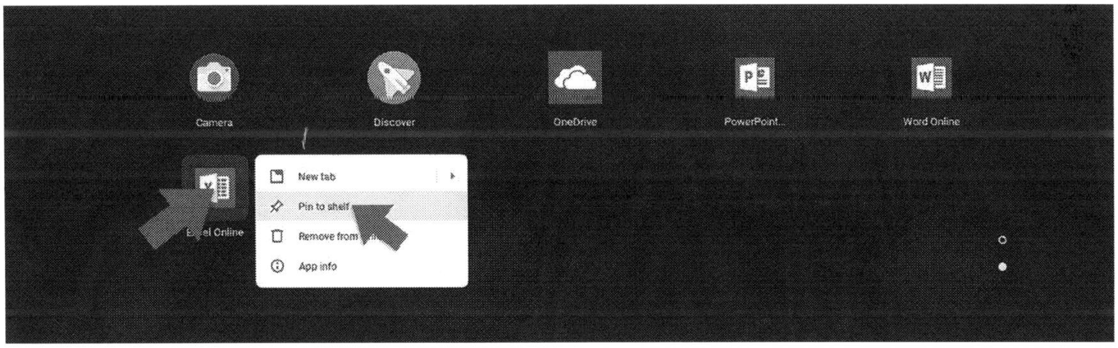

From the popup menu, click on 'pin to shelf'. You will see the app icon appear on the shelf at the bottom left of the screen, as shown below.

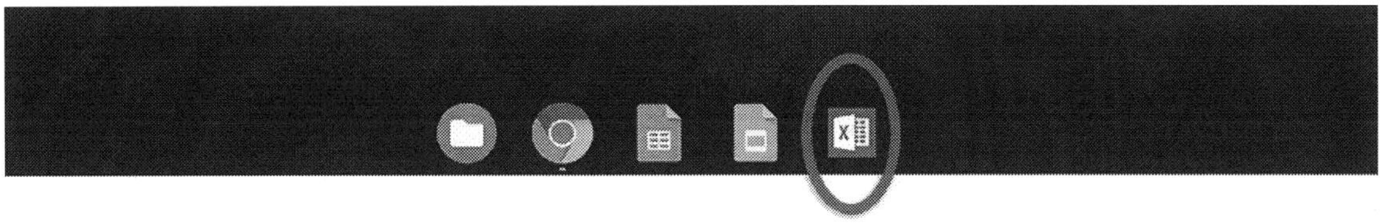

You can do this for all your most used apps, allowing you to quickly launch an app directly from the app shelf.

File Management

There are many different types of file types; files for photos, videos, documents, speadsheets, presentations and so on. You can access these files using the Files App. You'll find the Files App on your app launcher.

Along the left hand panel in the Files App, you'll see some folders.

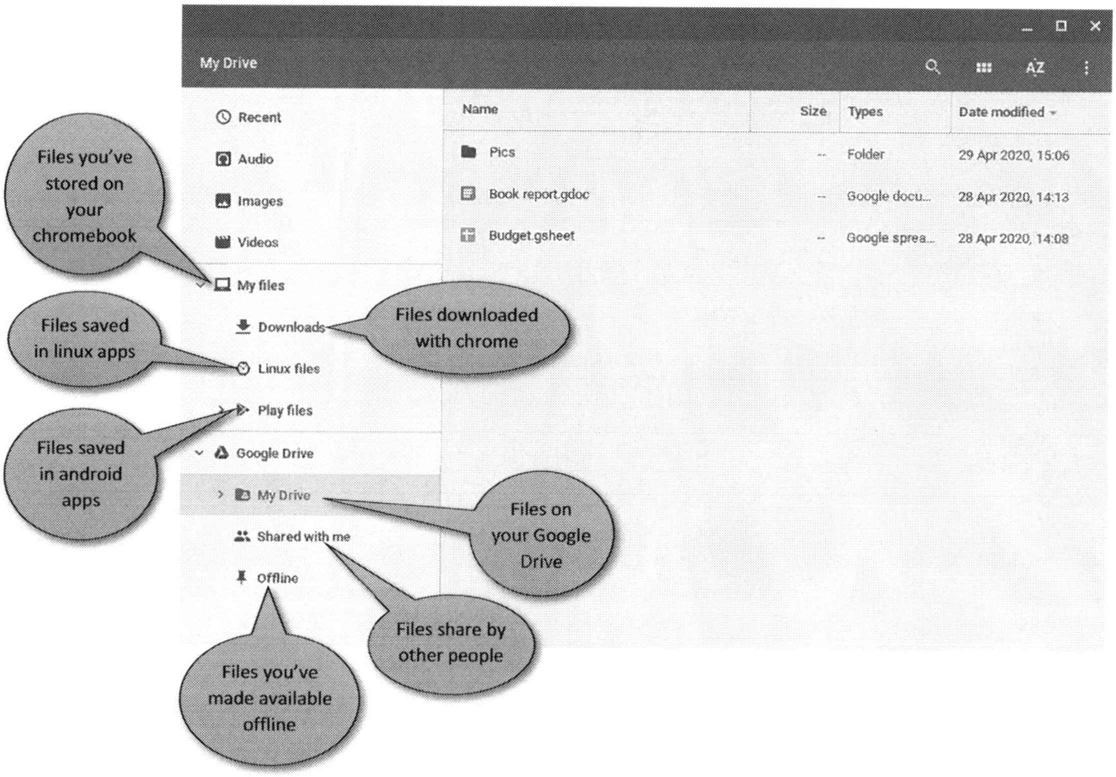

Along the top of the window you'll see some icons. These sometimes change depending what file or folder you've selected.

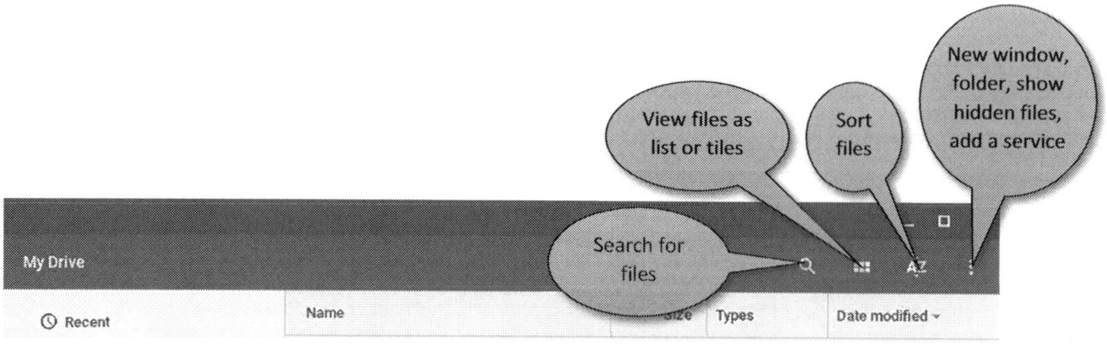

Creating Folders

To create new folders, navigate to the folder you want to create a new folder in using the panel on the left. Eg on google drive in 'my drive'.

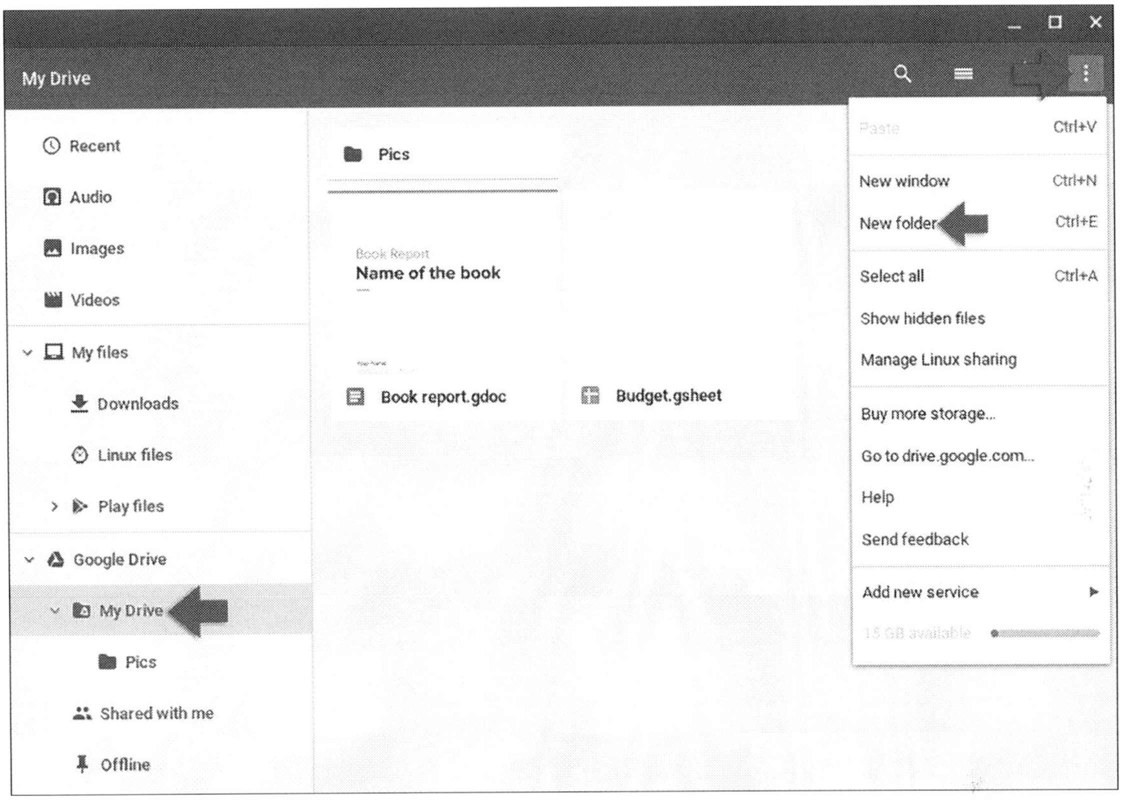

Click the three dots icon on the top right of the screen, then select 'new folder'.

Give the folder a meaningful name. Eg, 'work'.

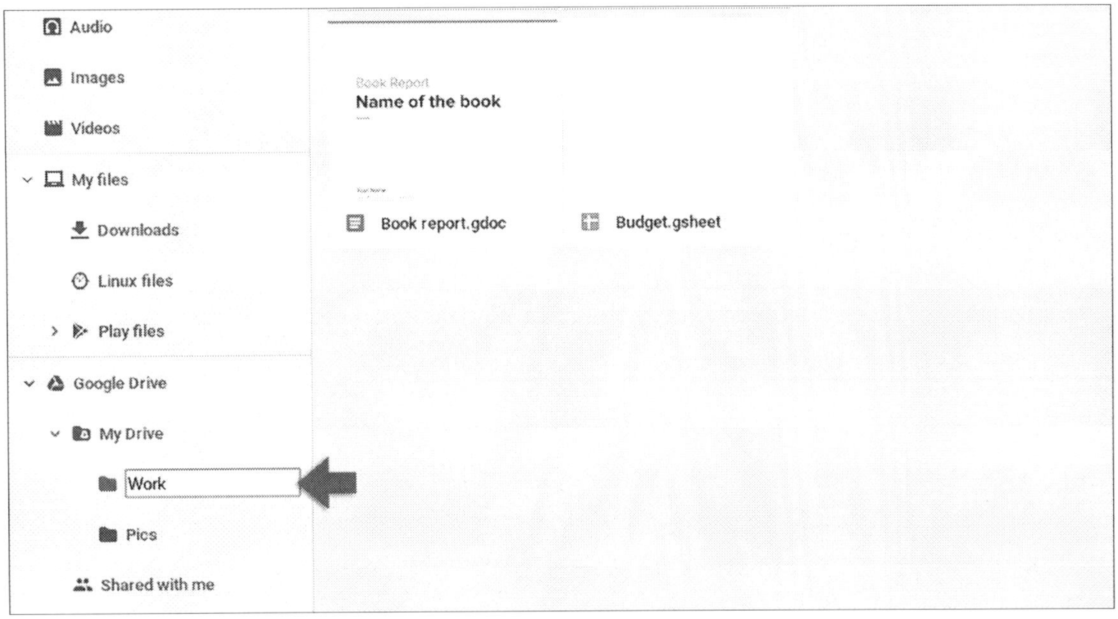

Moving Files

Select the files you want to move. Click the file icons to select multiple files, or click the tick box on the top left of the file thumbnail if you're viewing your files in thumbnail view.

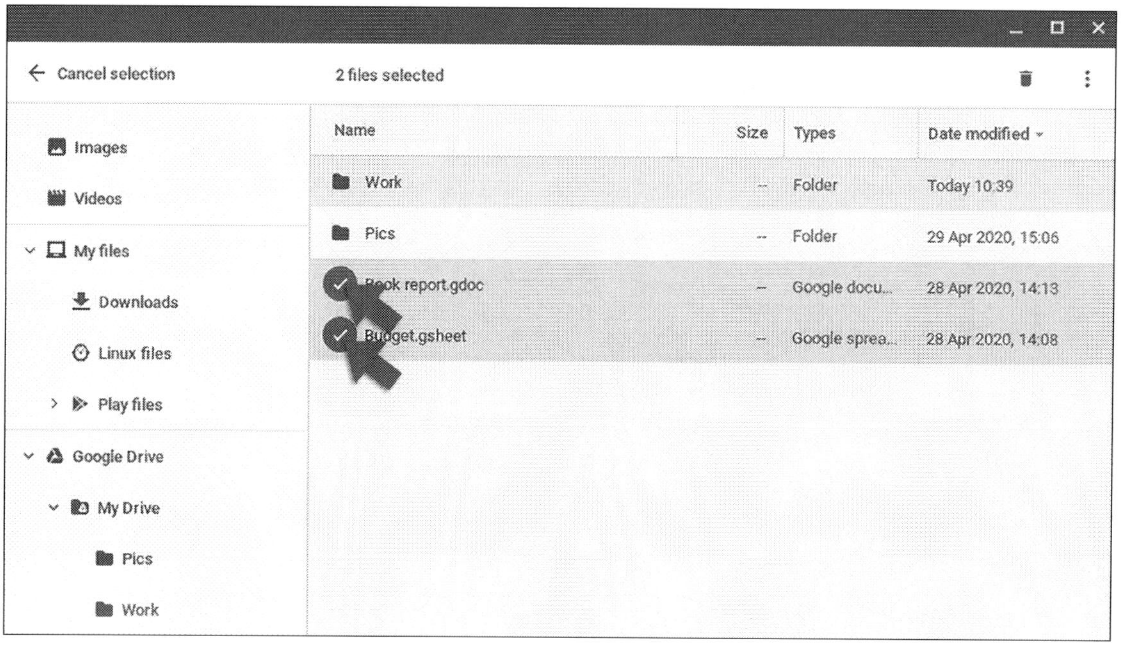

Click and drag the selection to the folder you want to move them to. In this example I'm moving my two files to the 'work' folder I created in the previous section.

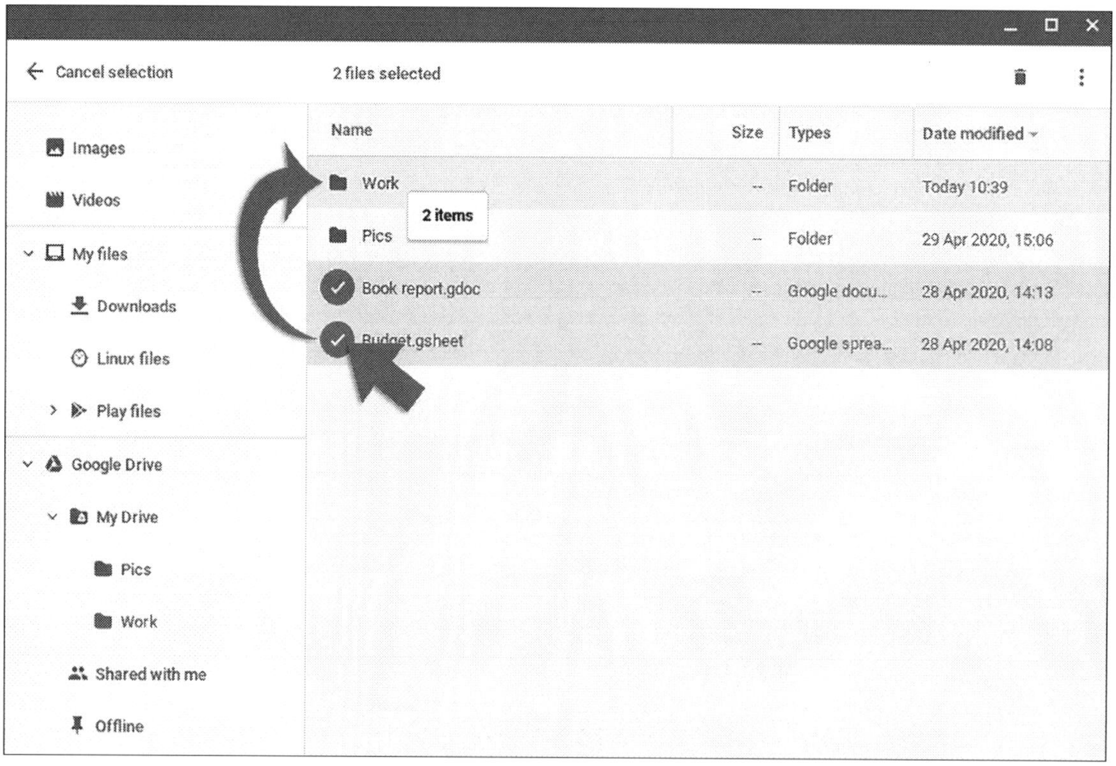

Copying Files

In the left hand pane, click the folder where the file you want to copy, is saved. Then click on the file(s) you want to copy to select them. Click the file icons to select multiple files, or click the tick box on the top left of the file thumbnail if you're viewing your files in thumbnail view. For example, lets copy an image from the 'images' folder.

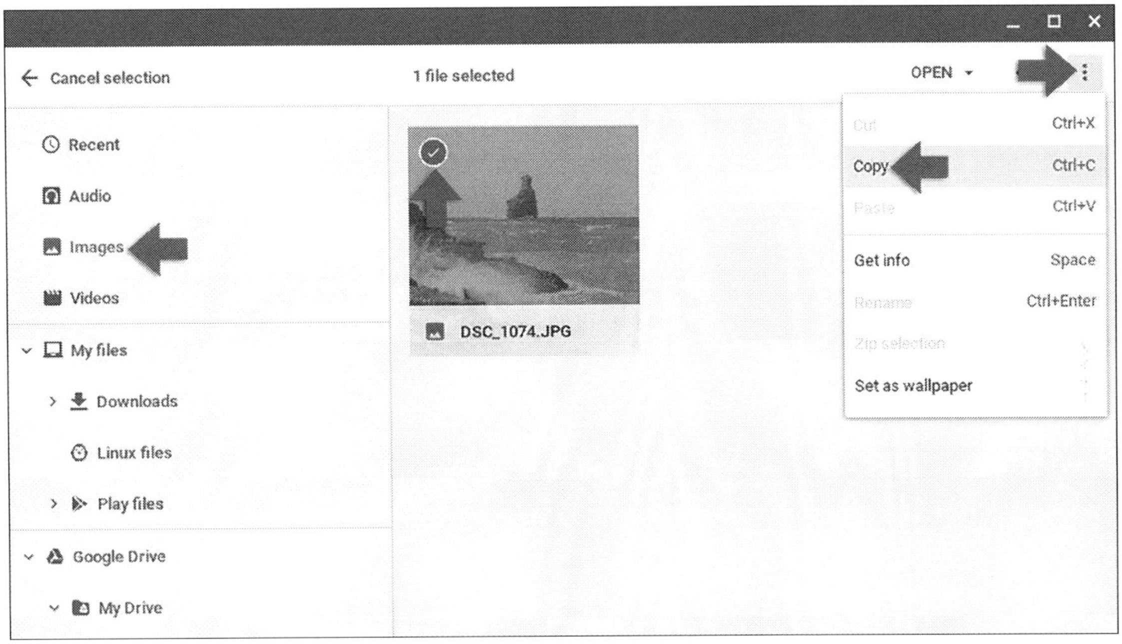

Using the left hand pane, navigate to the folder you want to copy the file to, eg google drive in 'my drive'.

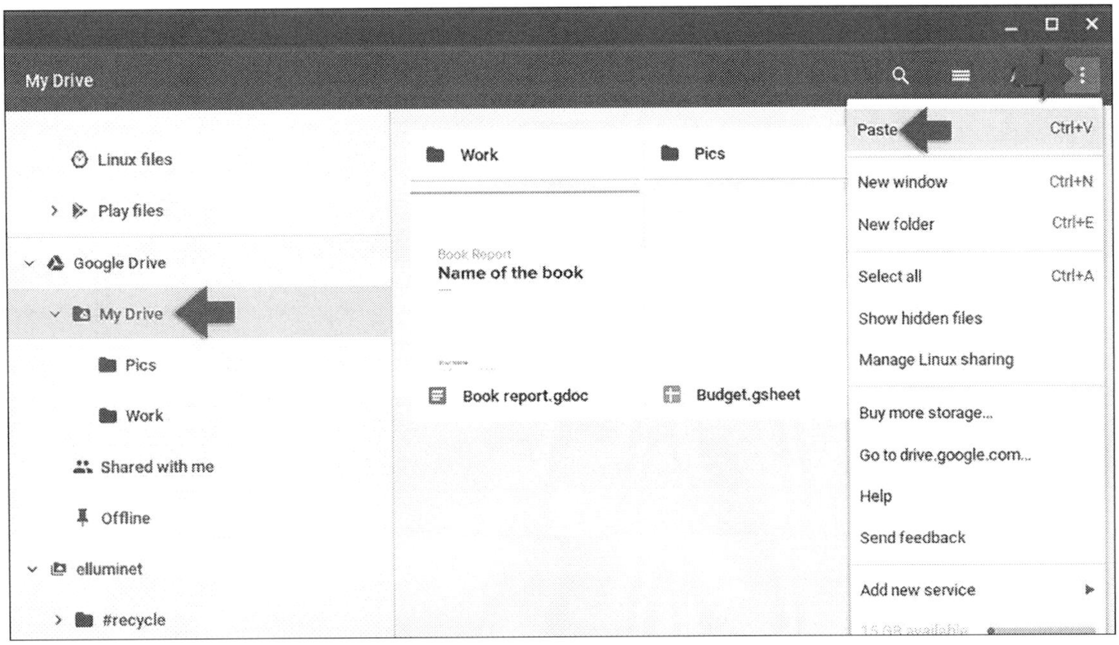

Click the three dots icon on the top right, select 'paste' from the menu.

Renaming Files

Navigate to the folder your file is saved in. In this demo it's in Google Drive. Right click on the file you want to rename, then select 'rename' from the popup menu.

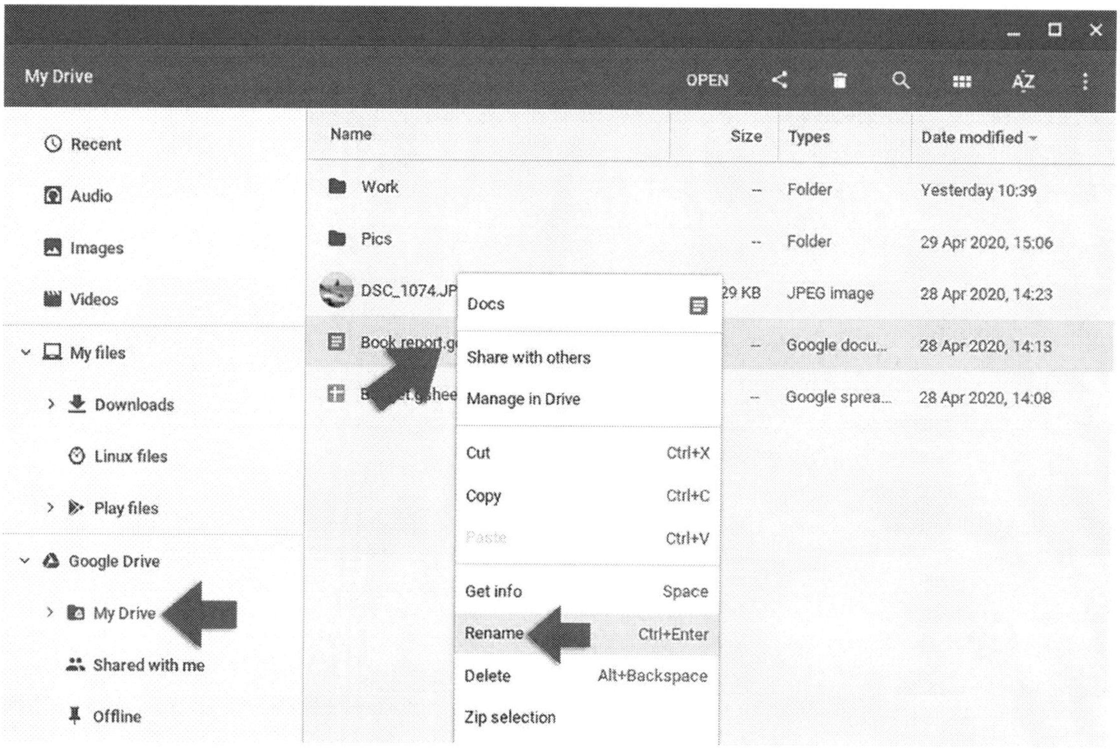

You'll see the name of the file highlighted in blue.

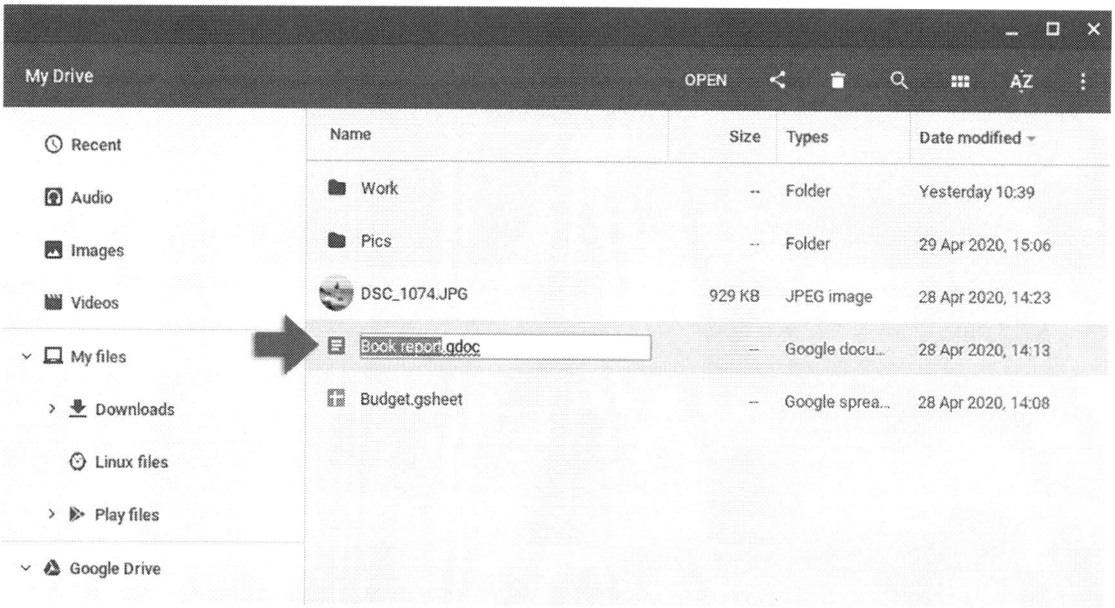

Now type in a meaningful name for the file. Press 'enter' on your keyboard when you're done.

Sorting Files

Within the files app, you can sort files alphabetically by name, or by size and date created. This makes it easier to find files especially when you have a lot of them in one folder. To sort your files, select the folder from the left hand side of the files app, eg, 'Google Drive'.

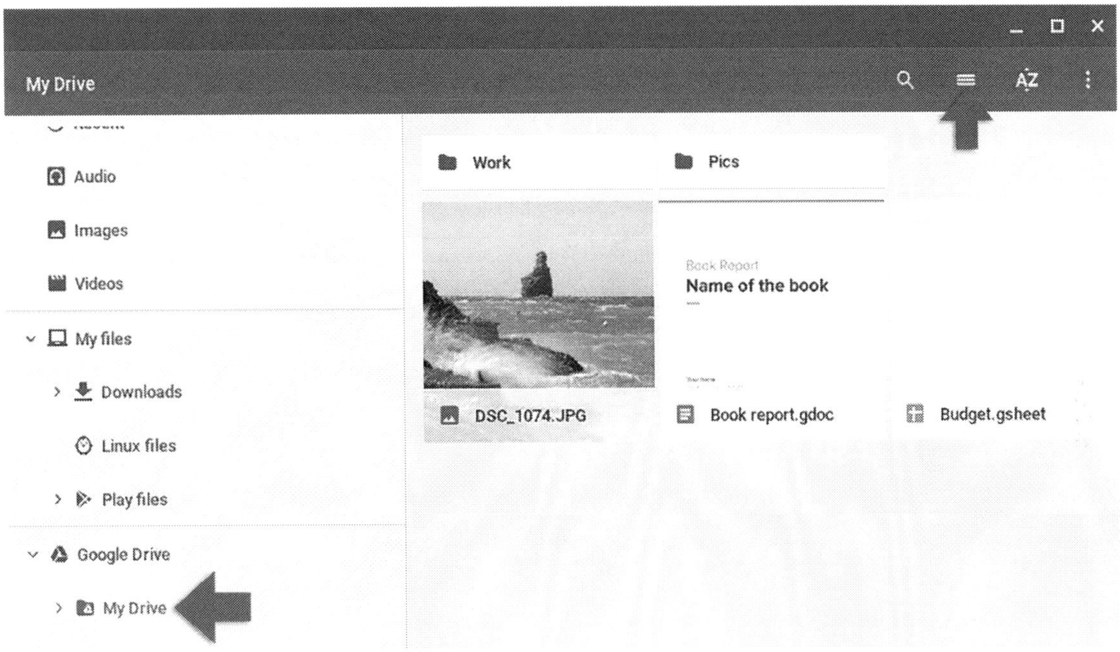

Switch to 'list view' - click the icon on the top right.

To sort the files, click the column headings. If you want to sort the files by name, click 'name'. To sort by file size click 'size', by file type click 'types', and by date modified click 'date modified'.

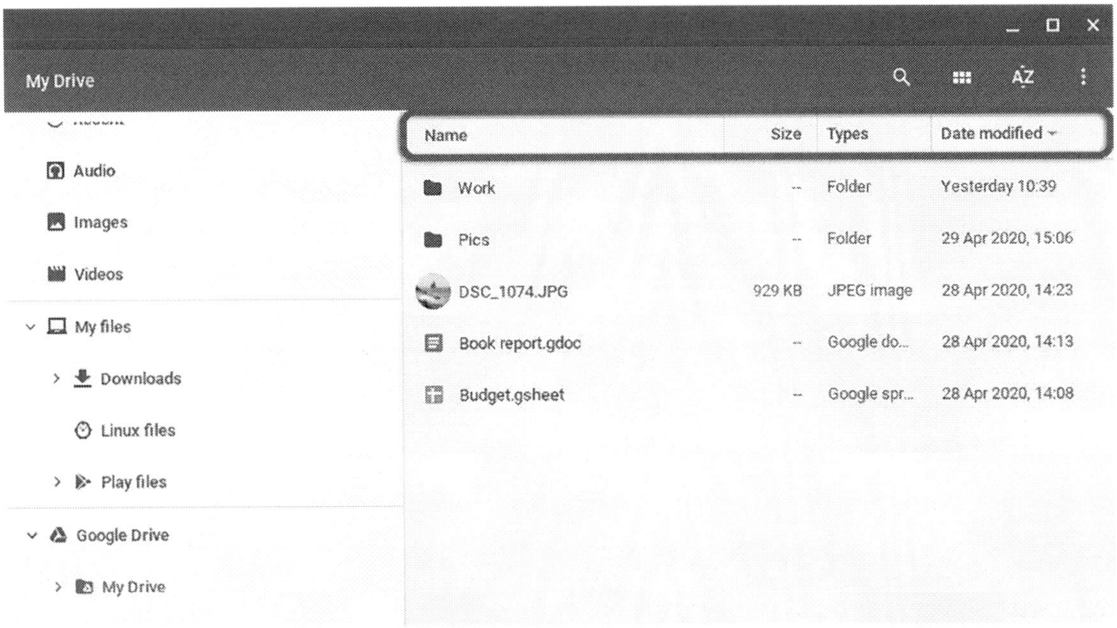

Searching for Files

You can search for files within the files app using the search icon on the top right of the window. First, select the location to search from, eg Google Drive.

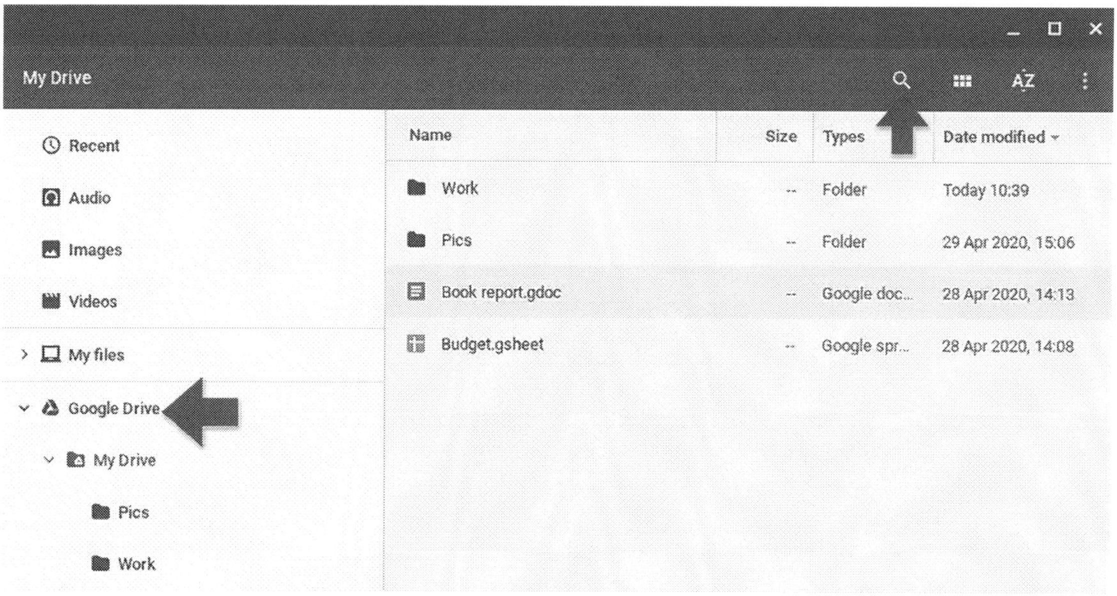

Click the search icon on the top right, then type your search keywords into the search field. You'll see a list of suggestions appear, to select, click on one in the list.

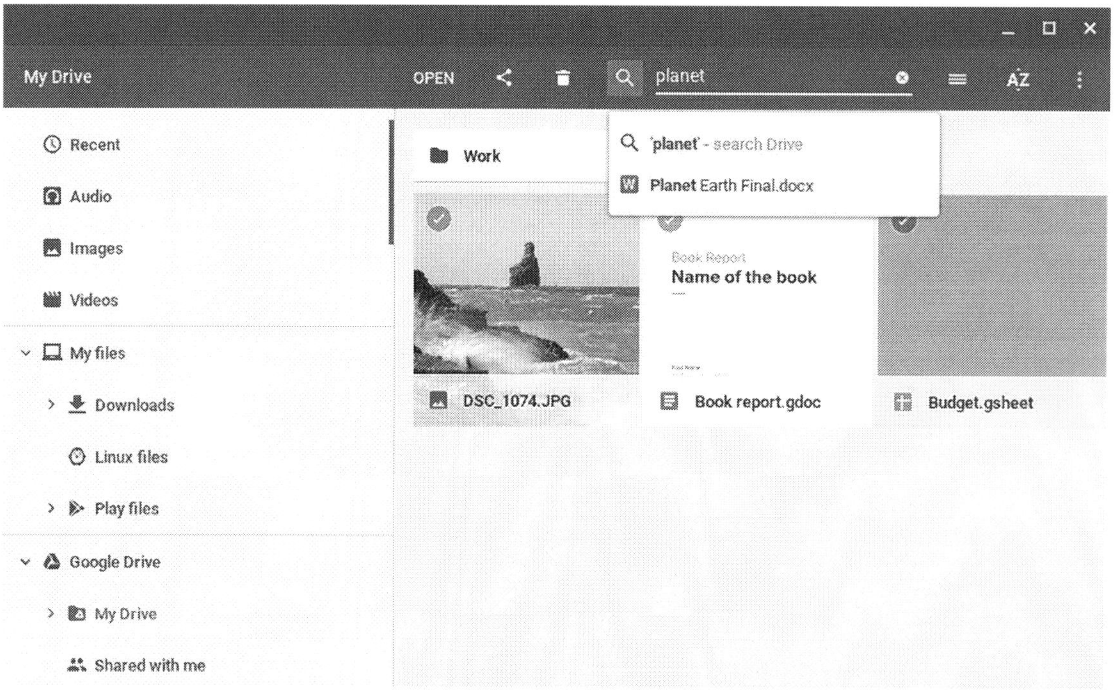

Select a file from the suggestions, or press enter on your keyboard to show all files.

External Drives

You can attach storage devices to your computer. The most common ones are memory sticks - also called usb keys, usb sticks, flash drives or thumb drives. The other type is the portable hard drive.

Memory sticks are usually smaller in capacity ranging from 1GB all the way up to 256GB. Portable hard drives can be larger than 1TB.

To read the drive, plug the device into a USB port on your chromebook, then select file explorer from the task bar.

To access the drive, open your files app. Your drive will show up in the panel on the left hand side of the screen. Click on the drive to view any files or folders on the drive.

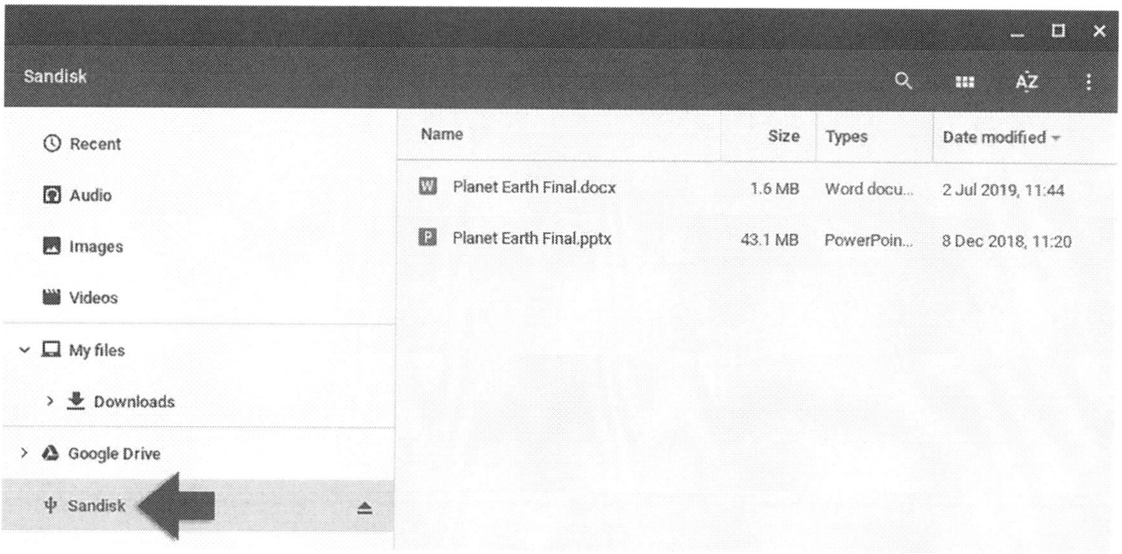

You can drag and drop files to and from your external drive. See moving and copying files on page 100.

Formatting External Drives

To format the drive, open your files app. Right click on the drive in the left hand panel then select 'format device'.

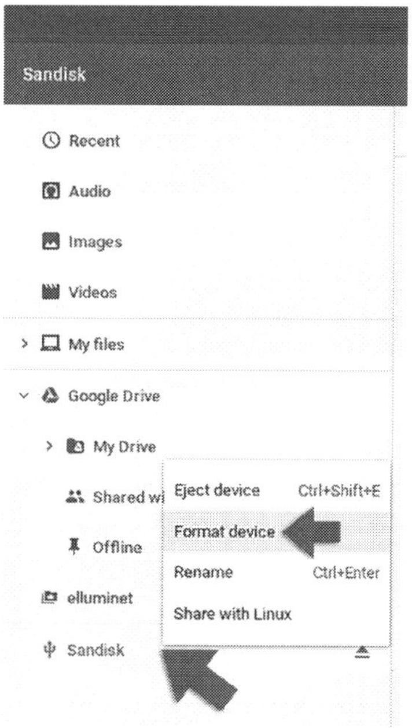

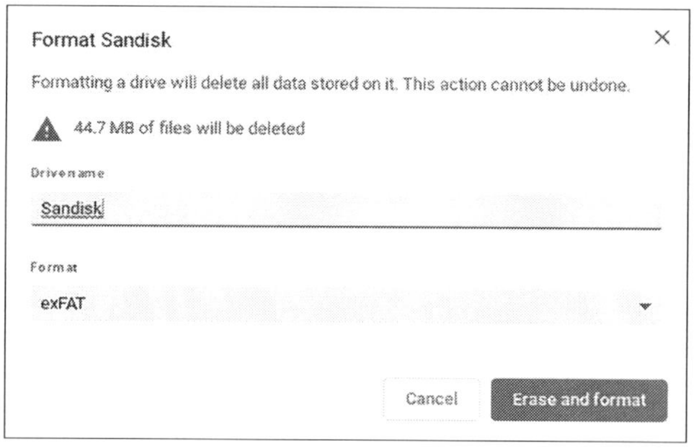

In the format window, give the device a name. In the 'format field' use exFAT for compatibility between platforms (windows, mac and chromebook).

SD Cards

You can expand your internal storage using an SD card. Find the SD card slot on your chromebook - usually on one of the side panels. This particular chromebook has a MicroSD card reader.

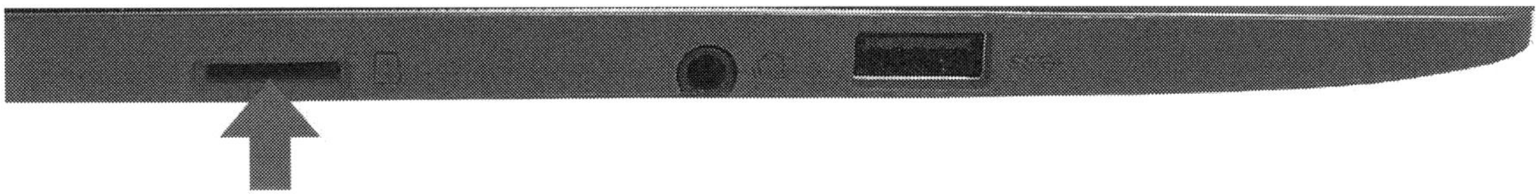

If you have a microSD card slot, then you'll need to insert a MicroSD card. Push the card in until it clicks in place.

Standard SD **Micro SD** **SD Card Adapter**

Your SD card will show up in your files app.

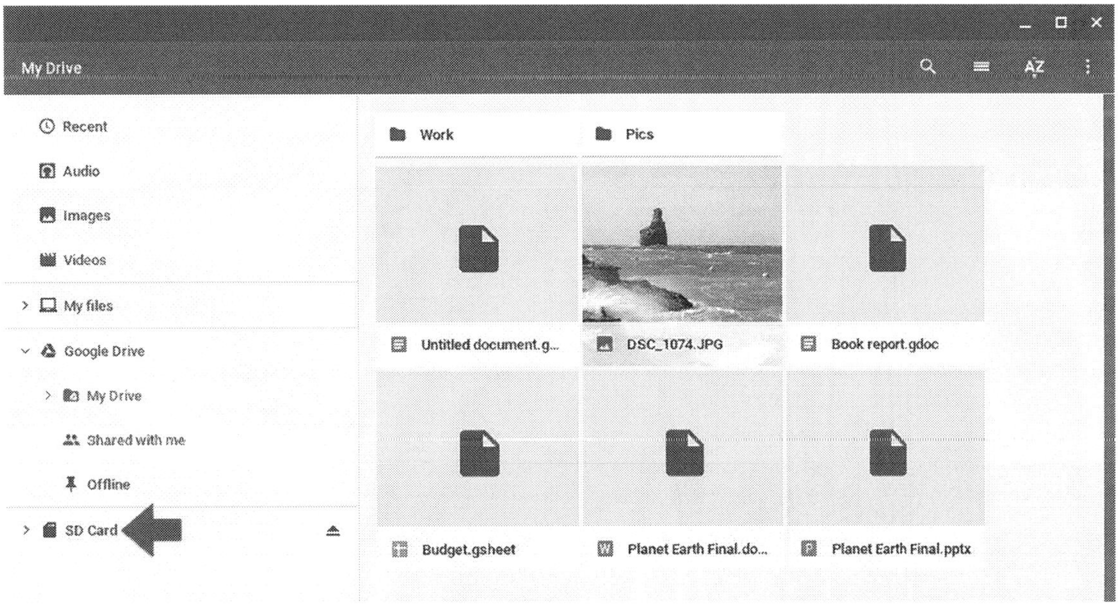

You can format the drive in the same way as any external drive. "Formatting External Drives" on page 106.

To move or copy files see page 100 and page 101.

Nearby Share

Nearby Share is a feature that uses Bluetooth and Wi-Fi to files between an Android device and a Chromebook.

Setup on Chromebook

Open the settings, then select connected devices.

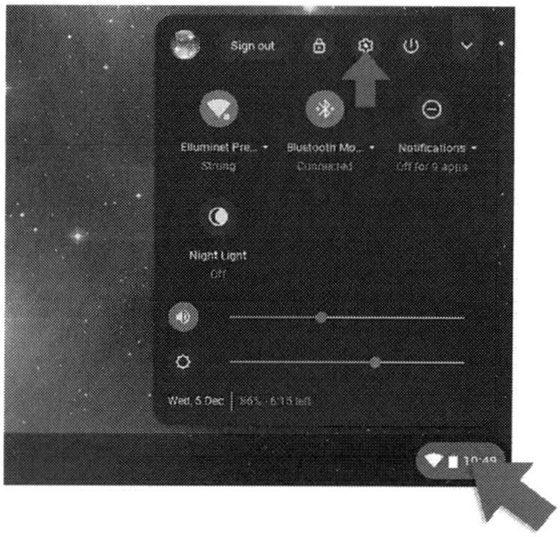

Scroll down to 'nearby share', then click 'setup'.

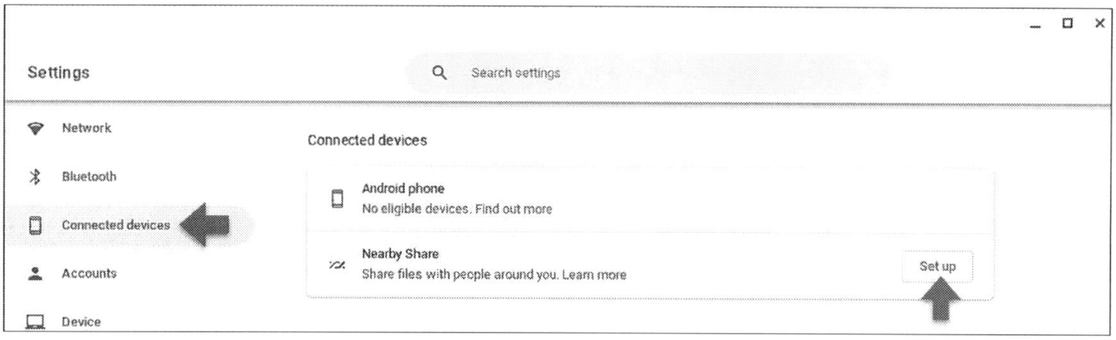

Give your device a name. This helps you identify your device when sharing.

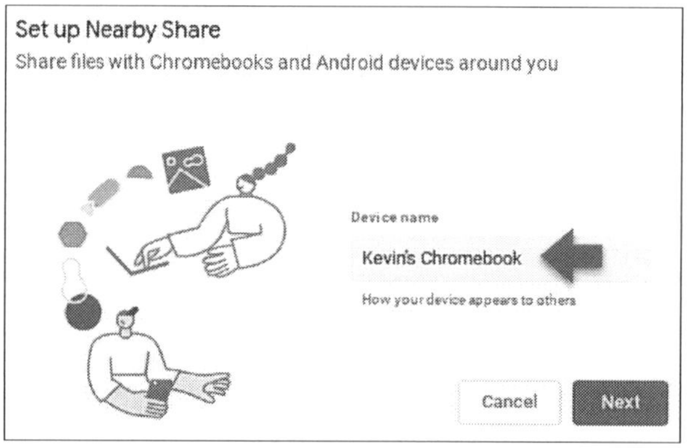

Choose who can see your chromebook and share files with you.

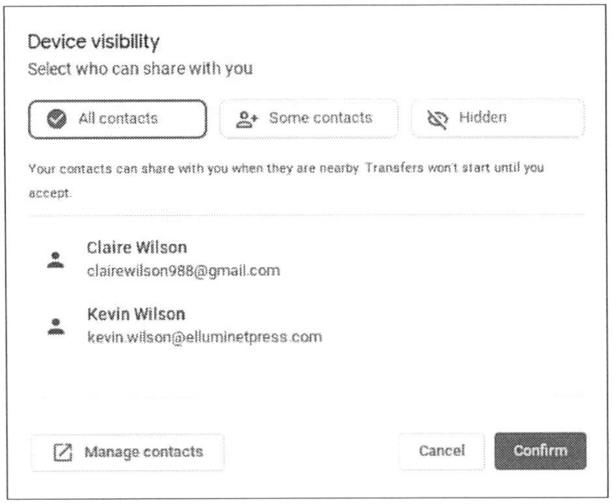

All Contacts. This means all of your contacts on your contacts list will be able to see your chromebook.

Some Contacts. This means you choose which contacts will be able to see your chromebook. To choose contacts, select 'some contacts' from the buttons along the top of the dialog box, then turn on the contacts you want to use. To add more contacts to your contacts list, select 'manage contacts'.

Hidden. No will be able to see your chromebook.

For this demo, I'm going to select 'all contacts'. Click 'confirm' when you're done.

Setup on Android Device

To set up nearby share on an android device, open the settings then select 'google'. Select devices and sharing

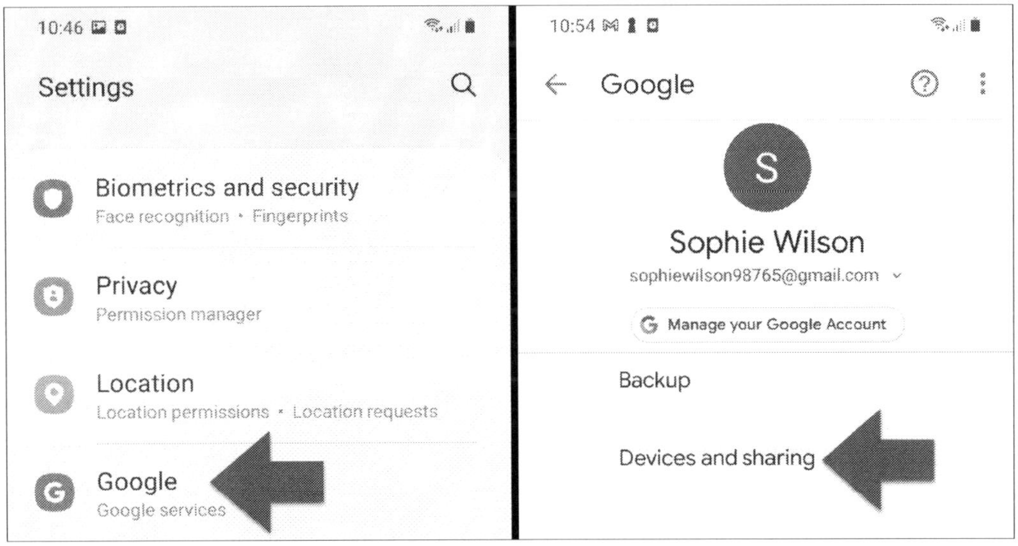

Select 'nearby share'. Click the switch to turn on the feature. Then underneath, click 'device name' to give the device a name so people can identify your device when they want to share something with you.

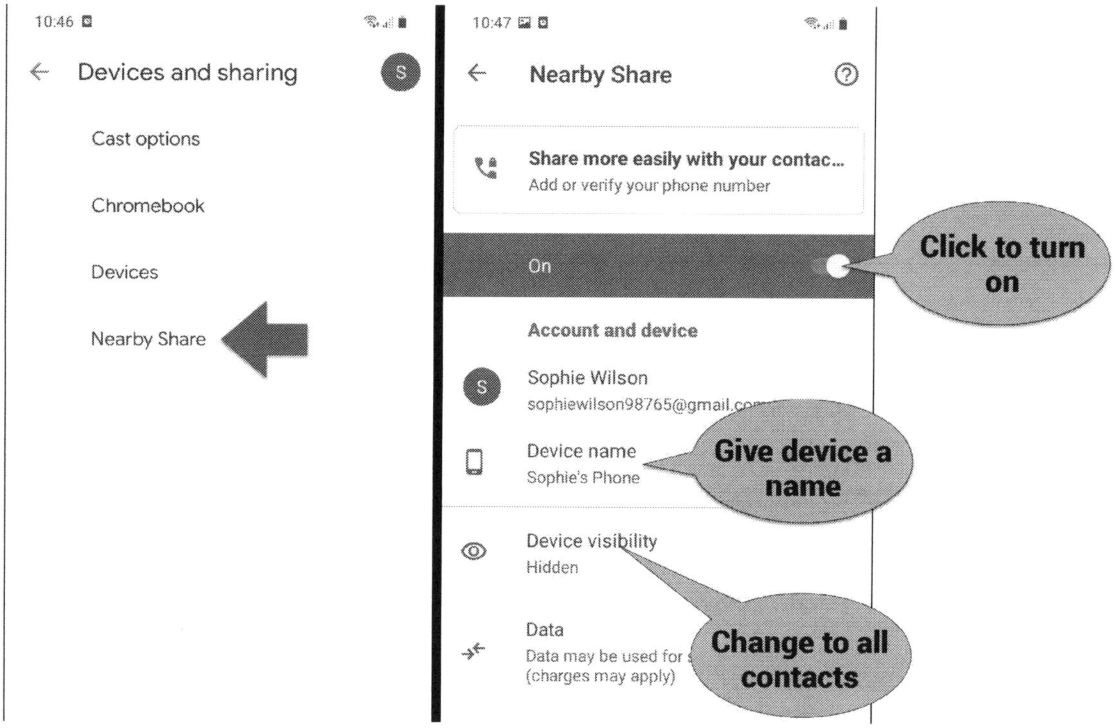

Next, click 'device visibility'. Choose who can see your chromebook and share files with you.

All Contacts. This means all of your contacts on your contacts list will be able to see your device.

Some Contacts. This means you choose which contacts will be able to see your device. To choose contacts, select 'some contacts' from the buttons along the top of the dialog box, then turn on the contacts you want to use.

Hidden. No will be able to see your device. For this demo, I'm going to select 'all contacts'.

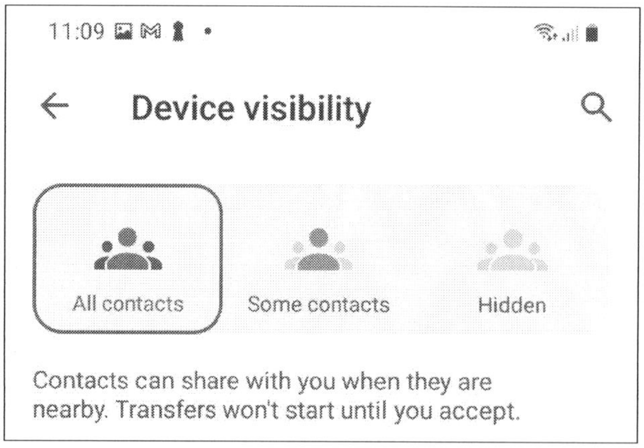

Sharing a File

To share a file, open the files app,

Select a file, then click the share icon on the top right of the window. Here, I'm going to share a file from my Google Drive folder on my Chromebook.

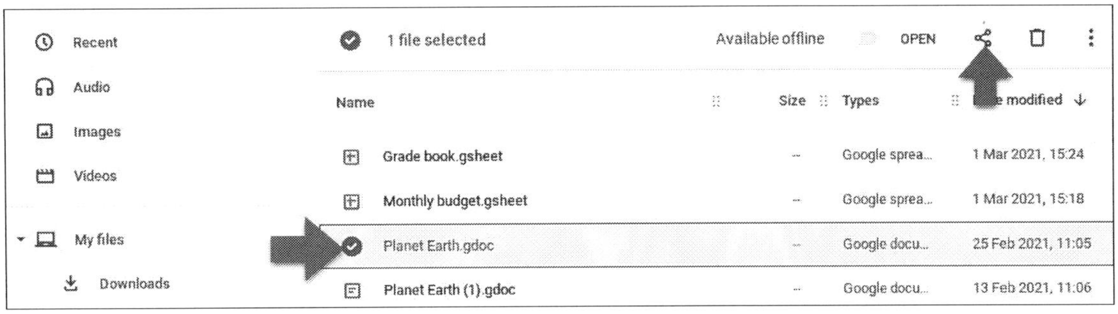

Select 'nearby share' from the share dialog box.

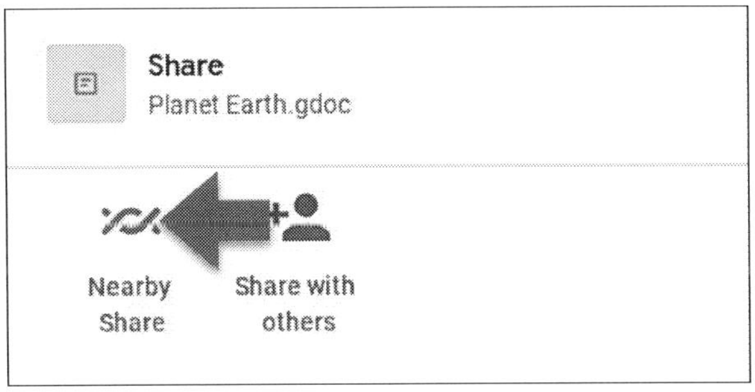

Your Chromebook will scan for nearby devices. Select the person's device from the list, click 'next'.

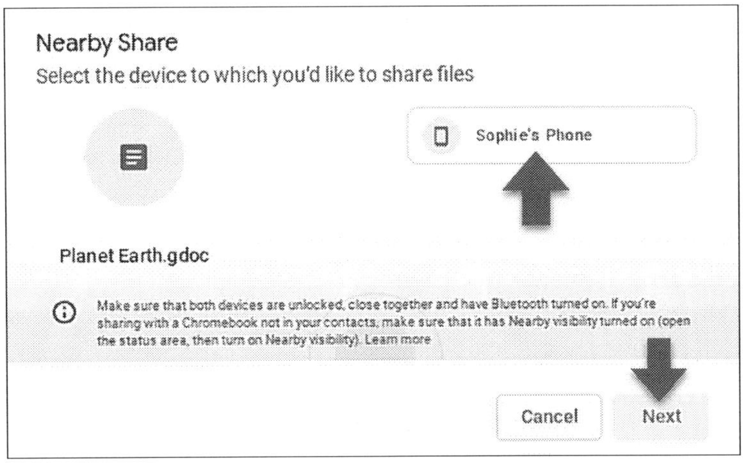

Make sure both devices are unlocked. Also make sure bluetooth is enabled on both devices.

The other person will get a prompt asking them to accept the transfer. They may also get a prompt asking them to "become visible" - tap on the prompt.

Once they tap 'accept', the file will send.

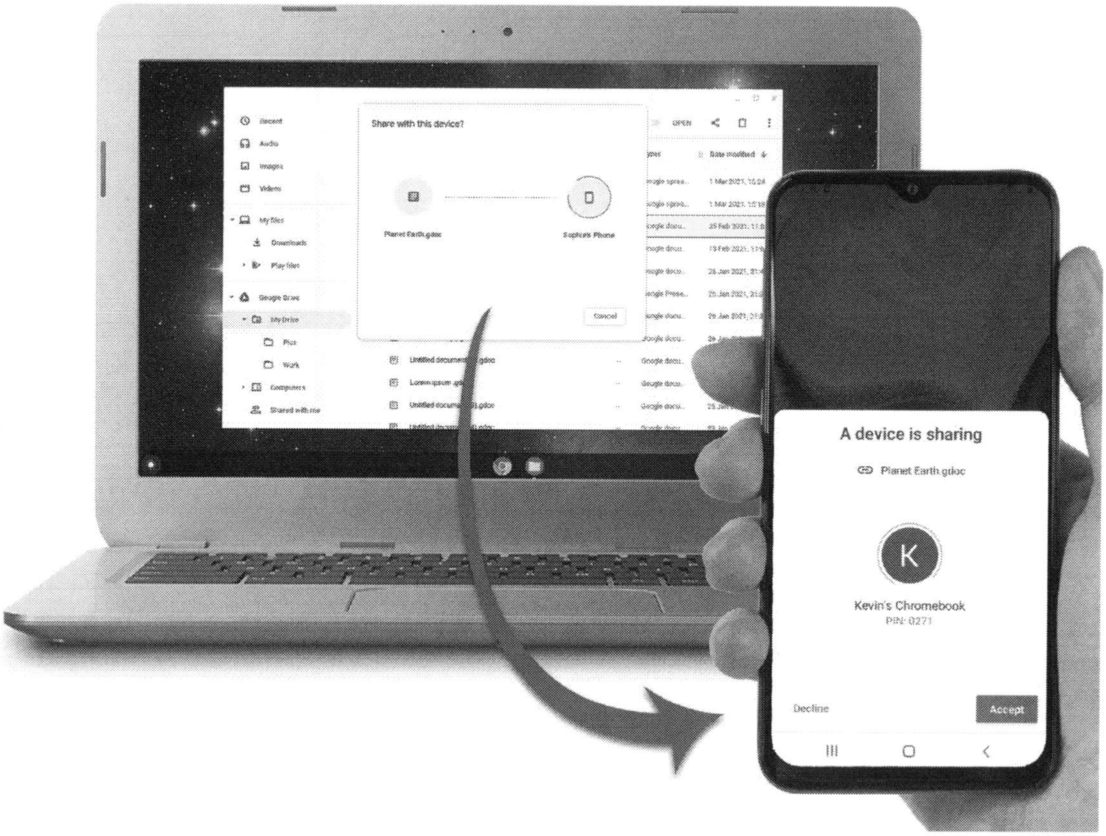

Screen Capture

You can take a screenshot or record your Chromebook's screen. You can then view, edit, and share the screen captures.

Screenshots

To take a screenshot, click the clock on the bottom right of the screen.

Select ‘screen capture’ from the options.

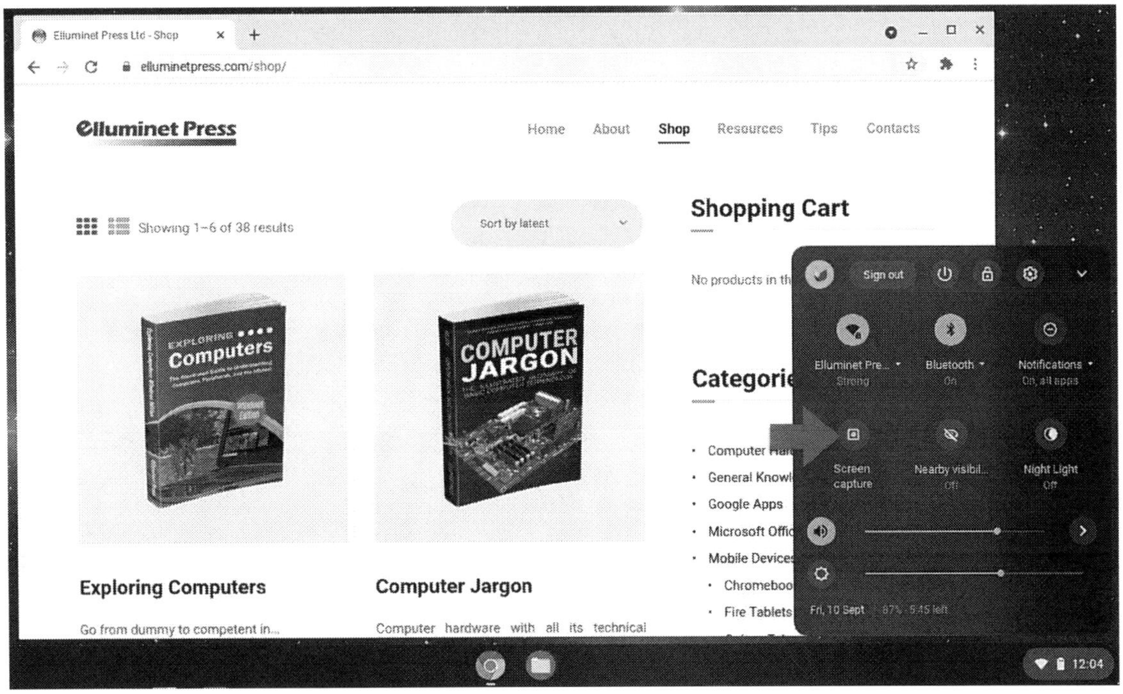

You’ll see the screen capture controls appear along the bottom of the screen.

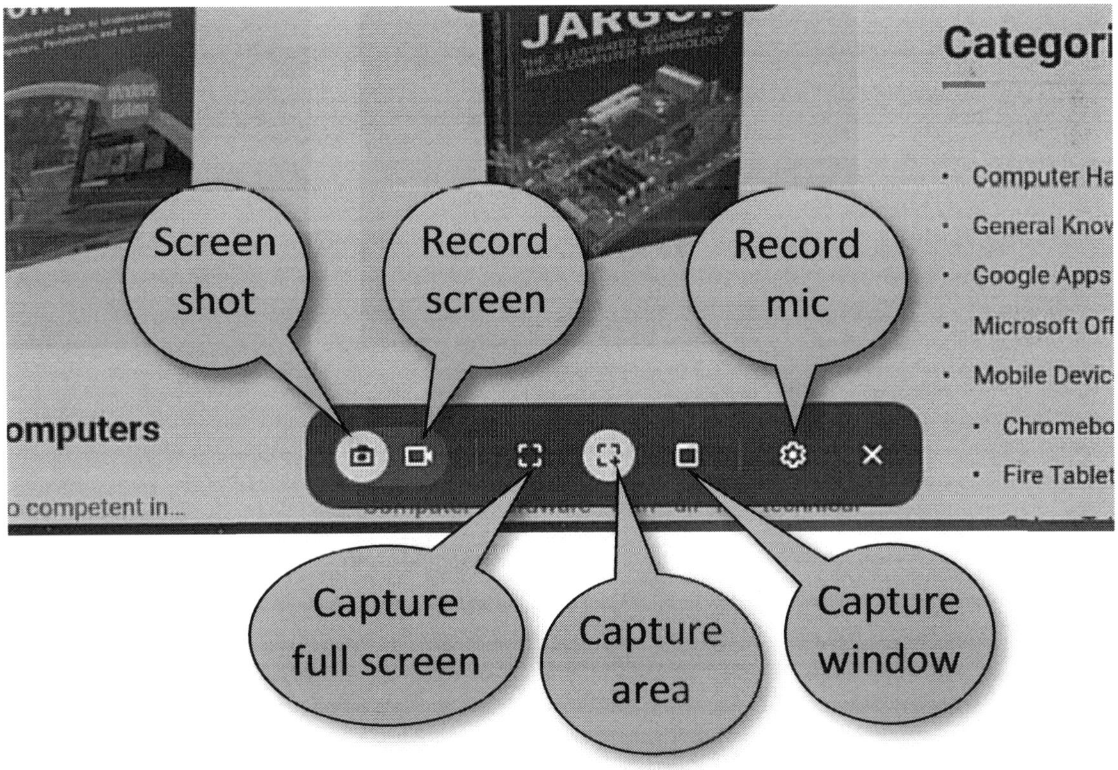

From the screen capture controls, select ‘screen shot’, then click ‘full screen’, if you want to take a screenshot of the whole screen.

Click 'capture area' if you want to take a screenshot of a part of the screen. Drag the selection box around the part of the screen you want.

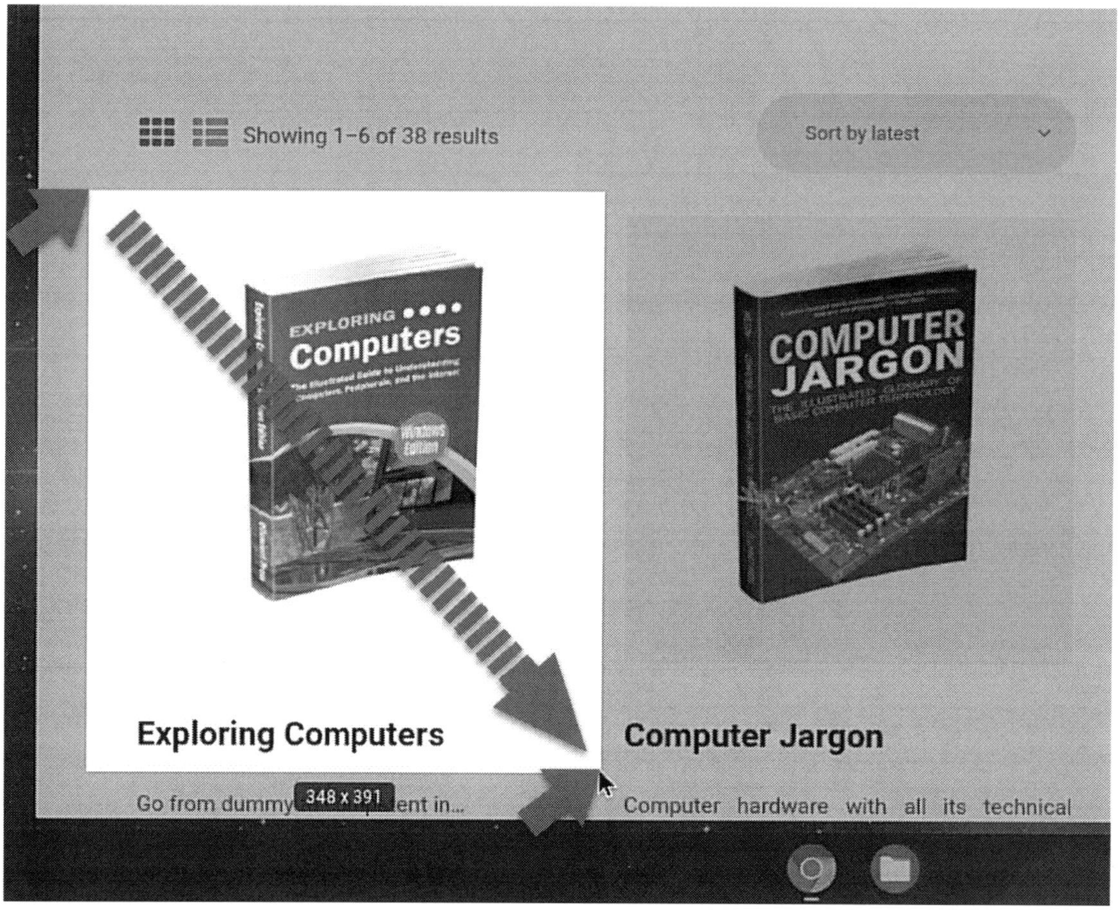

Click 'capture'.

The screenshot will appear in the 'pinned files' on the bottom right of the screen.

You'll also find them in the 'downloads' section in the files app.

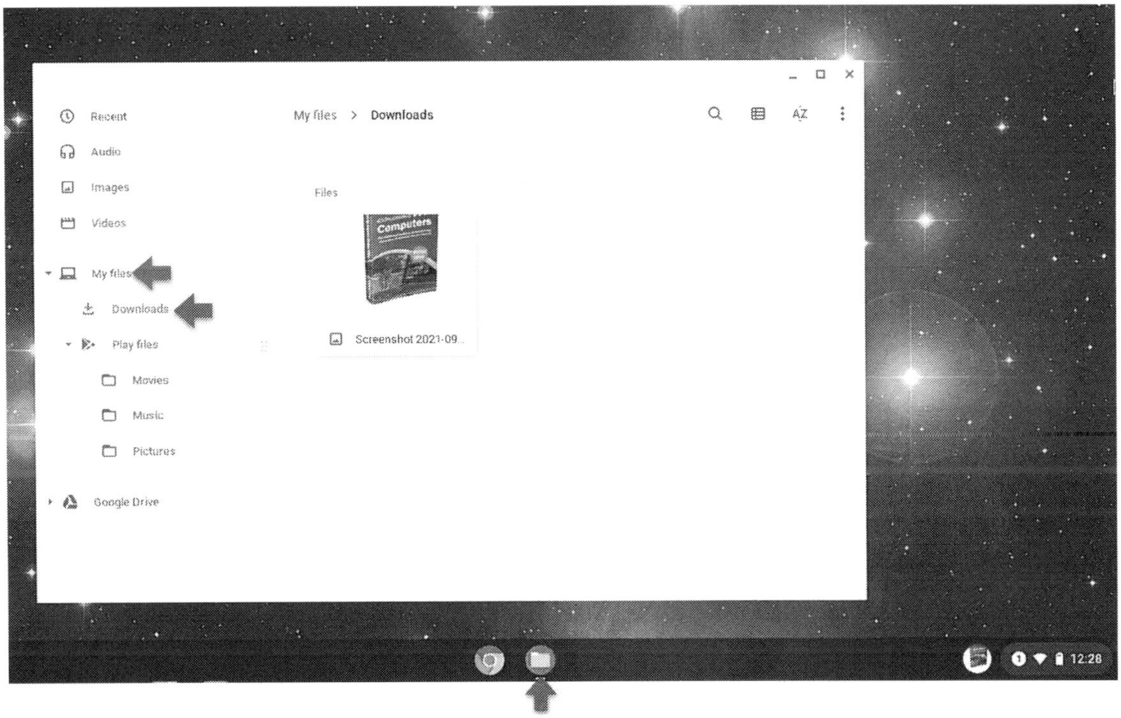

Record the Screen

You can record your screen and save it as a video file. To take a screenshot, click the clock on the bottom right of the screen.

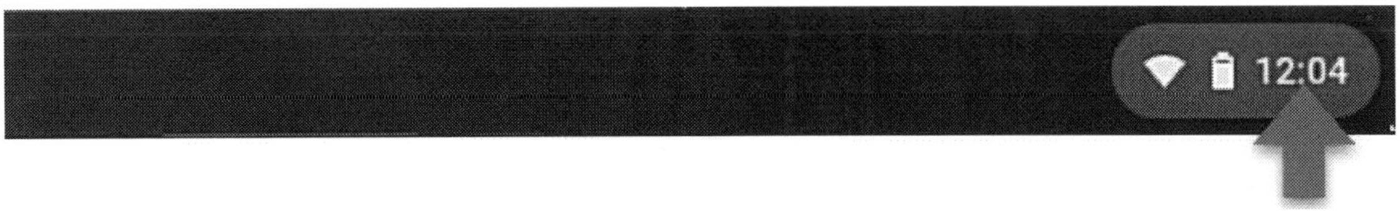

Select 'screen capture' from the options.

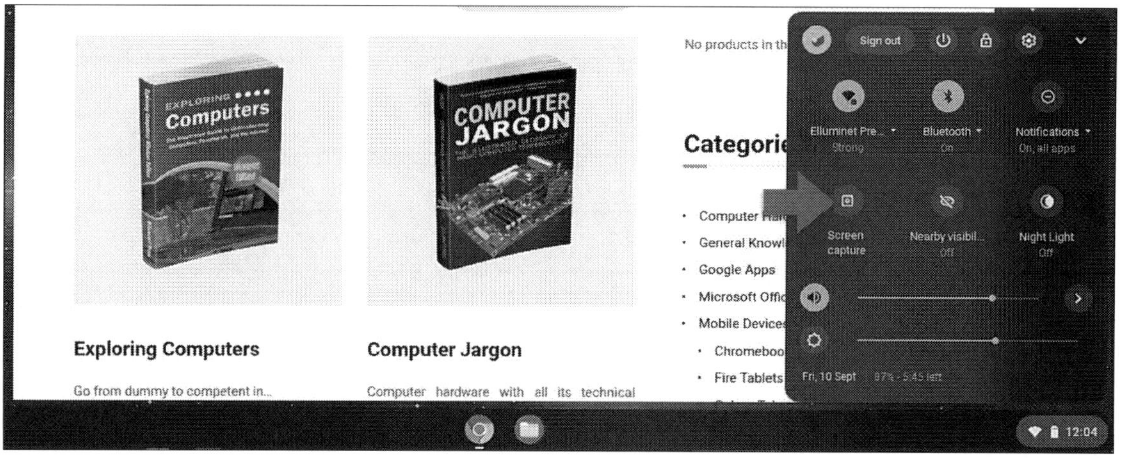

Select the record screen icon and the full screen icon from the screen capture controls.

Click anywhere on the screen to being recording. You'll see a 3 second countdown.

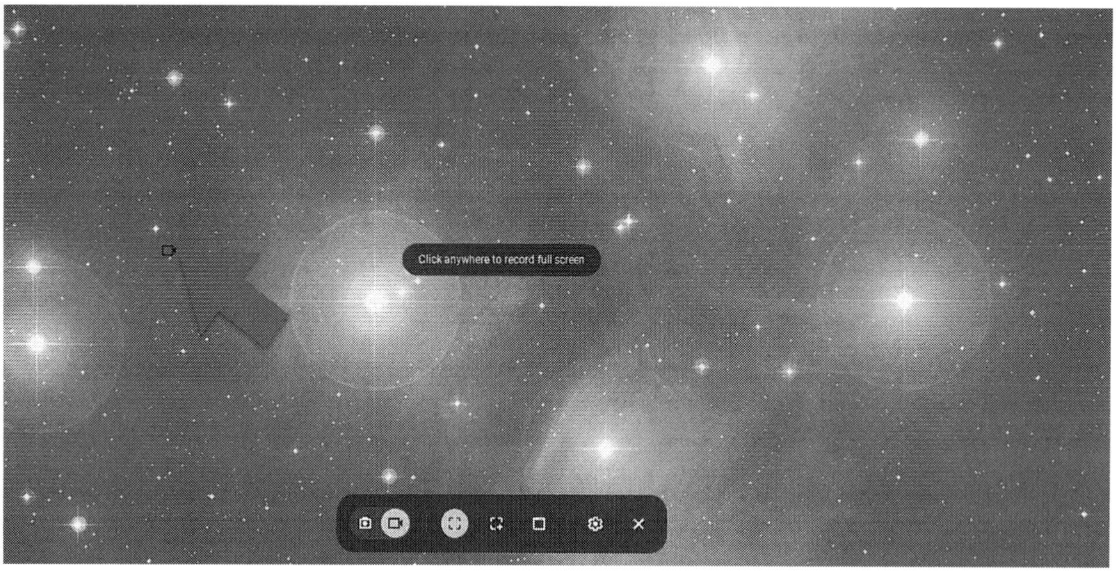

To stop recording, click the stop icon on the bottom right of the screen.

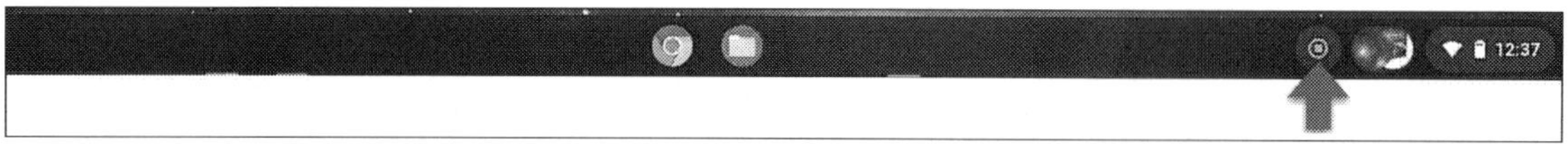

You'll find the recording in the 'downloads' section in the files app.

Talk to your Chromebook

The 'Google Now' voice assistant is integrated into Chromebook, but isn't always enabled by default.

To enable the feature, go to settings. Scroll down to 'Google Assistant'.

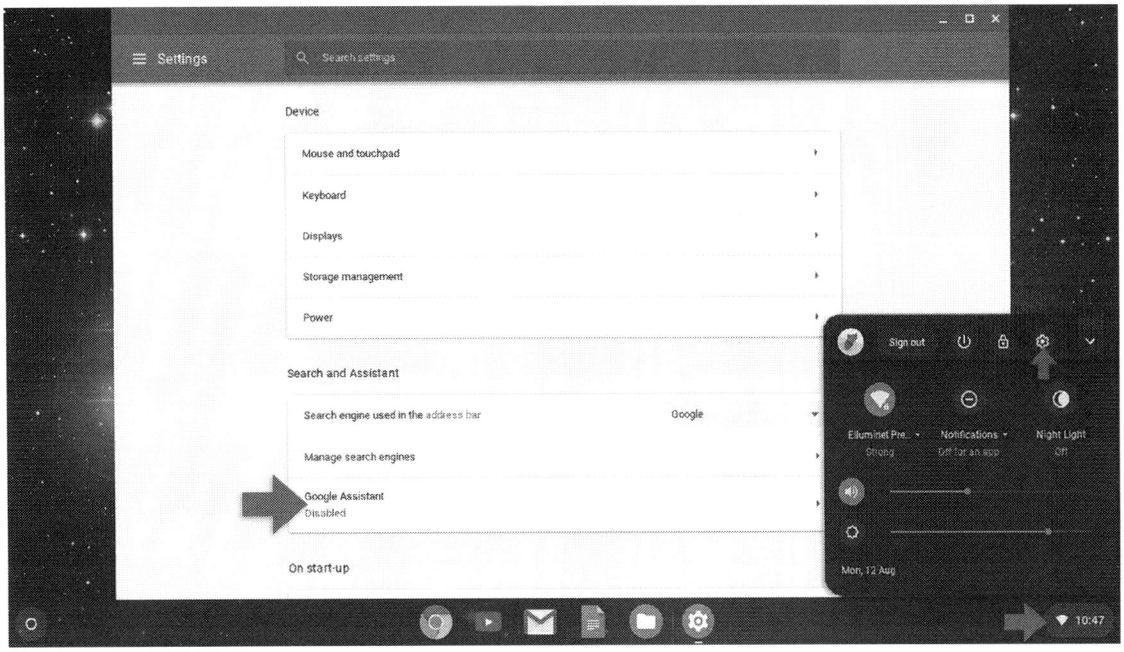

Turn on 'Google Assistant', also turn on 'OK Google'.

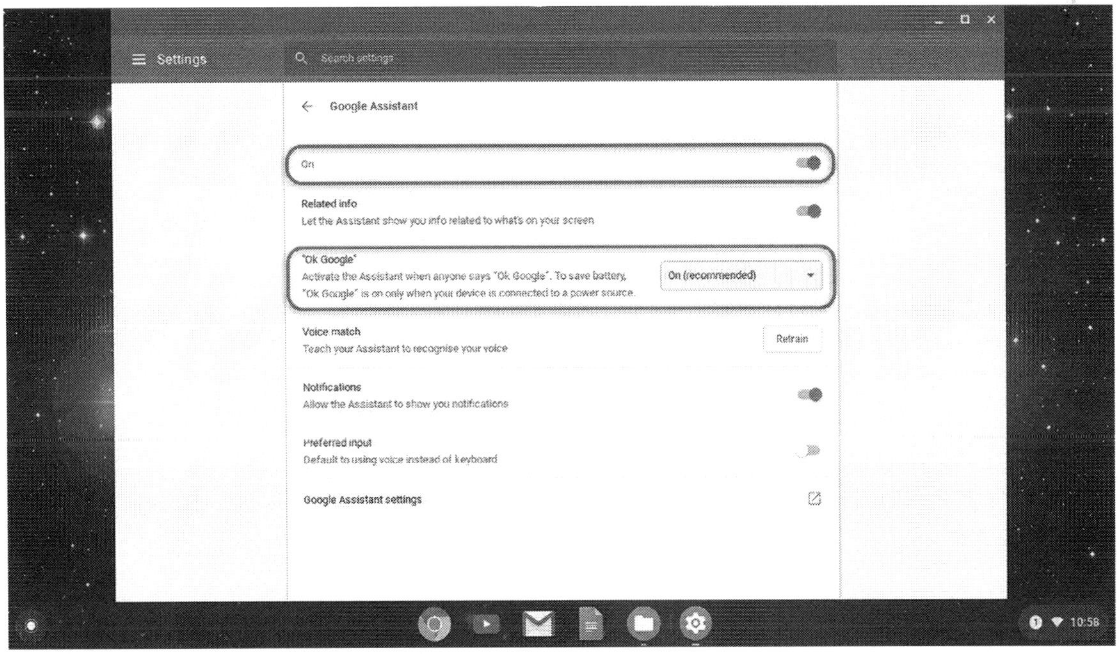

Go through the setup wizard to teach Google to recognise your voice.

Now, whenever you want something just say 'OK Google...'

4 Using Chrome Apps

There are two types of chrome app for the ChromeBook: a hosted app and a packaged app.

A hosted app, or Chrome app as it is sometimes called, is an app that runs within the Chrome Web Browser.

A packaged app is very similar in appearance to the traditional desktop apps we see in Windows and Mac operating systems and is capable of interacting directly with hardware and storage on your ChromeBook. These apps are available from the Chrome Web Store.

In your app launcher, chrome apps are indicated with a chrome symbol on the app icon, as you can see below:

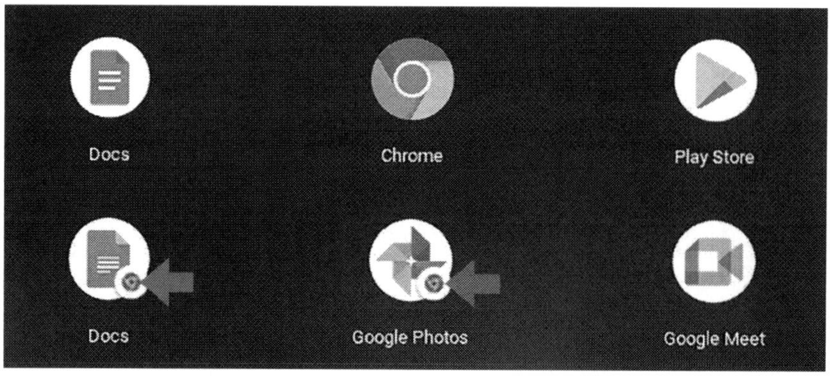

Chrome Web Store

This is where you can download countless apps for your ChromeBook. Many of these apps are free, but there are one or two that you will have to pay for.

To launch the website, open your app launcher

Click the arrow at the top to open the launcher fully. Click 'web store'.

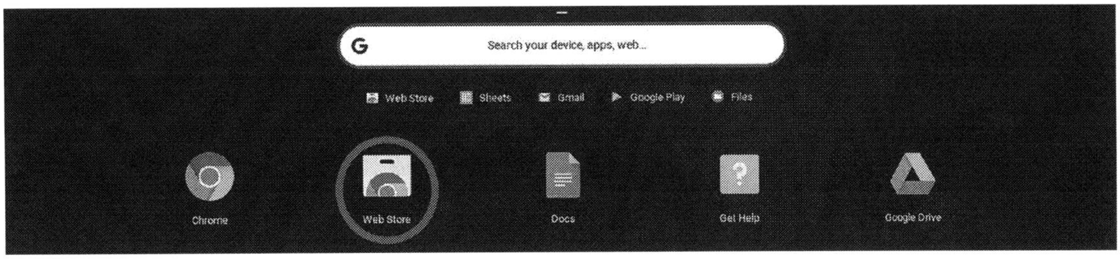

Once the web store opens, you'll see the home screen. Here, you can browse for apps and search for specific apps.

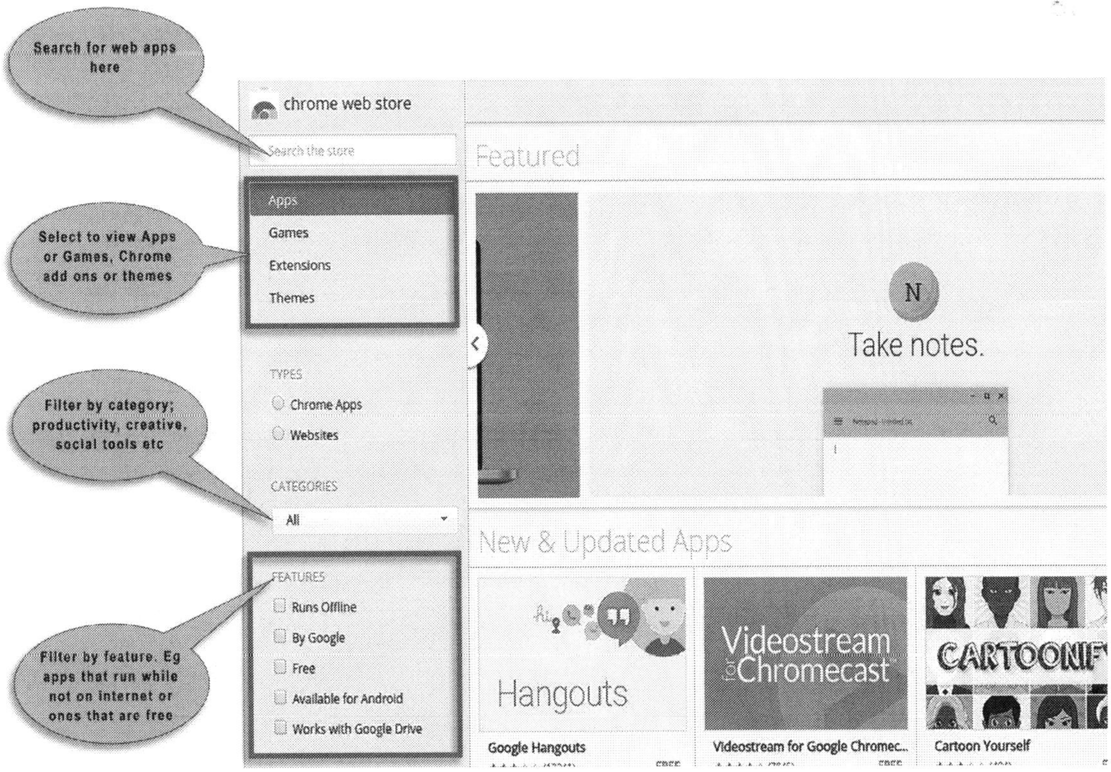

Browsing the Store

Down the left hand side of the Web Store, you'll see some options. Here you can select 'extensions', which are small apps that run within the Chrome Web Browser and extend the browser's features.

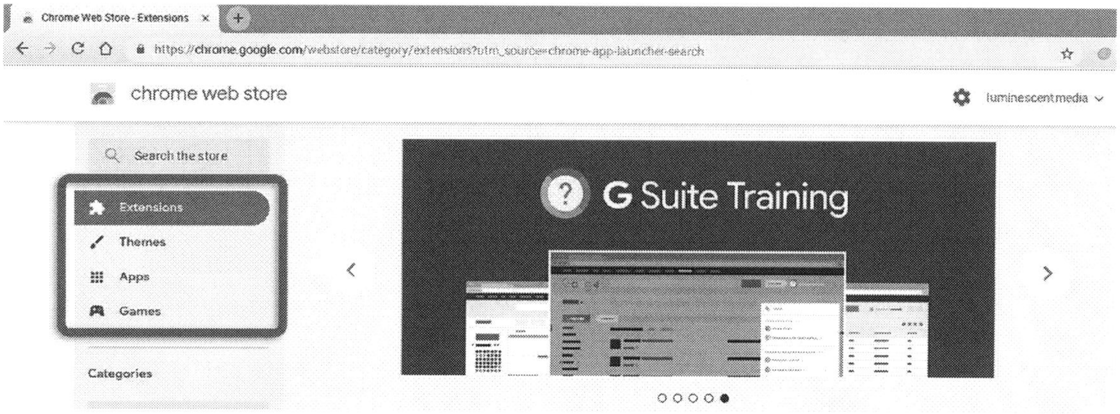

You can also select 'themes', which change the way your ChromeBook looks by changing the desktop wallpaper, toolbar colours, on screen fonts and so on.

You can select 'apps', such as Google Docs that either run on your ChromeBook itself or within the Chrome Web Browser.

You can also select 'games', which are gaming apps that run on your ChromeBook or Chrome Web Browser.

For the sake of this example, I'm going to select 'apps' from the options.

Underneath that, you can select various categories. To open the list of categories, click on the drop down box under 'categories' on the left hand side of your screen. Click on one of the categories. So if you are looking for productivity apps such as word processors, lifestyle apps such as social media, or educational apps, you'll find them here.

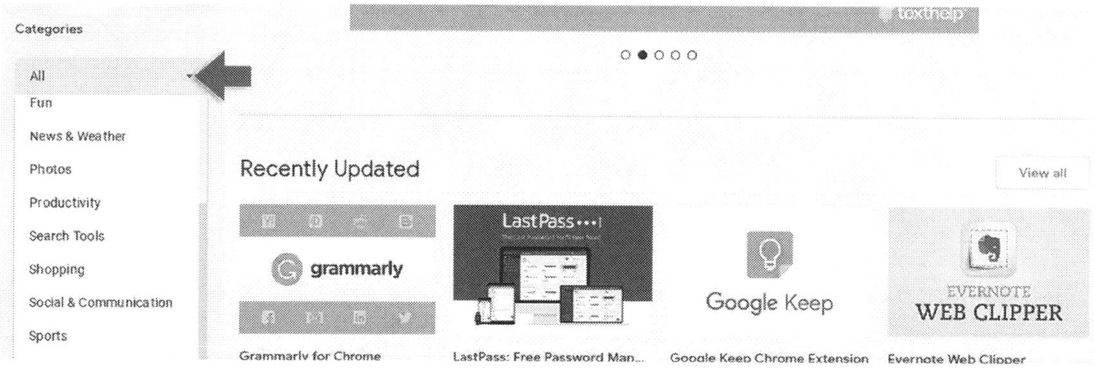

For this example, I'm going to select 'productivity' from the list of categories.

Many of the categories are divided into sub categories. So in our example, the productivity category is sub divided into 'creative tools' such as graphics and drawing, 'developer tools' such as coding and app development, 'office applications' such as word processors and spreadsheets, 'search & browsing tools' such as web browsers, and 'task management' such as todo lists.

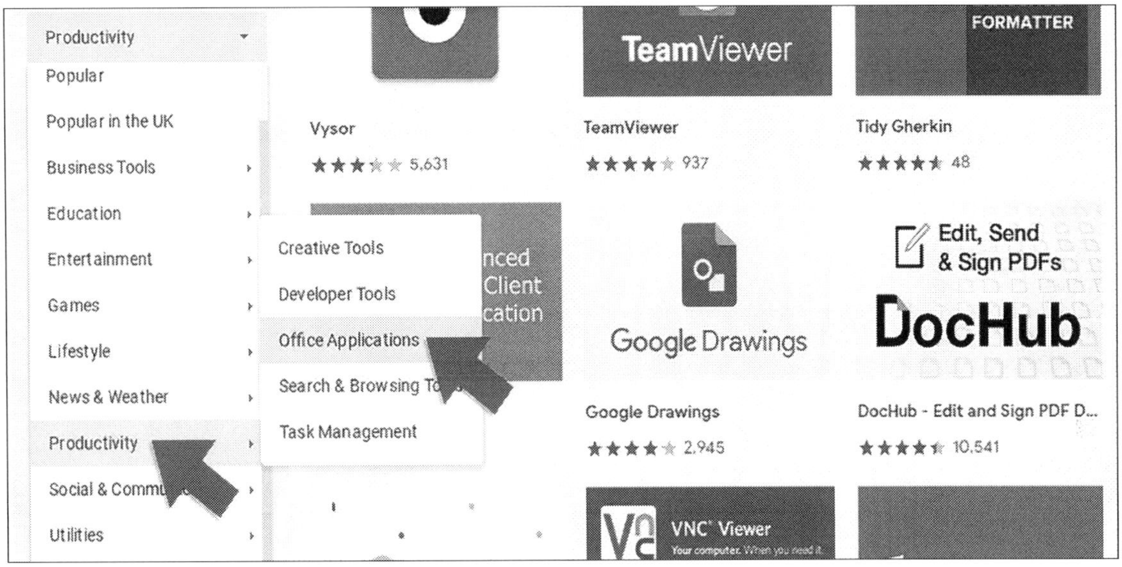

I'm going to select 'office applications'. Here, you'll see all your office applications such as word processors and any tools you need to get your work done on your ChromeBook.

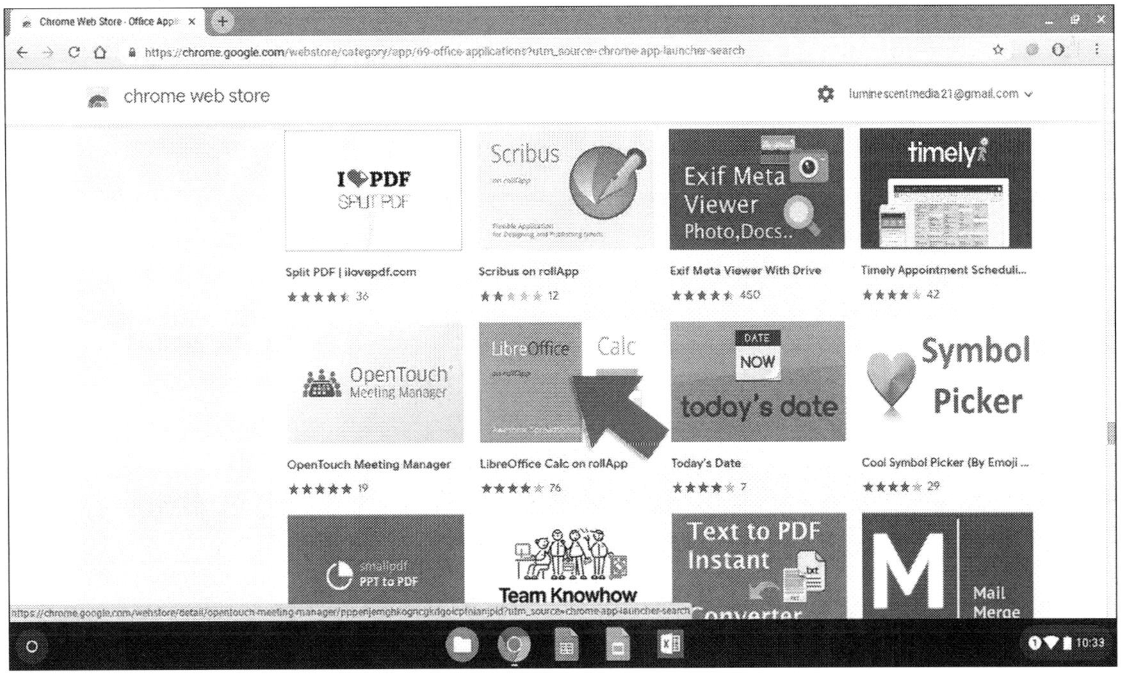

Scroll down and have a look at the apps. Just click on one of the thumbnails to see details on the app, and add it to your ChromeBook.

Searching the Store

On the top left hand side of the store, you'll see a search field.

Click in the search field and type what you're looking for. You can use the app's name if you know it, or you can type something more generic such as 'word processing', or 'social media'. You'll also see a list of suggestions appear as you type - you can click any of these. Press the enter key on your keyboard to execute the search.

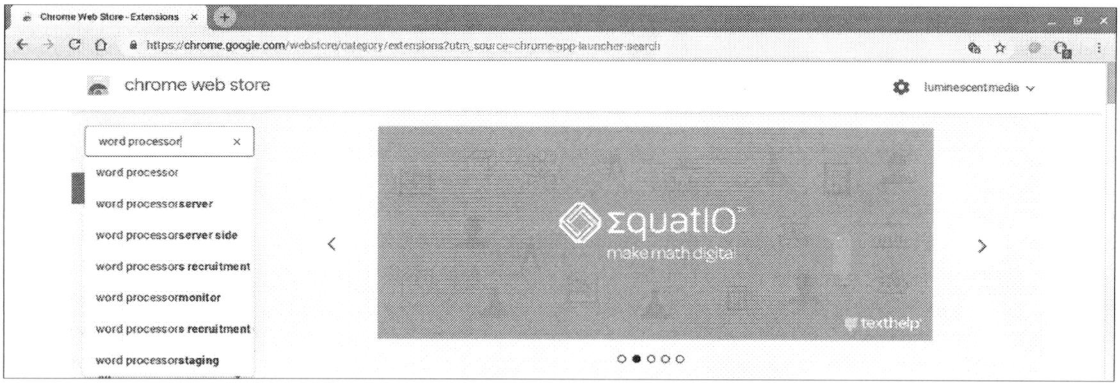

The Web Store will return a list of apps matching your search. You'll see the most popular apps in the list. To see all the apps, click 'more extensions' or 'more apps' on the top right of the screen.

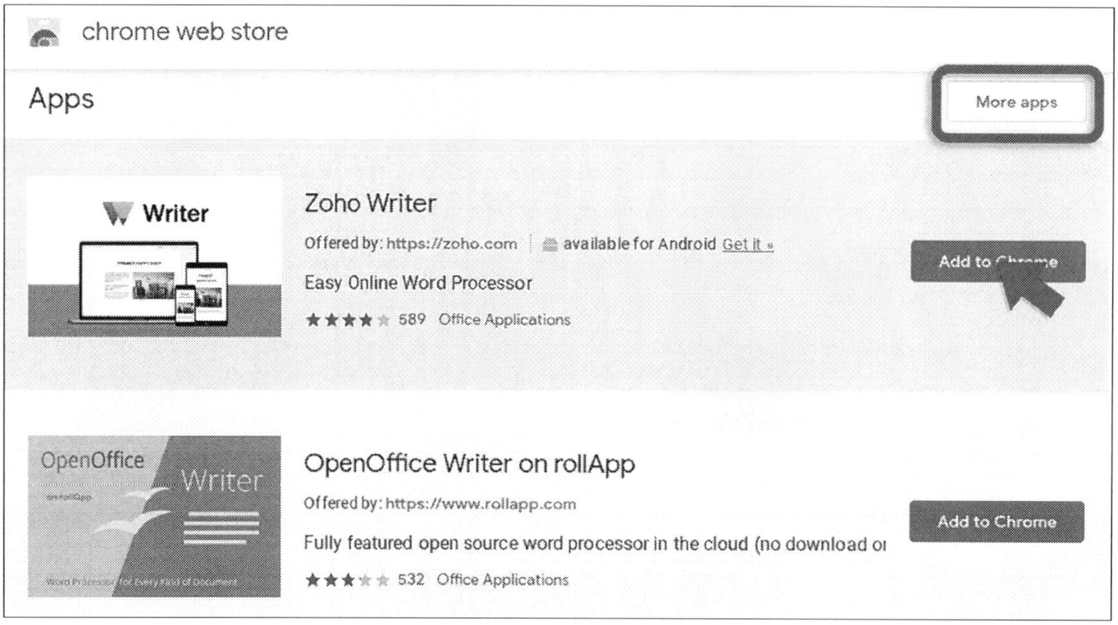

Downloading New Apps

Downloading new apps is fairly straightforward. Once you have searched for and found the app you want, click on the thumbnail icon.

Once the info screen appears, you'll see a write up of the app with some screen shots and features. On the top right of your screen, you'll see a couple of icons. To install the app tap 'add to chrome'

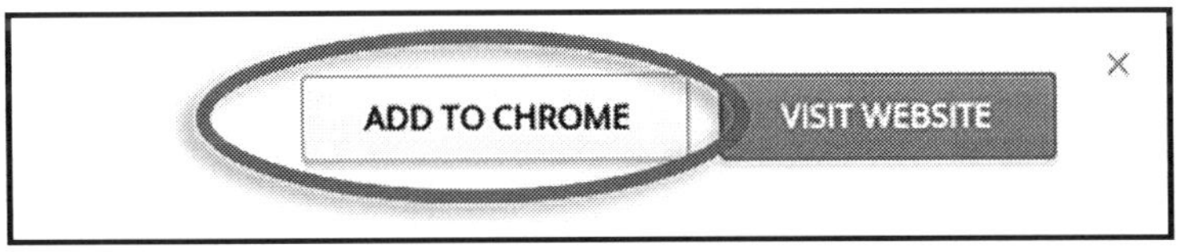

Then click 'add app' to install

You will see the app icon added to your App Launcher.

Removing Chrome Extensions

To remove a Chrome Extension, open the Chrome Browser from the app launcher.

Click the three dots icon on the top right. From the drop down menu, click 'more tools', then select 'extensions'.

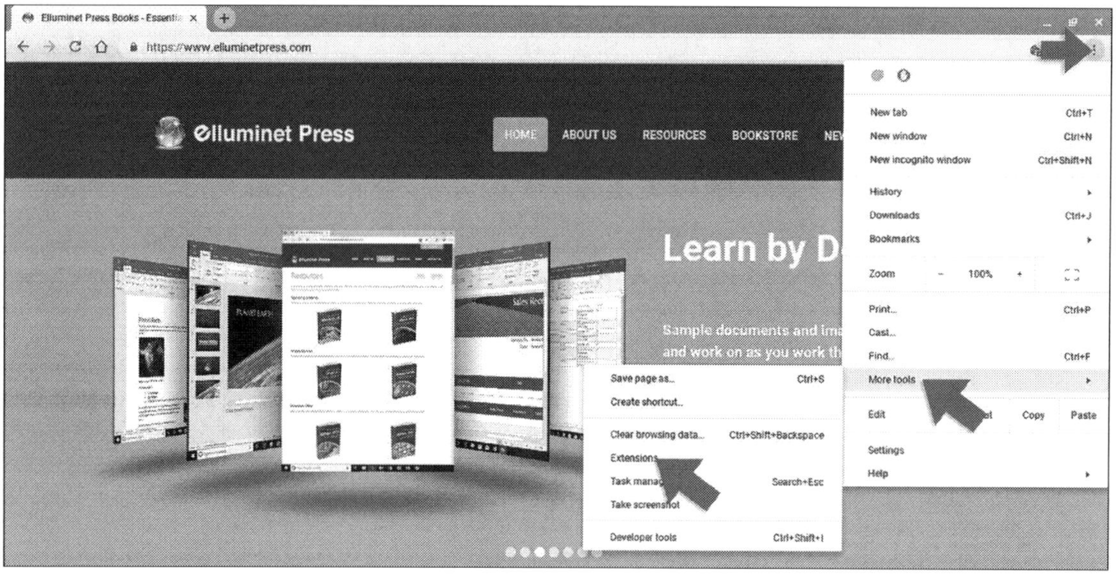

You'll see a list of all the extensions that have been added to Chrome.

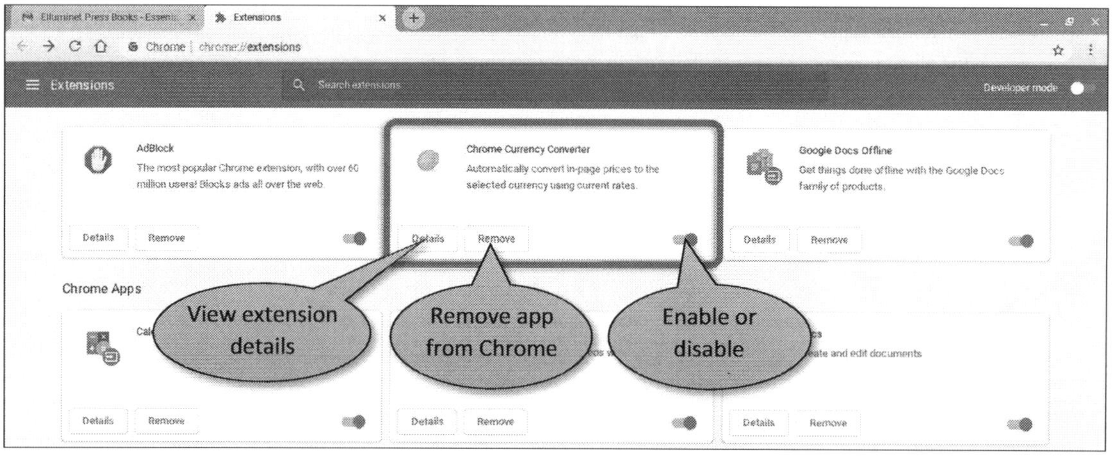

Click 'remove' under the extension you want to remove.

Useful Online Apps

Here are some useful apps you can download directly from the Web Store or by visiting the website.

Google Docs. A word processor included as part Google's free web-based office suite and is part of Google Drive.

`docs.google.com`

Google Sheets. A spreadsheet program included as part Google's free web-based office suite and is part of Google Drive.

`sheets.google.com`

Google Slides. A presentation program included as part Google's free web-based office suite and is part of Google Drive.

`slides.google.com`

Google Keep. An online, web based note-taking service developed by Google.

`keep.google.com`

Google Drawings. A web-based diagramming program for drawing charts and diagrams such as org-charts, mind maps and flowcharts.

`drawings.google.com`

Google Translate. An online translation program designed to translate wcbpagcs or tcxt into a givcn languagc.

`translate.google.com`

Pixlr Editor. A popular online photo editor. According to its author Pixlr supports all common image formats, including JPG, PNG, GIF, BMP, PSD and TIFF.

`pixlr.com/editor`

Grammarly. Allows you to check your English text for grammar, spelling, and punctuation errors.

`www.grammarly.com/grammar-check`

Microsoft Office. Free online versions of Microsoft Word, Excel, PowerPoint, OneNote, Outlook, and OneDrive. You'll need to sign up for a free Microsoft Account.

`www.office.com`

5 Using Android Apps

More recently, Google has added the ability to run Android Apps from the Google Play Store. The latest ChromeBooks are able to run these apps; older ChromeBooks may not run Android apps at all.

Most new ChromeBooks come with the Google Play Store already installed so you can download your favourite Android apps. If your Chromebook was released in 2017 or later, then you'll be able to run Android apps.

Enable the Google Play Store

You can install android apps from the Google Play Store directly onto your ChromeBook. The Google Play Store is currently only available on certain ChromeBooks.

First, you'll need to enable the feature. To do this, open settings.

Select 'apps' from the panel on the left hand side.

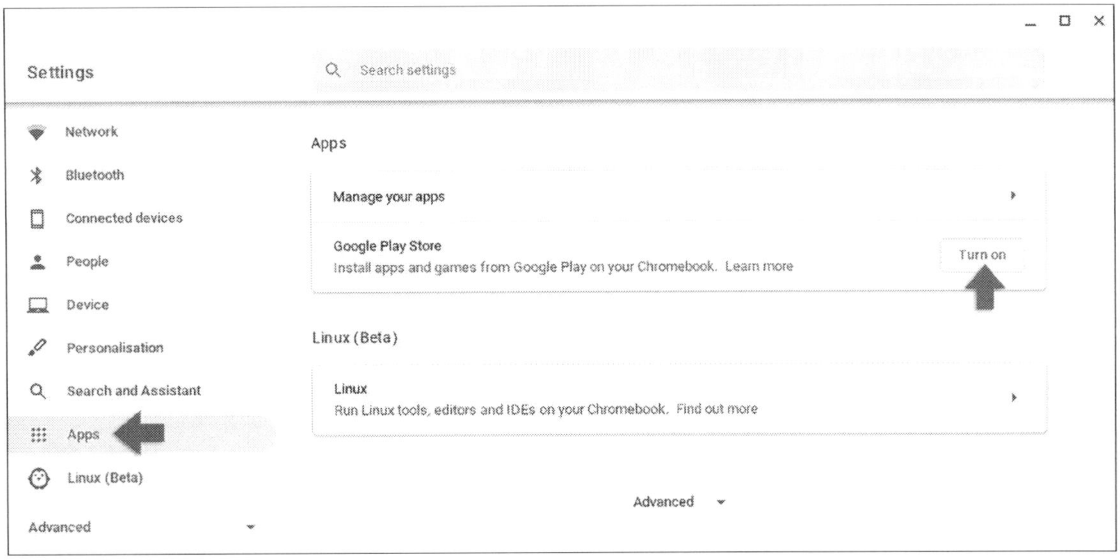

Next to 'google play store' click 'turn on'. Note: If you don't see this option, your Chromebook doesn't support Android apps.

Click 'more', then 'accept' on the 'google play apps and services' screen.

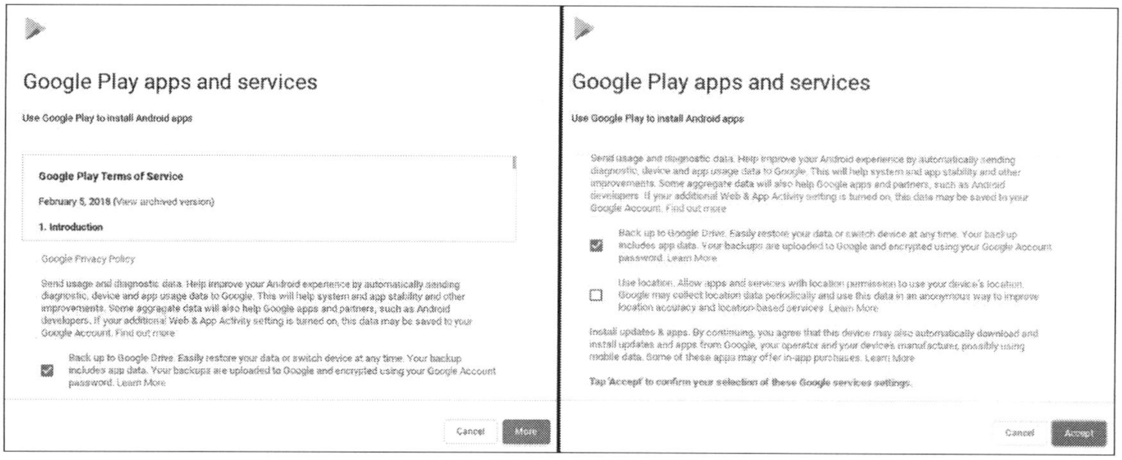

You'll find the google play store on your app launcher. Here, you'll be able to find and install all your favourite android apps.

Google Play Store

Using the Google Play Store, you'll be able to browse, search and download your apps.

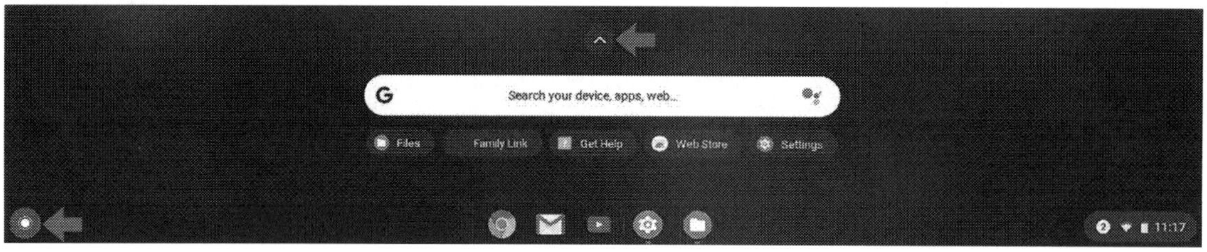

Select 'play store'.

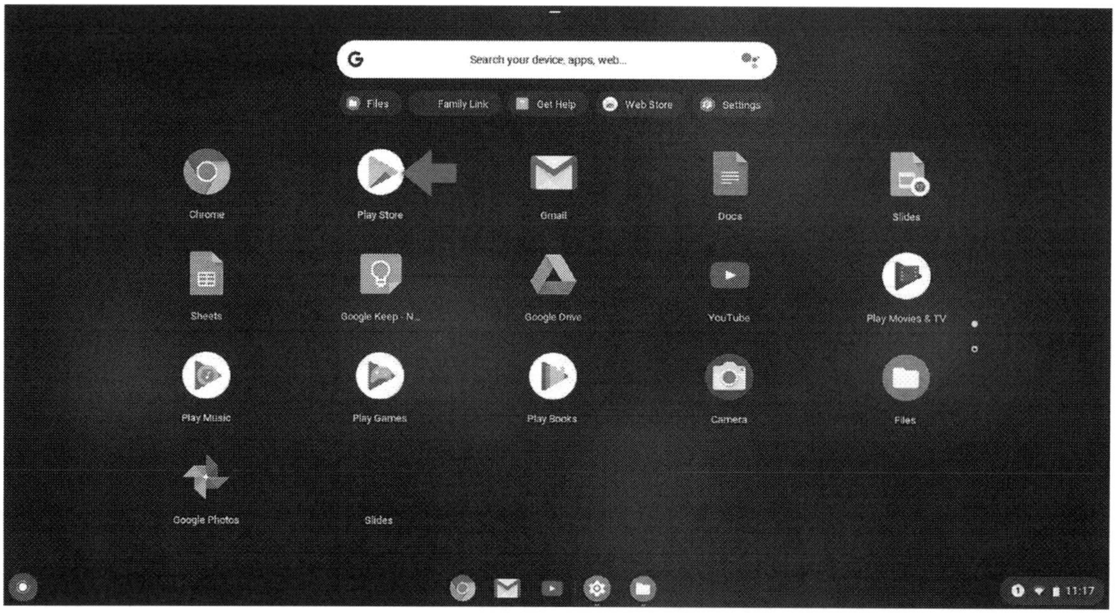

Browsing the App Store

Down the left hand side of the App Store, you'll see some categories. Here you can browse games, apps, movies, tv shows and books.

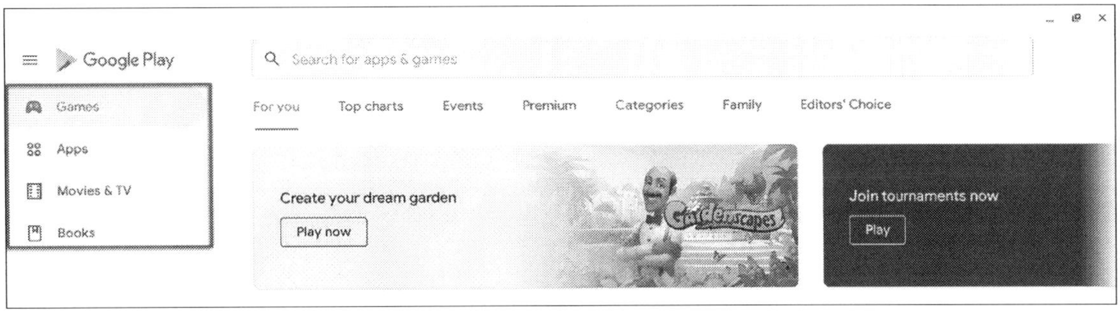

For this example, I'm going to select 'apps' from the list.

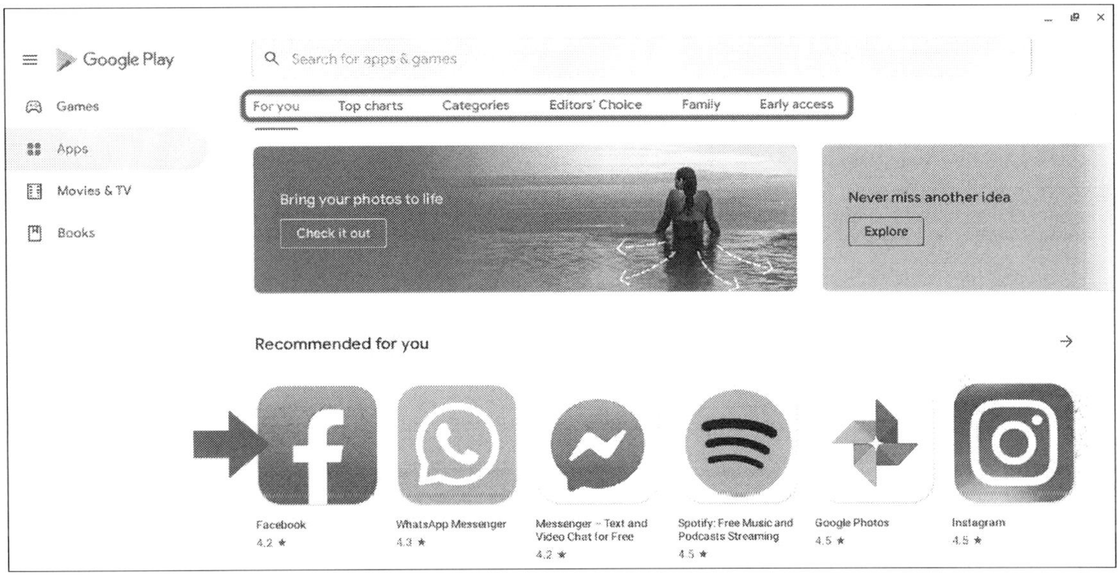

Here, you can browse apps selected 'for you', popular apps in 'top charts', various 'categories' off apps such as productivity, art design, educations and so on. You can also see 'editors choice' of apps, 'family' friendly apps, and 'early access' to apps not yet released.

Have a look through the sections. To install any of the apps, click on the icon, then select 'install'.

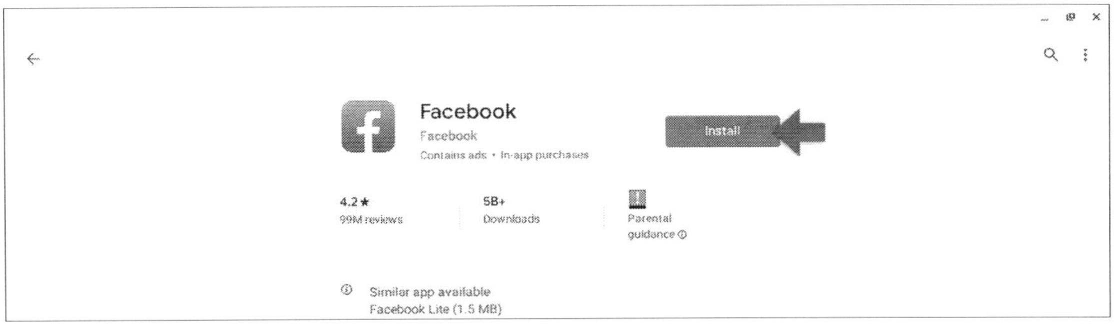

Search for Apps

To search for an app, type your search into the search field at the top of the screen.

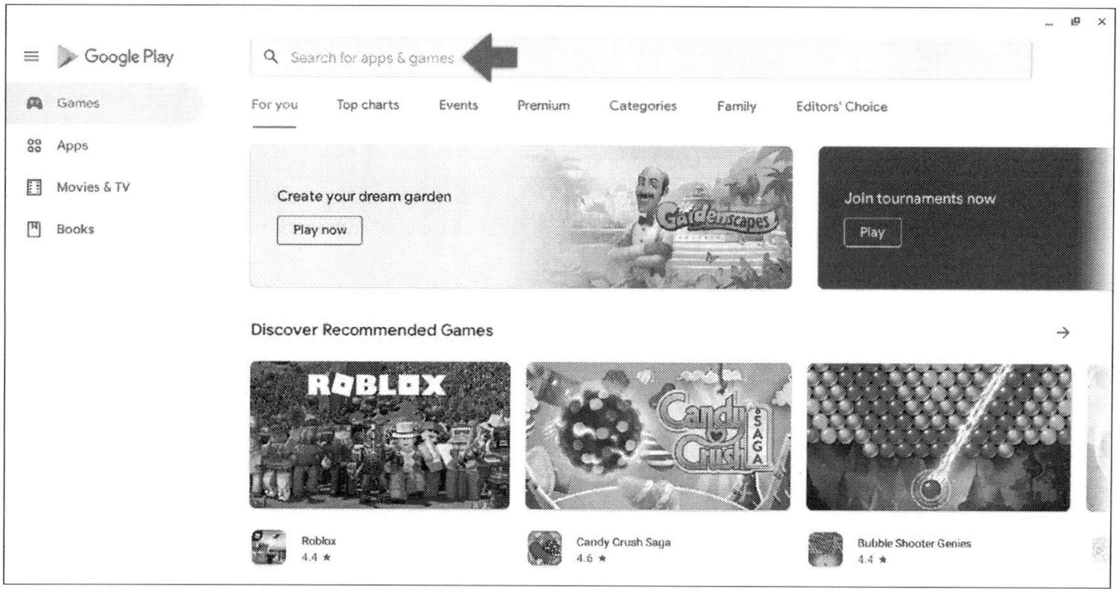

Select an app from the suggestions or press enter.

Click 'Install' (for free items) or the item's price to begin the installation.

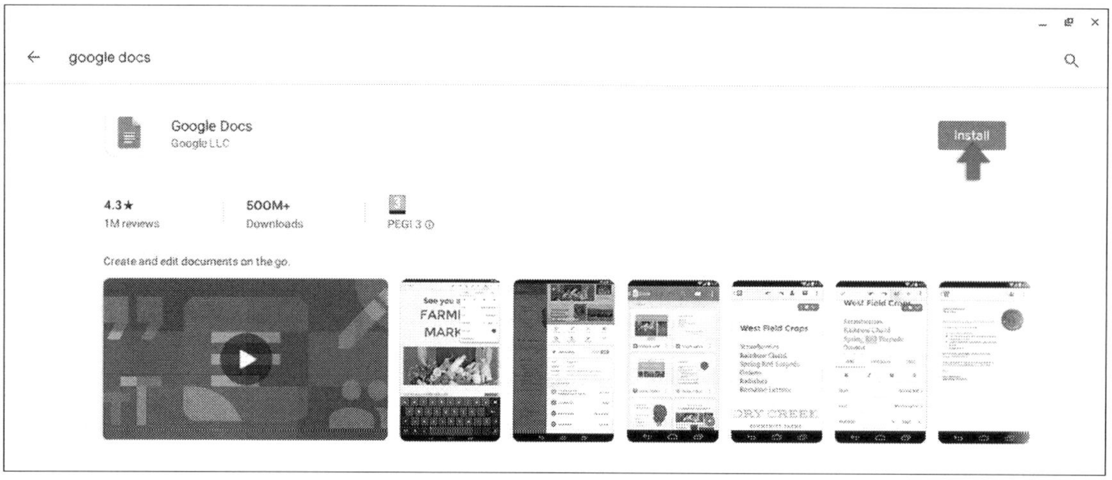

You'll find the app on your launcher.

Managing Apps

Over time, Apps and Chrome Extensions can start to fill up your ChromeBook, making it sluggish and unresponsive. It's a good idea to remove apps and extensions you don't use.

Removing Apps

To remove an app, open your app launcher from the bottom left hand side of the screen. Click the arrow in the centre to reveal all your apps.

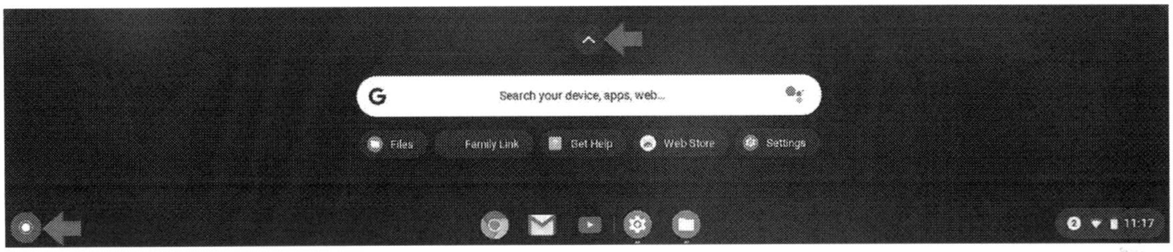

Right click on the app you want to remove.

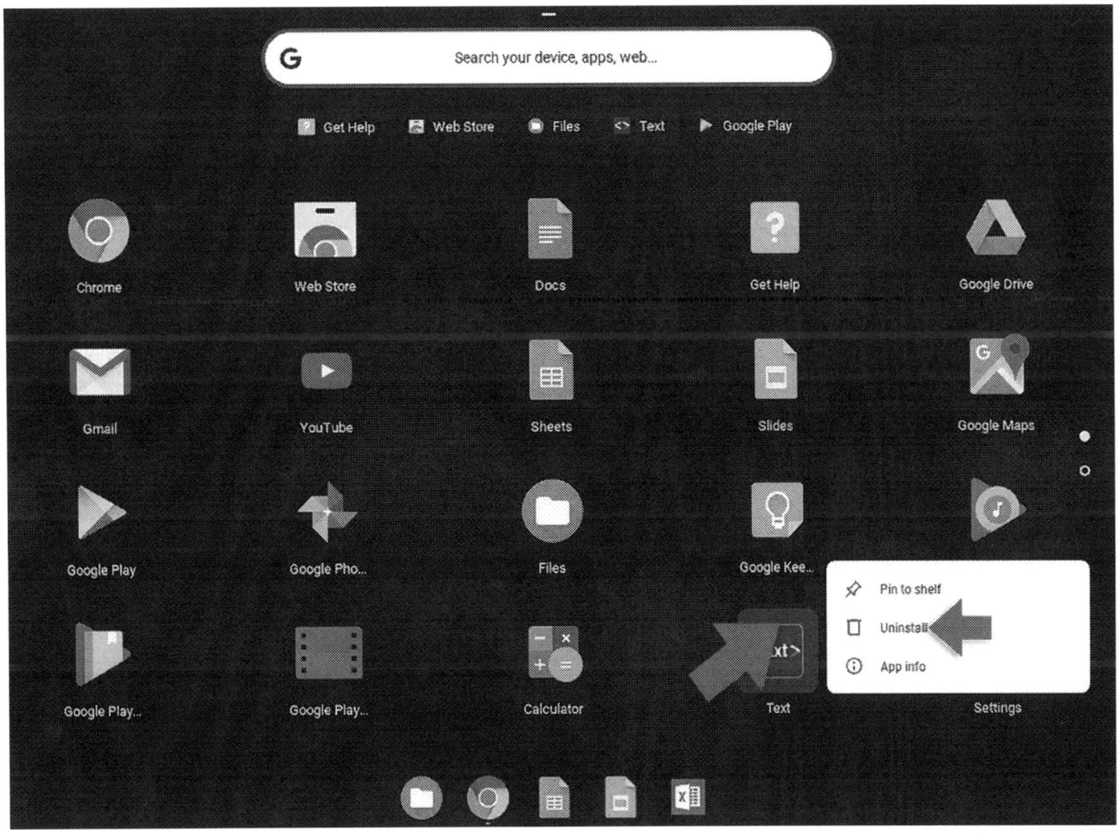

From the popup menu, click 'uninstall'.

Do this for all the apps you want to remove.

6

Using Linux Apps

More recently, Google has added the ability to run Linux Apps. Linux support is available in the latest stable version of Chrome OS

Linux is a free, open source operating system originally developed by Linus Torvalds, similar to the Unix operating system.

Linux has evolved to run on a wide variety of hardware from phones to PCs to supercomputers and is typically packaged in a Linux distribution. There are various distributions available such as Ubuntu, Redhat, SuSE, Centos, Raspbian to name a few.

Many Linux distributions and apps are available for free. Chrome OS itself is build on Linux.

Enable Linux Support

Linux support is currently only available on certain ChromeBooks. To use Linux apps, first you'll need to enable the feature. To do this, open settings.

Select 'linux' from the panel on the left hand side.

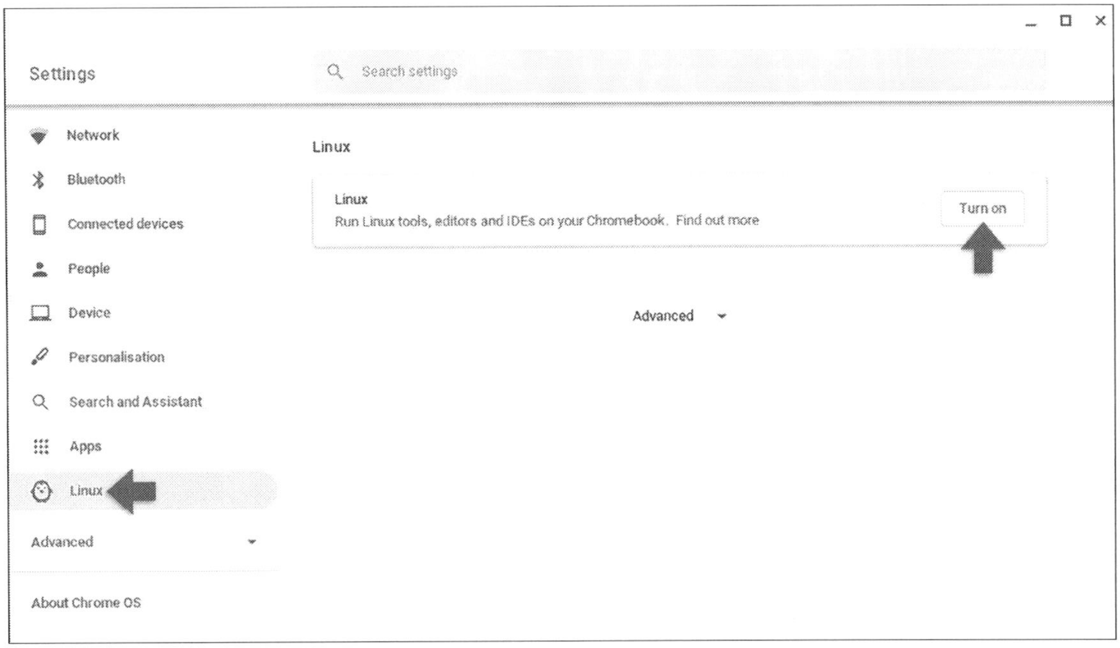

Next to 'linux, click 'turn on'.

Select 'install' from the 'setup' screen.

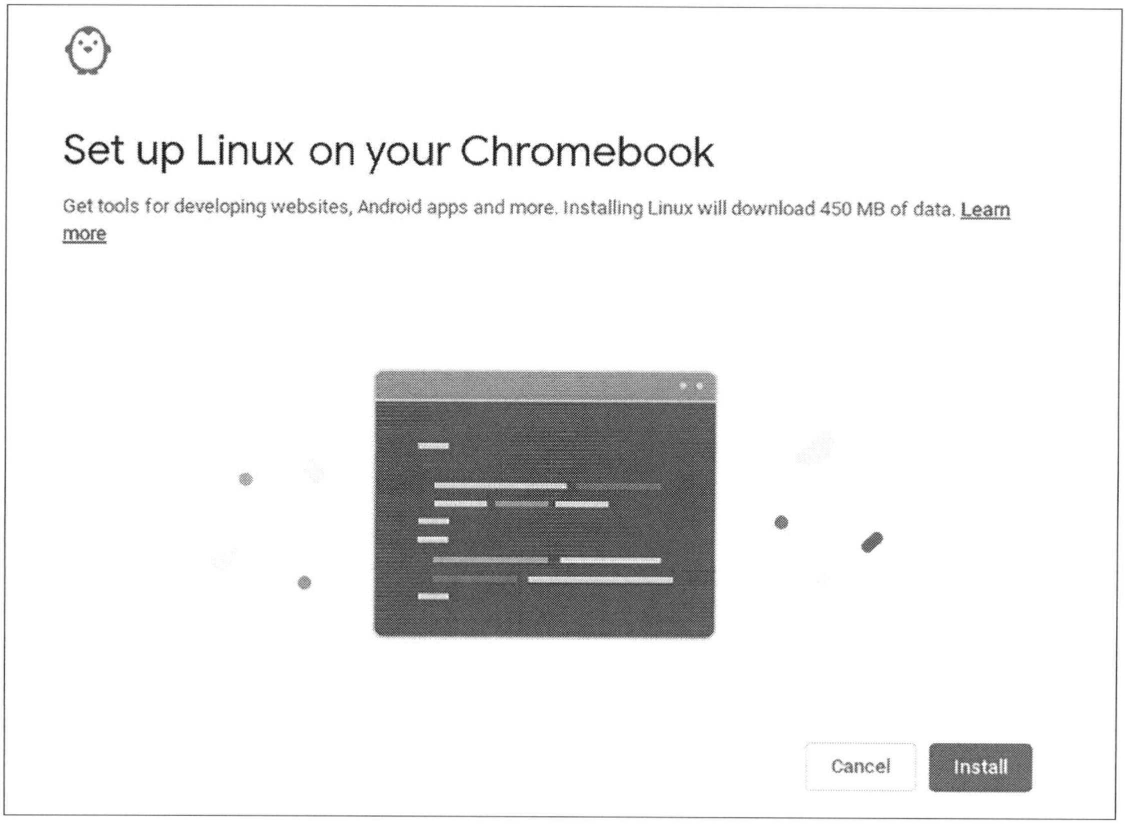

The installation will take a few minutes. Once complete, you'll find the linux terminal (command prompt) and other apps you install in the 'linux apps' group on your app launcher. Click the 'linux apps' group to open.

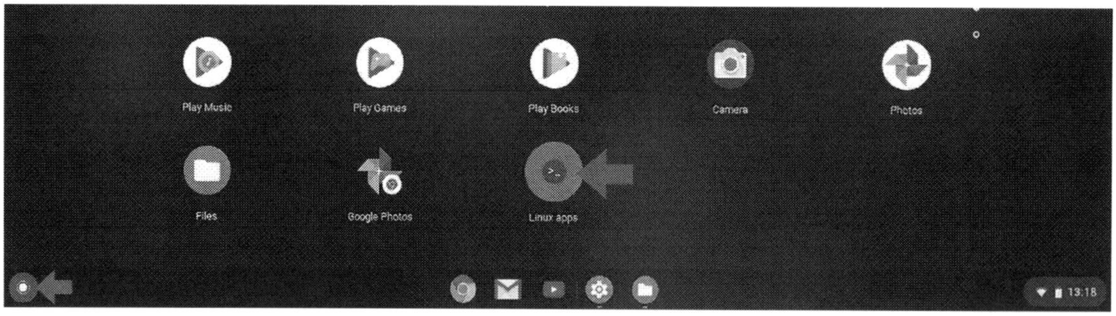

To open the terminal window, click 'terminal'.

Using Linux

To use linux, you'll need to open the terminal - as shown in the previous section.

```
kevwils10@penguin:~$ uname -r
4.19.98-08076-g24ab33fb8e14
kevwils10@penguin:~$ whoami
kevwils10
kevwils10@penguin:~$
```

This is a command line interface where you type in linux commands. Here are a few commands you can use...

Command	Function
ls	List files and directories
ls -a	List all files and directories
ls -l	Detailed list of files and directories
mkdir <dir-name>	Create directory
cd <dir-name>	Change to directory
pwd	Display the path of the current dir
cp <file> <destination>	Copy file to destination
mv <file> <destination>	Move file to destination
rm <file>	Delete file
rmdir <dir>	Delete directory
sudo <command>	Execute command with root privileges
su <username>	Switch user
sudo useradd <username>	Add new user
sudo groupadd <groupname>	Add new user group
sudo usermod -g <group> <user>	Change user's group
sudo passwd <username>	Change password of user
whoami	Show user currently logged in
netstat	Displays network state
ping	Check host is online
sftp [user-name]@[server]	Secure ftp connection to server
hostname	Display hostname or machine name
ssh [user-name]@[server]	Open a SSH connection to server

Give them a try...

```
kevwils10@penguin:~$ mkdir work
kevwils10@penguin:~$ ls -l
total 0
drwxr-xr-x 1 kevwils10 kevwils10 0 May 28 13:52 work

kevwils10@penguin:~$ mkdir pictures
kevwils10@penguin:~$ ls -l
total 0
drwxr-xr-x 1 kevwils10 kevwils10 0 May 28 13:52 pictures
drwxr-xr-x 1 kevwils10 kevwils10 0 May 28 13:52 work

kevwils10@penguin:~$ ping www.ell.com
PING www.elluminetpress.com (104.31.92.92) 56(84) bytes of data.
64 bytes from 104.31.92.92 (104.31.92.92): icmp_seq=1 ttl=57 time=8.30 ms
64 bytes from 104.31.92.92 (104.31.92.92): icmp_seq=2 ttl=57 time=9.31 ms
64 bytes from 104.31.92.92 (104.31.92.92): icmp_seq=3 ttl=57 time=9.07 ms
```

Install a Linux App

First make sure you're using the latest version of apt-get. To check type:

```
sudo apt-get update
```

To install programs on linux you need to type a command into the linux terminal.

```
sudo apt-get install [app-name]
```

Finding Apps

You can find a full list of linux packages at the following website.

`packages.debian.org/stable/`

Select a category (eg 'development'), then note the app-name in bold (eg if we wanted to install 'idle3'). This is the name you use in the `sudo apt-get install` command.

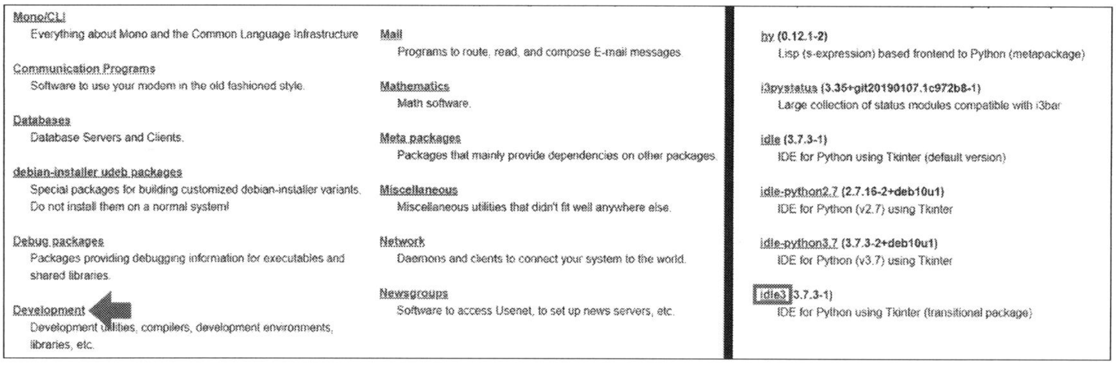

So in the example above, we insert the name 'idle3' in place of app-name. So...

```
sudo apt-get install [app-name]
```

Becomes...

```
sudo apt-get install idle3
```

Install FileZilla FTP

FileZilla is a free FTP program for transferring files using FTP or sFTP and is useful for uploading files to a web server. To install FileZilla, open the terminal window and type

```
sudo apt-get install filezilla
```

Install Audacity

Audacity is a free audio recording and manipulation program. To install Audacity, open the terminal window and type

```
sudo apt-get install audacity
```

Install Gimp Image Editor

Gimp is a free graphics program for image retouching and editing. To install Gimp, open the terminal window and type:

```
sudo apt-get install gimp
```

Install Libre Office

Libre Office is a free office package similar to Microsoft Office. To install Libre Office, open the terminal window and type:

```
sudo apt install libreoffice
```

Install Python

Python is an interpreted, high-level, general-purpose programming language. To install the python interpreter, open the terminal window and type:

```
sudo apt-get install python3.6
```

To install the integrated development environment, type:

```
sudo apt-get install idle3
```

Remove Linux Apps

To remove linux apps use the following command in the terminal window.

```
sudo apt-get remove [app-name]
```

Eg:

```
sudo apt-get remove idle3
```

Running Linux Apps

You'll find installed linux apps on your app launcher. Open your app launcher.

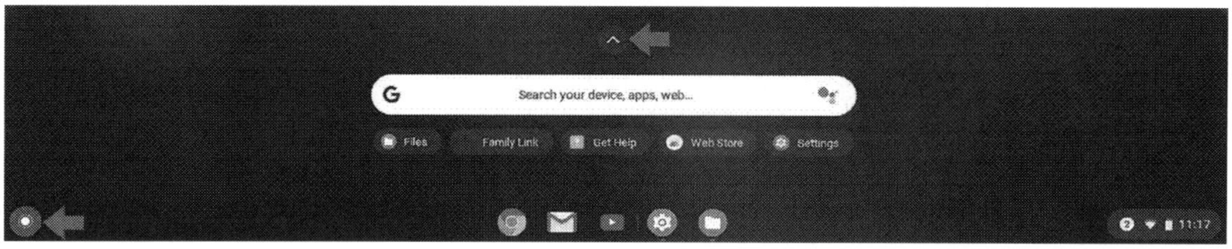

Select 'linux apps'.

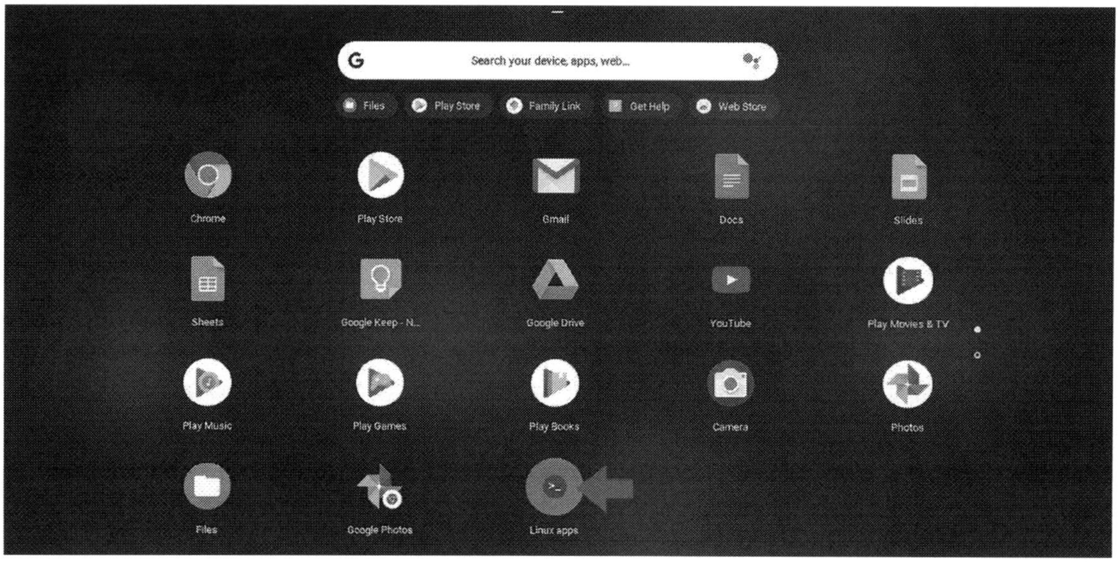

All the linux apps you install will appear in this group. Click on one of the icons to start the app.

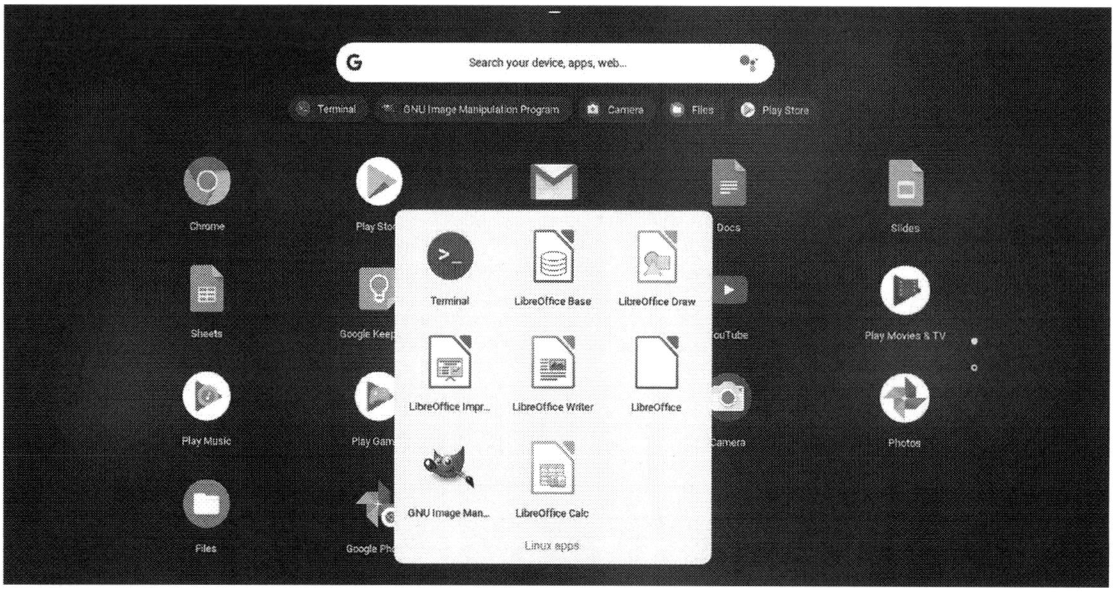

Here, I've started Gimp.

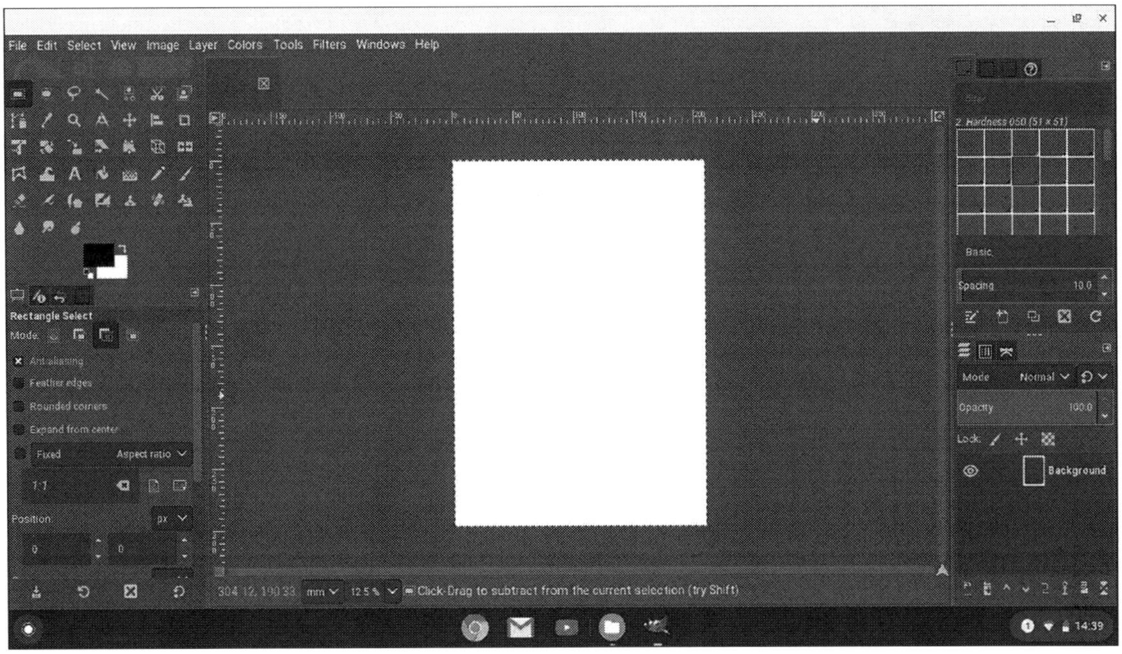

Note that when you save your files in a linux app, they are saved to the 'linux files' directory.

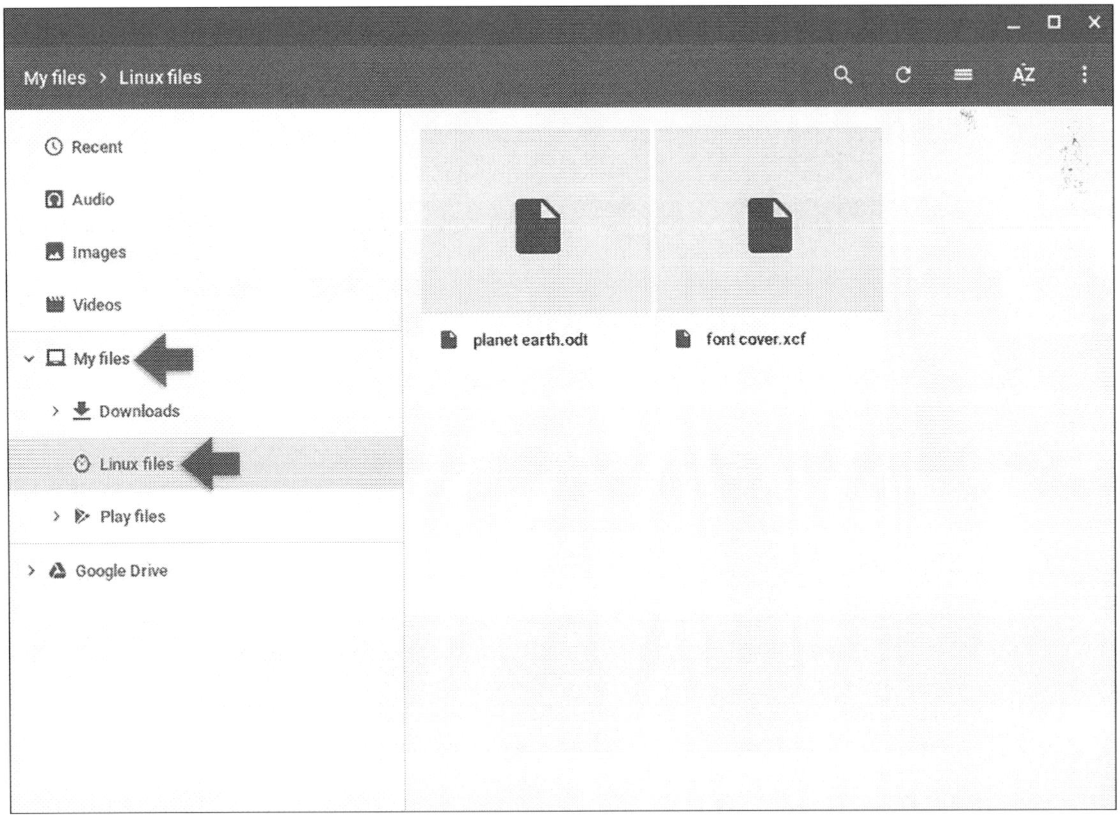

You'll find them in the files app under 'linux files' in the 'my files' section on the left hand side.

7

Web, Email & Communication

The Chromebook has numerous communication apps, such as email, teams, chat, duo and hangouts.

We'll take a look at how to use these apps, as well as using the Chrome web browser to browse the web.

For this section, have a look at the video resources. Open your web browser and navigate to the following website

`videos.tips/chromebook-comms`

To begin, let's take a look at the Chrome Web Browser.

Google Chrome

You'll find Google Chrome on your app shelf along the bottom of your screen.

You'll also find it on your app launcher.

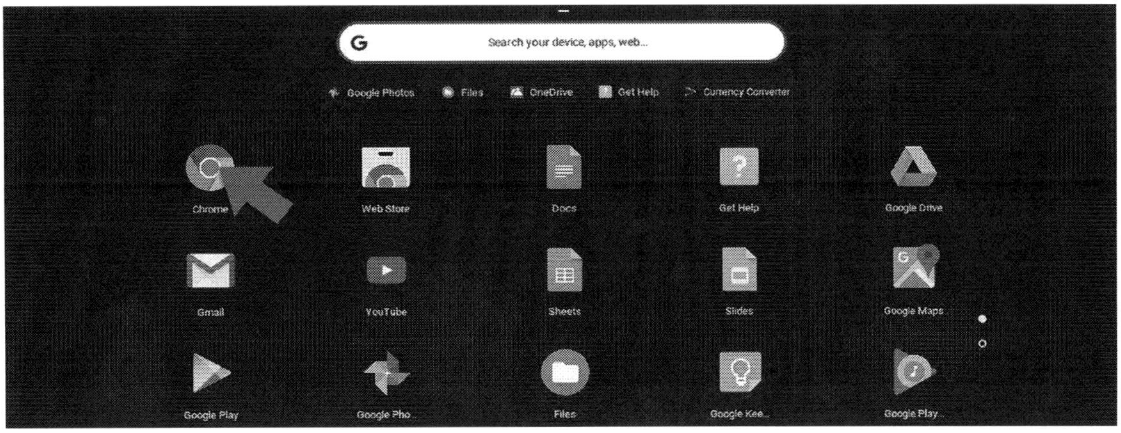

Once Chrome starts up, you'll see the main screen similar to the one below.

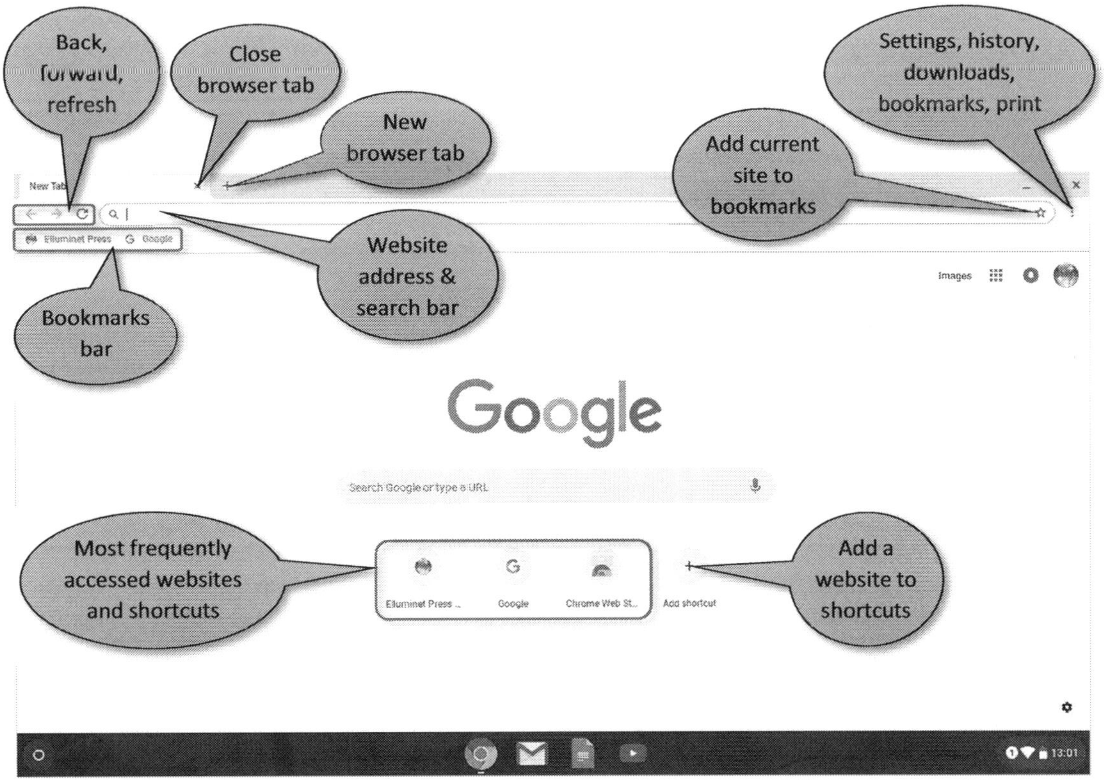

Browser Tabs

Browser tabs help you to keep track of websites you have open instead of having multiple browser windows open at the same time. This makes it easier to see what sites are open and switch between them.

You'll find your browser tabs along the top of the screen. In this example there are three different websites open in three different tabs.

When you want to open a new website, click on the new tab icon.

Enter the website address or Google search. You can also select one of your shortcuts under the Google search bar, or select a bookmark from the bookmarks bar along the top.

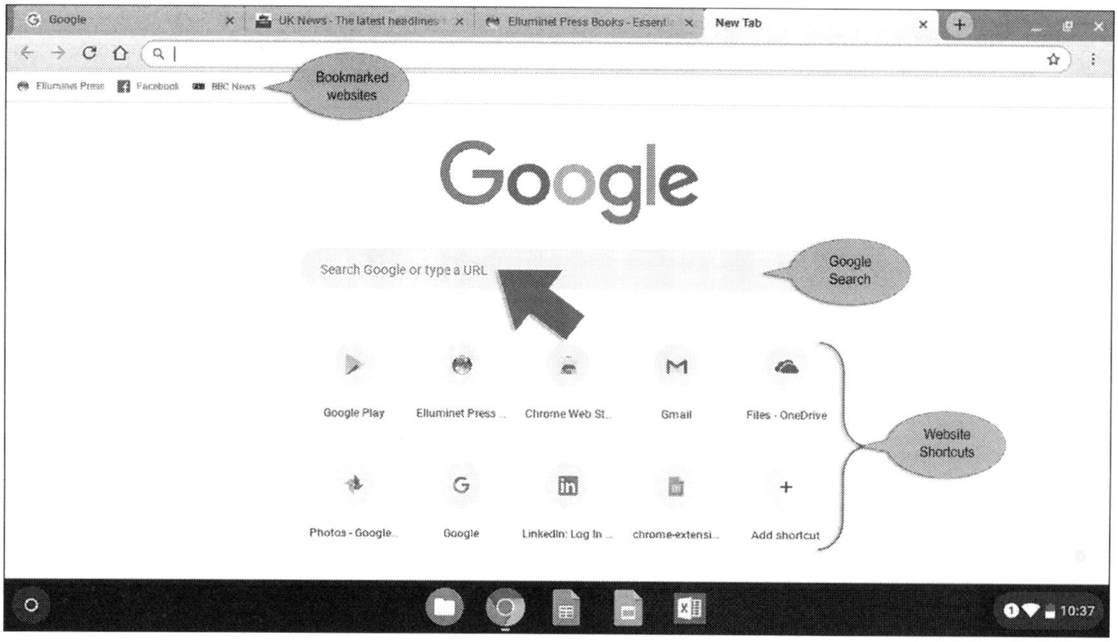

To return to any of the other websites, just click on the tab at the top of the screen.

To close a tab, just click the small x on the right hand side of the tab you want to close.

Browse Incognito

This mode is useful if you don't want Google Chrome on your ChromeBook to record your browsing activity, such as website history, cookies, site data, or information entered into forms. This mode doesn't hide your activity from your ISP, school/college, or employer.

To open an incognito tab, click the three dots icon on the top right of your screen

A new window will popup telling you you've gone icognito.

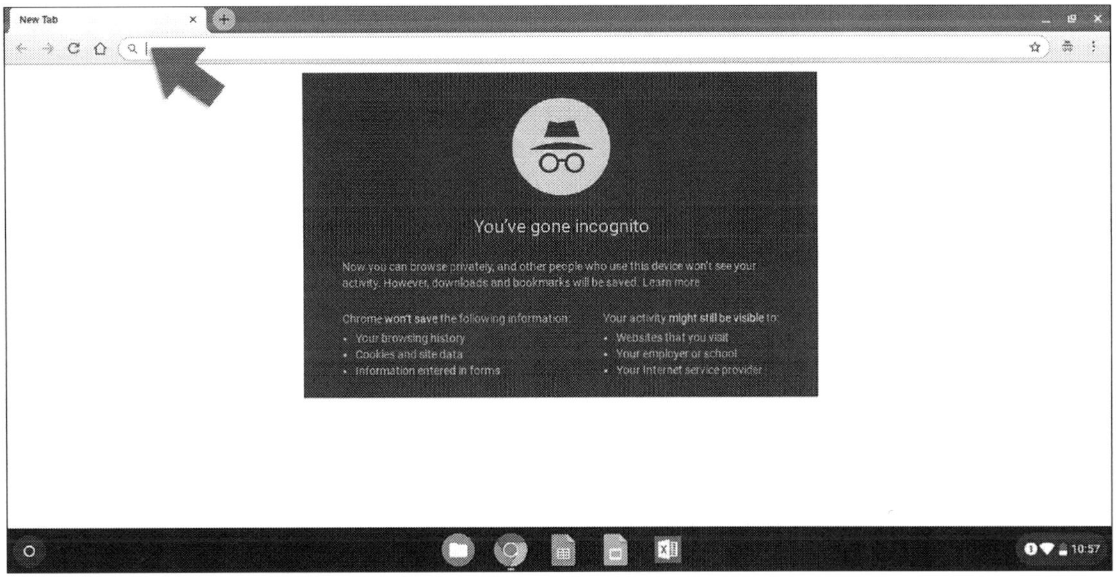

Type the web address of the site you want to visit, or a Google search into the field at the top of the screen.

Browsing History

The browsing history keeps a list of all the websites you've visited with Google Chrome. To find your browser history, click the three dots icon on the top right of your screen and select 'history' from the drop down menu.

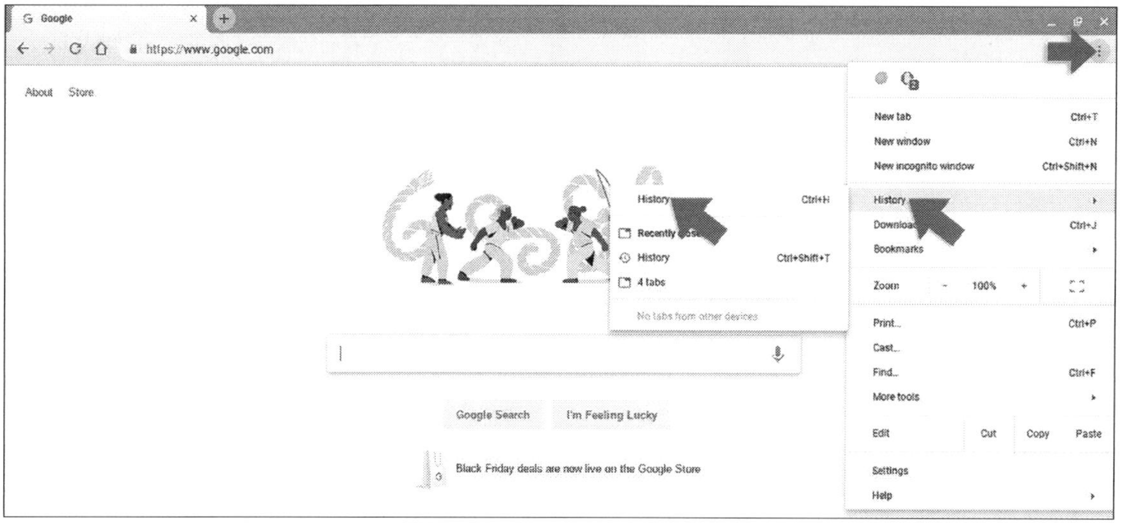

A new tab will pop up. From here, you can scroll down and click any site to revisit.

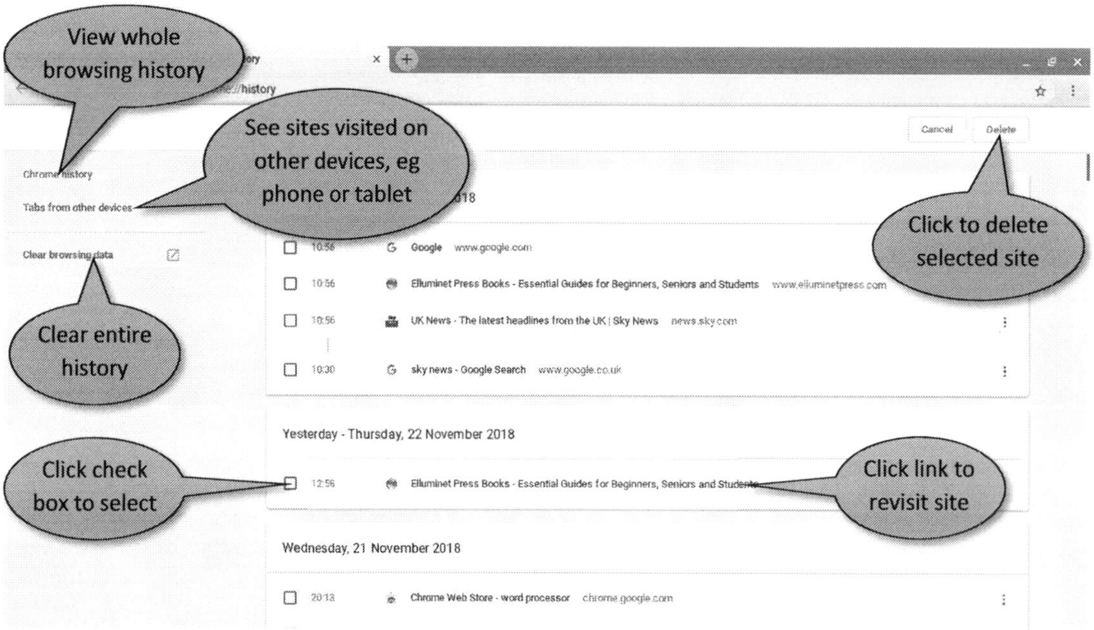

To delete a site from the history, click the tick box next to the website in the list, then click 'delete' on the top right.

Click 'clear history' to clear the list of visited websites, cache, cookies, and other site data.

Bookmarking a Site

It is useful to bookmark, or favourite a site you visit frequently. To do this, navigate to the website you want to bookmark, then click the small star icon to the right of the address bar at the top of your window.

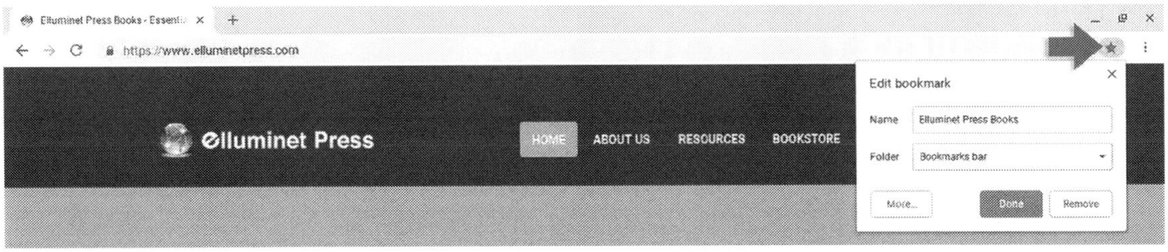

Enter a meaningful name in the 'name' field, if there isn't one. Add your bookmark to the bookmarks bar along the top of your screen.

Click 'done' when you're finished.

Notice that your bookmarks bar isn't enabled by default. To enable the bar, click the three dots icon on the top right of the screen. From the drop down, go to 'bookmarks', then from the slideout menu, select 'show bookmarks bar'.

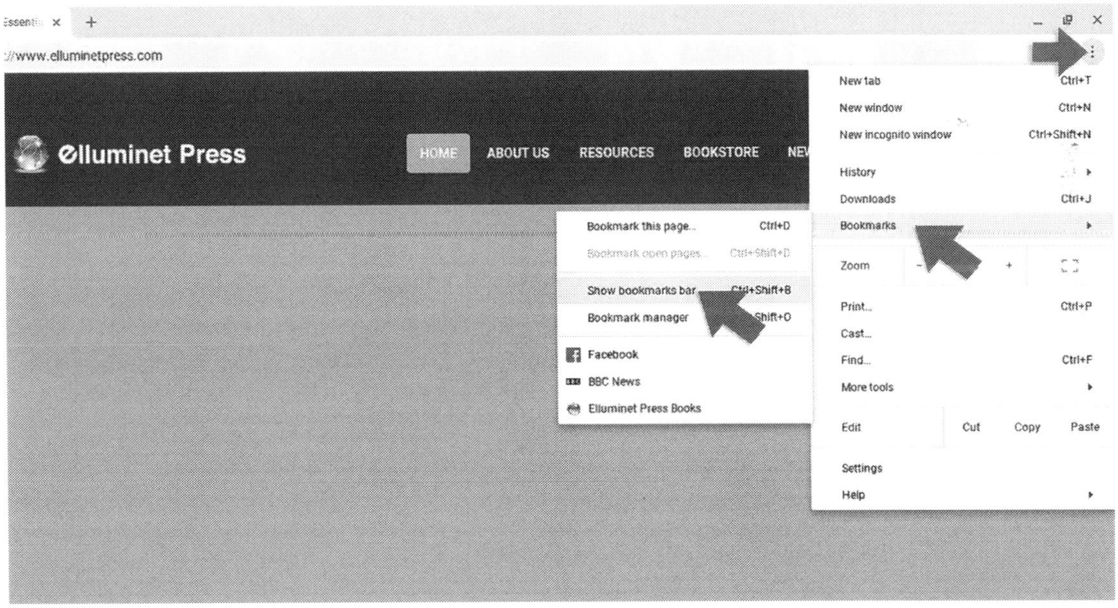

The bar will appear along the top of the screen underneath the address bar.

Bookmark Folders

If you have a lot of bookmarked sites, the bookmarks bar can become very cluttered. To get around this, you can create folders on your bookmarks bar, to make it easier to find sites.

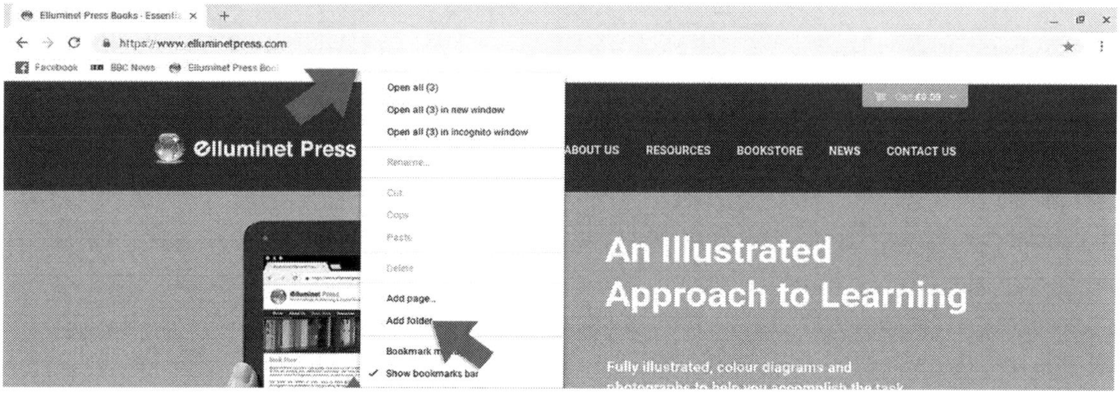

In the dialog box, type in the name of the folder and select 'bookmarks bar'.

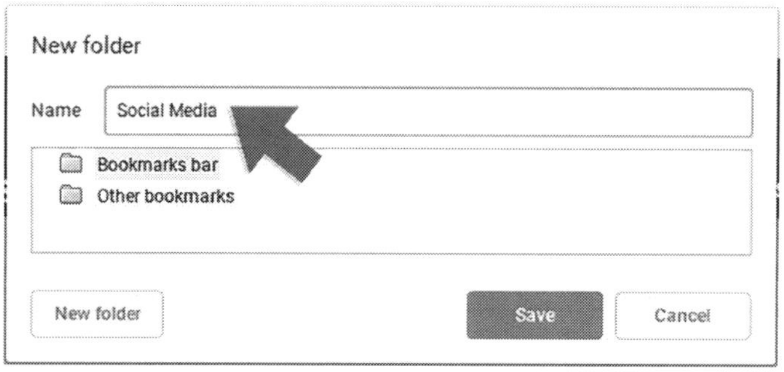

Click 'save' when you're done. You'll see your folder appear on the bookmarks bar.

Now you can drag the site bookmarks you want to put in this folder. For example, I'm going to add 'facebook' to the social media folder.

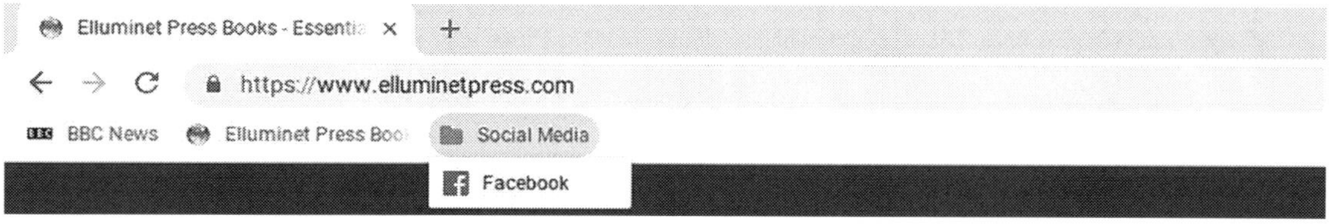

Site Shortcuts

Site shortcuts appear on your home page - the page that appears when you open Chrome or when you open a new tab.

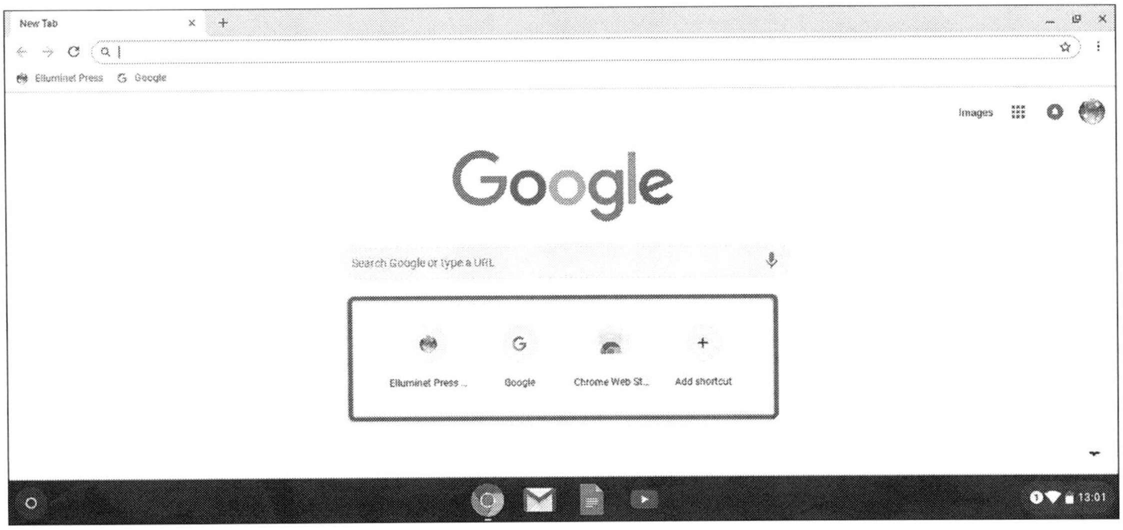

To add a shortcut, you need to know the websites address or URL. For example, I want to add the Elluminet Press website to the shortcuts. To do this, click 'add shortcut' from Chrome's home screen. In the dialog box that appears, type in the website's name and address.

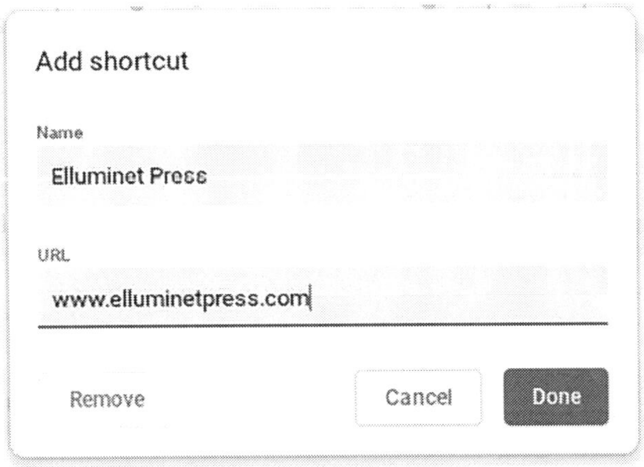

To delete a shortcut, hover your mouse pointer over the shortcut's icon on the Chrome home screen. You'll see three dots appear on the top right. Click on this icon.

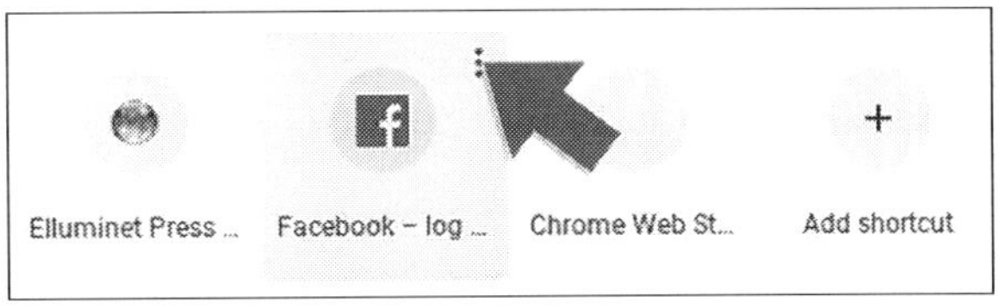

From the popup, click 'remove'.

Downloads

If you have downloaded photos, files, or web pages for offline viewing, you'll find them here in the downloads folder. To get to your downloads, click the '3 dots' icon on the top right. From the menu that appears, select 'downloads'.

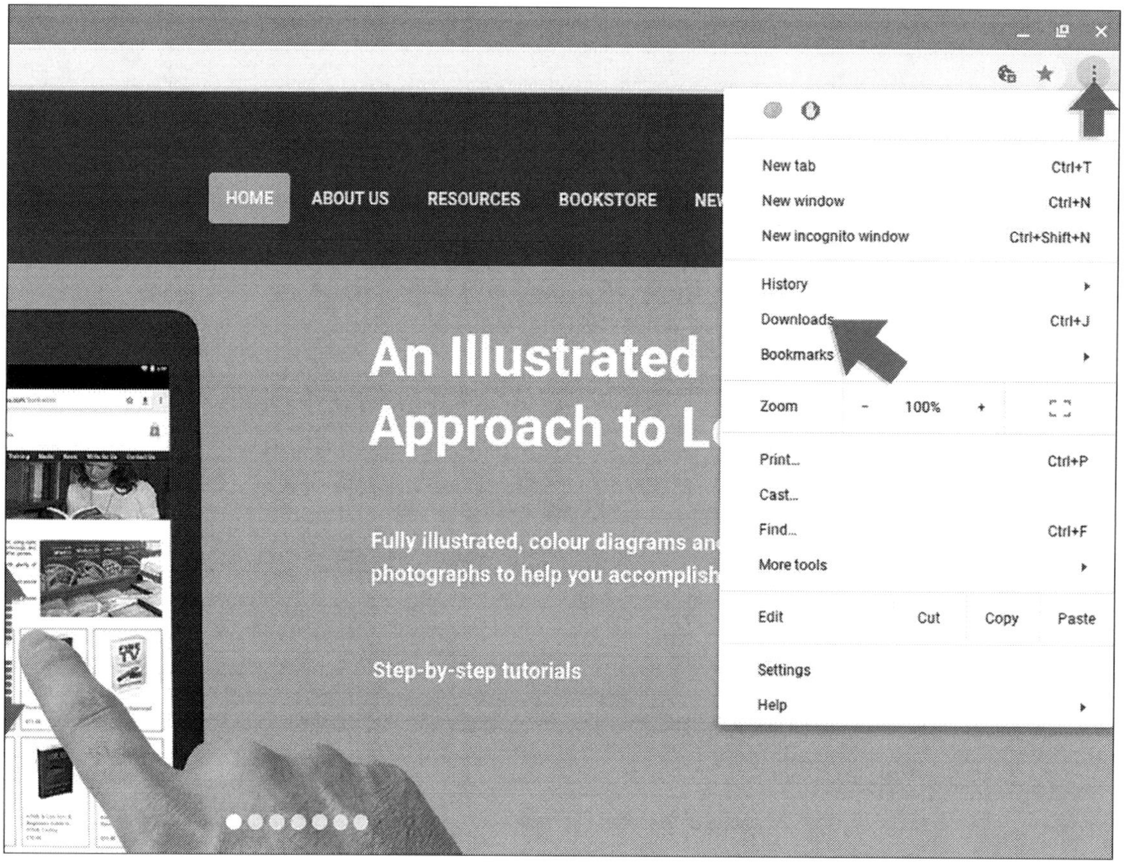

Here you'll see a reverse chronological list of items you've downloaded.

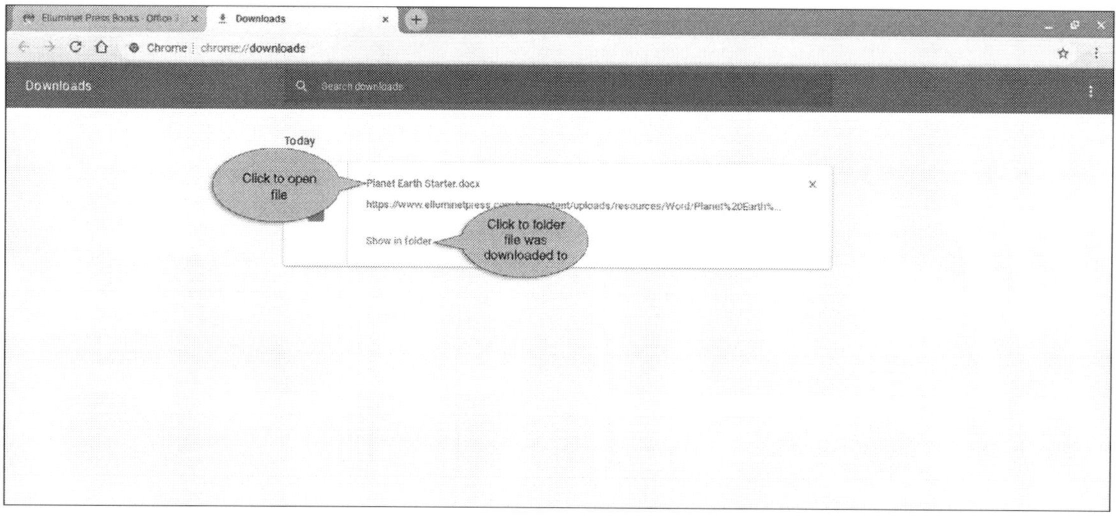

Click on an item in the list to open it up.

Printing a Webpage

To print a webpage in Chrome, click the three dots icon on the top right of your screen, then from the drop down menu, select 'print'.

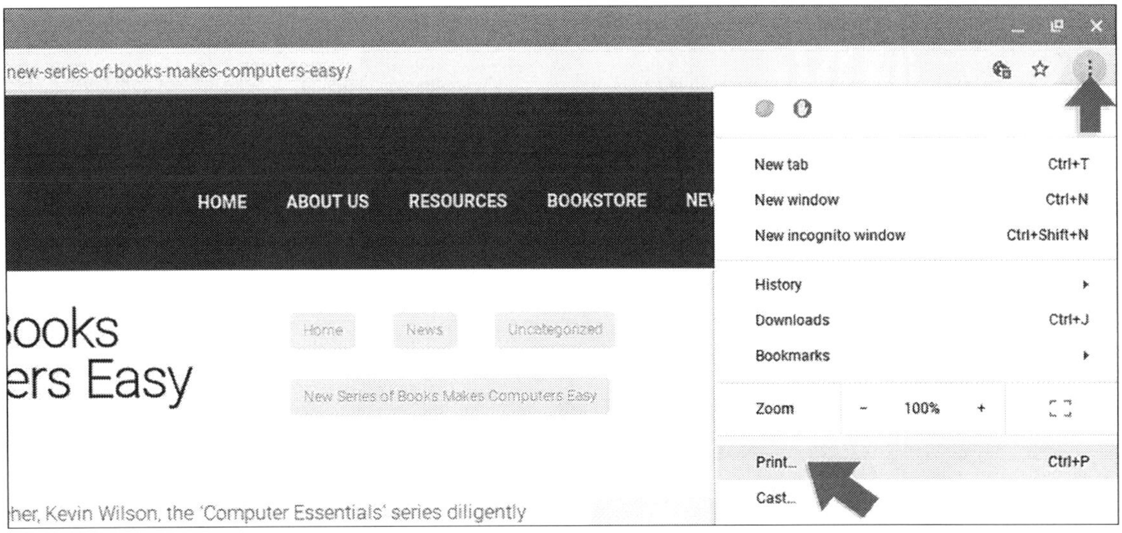

Check the printer 'destination', make sure your printer is selected. Click 'change' if you need to change this. Enter the pages you want to print, or leave it blank to print all of them. Enter the number of copies you want.

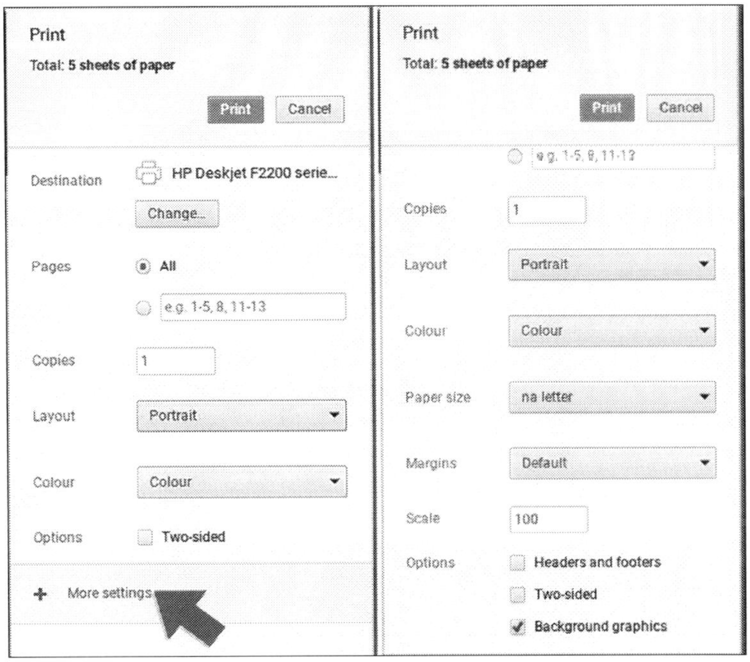

Click 'more settings'. Select the paper size if needed. Change the margins if the website doesn't fit on the page. Click 'background graphics' - this ensures all the graphics will print.

Click 'print' when you're done.

Saving Passwords

When you sign into a website or for the first time, you will receive a prompt asking you whether you want to save your login details.

Sign in, in the normal way - enter your username and password. Once you sign in successfully, Chrome will prompt you to save the password. If this prompt doesn't show up, click the small 'key' icon on the top right of your screen.

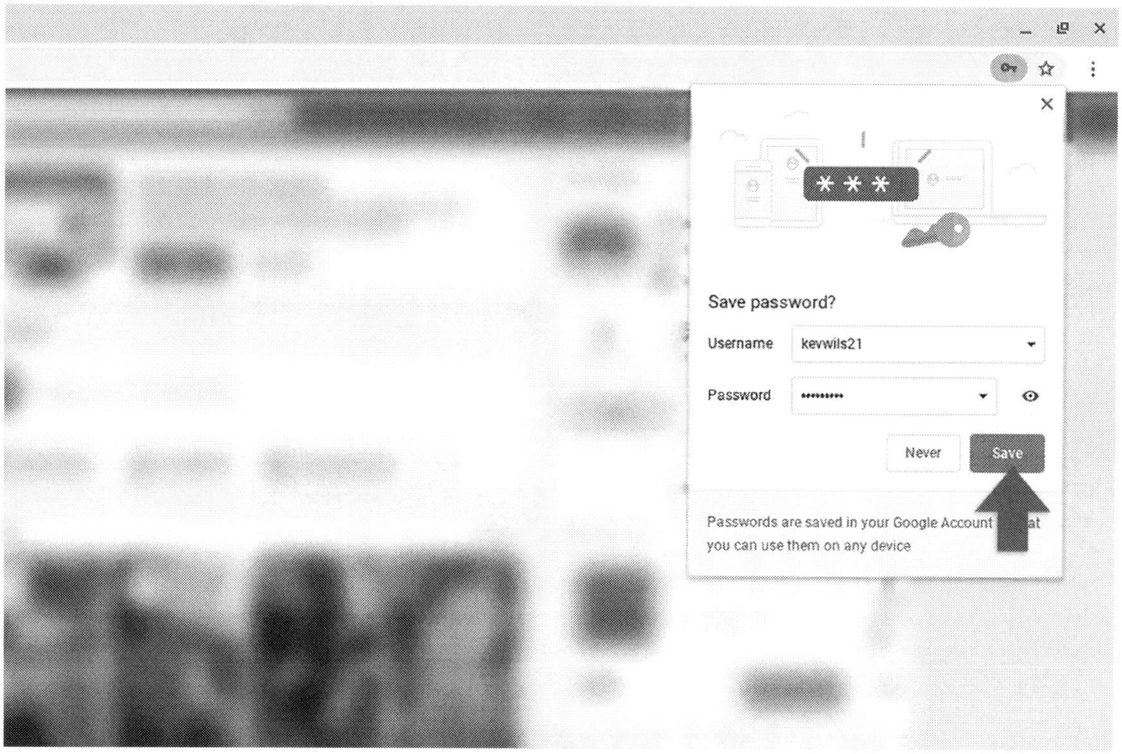

Click 'save'. This will save your password so you don't have to type it in each time.

To sign in the next time, just click in the username or password field.

Select the username from the drop down list, click 'log in' or 'sign in'.

Managing Passwords

You can save passwords to your password list from various different websites so you don't have to remember them all. Top open password manager, click the three dots icon on the top right. From the drop down menu, click 'settings'.

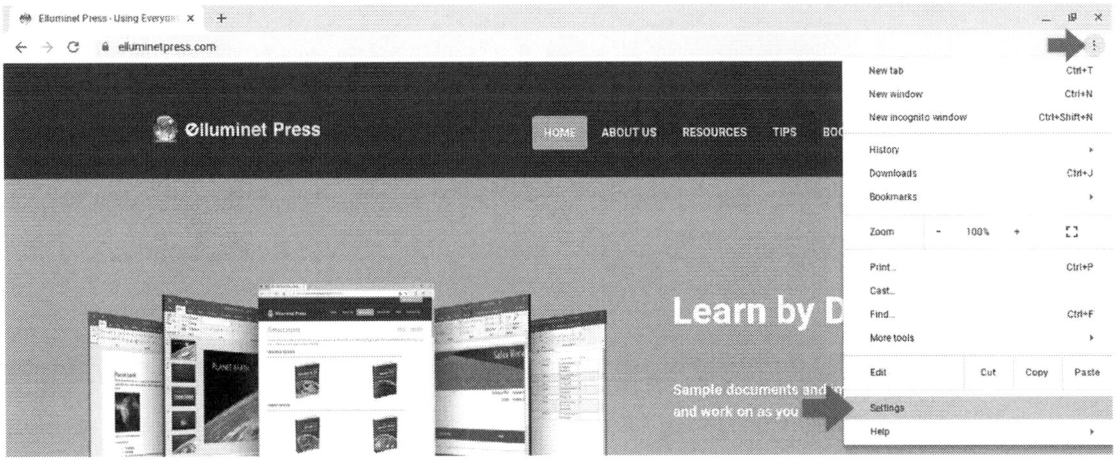

Scroll down to the 'auto fill' section, then click 'passwords'.

Along the top section you can turn on/off auto sign in or the password save option. If you turn these off, Chrome will no longer save your passwords.

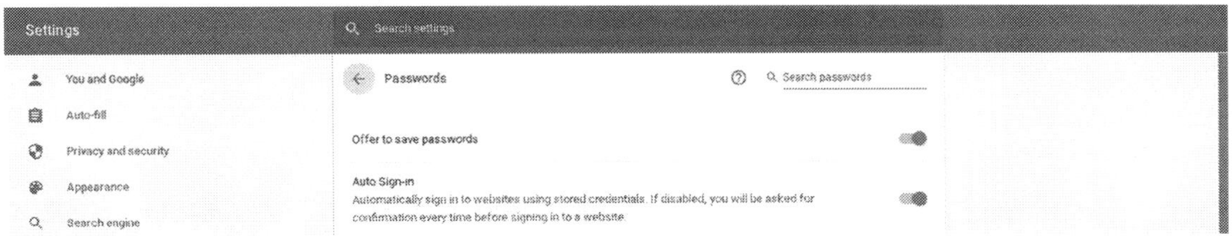

Underneath, you'll see a section called 'saved passwords'. This is the list of all sites you've allowed Chrome to save the password. Click the various icons indicated below to manage your passwords.

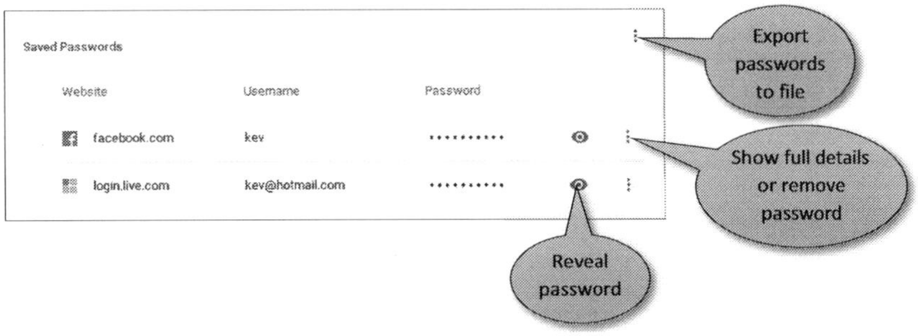

Generate Automatic Strong Passwords

Strong passwords are a must these days. To help you generate good passwords, chrome can automatically generate them for you when you use it to sign up or open an account on any website - whether it's Facebook, Google, Microsoft, yahoo and so on.

To start, go to a website where you where you want to sign up for an account. In this example I'm going to sign up to Facebook.

Fill in the 'create account' form with your details. Click in the password field.

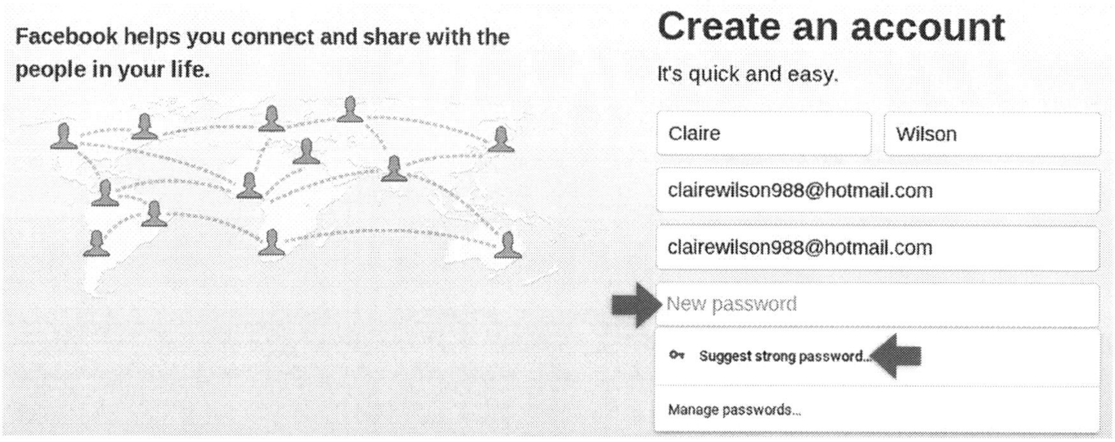

Click 'Suggest Strong Password'.

Chrome will automatically generate a strong password for you. You'll see the password listed on the right of the drop down box.

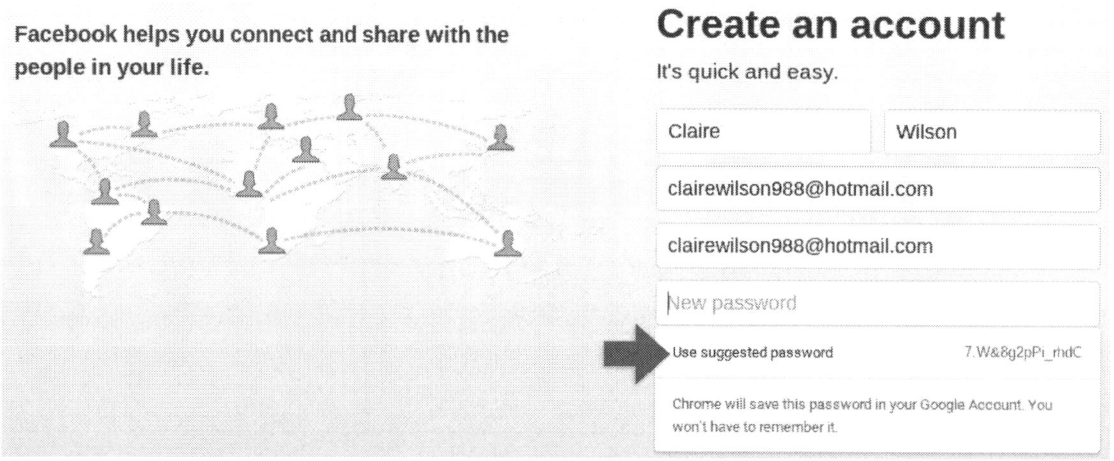

Click 'use suggested password'. This will save the username an password for this website.

The next time you need to sign into the site, just click in the password field and select the username & password for that site.

Chrome Security

In Chrome, click the three dots icon on the top right, then select 'settings' from the menu.

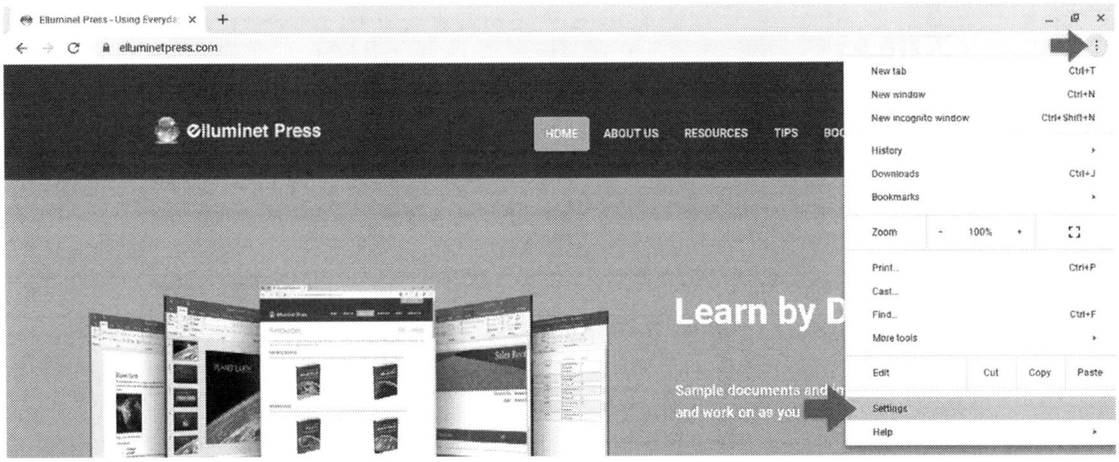

Scroll down to 'privacy & security'. Click 'site settings'.

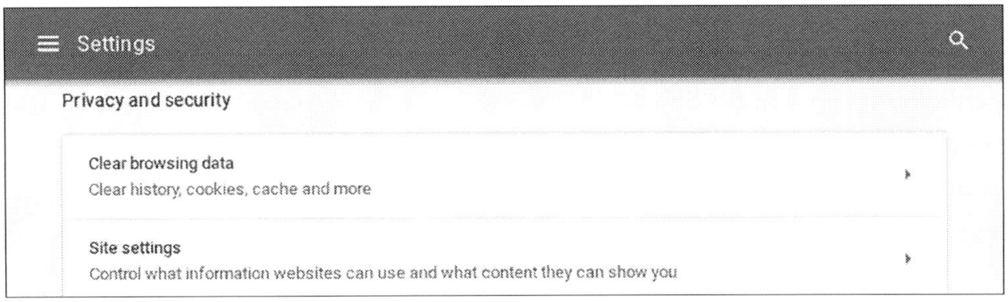

Here you can adjust security permissions for websites. You can allow or deny permission to your location, camera, as well as cookies and other site data. Scroll down the list, select from the list to change the settings.

For example, If you wanted to block irritating ads on websites click 'popup ads and redirects'

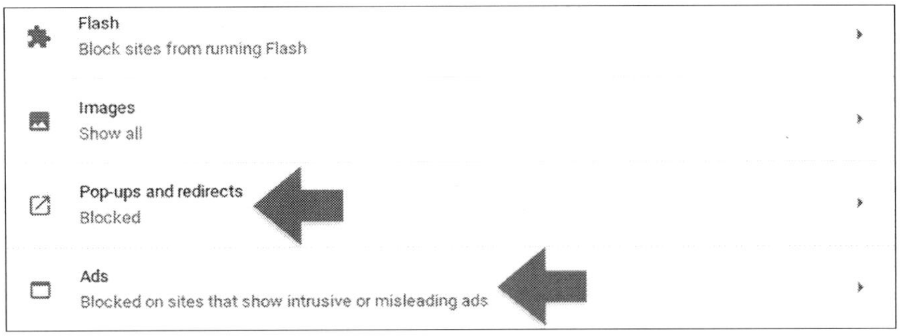

On the following page, turn the switch on the right to blocked.

Gmail App

The Gmail app is where you'll be able to check your email. You'll find Gmail on your app launcher.

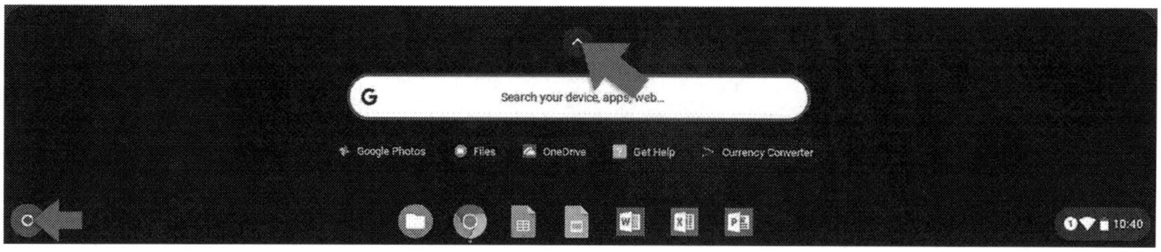

Open the app launcher fully and click the Gmail icon. Make sure you run the Android version of the app.

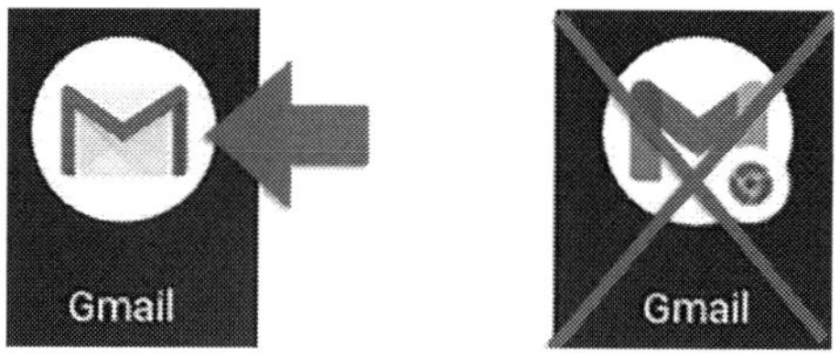

On some Chromebooks you might see two icons - one is an Android App and one is a Chrome App. You can tell the difference by the app icon - the Chrome App has a Chrome symbol on the bottom right of the icon. Chrome Apps are being discontinued in favour of the Android Apps.

Once the app opens, you'll land on the home screen. Lets take a look around.

The three small icons on the left allow you to filter emails. The top icon is your inbox and will contain messages sent to you by people you know and new email. The next icon down will contain email notifications from social media sites, and the bottom icon will contain any promotional message from any other site.

Reading Email

When you open Gmail it will check for any new messages. These will appear in your inbox. Of the three small icons on the left, make sure you've selected your inbox. In the next pane across, click on the message you want to read. The contents will be displayed in the main window.

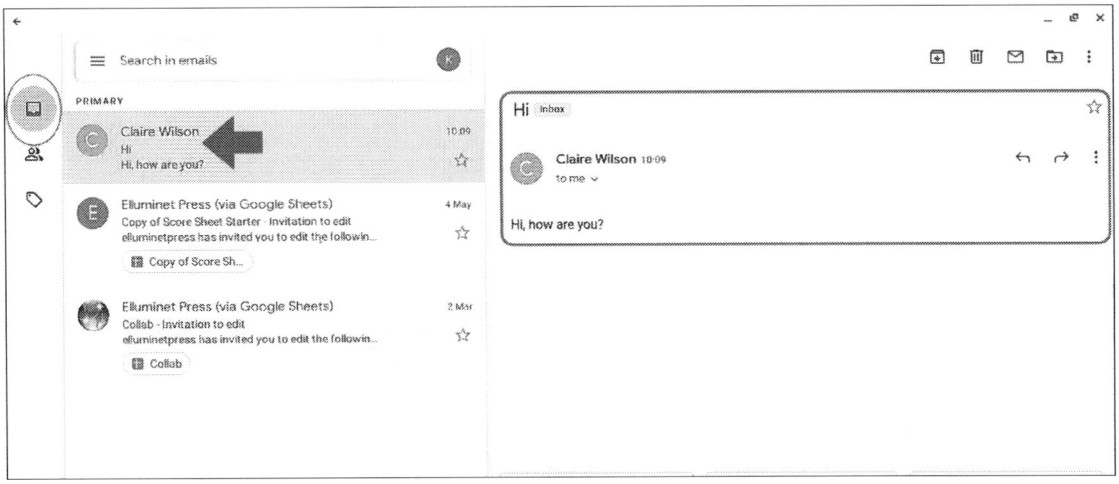

Reply

To reply to a message, select it from your inbox.

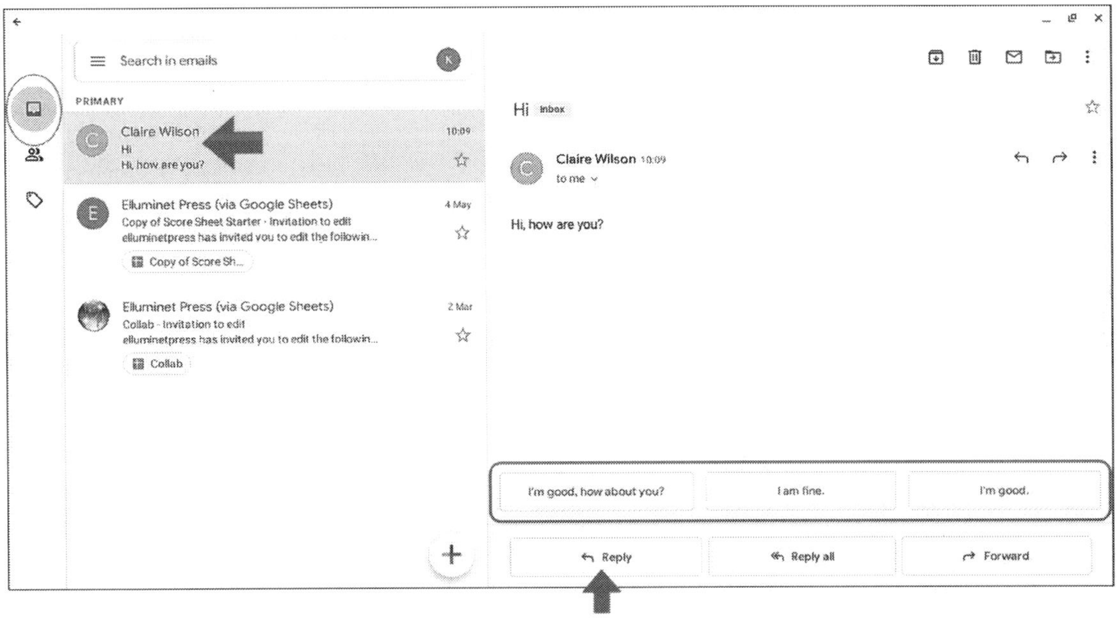

At the bottom of the message you'll see some quick reply options. This is Gmail's way of trying to help you by generating some suggested responses to the email. Click on one if you want to use it, otherwise click the reply icon to compose your own reply.

Here you can type in your message. Your message will appear under the message you're replying to, as shown below.

When you're done, click the send icon on the top right of the screen.

Writing a New Message

To start a new message, click '+' icon on the bottom of the main screen.

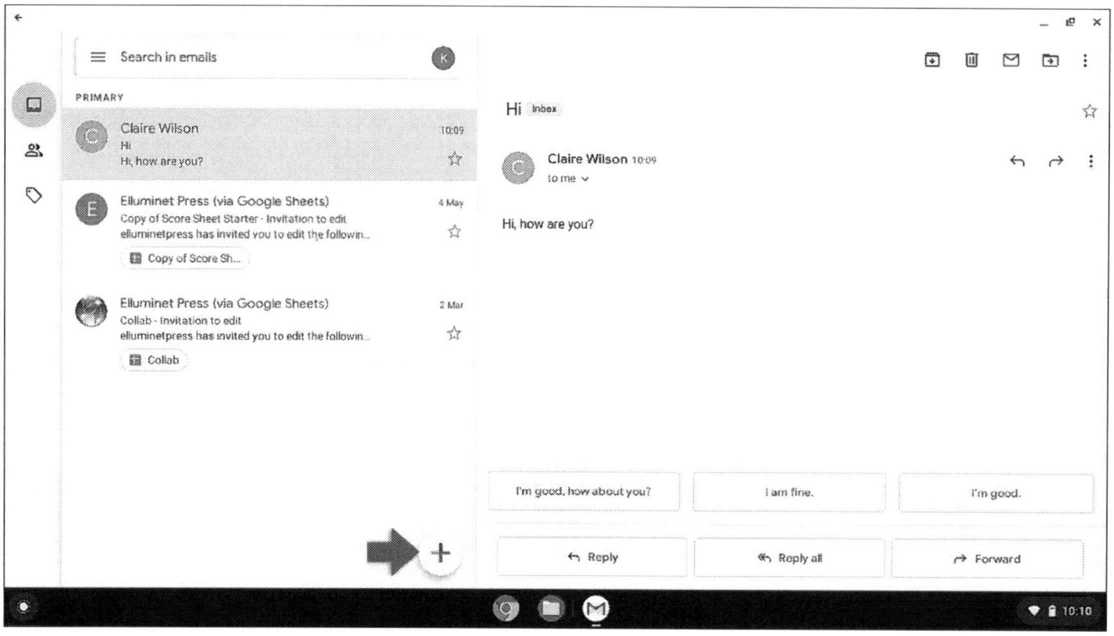

Type the person's email address in the top field. Select the email address from the suggestions.

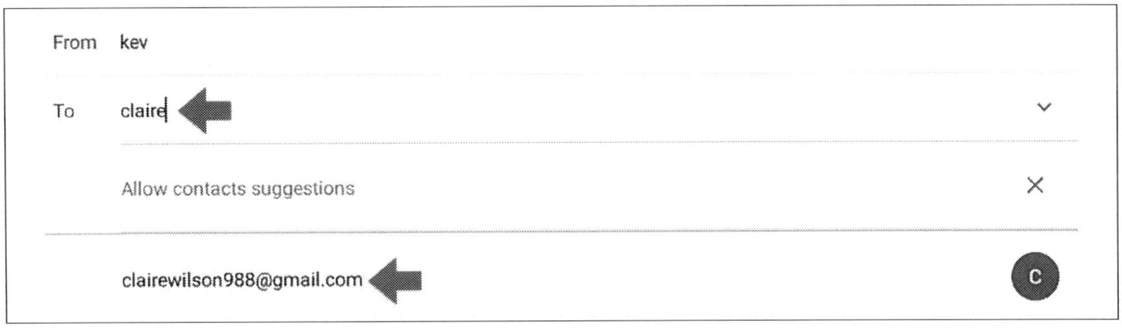

Enter your message, then click send on the top right.

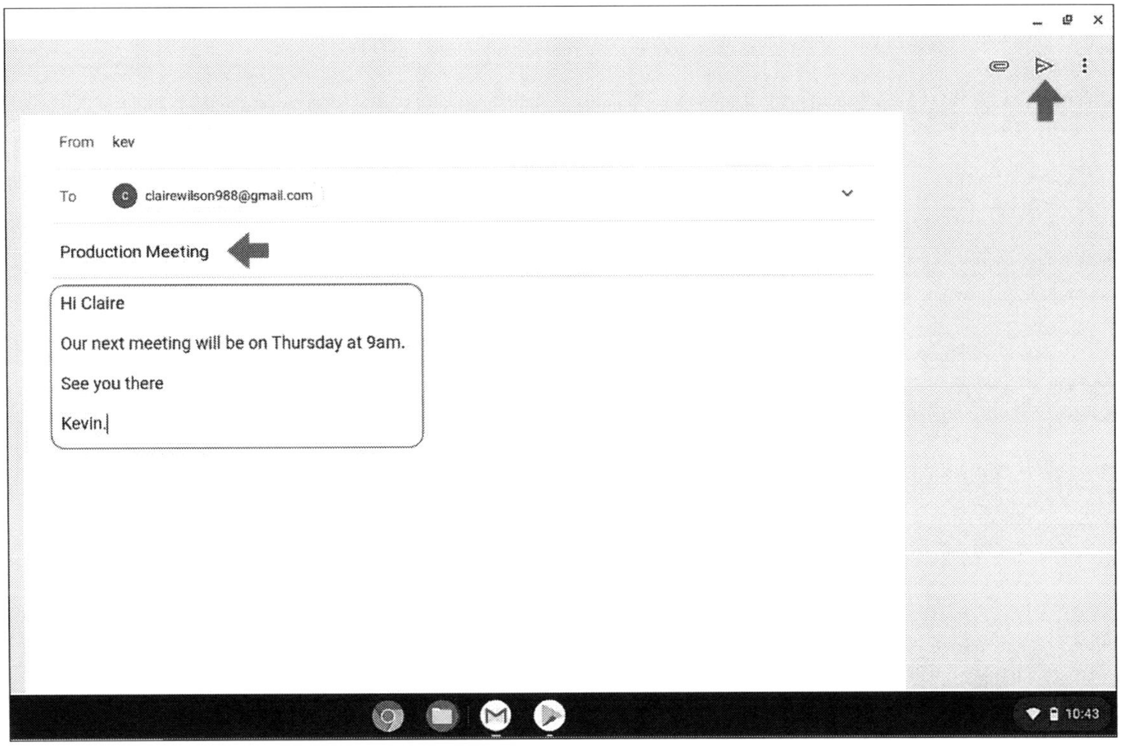

Adding Attachments

To attach a file, click the paperclip icon along the bottom of your message. Use this option to attach files such as documents, videos, music, or multiple photos.

From the popup select 'attach file'. From the dialog box, click on the file(s) to attach. Hold down the control key on your keyboard to select multiple files. Click 'open' when you're done.

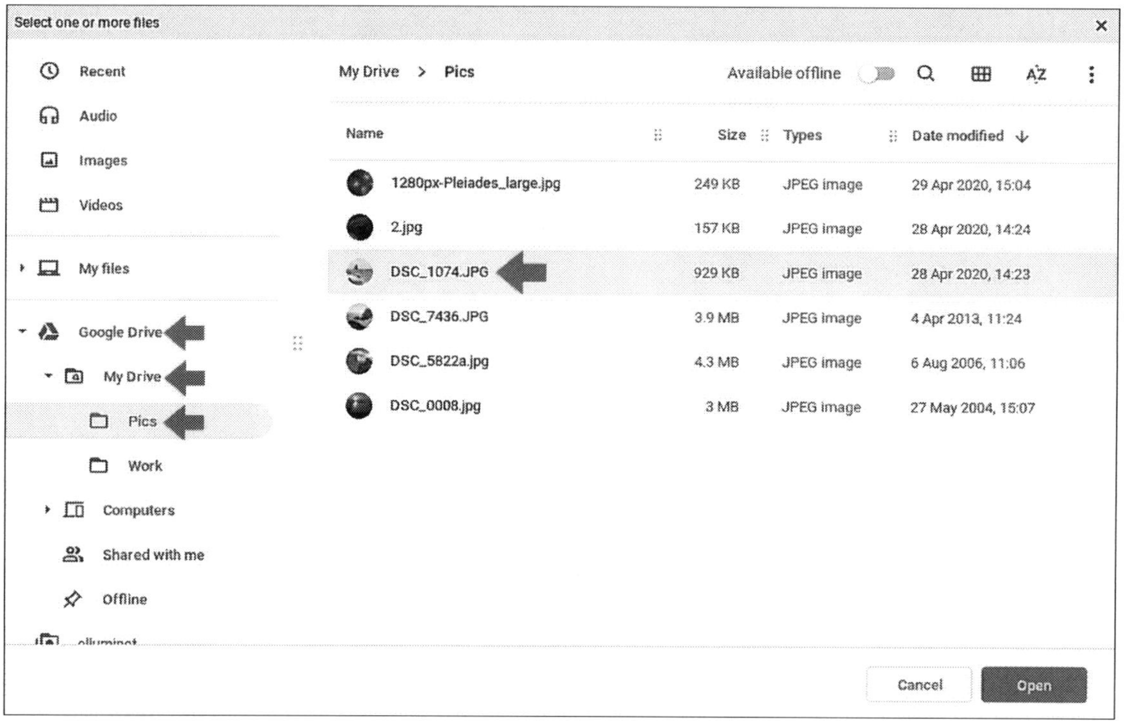

These attachments will be added to the end of the email.

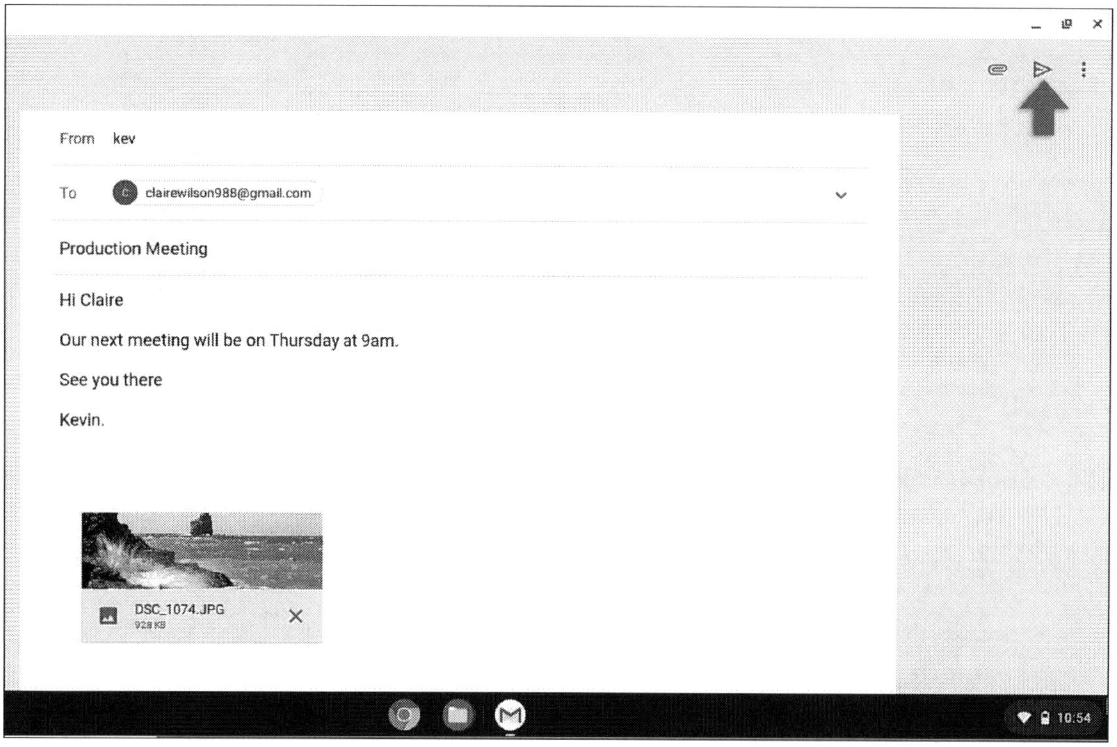

Once you are done, click 'send' on the bottom left.

Recover Deleted Messages

Click the hamburger icon on the left hand side to open the side panel.

Scroll down the list then select 'bin'.

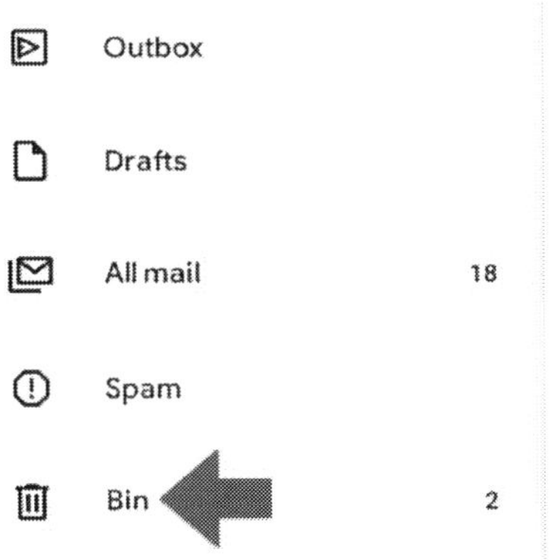

Select the messages you want to restore, then click the three dots icon on the top right, select 'move to'.

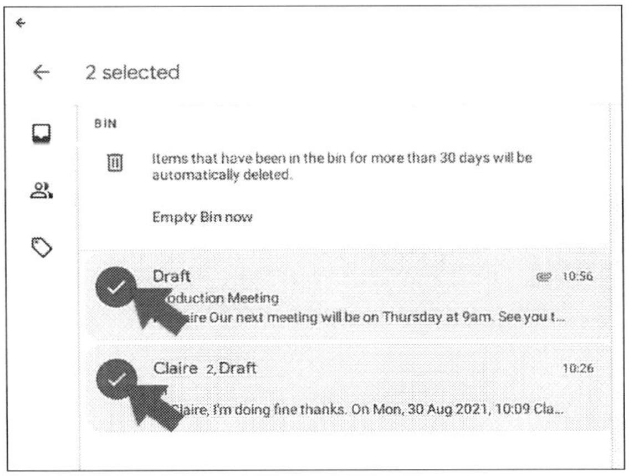

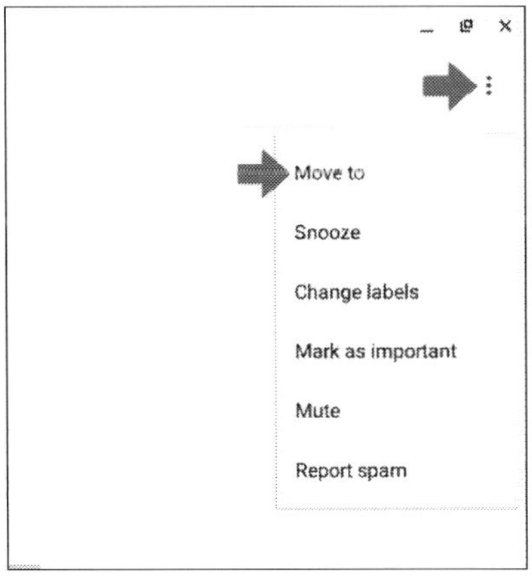

Select 'primary' from the popup dialog box.

Search

Type what you're searching for into the search field at the top of the screen.

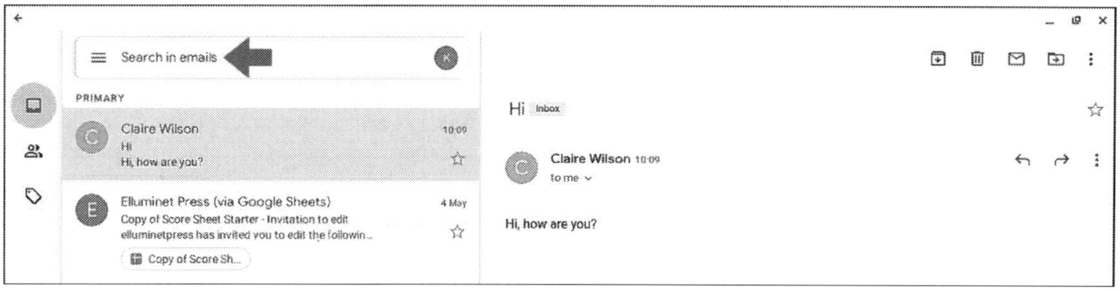

You can narrow down your search using different criteria. If you want to search for all emails from a specific person use 'from' followed by the person's name or email address. So if I wanted to find all emails sent by Claire, I could type:

from:<u>claire</u>

This will return all emails sent by Claire

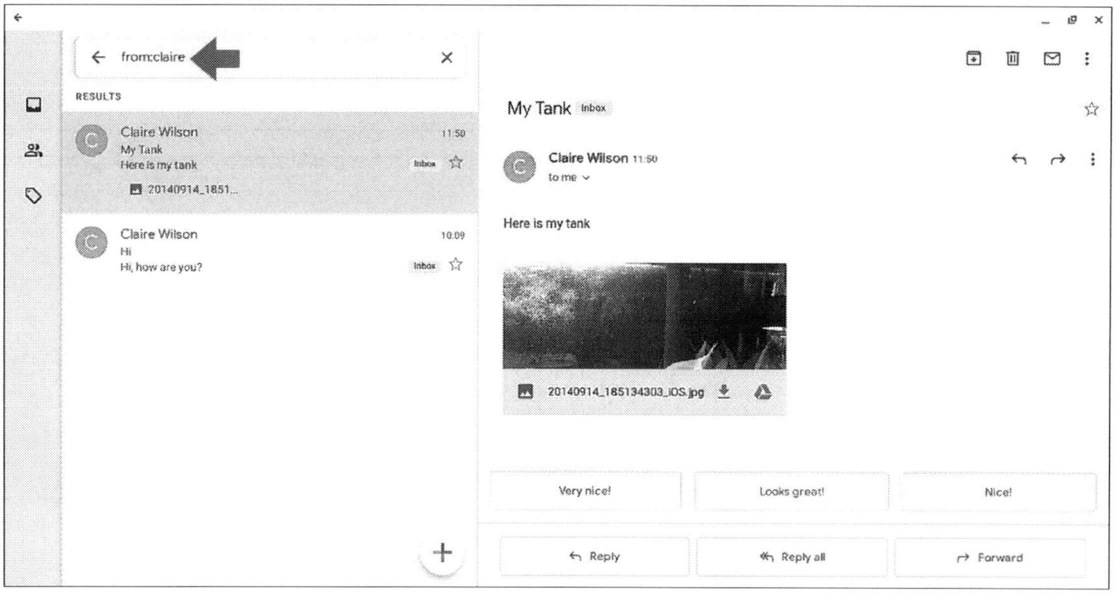

If you want to search for emails sent to a specific person use 'to' followed by the person's name

to:<u>claire</u>

If you want to find emails of on a particular subject use 'subject' followed by the email subject

subject:<u>production meeting</u>

If you want to search for messages containing an attachment add 'has:attachment'

```
has:attachment
```

So if I wanted to search for all emails sent by Claire containing an attachment, I'd type:

```
from:claire has:attachment
```

This will return all emails sent by Claire containing an attachment such as a photo or document.

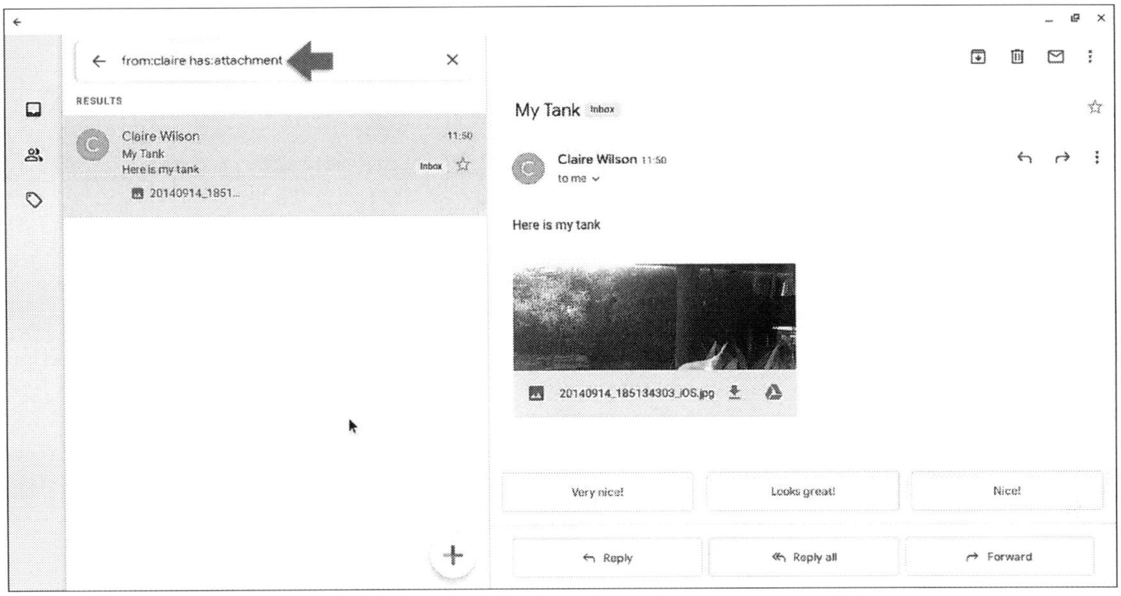

Or attachments with a certain name or file type add 'filename' followed by the name of the file.

```
filename:exploringchromebook.pdf
```

Adding Other Email Accounts

Click the hamburger icon on the left hand side to open the side panel.

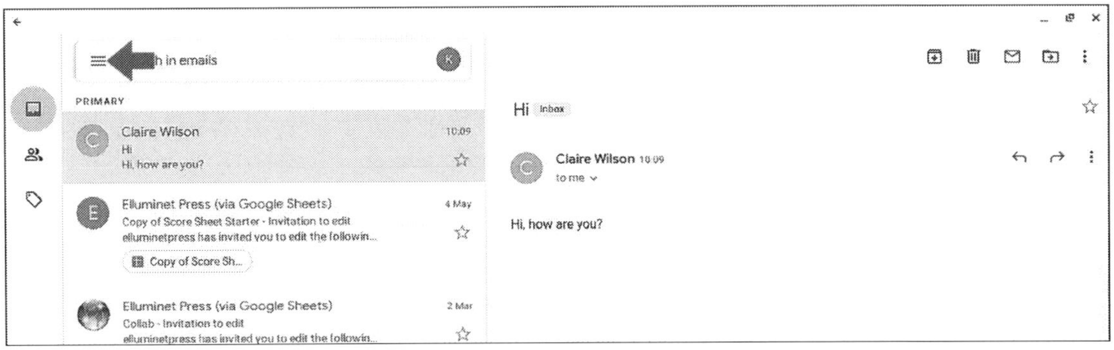

Scroll down the list on the left, then select 'settings'.

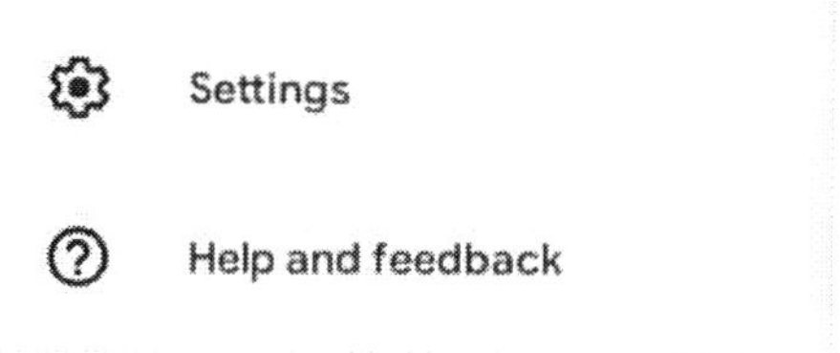

On the left hand side, you'll see a list of currently added email accounts. To add a new one, select 'add account'.

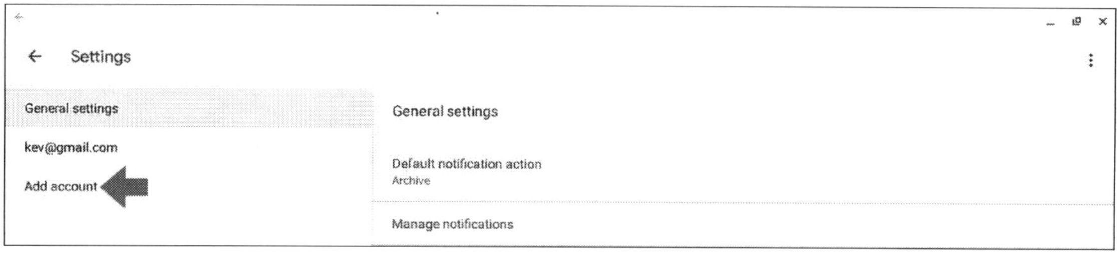

Select the type of account you want to add. This could be Yahoo, Hotmail, or another Google Mail account.

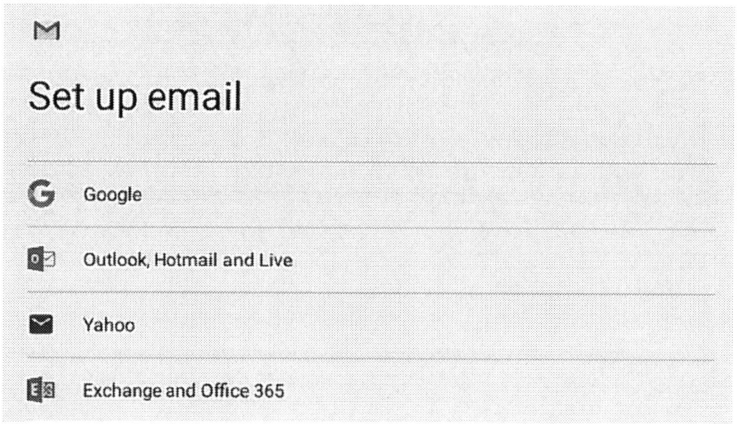

Select an option, then follow the prompts on the screen to enter the email account details such as email address and password.

On the top left of the main screen, you'll see a new icon appear called 'all inboxes'. This is where you'll find the email from all the accounts you've added.

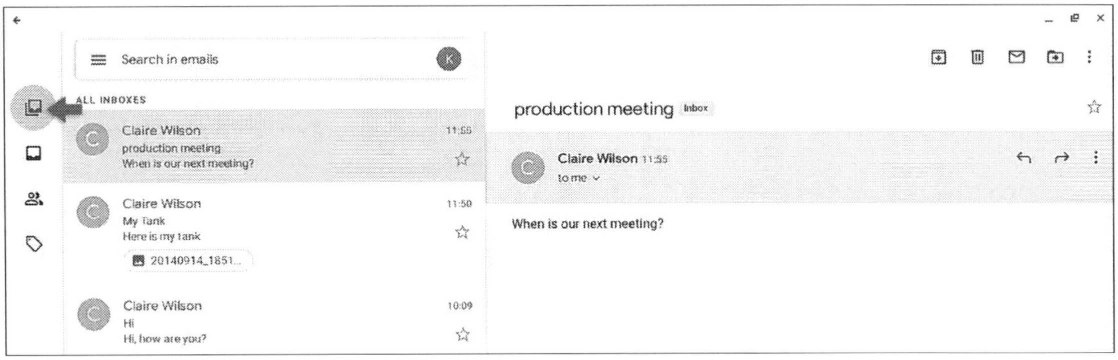

Contacts

This is your address book and stores all your email, phone numbers, and addresses that you can access from the contacts app itself or through your email, Teams, Duo, or Chat.

Starting

You'll find the contacts app in the Gmail app. Open the Gmail app, then click the hamburger icon on the top left.

Scroll down the list, select 'contacts'.

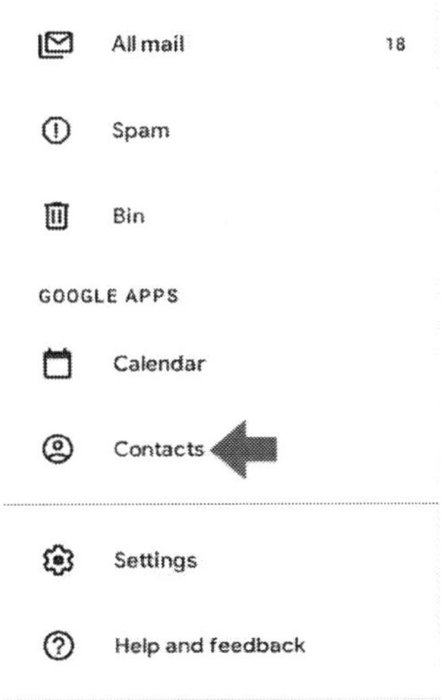

New Contact

To add a new contact, click the '+' icon on the bottom right of the window.

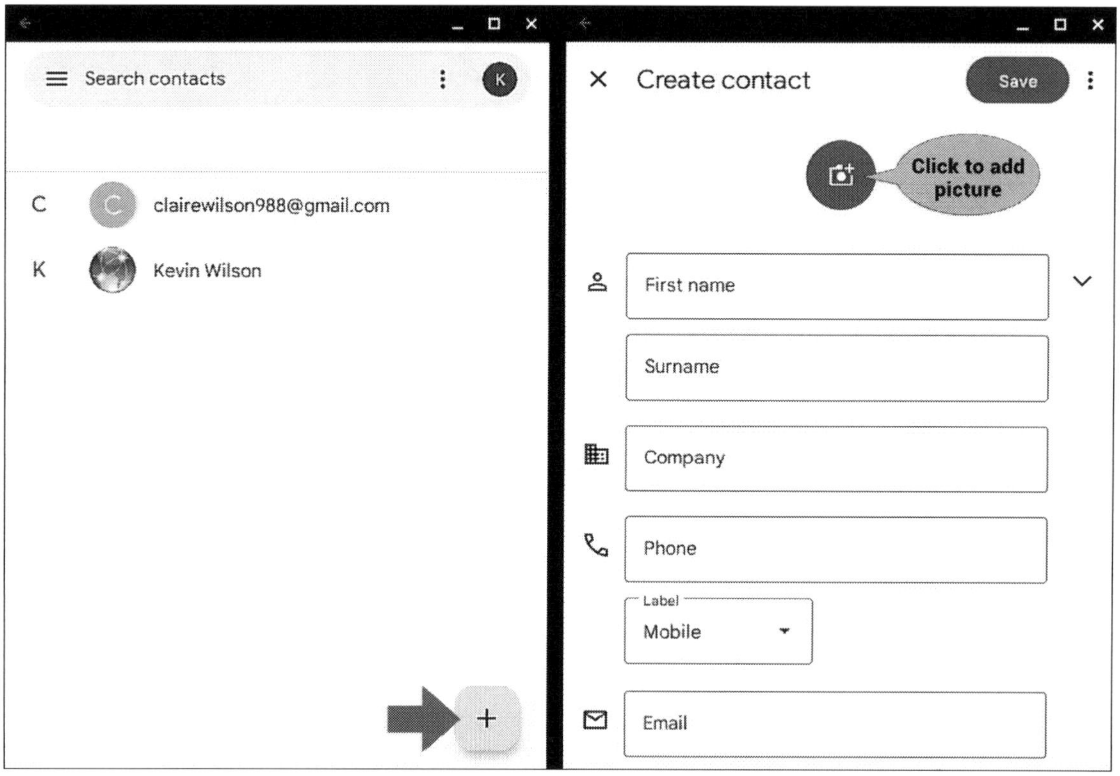

Fill in the person's contact details, then click 'save'.

Edit Contact

To edit a contact's details, click on the person's name in the list.

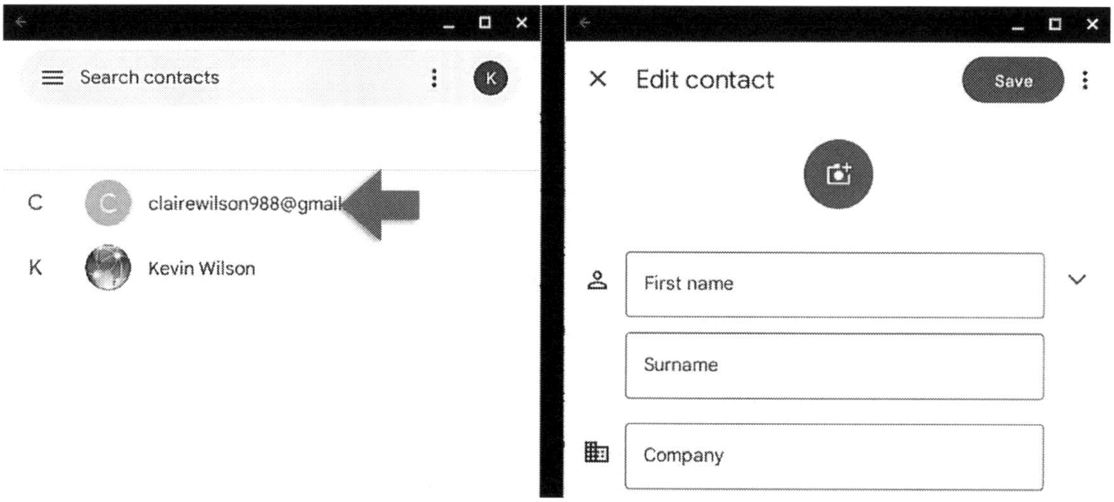

Amend the details, click 'save' when you're done.

Calendar App

This app is useful for scheduling appointments, events, meetings and so on. To start the calendar app, open your app launcher, then click the calendar icon.

Let's take a look around the main screen.

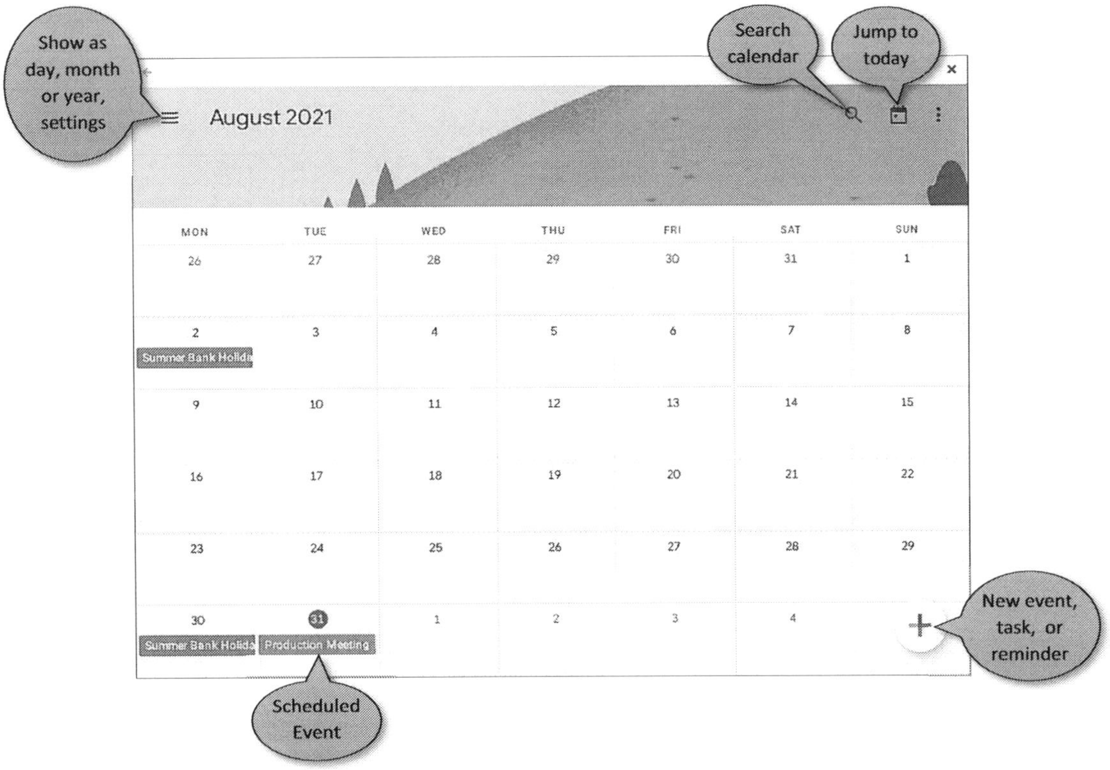

From here, you can add events, reminders, goals and tasks. Just click on the '+' icon on the bottom right, then select an option.

Events can be appointments, meetings, or even social events.

Reminders allow you to remind yourself to do something at a particular time or day.

Tasks allow you to create 'to-do' lists, and goals allow you to set goals to learn something new, exercise, or organise your life.

Adding Events

To add an event, click the '+' icon on the bottom right.

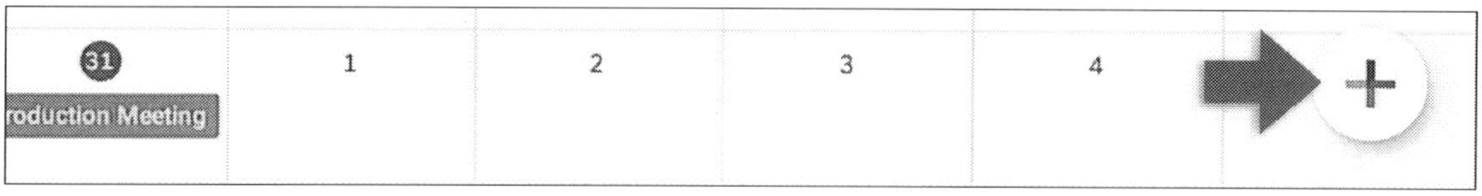

Select 'event' from the popup menu.

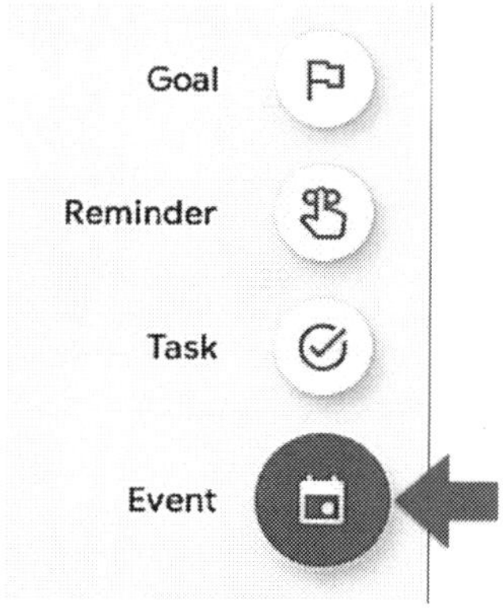

Fill in the details of the event

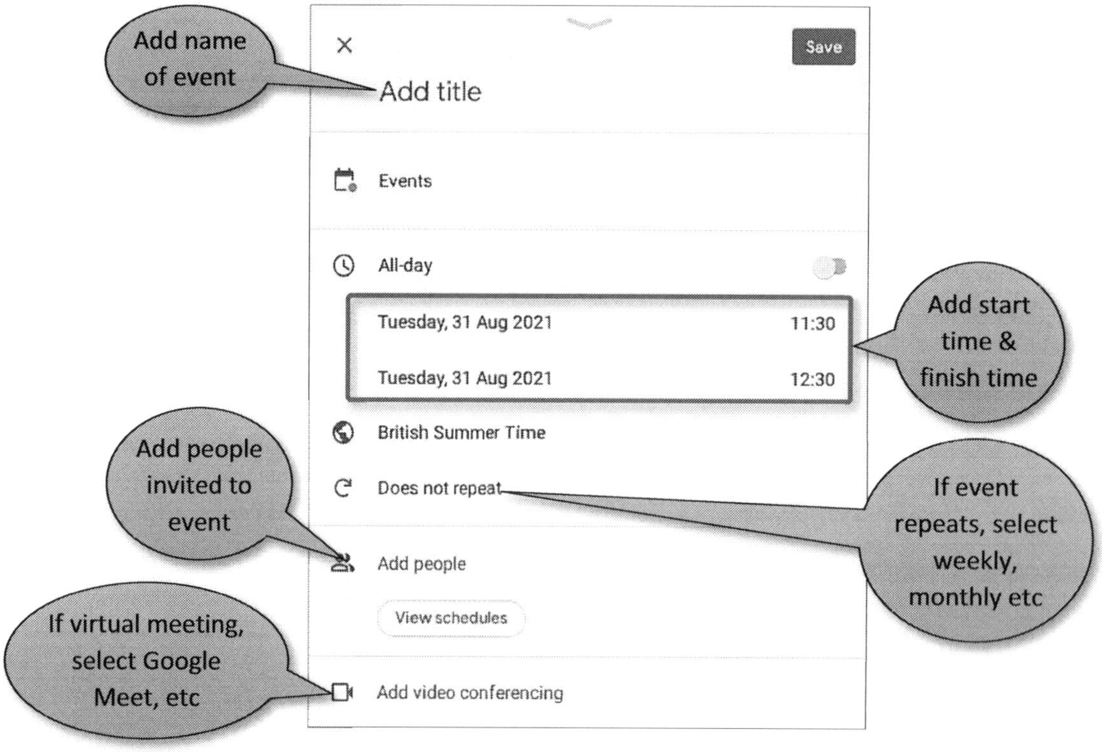

Scroll down, add a reminder and description.

Click 'save' when you're done.

Adding Reminders

To add a reminder, click the '+' icon on the bottom right.

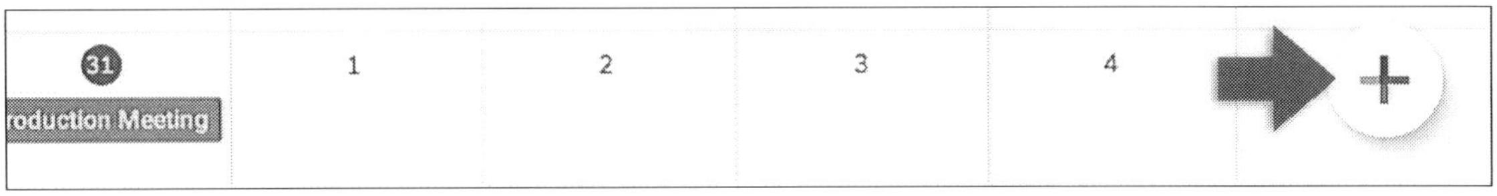

Select 'reminder' from the popup menu.

Fill in the details.

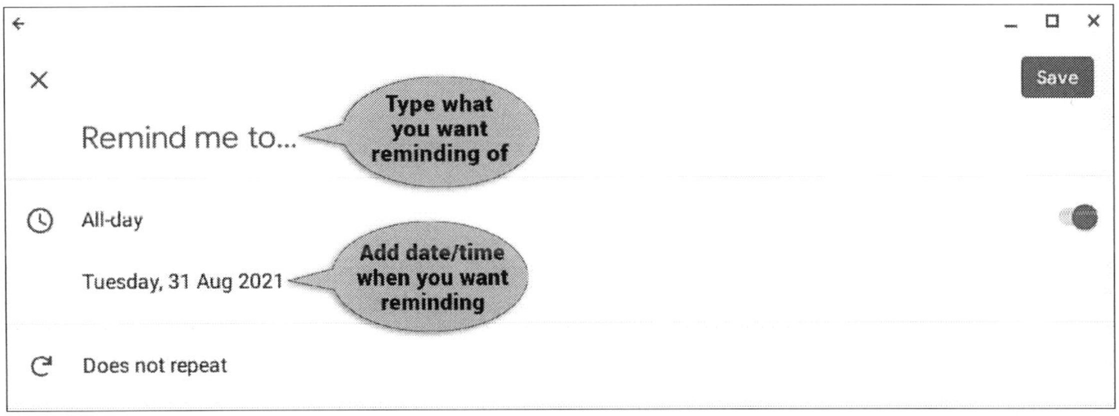

Click 'save' when you're done.

Adding Tasks

To add a task, click the '+' icon on the bottom right.

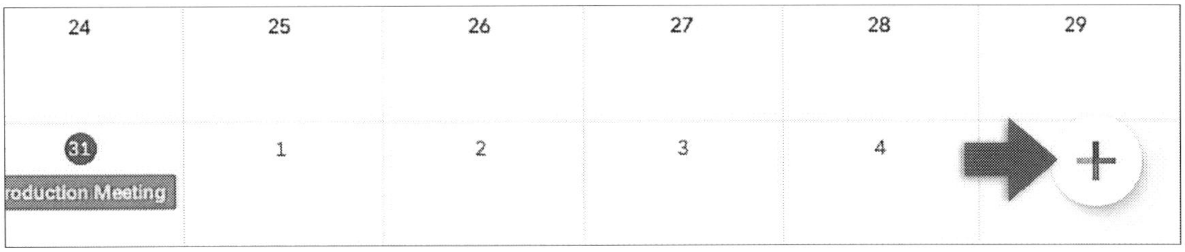

Select 'task' from the popup menu.

Fill in the details.

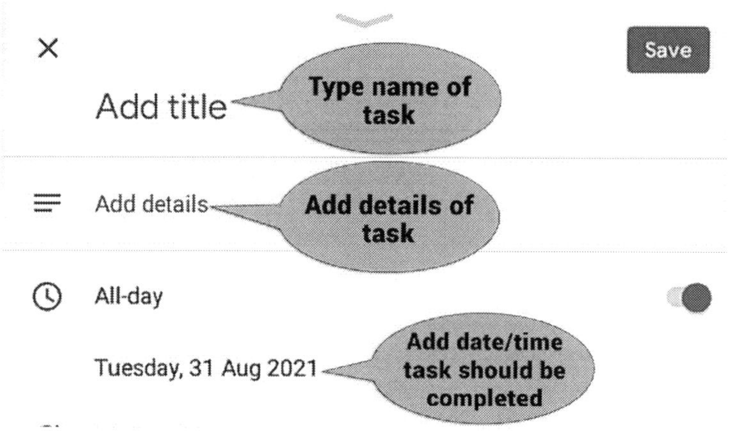

Click 'save' when you're done.

Add a Goal

To add a goal, click the '+' icon on the bottom right.

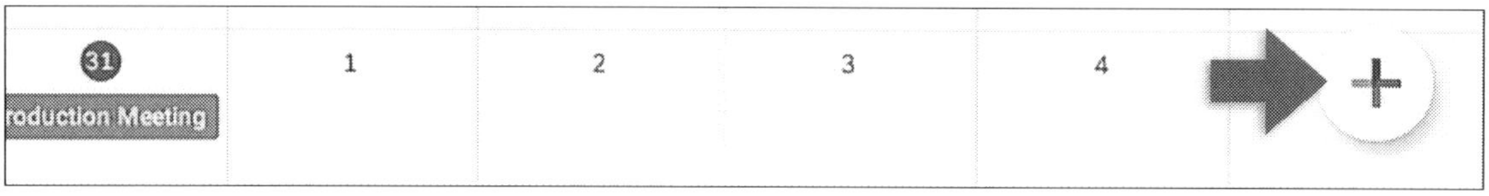

Select 'goal' from the popup menu.

Select a goal from the list. For example, I want to build a new skill. Then select a skill, eg 'learning to code'.

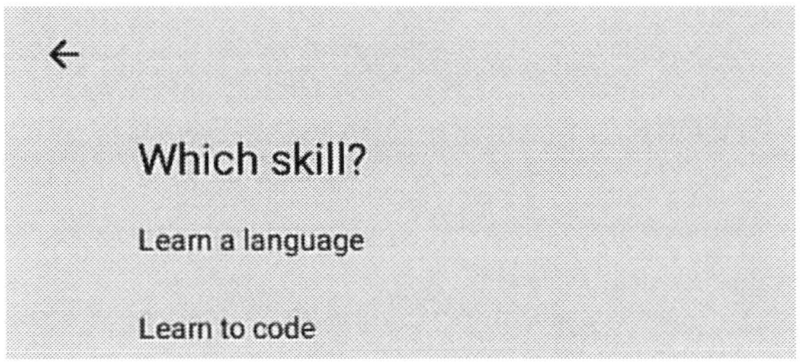

How many times a week do you want to spend learning the skill? Select and option. Eg once a week. How long do you want to spend learning the skill? Eg 1 hour.

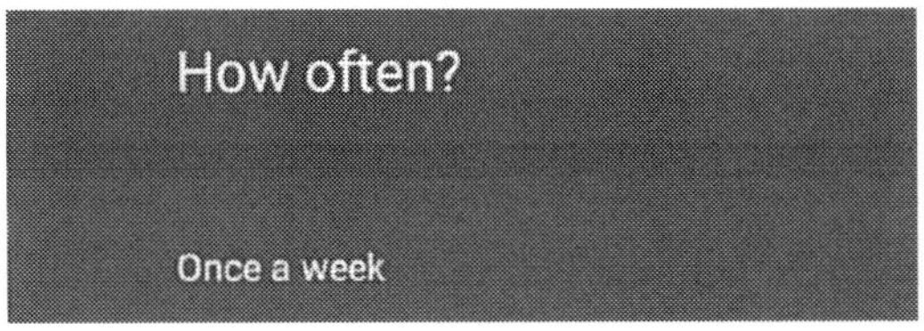

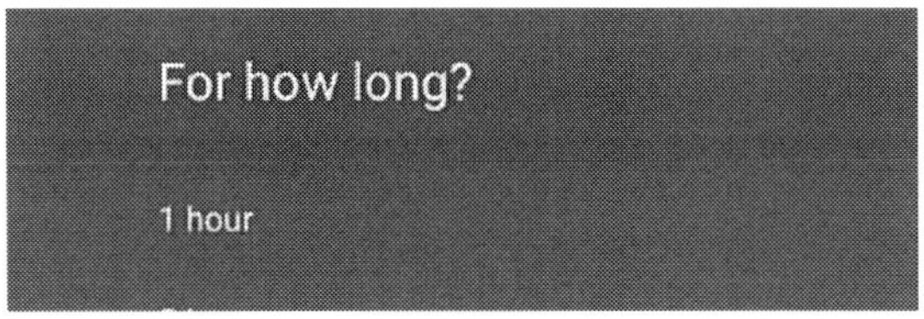

What time of day? Click the blue tick to confirm.

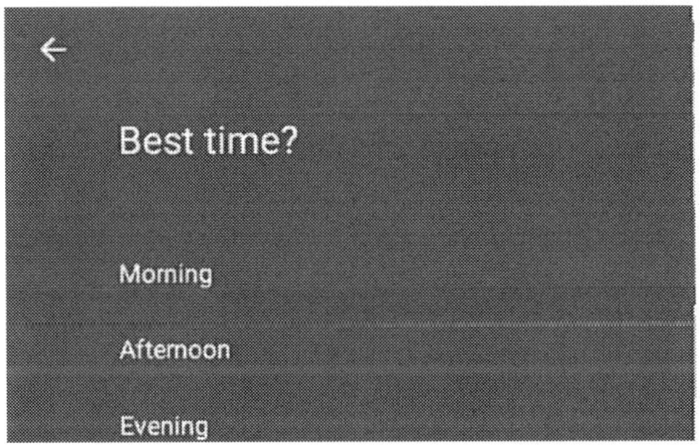

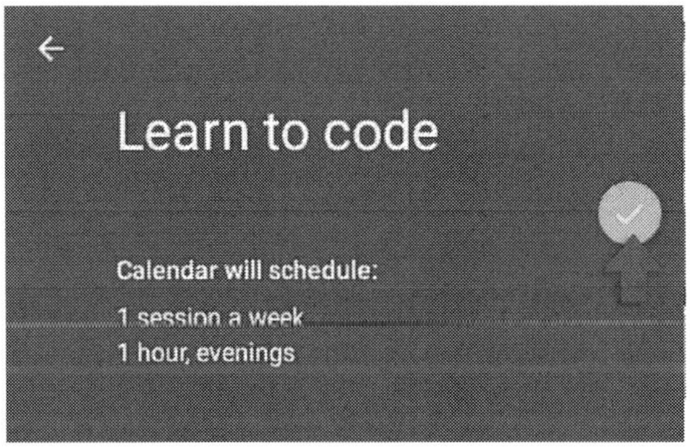

You'll see the goal is now scheduled on your calendar.

Select 'looks fine' from the message on the bottom right of your screen.

Gmail on the Web

If you are on a Windows machine, a Mac, or even your Chromebook, you can check your email using a web browser. Navigate to the following website

```
mail.google.com
```

Type the address into the address bar along the top of the browser.

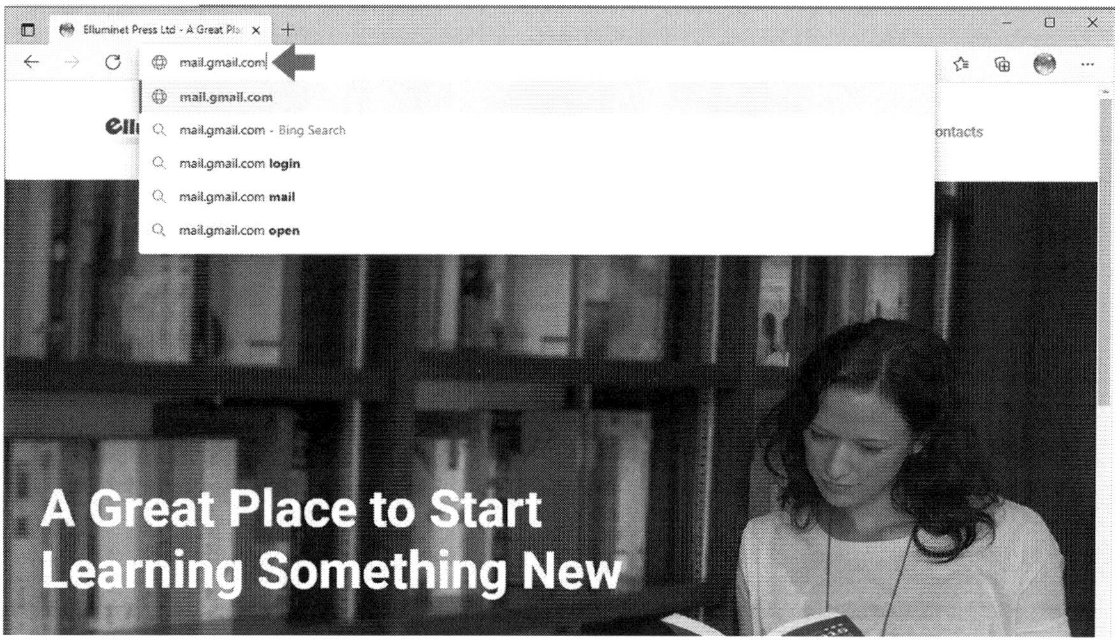

Once Gmail opens, you'll be able to see the email messages sent to your Google Account email address. Let's take a look at the main screen.

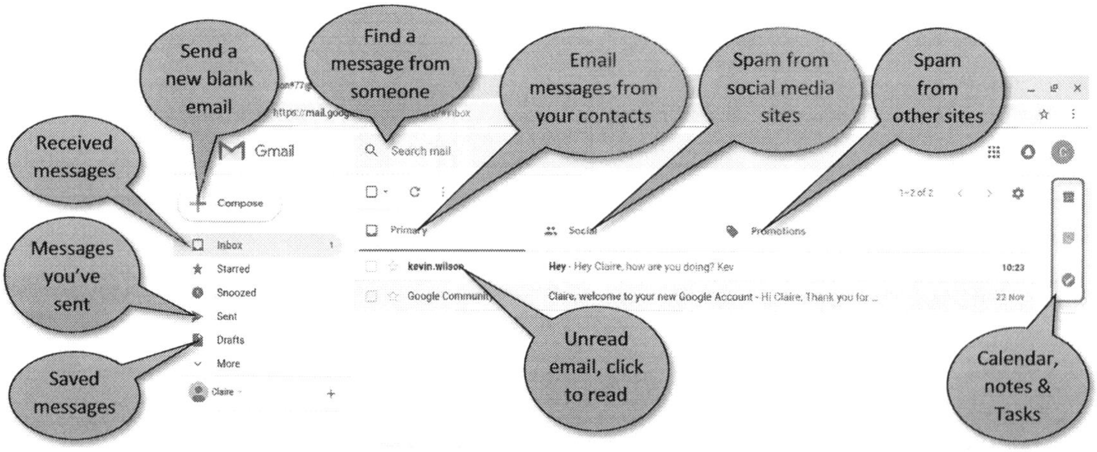

Down the lest hand side you'll see your mailboxes. Inbox is where all your new messages will appear. Starred messages are messages you've marked as important. Snoozed messages are you don't want to be notified about. Spam is what Google detects as spam or junk email.

Reading Mail

When you open Gmail it will check for email, any new messages will appear in your inbox. Click on the message in your inbox. The contents will be displayed in the main window.

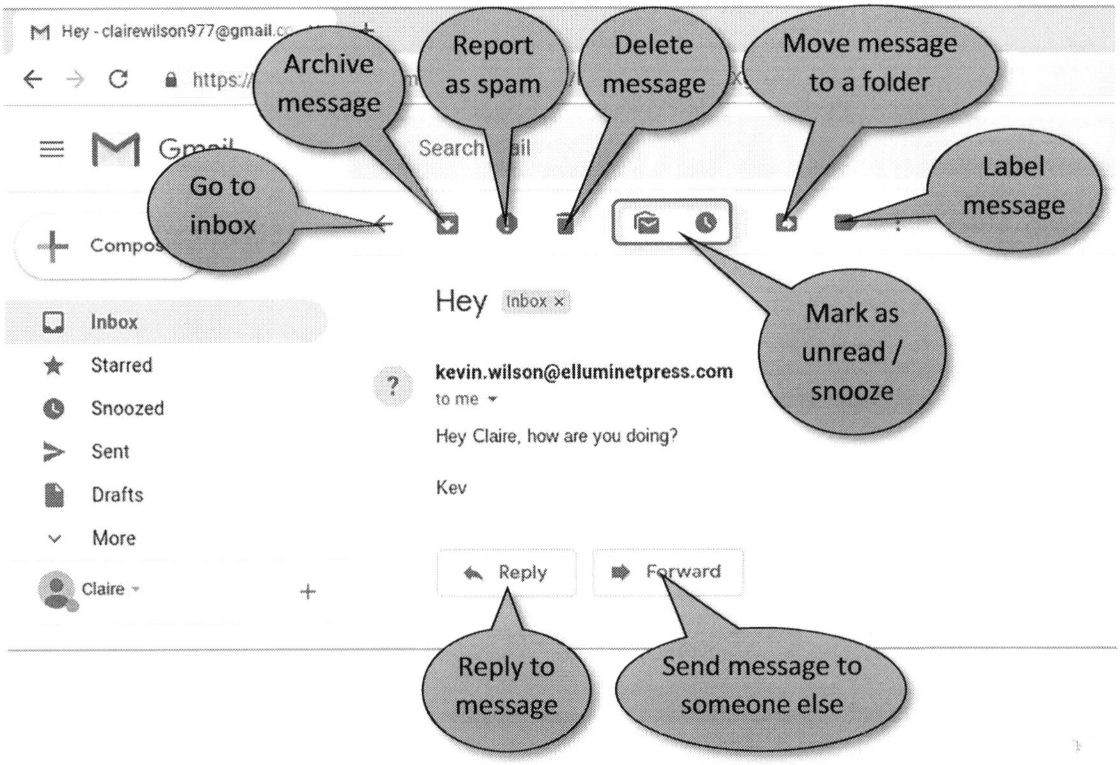

Writing a New Message

To start a new message, click 'compose' on the top left hand side of the main screen.

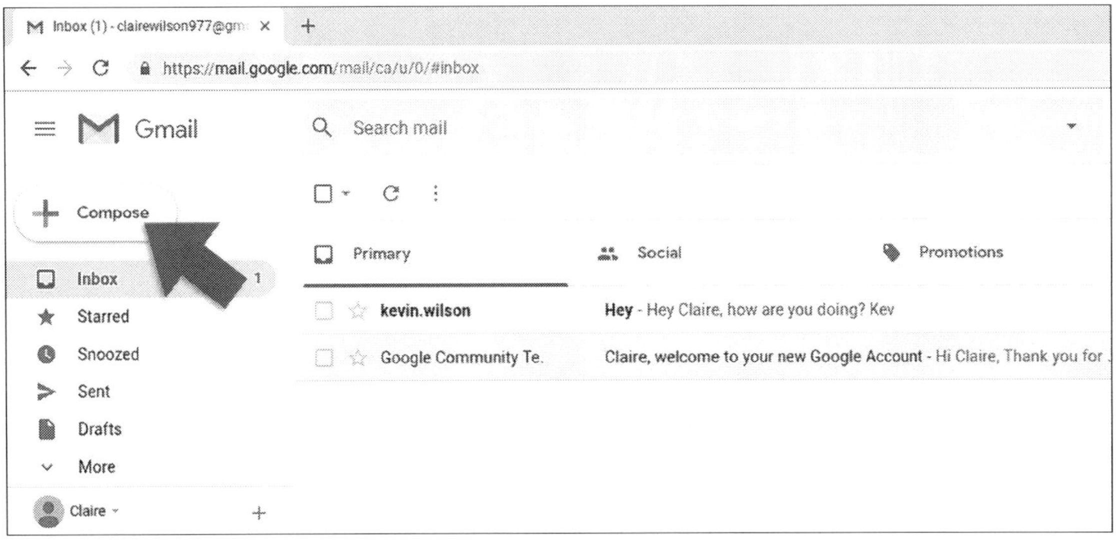

In the message popup window, you will need to enter the person's email address in the 'To' field.

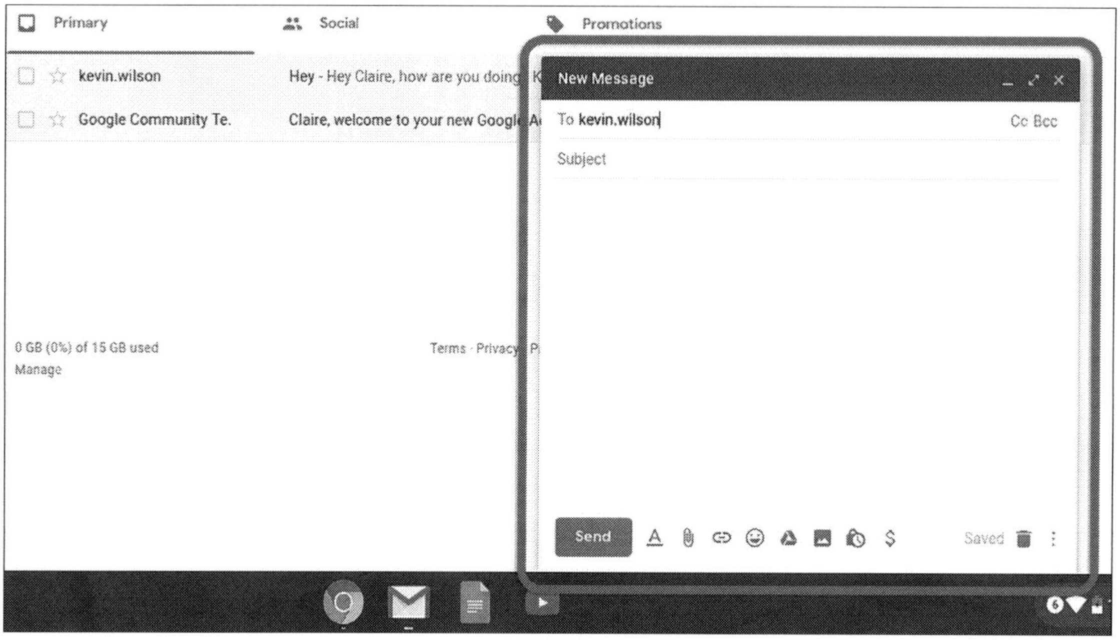

Add a subject, then type your message in the body section.

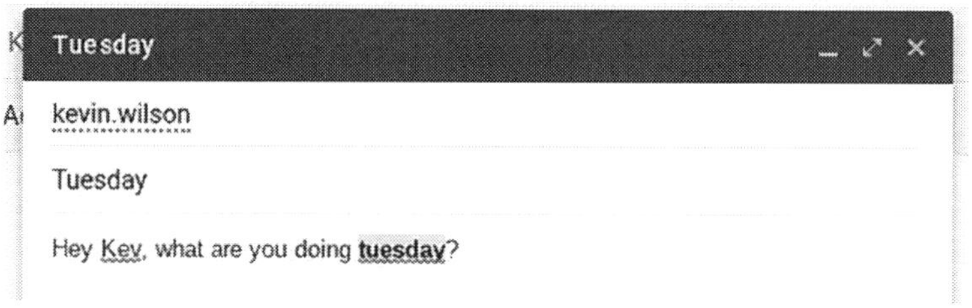

In the body section, you can use the normal text formatting tools such as bold, change the font colour or size and so on, using the format tool bar as you can see below.

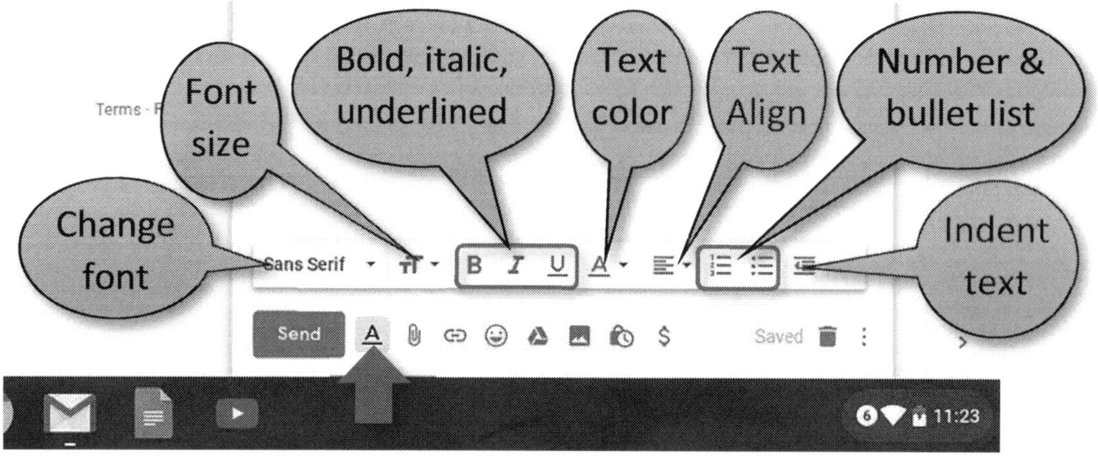

Hit 'send' on bottom left to send your message.

Reply to a Message

To reply to the message, click the reply icon on the bottom of the email.

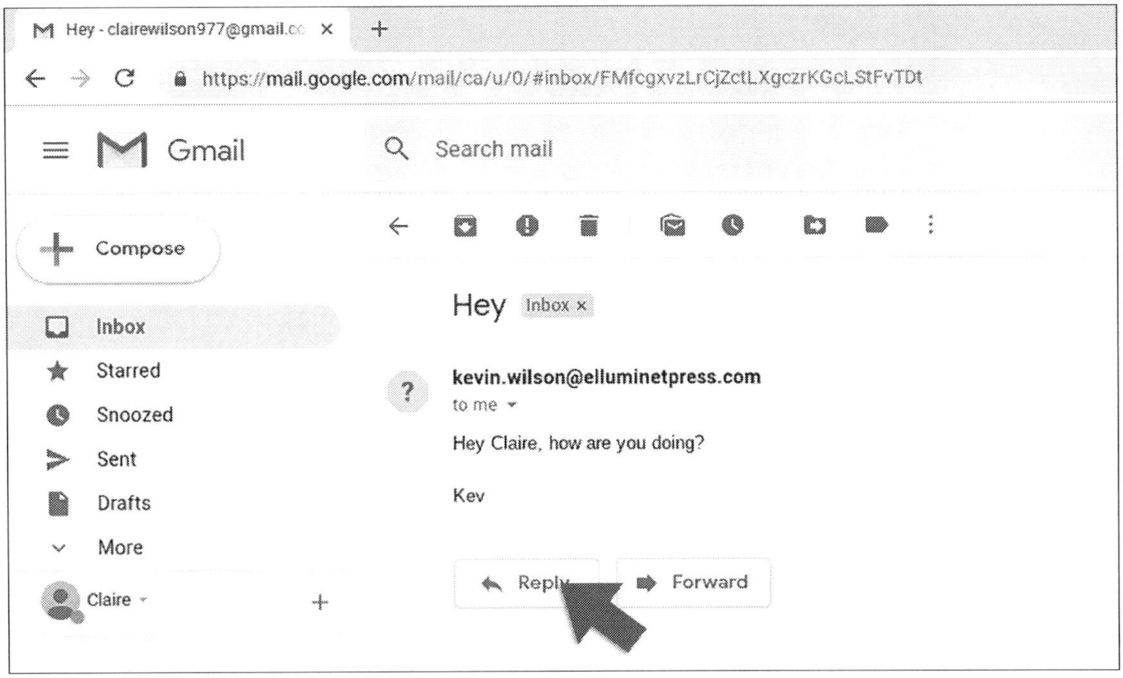

You'll see a screen that looks a bit like a word processor. Here you can type in your message. Your message will appear under the message you're replying to, as shown below.

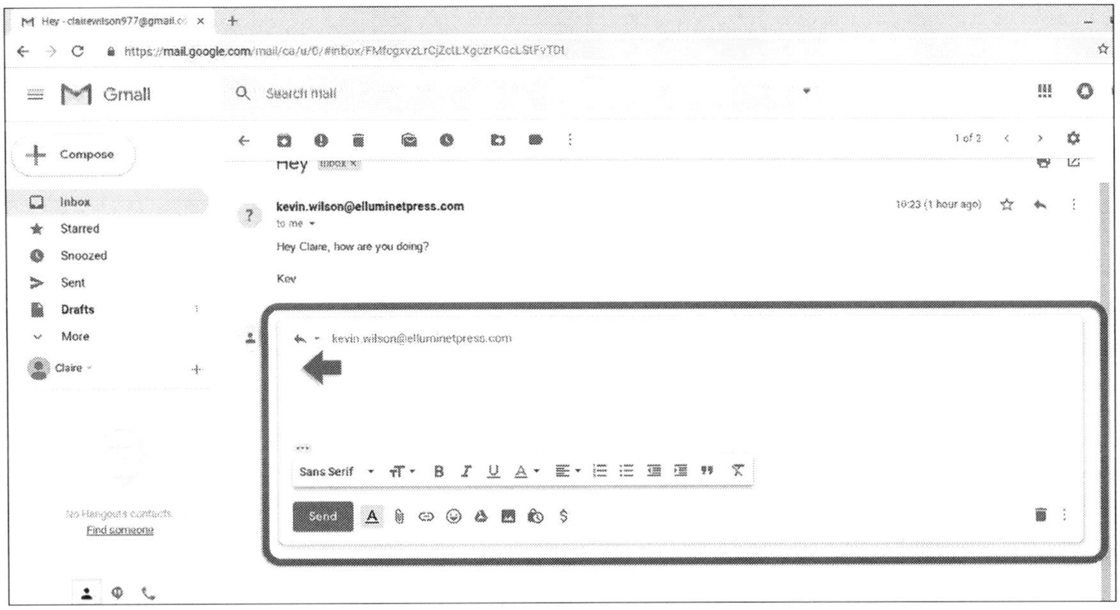

You can use the basic formatting tools. You can make text bold - select the text and click the 'A' icon on the toolbar.

Click 'send' when you're done.

Adding Attachments

To attach a file, click the paperclip icon along the bottom of your message. Use this option to attach files such as documents, videos, music, or multiple photos.

Select your file from the dialog box. Click the tick box on the top left of the images to select multiple files. Click 'open' when you're done.

These attachments will be added to the end of the email.

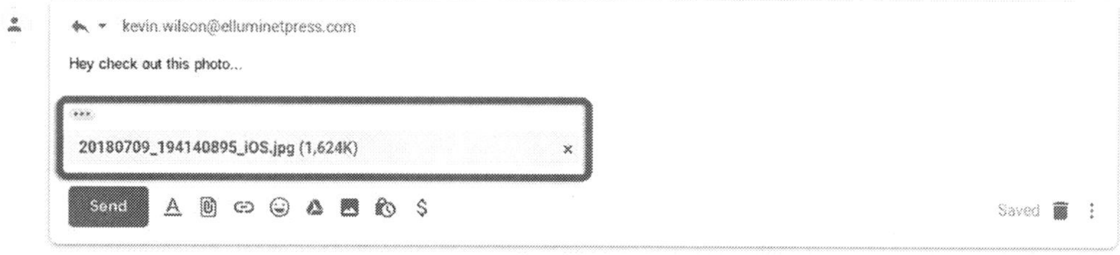

Once you are done, click 'send' on the bottom left.

Inserting Images

Inserting images is a little different from adding an attachment. When you insert an image, you insert it into the body of the email message so it appears inline with the text.

In your email message, click the images icon from the bottom of your message.

Click 'upload' along the top of the window, if it isn't already selected. Select 'inline' from the two options on the bottom right of the window.

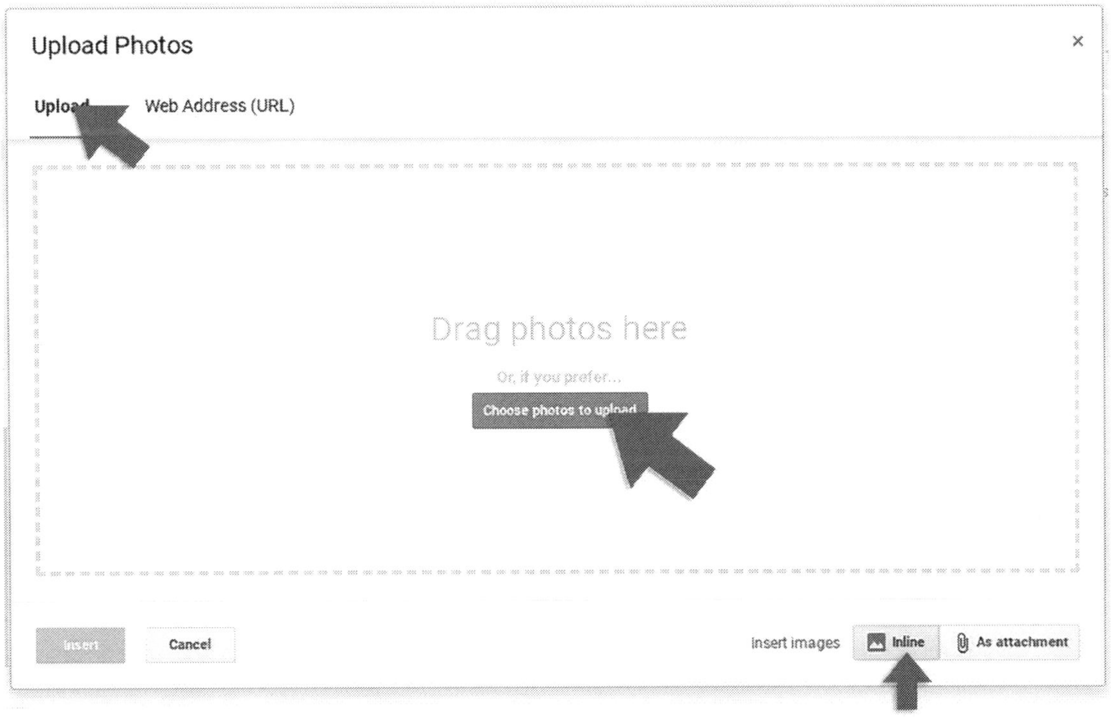

Click 'choose photos to upload'.

Select your file from the dialog box. Click the tick box on the top left of the images to select multiple files. Click 'open' when you're done.

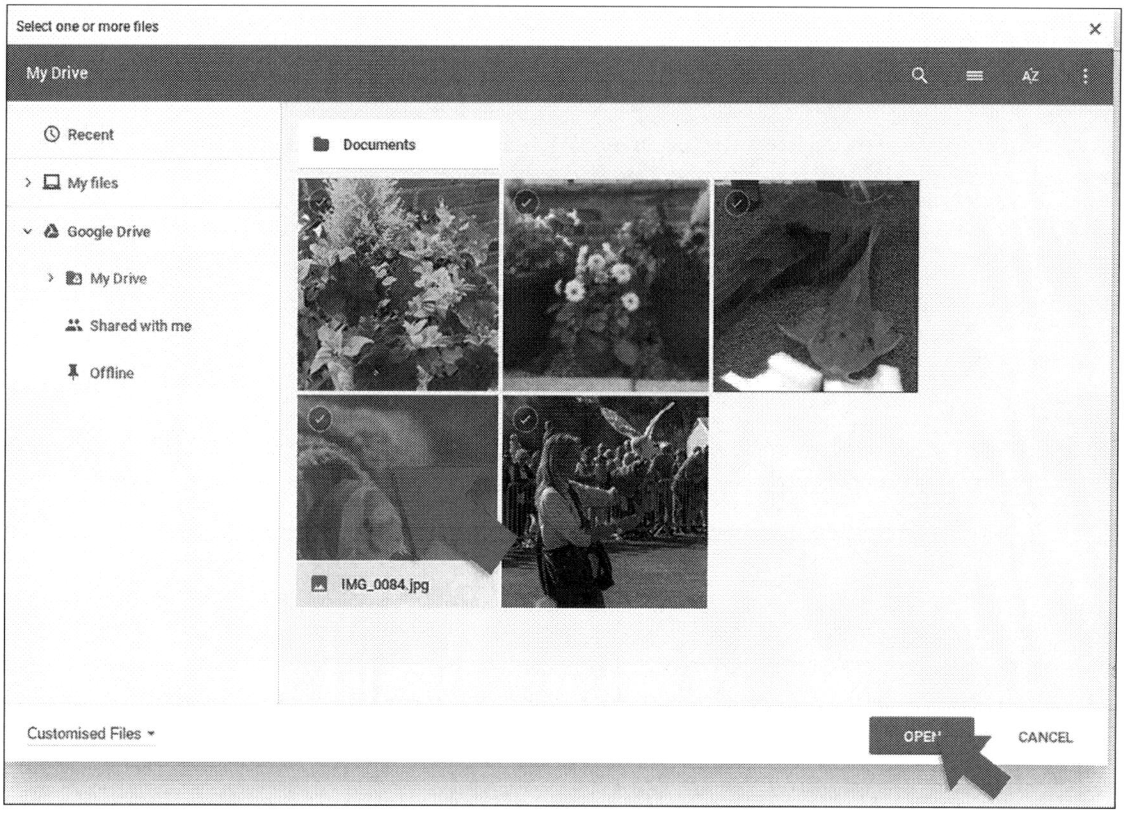

Notice the photo has been inserted within the text body of your email, rather than just attached to the end as an attachment.

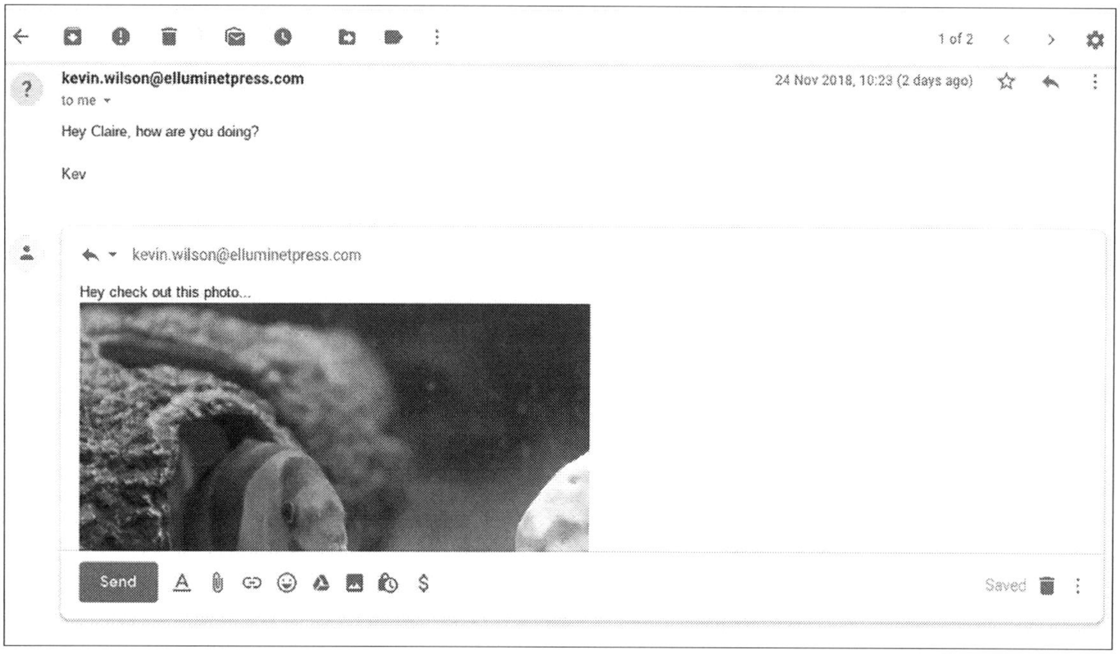

Click the 'send' icon on the top right when you're done.

Sending Money

You can send money to someone using Google Pay. To use this feature, you'll need to have a payment method set up on your Google Account.

To send money, click the $ or £ icon on the bottom of your message.

Enter the amount you want to send and choose a payment method or add a new one.

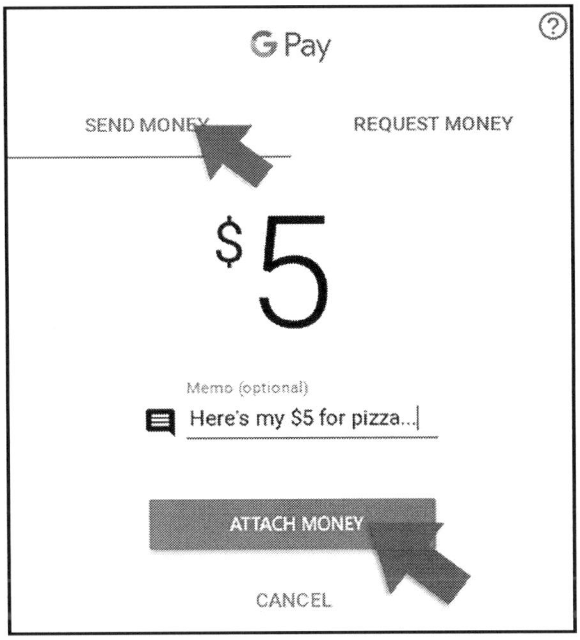

Click 'attach money'. If you don't have a payment method set up on your Google Account, click 'add debit card' then enter your card details.

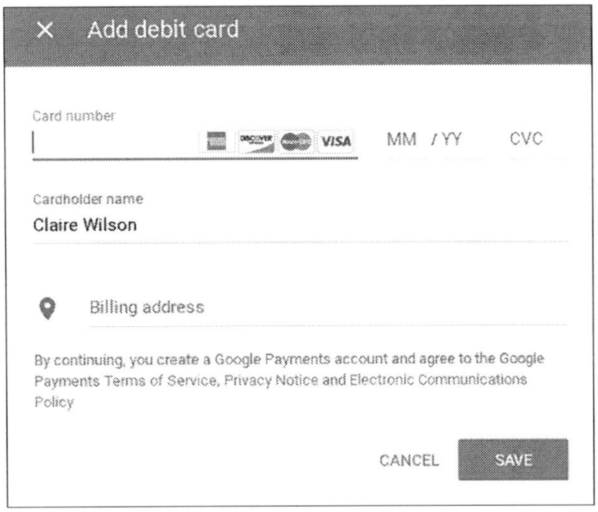

You'll see the Google Pay attachment at the bottom of your email. Click 'send' on the bottom left to send the message.

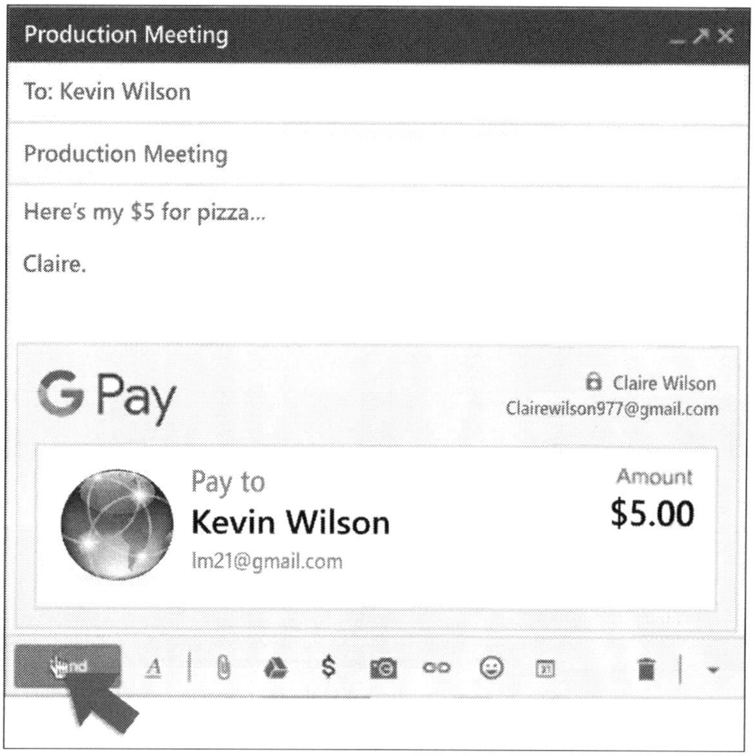

Now, when the recipient checks their email, they'll get a message like this in their inbox.

To claim the money, click 'claim money' at the bottom of the message.

Once you've claimed your money, it will be available in your Google Pay Balance. Go to

`pay.Google.com`

From here you'll be able to send money to other people, transfer to your bank account, or use it on the Google Play Store.

Adding Other Email Accounts

In the top right, click the 'settings' icon, then select 'settings' from the menu.

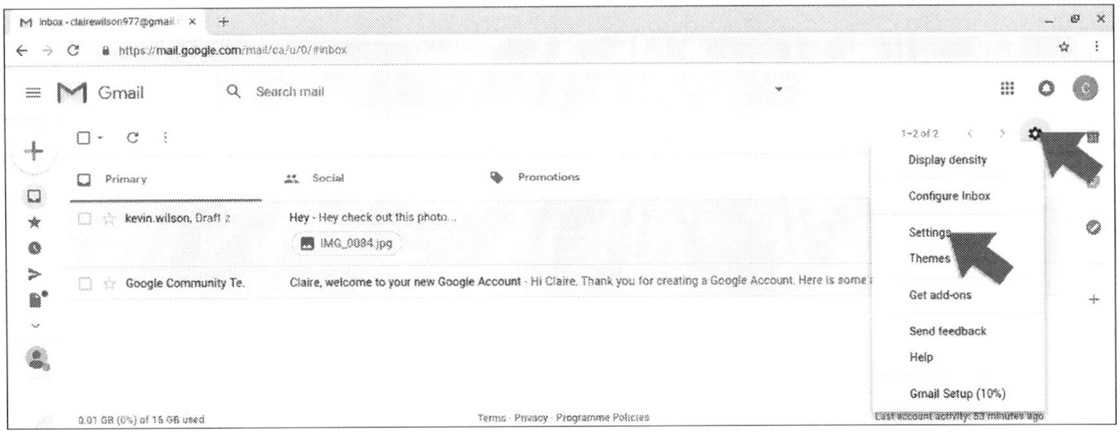

Click 'accounts and import', then select 'add an email account'.

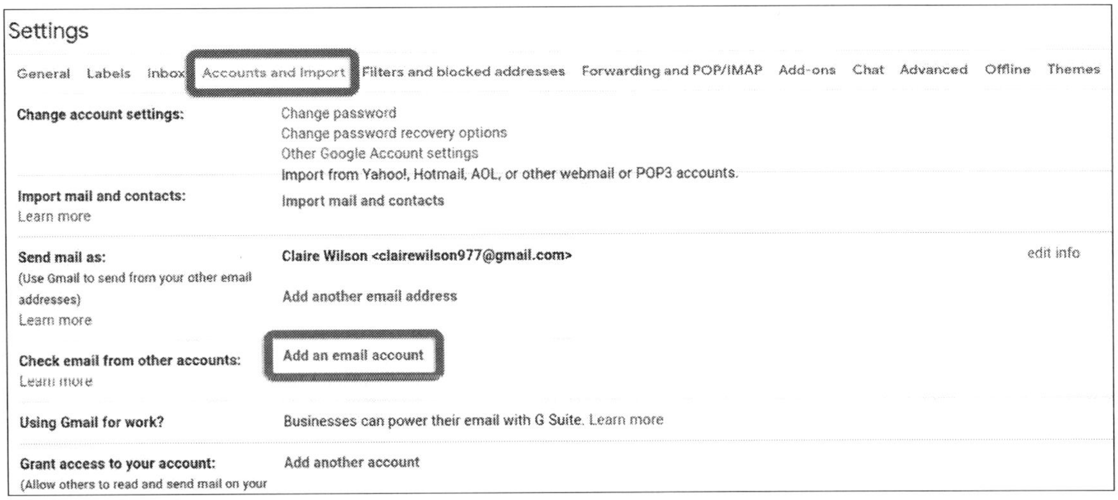

In the dialog box that appears, enter the email address of the account you want to add.

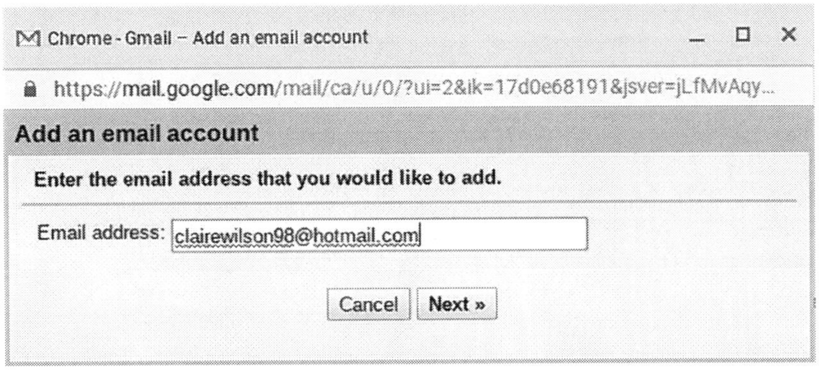

Click 'next'.

Select 'link accounts with Gmailify' if available, then click 'next'.

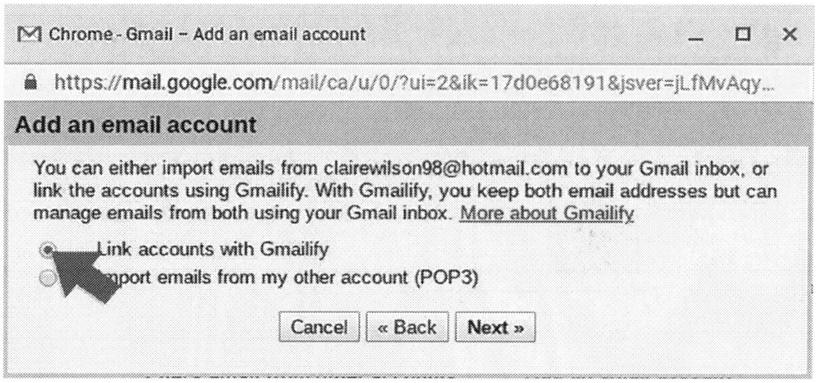

Sign in with the password for the account you're adding.

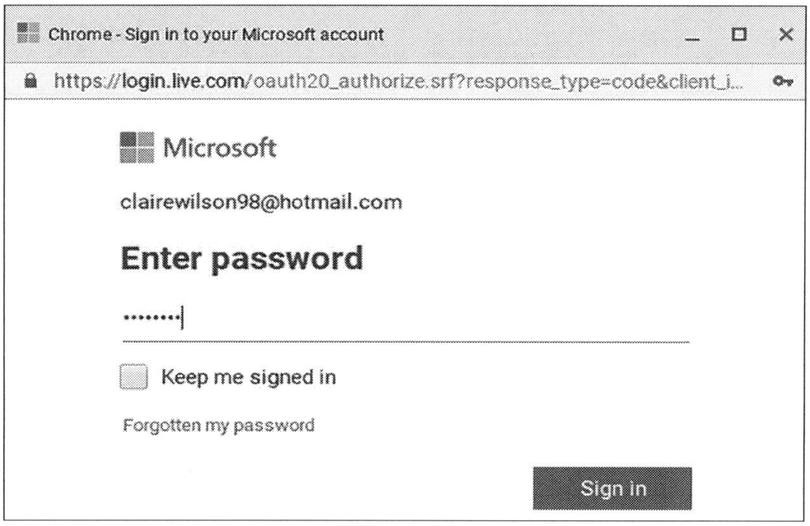

Click 'yes' to grant access to the email account you're adding.

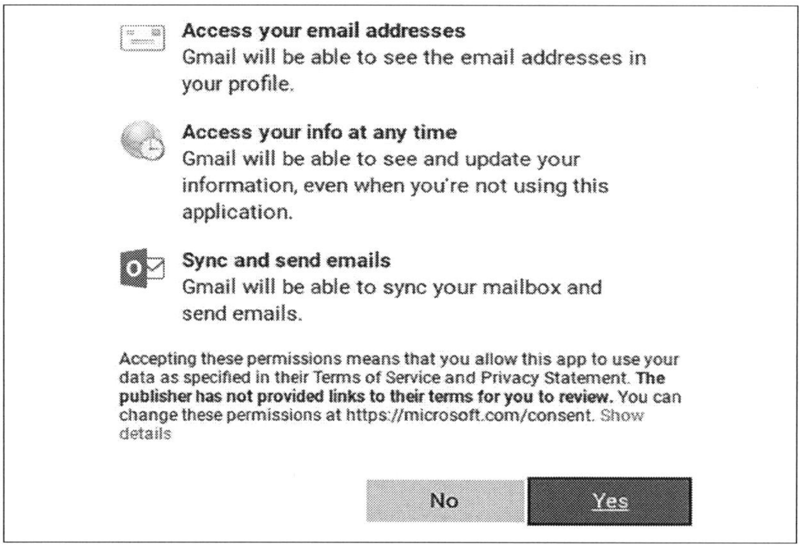

Click 'close' on the last dialog box, and you're done.

Contacts Web App

The contacts app is your address book and contains your contact's email addresses, phone numbers and addresses.

Click the apps icon on the top right of your screen

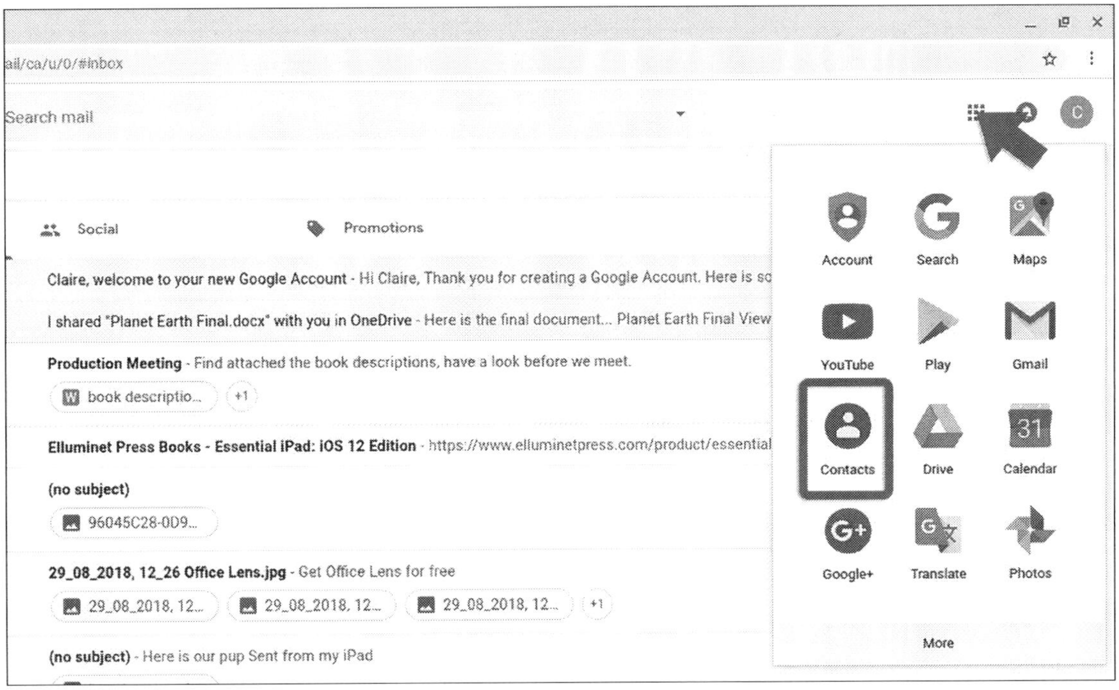

Click on the contacts icon.

View Contact Details

Once the contacts app opens, you'll see a list of all the people you have contact information for. Click on one of the names to view or edit the details for that person. I'm going to click on my contact 'Sophie' in the list.

The person's details will open up on your screen.

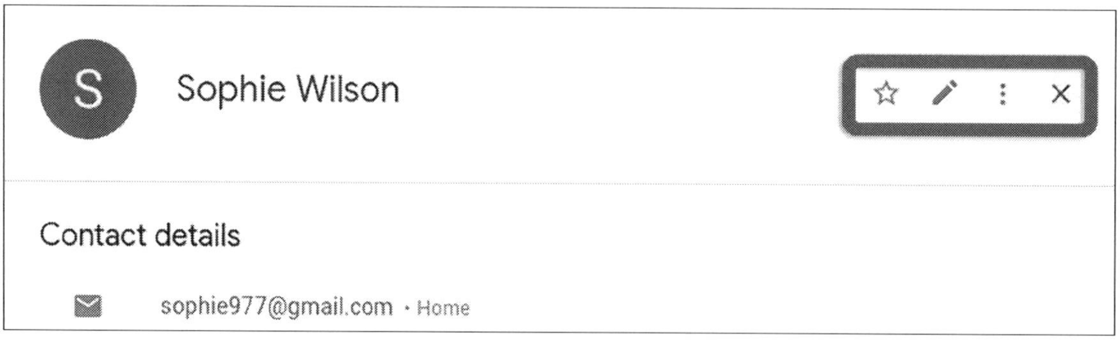

Along the top you'll see three small icons on the right hand side. Here you can add the person to your favourites - the star icon. This is similar to your 'speed dial' on your phone, where you can quickly send messages to people you correspond with the most.

Click the pencil icon to edit the person's details, eg if they've changed their number or email address.

Use the three dots icon to open the drop down options menu. Here you can delete the contact, export, hide, or print the details.

Edit Details

Click on the name of the person in the list whose details you want to change.

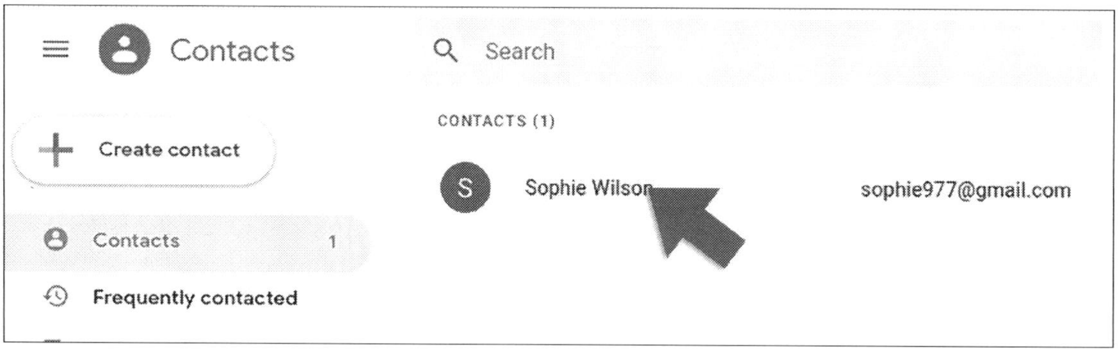

Click the pencil icon on the top right of the dialog box.

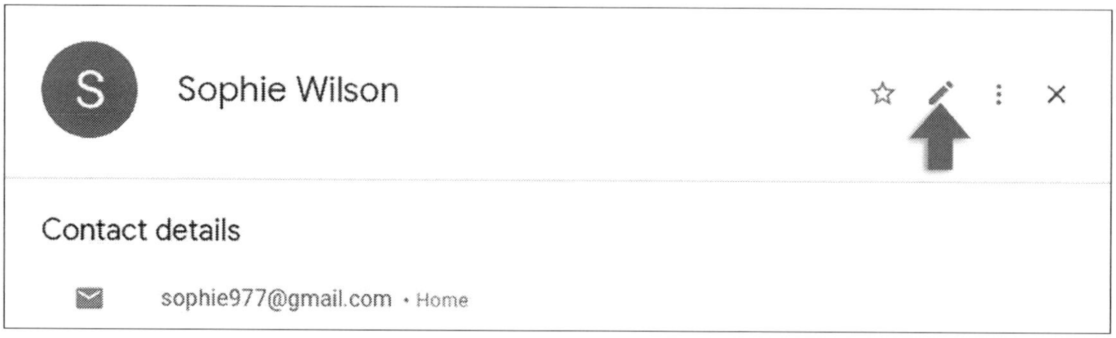

Click on the field you want to change. In this example I'm adding a mobile phone number.

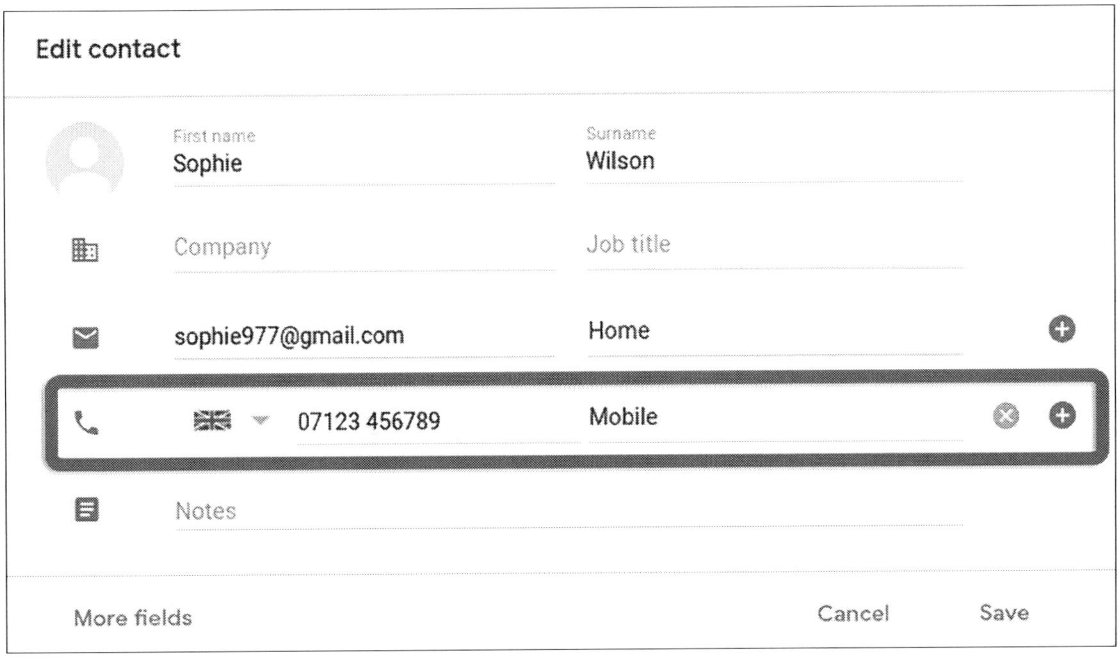

Make any other changes you need to, then click 'save'.

Add New Contact

You can add a new contact from scratch using the contacts app. To do this, click 'create contact' on the top left of your screen.

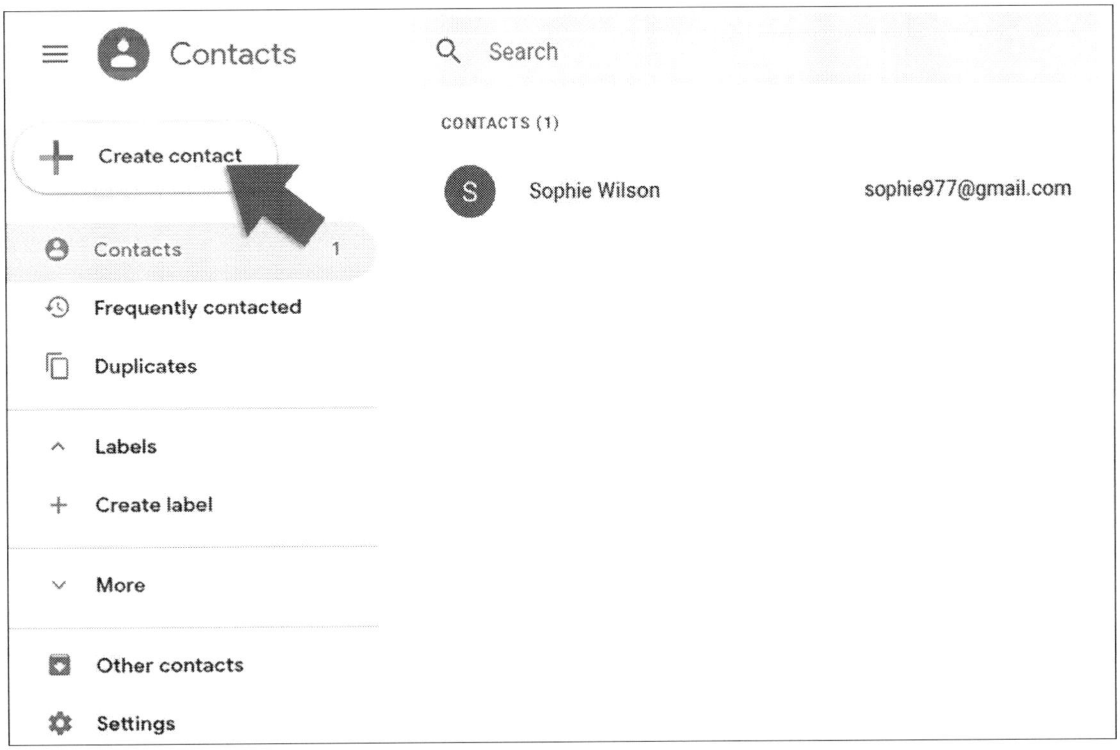

Enter the details into the appropriate fields, as shown below.

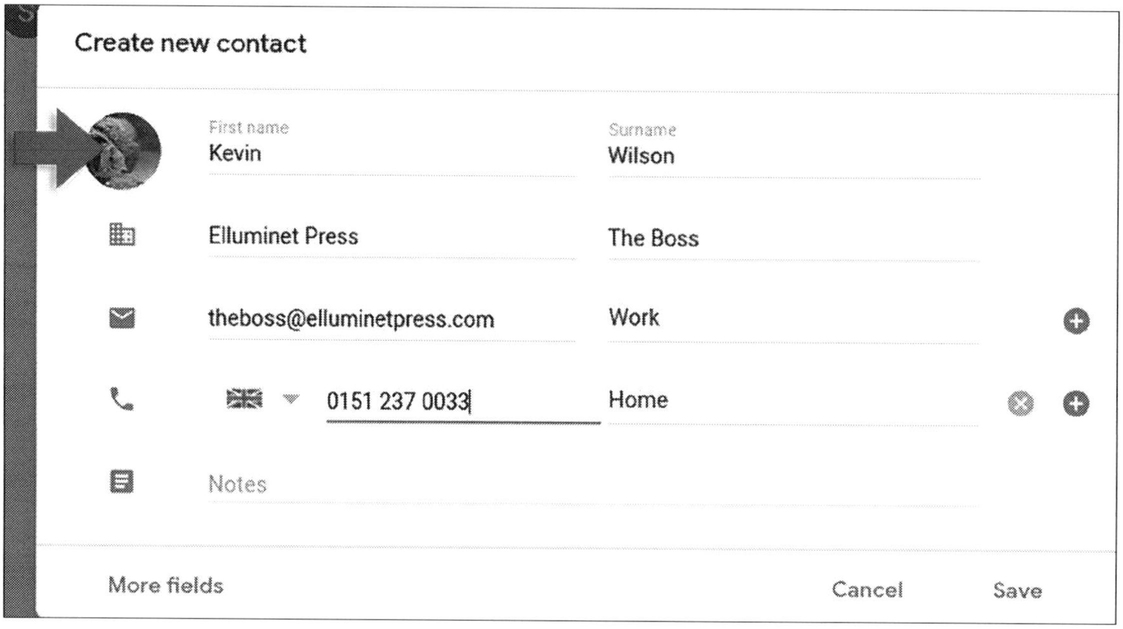

Click on the image on the top left to add a profile picture.

Click 'save' when you're done.

Add Contact from Message

You can add a new contact from the Hangouts App or the Gmail App

Open the email.

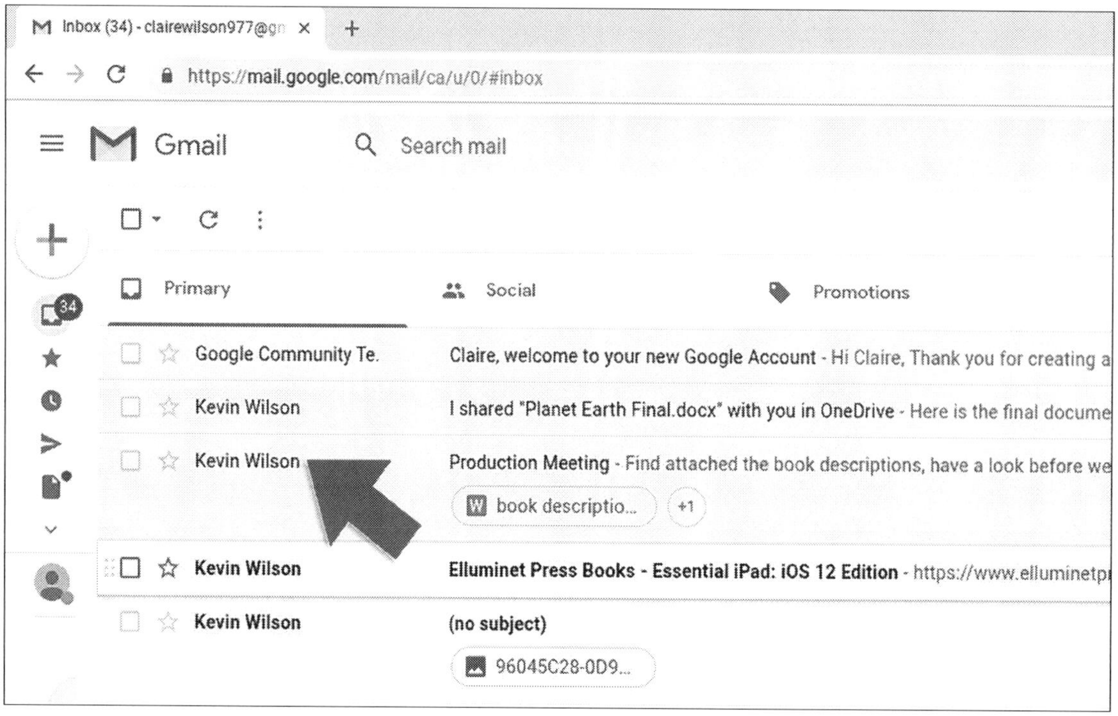

Click on the three dots icon on the top right of your email message, then select 'add ... to contacts list'.

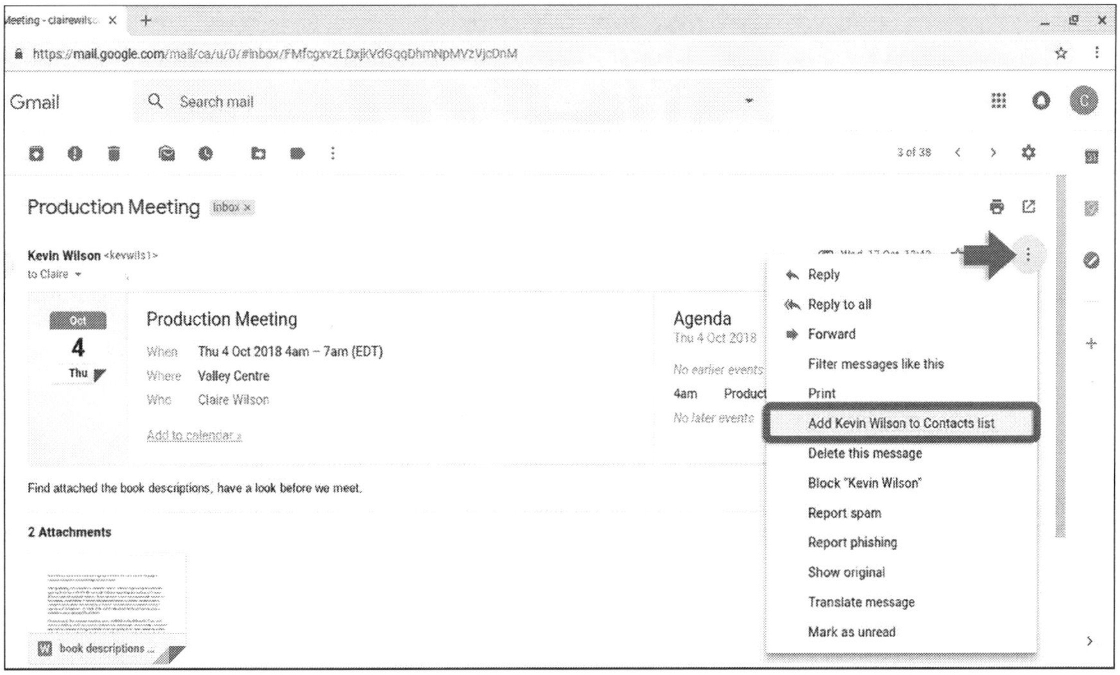

The email address and the person's name will be added to your contacts. Click on the contact's name in your contacts app to edit any details.

Calendar Web App

The calendar app allows you to keep track of events and appointments. You can add reminders, create appointments and events, so you never miss anything.

Click the apps icon on the top right of your screen, then select 'calendar'.

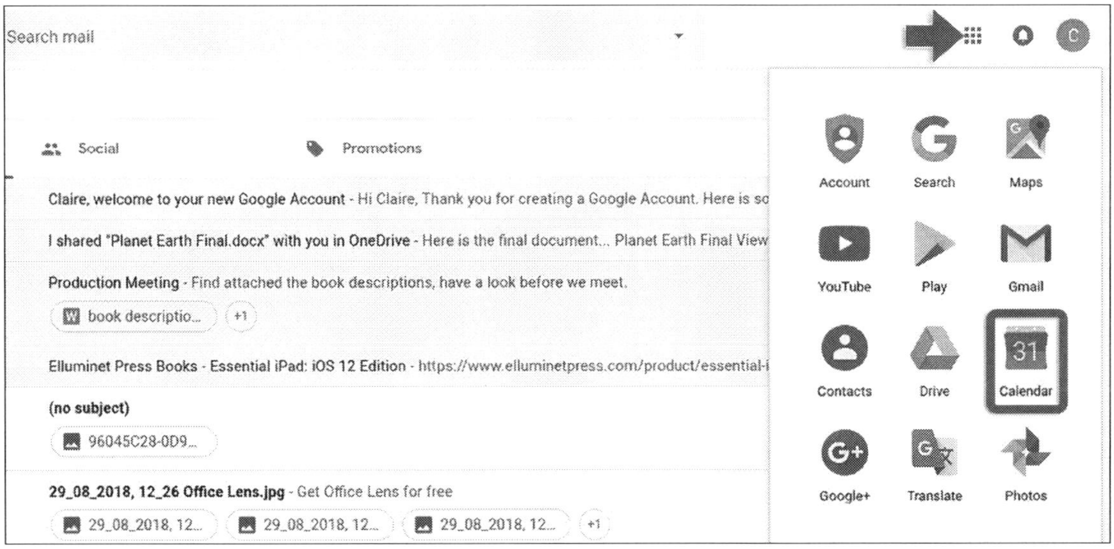

Calendar View

You can change the calendar view to show appointments and events by month, week or day - as shown below.

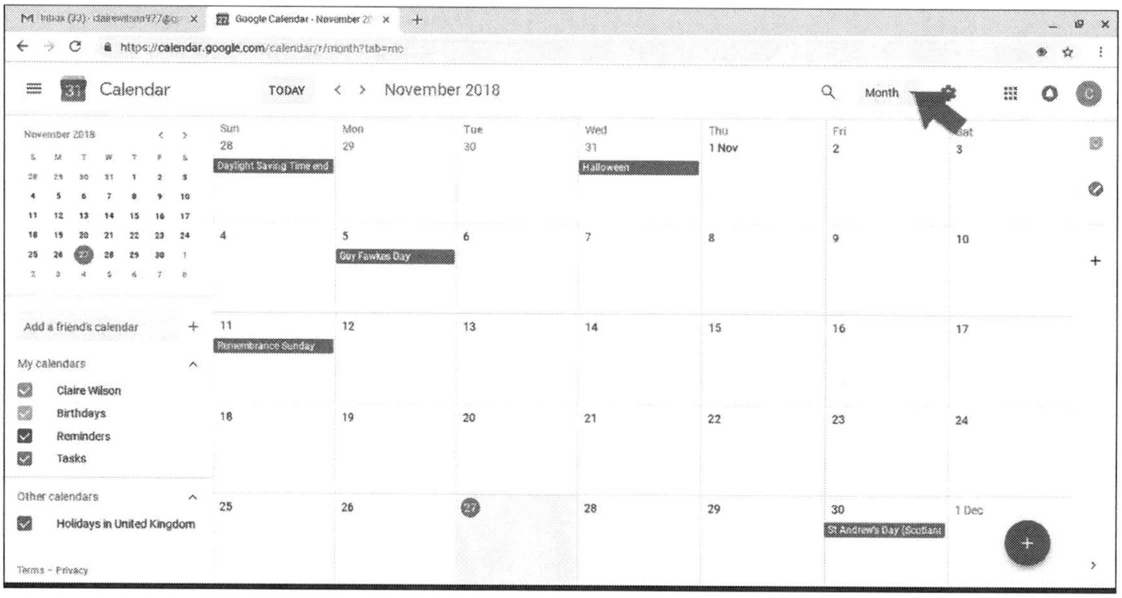

To do this, click the icon on the top right of the screen.

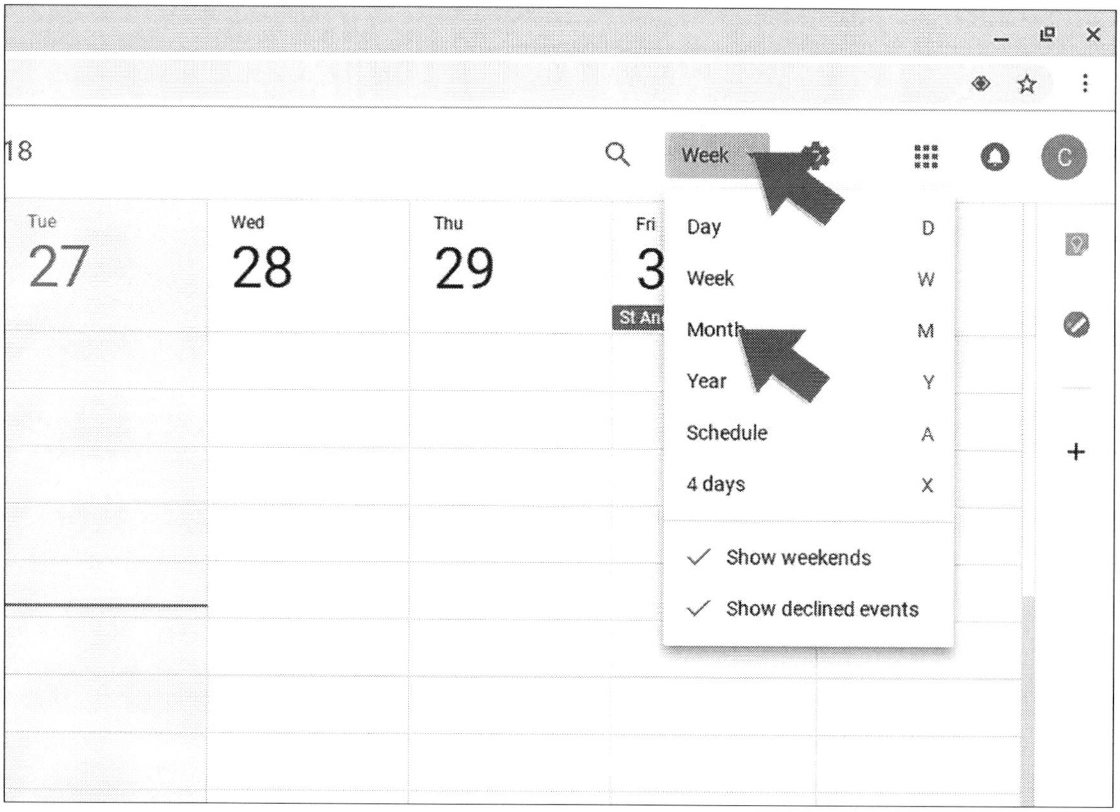

From the drop down menu, select 'day', 'week' or 'month', depending on how you want to view your events/appointments.

Add Event

To add a new event, reminder or appointment, in month view, click on the day the appointment falls on.

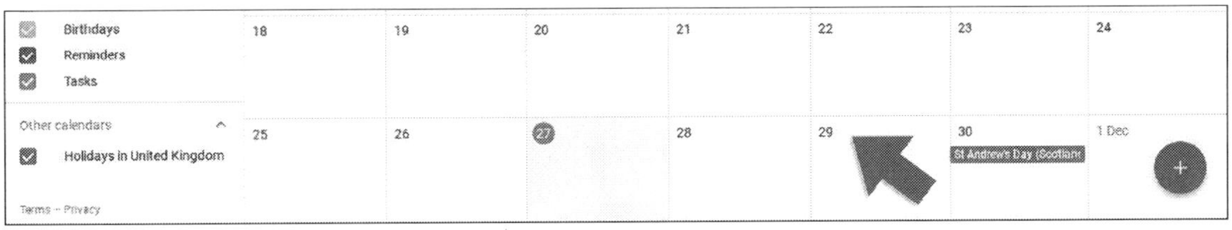

In the popup box, start typing in the name of the event or appointment in the field at the top. Eg “production meeting”, “coffee with claire”, and so on. Select ‘event’, then click ‘more options’.

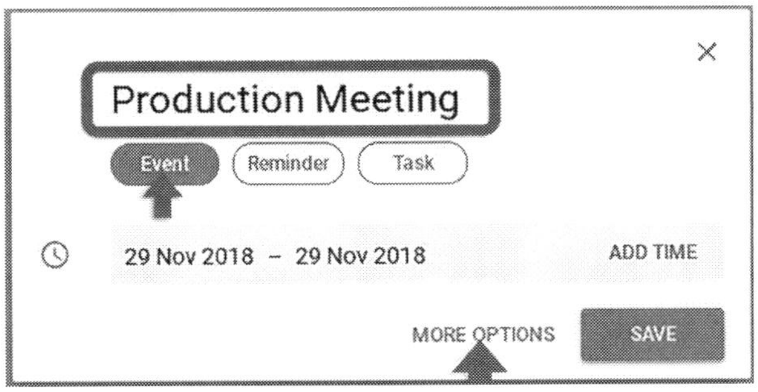

Remove the tick from ‘all day’ and enter the start and finish times of the event.

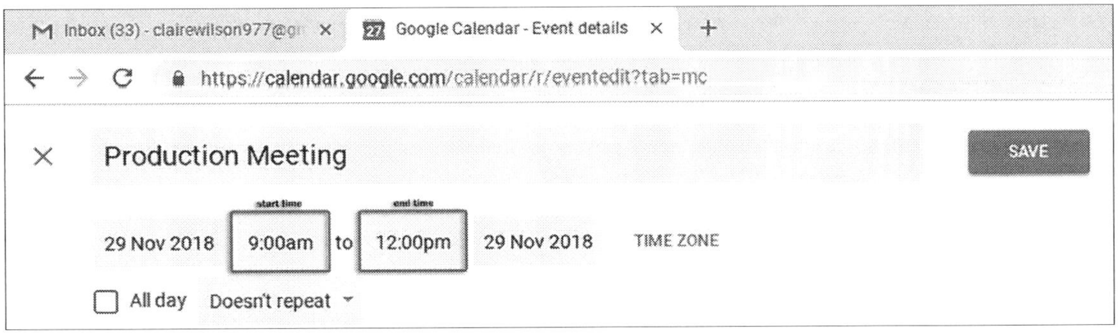

If this event repeats, for example, a weekly meeting, click where it says ‘doesn’t repeat’ and from the drop down, select how often the event repeats. This event occurs every week, so I’m going to select ‘weekly’.

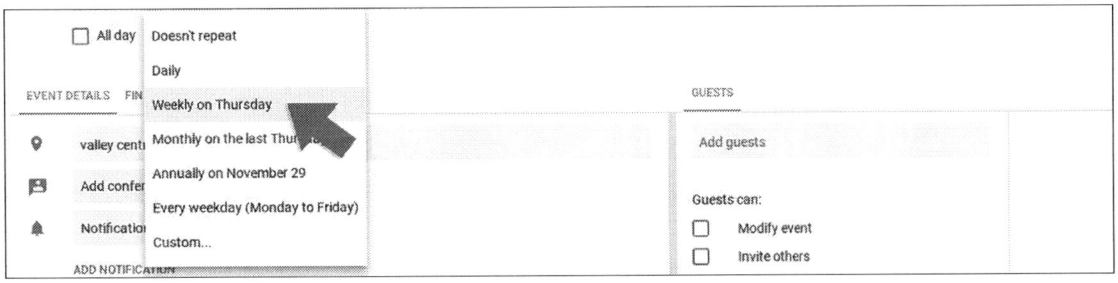

Now select where the event/appointment will be held. Type in the location.

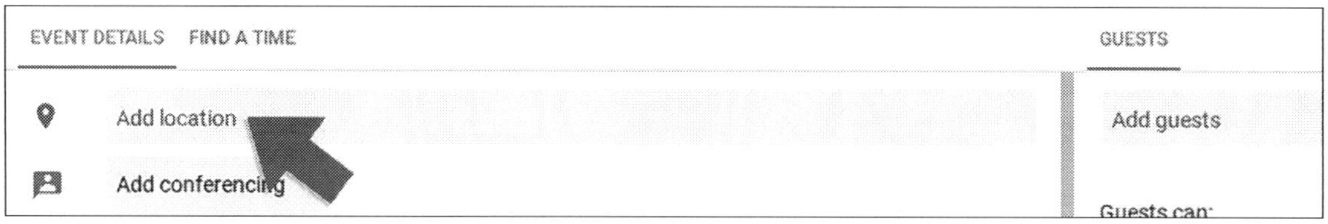

Google will search for places you've been, go to frequently, or places nearby. Click on one of these. So if we were meeting at the Valley Centre, I'd click on 'valley centre' in the list.

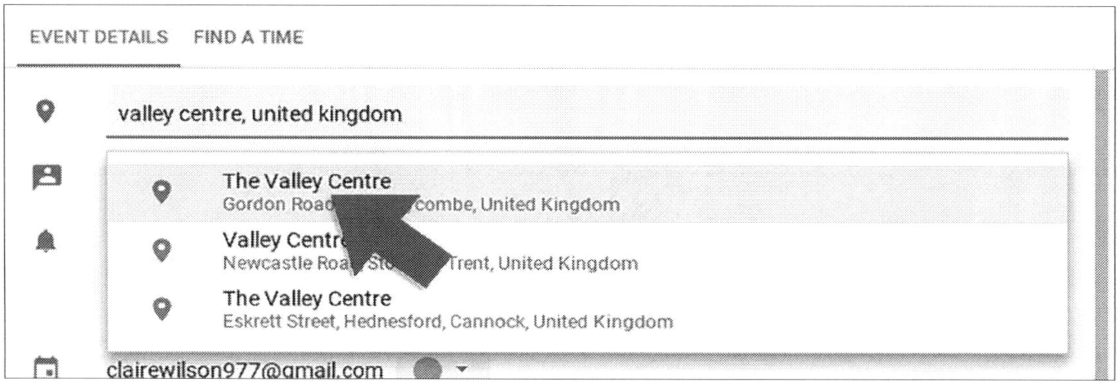

You'll see a summary of the appointment. Here you can amend any details, set a reminder - where it says 'notification', change the times - select how far in advance you want to be reminded. In this example, I've set it to remind me a day before. You can also set it to 30 mins before, an hour before, and so on.

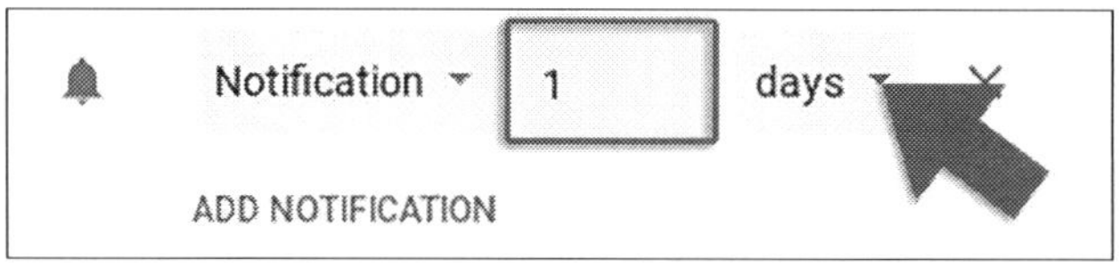

Now we need to say who we are meeting. Click where it says 'add guests' on the right hand side.

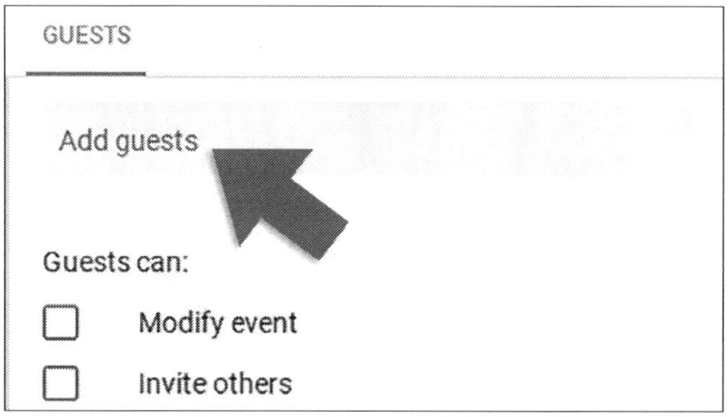

Start typing in the names of the people you want to send an invite to.

You'll see a list of your contacts - select their name.

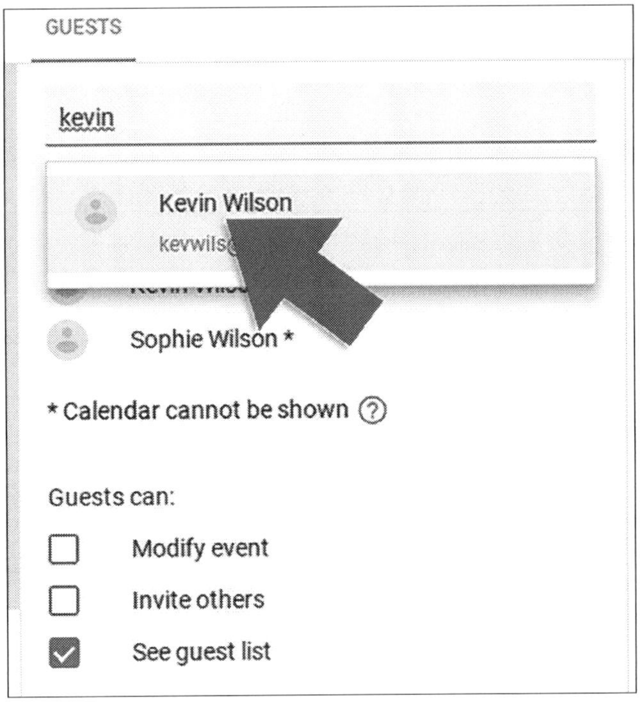

Underneath where it says 'guests can', remove the ticks from the permissions to prevent your guests from making changes to the event invitation. You can allow them to 'see the guest list' so they can see who is attending.

At the bottom left, where it says 'add description'. Add a message, and any attachments, or documents needed for the event. These could be minutes, meeting notes, programmes, and so on. To add an attachment, click the paper-clip icon, then select a file to attach.

Click the blue 'save' button on the top right when you're done.

Click 'send' to send the invitations to your attendees if you added any guests.

Click 'invite' to allow your attendees to access any files you attached.

Google Meet

Google Meet is a video-communication service where you can host meetings, share your desktop, and presentations with friends, colleagues, large groups, and customers.

The free version of Google Meet allows 1 to 1 meetings up to 24 hours, and group meetings with three or more participants for up to 1 hour at a time. You can purchase Google Workspace Individual or Google Workspace Enterprise depending on your needs. Go to the following website for more up to date information.

`apps.google.com/meet/pricing`

Starting Google Meet

You can open the Google Meet app on your app launcher. *If you don't see it, go to the Google Play store and download it.*

Or open Google Chrome Web Browser then navigate to the following website:

`meet.Google.com`

Once the app loads up, you'll land on the home screen. From here, you can start a new meeting - click 'new meeting' or you can join a meeting using a code or link someone has sent you - just paste it into the 'enter a code or link' box.

From the settings icon on the top right, you can setup your camera, speakers, and microphone.

Create Meeting for Later

Create a meeting for later sets up a meeting and generates a link you can send to other people. No meeting is actually scheduled.

To create a meeting for later, click 'new meeting', then select 'create meeting for later' from the drop down menu.

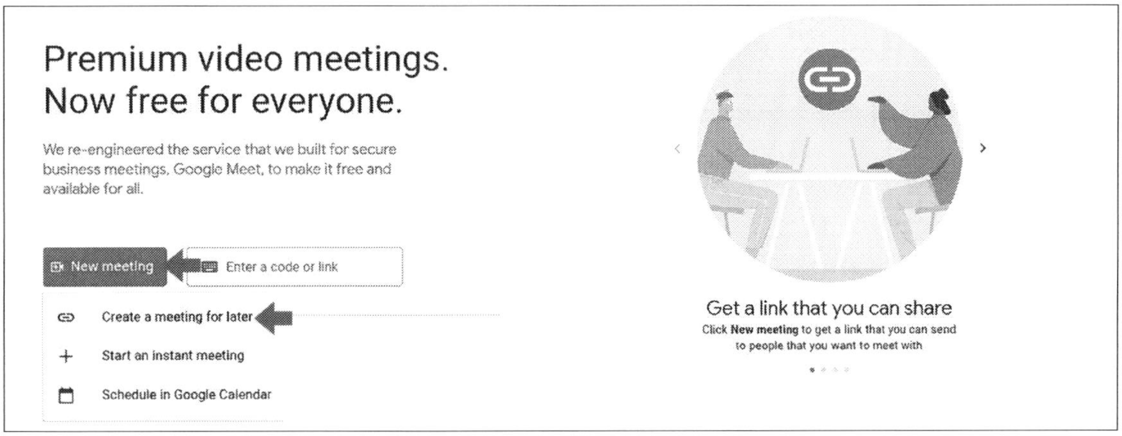

A popup box with a link will appear. Click the clipboard icon on the right to copy the link.

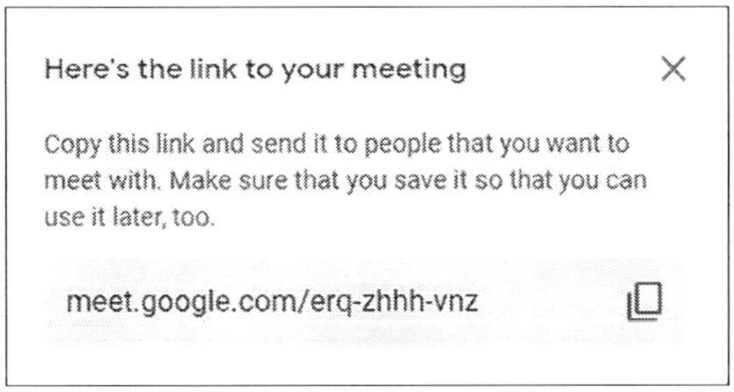

Now you can paste the link into an email or text message.

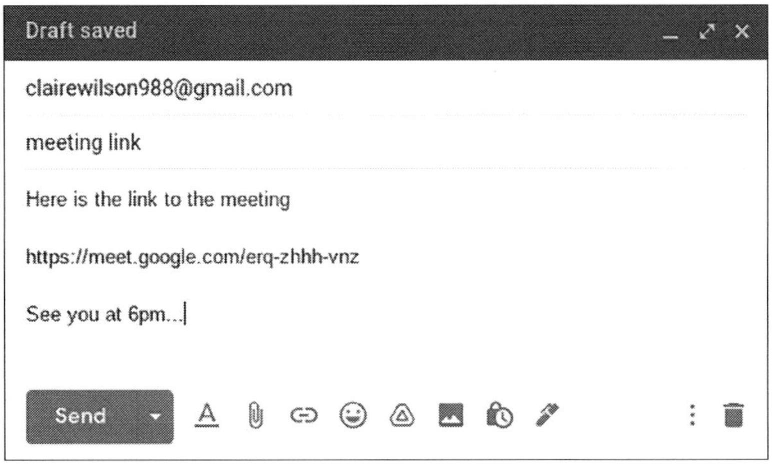

Make sure you keep a copy of that link so you can join the meeting too. A good way to do this is send yourself a copy of the email.

Start Instant Meeting

Start an instant meeting sets up a meeting room for you and opens it up. It then generates a link you can use to invite other people.

To start an instant meeting, click 'new meeting', then select 'start an instant meeting' from the drop down menu.

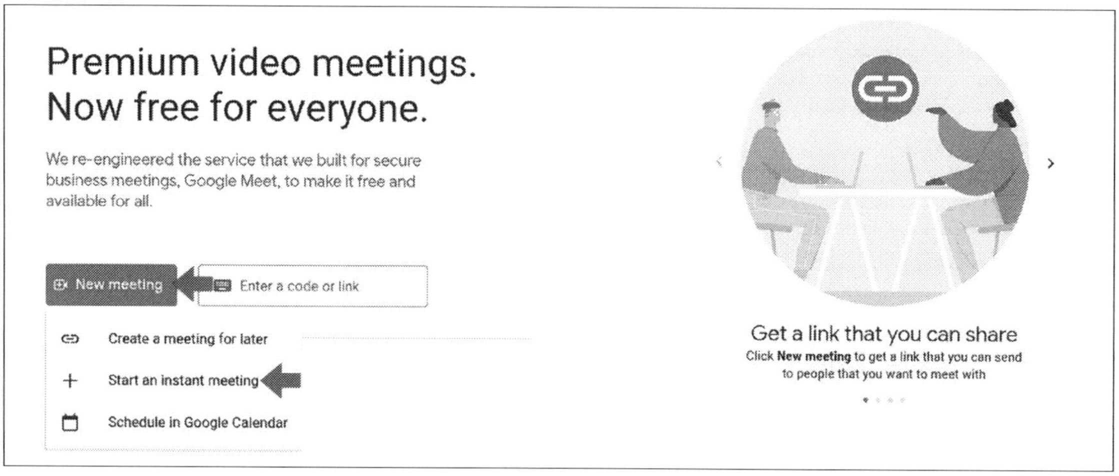

Your meeting will open up in the in call chat window. Allow access to your cam and mic if prompted. On the top right of the screen, you'll see and invite box.

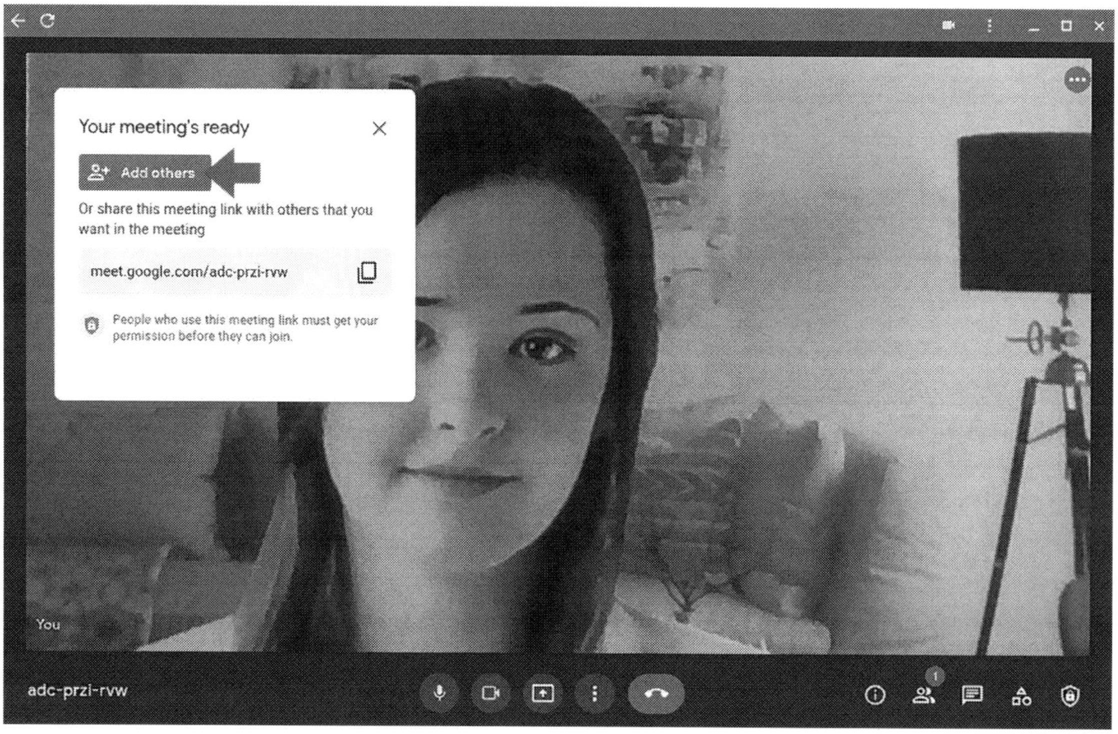

Click 'add others' to invite someone to the meeting you just created. You can also copy the link at the bottom of the invite box and send it to the person you want to invite.

Add the email addresses in the field at the top. If you want to type more than one email address, separate them with a comma. Then click 'send' when you're done.

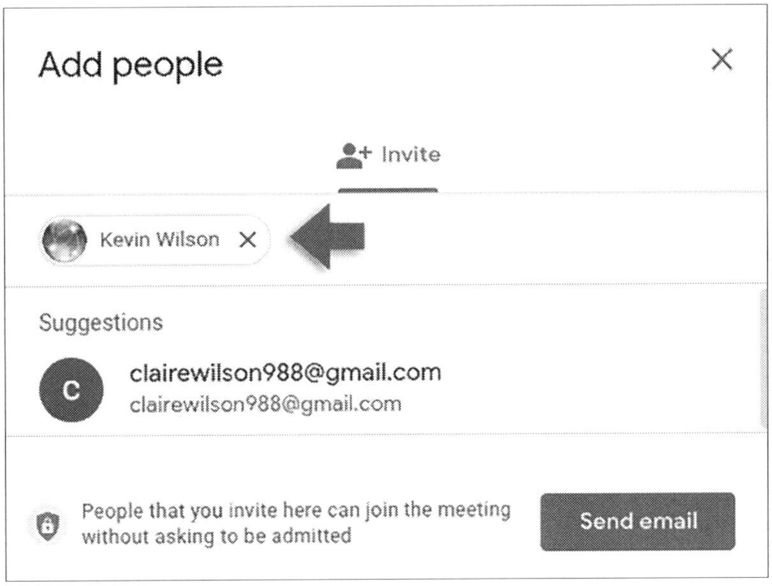

The other person will receive an email with a link.

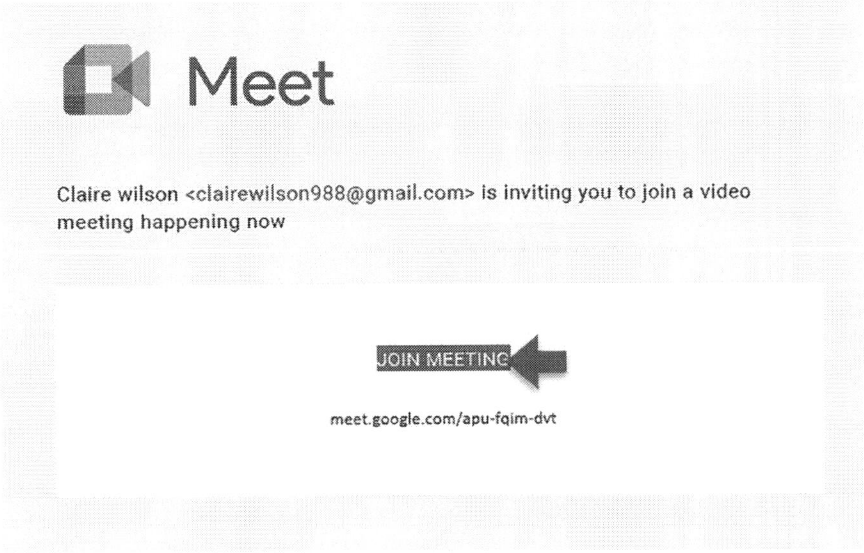

Once they click the link, you'll get a notification allowing you to admit the person to your meeting.

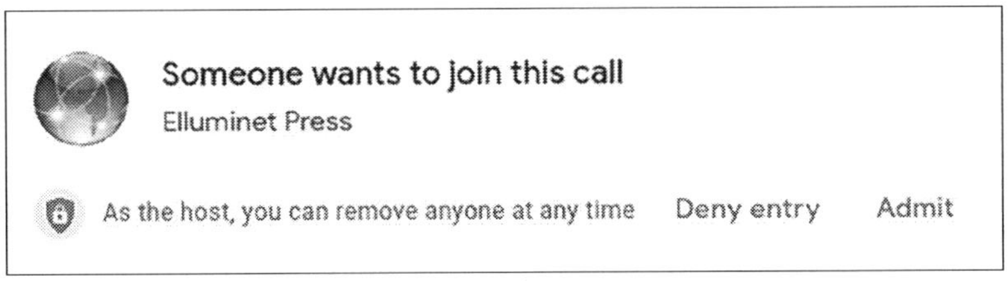

Click 'admit' to let them in.

Schedule Meeting in Calendar

Schedule a meeting allows you to open up your calendar app and schedule a meeting at a later date. Google Meet also generates an email with a link you can use to invite people to the meeting.

To schedule a meeting, click 'new meeting', then select 'schedule in Google calendar' from the drop down menu.

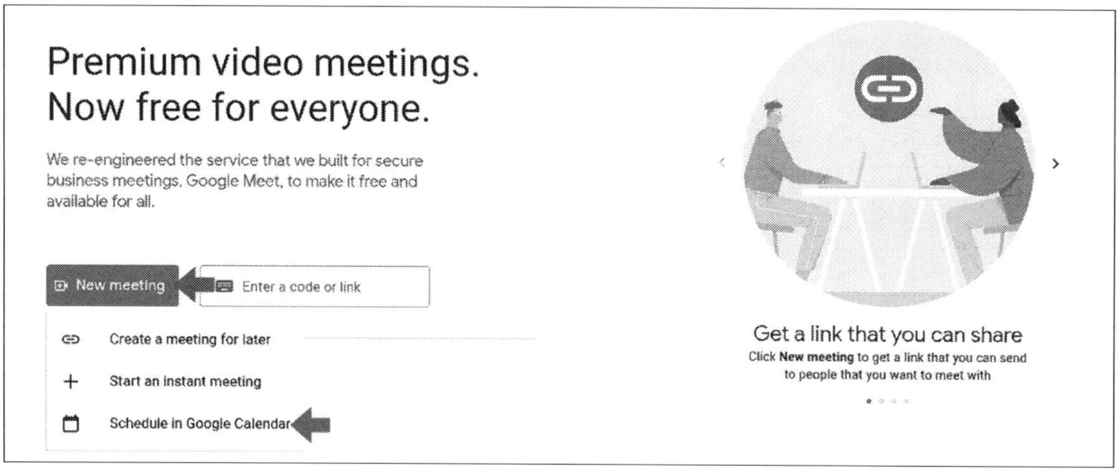

When your calendar opens, fill in the details to create an event. Add the meeting name at the top.

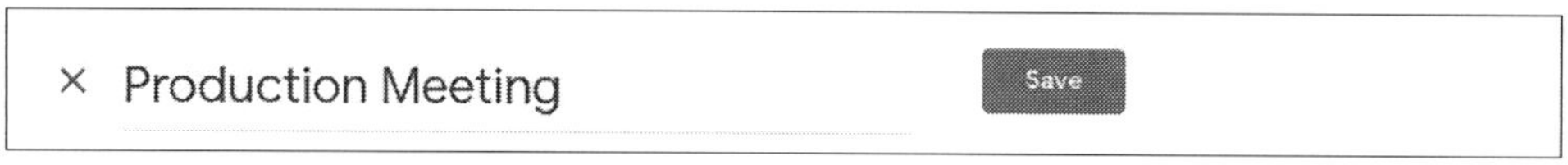

Underneath, add the date of the meeting, with the start and end times.

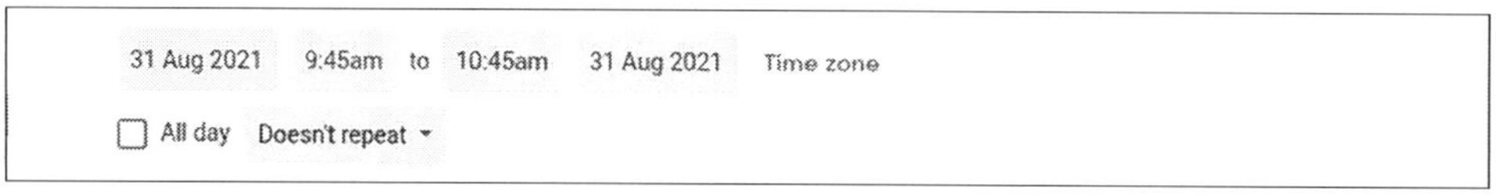

Under 'event details' add a location if required. This could be a street address, or venue if the meeting is held elsewhere.

Click 'add notification' to add a reminder notification, if you want to be reminded of the event. Select how long before the event you want the notification to appear.

Select which calendar to add it to if you have more than one, then select a highlight colour. This is the colour the event is marked as on your calendar. Next, select if you want your calendar to show you as busy or free during the event, and the visibility (public or private). Add a message to include in the invite to your participants.

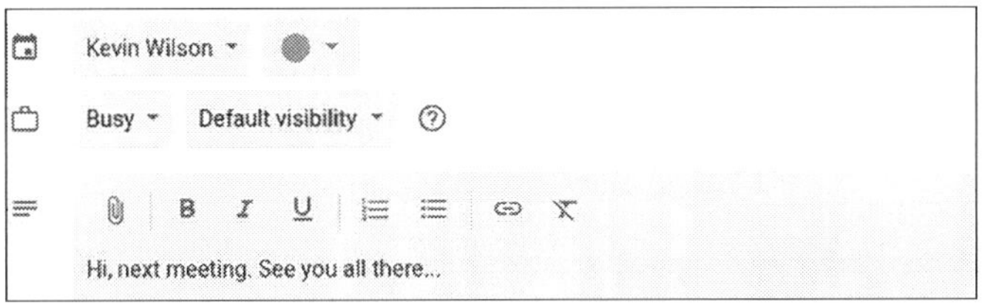

To invite participants to the meeting, click 'add guests' on the right hand side of the screen.

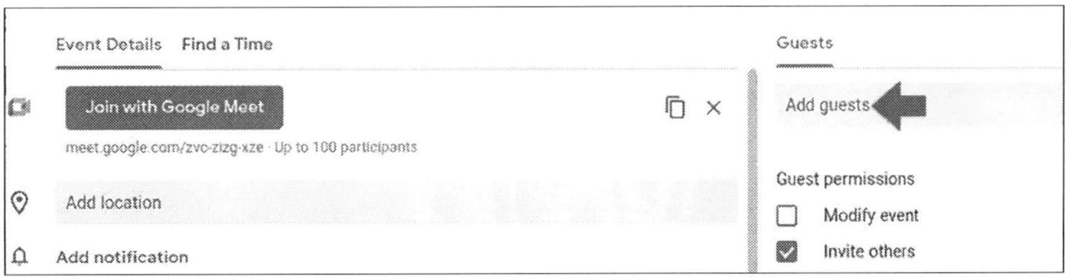

Enter the names or email addresses of the people that you want to invite - these are your participants. Click 'save' when you're done.

Click 'save' on the top right of the screen.

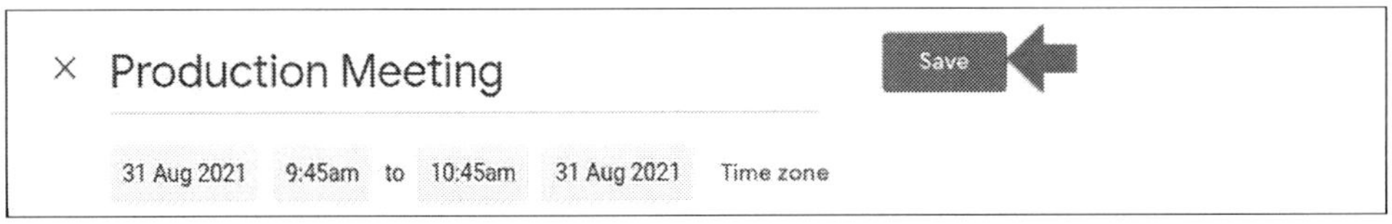

Then click 'send' to email the notification to your participants.

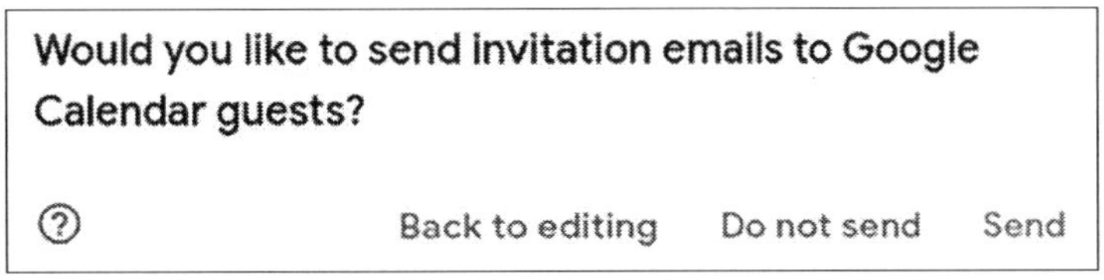

Joining a Meeting

If someone has sent you a meeting link in an email, click the link to join the meeting.

If someone has sent you a code such as `erq-zhhh-vns`, open Google Meet, then type or paste the code into the 'enter a code or link' box, click 'join'.

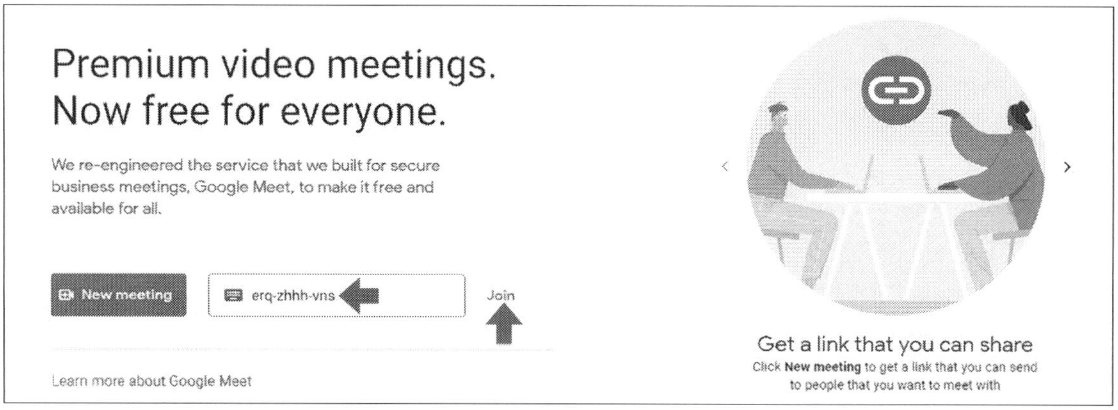

Click 'ask to join' if prompted. Once the host lets you in, the meeting will open up in the in call chat window. Allow access to your cam and mic if prompted.

In Call Options

When you're in a call, you'll see the other participants tiled along the top of your screen. At the bottom, you'll see your own camera. In the screenshot below, you can see our friend Nadia chatting to Sophie and Claire. Let's take a look around the window.

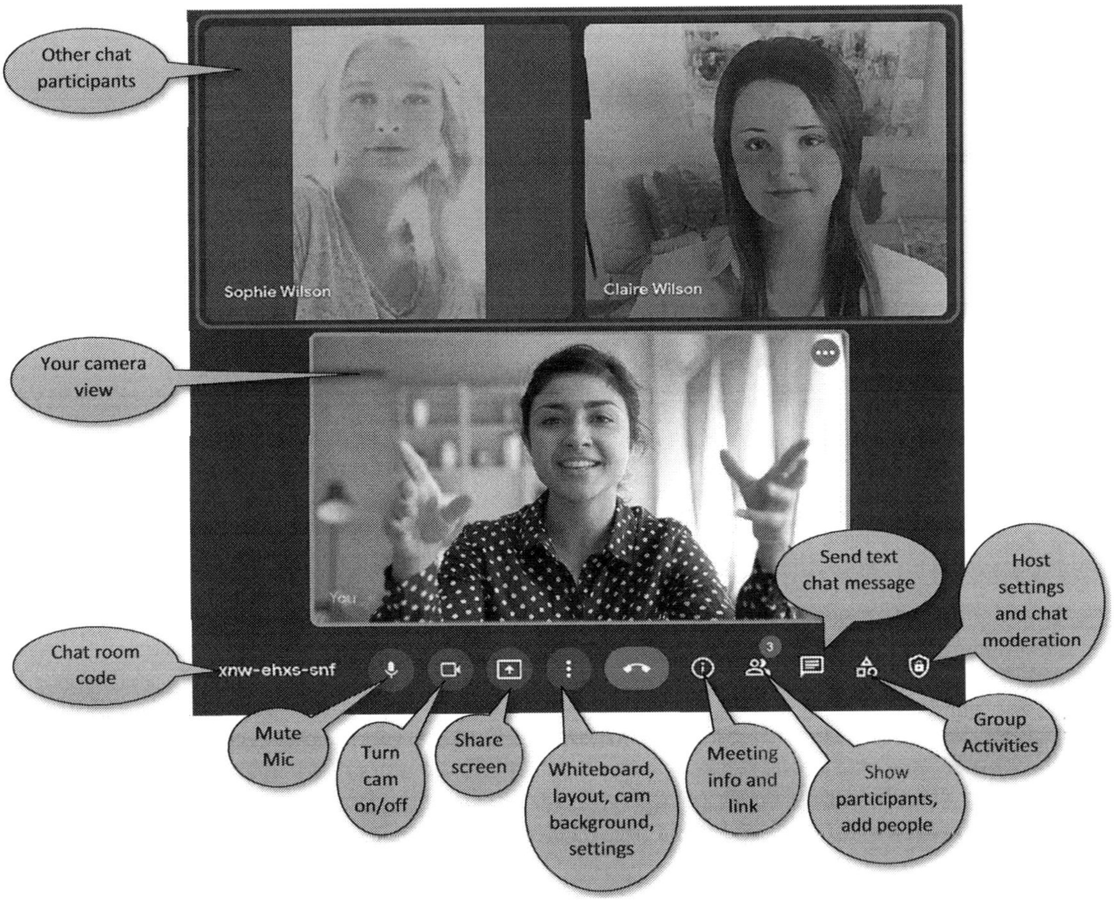

Along the bottom of the window, you'll see some tools and options. Here, you can mute your mic and turn off your camera.

The third icon from the left allows you to share your screen, a window, or a browser tab. With the next icon, the three dots, you can open whiteboard, change your cam background or the screen layout.

The large red icon in the middle hangs up your call - click this when you're finished your meeting.

The next icon shows you meeting info, here you'll find the meeting link you can use to invite others to your meeting. With the show participants icon, you can view a list of all the people participating in your meeting. You can also mute all, add people, search for people, and turn on/off host controls (allow people to share their screen or send messages).

Host settings allows you to allow/disallow any of your participants to share their own screens or send chat messages. You'll only see these options if you are hosting the meeting.

Present & Share Desktop

You can share your whole screen with your participants, or you can share an app (in a window), or a browser tab. This is useful if you want to show your participants something such as a presentation, a website, or a video.

To share your desktop, select the 'present' icon from the toolbar along the bottom of the 'in call' screen.

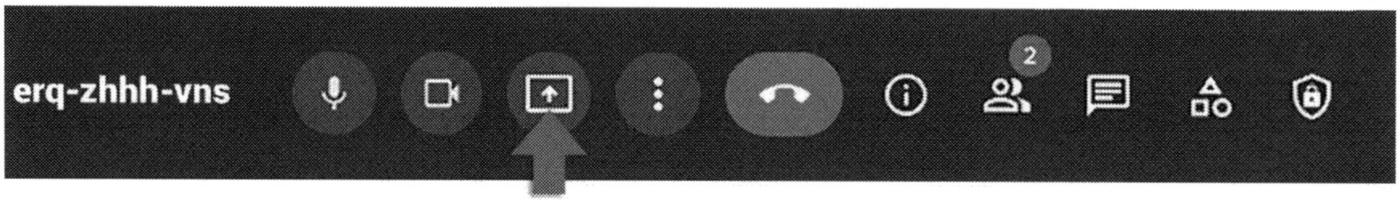

Select 'a window' from the popup menu. You can also share your entire screen, however your participants will see every app open and your desktop background, so make sure you haven't got anything open that you don't want people to see. You can also share a browser tab from Chrome.

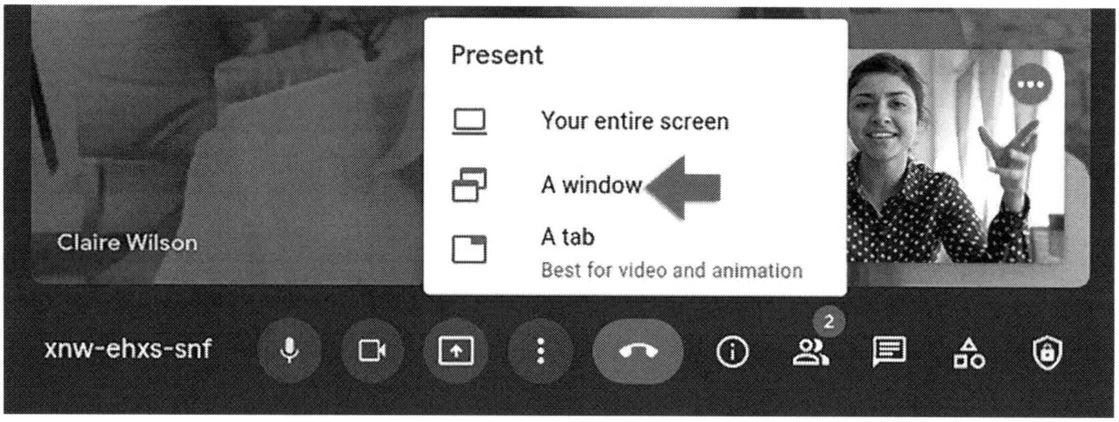

Open the app you want to present, if you haven't already done so. You can do this using the app launcher. Here, I've opened Google Chrome as I want to show a website.

Click on the Google Meet icon on the app shelf along the bottom to switch back to the app.

Select the app from the 'share application window', then click 'share'.

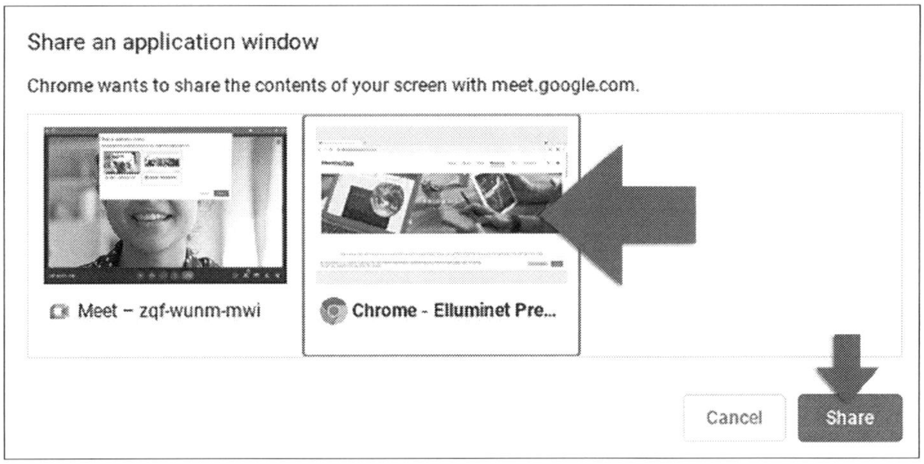

Now, the other participants in your meeting will be able to see the app your just shared. You can use it to show what you want to show.

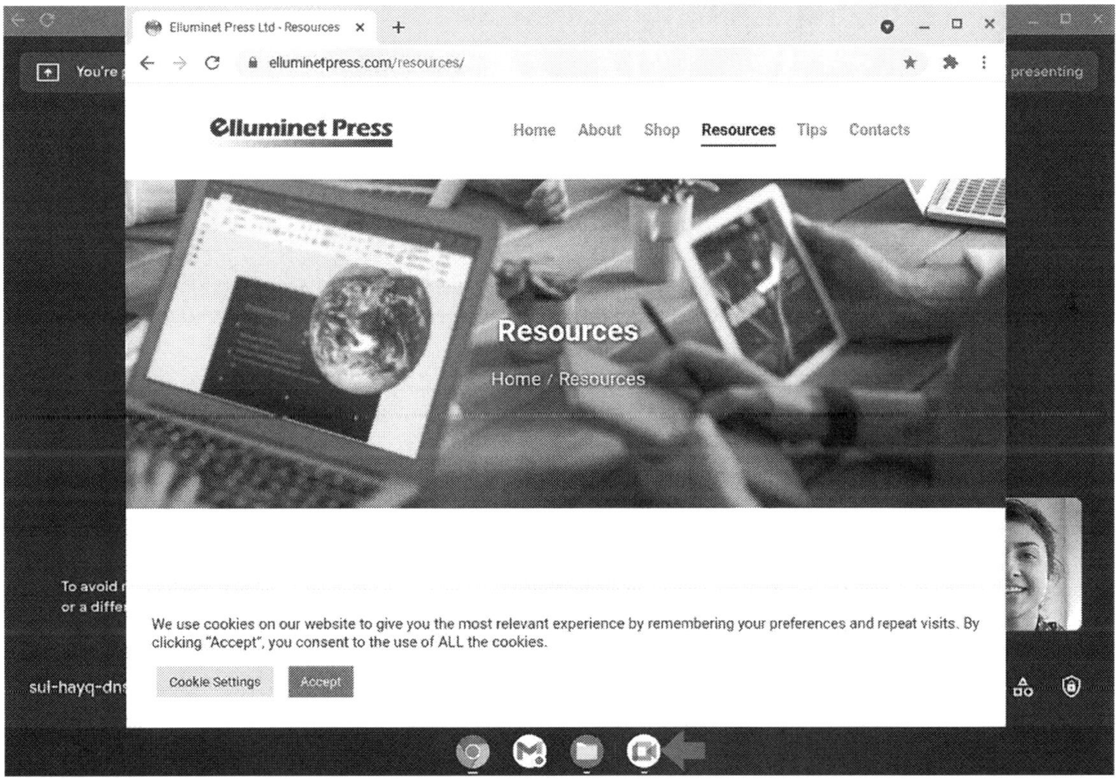

To stop sharing your screen, click on the Google Meet icon on the app shelf along the bottom. Select 'stop presenting' on the top right of Google Meet 'in call' window.

Whiteboard

You can open a whiteboard and share it with your participants. This is useful if you want to illustrate something. This feature works best if you are using Google Meet on a chromebook or tablet with a touchscreen where you can use a pen.

To open your whiteboard, click the three dots icon in the middle, then select 'whiteboard' from the popup menu.

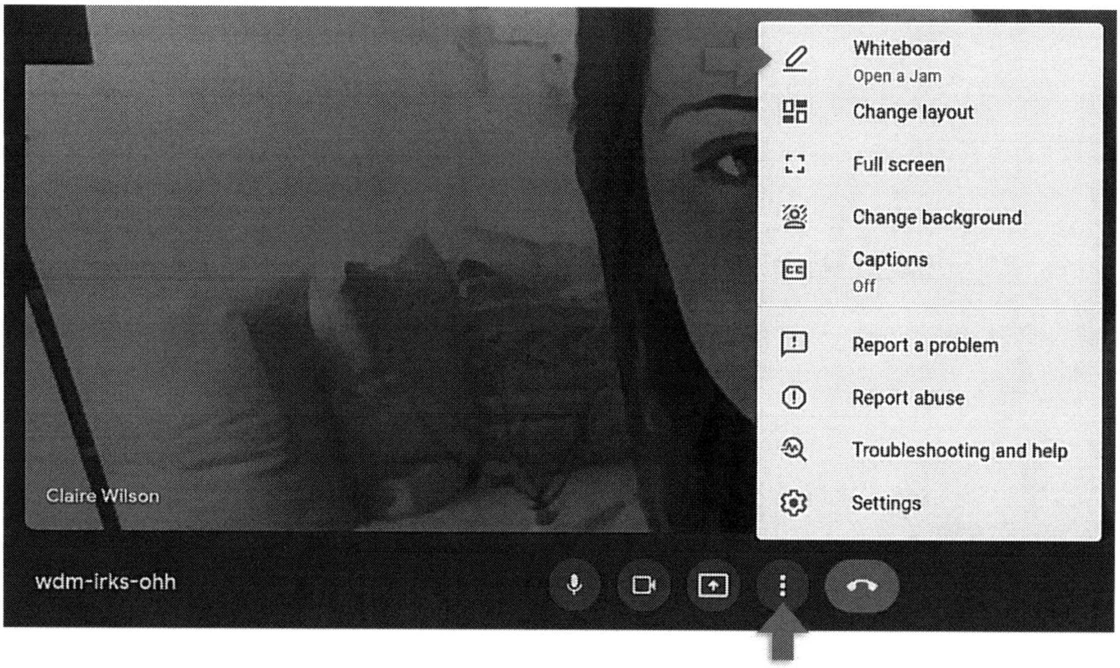

Click 'choose from drive' to load a saved whiteboard from Google Drive, or click 'start a new whiteboard' to create a blank board.

Click 'send' to send the access invitation to the person.

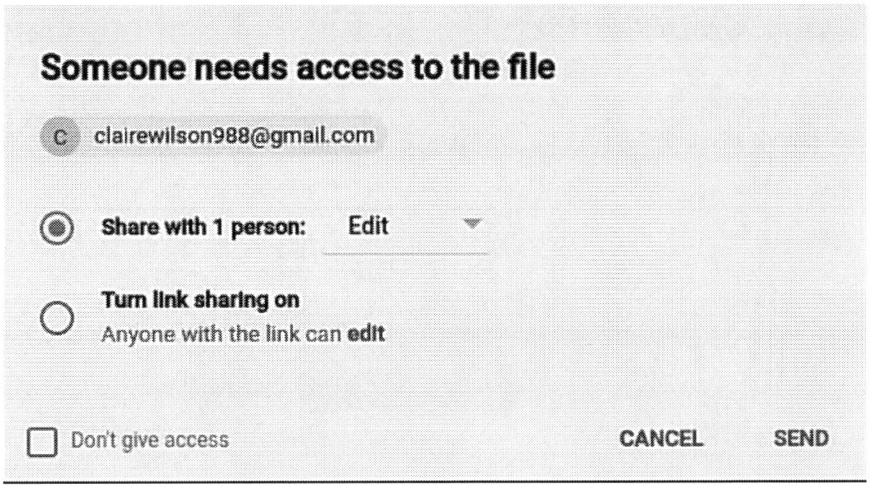

When your whiteboard opens, select a pen from the icons on the left, then choose a colour. If you have a touchscreen on your Chromebook, or you're running Google Meet on a tablet, use your pen to write on the whiteboard.

To present your whiteboard to your team, click the present icon on the toolbar at the top of the screen.

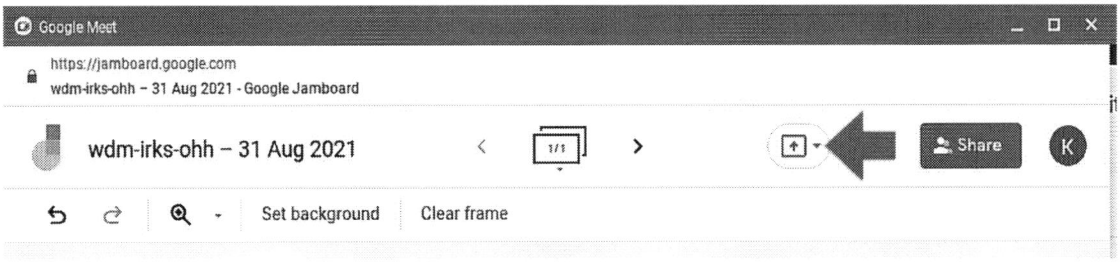

Select 'present tab to meeting' from the drop down menu.

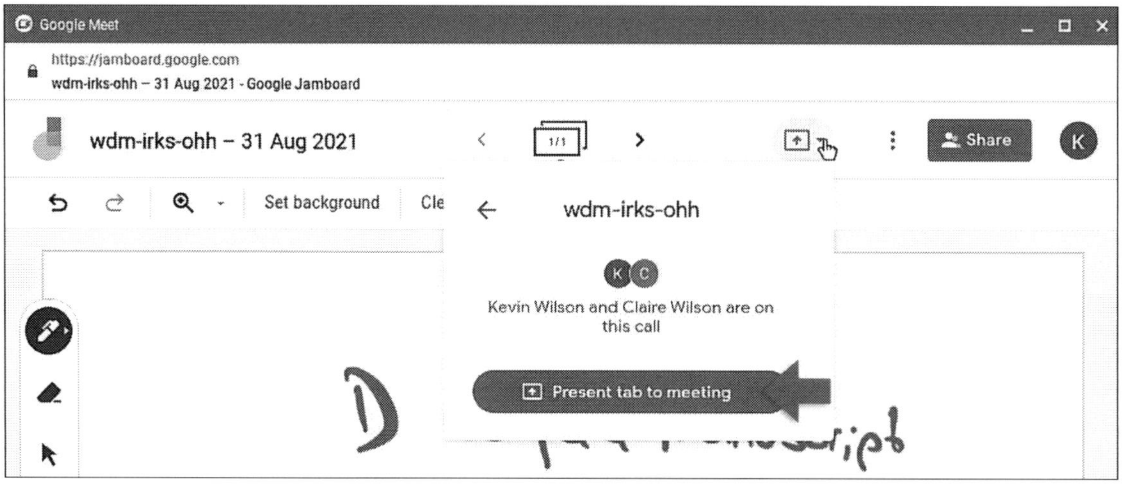

Select the whiteboard under 'this tab' from the share options. Click 'share'.

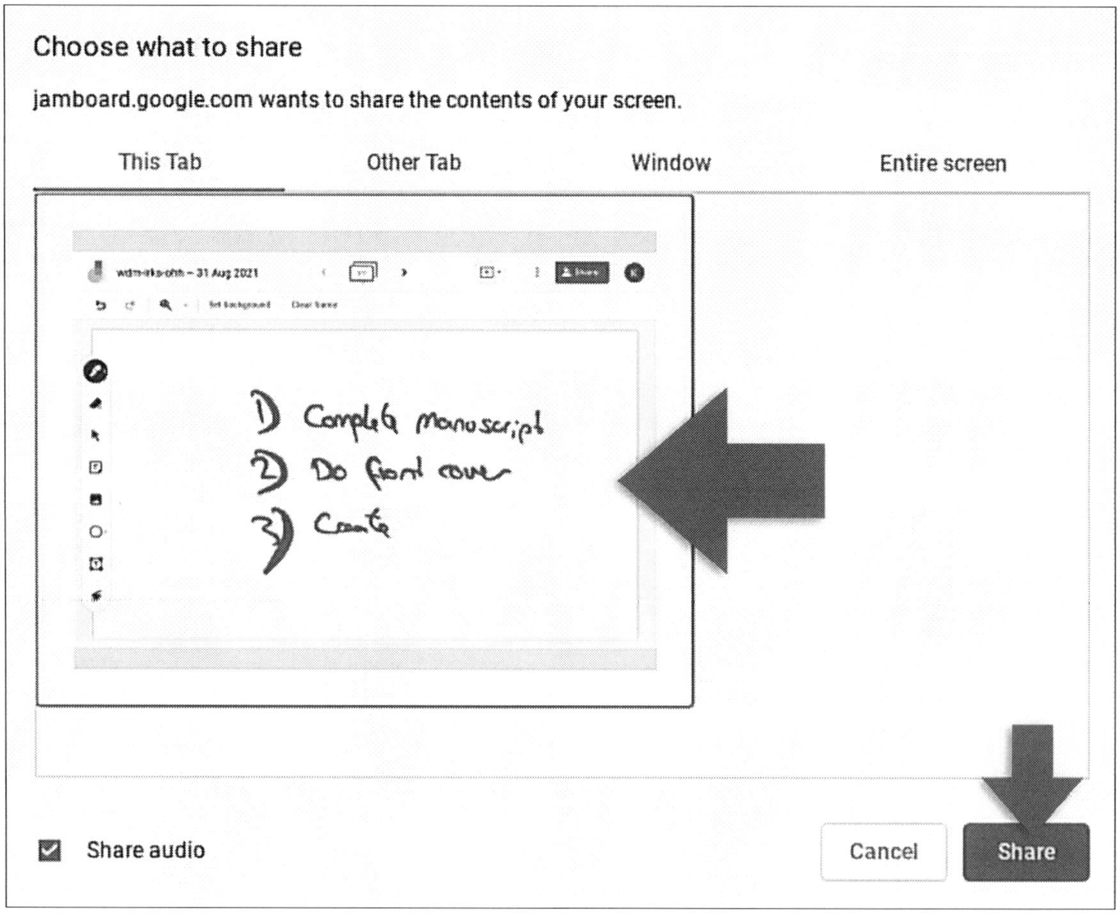

Now, your participants will be able to see the whiteboard. You can draw more ideas on your board as your meeting progresses.

To stop sharing, click 'stop' at the top of the whiteboard window.

Change Background

To change the background, click the three dots icon, then select 'change background' from the popup menu.

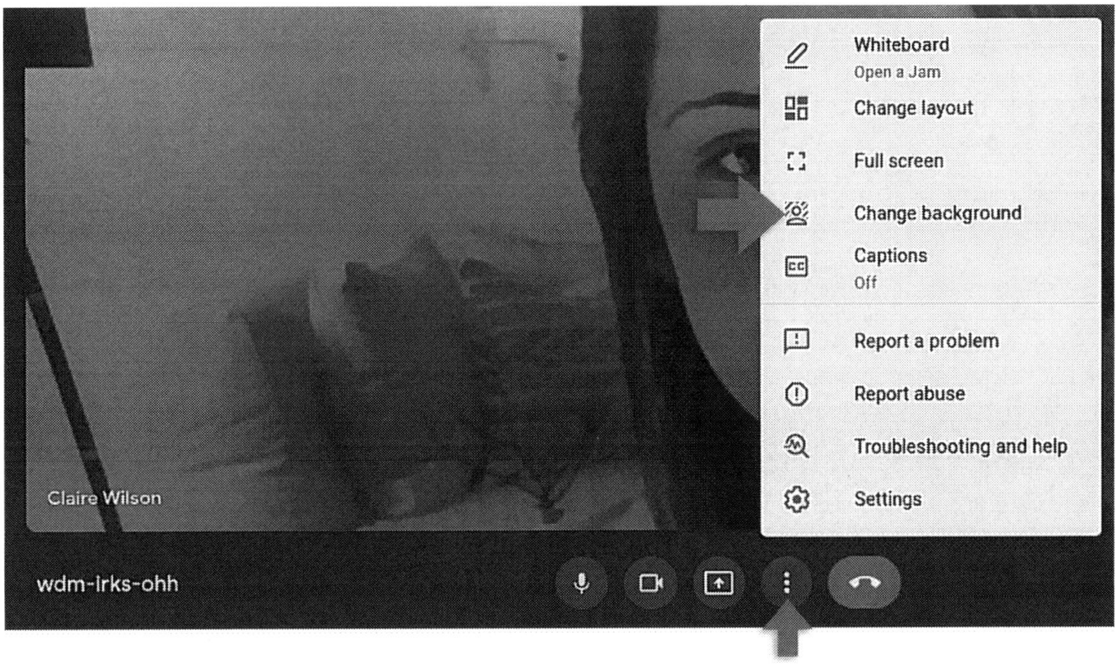

Choose a background from the pre-designs or click the + icon to add an image of your own as a background.

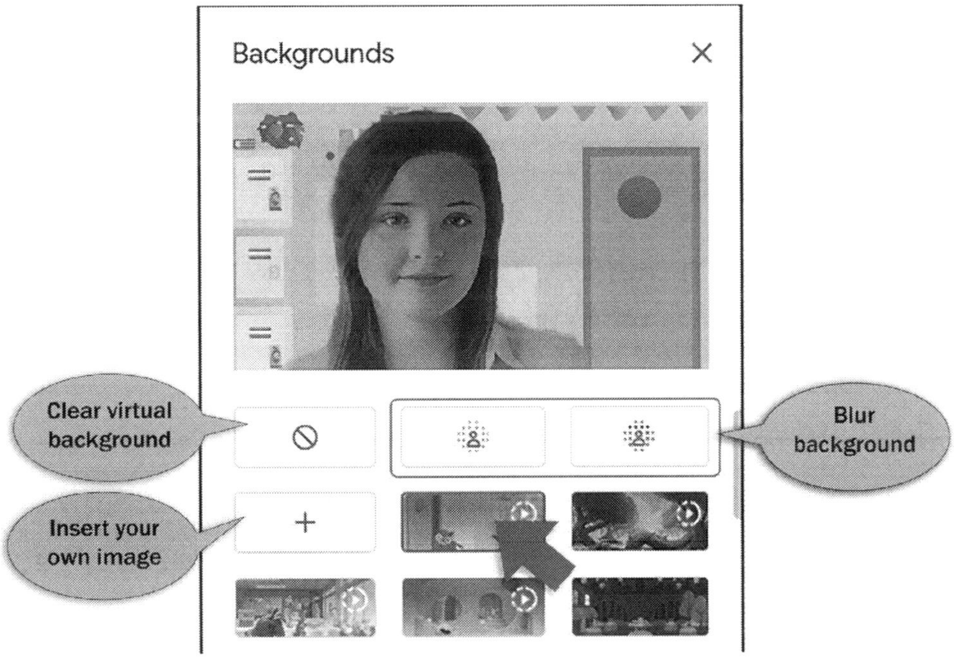

For best results, make sure you sit in-front of a plain background in a well lit room for the effect to work

Captions

Captions are useful if you happen to be hard of hearing have no sound. To turn them on, click the three dots icon in the middle, select 'captions' from the popup menu.

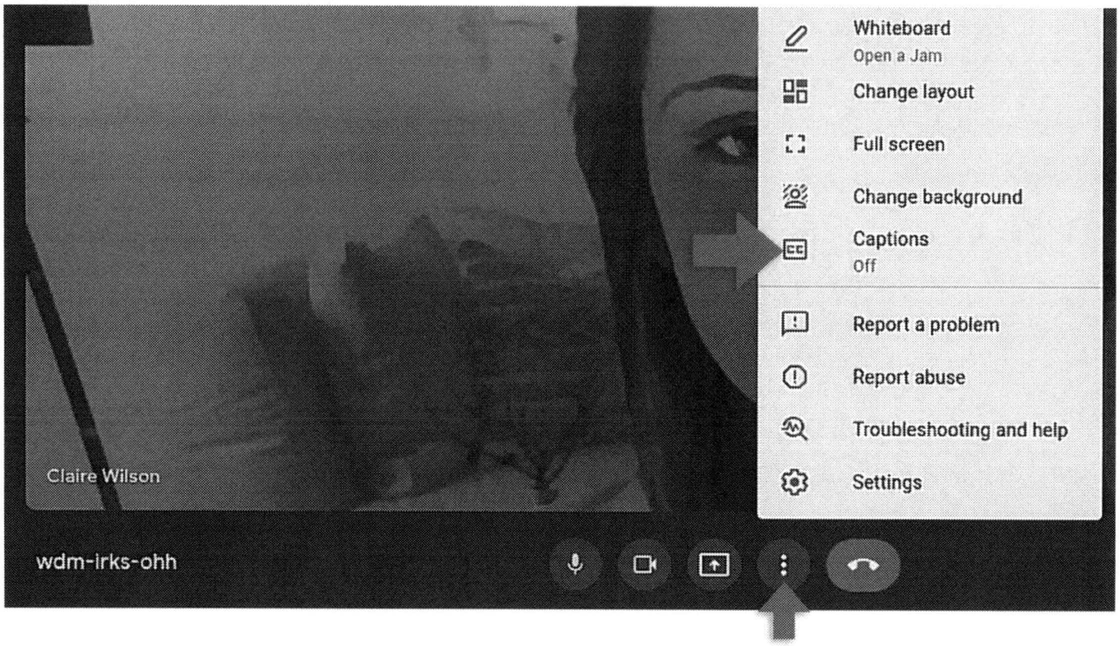

Choose your language from the list.

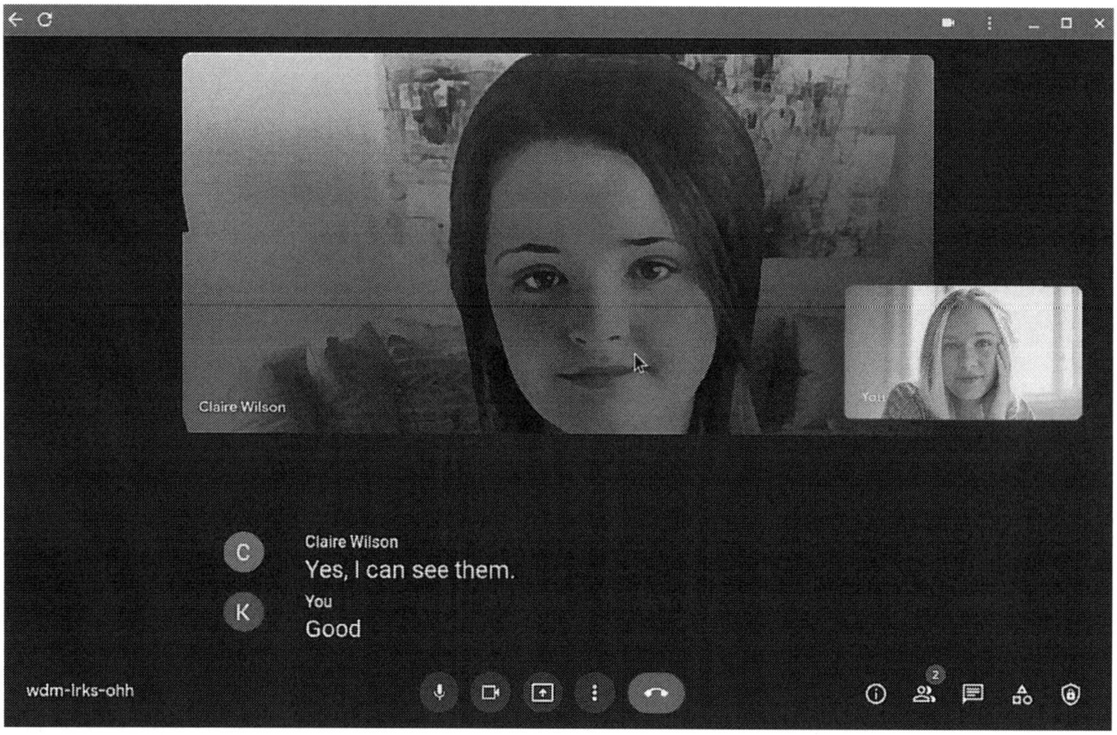

You'll see auto generated captions appear at the bottom of your window.

Google Chat

Google Chat makes it easy to collaborate with your team, colleagues, friends or family. You can create chat rooms, send messages, share files in Google Docs, Sheets, and Slides. Google Chat does not have video/audio calling or screen sharing options, however you can link with Google Meet for this.

Starting Google Chat

You can open the Google Chat app on your app launcher. *If you don't see it, go to the Google Play store and download it.*

Or open Google Chrome Web Browser then navigate to the following website:

`chat.google.com`

Once the app loads up, you'll land on the home screen. From here, you can start a group conversation or create a chat room.

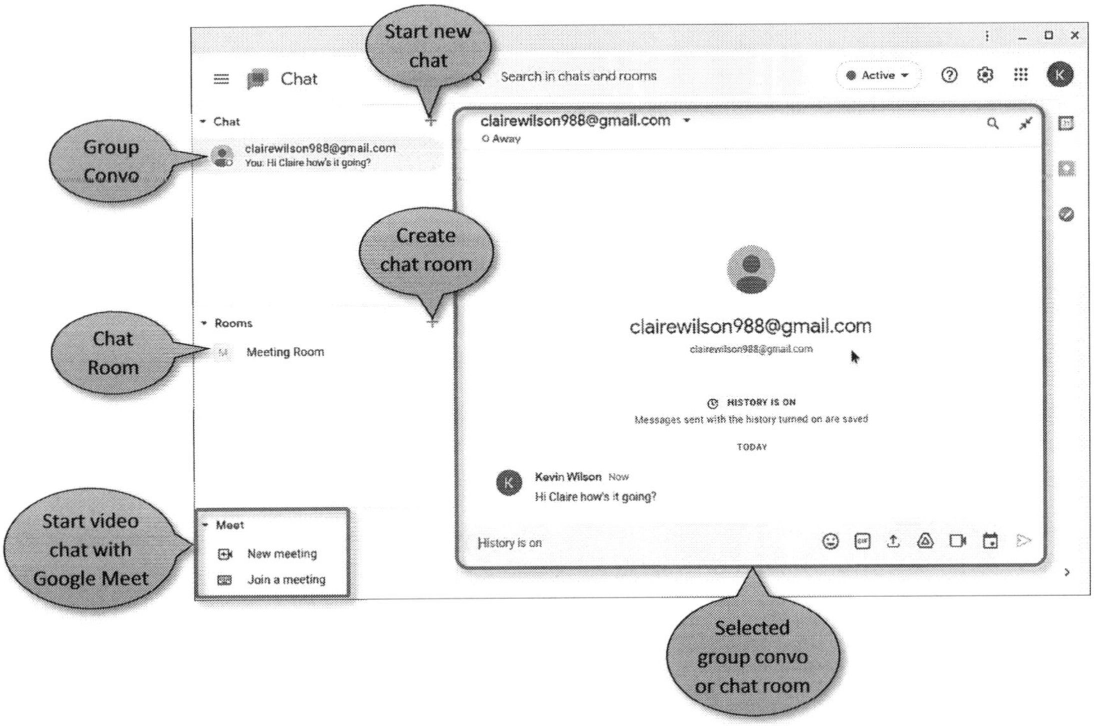

On the left hand side, under 'chat', you'll see all your previous or current group conversations. When you select a conversation, it will open up in the main window on the right. Same with 'rooms' - lists your chat rooms.

Group Conversations

To create a group chat conversation, click the '+' icon next to 'chat' on the left hand side of the screen. Select 'start group conversation' from the popup menu.

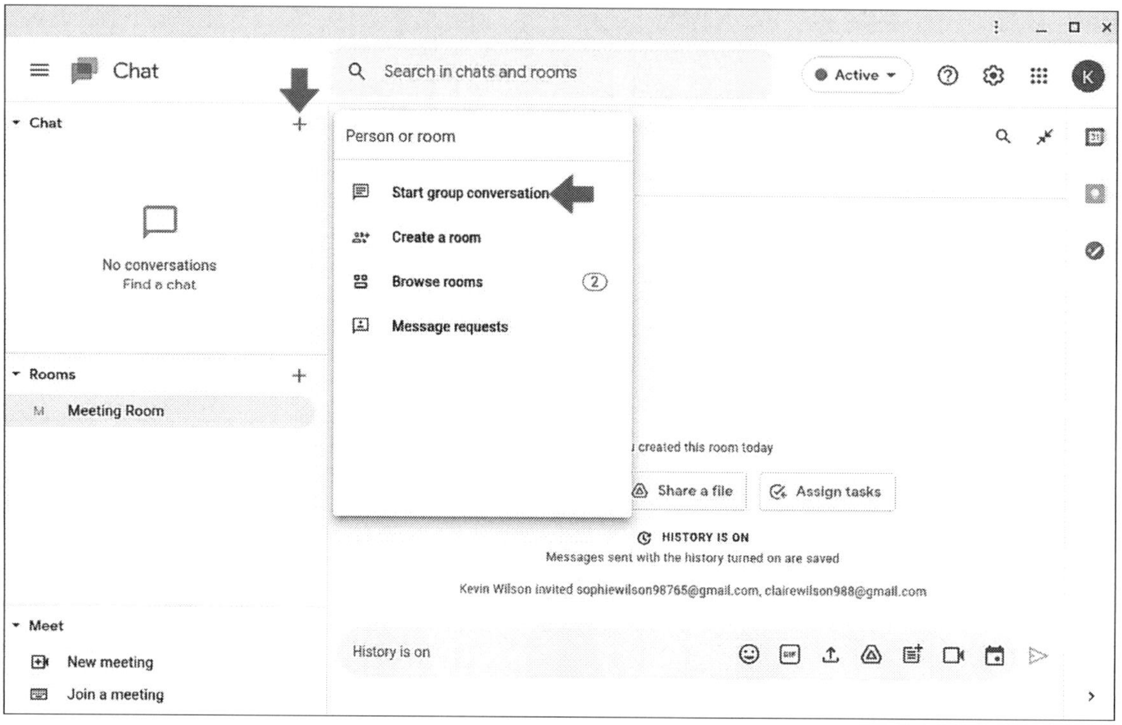

Enter the email addresses of the people you want to invite. Click the blue tick icon when you're done.

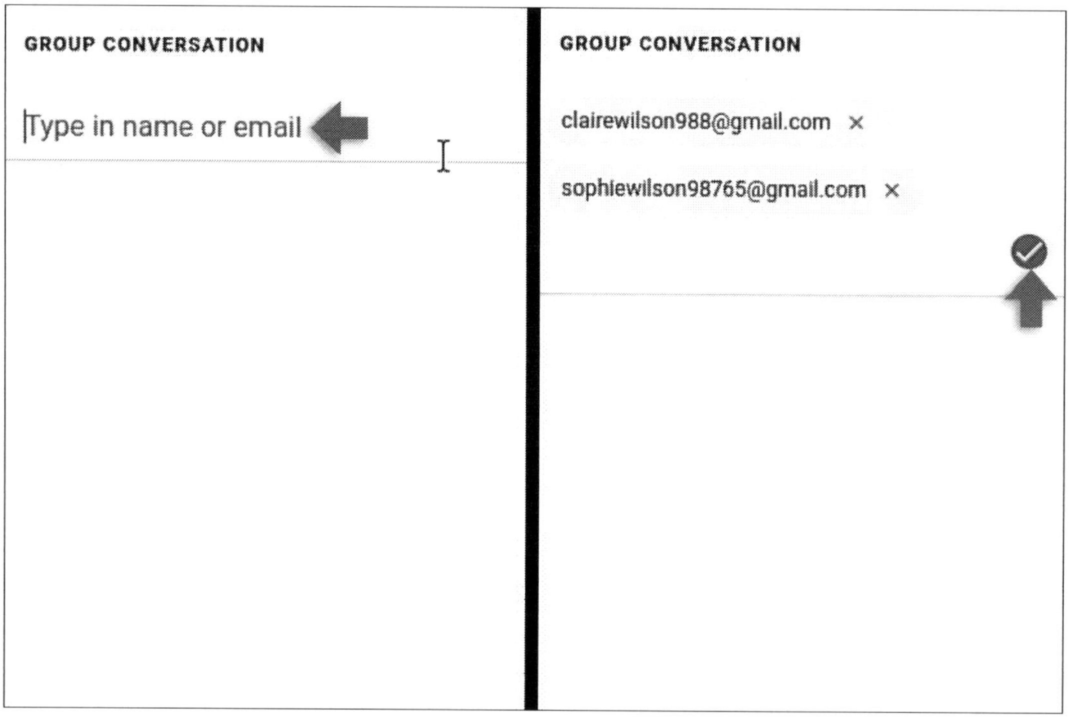

Once your participants accept the invite, they'll enter your group conversation.

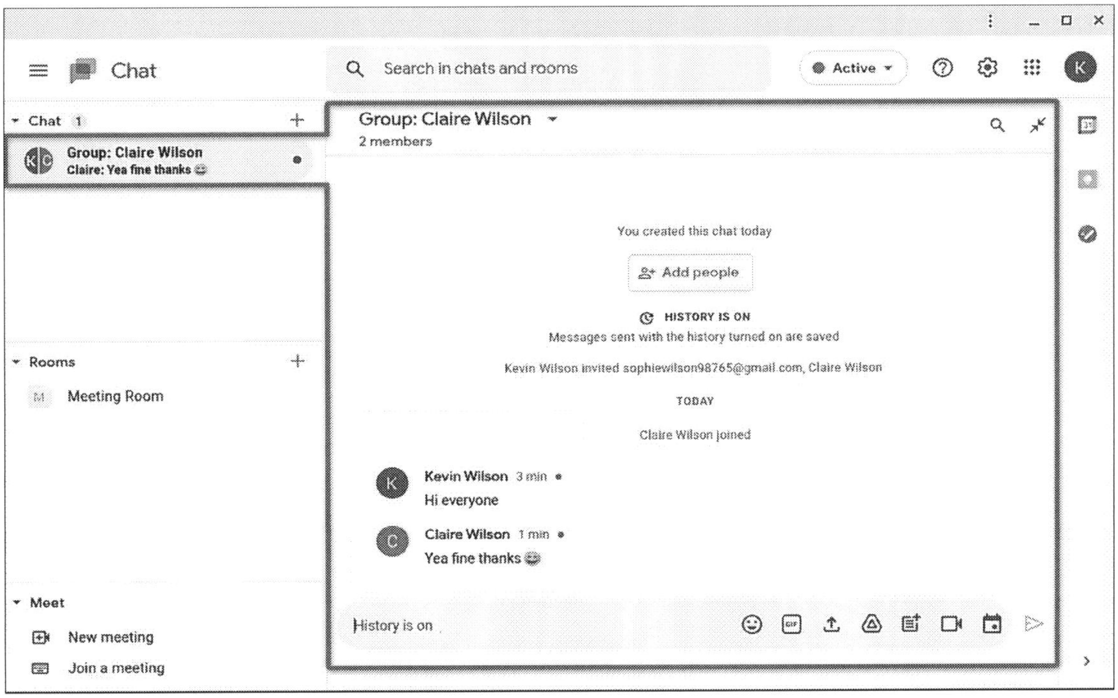

You'll see messages from your participants appear in the main chat window. In the grey bar along the bottom of the window, you can type your message. Press enter to send.

To the right on the grey bar, you'll see some icons. Lets take a look at what these icons do.

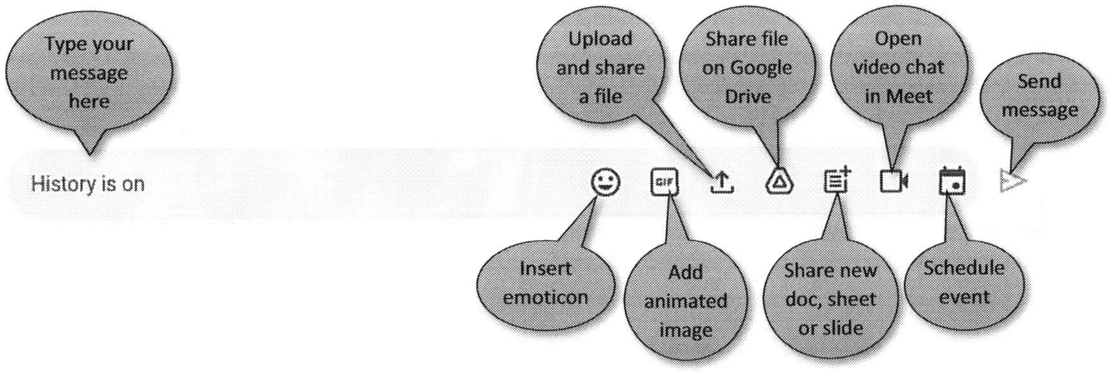

You can use these to insert emoticons such as smileys, and animated gifs - little animated images you can send to people. You can upload a file from your device or Google Drive and share it with the group.

You can also create a new Google Docs document, spreadsheet or slide to share with the group.

Finally, you can open a chat in Google Meet or schedule an event.

Chat Rooms

Chat rooms are similar to group conversations, except you can post files and assign tasks to participants. Chat rooms are better suited to long term collaboration or meetings and has separate sections for chat, files shared, and tasks assigned.

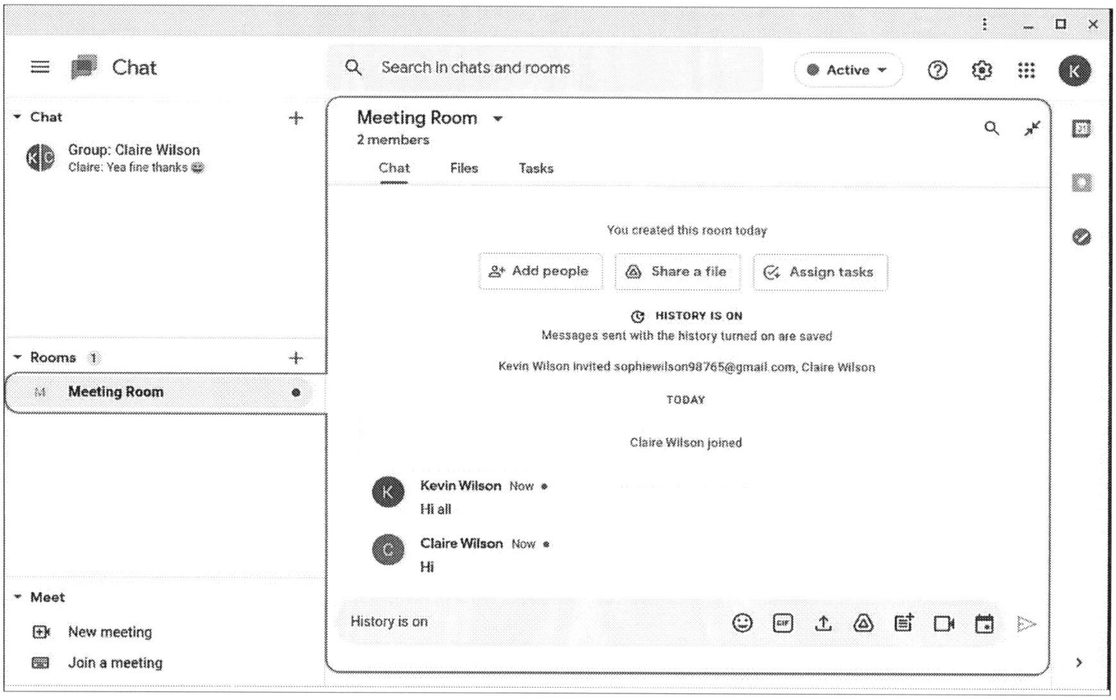

Creating a Room & Chatting

To create a room, click the '+' icon on the top right under the 'rooms' section. Select 'create a room' from the popup menu.

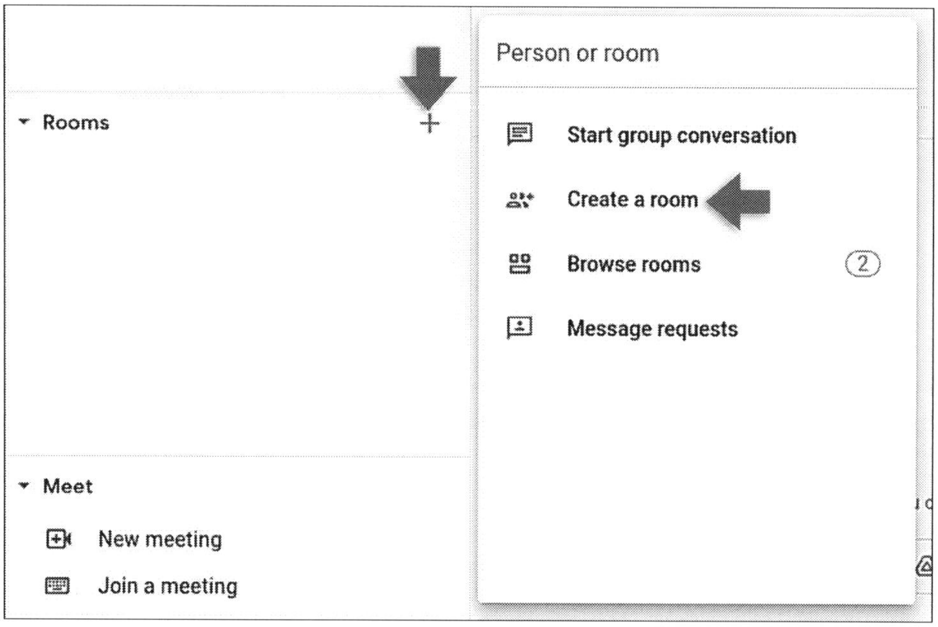

Add a name in the top field. Then enter the email addresses of the people you want to invite. Click 'create' when you're done.

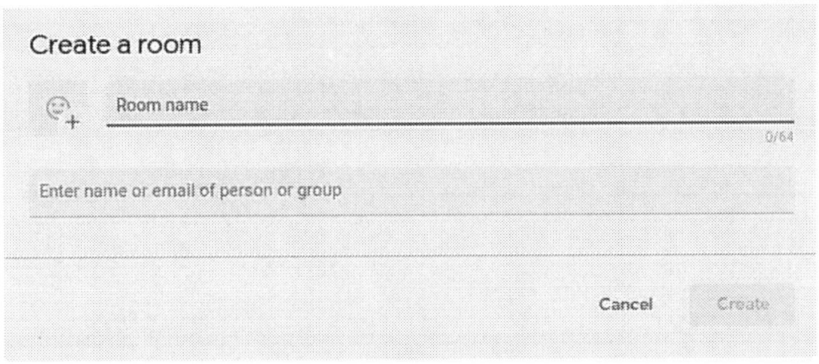

You'll see your new room appear under 'rooms' on the bottom left of the screen. Let's take a look around the room.

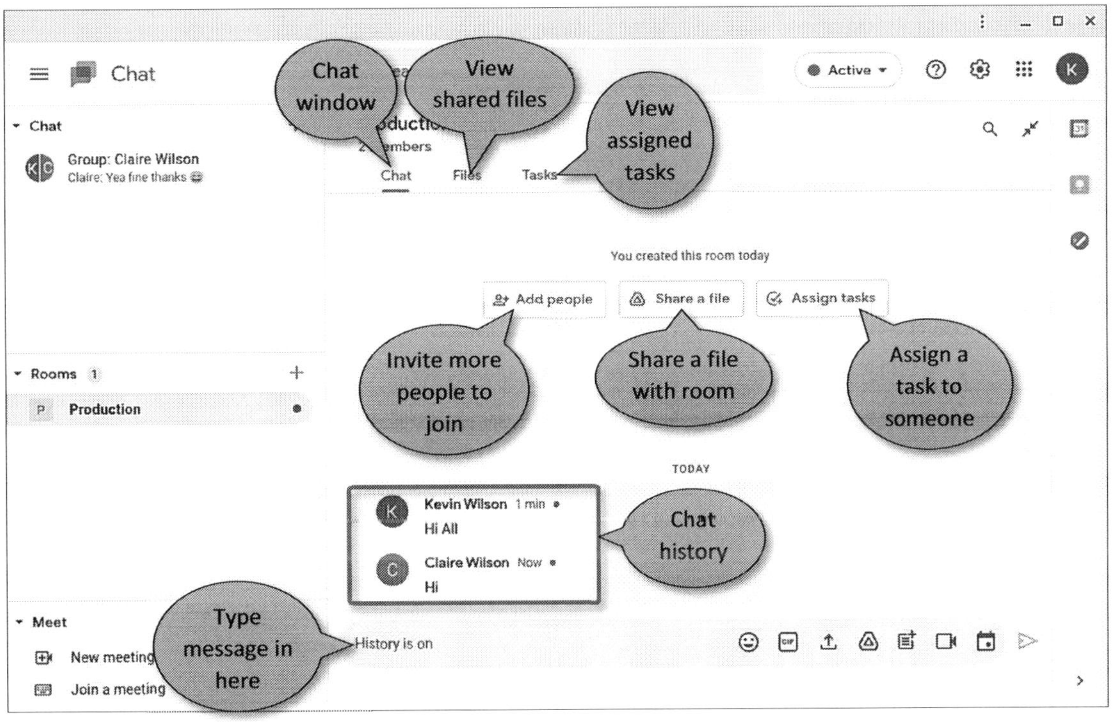

To the right on the grey bar at the bottom of the screen, you'll see some icons. Lets take a look at what these icons do.

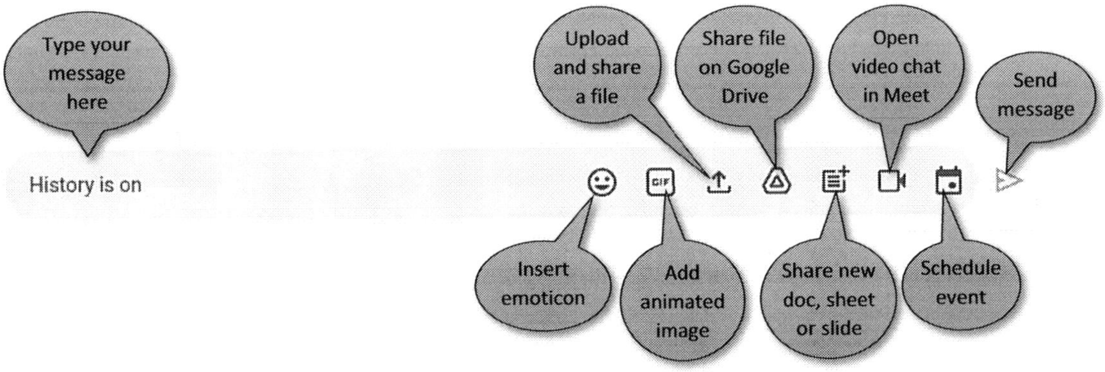

Share a File

To share a file, select the 'files' tab along the top of the room window. Click 'add file'

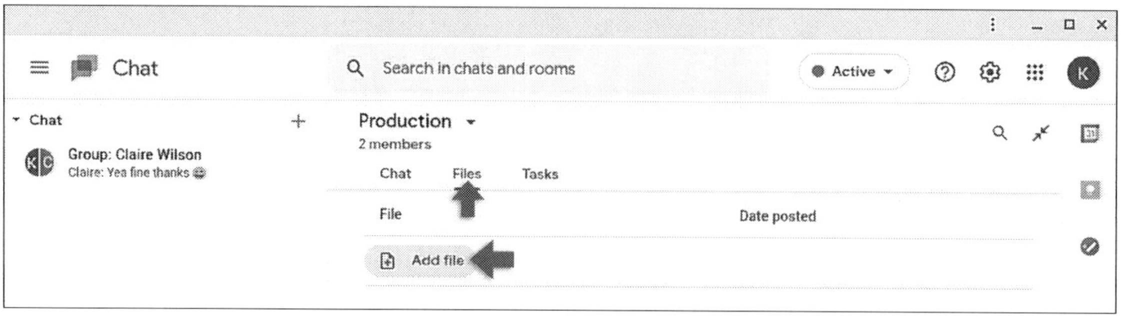

Select where the file is saved - your device (upload), or Google Drive. Then select the file, click 'insert'.

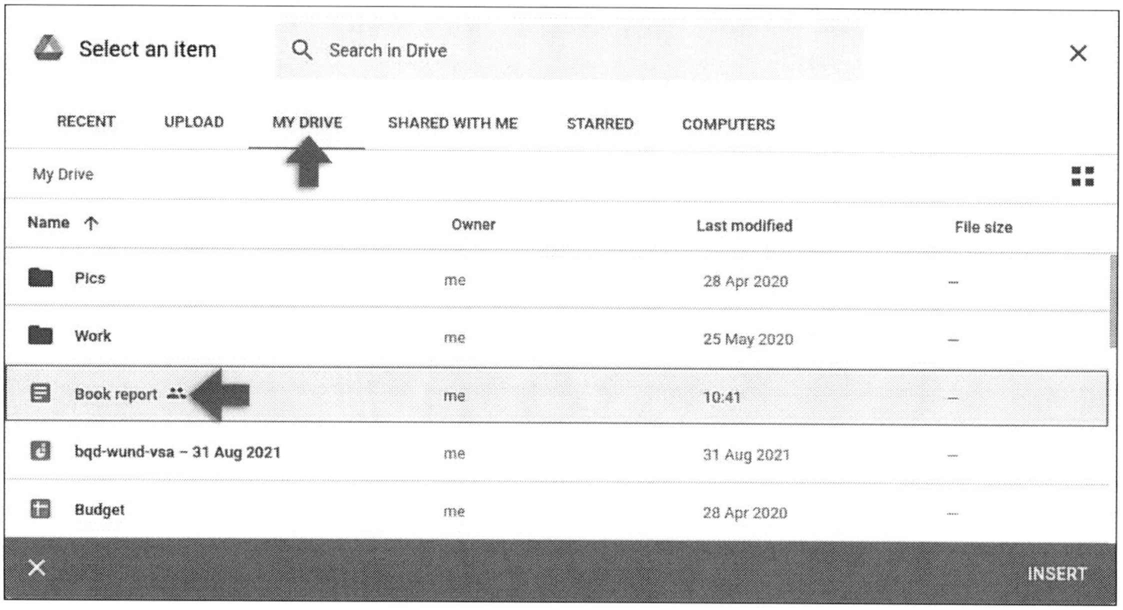

Click the send icon to share with the room.

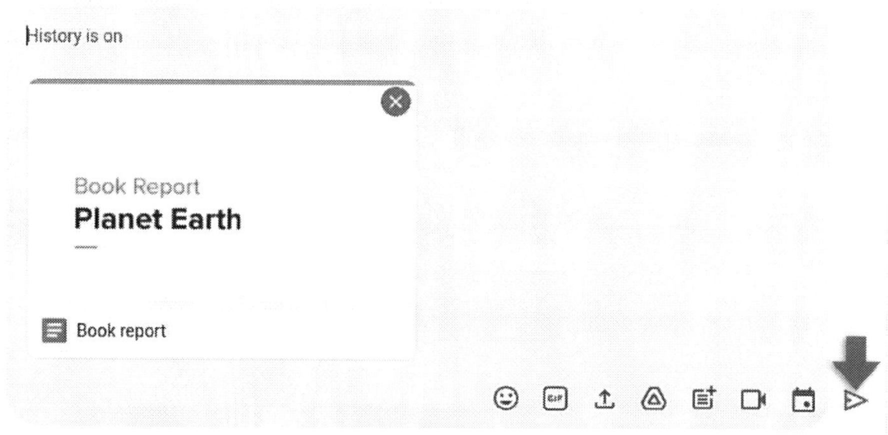

Assign a Task

To share a task with the room, select the 'tasks' tab along the top of the room window.

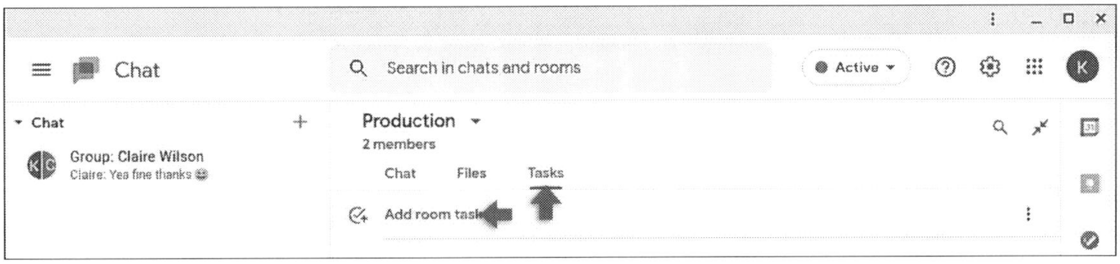

Enter the task title, the date task is to be completed by.

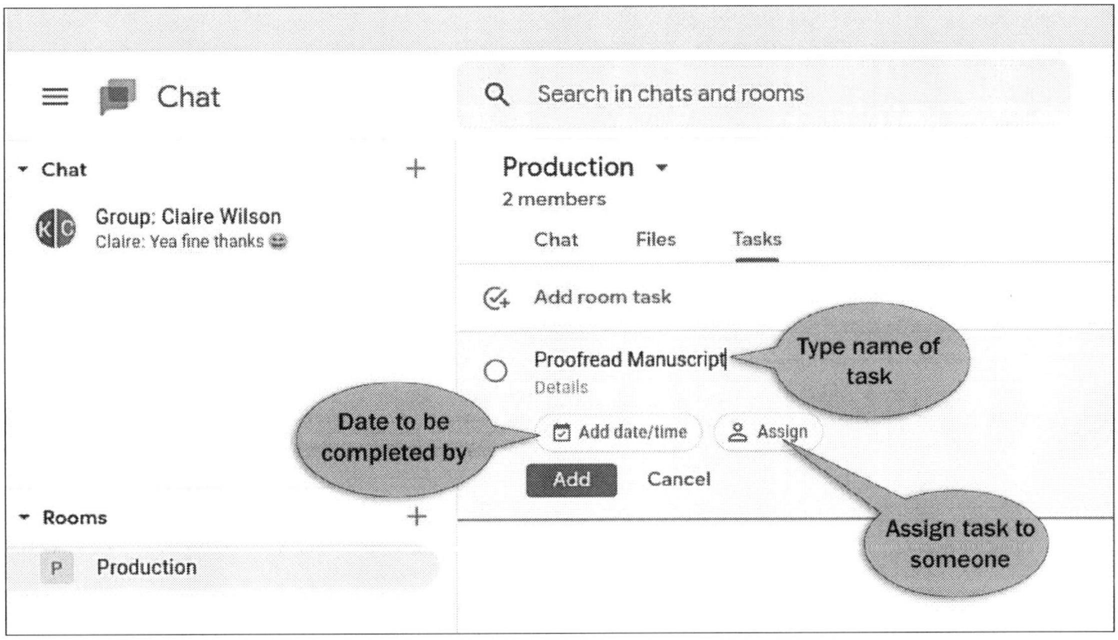

To assign the task to someone, click 'assign' then select the name of the person. Click 'add' when you're done.

Tasks will appear in the 'tasks' tab. When the person has completed the task, they can click on the circle to the left of the task. This marks the task as complete.

Google Duo

Is a person-to-person video calling app. If you want to video call friends, use Google Duo. It's great for personal communication, with support for small groups.

Starting Google Duo

You can open the Google Duo app on your app launcher. *If you don't see it, go to the Google Play store and download the app.*

Or open Google Chrome Web Browser then navigate to the following website:

`duo.google.com`

Once the app loads up, you'll land on the home screen. Lets take a look around the screen.

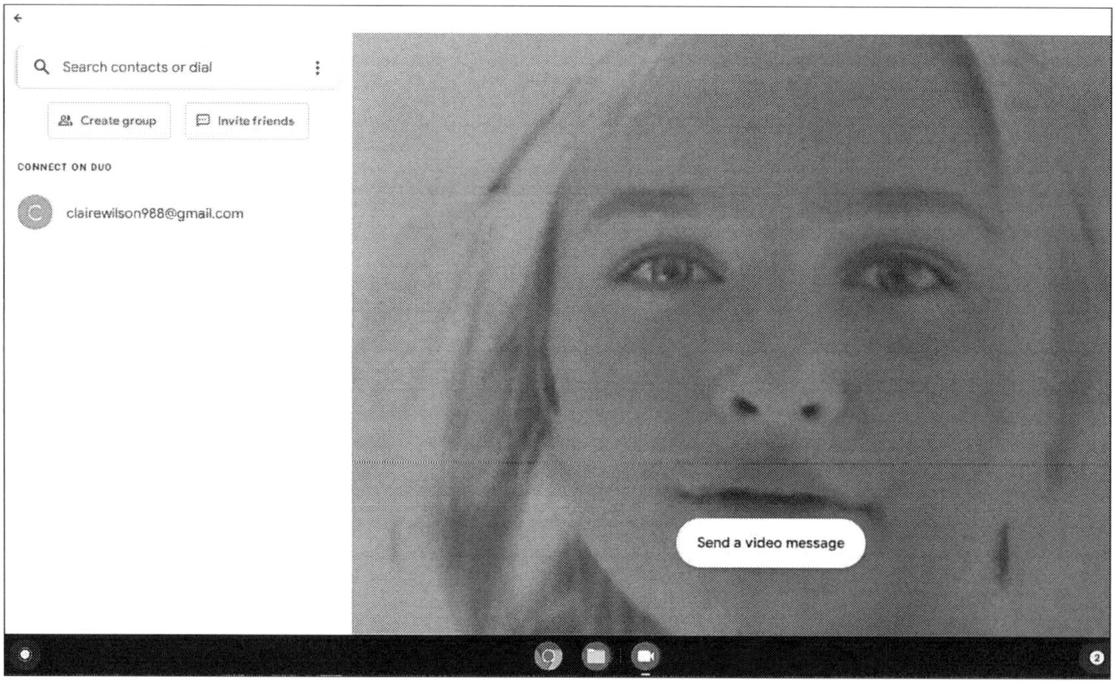

On the left hand side of the screen, you can search for contacts, create a chat group and invite friends.

Under that, you'll see a list of people you've been in contact with.

On the right hand side, you'll see a preview of your camera, where you can also record and send a video message.

Setup

Open the app from your app launcher. Sign in with your Google Account if prompted, then click 'give access' to your microphone and camera.

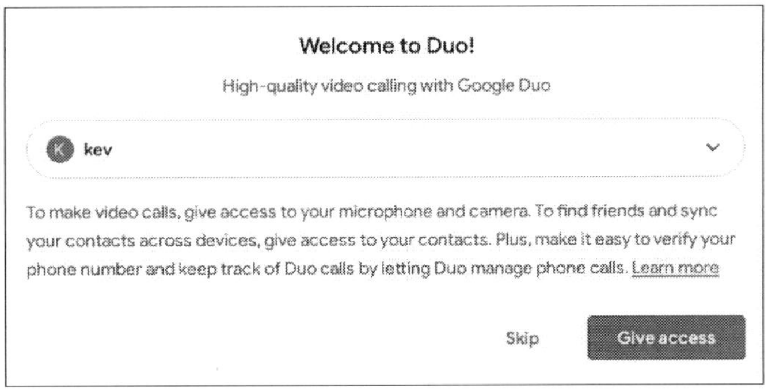

Click 'allow' on any access prompts for contacts, mic and camera you may get.

Click 'add phone number'. Enter your phone number.

Check your phone for a text/sms message. Type in the code you receive.

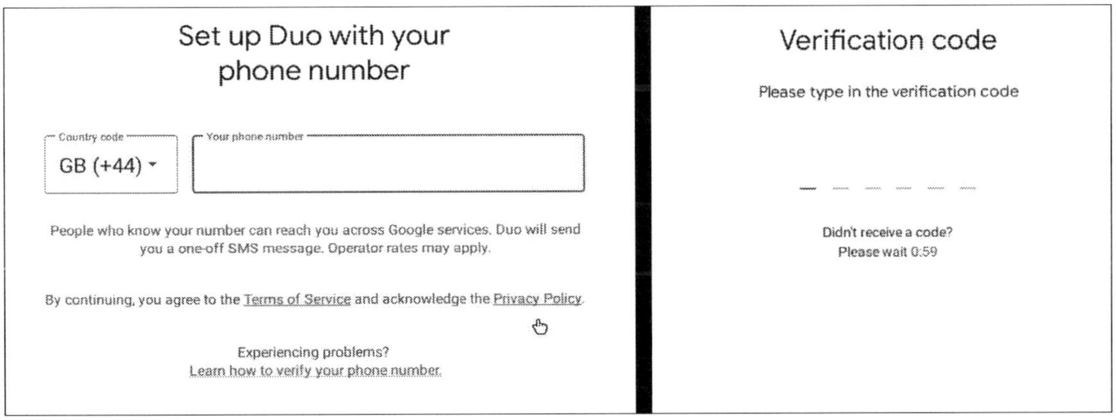

Start a Conversation

From the main screen select a contact to call from the list on the left. You'll see your recent calls at the top. If you don't see their name, type their Google Account email address or phone number into the search field at the top of the screen.

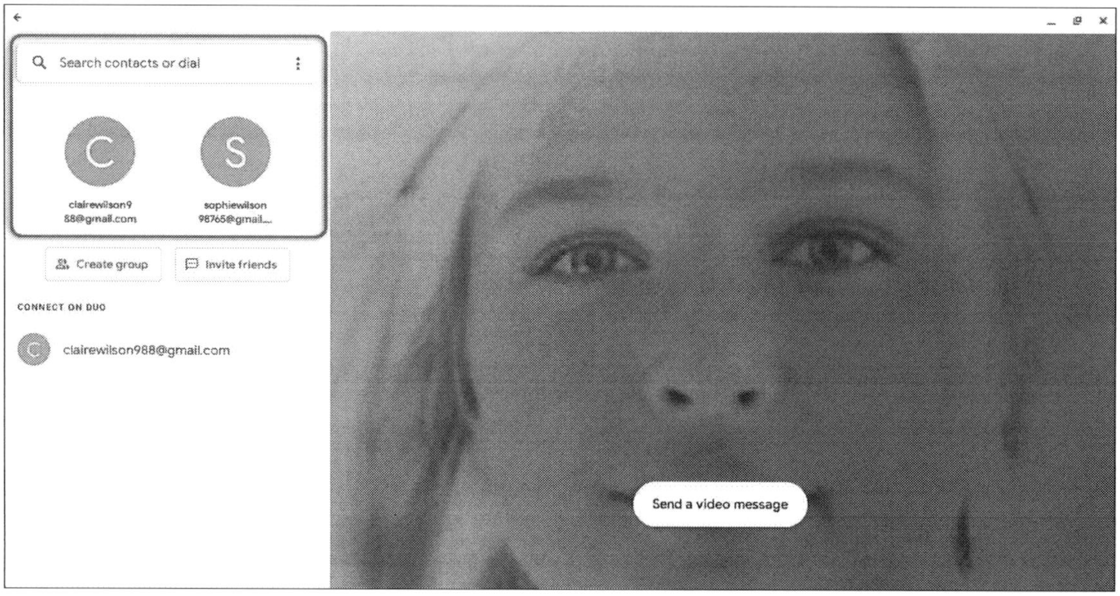

Select 'video call' at the bottom of the screen, then wait for the other person to answer.

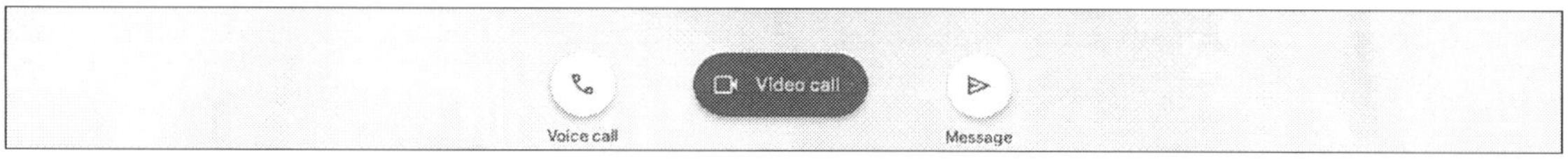

Once the other person answers, you'll see their camera in the main view. You'll also see your own camera on the bottom left.

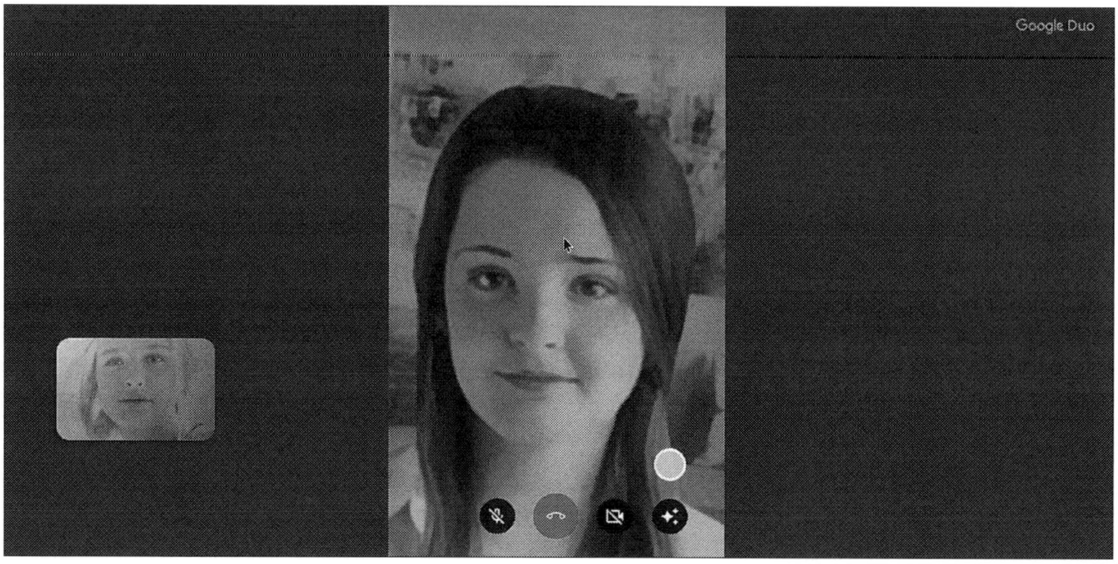

Group Conversations

To create a group, click 'create group'.

Add the participant's email addresses or phone numbers. Type these into the search field at the top of the window. Click 'done' when you're finished.

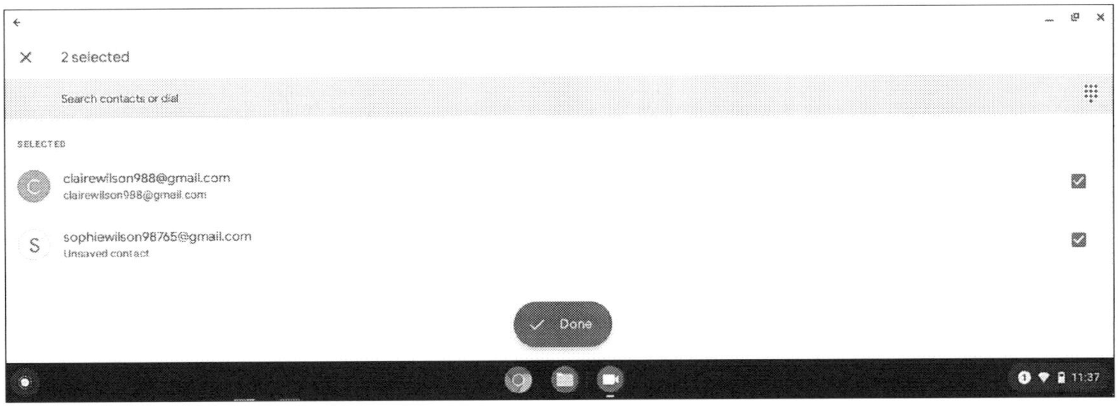

Wait for your participants to join the group.

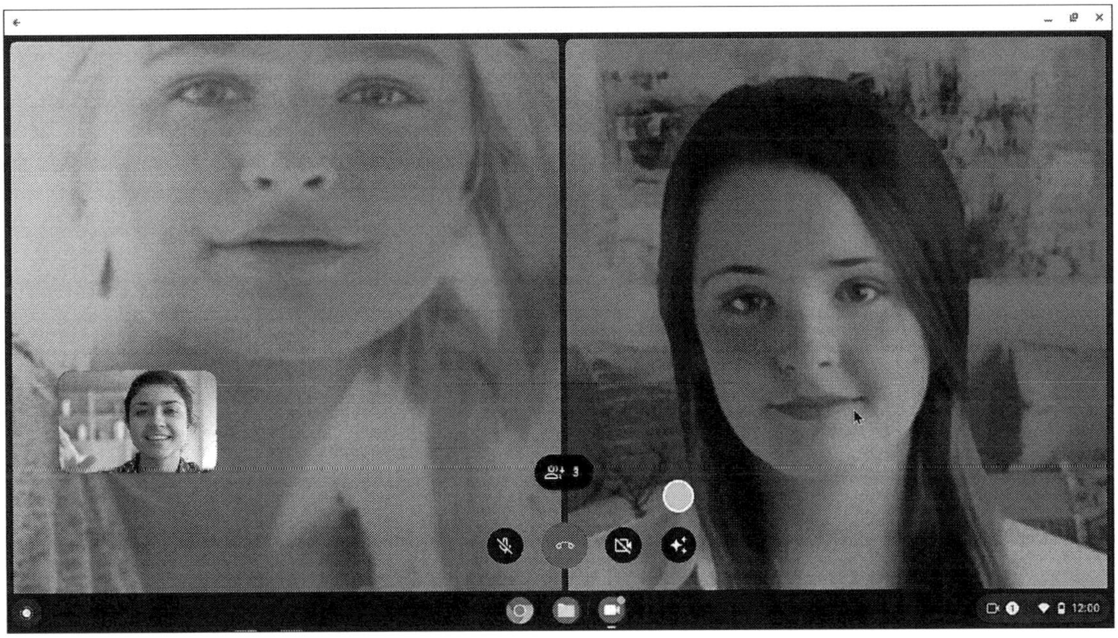

Invite Friends

To invite people to Duo, click 'invite friends' on the top left of the screen.

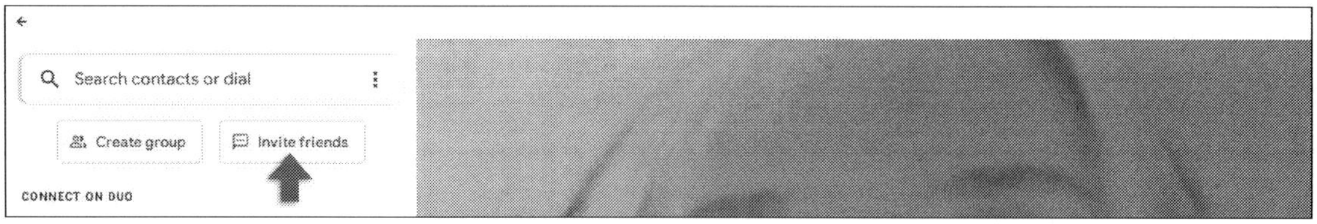

Type in the person's Google Account email address, or the person's phone number.

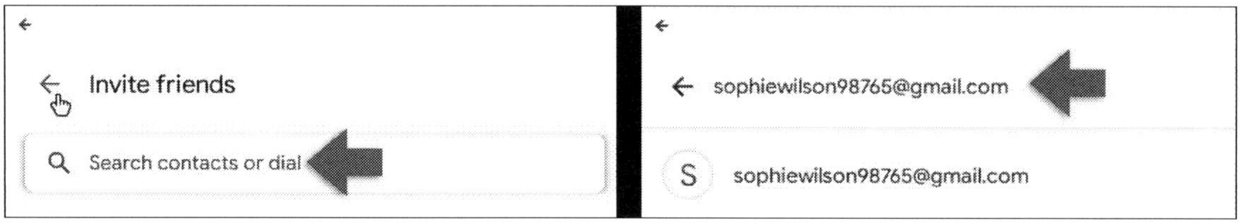

Click compose invitation

Select the app you want to use to send the invitation eg Mail.

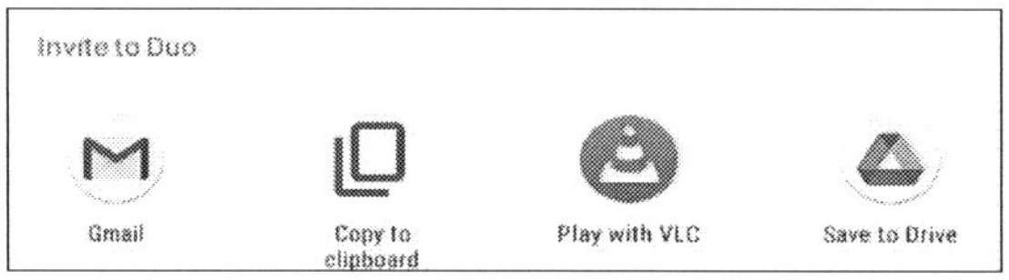

Type in a message, click the send icon on the top right.

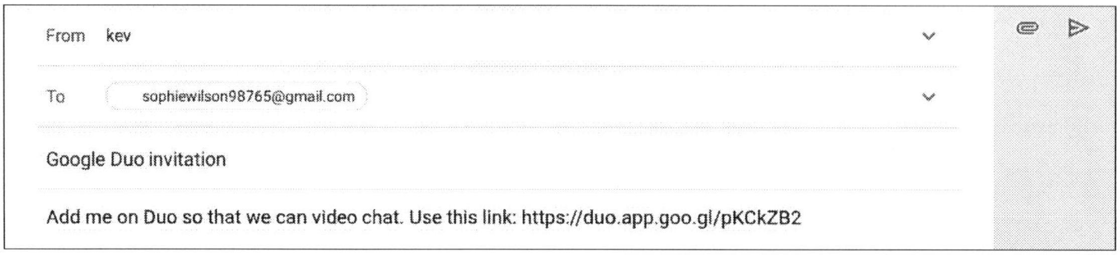

Google Hangouts

Google hangouts is being discontinued and is to be replaced with Google Chat and Google Meet.

You can call anyone on a tablet, ChromeBook, laptop, phone or pc that has Google hangouts and a webcam on the device. You can also send instant messages, photographs and videos.

To start the Google hangouts, open Google Chrome and navigate to:

`hangouts.google.com`

When hangouts opens up, you'll see a list of contacts you've been in contact with listed down the left hand side.

If you use hangouts a lot, you'll find all your most recent contacts listed here. Click on the names to see the conversations you've had with these contacts.

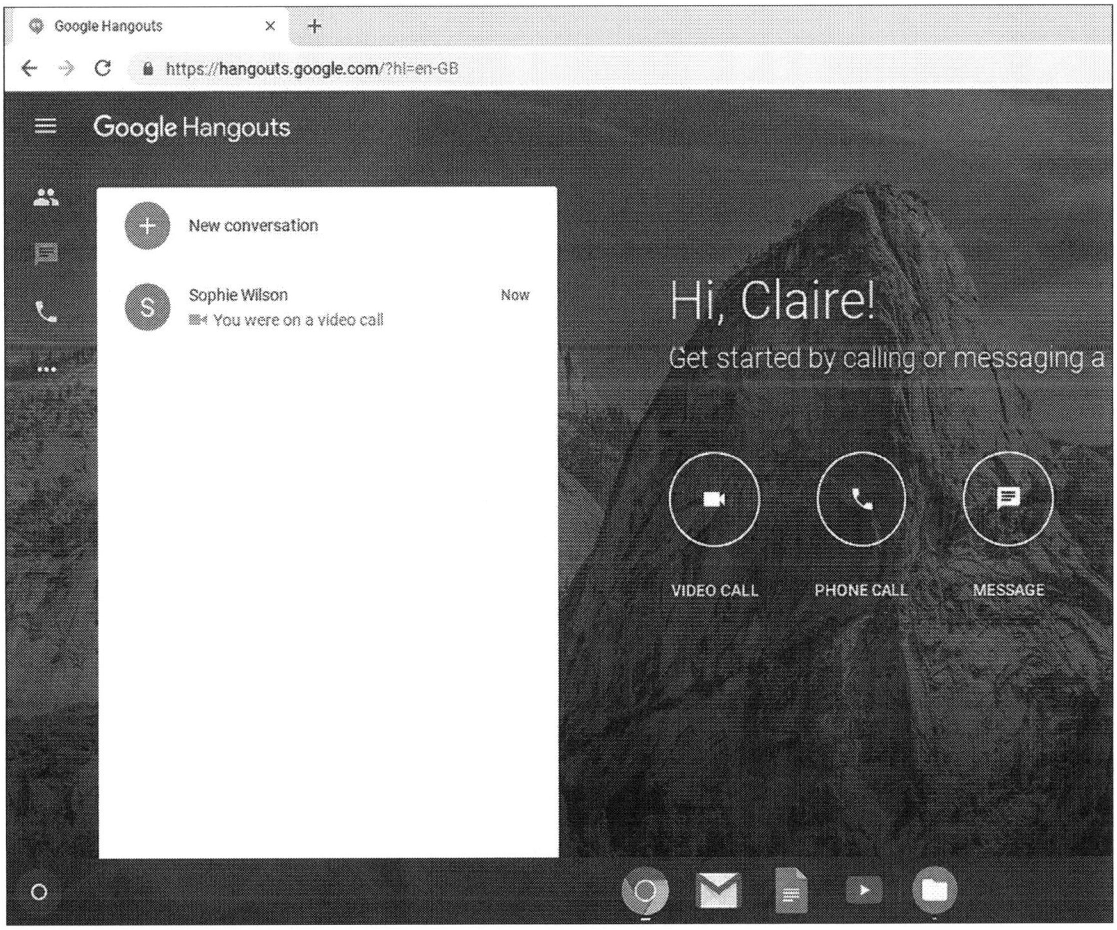

In the middle of the screen, you'll see three buttons. Here you can make a video call, a phone call, or send an instant message.

Messaging New Contacts

To contact someone new, click 'new conversation' on the top left of your screen.

Type the person's name in the field, then select from the contact list that appears.

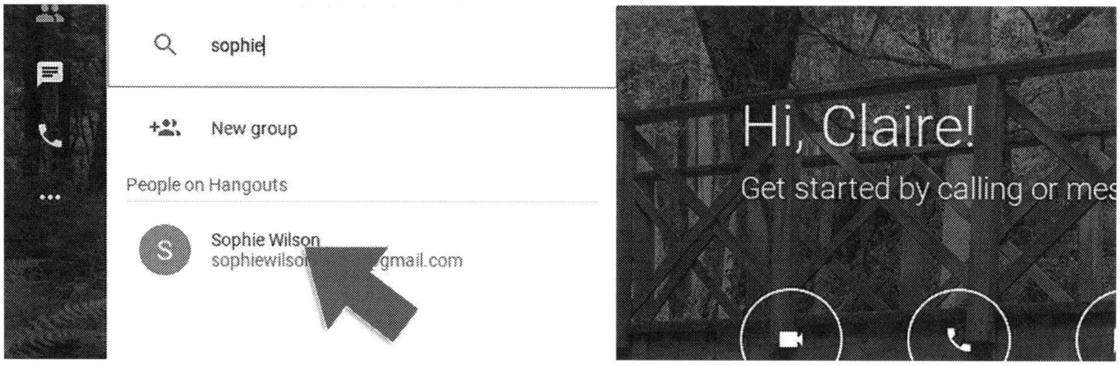

You'll see an instant message window pop up on the right hand side of your screen. Here, you can send instant text messages, as well as start video and audio chats. Just type your message in using the field at the bottom of the window.

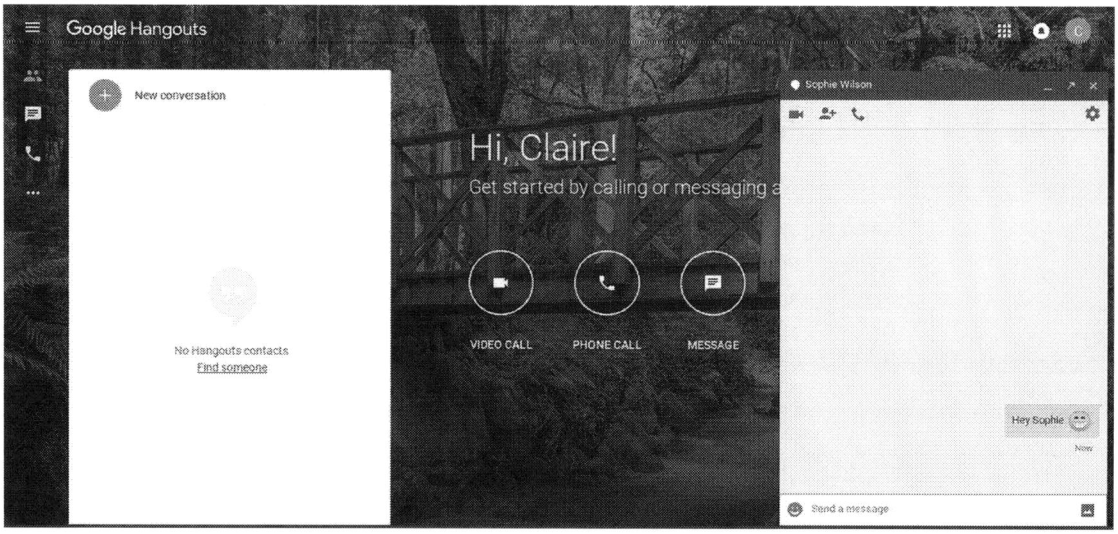

Calling Someone New

To place a new video call, click the video icon in the middle of the screen.

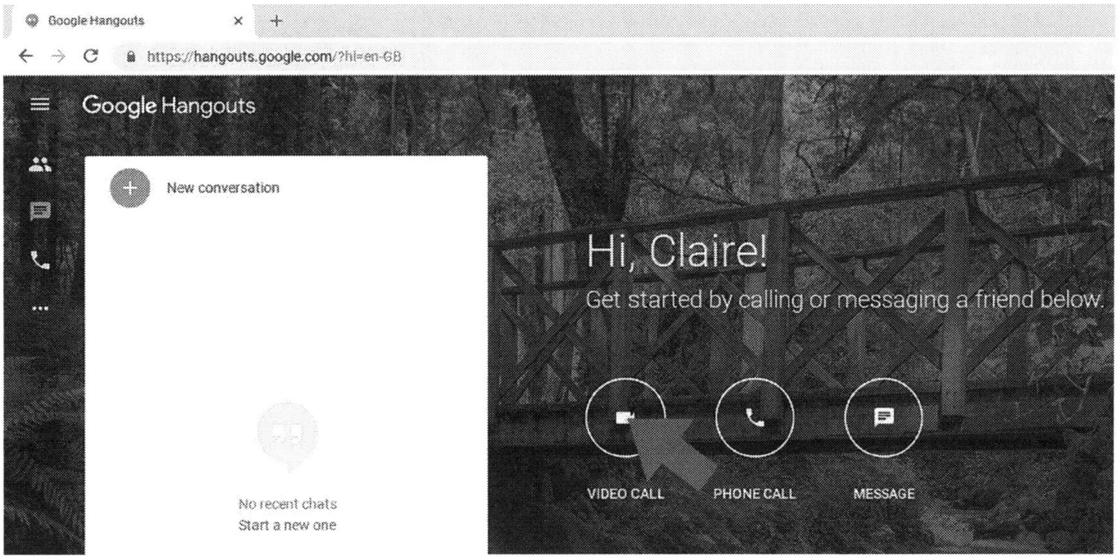

Enter the name or Gmail address of the person you're calling. Click the correct name from the drop down list.

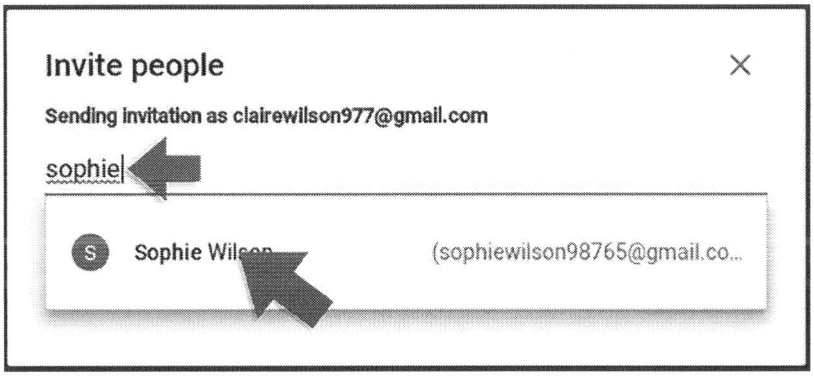

Click 'invite'.

The other person will get a prompt on their hangouts window.

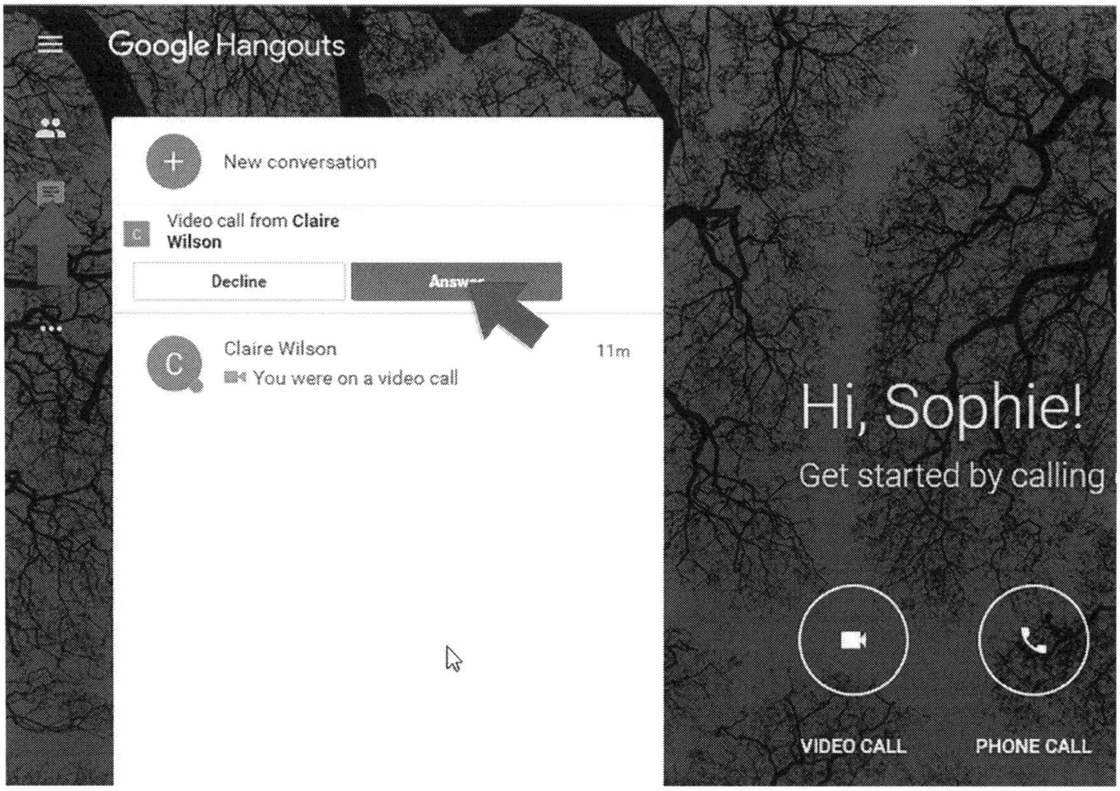

Now you can have a video conversation with that person.

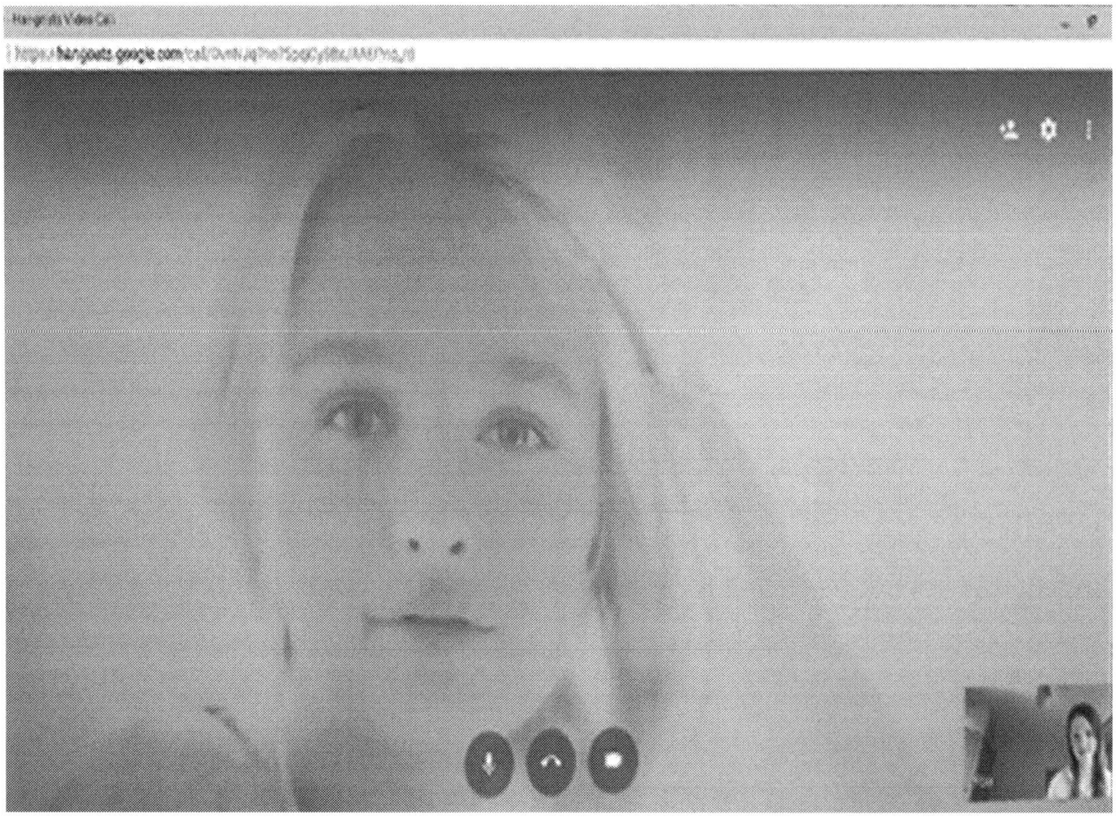

Calling Someone in Conversation Window

If you've had a conversation with someone before, you'll see their name listed in the recent contacts list when you open hangouts. Click on one of these names to see the conversations you've had.

This will open up your conversation window with that person. To place a video call, click the small camera icon on the top left.

When you place the call, you'll see an image of your webcam in the main viewer while you are waiting for the other person to answer.

The other person will get a prompt allowing them to either answer or decline the call.

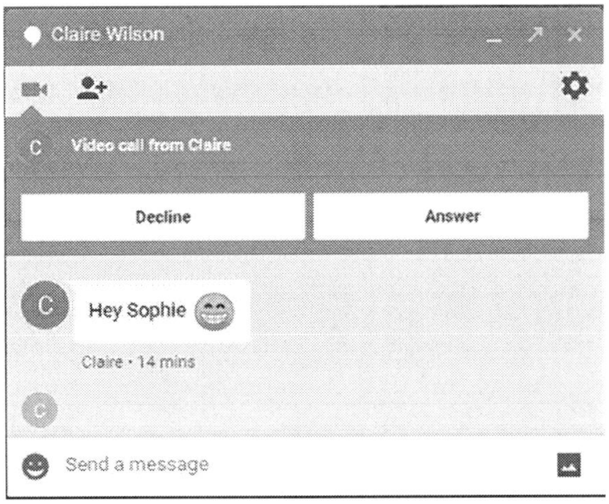

To answer, just select 'answer' from the prompt.

When the other person answers, you'll see their webcam in your main viewer. You'll also see a preview of your own camera on the bottom right of your screen, as you can see below.

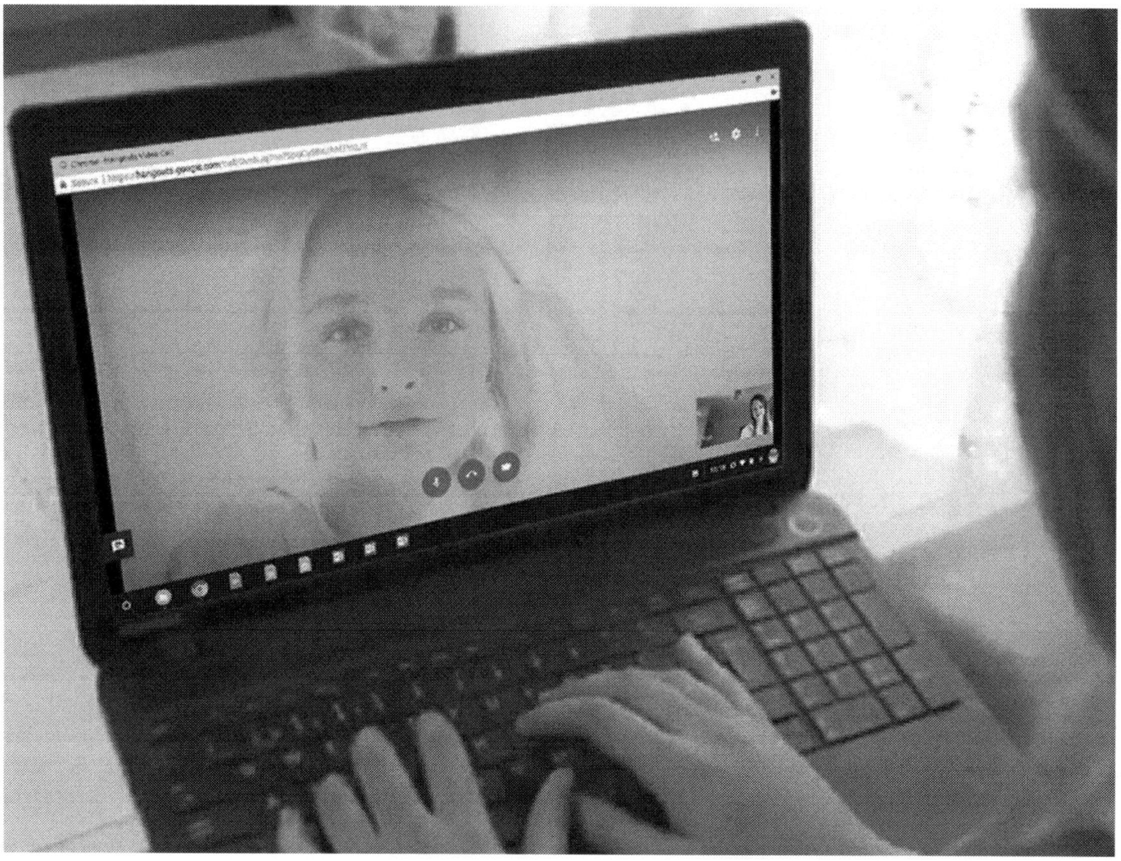

Along the bottom of your screen, you'll also see three buttons. These usually disappear during a call - just click the screen to bring them up.

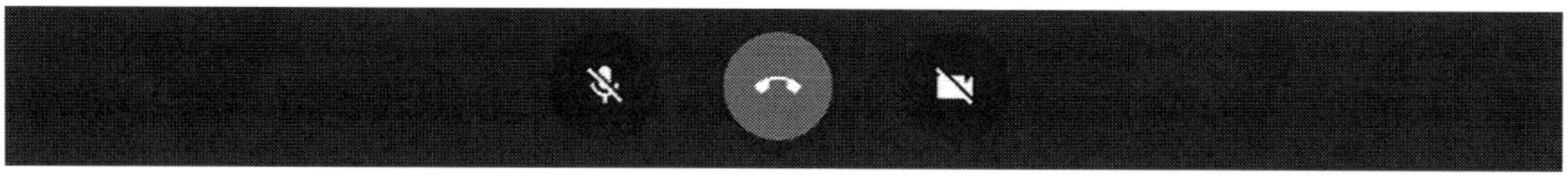

The button on the far left mutes your microphone so the person you're talking to can't hear you. Similarly the icon on the far right turns off your camera. Useful if you want a moment's privacy.

The red button in the middle closes your video call.

This is useful for keeping in touch with friends and family all over the world.

These calls are also free to make and you can chat as long as you like - you'll still have to pay for your internet connection though, whether that is through cable, broadband, wifi or cellular depending on your service provider.

Sending Images

You can send files such as photos using the conversation window.

To send an image, click the image icon on the bottom right of the conversation window.

Select 'upload photos'. Then click 'select a photo from your computer'.

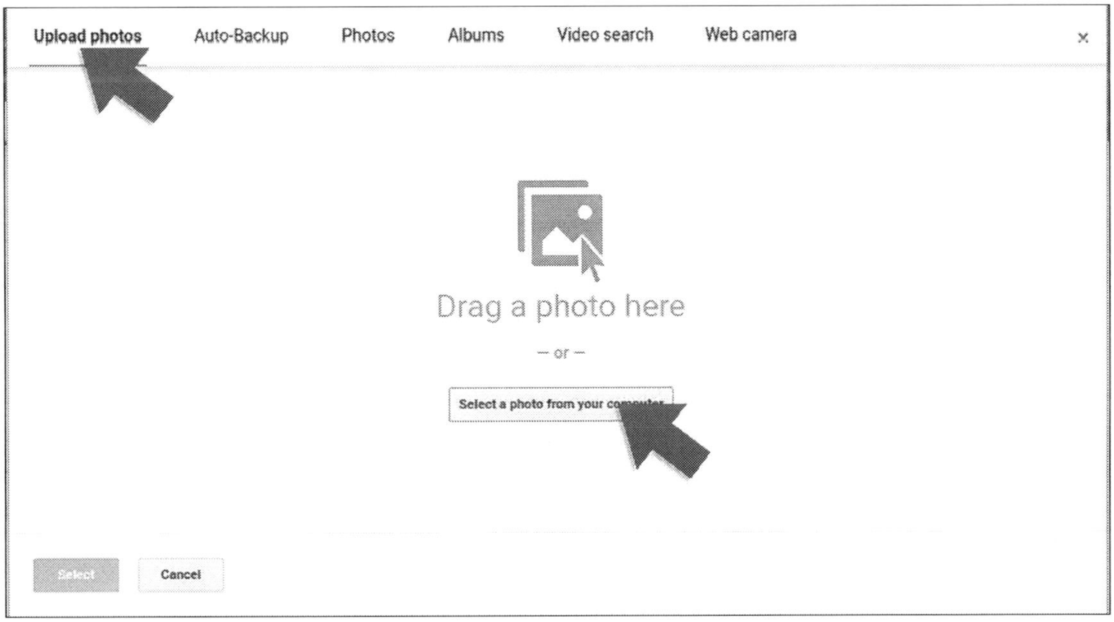

You can also send photos from Google Photos, albums, video search on the web, or the web cam on your ChromeBook.

Select 'Google Drive', or 'My Files', depending on where the image you want to upload is stored.

Click 'open', when you're done.

You'll see a preview of the image in the conversation window. Click the 'send' icon in the middle of the image to send.

Sending Emoticons

You can send smilies and all sorts of other emotes in the conversation window.

To do this, click the smiley face icon on the bottom left hand side of the window.

Select a category of emoticons or stickers using the row of icons along the top.

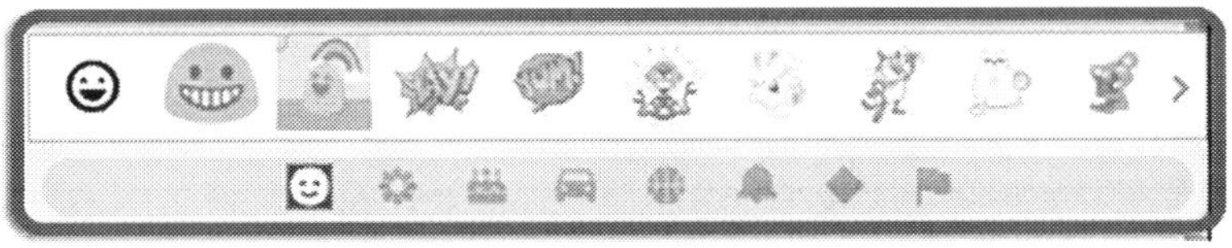

Then click an emoticon or sticker from the list, to send or insert into your message.

8 Entertainment

Your ChromeBook has a large collection of multimedia apps available. You'll find these apps on your app launcher, and many more can be downloaded from the play store.

In this section we'll take a look at taking photos with your camera app, downloading apps, ebooks, movies, tv programmes and listening to music.

For this section, have a look at the video resources. Open your web browser and navigate to the following website

`videos.tips/chromebook-mm`

Google Play Store

Google Play allows you to search for and download digital media such as music, books, movies, and television programs, as well as apps and games.

You'll find the play store on your app launcher. Click the app launcher icon on the bottom left, then click the arrow in the top middle to open it up fully.

Click the play store icon to start the app.

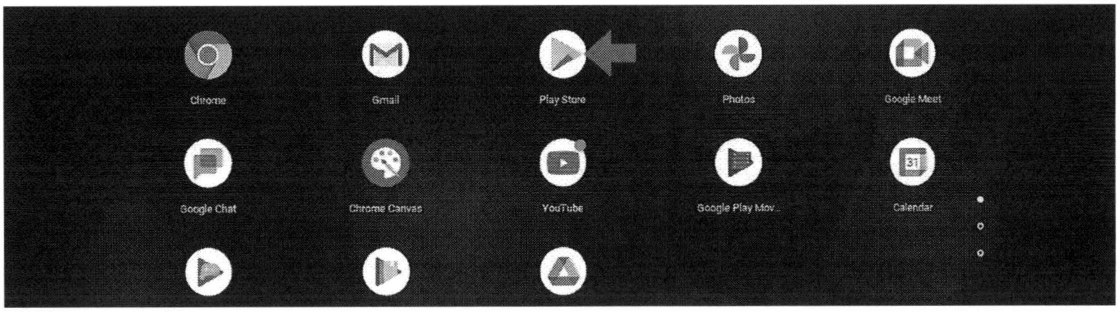

The play store will open. Along the top of the screen, you can search for apps, games, tv/movies and books.

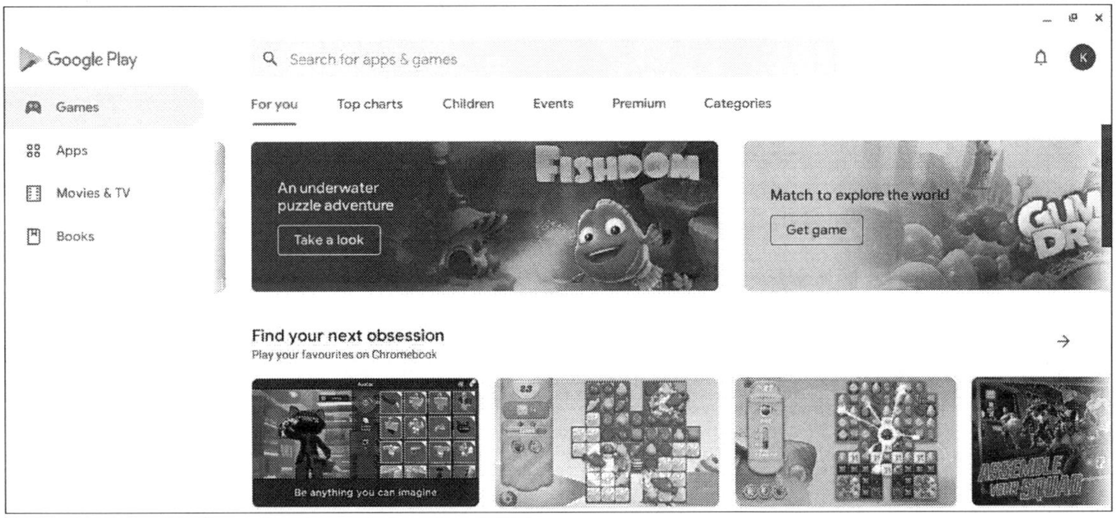

Down the left hand side, you can browse by category: games, apps, movies & tv or books.

Google Photos

With the photos app you can manage, store and enhance the photographs you take with your camera. You can also share photos on social media, or send them to friends and family.

Click the app launcher icon on the bottom left, then click the arrow in the top middle to open it up fully.

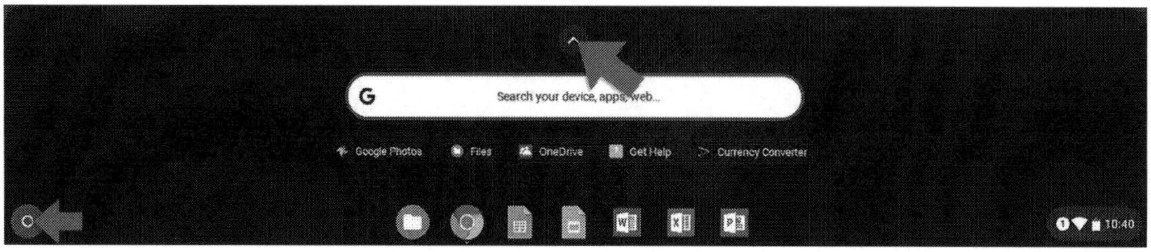

Click the Photos icon to start the app. Make sure you run the Android version of the app.

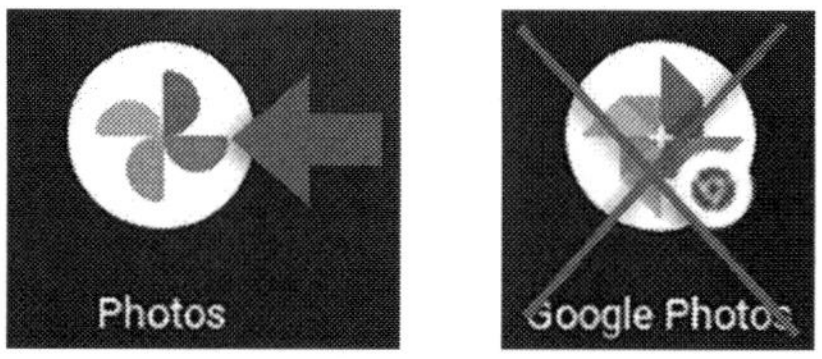

On some Chromebooks you might see two icons - one is an Android App and one is a Chrome App. You can tell the difference by the app icon - the Chrome App has a Chrome symbol on the bottom right of the icon. Chrome Apps are being discontinued in favour of the Android Apps.

Once the app opens, you'll land on the home screen.

Viewing Photos

To browse through all your photos, click the photos icon on the left hand side.

Scroll up and down, you'll see your photos listed in reverse chronological order. Click on one of the thumbnails to view the image in full.

Search

Google Photos uses an intelligent image recognition search that scans your photos for recognisable patterns, shapes and objects. To search for photos, type your keywords into the search field at the top of the screen.

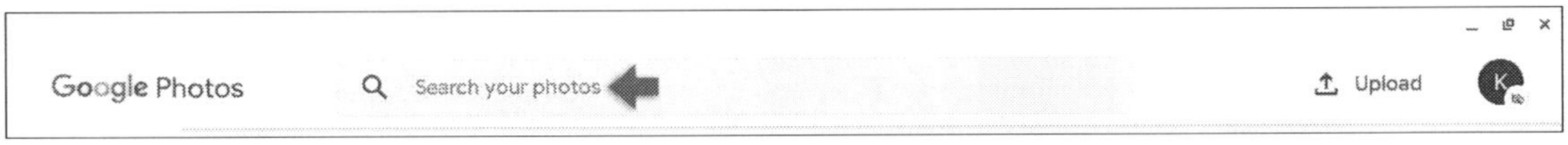

In this example, I'm searching for all photos taken by the sea.

Adjusting Photos

You can adjust the brightness, contrast, bring up detail in shadows or highlights, as well as crop, and straighten up photos.

Open a Photo

To adjust a photo, select it from the photos section or album. The photo will open up.

Select 'edit' from the icons along the bottom of the screen.

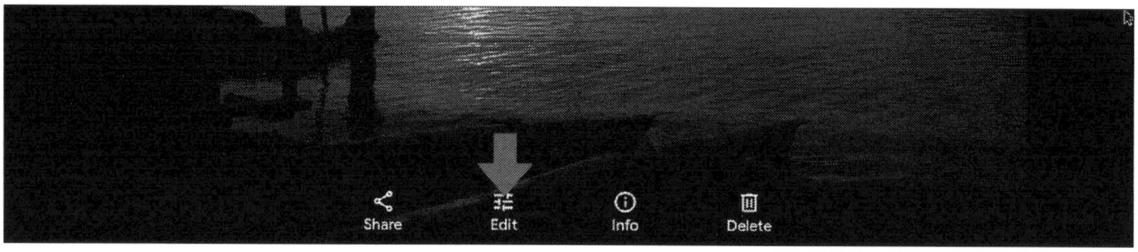

Brightness & Contrast

To change the brightness, contrast, shadows, highlights and so on, open the photo, select 'adjust' from the list along the bottom of the screen.

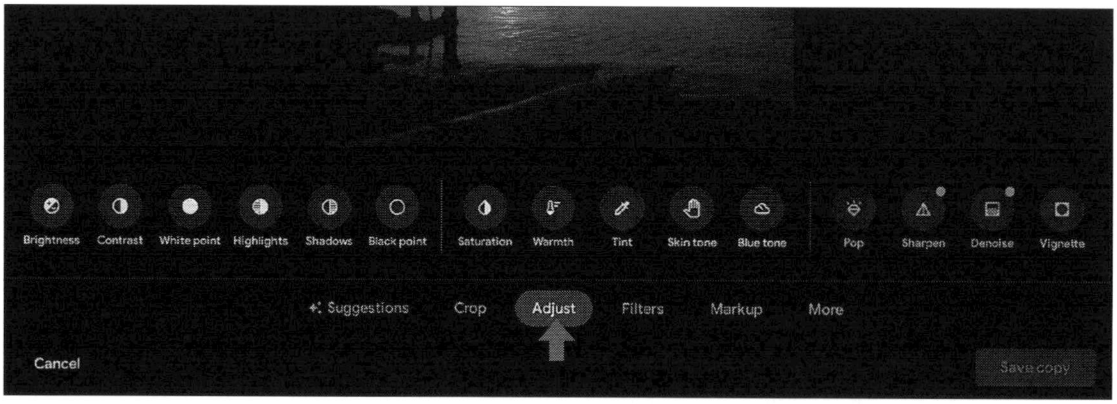

You'll see a whole list of adjustments you can make. Click on one of the options to make adjustments.

Lets take a look at what each adjustment does:

- **Brightness** changes the overall brightness of the image. You can make the whole photo lighter or darker.
- **Contrast** is the difference between the dark and light parts of the image. Increasing the contrast can make parts of your image stand out.
- **White Point** adjust the brightest part of the image such as objects that appear mostly white.
- **Highlights** adjust the bright parts of the image. Eg you could darken the sky in a photo if it's too bright.
- **Shadows** adjust the dark parts of the image. Eg you could lighten up the shadows of a photo.
- **Black Point** adjusts the darkest part of the image such as objects that are mostly black.
- **Saturation** adjusts the intensity of the colours. For example, if you turn up the saturation, the colours become darker and more intense.
- **Warmth** adjusts the colour cast of the image. If you increase the 'warmth' the photo becomes more orange, and if you decrease the warmth, the photo becomes more blue. This is useful if your photographs have come out too orange or too blue. If you photo is too orange (ie too warm), just turn the 'warm' slider towards the left.
- **Tint** adjusts how much white is added to the photo
- **Skin Tone** enhances 'skin colours' in the photograph. This can help make people look a bit more natural in the photo.
- **Blue Tone**, is useful for oceans, skies, and anything that is blue.
- **Pop** makes the image stand out more by enhancing the edges of objects.
- **Sharpen** sharpens the image and attempts to remove blur.
- **Denoise** removes image noise from the photograph. Noise usually appears in photos taken in low light.

In this example, I'm going to increase the shadows. To make your adjustment, drag the slider

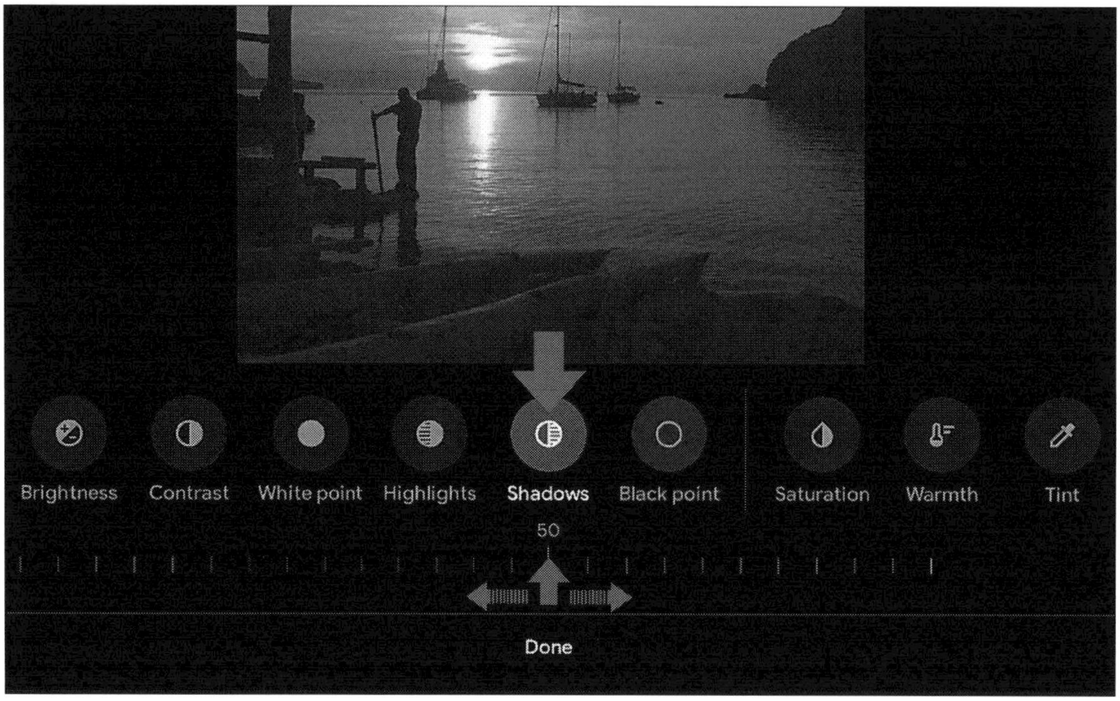

Click 'done' when you're finished.

Crop & Rotate

To crop, open the photo, select 'crop' from the list along the bottom of the screen.

To crop the image, drag the small white circles around the part of the image you want to keep.

You can also crop to a preset size. To do this, click the preset icon on the bottom left. Select a size from the popup menu. Click and drag the image so it fits inside the crop box.

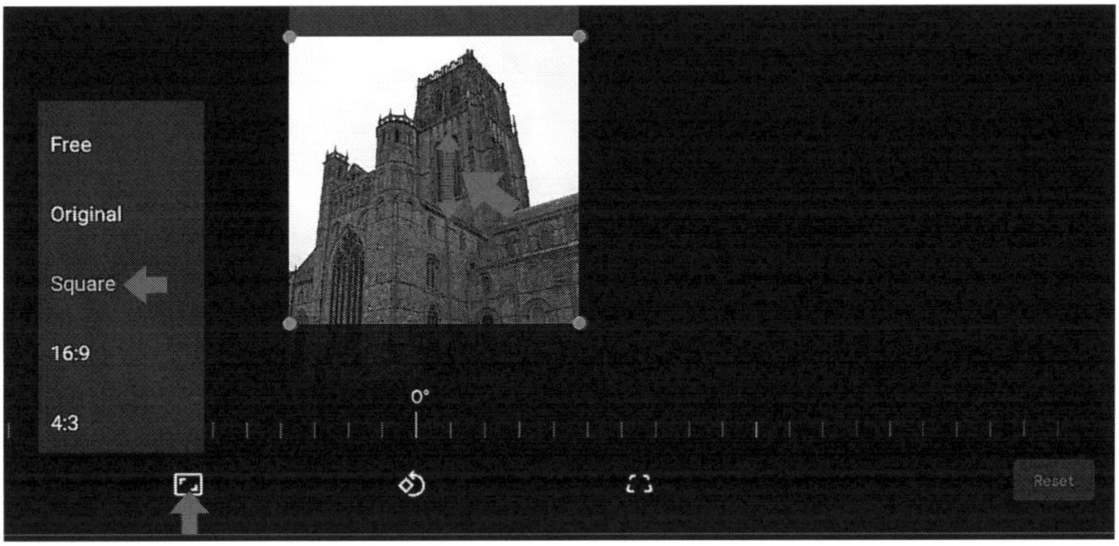

If you want to rotate the image. Click the rotate icon in the middle. Each click will rotate the image 90° counter-clockwise.

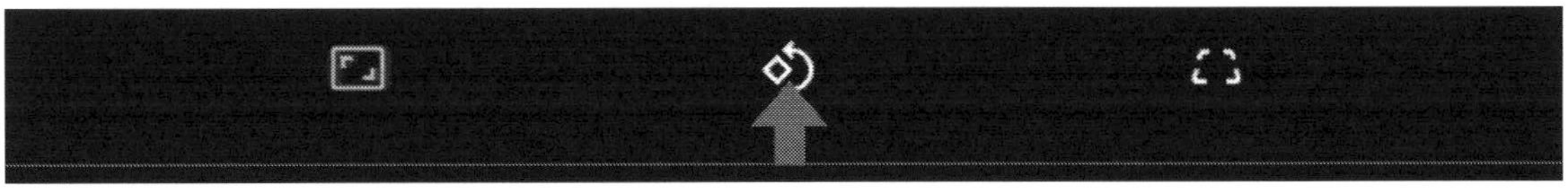

Click 'save a copy' on the bottom left when you're done. To go back to your photos, click the back arrow on the top left of the screen.

Straighten

To straighten the photo, click and drag the dial at the bottom of the screen.

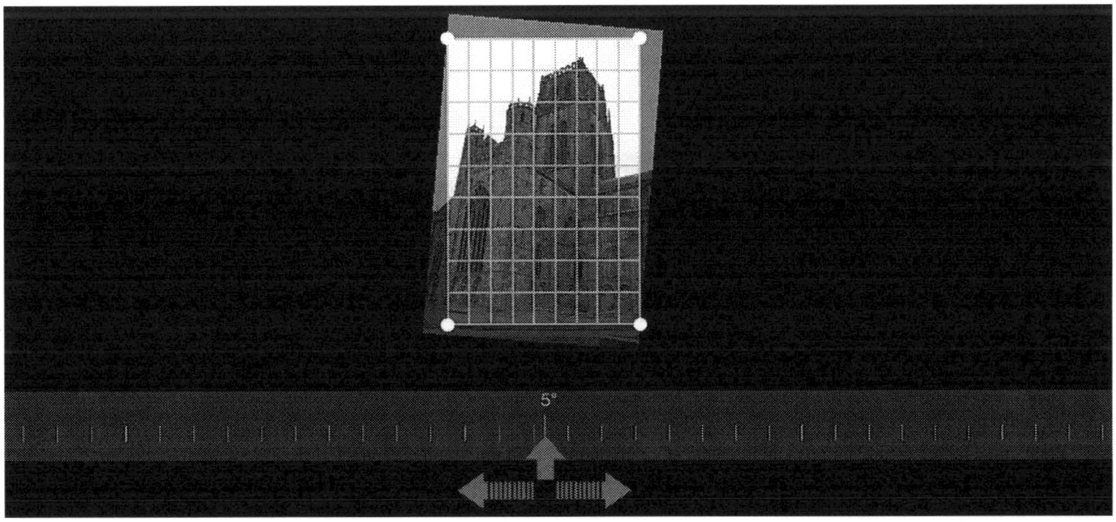

Photo Albums & Collages

You can create albums to keep your photos together, create collages and share them with people.

Creating

Select the photos you want to add to your album - click the 'tick' icon on the top right of the photo. Click the '+' icon on the top right, then select 'album' from the popup menu.

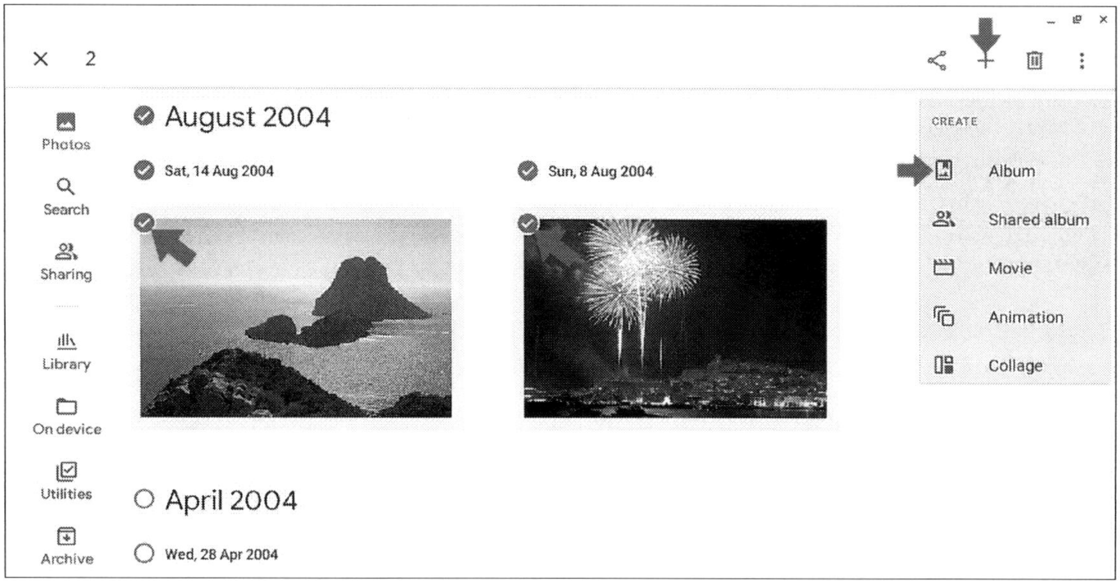

Give your album a name, then click the blue 'tick' icon on the top left of the screen.

You'll find all your albums in your 'album' section of Google Photos. Select 'library' from the panel on the left hand side of the screen.

Collage

A photo collage is a composition made up of various different photographs assembled together. These are useful for posting to social media.

To create a collage, select the photos you want to use from an album or the photos section. Choose six good ones. Click the '+' icon on the top right of the screen. From the drop down menu select 'collage'.

Click the adjustments icon to add a filter, or adjust the colour and brightness.

Click the share icon at the top to post your collage to social media, or send to a friend using email.

You'll find all collages you have created in your albums section.

Sharing Photos

Select the photo(s) you want to share from the photos section in Google Photos.

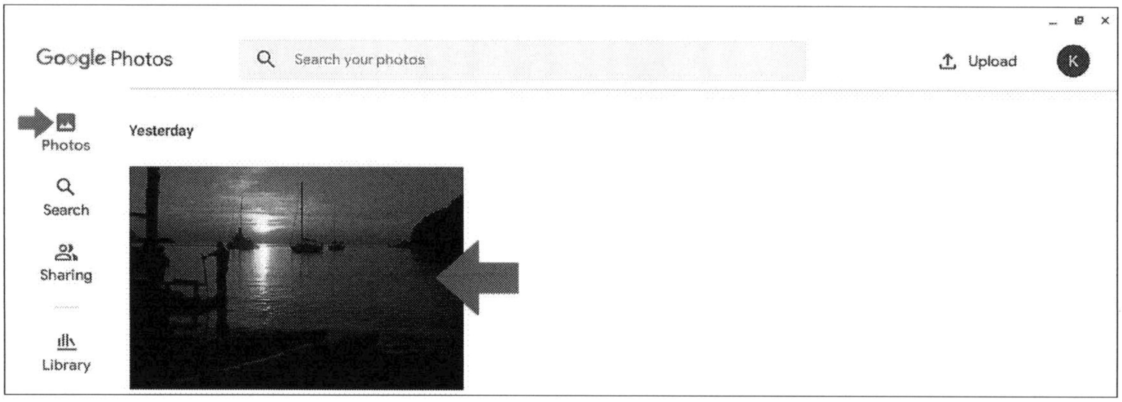

Click the ‘share’ icon on the bottom of the screen.

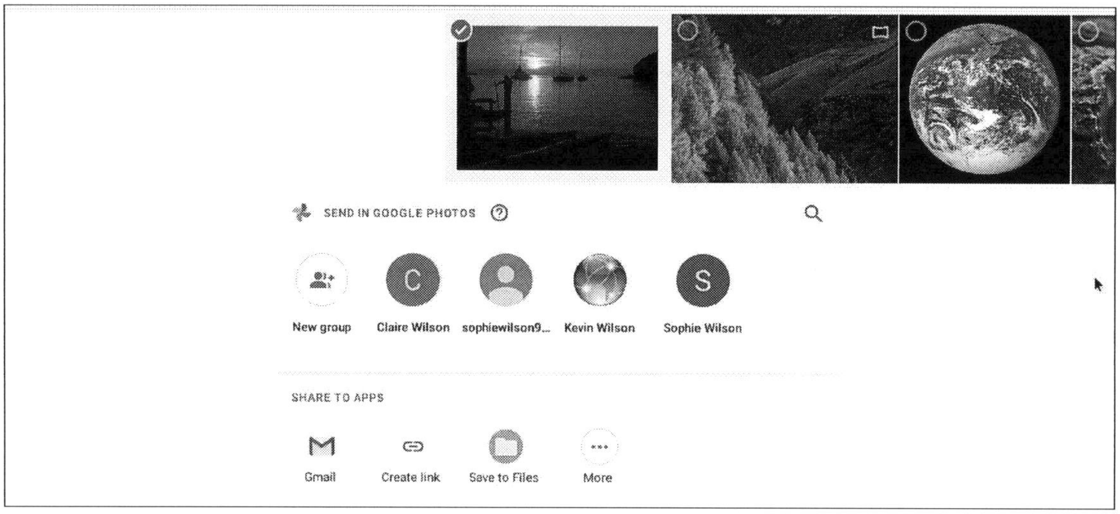

Select the people you want to share the photos with. If their name isn’t there, select an app to send the photo. Eg Gmail.

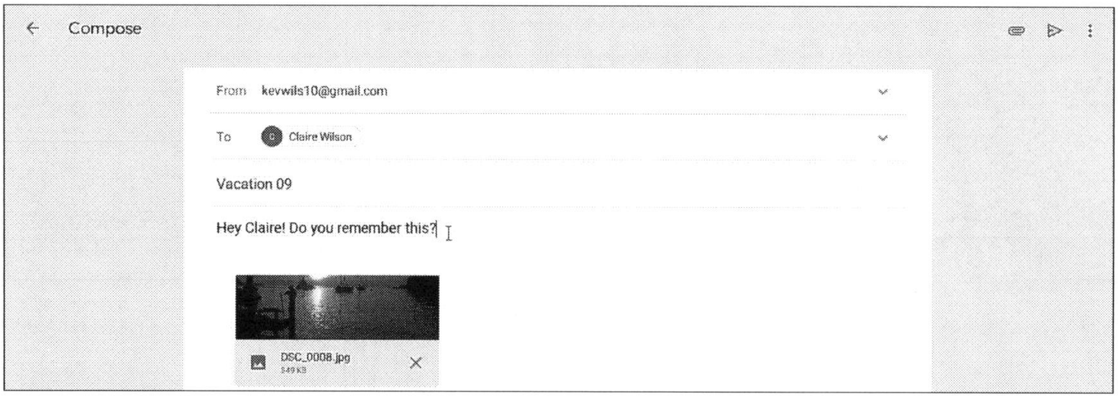

Type in a message if you want to, then click the send icon.

Sharing Albums

You can share an album on social media such as facebook or via email. To do this, select 'library' from the icons on the left hand side of the screen.

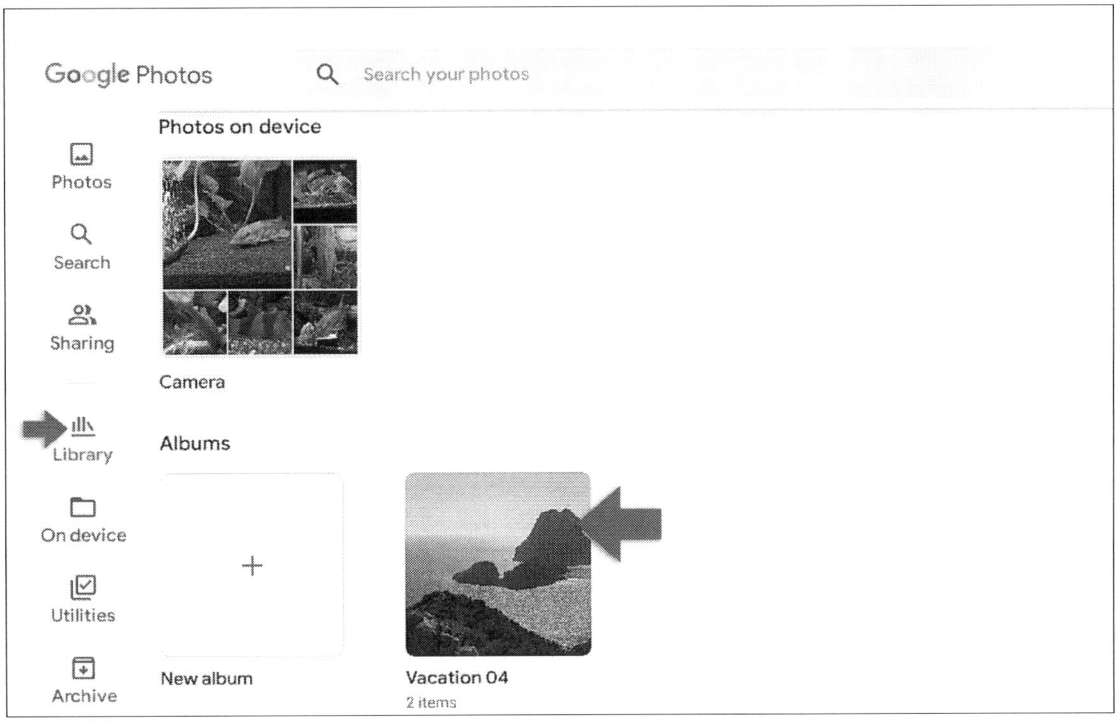

Select the album you want to share.

Click 'share'.

Select the people or person you want to share your album with from your contact list, or enter their email address.

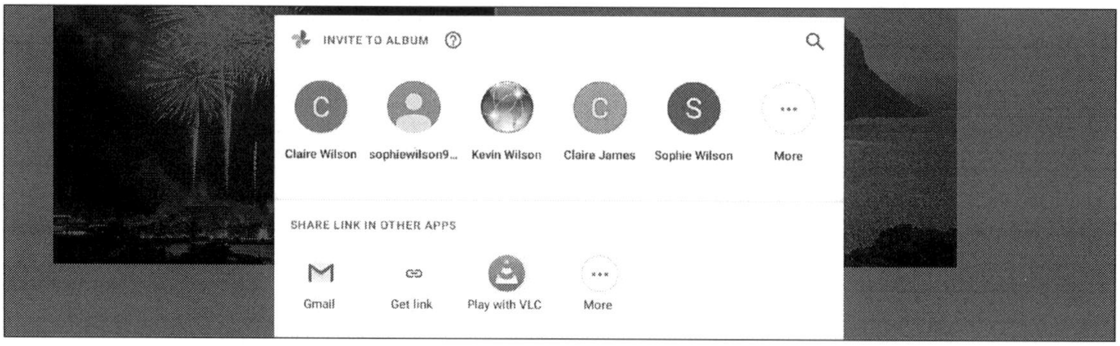

Click 'send' on the bottom right.

This will send an email invitation with a link to your album.

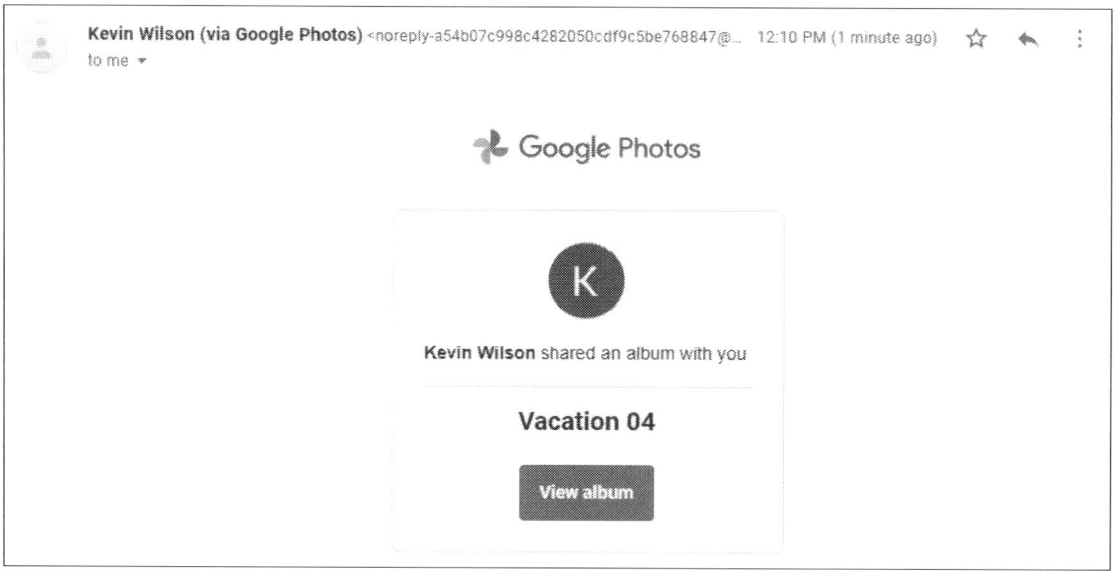

Spotify

You can stream millions of songs from spotify. To get started, you'll need to download the app from the Google Play Store. Open the Play Store and search for 'spotify'. Select 'spotify' from the search results.

Click 'install'.

Once downloaded and installed, you can start the spotify app from your app launcher. You'll need to sign up for a free account. Click 'sign up for free' and fill in your details. If you already use spotify, click 'log in'.

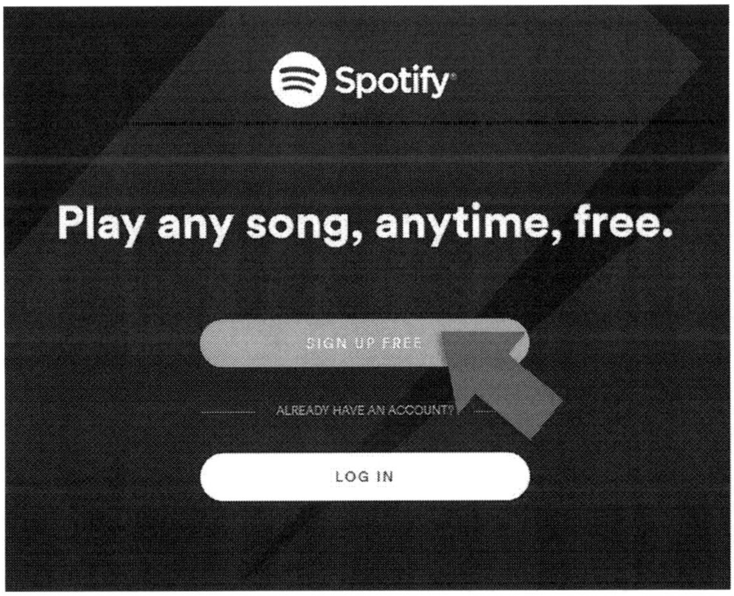

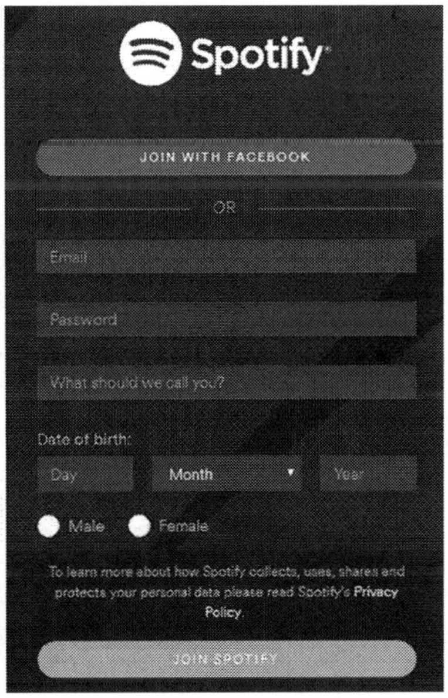

Click 'join spotify' when you're finished.

With spotify, you can search for any song, album or artist you like. Just type it into the search field at the top of the screen.

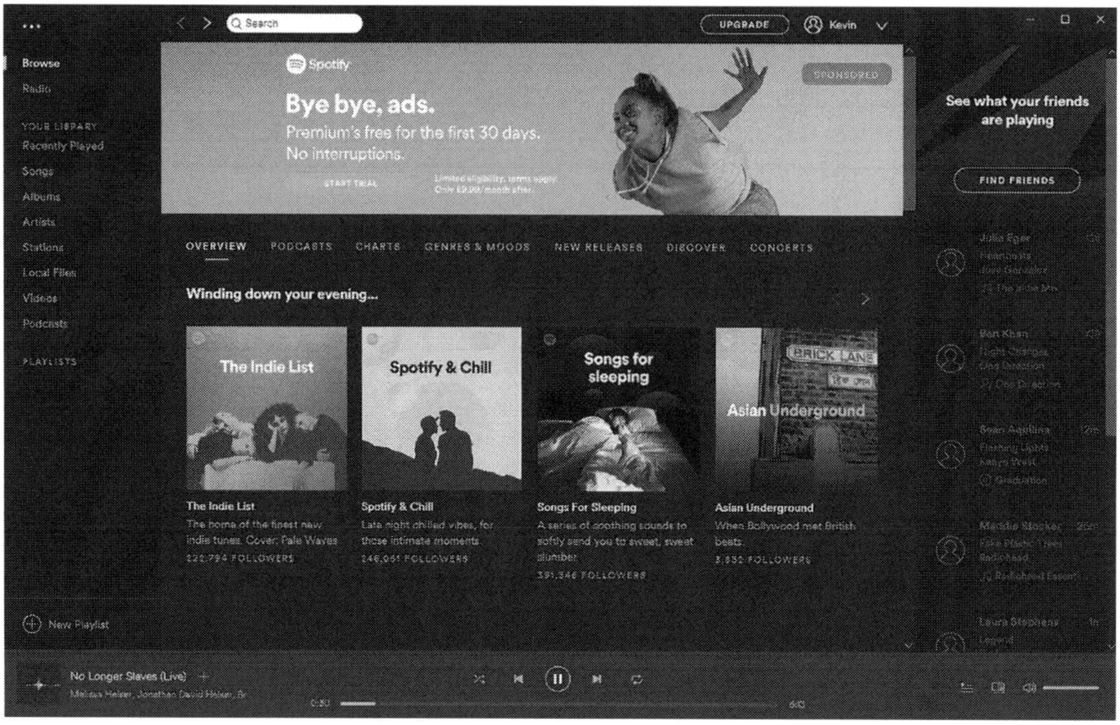

You can scroll down the main page and browse through the genres. Once you've found a song, either by searching or browsing through your favourite genres, you can add them to your library. To do this, click the '+' sign to the left of the track name.

You'll find the tracks in your library on the top left of the main screen

Click on the track to play.

YouTube Music

YouTube Music is free to download and use, however viewers can also subscribe to a premium membership to get an ad-free experience that also allows them to download music to listen offline or without video.

You can download the app from the Google Play Store. Just search for 'youtube music'.

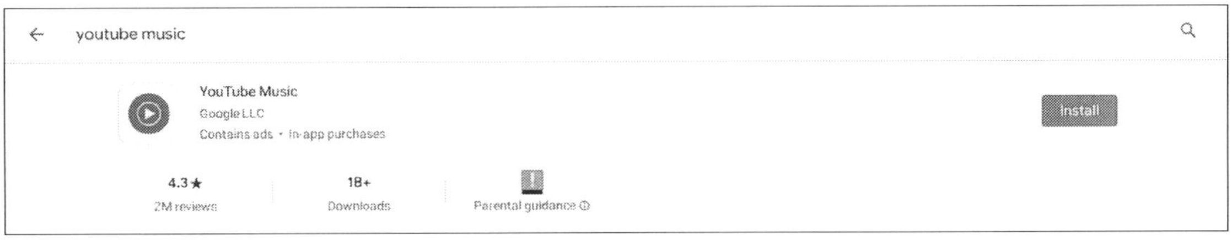

Once you've done that, it will appear on your app launcher.

Once you start the app, you'll land on the home screen. Let's take a look.

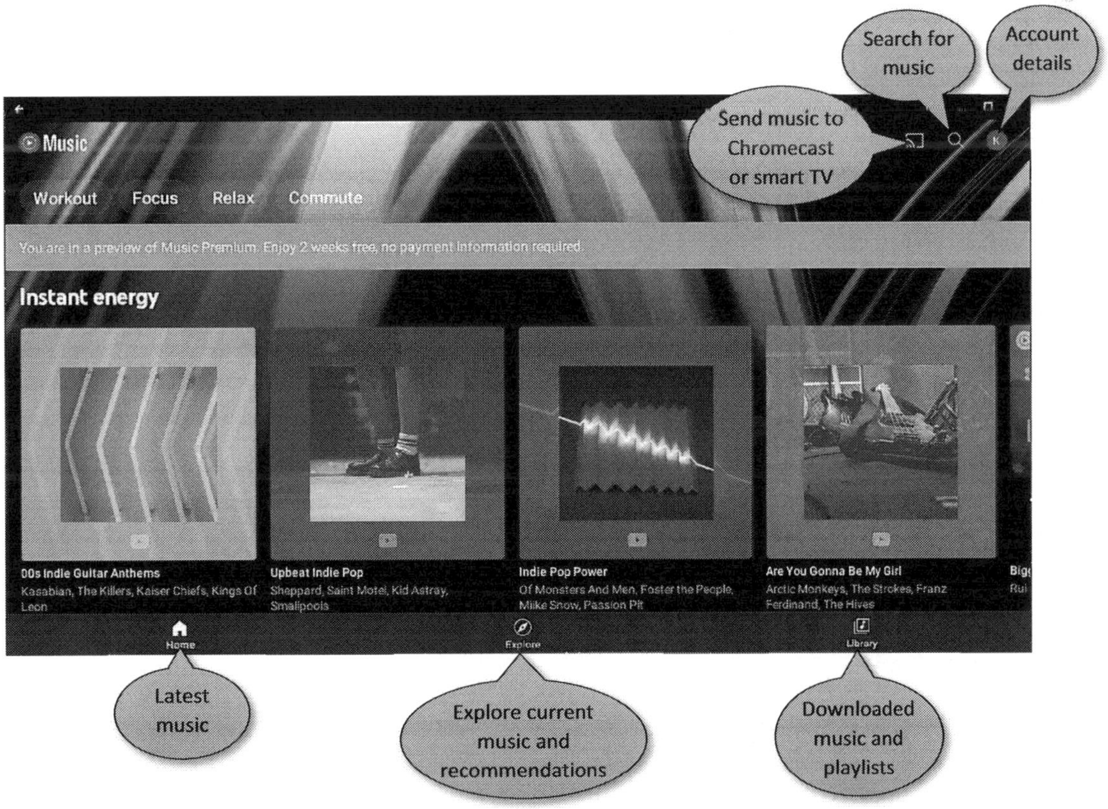

Listening to Music

The easiest way to find music you like is to search for it.

Search

To do this, click the search icon on the top right of the screen.

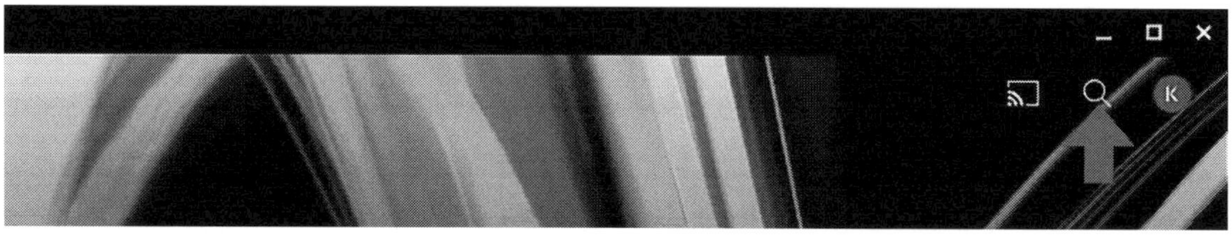

Type in the band name, artist, or song title. Then select from the list to narrow down the search. If you want to view songs click 'songs', if you want to see albums, click 'albums', and so on.

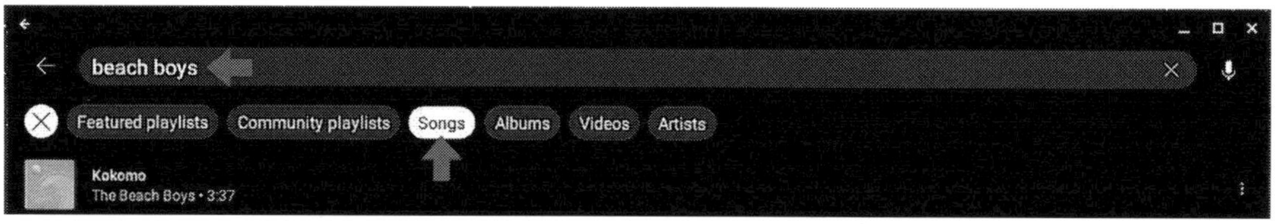

In the list of songs click on one to play.

You'll see the play screen appear.

Add to Playlist

You can create your own playlists. You can create private playlists - ones only you can see, or you can create public playlists you can share with others.

To add a song to a playlist, open the song in they play screen. Right click on the album, then select the 'playlist' icon from the popups.

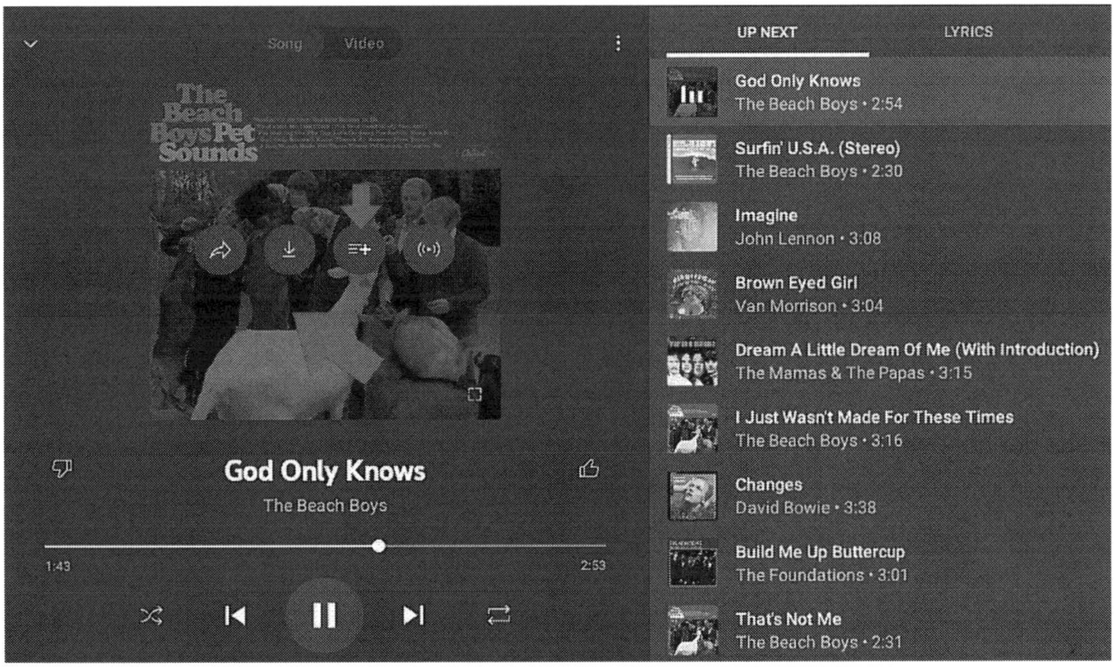

Select the playlist you want to add the song to. If there is no playlist, click 'new playlist'.

Add a name, then select your privacy settings. If you just want to listen to the songs yourself, click private. If you want to share with others, select public.

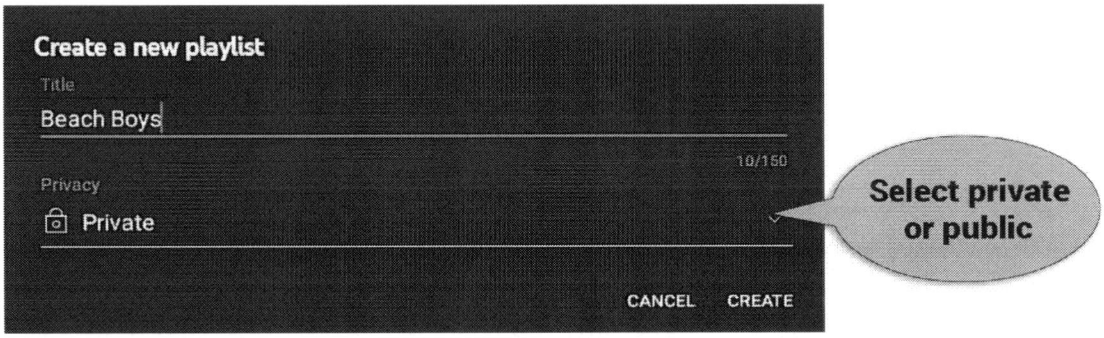

Open Playlist

You'll find your playlists in your library. Click the 'library' icon on the bottom right of the screen.

Scroll down the screen, then select 'playlists'

Click on the playlist you want to listen to.

Click 'play'.

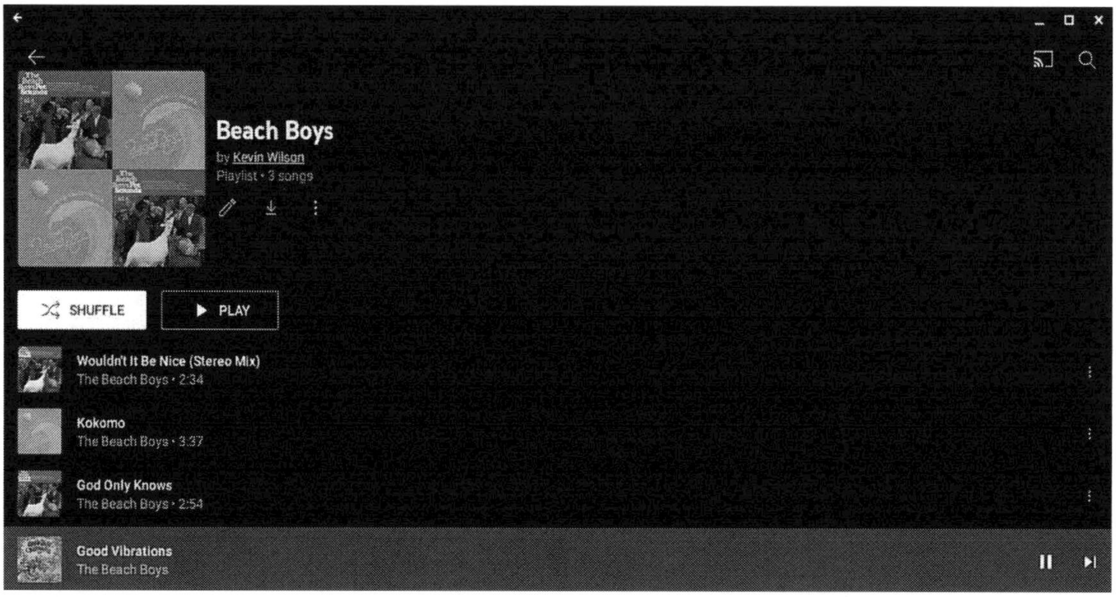

Share a Playlist

If you set your playlist privacy to public, you can share the playlist with other people.

Open your playlist, as shown in the previous section. Click the three dots icon underneath the playlist title. Select 'share' from the menu.

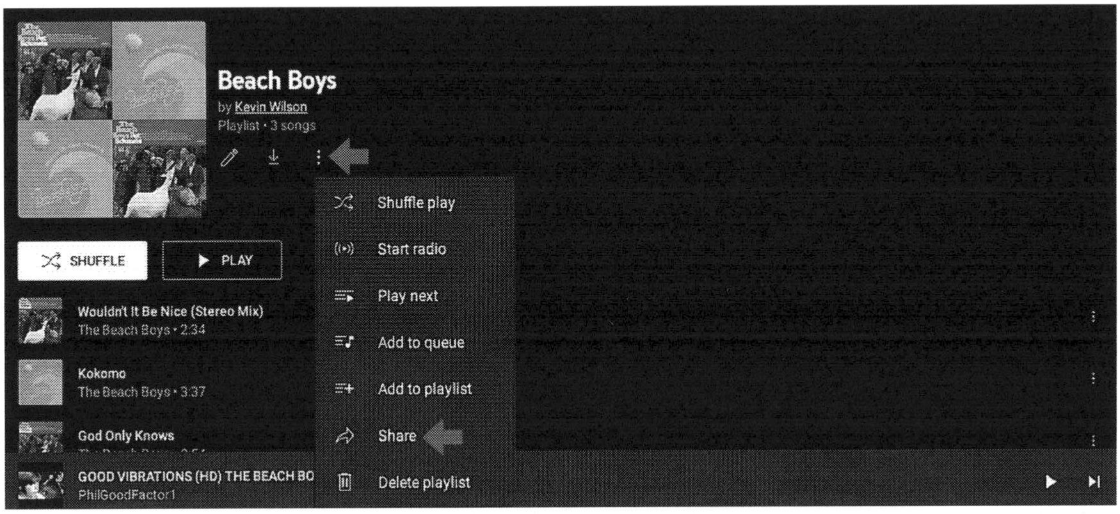

Click 'switch' if your playlist was set to private. Playlists need to be public before you can share them.

Set the privacy setting to 'public', then click 'done' on the top right of the screen.

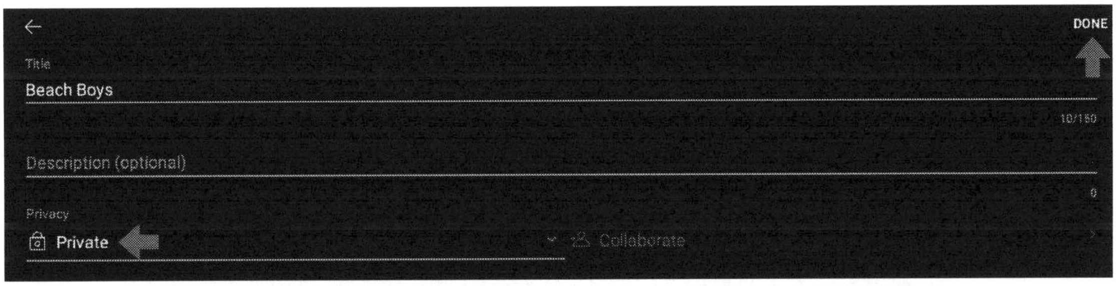

Select the app you want to use to send the link, eg email.

Type the person's email address in Gmail, click send.

YouTube

YouTube is an online video sharing and streaming website that allows users to upload, view, share and comment on videos. It offers a wide variety of user-generated content as well as content from TV channels and other corporate media. You'll be able to search for video clips, music videos, movie trailers, live streams, video blogs, short original videos, educational videos, self help and how-to videos.

Open the Play Store and search for 'youtube'. Select 'youtube' from the search results. Click 'install'.

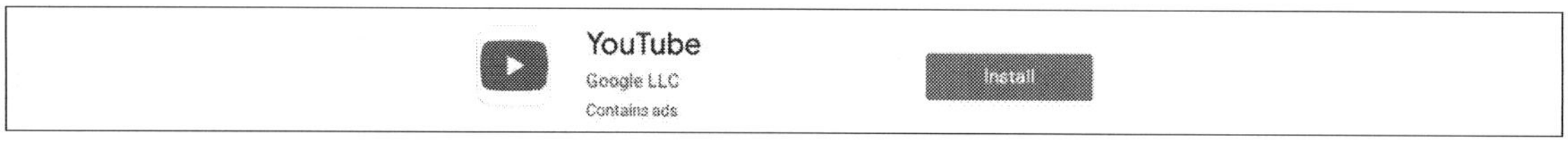

Once downloaded and installed, you can start the youtube app from your app launcher.

Search for any content you want to watch. Click the magnifying glass icon on the top right. Type in your search.

In the search results, click on the thumbnail to view.

Click play icon.

Google Play Movies & TV

Using the play movies app you can purchase or rent movies from the play store.

Click the app launcher icon on the bottom left, then click the arrow in the top middle to open it up fully.

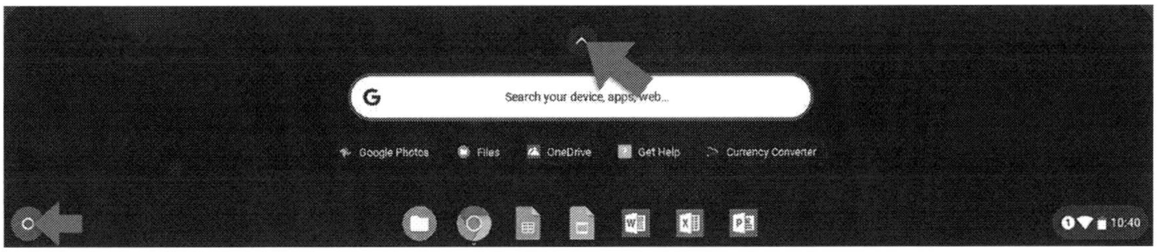

Click the Google play music & TV icon.

Google play movies & TV app will open.

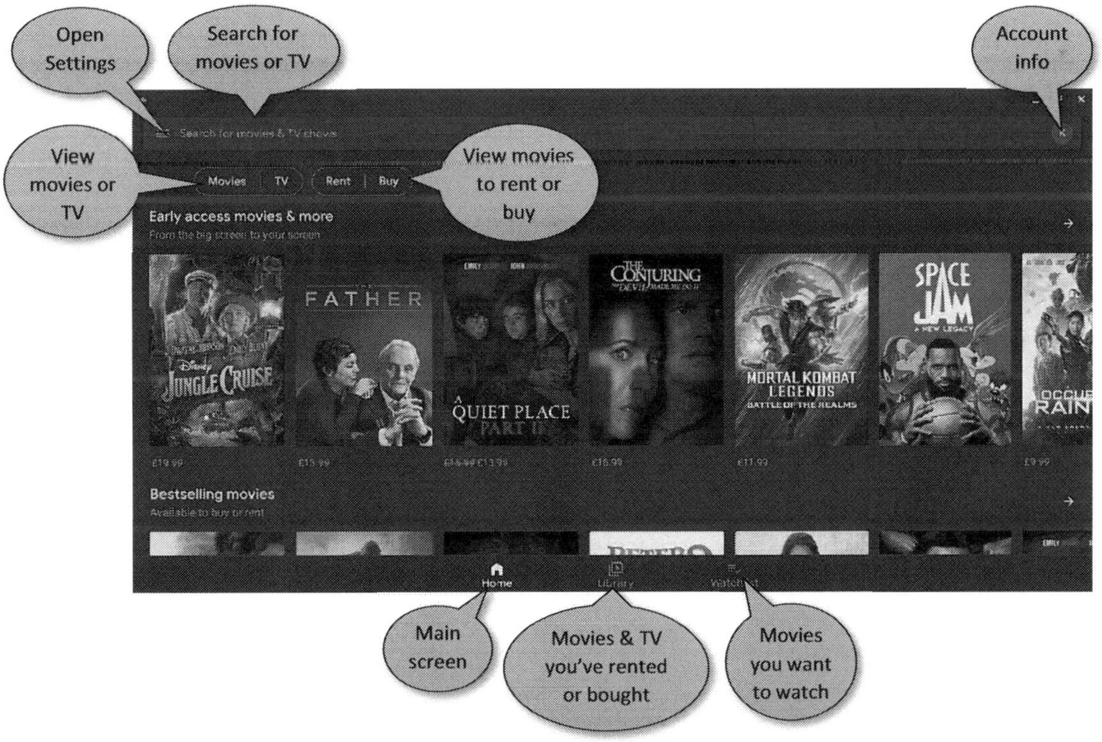

Here you'll see any movies or tv programmes you have downloaded, as well as the latest movies and tv shows for you to buy.

Browsing the Store

To get new movies, you'll need to go the home screen. Here, you can browse through latest releases. You can browse movies, or tv programmes. You can also browse movies or TV programmes that are available to rent or buy.

Scroll down the home page, you'll see a list of genres you can browse by: action, comedy, sci-fi etc.

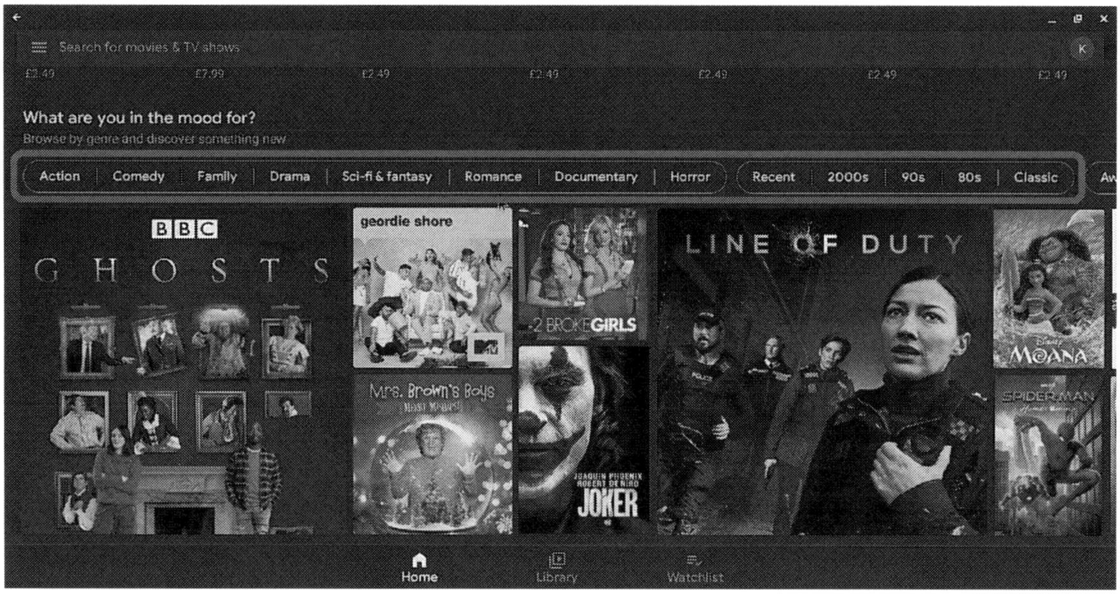

Click on one of the movies, or TV programmes to view details

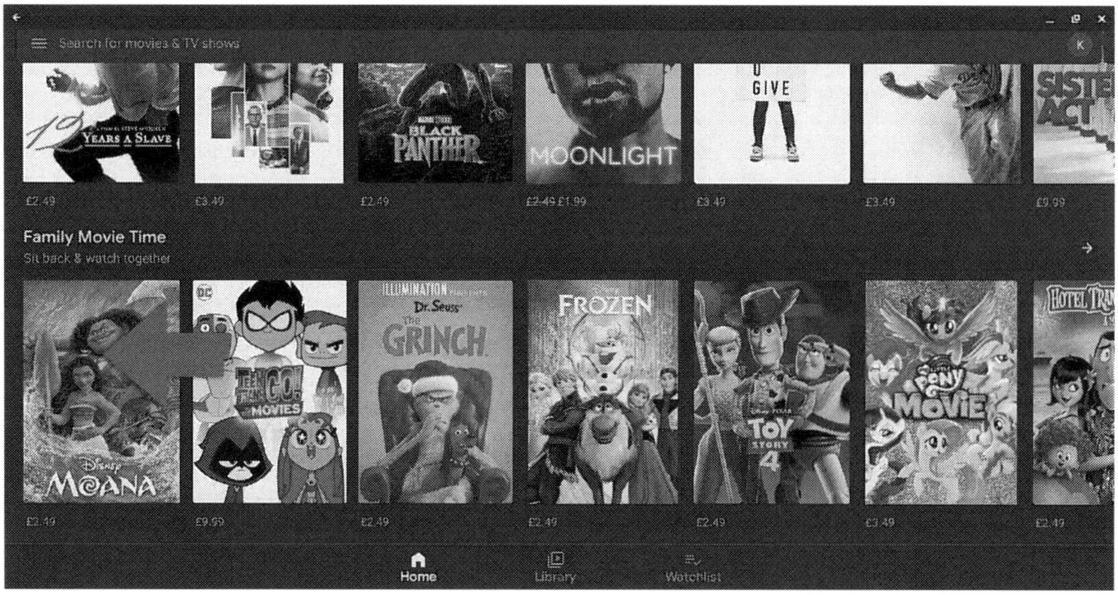

Here, you can watch a trailer, view a write up of the movie.

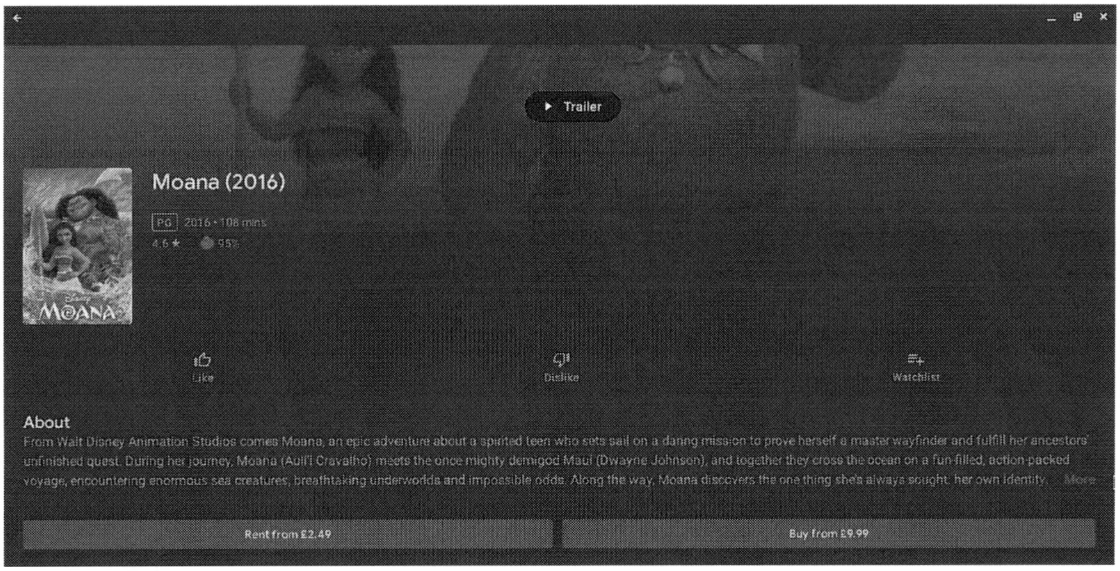

To rent the movie, click 'rent', to buy it click 'buy'. You'll need to add a payment method to do this.

Select the quality you want. If your Chromebook can play back HD quality, or you intend to watch the movie on an external screen or projector then Choose HD. If not, choose SD.

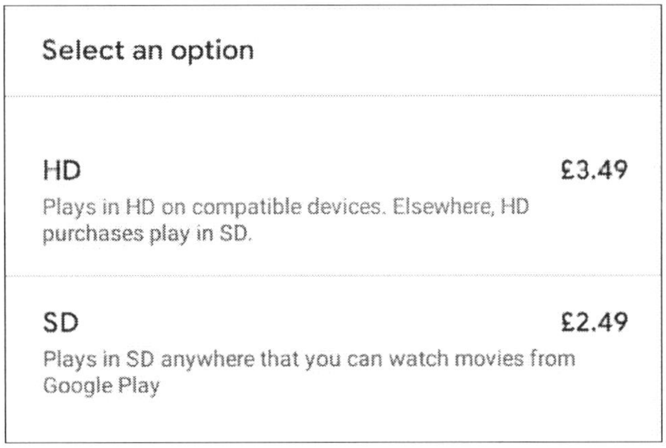

You'll find your movie in your library.

Searching for Movies or TV Programmes

To search for movies or TV programmes, use the search field at the top of the screen.

Type in the name of the movie, TV programme, or actor.

Select the movie from the search results.

Here, you can watch a trailer, view a write up of the movie.

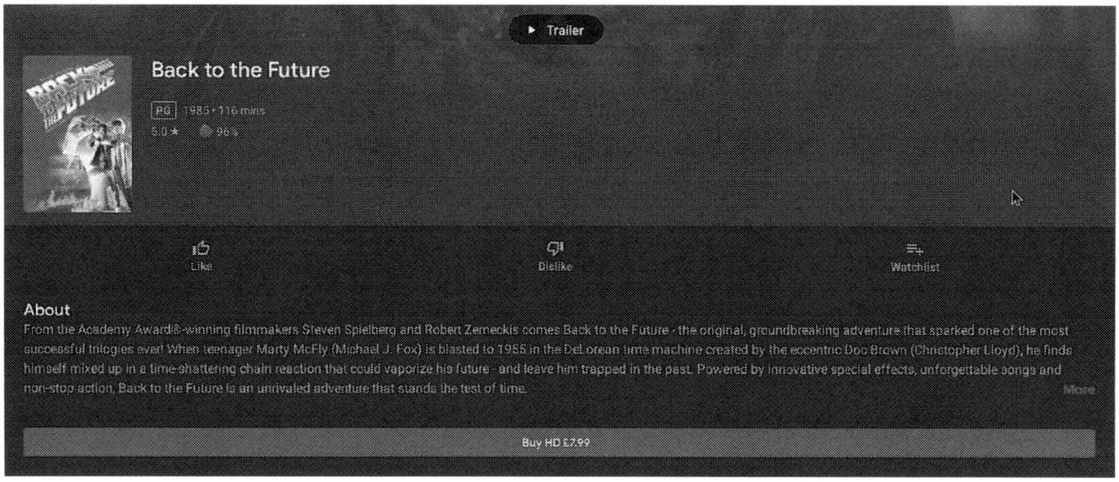

To rent the movie, click 'rent', to buy it click 'buy'. You'll need to add a payment method to do this.

Select the quality you want. If your Chromebook can play back HD quality, or you intend to watch the movie on an external screen or projector then Choose HD. If not, choose SD.

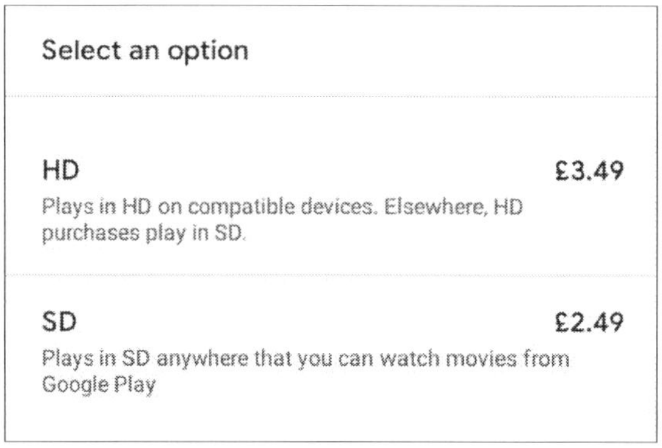

You'll find your movie in your library.

Watching Movies

Once you've rented or purchased your content, you'll find it in the 'library' section of the app.

Click the thumbnail cover of the movie you want to watch.

On the movie details page, click 'play' to start your movie.

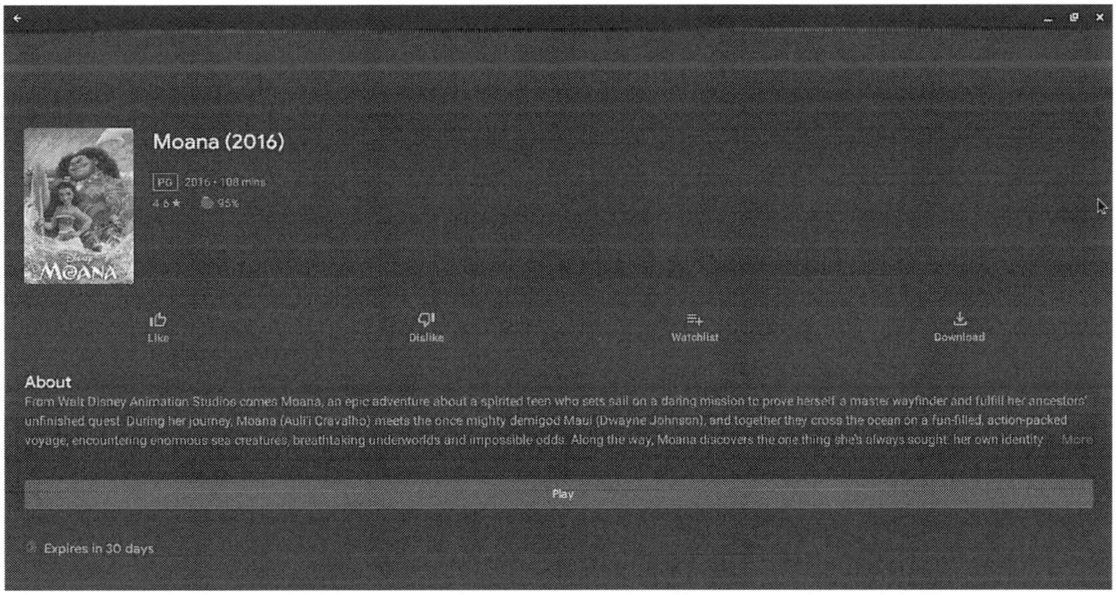

To watch the movie, you'll need a good internet connection. If your connection isn't that good or if you want to watch the movie offline, click 'download'.

Press the full screen button on the keyboard, then enjoy your movie.

You can also watch your movie to a TV or Projector, you can connect to it using an HDMI cable, and watch your movie on a big screen.

Netflix

Netflix is a subscription-based streaming service that offers an online library of films and television programs. A free trial is available but you'll need to sign up and subscribe to the service for £8.99 a month.

Open the Play Store and search for 'netflix'. Select 'netflix' from the search results.

Click 'install'

Once downloaded and installed, you can start the netflix app from your app launcher.

When you start netflix, you'll need to either sign up for an account or log in with an existing account.

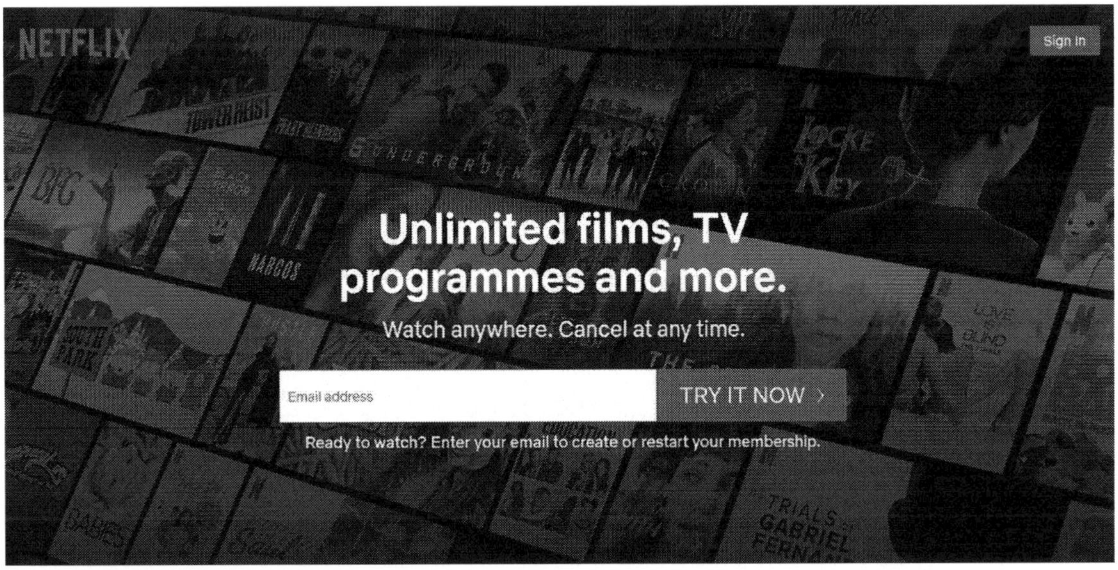

To sign up, click 'try it now', then follow the instructions on the screen to open your account.

You can browse through TV Shows and Films. Use the categories along the top of the screen, scroll down the home page to view latest films and TV shows. Click the one you want to watch.

You can also search for content using the search icon on the top right.

Type in your search. Click on a TV show or movie in the search results.

Here, you'll see details of the show or movie. Select an episode, click the play button to play.

If you have a smart TV or Chromecast, click the cast icon to watch the film on your TV.

Prime Video

Prime Video is a streaming video service provided by Amazon and is included with an Amazon Prime membership.

Open the Play Store and search for 'prime video'. Select 'prime video' from the search results. Click 'install'.

Once downloaded and installed, you can start the amazon prime video app from your app launcher.

Sign in with your amazon account.

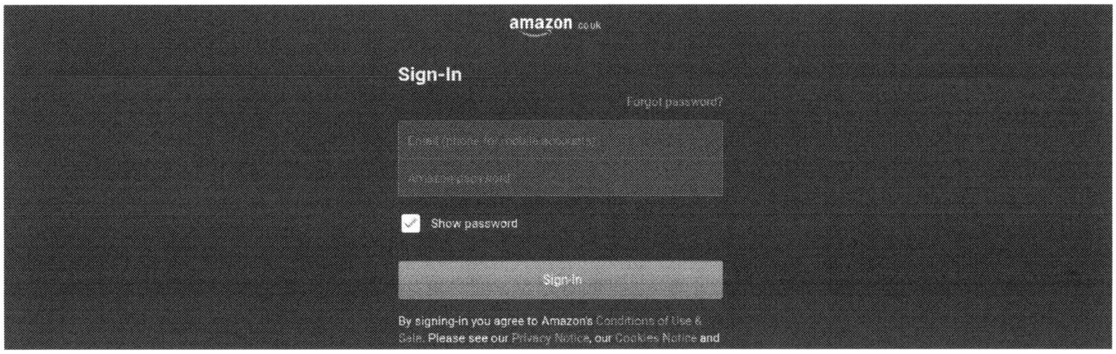

Here, you can rent movies, watch TV shows, just select what you want to watch.

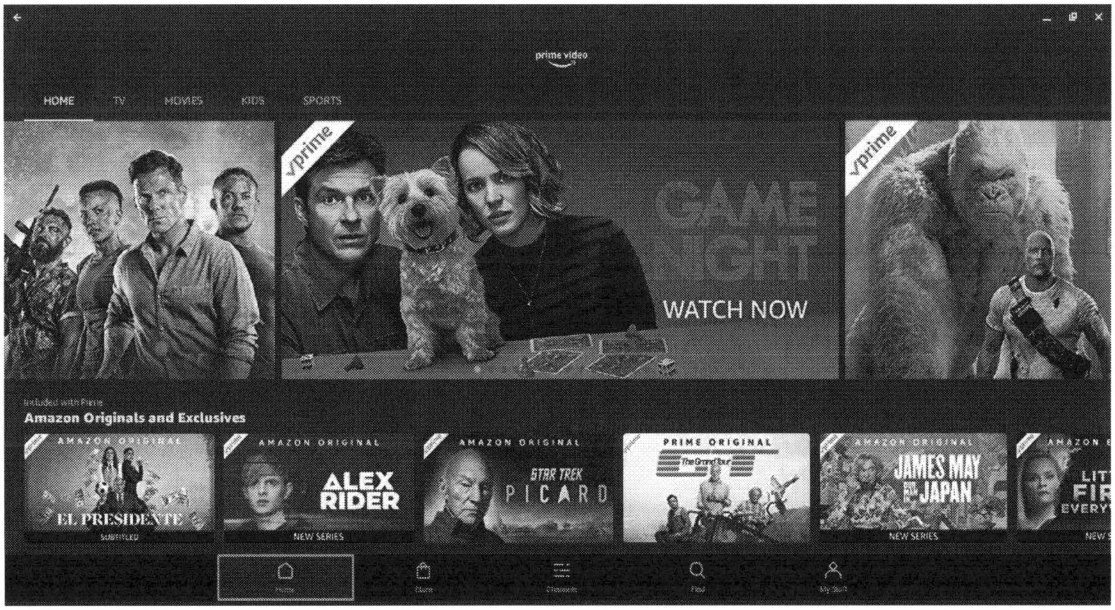

Projectors & TVs

You can hook your ChromeBook up to a digital projector or television. You can also cast your video wirelessly to a ChromeCast device plugged into your TV or projector.

HDMI

Your ChromeBook has an HDMI port on the side that will enable you to connect to a TV or projector. Most modern TVs & projectors will have at least 1 HDMI port on the back.

You can buy an HDMI cable from most electronic stores and online. An HDMI cable looks like the one below.

Plug one end into an HDMI port on your TV or projector, then plug the other end into the HDMI port on your ChromeBook.

ChromeCast

To use ChromeCast, first you'll need to buy a ChromeCast device, and plug it into an HDMI port on your TV or projector.

With ChromeCast you can stream from Netflix and YouTube, as well as any movie, TV show, or app from the Google Play Store. You can also use it to stream anything from Chrome browser on your ChromeBook.

Both your ChromeCast device and your ChromeBook will need to be on the same wifi network for it to work.

To cast a video, open the Google Play Movies & TV app.

Select the movie you want to watch.

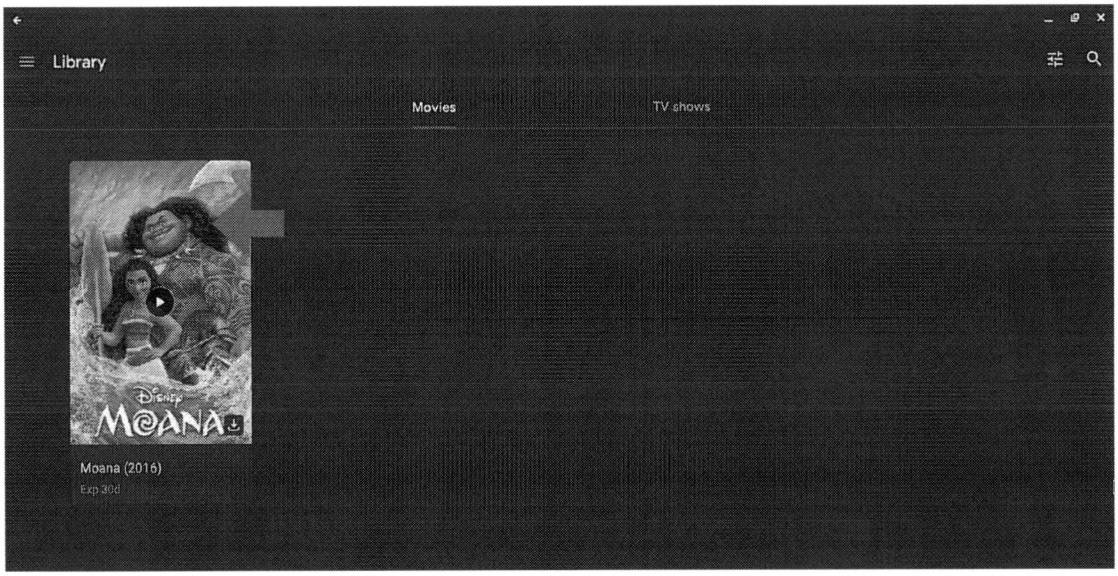

Click 'play' on the summary screen.

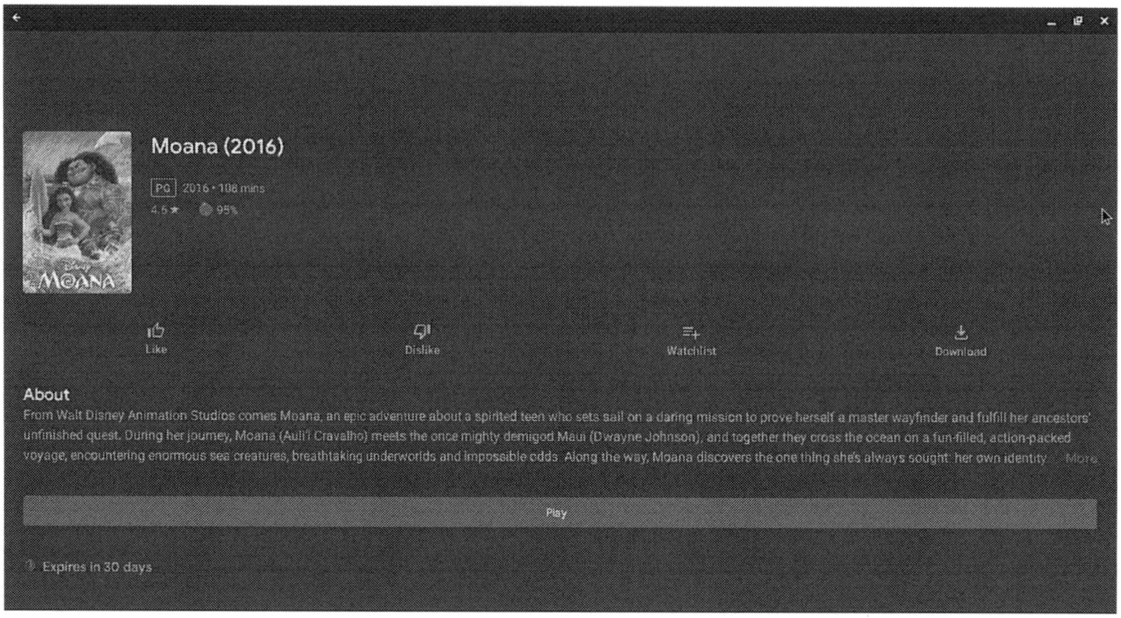

As you hover your mouse over the video, you'll see some icons. Tap the 'cast' icon on the top right hand side of the screen, then select your Chromecast device from the device list.

You can do the same for any movie or TV show you have downloaded from the Google Play Store.

The cast icon will only appear if your Chromecast device is plugged in, powered on, and connected to the same wifi network as your Chromebook.

Google Play Books

With the books app you can buy and read ebooks in a wide variety of different genres from the play store.

Click the app launcher icon on the bottom left, then click the arrow in the top middle to open it up fully.

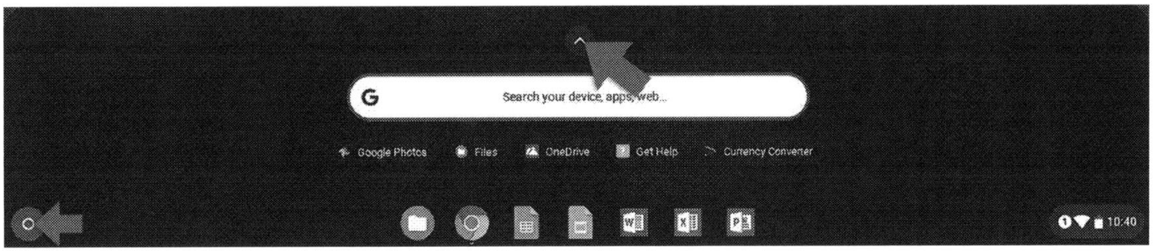

Click the Google play books icon.

Google play books will open up on the main screen.

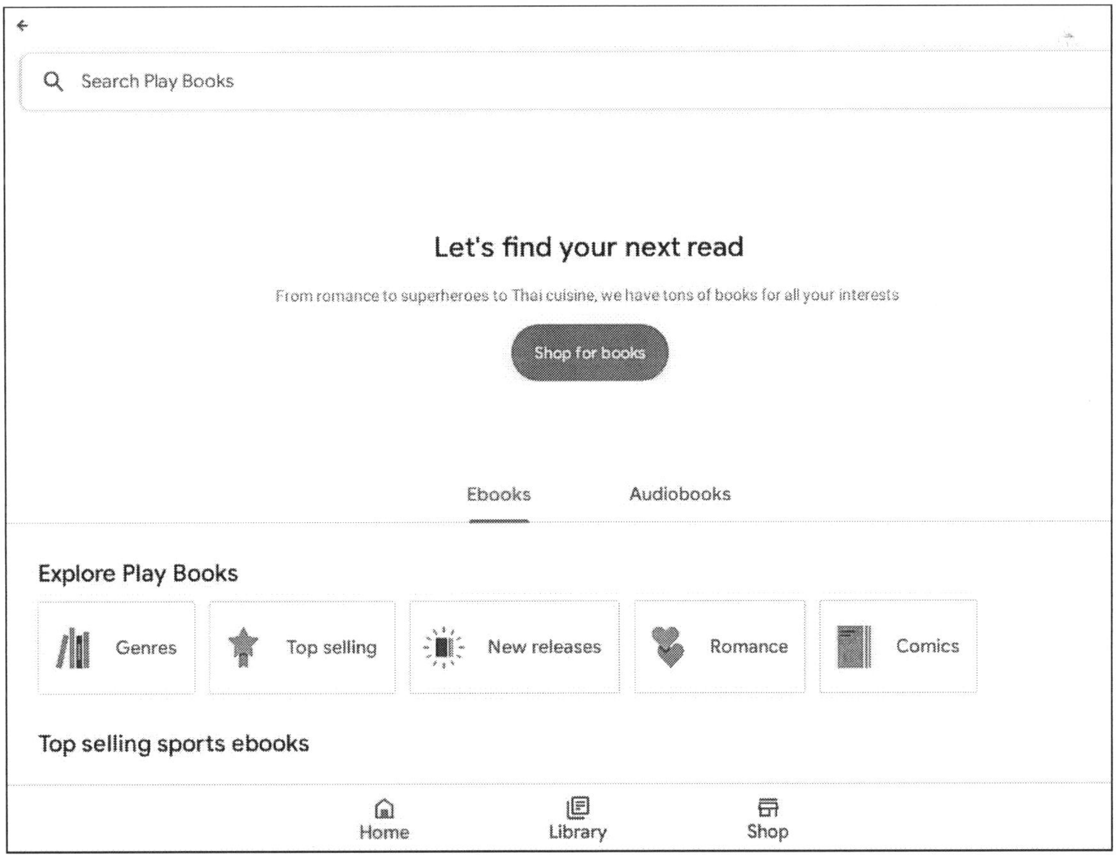

Downloading eBooks

To download new eBooks, click 'shop' on the bottom right of the screen.

From here, you can browse through the latest releases and best selling books in various genres.

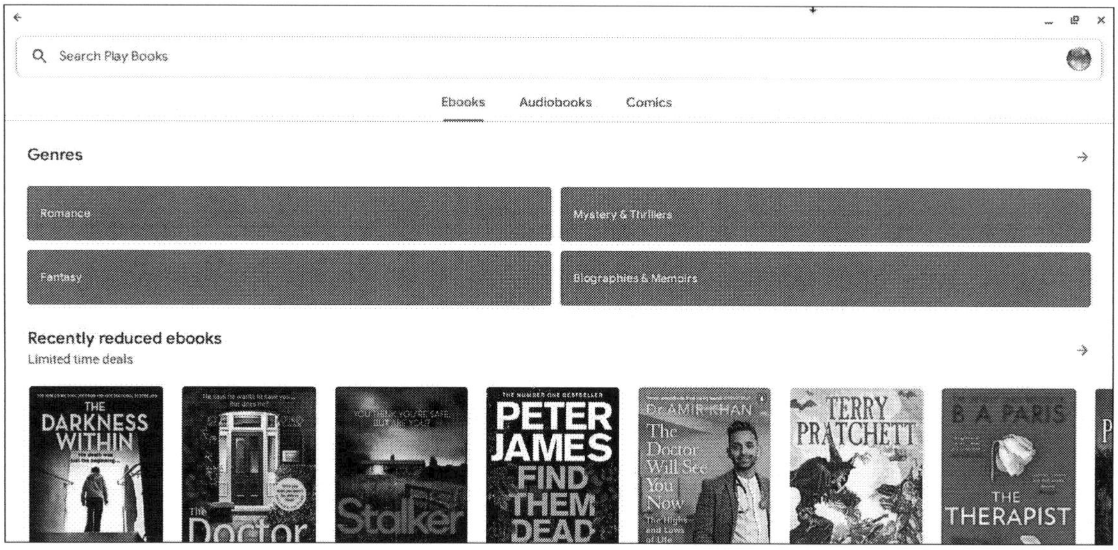

You can also use the search field at the top of the screen to find book titles or authors you want. Press enter on your keyboard to execute the search.

Browse through the search results, click on a book cover thumbnail to view details of the book.

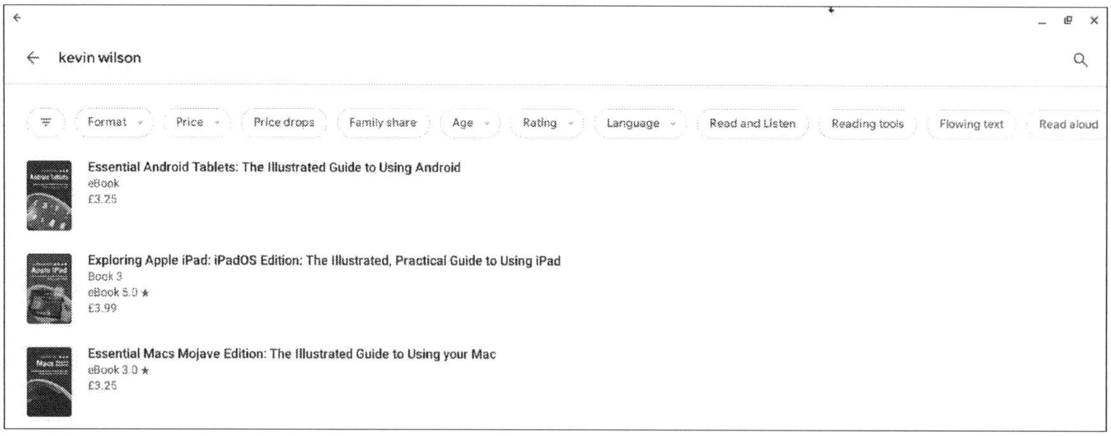

From here you'll be able to read a write up of the book, see reviews and other technical information. Click 'free sample' to read a sample of the book, or click the price tag, to buy and download the book.

Select your payment method if needed, then click 'buy ebook' to confirm.

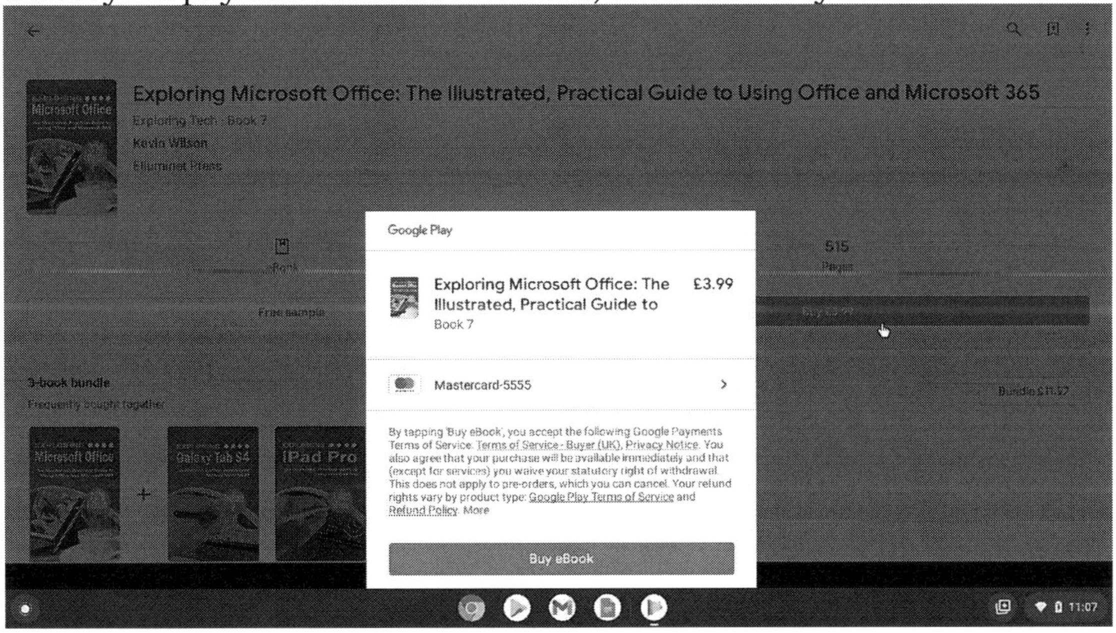

Click 'read' to start reading your book

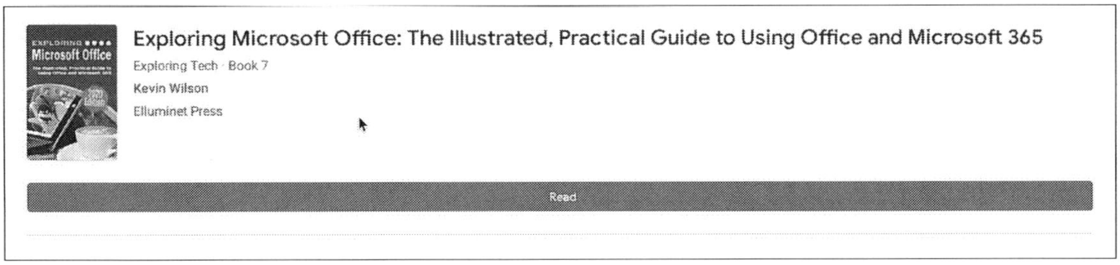

Library

Open Google Play Books if you haven't already done so, click 'library' on the bottom of the screen.

Here, you'll find the books you've downloaded. Click on the book cover to open it up.

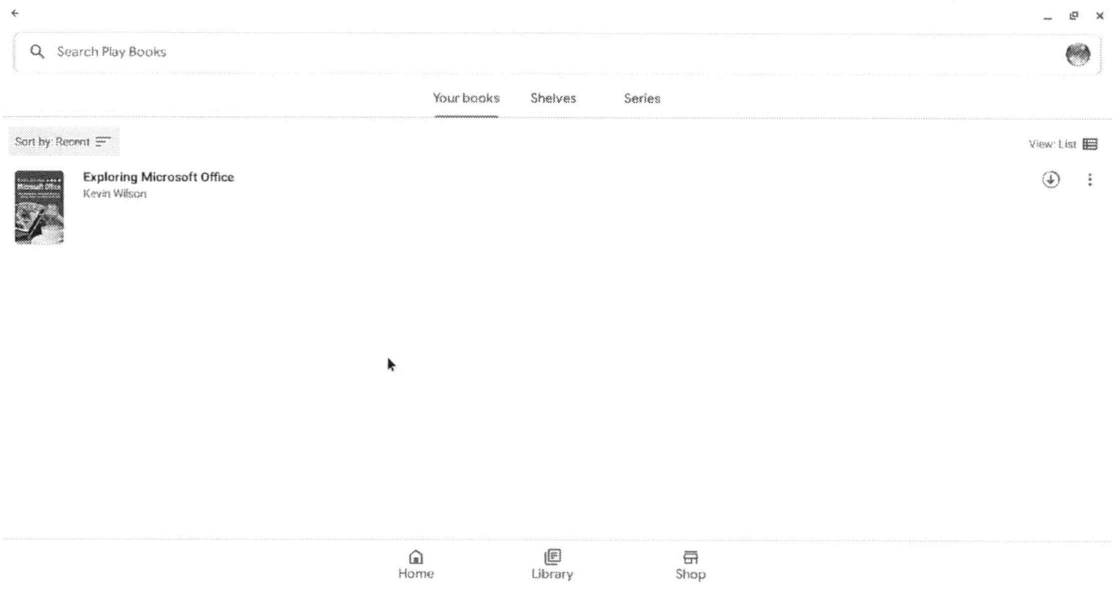

Swipe with two fingers left or right on the trackpad to turn the pages.

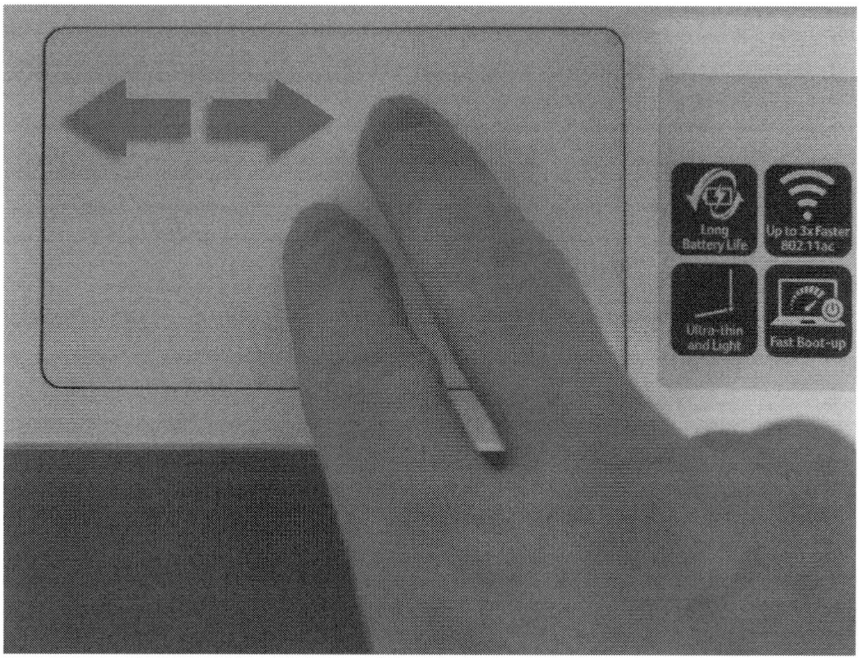

Click on a page to open up the options. On the top right, you can search for keyboards, or change the text size.

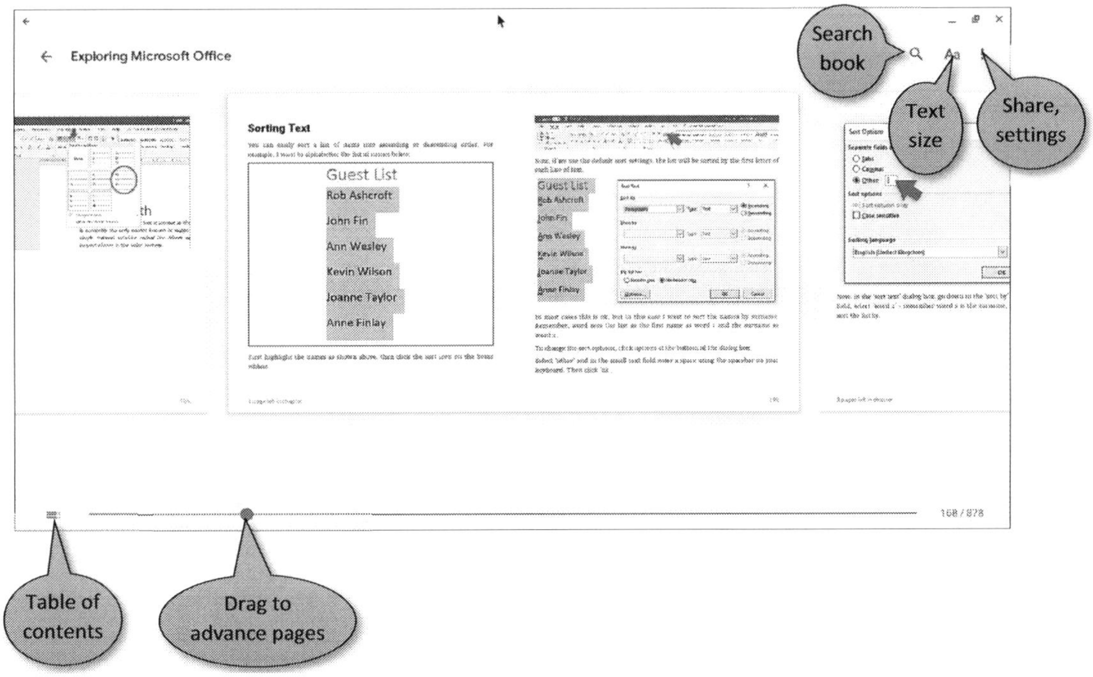

On the bottom left, you can open up the table of contents, bookmarks or notes. You can drag the blue slider to advance pages.

Right click on a word, here you can add a note, translate the word, search the book for the word, or highlight the word in a colour.

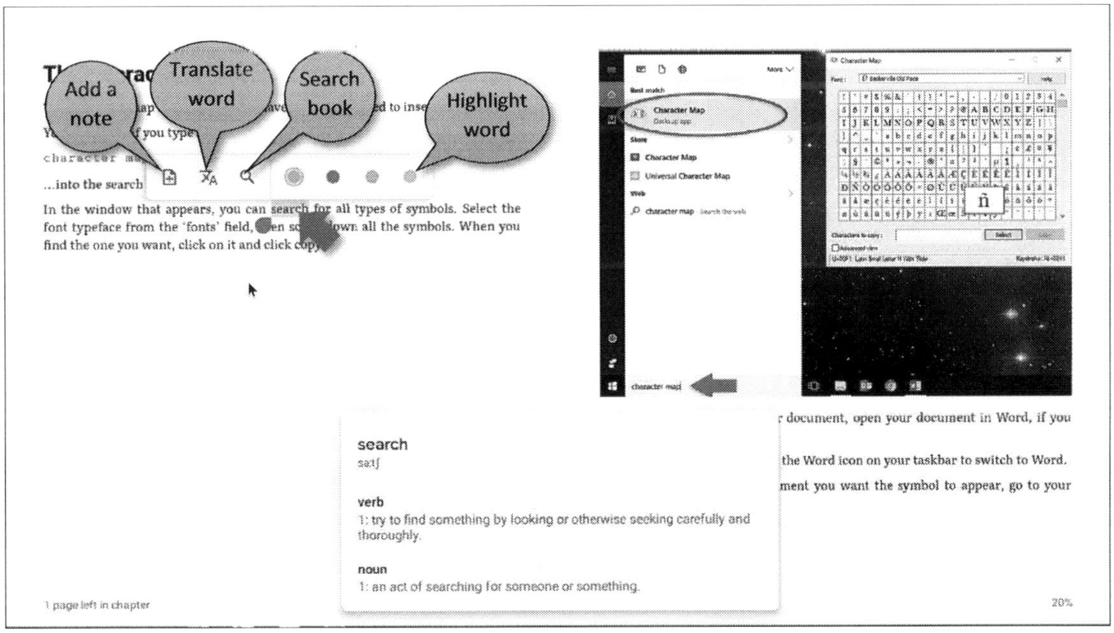

Underneath you'll see a definition of the word you've selected. You'll find a list of all your notes in the notes section of the table of contents.

9 Google Docs

Google Docs is an online word processor much like Microsoft Word and is included as part of a free, web-based office suite developed by Google.

Google Docs allows you to do many of the same things as Microsoft Word but lacks some of the more advanced features.

However, Google Docs is a great alternative and works well on a ChromeBook.

In this section, we'll take a brief look at Google Docs. For more detail, check out our other book 'Understanding Google Docs'.

ISBN: 9781913151454

Getting Around Google Docs

I find the best version of Google Docs to use is the web based version rather than the Android Version you might find on your Chromebook. To start the web based version of Google Docs, open your app launcher, then click on Google Chrome.

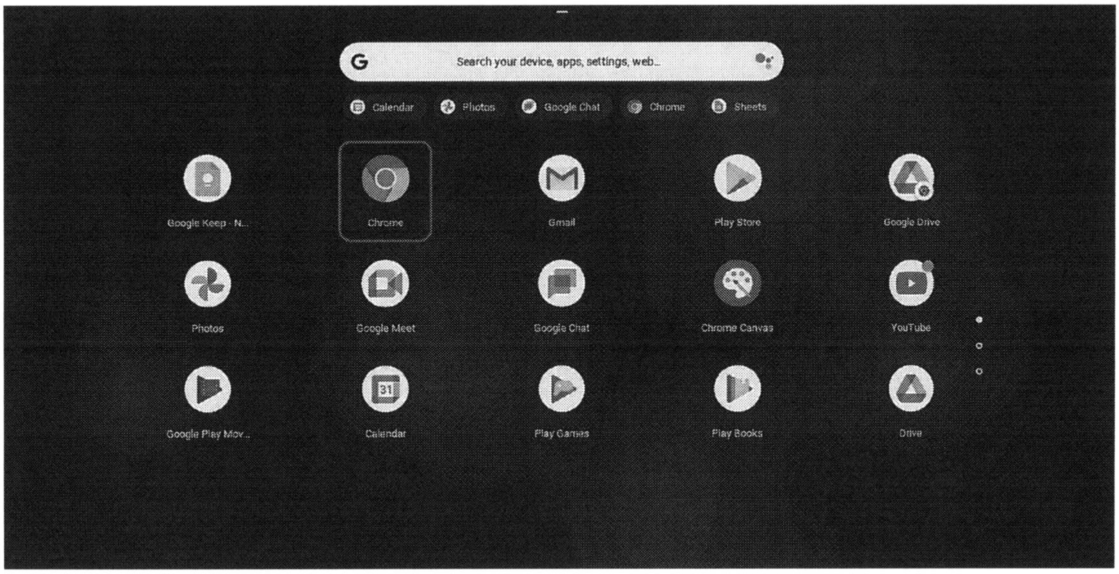

Navigate to the following website:

```
docs.google.com
```

When Google Docs opens, you'll see the documents you have been working on recently. You can click any of thcsc to rc-opcn thcm. To create a new document, click blank on the top left of the screen.

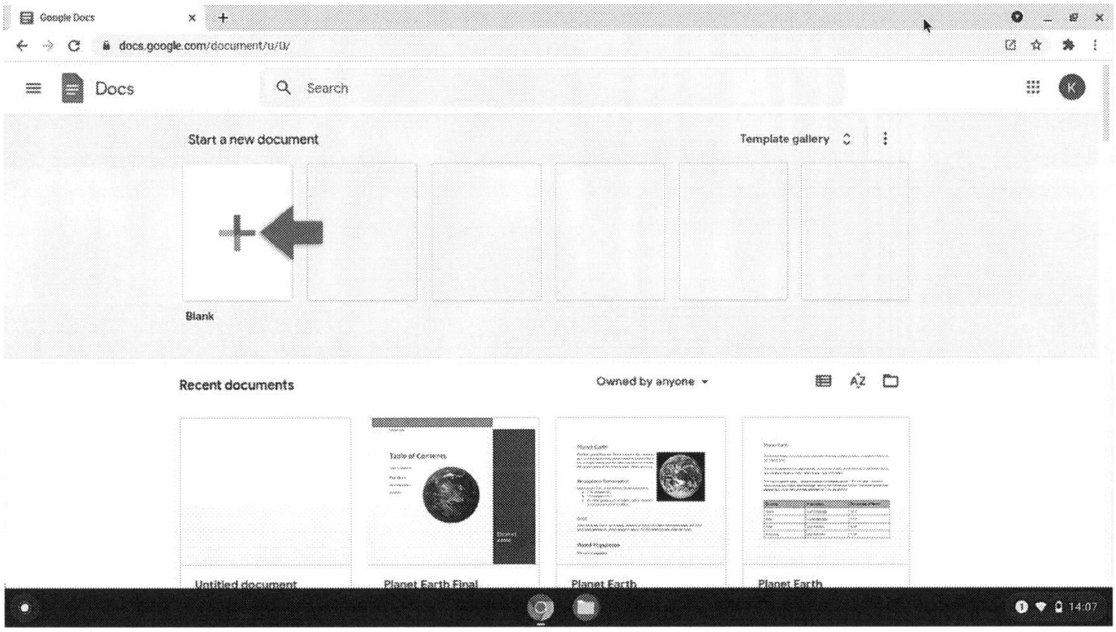

Google Docs will open the main window where you can create your document.

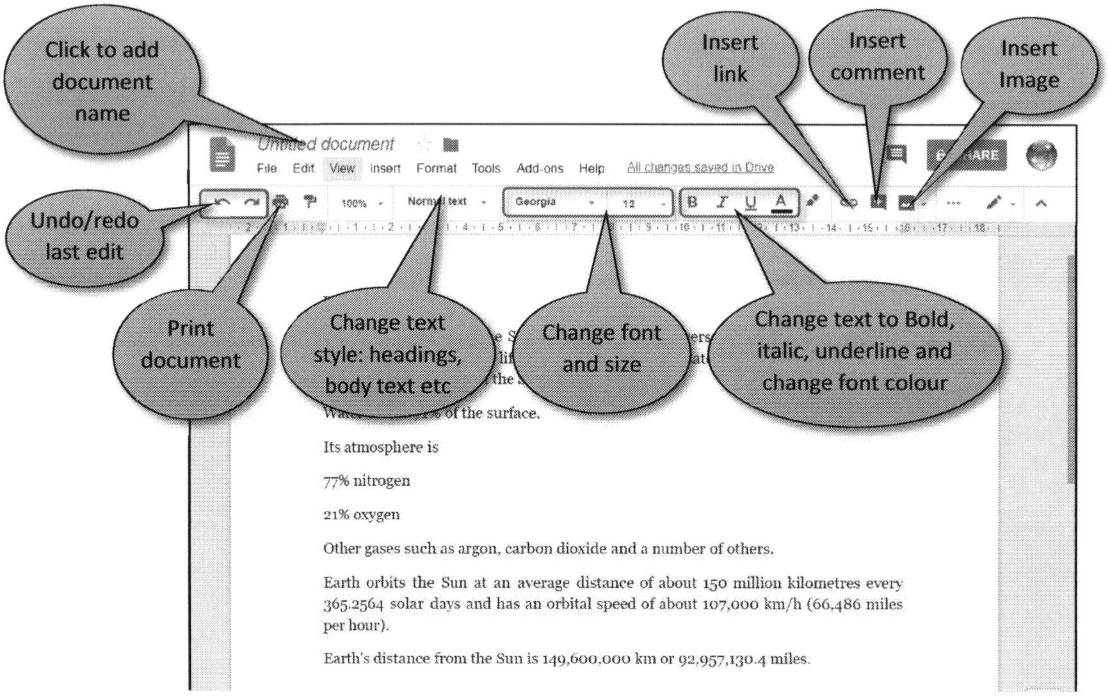

Along the top you'll see the document name. It's a good idea to rename this to something more meaningful that 'untitled document'. Click on the text and type in a name.

Underneath are the menus. This is where you'll find tools that are not represented as icons on the toolbar.

Under the menus you'll see the toolbar. This is where you'll find most of the tools you'll need to create and format your documents.

Using Paragraph Styles

Google Docs has several paragraph styles that are useful for keeping your formatting consistent.

For example you can set a font style, size and colour for a heading or title style...

Headings

To set the styles for a heading or paragraph, just highlight it with your mouse and click the drop down box 'normal text'.

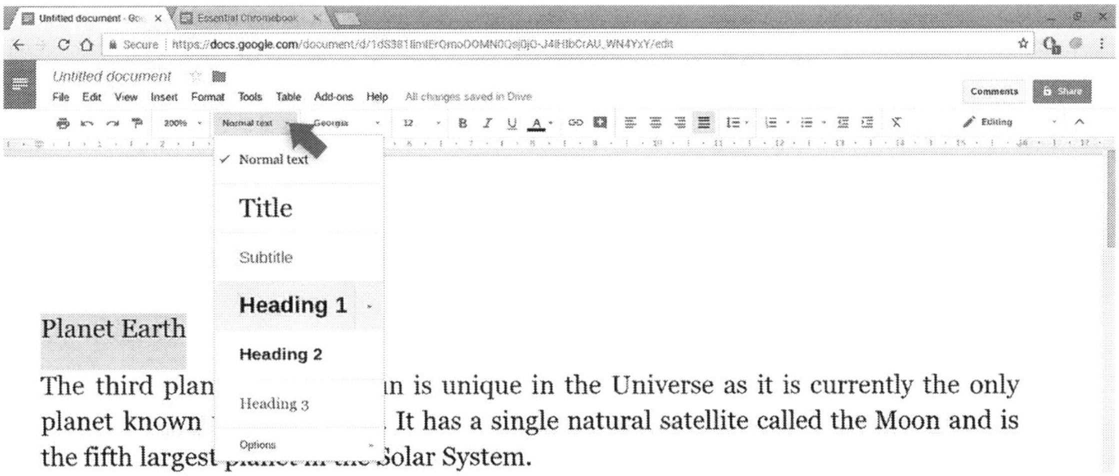

Bold, Italic, Underlined

To make text **bold**, *italic,* or <u>underlined</u>, highlight the text with your mouse and select the bold, italic, or underline icon from the toolbar.

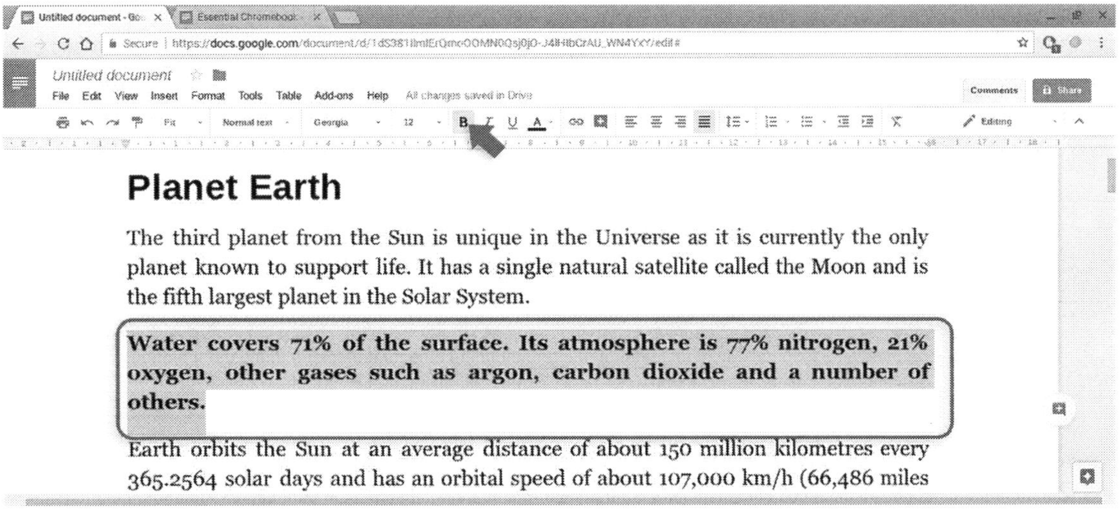

Changing Fonts

Google Docs has a variety of fonts to choose from. To apply a different font to your text, highlight the text, then click the font style drop down box as shown below.

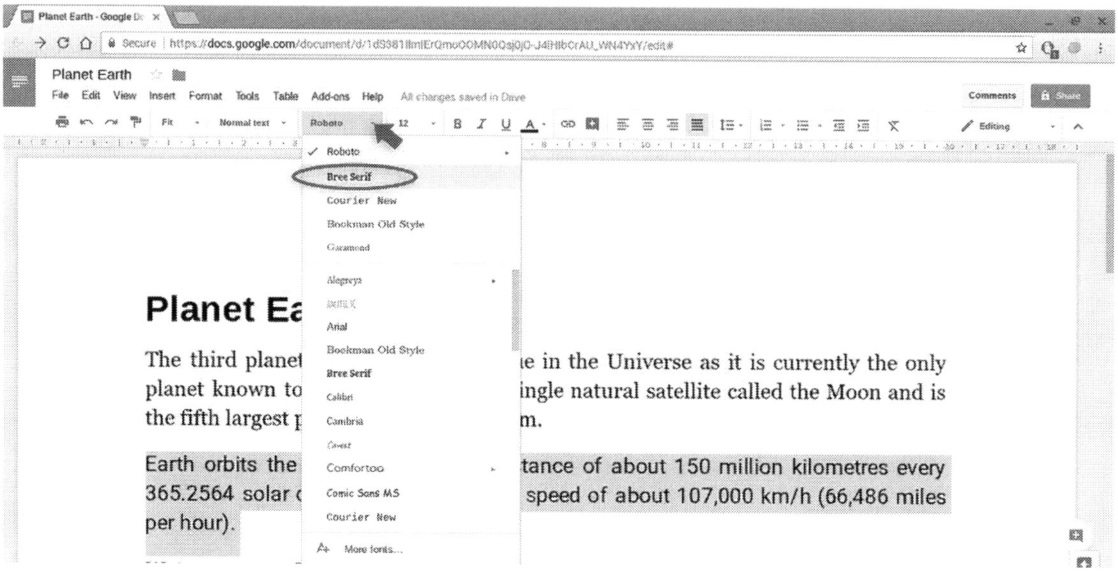

Font Colour

To change the colour of the text, first highlight it with your mouse. In the example below, I want to change the text colour of the second paragraph. To do this, click before the word 'Earth' and drag across the paragraph, to the end after '...miles per hour', to highlight it.

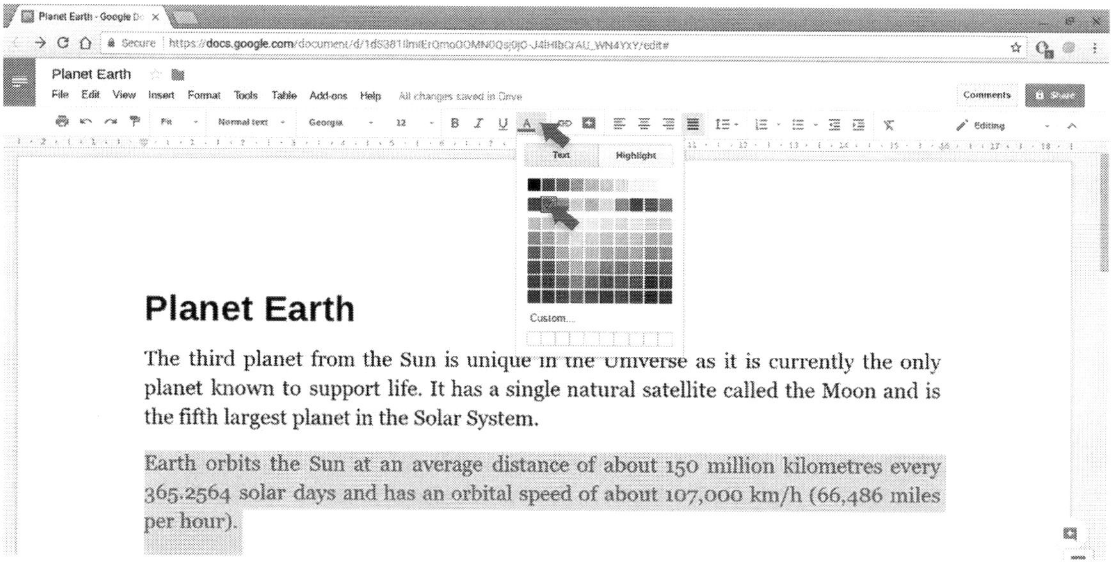

From the toolbar, select the font colour icon and from the drop down choose a colour. In this example I'm using red.

Justify Text

You can align text to different margins: left align, centred, right align, and fully justified.

The third planet from the Sun is unique in the Universe as it is currently the only planet known to support life. It has a single natural satellite called the Moon and is the fifth largest planet in the Solar System.

The third planet from the Sun is unique in the Universe as it is currently the only planet known to support life. It has a single natural satellite called the Moon and is the fifth largest planet in the Solar System.

The third planet from the Sun is unique in the Universe as it is currently the only planet known to support life. It has a single natural satellite called the Moon and is the fifth largest planet in the Solar System.

The third planet from the Sun is unique in the Universe as it is currently the only planet known to support life. It has a single natural satellite called the Moon and is the fifth largest planet in the Solar System.

In this example, I want right justify the first paragraph. This means the text is aligned to the right hand margin. To do this, click before the word 'The' and drag across the paragraph, to the end after '...solar system as shown above to highlight it.

The third planet from the Sun is unique in the Universe as it is currently the only planet known to support life. It has a single natural satellite called the Moon and is the fifth largest planet in the Solar System.

Select the right align icon from the toolbar.

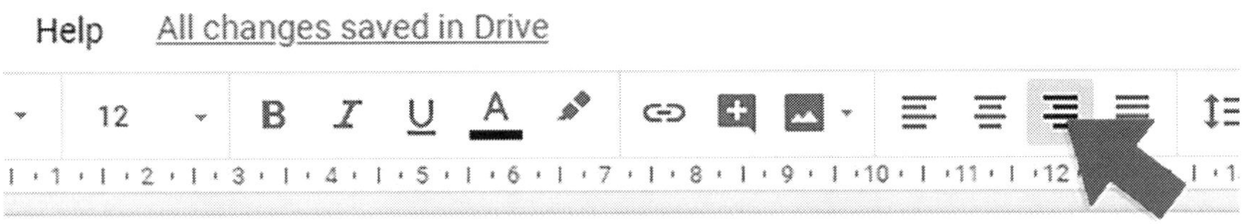

The selected text will move to the right hand margin.

The third planet from the Sun is unique in the Universe as it is currently the only planet known to support life. It has a single natural satellite called the Moon and is the fifth largest planet in the Solar System.

Bullets Lists

Select the text using your mouse as shown below.

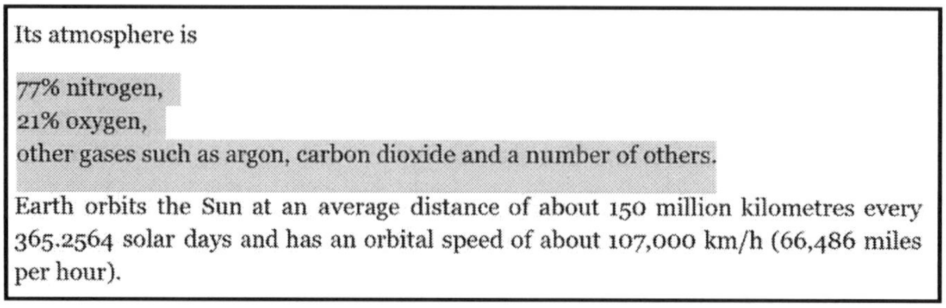
Its atmosphere is

77% nitrogen,
21% oxygen,
other gases such as argon, carbon dioxide and a number of others.

Earth orbits the Sun at an average distance of about 150 million kilometres every 365.2564 solar days and has an orbital speed of about 107,000 km/h (66,486 miles per hour).

Then from the toolbar, click the bullet points icon on the right hand side.

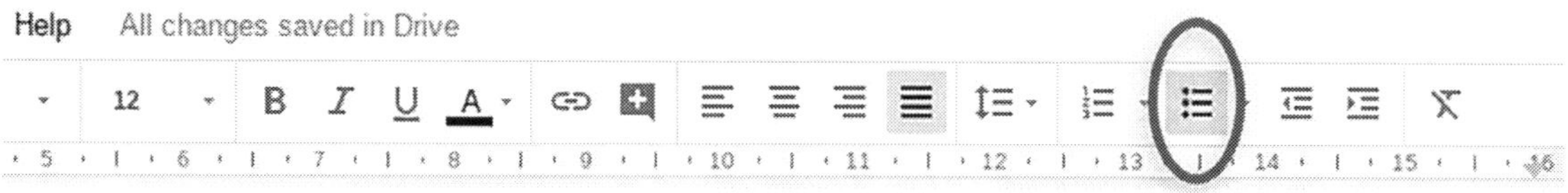

You can also have different styles of bullets such as ticks, stars and so on. To get the drop down menu, click the small down arrow next to the bullet icon.

Bullet points will be added to the selected text.

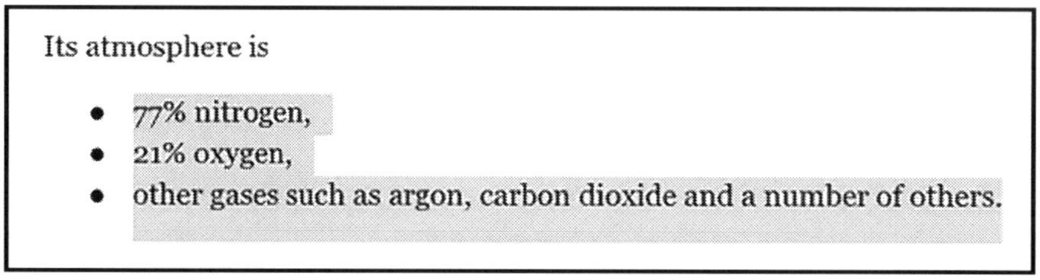
Its atmosphere is

- 77% nitrogen,
- 21% oxygen,
- other gases such as argon, carbon dioxide and a number of others.

Numbered Lists

Sclcct thc tcxt using your mousc as shown below.

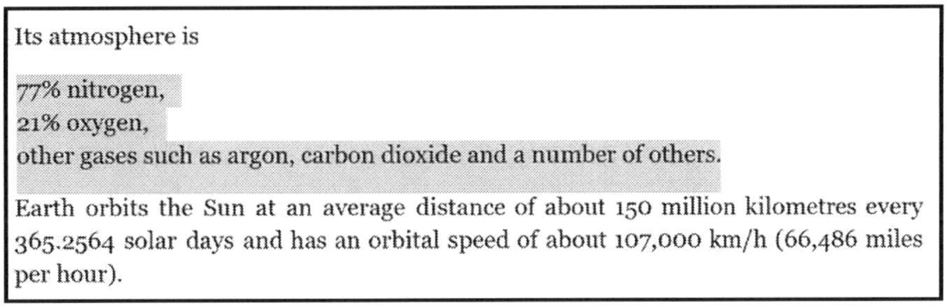
Its atmosphere is

77% nitrogen,
21% oxygen,
other gases such as argon, carbon dioxide and a number of others.

Earth orbits the Sun at an average distance of about 150 million kilometres every 365.2564 solar days and has an orbital speed of about 107,000 km/h (66,486 miles per hour).

Then from the toolbar, click the numbered points icon on the right hand side.

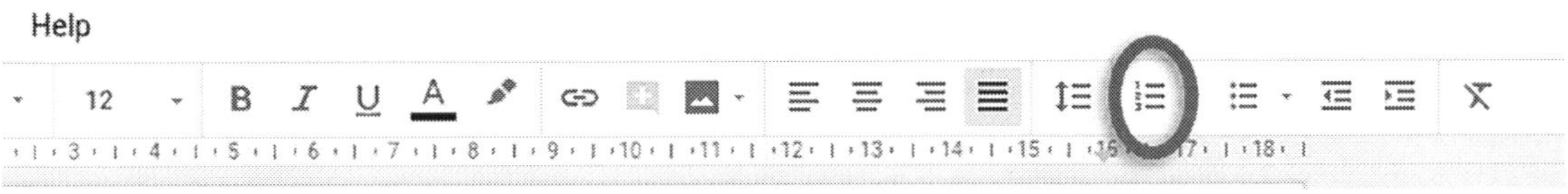

You can also have different styles of numbers such as roman numerals, letters, and so on. To get the drop down menu, click the small down arrow next to the numbered icon.

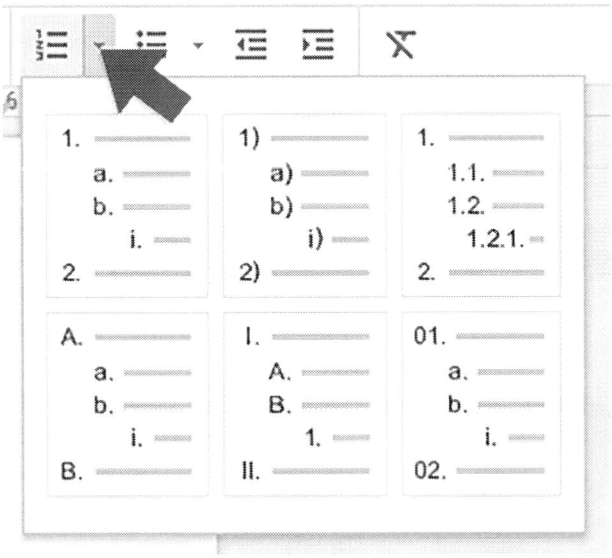

Numbers will be added to the selected text.

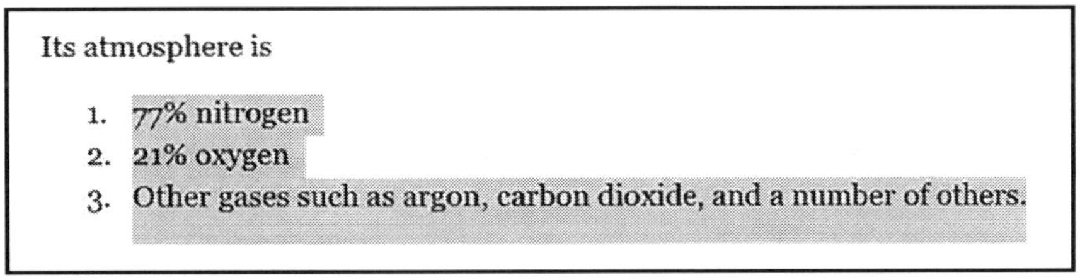
Its atmosphere is

1. 77% nitrogen
2. 21% oxygen
3. Other gases such as argon, carbon dioxide, and a number of others.

Cut, Copy & Paste

To ease editing documents, you can use copy, cut, and paste to move paragraphs or pictures around on different parts of your document.

First select the paragraph you want to cut or copy with your mouse. I'm going to cut the last paragraph in the document below.

Click before the word 'Earth', and dragging your mouse across the line towards the end of the line, as shown below.

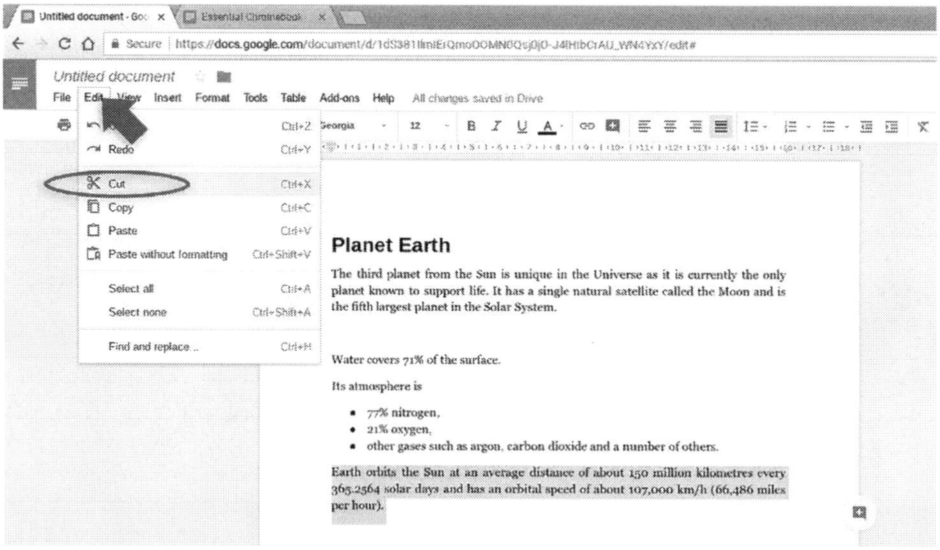

From the edit menu, select 'cut'. Now click on the position in the document you want the paragraph you just cut out to be inserted.

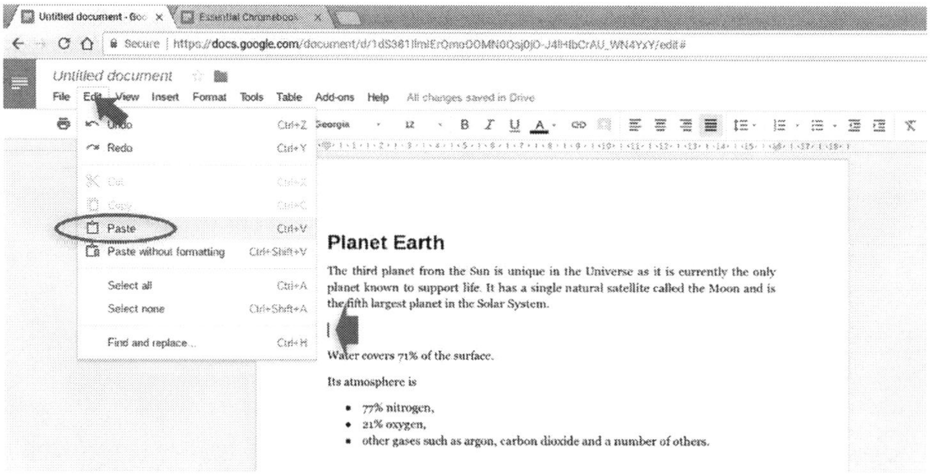

Once you have done that, click the 'edit' menu and select 'paste'.

If you wanted to copy something ie make a duplicate of the text, then use the same procedure except select 'copy' instead of 'cut' from the edit menu.

Adding Images

You can insert images from your Chromebook, from the web, Google Drive, your Photos App or directly from the onboard camera.

From your Chromebook

Click on the line in your document where you want your photograph or image to appear.

Go to your insert menu and click on 'image'. From the slideout menu select 'upload from computer'.

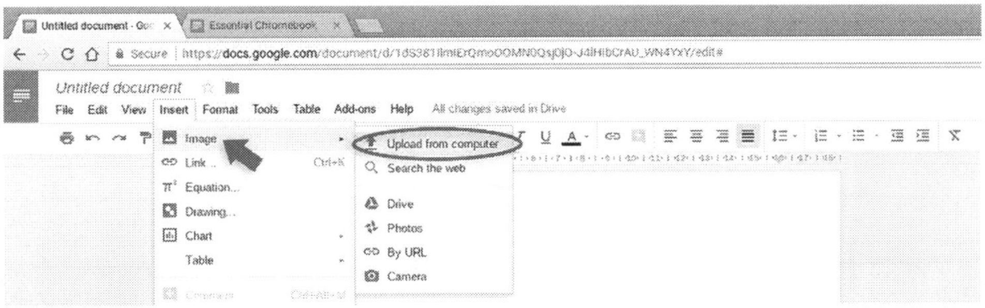

Choose the picture or photo you want on your Google Drive, from the dialog box that appears.

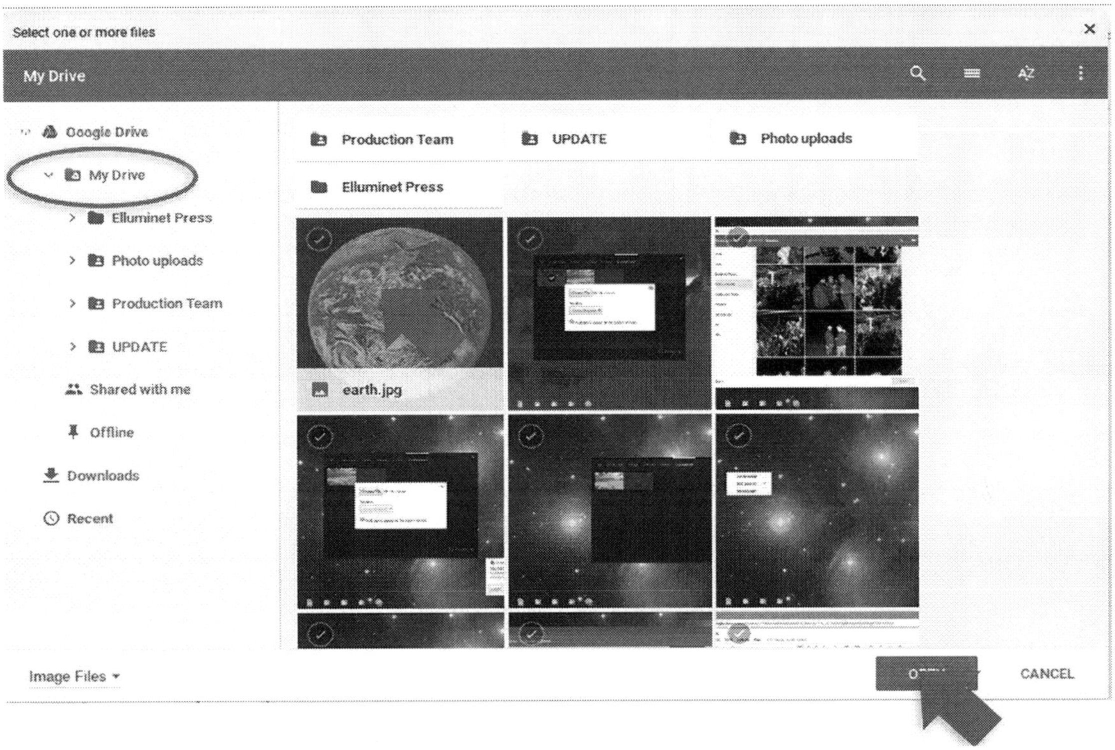

Click 'open' to insert the image.

From the web

You can add images from a Google Image search. To do this, click the 'insert' menu, then select 'image'. From the slideout select 'search the web'.

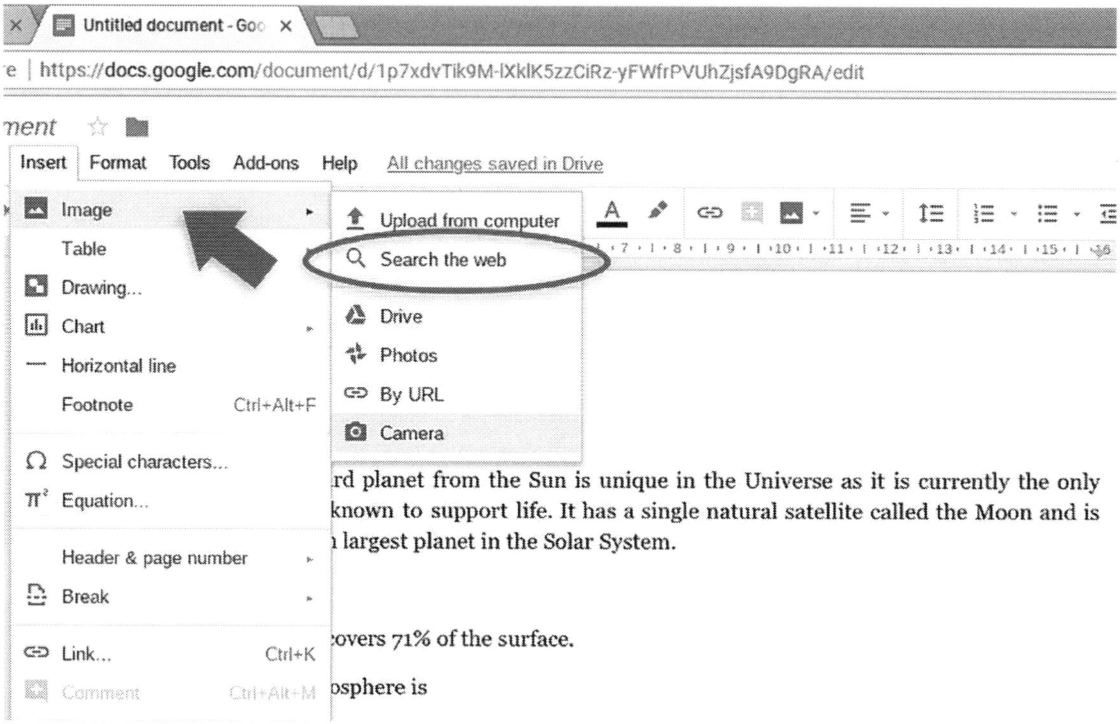

You'll see a search box appear on the right hand side of the screen. Type in the name of what you're searching for. In this example I need an image of the earth, so I'm going to type in 'planet earth'.

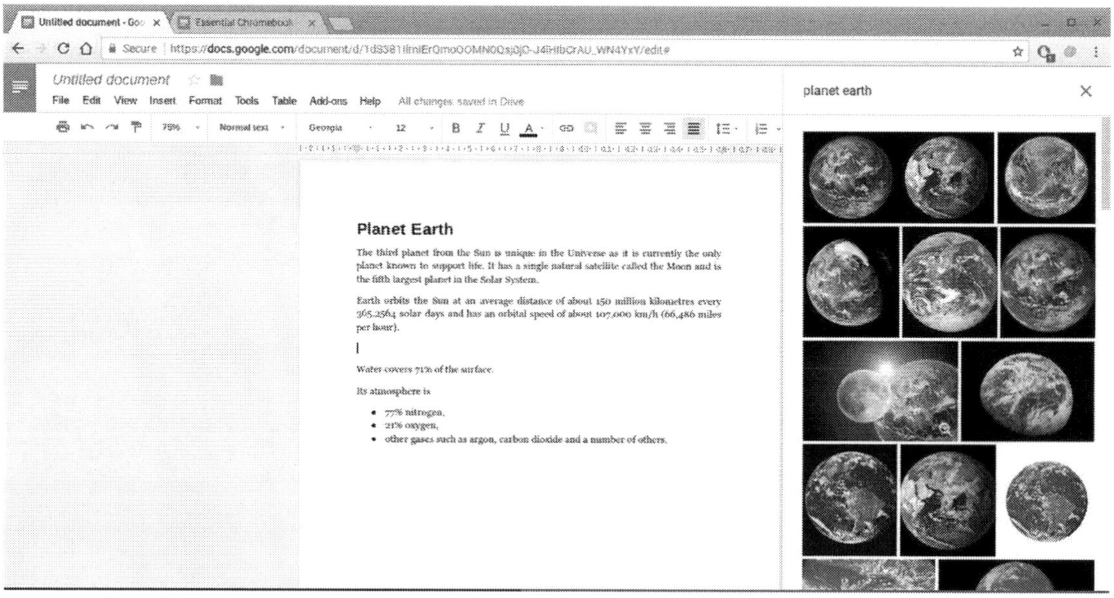

Click on one of the images to insert it into your document.

From your Photos

You can add images from your Google Photos App. To do this, click the 'insert' menu, then select 'image'. From the slideout select 'photos'.

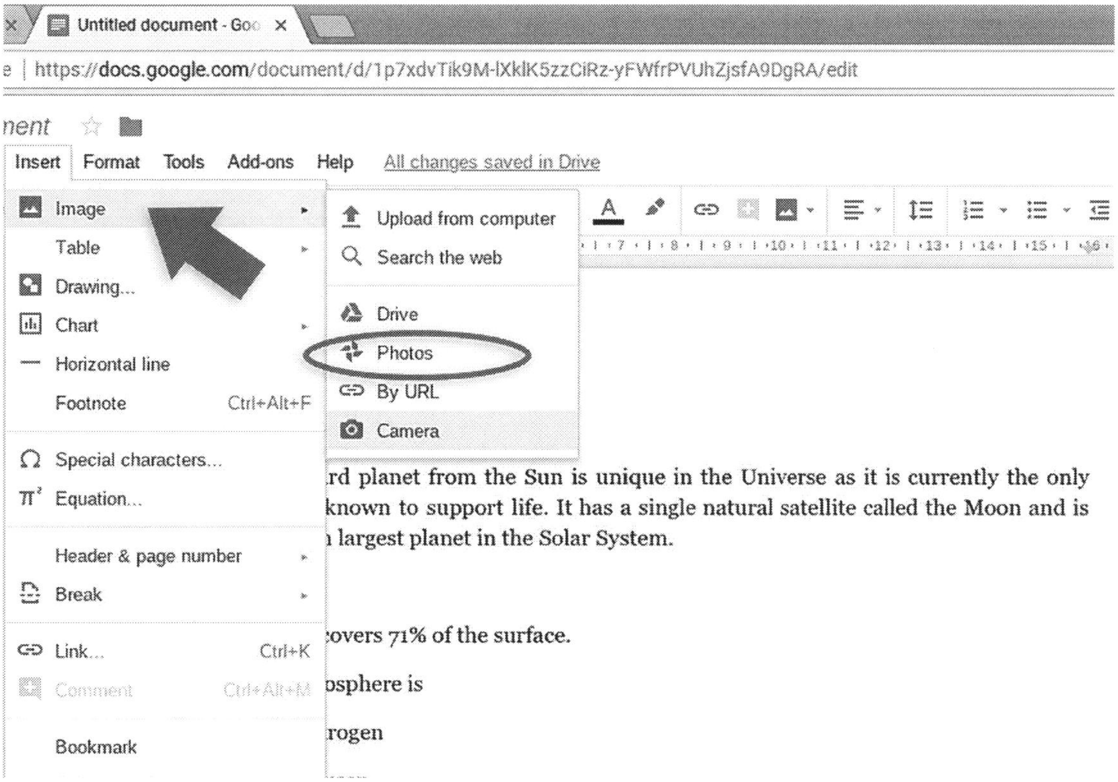

You'll see the Google Photos Panel appear on the right hand side of the screen.

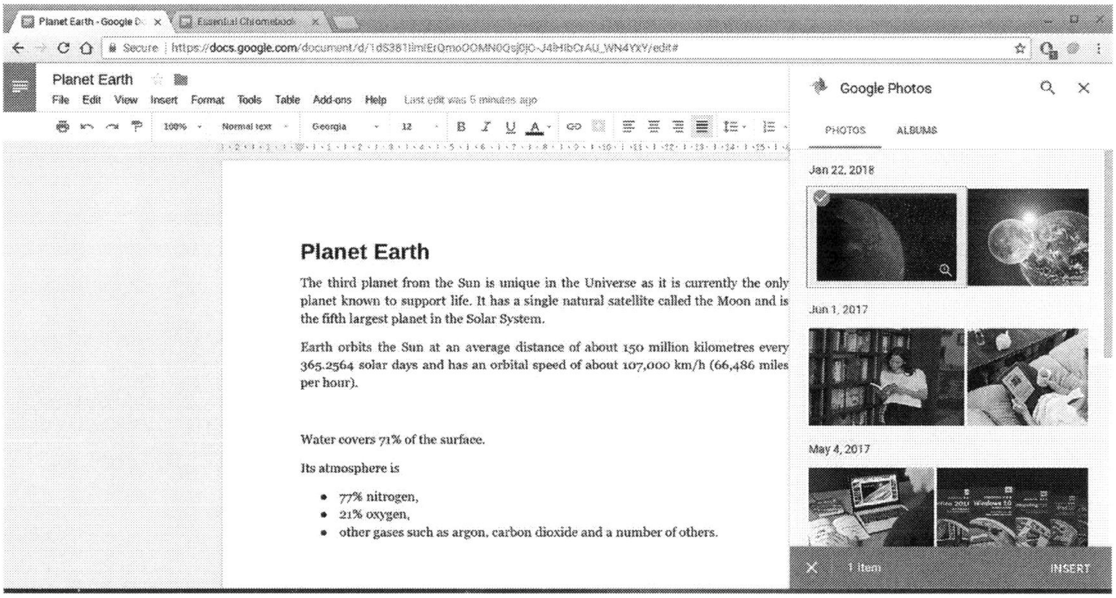

Browse through the photos and select the one you want to insert.

From your Camera

Probably works better on an android tablet, but can still be achieved using the onboard camera that comes with your Chromebook.

Go to the insert menu, click image, then select 'camera' from the slideout.

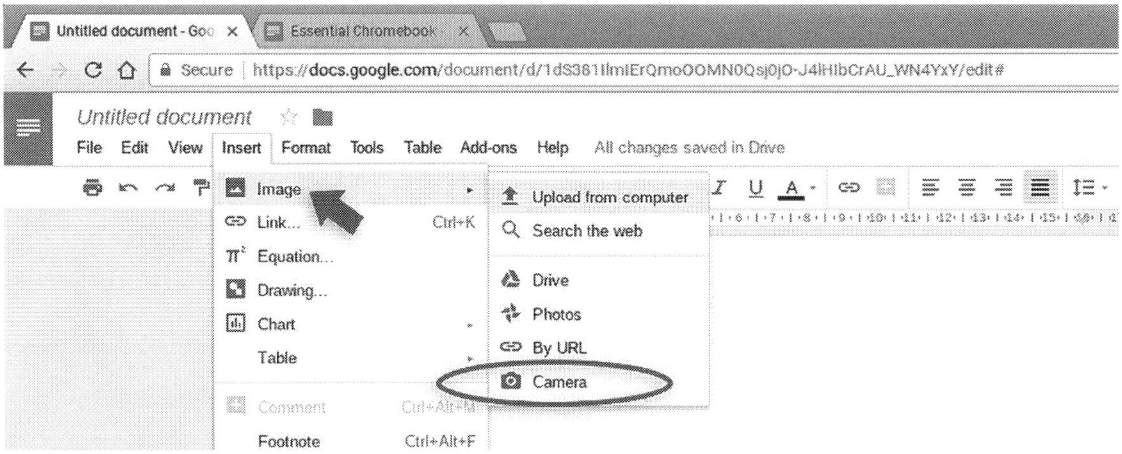

Click the yellow camera icon to take the photo.

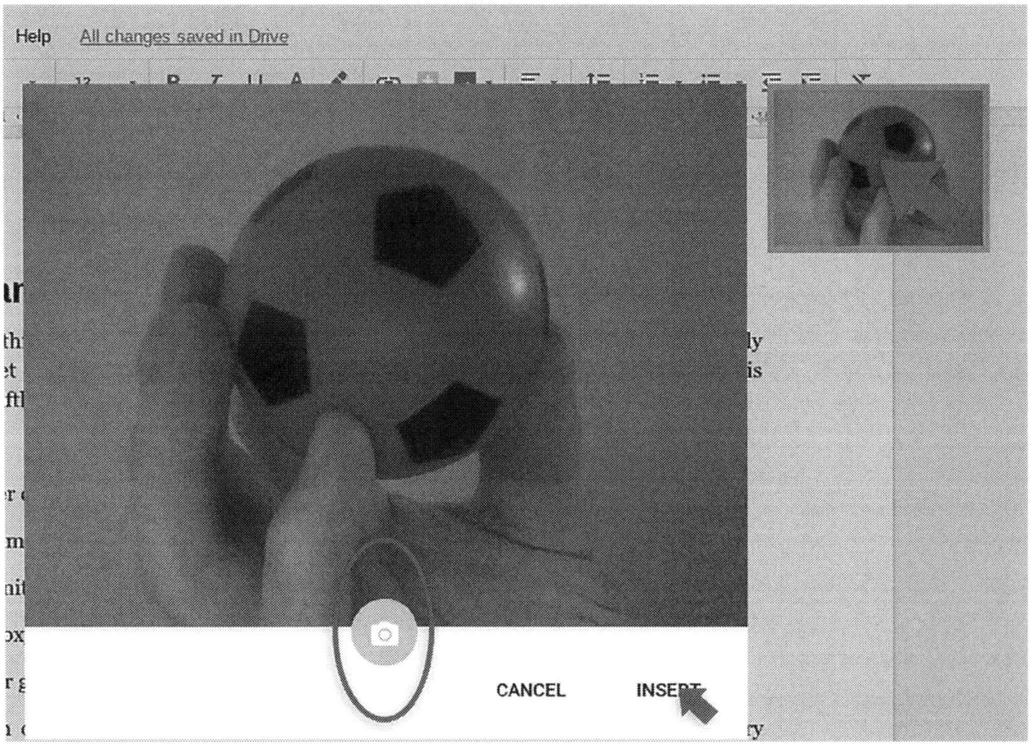

If you took more than one photo, select the one you want from the small thumbnails on the right.

Click 'insert' to add the image to your document.

Formatting Images

Right click on your image and select 'image options' from the popup menu.

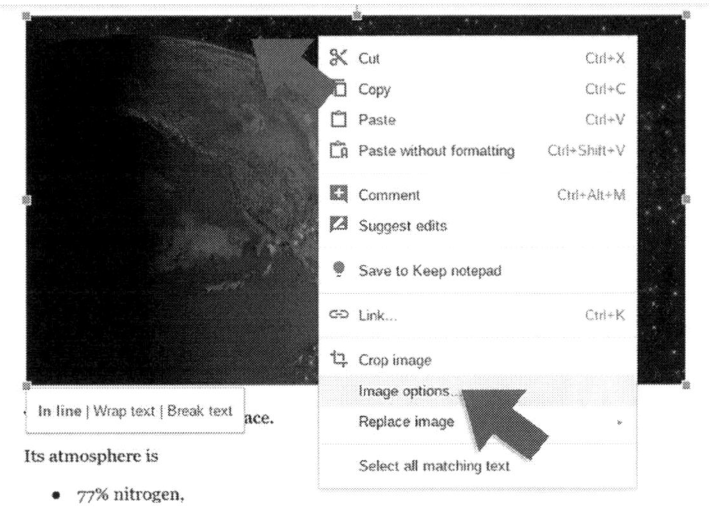

On the right hand side of the screen, you'll see the image options panel open up. From here you can recolour the image - that is give it a red, blue, green, or yellow hue, or turn it into black and white.

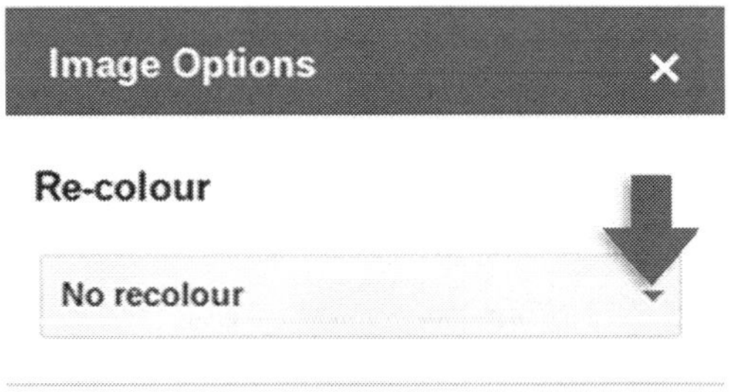

You can adjust the transparency of the image, as well as the brightness and contrast of the image using the sliders.

Cropping Images

To crop an image, right click on it and from the popup menu, select 'crop image'.

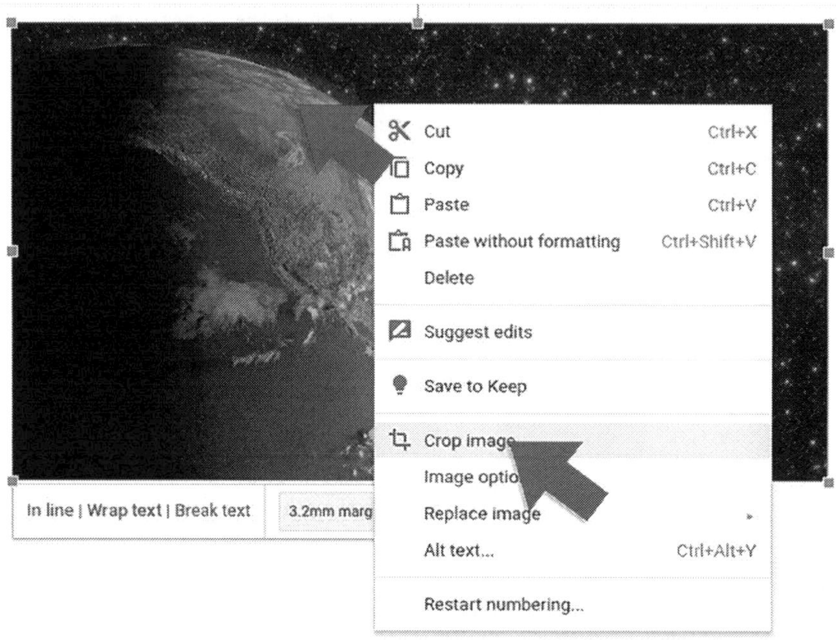

You'll see black crop handles appear on the corners and sides of the image. Click and drag these inwards, around the part of the image you want to keep as illustrated below.

Click anywhere outside the image to execute the crop.

Adding Tables

First click the position in the document you want the table to appear.

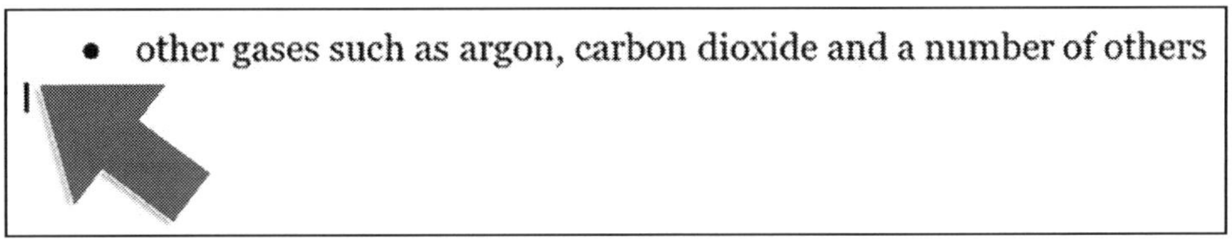

To add a table, click the 'table' menu and select 'insert table'. From the slideout, select how many rows and columns you want in your table.

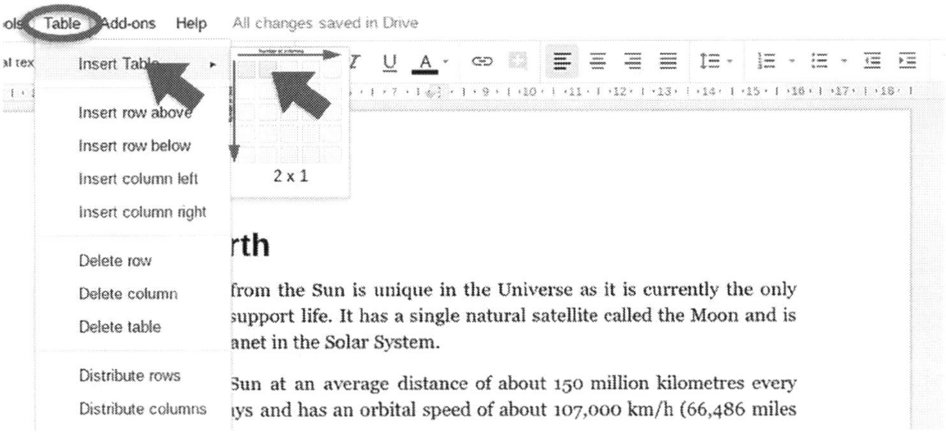

Inserting Rows & Columns

To insert a row or column, right click on the position in the table where you want to insert the row or column.

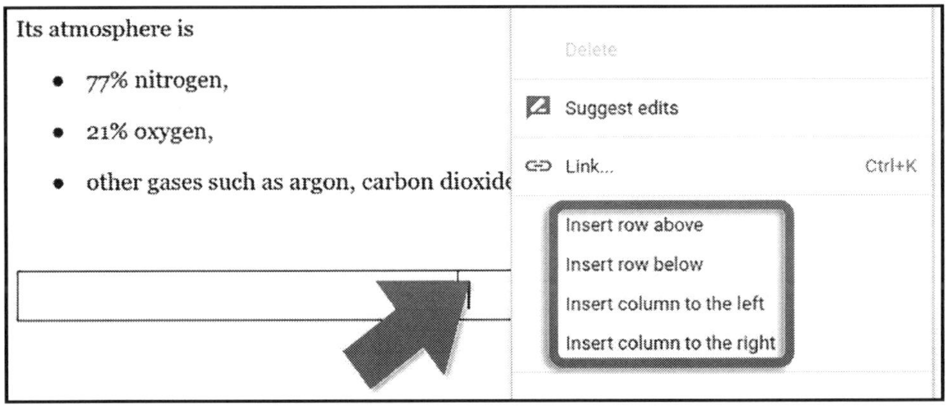

If you want to insert a row below the row selected, click 'insert row below'.

If you want to insert a column after the column selected, click 'insert column to the right'.

Saving Documents

Documents are automatically saved to your Google Drive. Make sure you give your document a name. You will see the document name on the top left of the screen. If you haven't given your document a name you'll see "untitled document" in the title.

Click on this title and type in a name for the document.

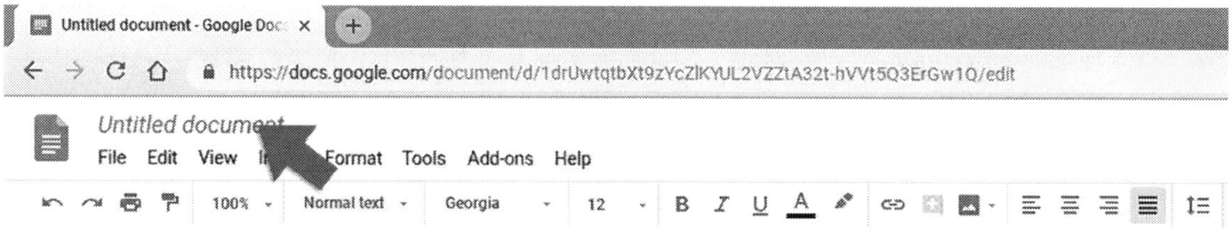

This will save it in Google Drive. To save in another folder on Google Drive, click 'my drive' then select the folder you want to save in.

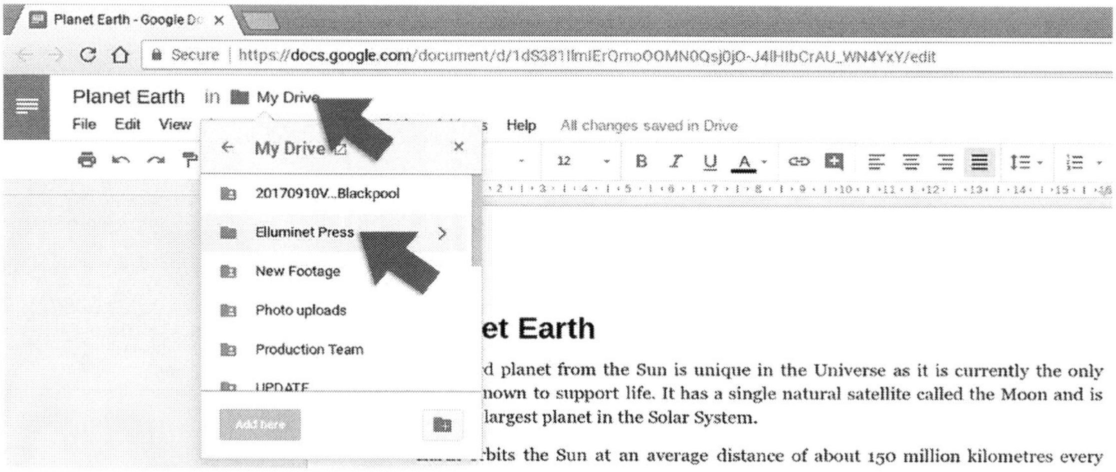

If you want to create a new folder, click the 'new folder' icon on the bottom right of the drop down.

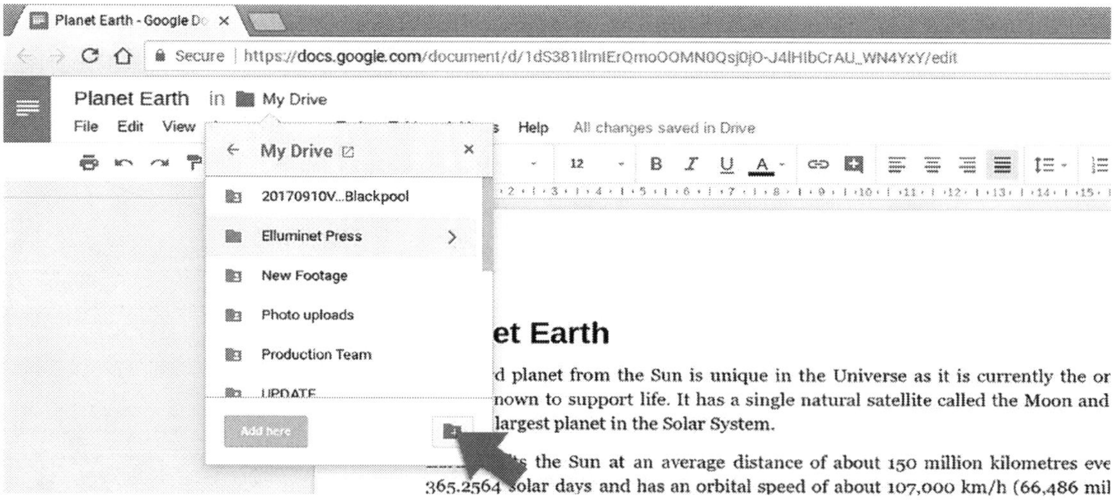

Opening Saved Documents

To open a document from Google Drive, double click on the document.

When you open Google Docs, you'll see a list of documents you've recently opened. Click on one of these to open it up.

To open a document within Google Docs, click the file menu, then select 'open'.

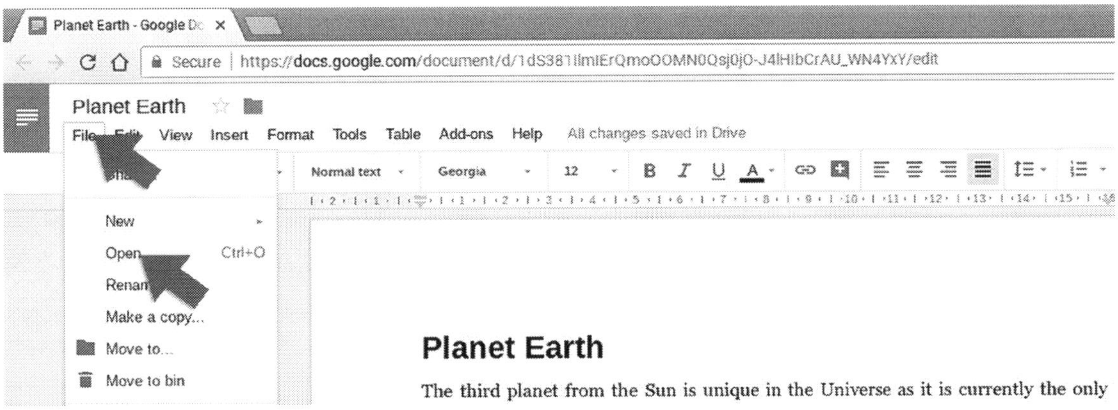

From the dialog box, select the file you want to open. Select 'my drive' to open a file saved on your Google Drive. Click 'shared with me' to open files other users have shared with you. Click 'recent' to open a file you've recently worked on.

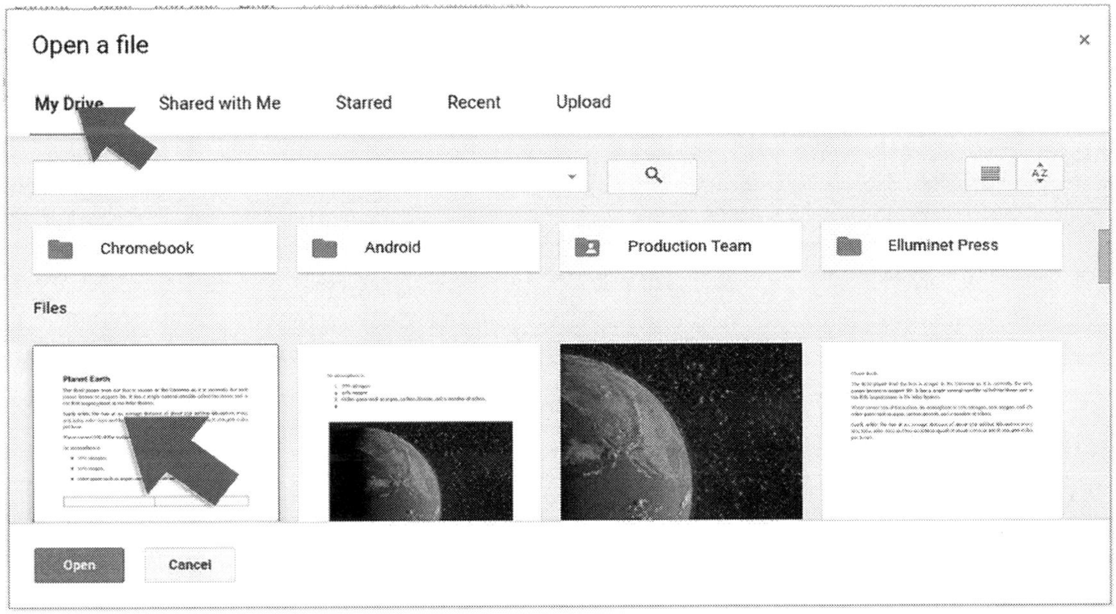

You can also search for the file using the search field at the top of the screen.

Click on a file to select it, then click 'open'.

Printing Documents

To print a document from within Google Docs, click the file menu, then select 'print'.

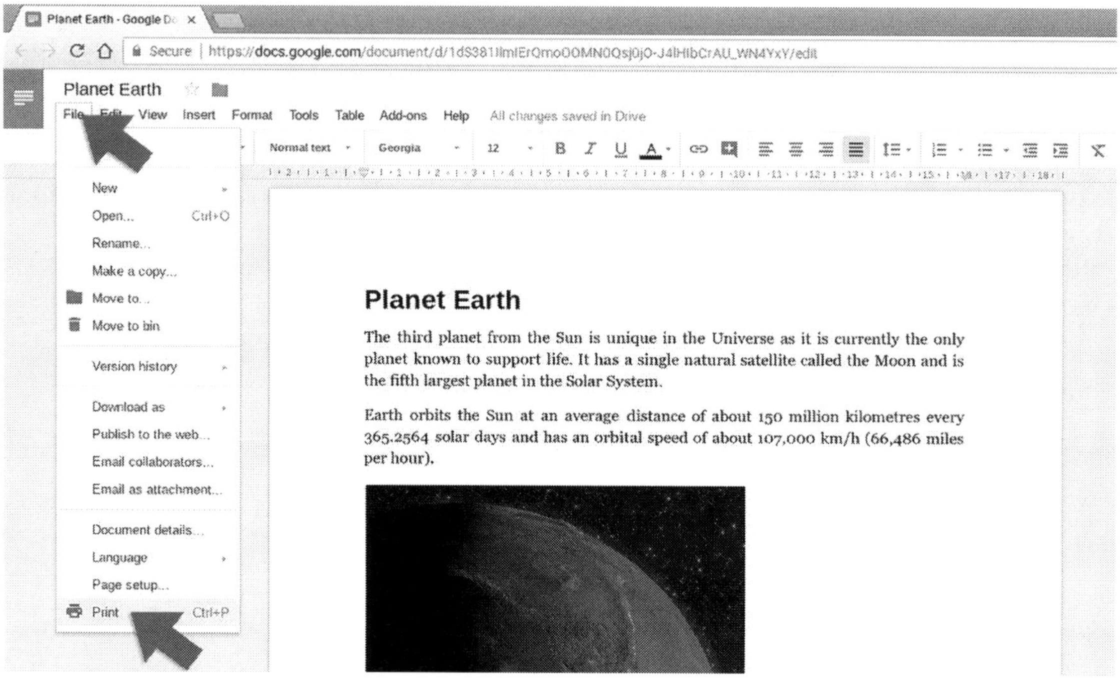

From the dialog box, select the printer you want to print to. To do this click 'change', then select a destination.

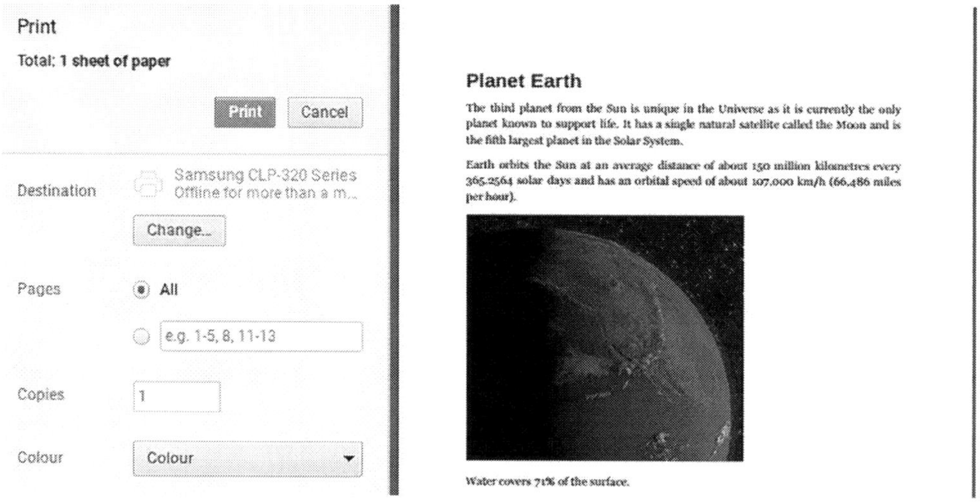

Enter which pages you want printed, or leave the option on 'all' if you want the whole document.

If you want the document in black and white, click 'colour', then change the setting to 'black and white'.

To print the document click 'print' at the top of the dialog box.

Sharing Documents

You can share your document using email and Google Drive's collaboration features.

To do this, click the 'share' icon on the top right of the screen.

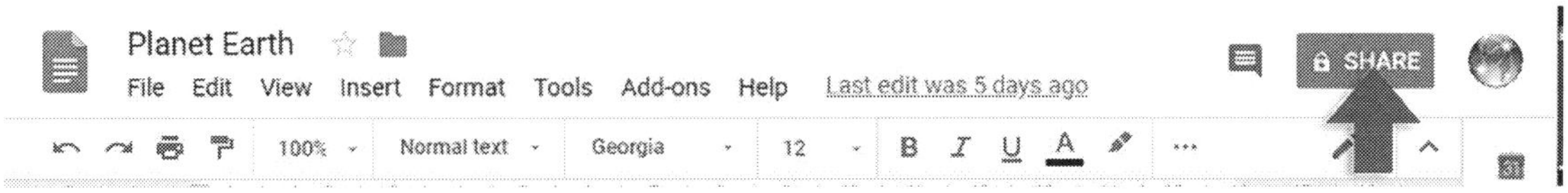

Enter the names of the people you want to grant access to in the 'add more people' field.

Click the pencil icon to the right of the field and select 'can edit' if you want these people to be able to edit your document, if not select 'can view'.

Click 'send' when you're done.

If you just want a link to the document, click 'get shareable link'.

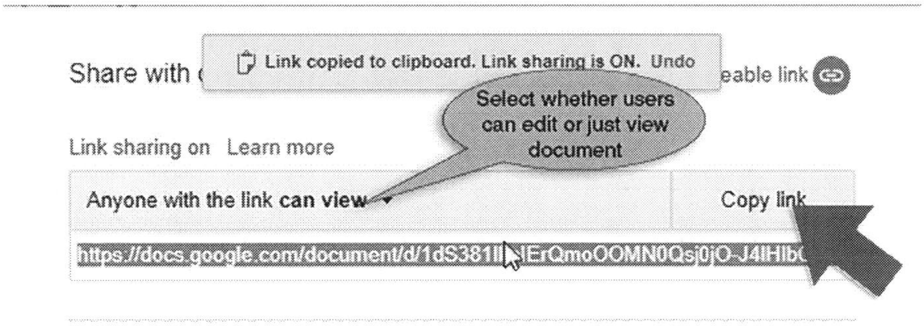

The link will be copied to your clipboard. From here you can paste into an email or another document.

10 Google Sheets

Google Sheets is an online spreadsheet programme much like Microsoft Google Sheets and is included as part of a free, web-based office suite developed by Google.

Google Sheets allows you to do many of the same things as Microsoft Excel but lacks some of the more advanced features.

However, Google Sheets is a great alternative and works well on a ChromeBook.

In this section, we'll take a brief look at Google Sheets. For more detail, check out our other book 'Understanding Google Sheets'.

ISBN: 9781913151478

What is a Spreadsheet

A spreadsheet is made up of cells each identified by a reference. The reference is made up by using the column, eg D, and the row, eg 10. So for a particular cell, you look to see what column it's in (D), then what row it's in (10). Put them together and you get the cell reference for that cell.

```
[COLUMN] [ROW]
```

So the highlighted cell in the illustration below would be D10.

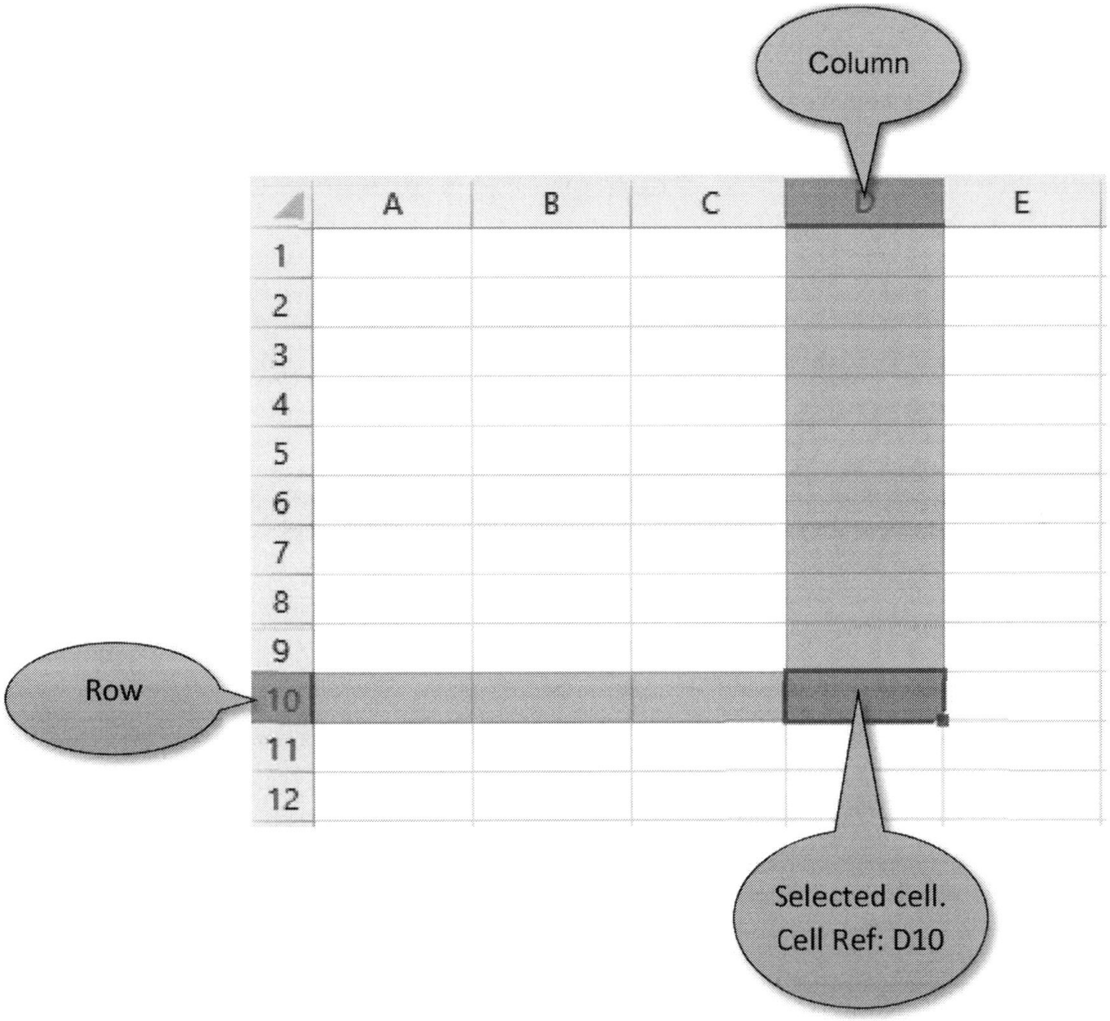

You can also select multiple cells at the same time. A group of cells is called as a cell range. You can refer to a cell range, using the cell reference of the first cell and the last cell in the range, separated by a colon.

```
[FIRST CELL in RANGE] : [LAST CELL in RANGE]
```

For example, this cell range would be A1:D10 (firstcell : lastcell).

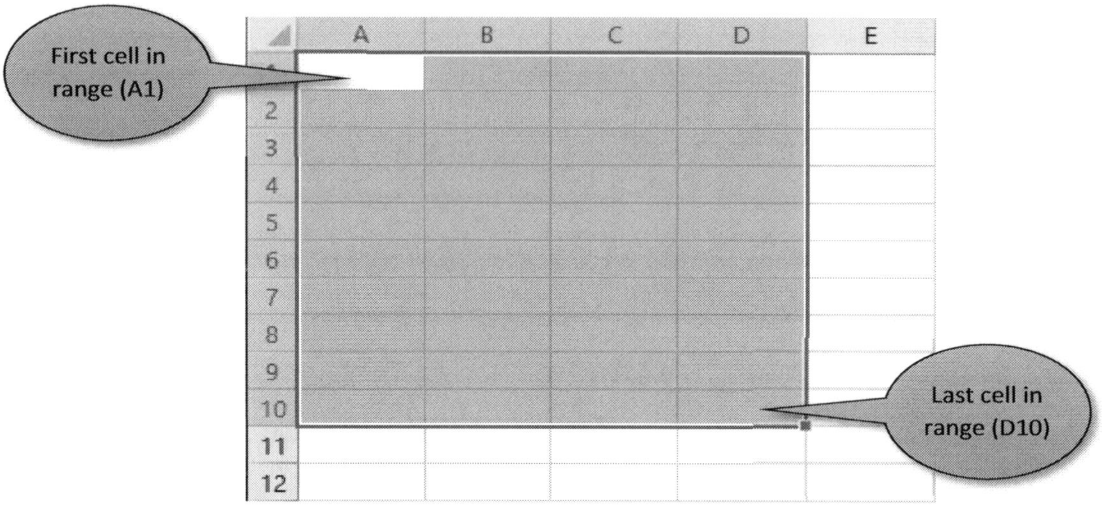

Cell references are used when you start applying functions to the numbers in your cells.

In the example below, to add two numbers together, you can enter a formula into cell C1.

Instead of typing in **=5+5** you would enter **=A1+B1**.

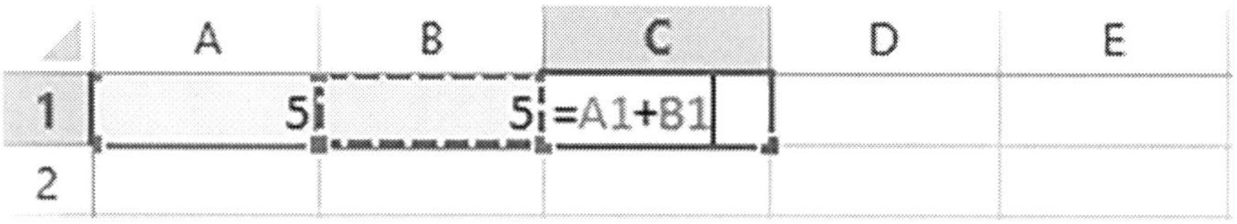

The theory is, if you enter the cell reference instead of the actual number, you can perform calculations automatically and Google Sheets will recalculate all the numbers for you should you change anything.

For example, if I wanted to change it to **5+6**, I would just change the number in cell B1 without rewriting the formula in C1.

Now you can type any number in either cell A1 or B1 and it will add them up automatically.

This is a very basic example but forms the building blocks of a spreadsheet. You can use these concepts to build spreadsheets to analyse and manipulate data, as well as allow changes to the individual data and other parts of the spreadsheet without constantly changing formulas and functions.

Now that we understand the basics of what a spreadsheet is, lets take a look at Google Sheets.

Getting Around Google Sheets

I find the best version of Google Sheets to use is the web based version rather than the Android Version you might find on your Chromebook. To start the web based version of Google Sheets, open your app launcher, then click on Google Chrome.

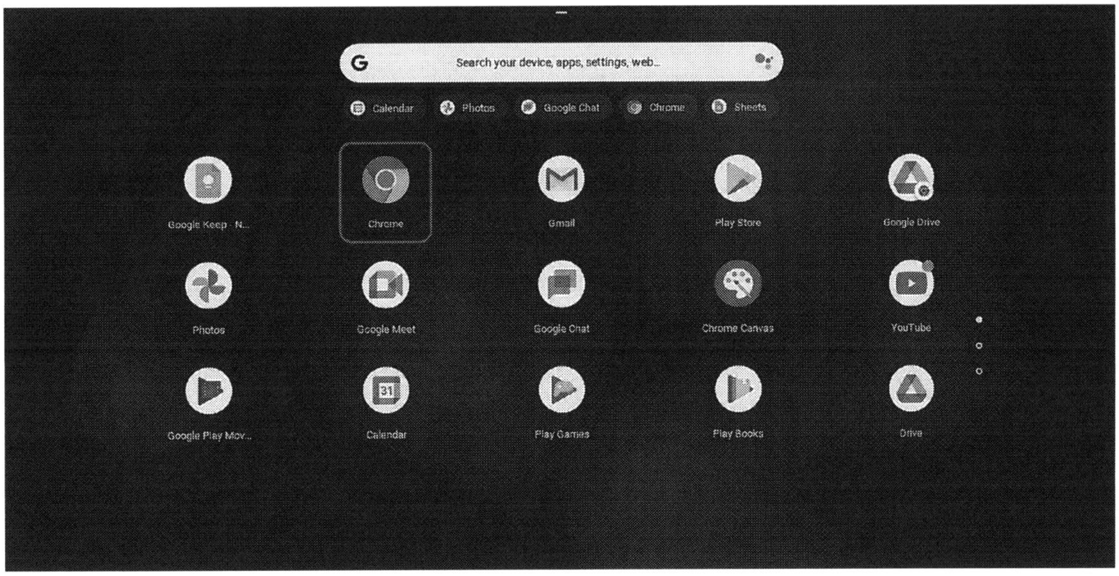

Navigate to the following website:

`sheets.google.com`

When Google Sheets opens, you'll see the sheets you have been working on recently. You can click any of these to re-open them. To create a new sheet, click 'blank' on the top left of the screen.

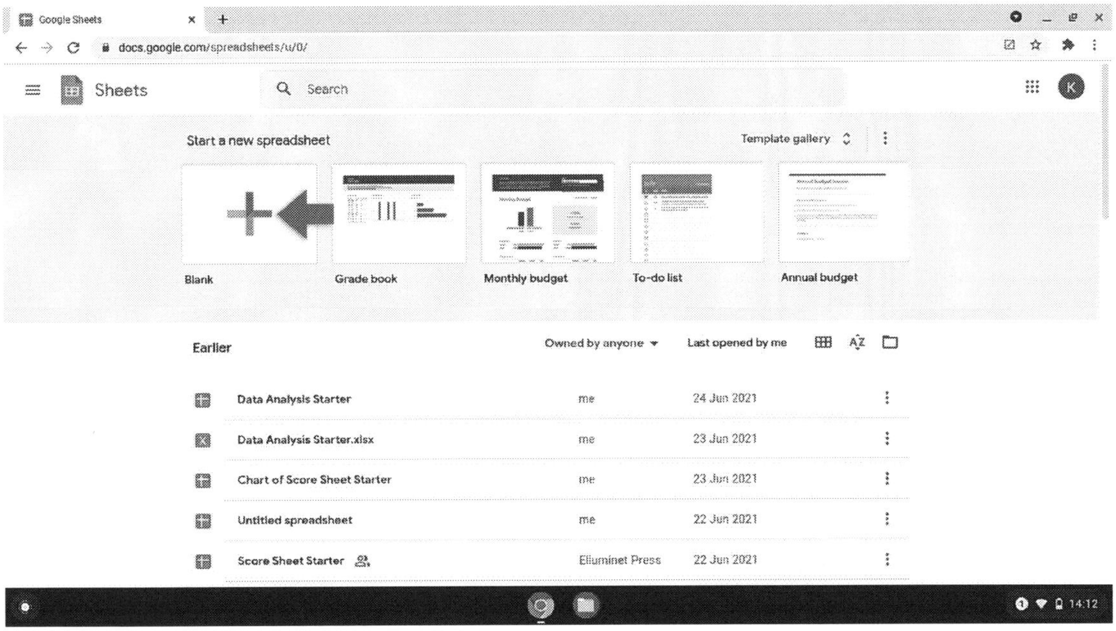

Google Sheets will open the main window where you can create your spreadsheet.

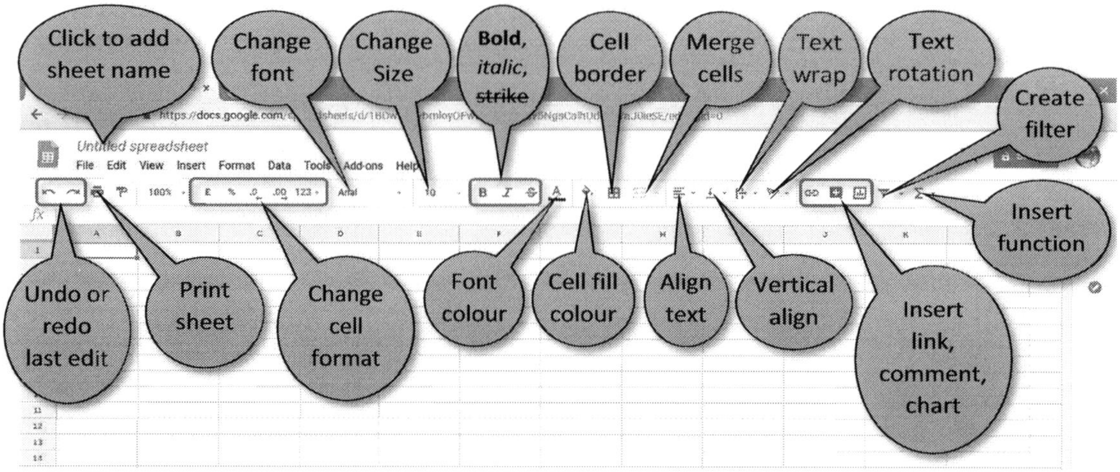

Along the top you'll see the spreadsheet name. It's a good idea to rename this to something more meaningful that 'untitled spreadsheet'. Click on the text and type in a name.

Underneath are the menus. This is where you'll find tools that are not represented as icons on the toolbar.

Under the menus you'll see the toolbar. This is where you'll find most of the tools you'll need to create and format your spreadsheets.

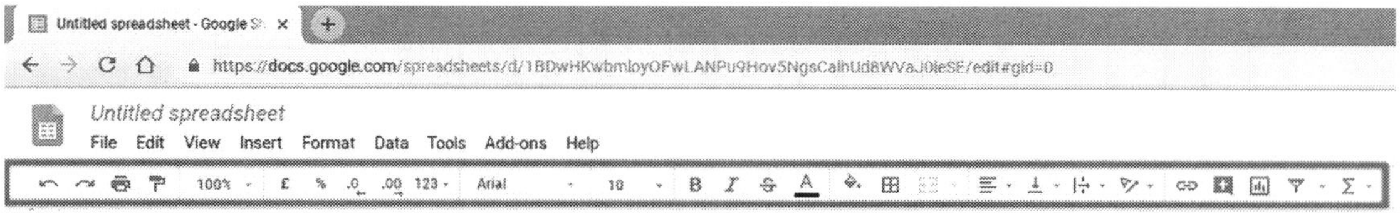

Then you have the formula bar *(fx)*. Here, you'll be able to see and add any functions or formulas in the selected cell.

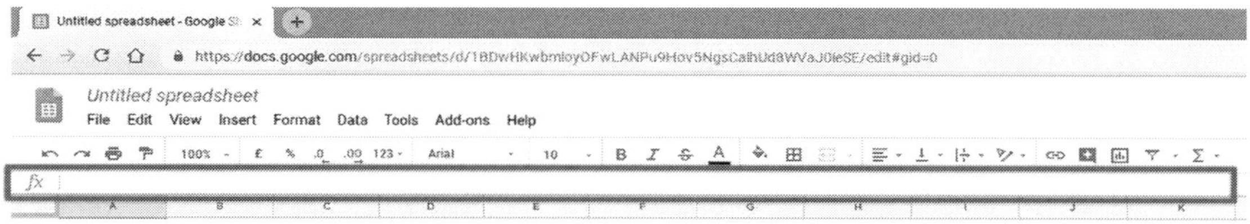

Simple Text Formatting

In this example we are doing a basic scoring sheet. Enter the sample data into the spreadsheet as shown below.

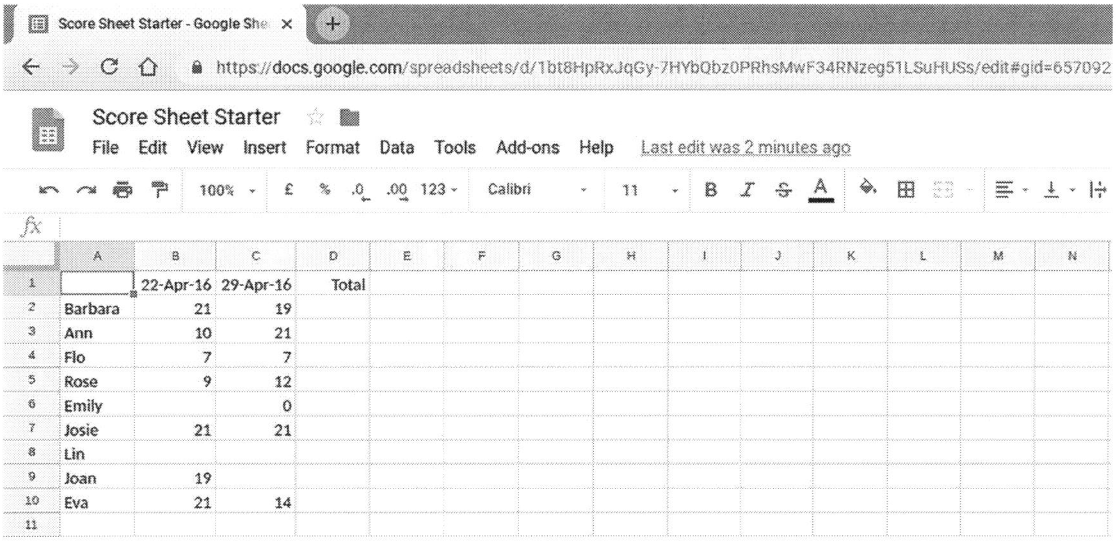

Bold, Italic, Strike & Underlined

Sometimes it improves the readability of your spreadsheet to format the data in the cells.

For example, we could make the column headings and the player's names bold.

First, select the cells you want to apply the formatting to, click the bold icon from the toolbar.

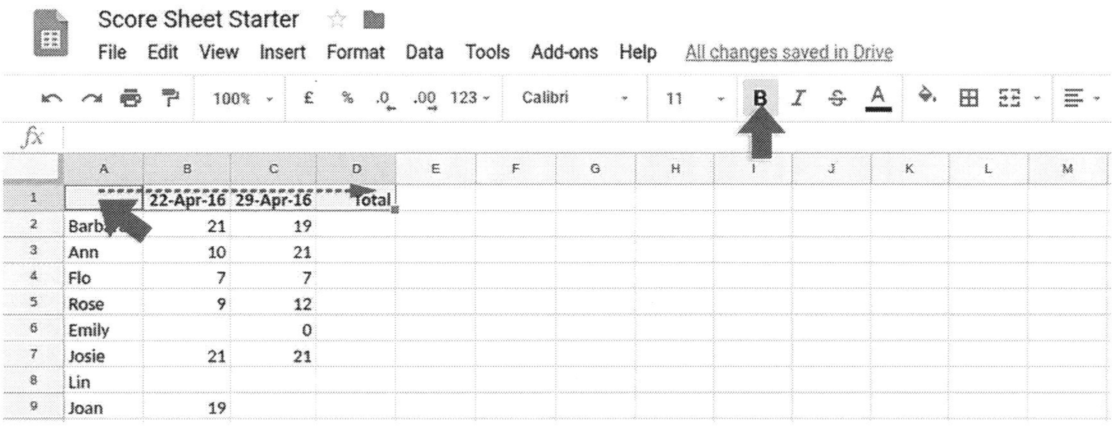

If you want *italic* text, click the '*I*' icon on the toolbar. If you want ~~strike~~ text, click the '~~S~~' icon. If you want <u>underlined</u> text, you'll need to go to the format menu and select 'underlined'.

Changing Fonts

First, select the cells you want to apply the formatting to.

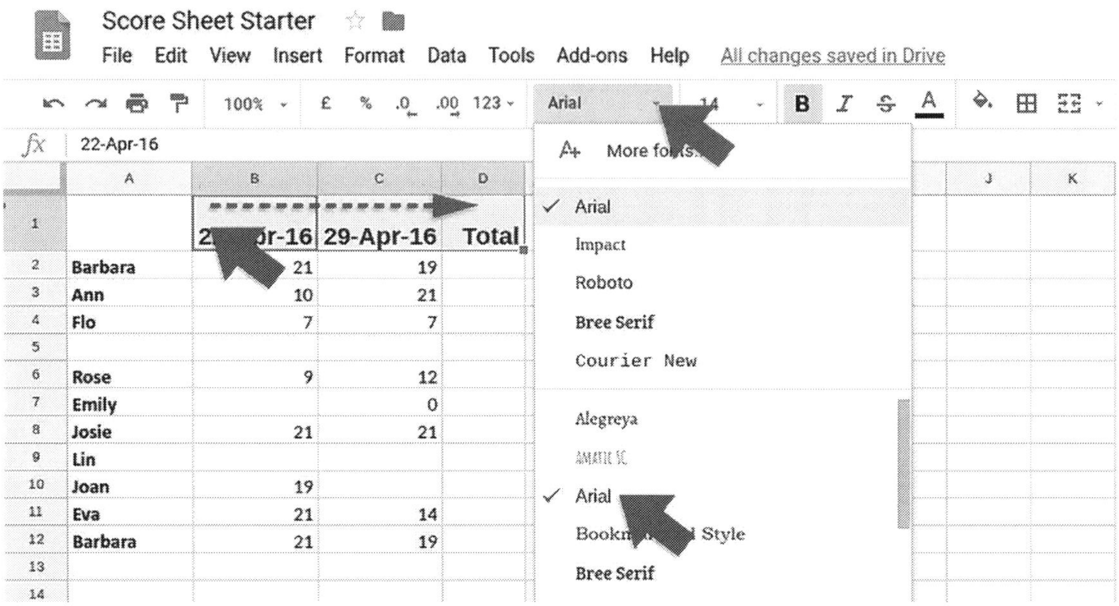

Click the font selector from the toolbar, and select a font from the drop down box.

Font Size

First, select the cells you want to apply the formatting to.

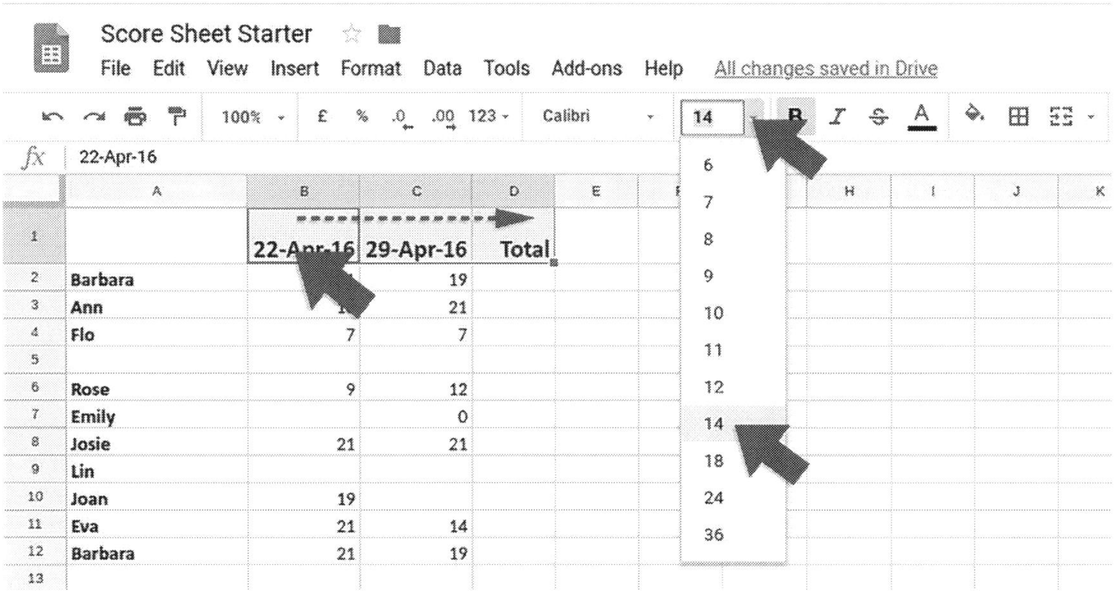

Click the font size selector from the toolbar, and select a size from the drop down box.

Cut, Copy & Paste

You can copy and paste a cell or cell range and paste it into another worksheet or in a different location on the same worksheet.

To perform a basic copy, select the cells you want to copy.

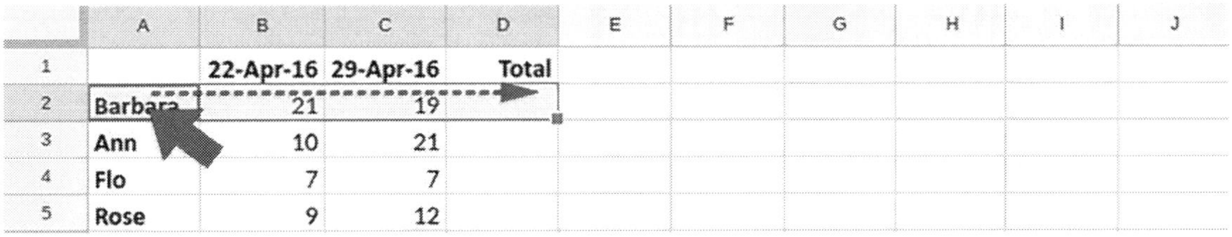

Right click on the selection, then select 'copy' from the popup menu.

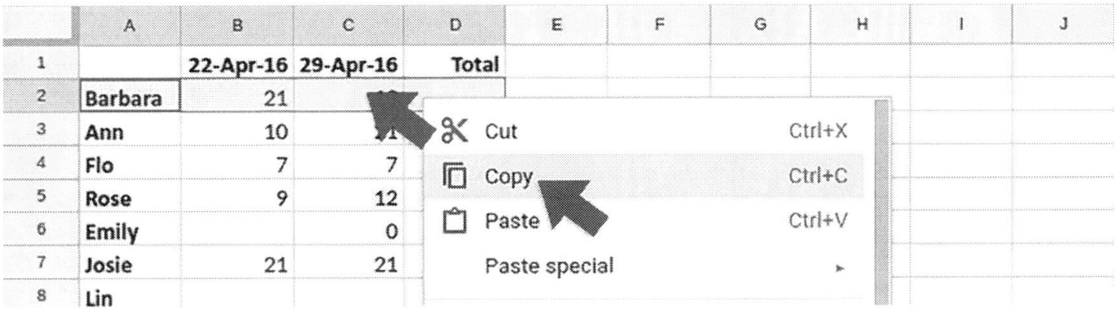

Right click the cell where you want the cells to be copied to. I'm going to paste the cells at the end of the table. From the popup menu, select 'paste'.

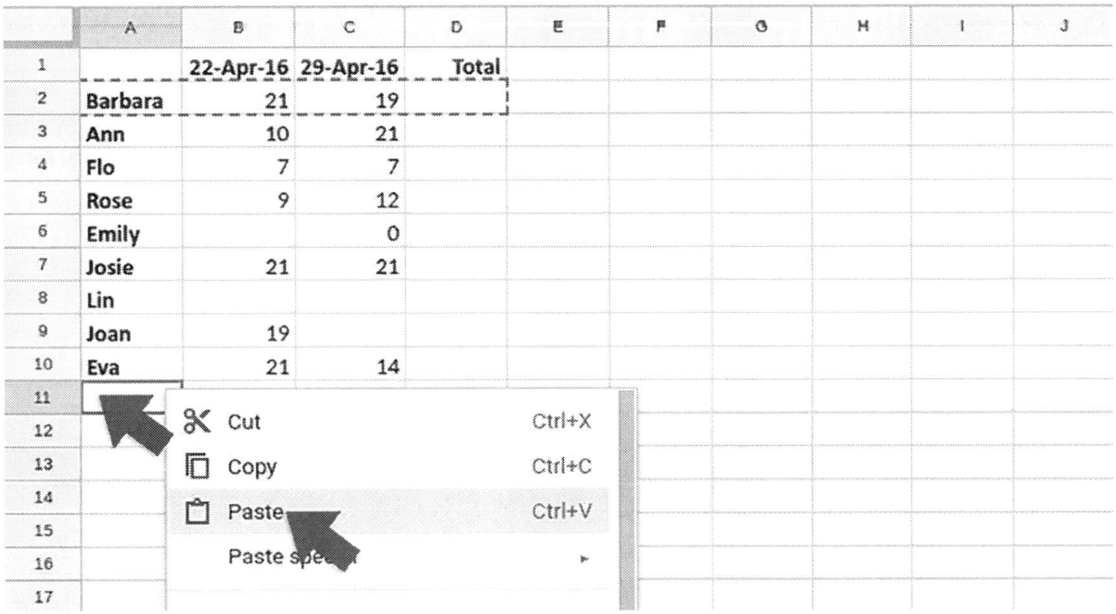

Do the same for 'cut', except choose 'cut' from the menu instead of 'copy'.

Resizing Rows and Columns

You can resize a column or row by clicking and dragging the column or row divider lines as shown below.

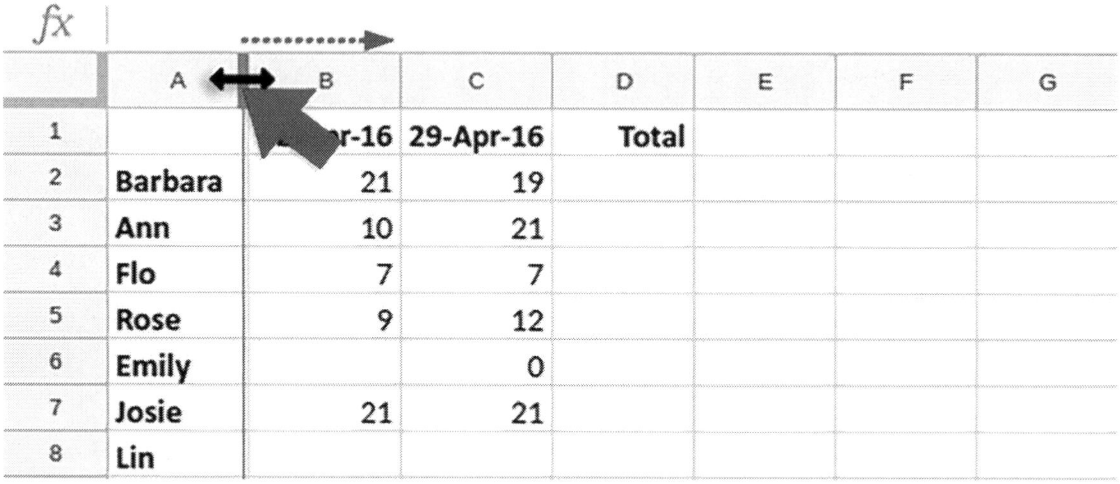

You can also double click on these lines to automatically size the row or column to the data that is in the cell.

Inserting Rows & Columns

To insert a row between Flo and Rose, right click your mouse on the row 'Rose' is in. In this case row 5

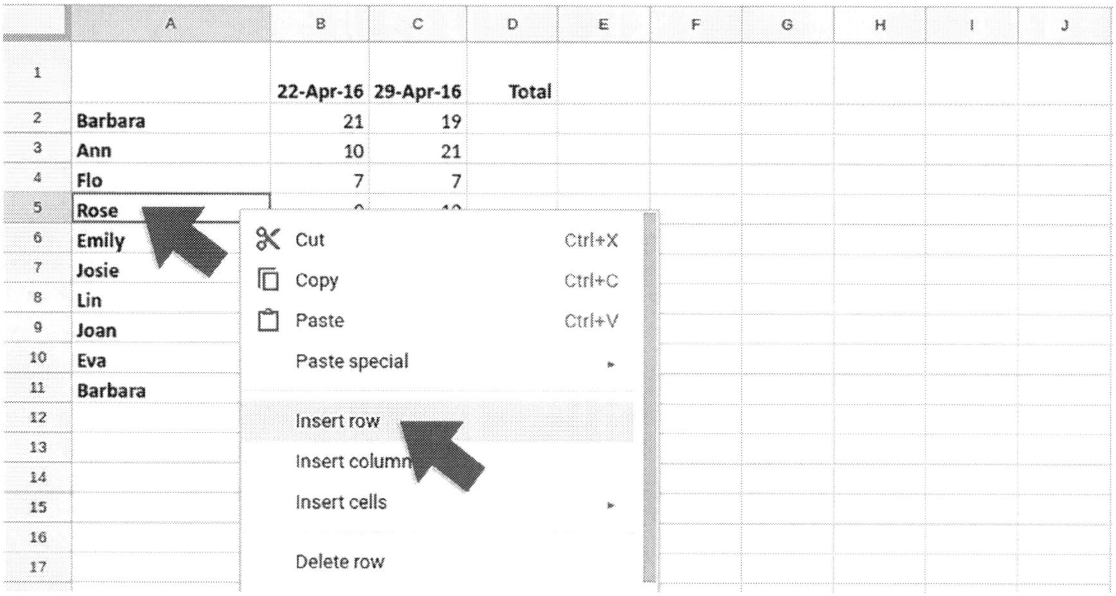

Remember, Google Sheets always adds a row or column before the one you've selected.

Cell Alignment

This helps to align your data inside your cells and make it easier to read. You can align data in the cells to the left, center, or right of the cell.

To do this highlight the cells you want to apply the alignment to, then select the alignment icon on the toolbar. From the drop down box, click the centre icon to align everything to the centre of the cell, click the right hand icon to align everything to the right of the cell.

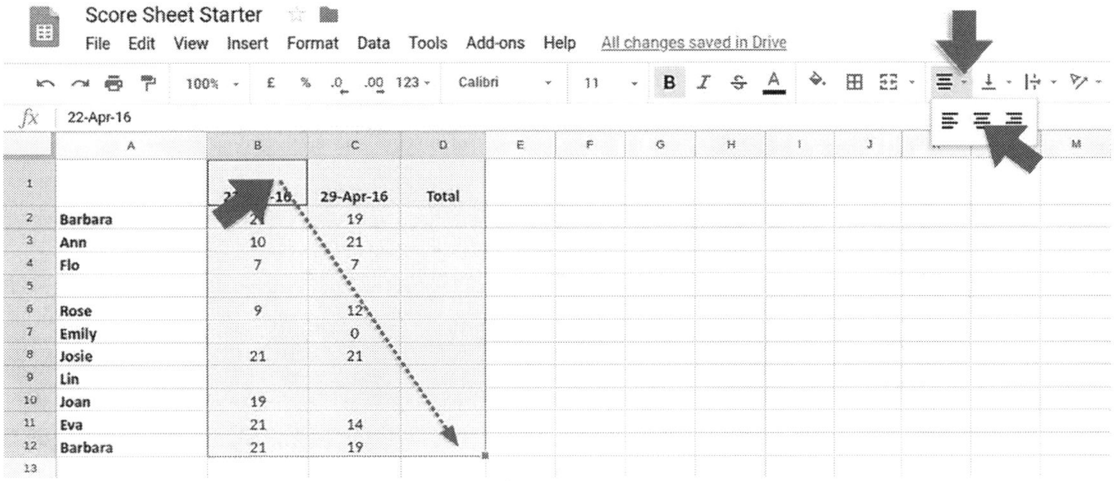

You can also align data vertically in the cell: top, middle, bottom. To do this highlight the cells you want to apply the alignment to, then select the vertical alignment icon on the toolbar.

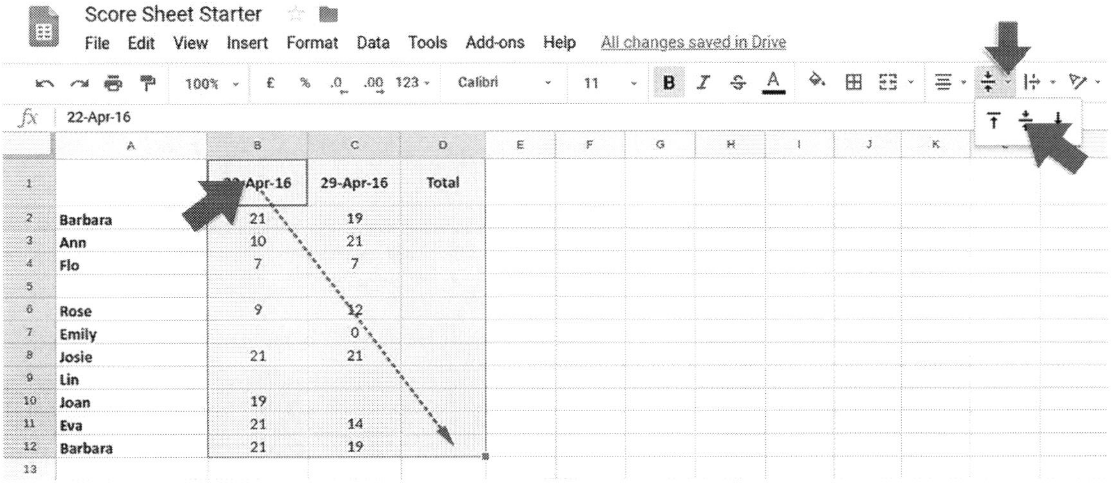

From the drop down box, click the left icon to align everything to the top of the cell, click the centre icon to align everything to the middle, and click the right hand icon to align everything to the bottom of the cell.

Cell Borders

To apply borders to your spreadsheet, with your mouse select the cells you want to format. In this case, I am going to do the whole table.

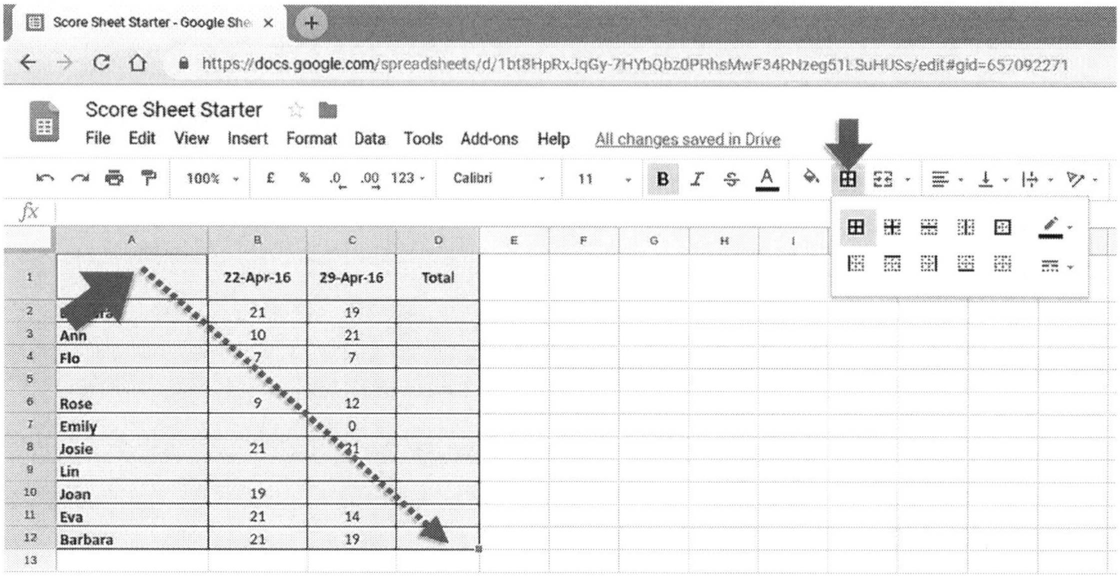

Select the borders icon from the toolbar. Lets take a look at the options on the borders drop down box.

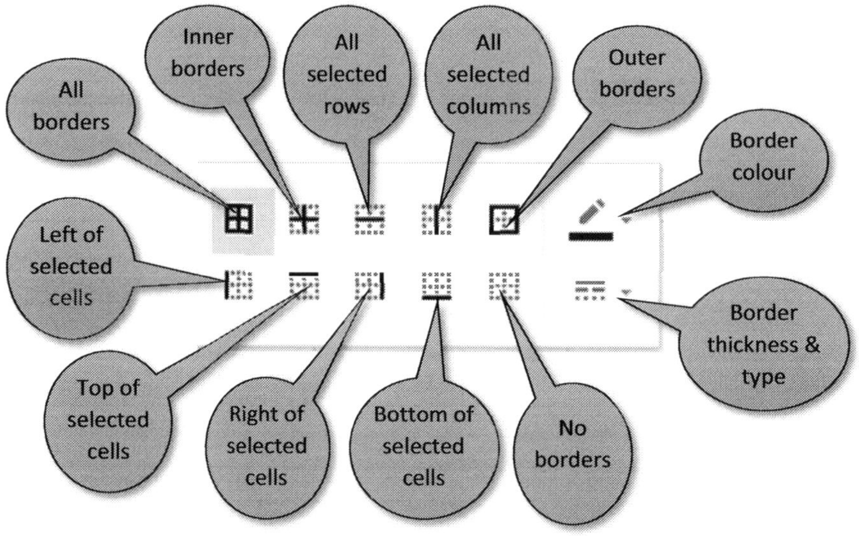

In the example, I want the borders around all the cells both inside and the outline. So from the dialog box click the 'all borders' icon.

To change the thickness, click the 'border thickness & style' icon and select an option.

To change the colour of the border, click the 'border colour' icon, and select a colour.

Using Formulas

If I wanted to add up all the scores in my score sheet, I could add another column called total and enter a formula to add up the scores for the two weeks the player has played.

To do this, I need to find the cell references for Barbara's scores.

Her scores are in row 2 and columns B and C circled below.

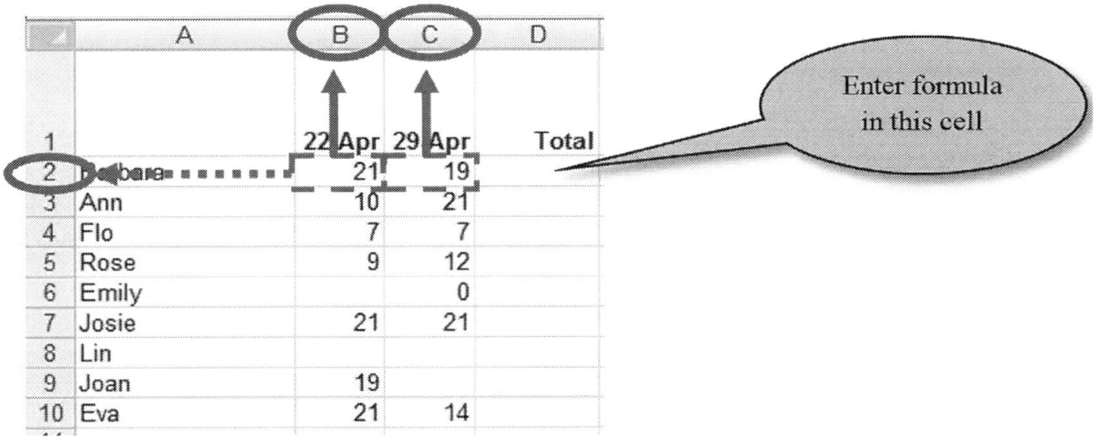

So the cell references are B2 for her score of 21, and C2 for her score of 19.

So we enter into the cell under the heading 'total'

    = B2+C2

Remember all formulas must start with an equals sign **(=)**.

To save you entering the formula for each row, you can replicate it instead.

If you click on the cell D2, where you entered the formula above, you will notice on the bottom right of the box, a small square handle.

I've enlarged the image so you can see it clearly.

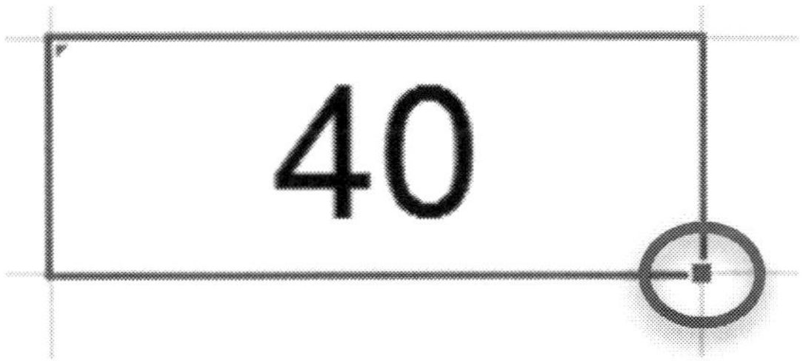

Drag this handle down the rest of the column to replicate the formula.

Using Functions

A function is a pre-defined formula. Google Sheets has hundreds of different functions all designed to make analysing your data easier.

Count

Say I wanted to count the number of games played automatically. I could do this with a function.

Insert a new column after "29 Apr" into the spreadsheet and call it "Played". To do this, right click on the D column (the 'Total' column) and from the menu click 'insert column'.

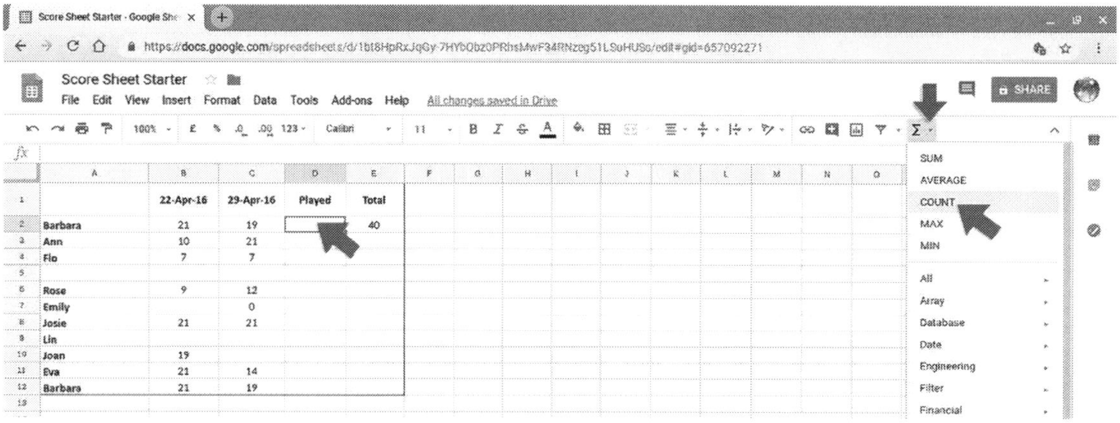

Make sure you have selected the cell you want the formula to appear in, then click 'insert function' icon on the toolbar.

Now, click and drag across the row of cells you want to apply the function to. In this example, I want to count the number of games a player has played, so I'd drag the selection box across the two scores in cells B2 to C2.

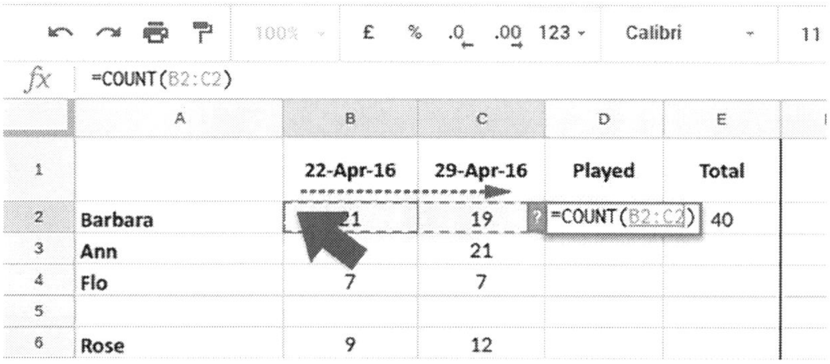

Press the enter key on your keyboard to execute the function. Drag the handle, down to replicate the formula down the column as normal, as shown in the previous example.

Auto Sum

Auto sum, as its name suggests, adds up all the values in a row or column.

To add up a row, click on the cell you want the total to appear in.

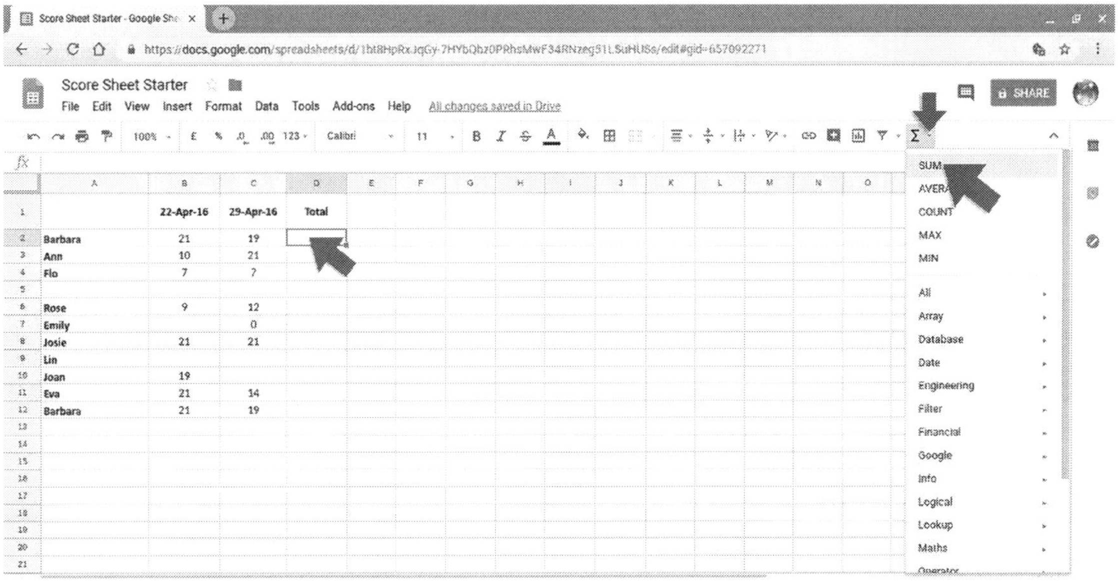

Now, click and drag across the row of cells you want to apply the function to. In this example, I want to add up the scores for each player, so I'd drag the selection box across the two scores in cells B2 to C2.

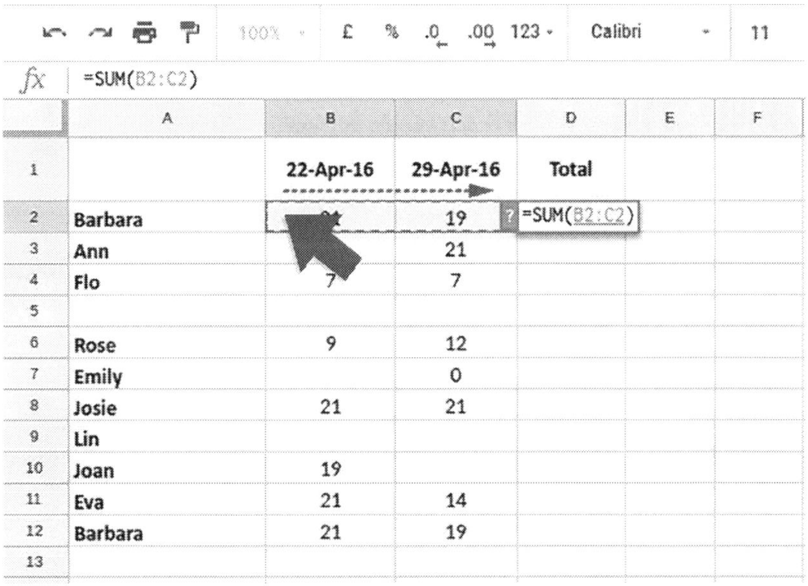

Press the enter key on your keyboard to execute the function. Drag the handle, down to replicate the formula down the column as normal, as shown in the previous example.

Types of Data

There are several different types of data you will come across while using Google Sheets. These data can be numeric such as whole numbers called integers (eg 10), numbers with decimal points (eg 29.93), currencies (eg £4.67 or $43.76), as well as date and time, text and so on.

Going back to our scoring spreadsheet, we need another column for the average scores. Insert a new column and type the heading 'Average' as shown below.

	A	B	C	D	E	F	G	H	I
1	**Name**	**22-Apr-16**	**29-Apr-16**	**Played**	**Total**	**Average**			
2	**Barbara**	21	19	2	40				

We are going to work out the average scores over the number of games the players have played. In the Cell F2 enter the formula

```
Average = Total Score / Total number of Games Played
```

The total score is in E2 and the total number of games played is in D2.

So we enter into F2:

```
= E2 / D2
```

Replicate the formula down the column as we did previously in the example.

Now we need to change the data type of the average to a number with two decimal places. To do this, select the values in the column, then click the data type icon from the toolbar.

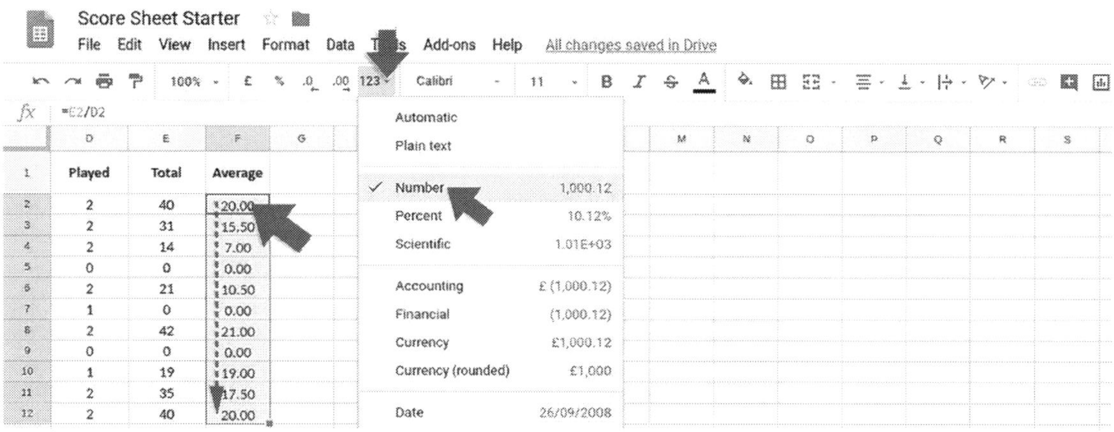

Select 'number' from the drop down menu.

It would be the same for recording the fees paid by the players. Insert another column and call it ‘fee’. Say the fees are 4.50. When we enter 4.5 into the cell, Google Sheets thinks it’s just a number, so we need to tell Google Sheets that it is currency.

Select all the data in the fee column. You don’t need to include the heading row.

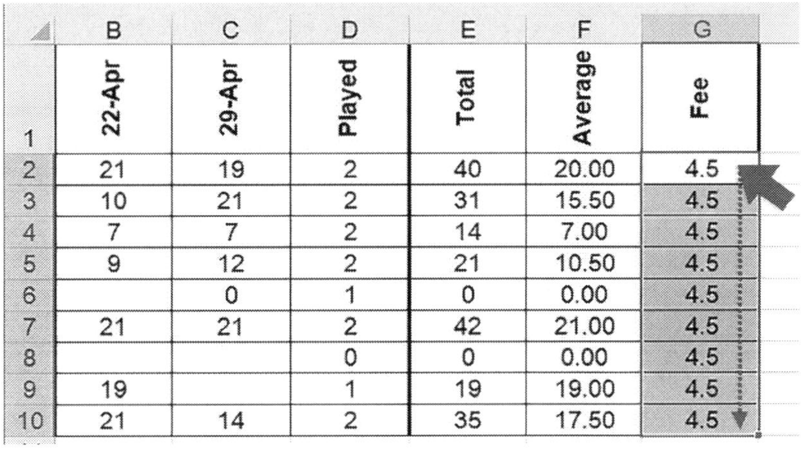

	B	C	D	E	F	G
1	22-Apr	29-Apr	Played	Total	Average	Fee
2	21	19	2	40	20.00	4.5
3	10	21	2	31	15.50	4.5
4	7	7	2	14	7.00	4.5
5	9	12	2	21	10.50	4.5
6		0	1	0	0.00	4.5
7	21	21	2	42	21.00	4.5
8			0	0	0.00	4.5
9	19		1	19	19.00	4.5
10	21	14	2	35	17.50	4.5

Click the data type icon on the toolbar.

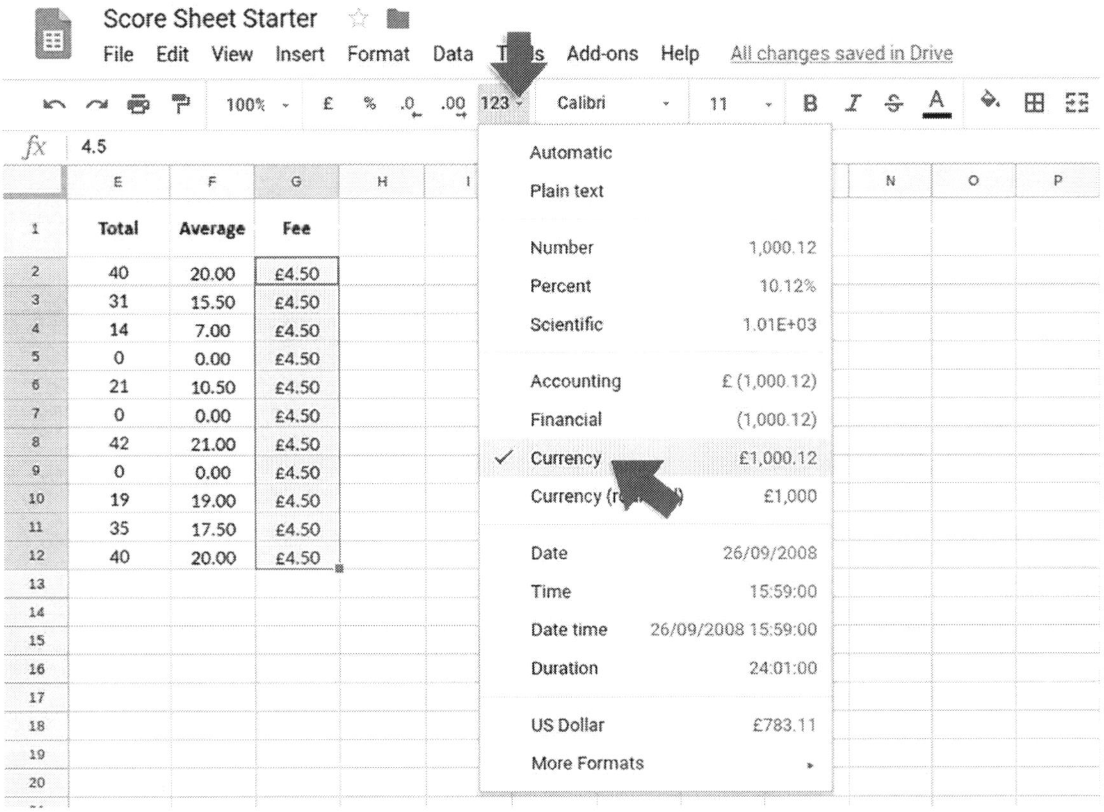

From the drop down menu click currency. This will format all the numbers as a currency.

Adding a Chart

There are many different types of charts to choose from, here are a few examples of some common ones.

First select all the names in the first column. This will be the X-Axis on the chart.

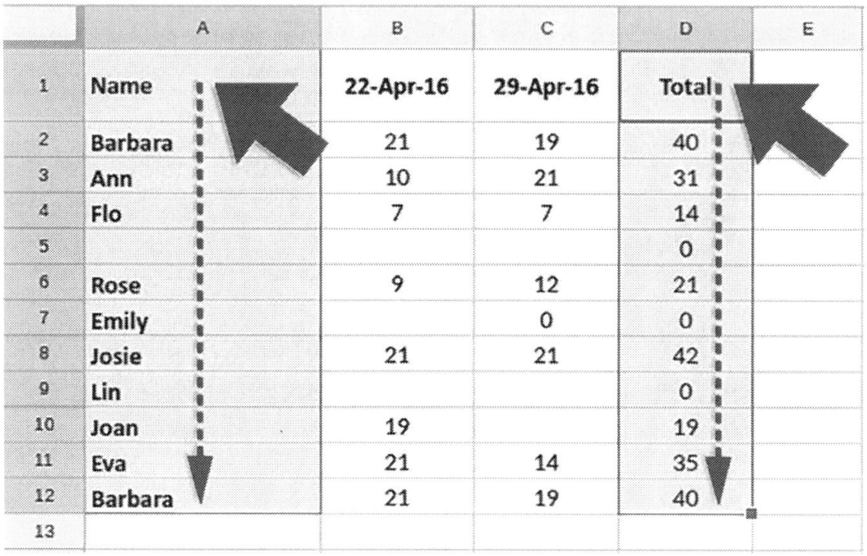

Now hold down the control key (ctrl) on your keyboard. This allows you to multi-select. While holding down control, select the data in the total column with your mouse. This will be the Y-Axis on the chart. Note the data in the names column is still highlighted.

Click the chart icon on the toolbar.

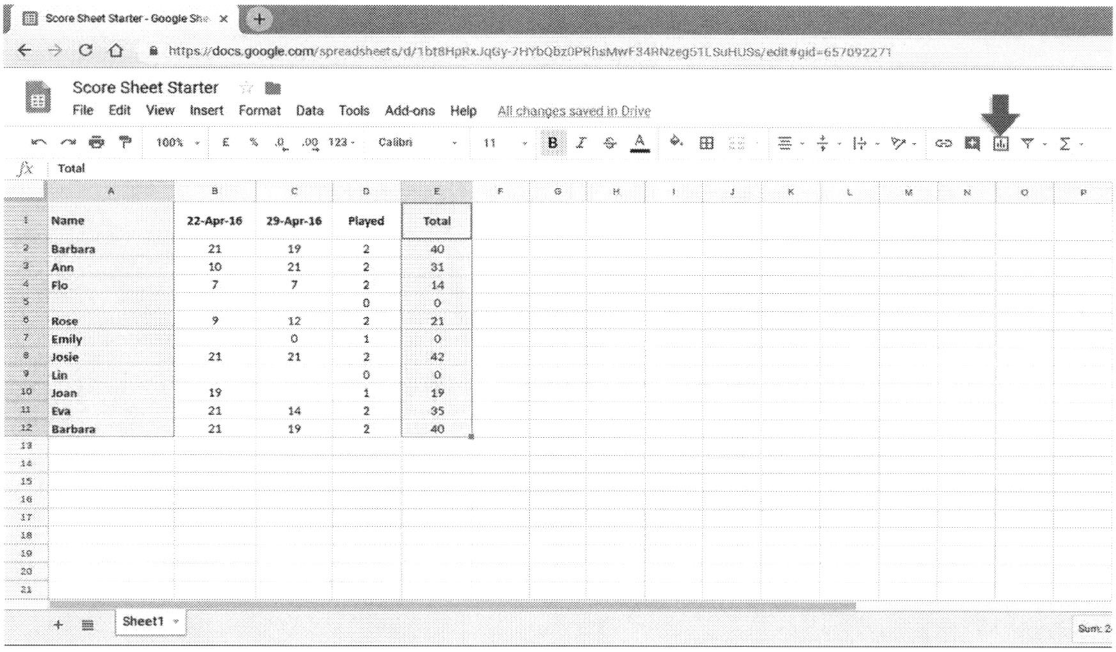

From the chart editor that appears on the right hand side, select the chart type you want. You can change it to a line chart, bar chart, column chart, pie chart, and so on.

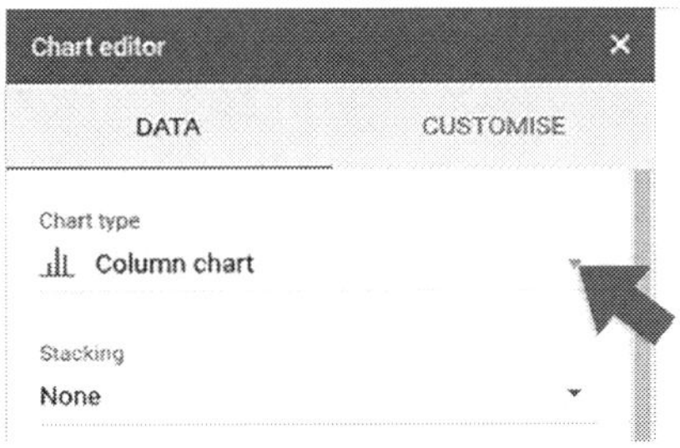

To edit the chart title, click the title on the chart and type in a name. On the chart editor on the right hand side, you can change font, size, and alignment using the controls.

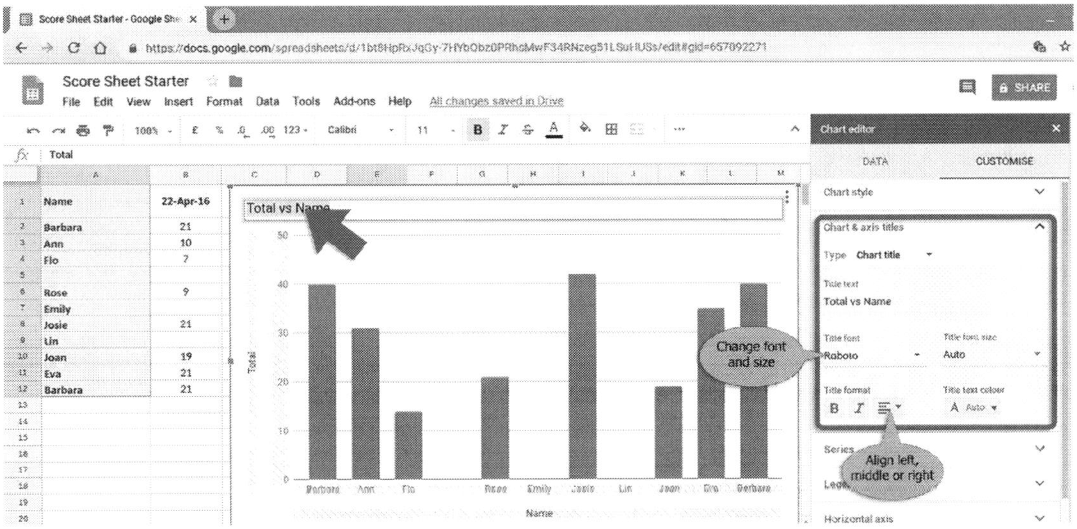

To change the x and y axis labels. Click the label on the chart.

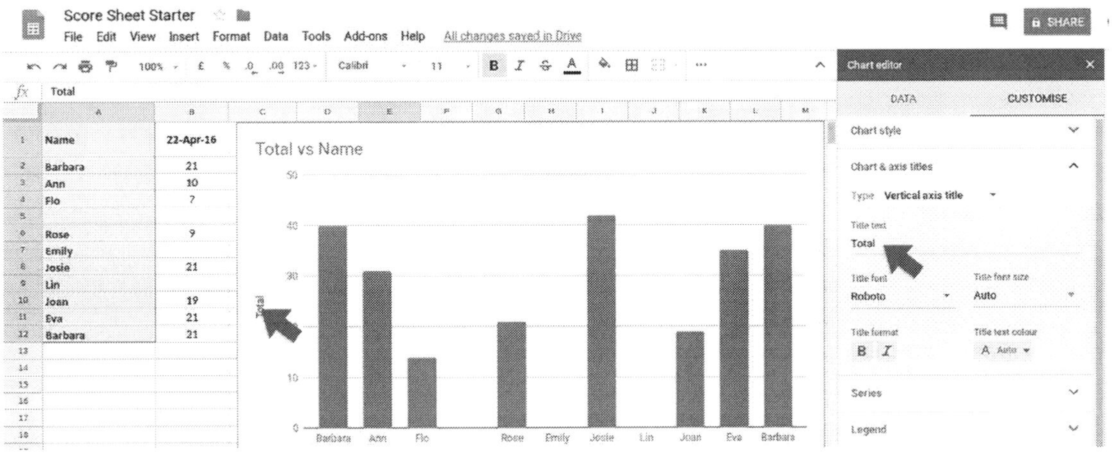

In the chart editor that appears on the right hand side, click 'title text' and type in a label.

11 Google Slides

Google Slides is an online presentation programme much like Microsoft PowerPoint or Apple Keynote and is included as part of a free, web-based office suite developed by Google.

Google Slides allows you to do many of the same things as Microsoft PowerPoint but lacks some of the more advanced features.

However, Google Slides is a great alternative and works well on a ChromeBook.

You can also connect your ChromeBook to a projector or TV screen to give your presentation.

Getting Around Google Slides

I find the best version of Google Slides to use is the web based version rather than the Android Version you might find on your Chromebook. To start the web based version of Google Slides, open your app launcher, then click on Google Chrome.

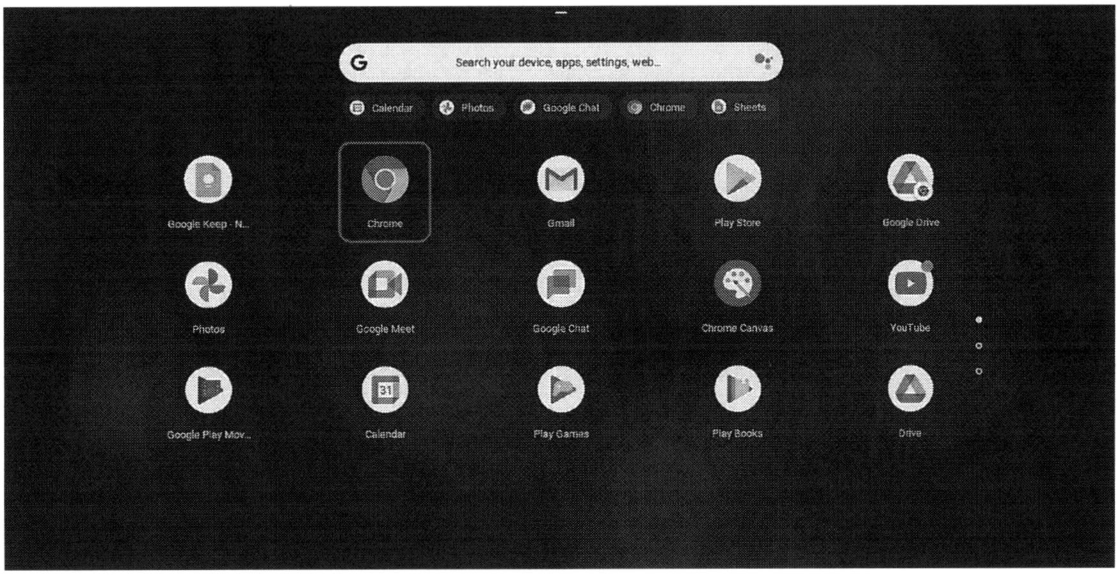

Navigate to the following website:

```
slides.google.com
```

When Google Slides opens, you'll see the presentations you have been working on recently. You can click any of these to re open them. To create a new presentation, click blank on the top left of the screen.

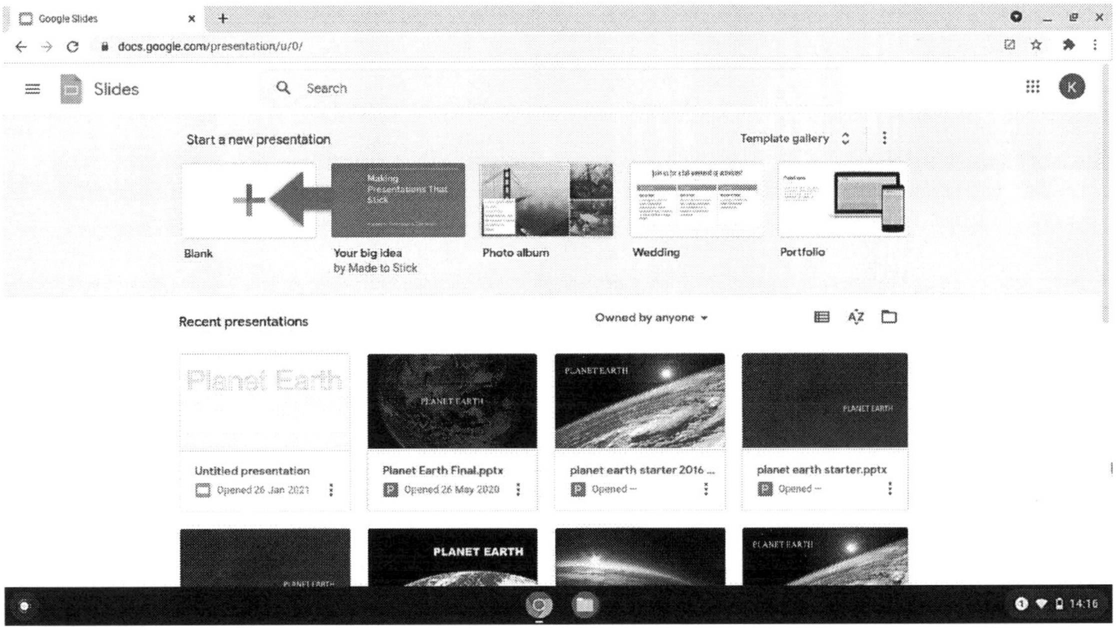

Google Slides will open the main window where you can create your presentation.

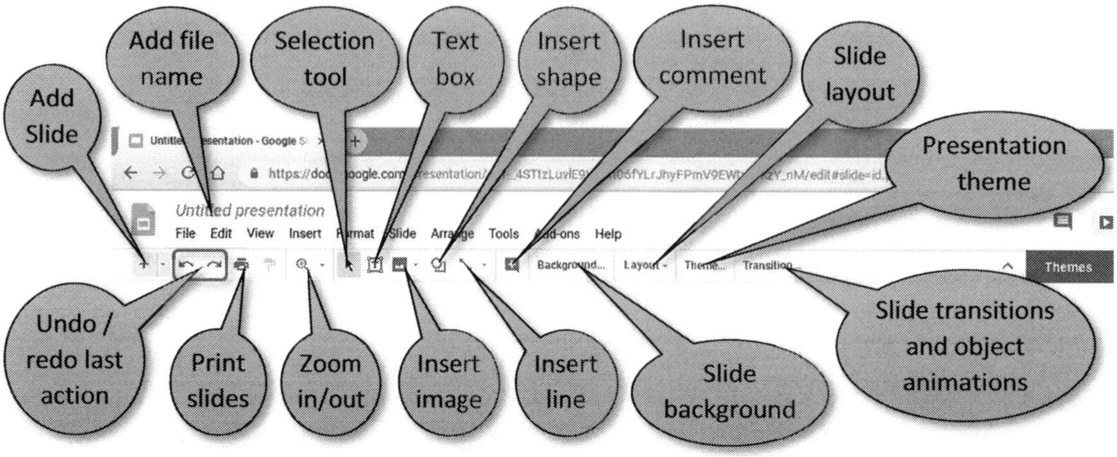

Along the top you'll see the presentation name. It's a good idea to rename this to something more meaningful than 'untitled presentation'. Click on the text and type in a name.

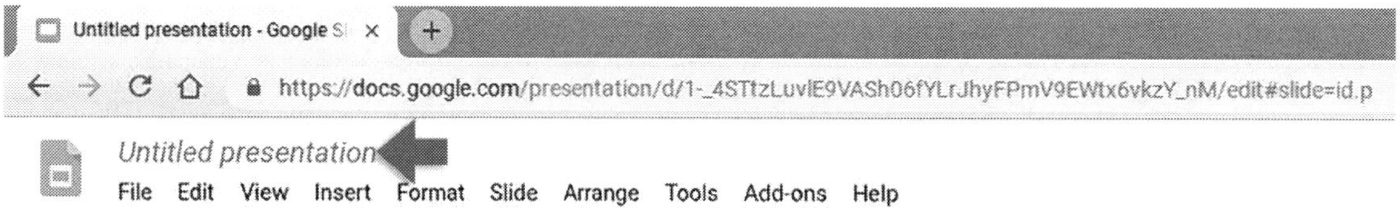

Underneath are the menus. This is where you'll find tools that are not represented as icons on the toolbar.

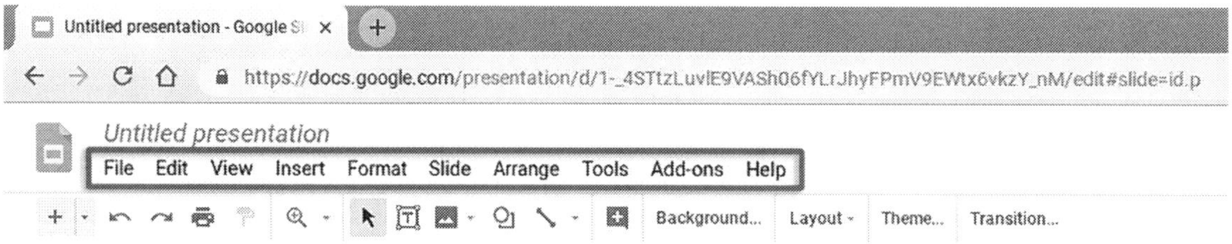

Under the menus you'll see the toolbar. This is where you'll find most of the tools you'll need to create and format your presentations.

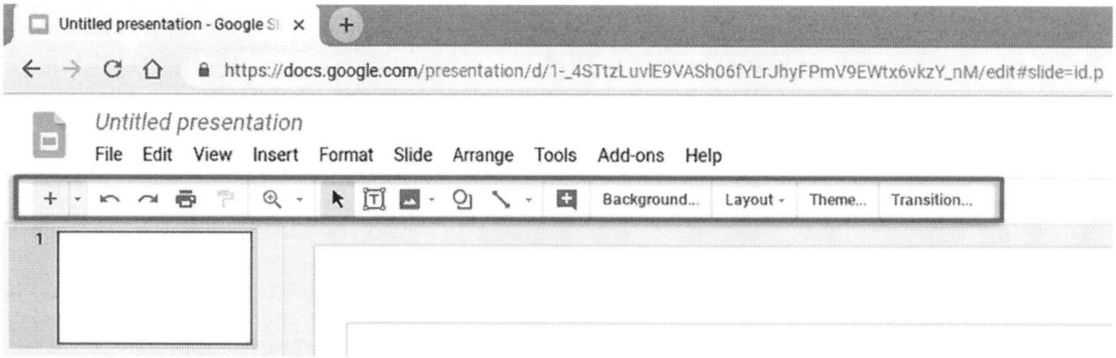

Designing a Slide

Let's begin by adding the title to our first slide. First, select a theme from the templates on the right hand themes panel. Once you have selected a theme, click the white cross on the top left of the panel to close it.

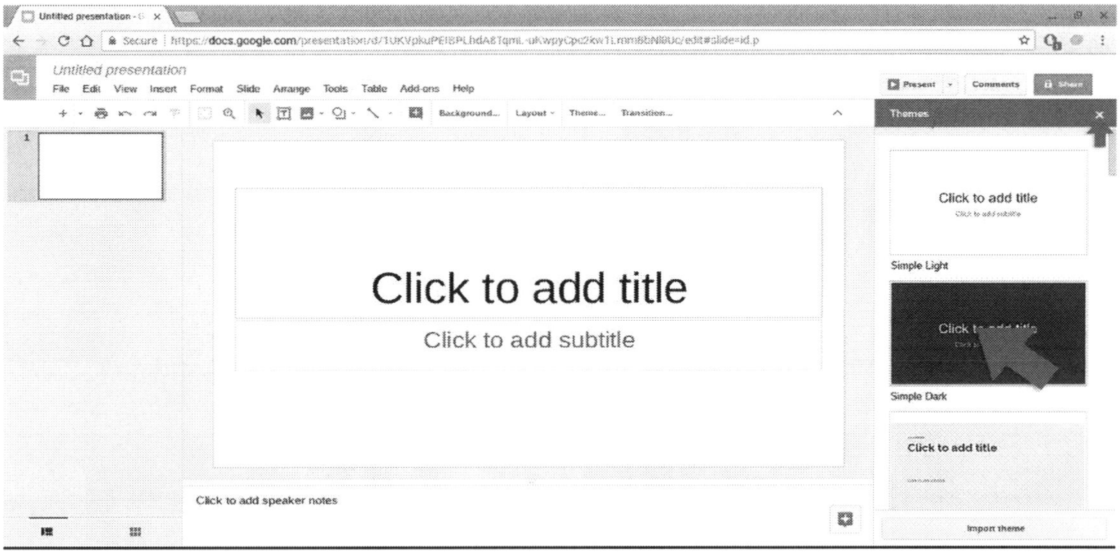

On your slide, click where it says 'click to add title'. This is a place holder for you to enter a title.

Enter the title 'Planet Earth'.

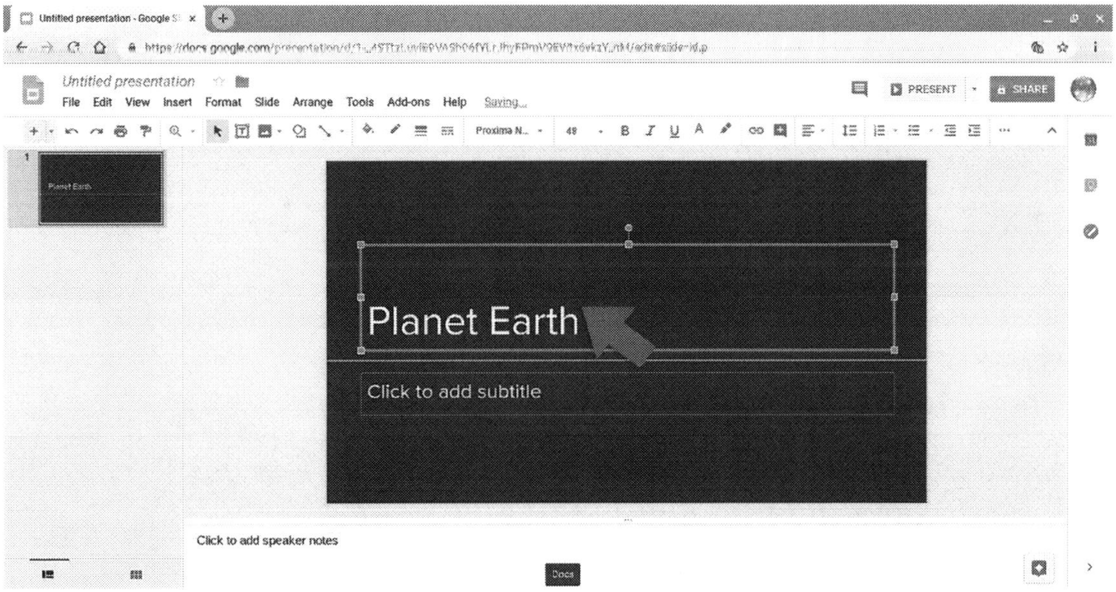

In this example, we won't be adding a subtitle, but you can add one if you want to.

Lets add some images to spice our title slide up a bit.

Add an Image

To add an image, select the slide you want to add the image to using the slide selector on the left hand side. Go to the insert menu then select 'image'.

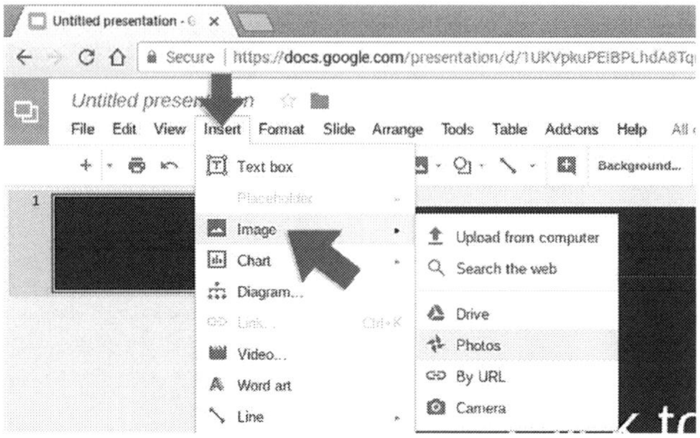

Now, from the slideout menu, select where you are adding the image from. This can be uploaded from your computer, the web, Google Drive, Google Photos, a direct weblink, or from your on-board camera.

From Photos

To add an image from Google Photos, select 'photos' from the image slideout menu. Google Photos contains photos you've taken with your android phone, or any other tablet you've signed into with your Google Account.

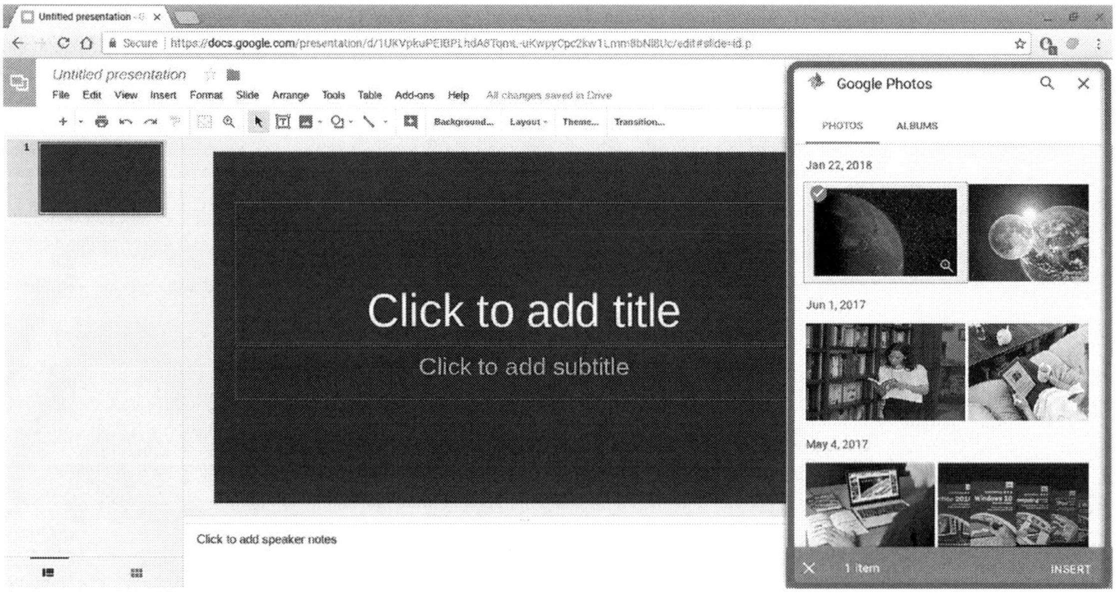

Google Photos will open in a panel on the right hand side, scroll through, click a photo then click 'insert'.

From the Web

To add an image from the web, select 'the web' from the image slideout menu. Google Search will open up in the panel on the right hand side. Type in your search into the field at the top

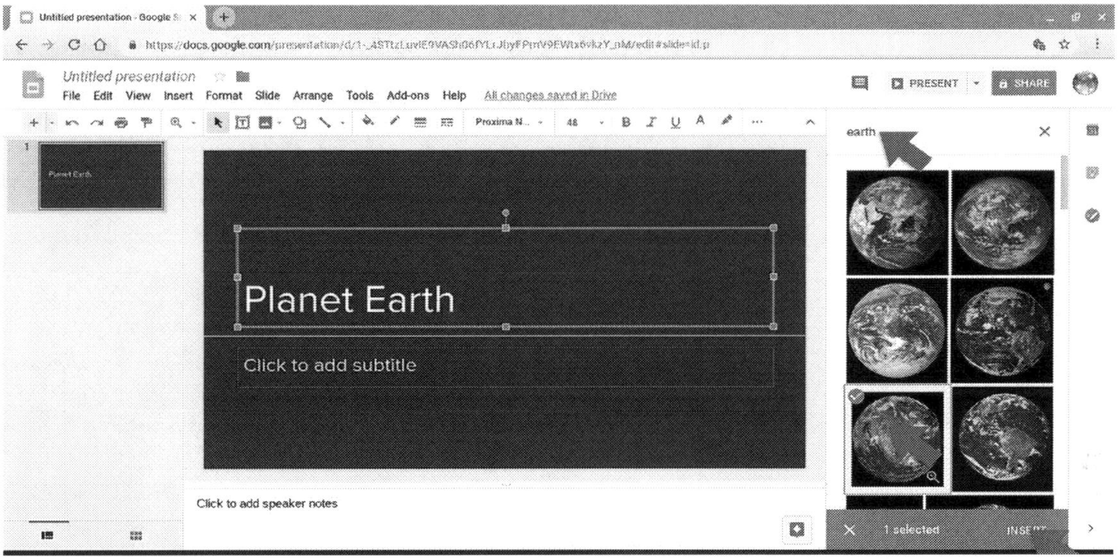

Click on the image you want then click 'insert'.

From your Google Drive

To add an image from your Google Drive, select 'Drive' from the image slideout menu. In the panel on the right hand side click 'my drive'. Any images stored on your Google Drive will open up in the panel on the left hand side.

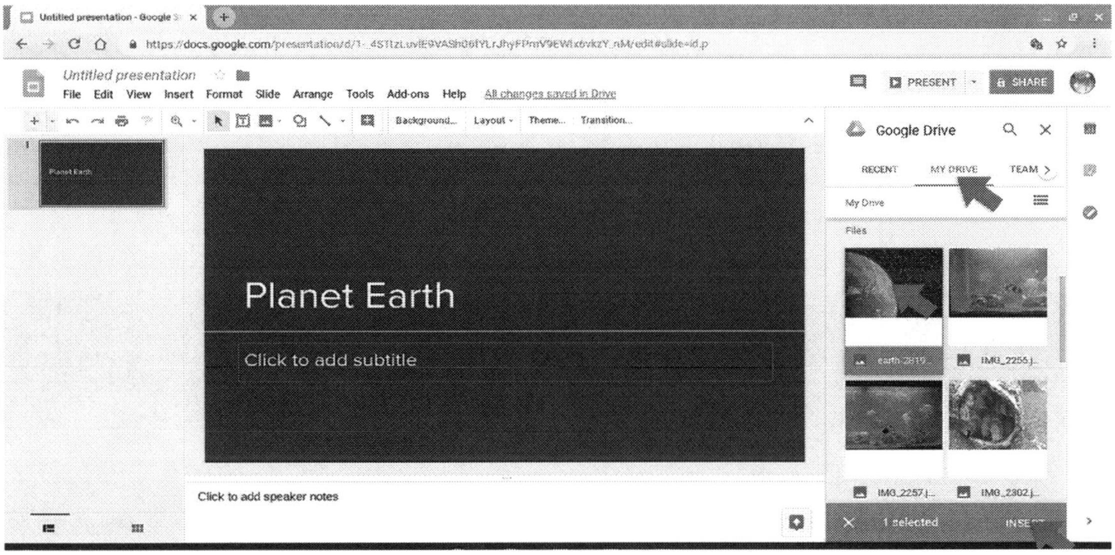

Click on the image you want then click 'insert'.

Resize an Image

When you click on an image on your slide, you'll see some resize handles appear around each corner.

Click and drag these resize handles to resize the image.

You may need to move the image into position. To do this, click and drag the image into position.

Crop an Image

Click on the image you want to crop, then from the toolbar, select the 'crop' icon.

You'll see some crop handles appear around each corner.

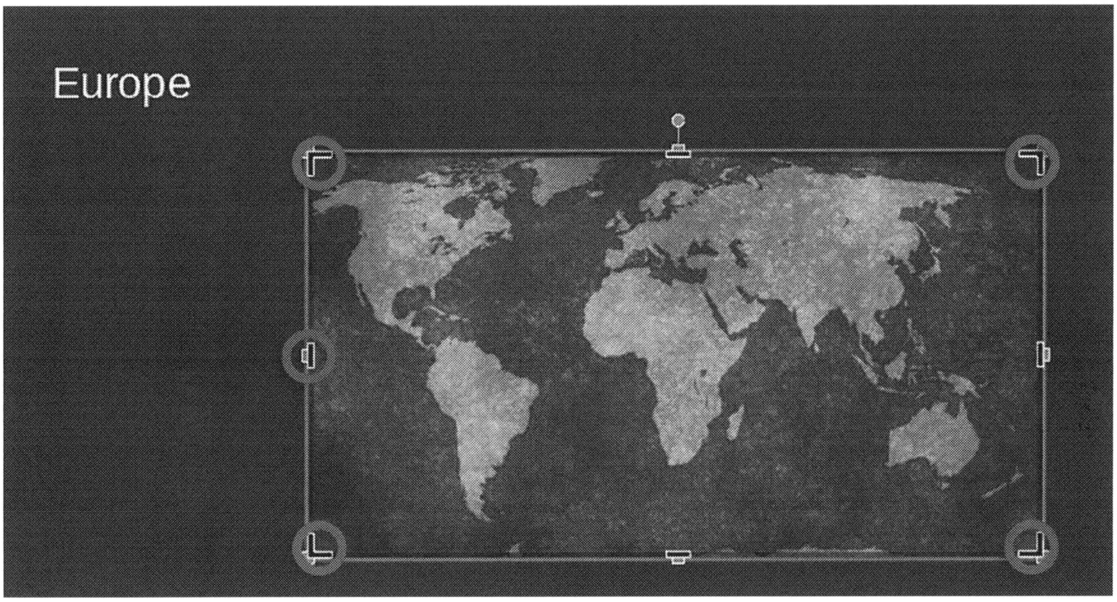

Click and drag these crop handles around the part of the image you want to keep. In this example, I only want to highlight Europe on this map.

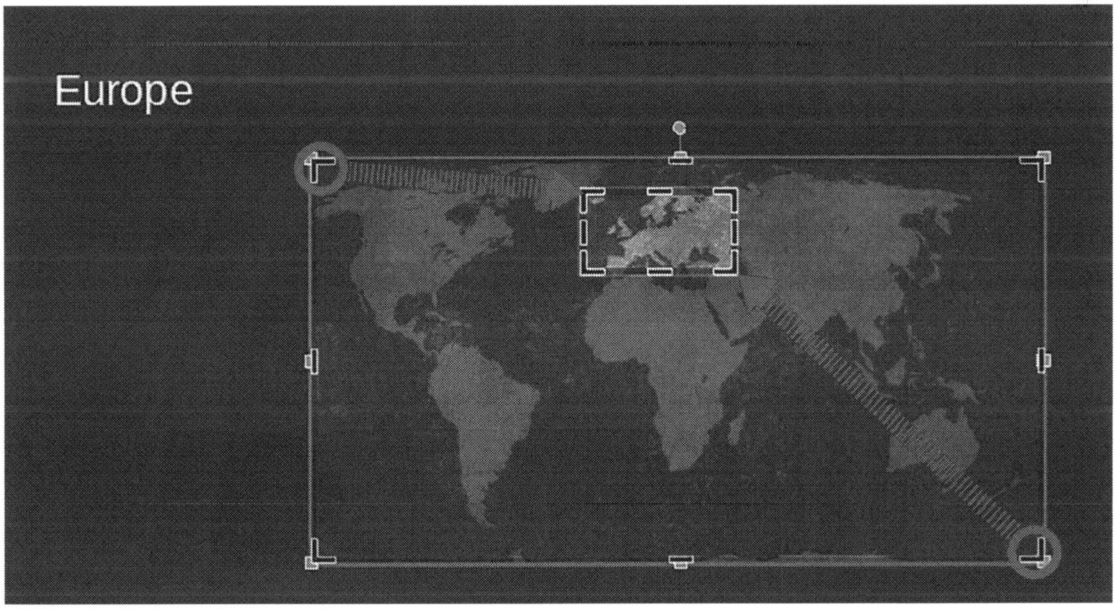

You may need to move the image into position. To do this, click and drag the image into position. Resize the image if needed.

Add a Video

You can add YouTube videos, or your own videos stored on Google Drive.

To do this, select the slide you want to add your video to, from the slide selector on the left hand side. From the insert menu, select 'video'.

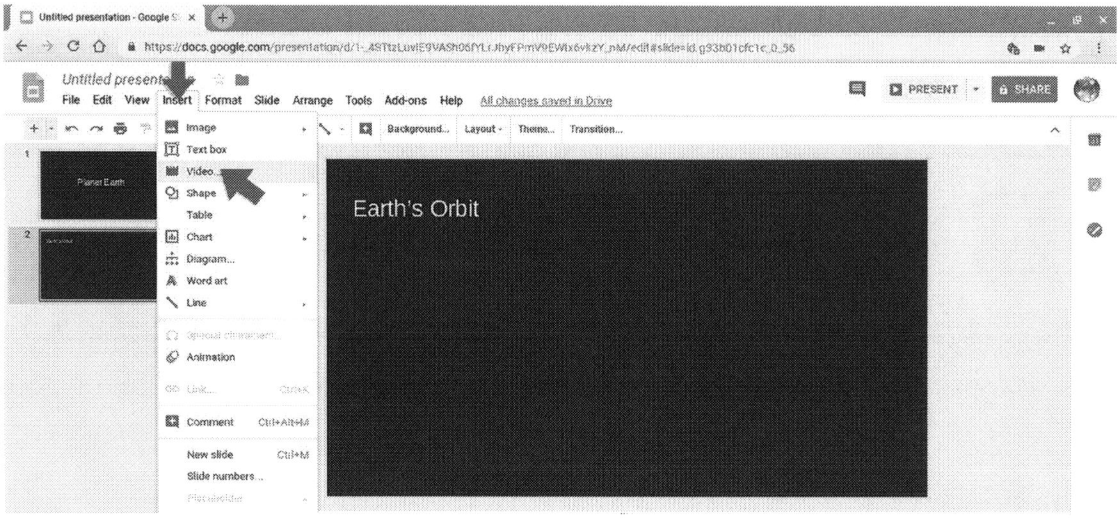

From the dialog box that appears, select 'search' to search the web for a YouTube video, or click 'Google Drive' to use one of your own videos.

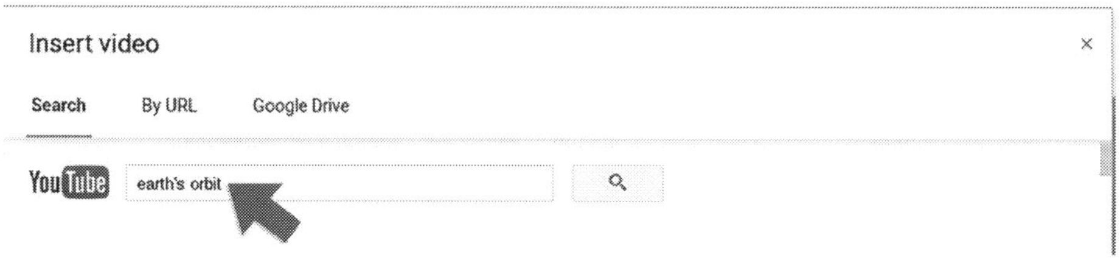

In the search field at the top of the screen, type in your search and press the enter key on your keyboard.

From the search results, select the video you want to insert, then click 'insert'.

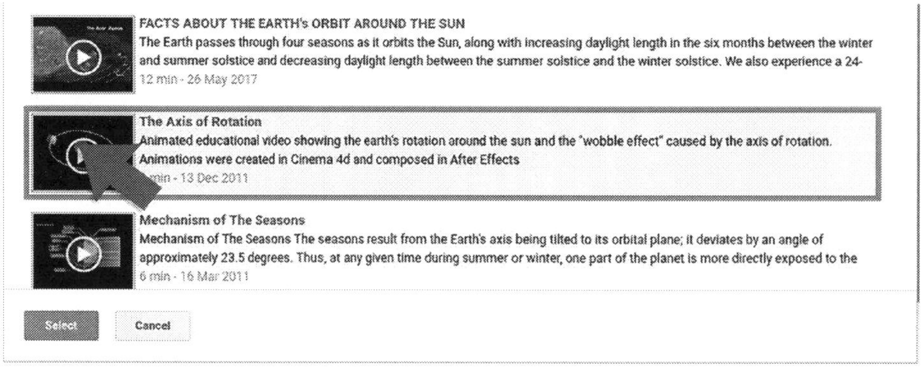

Videos on YouTube have a lot of rubbish in them that you don't need. You can trim the beginning and end of the video, so it starts and ends exactly in the right place. To do this, right click on the video on the slide. From the popup menu, select 'format options'.

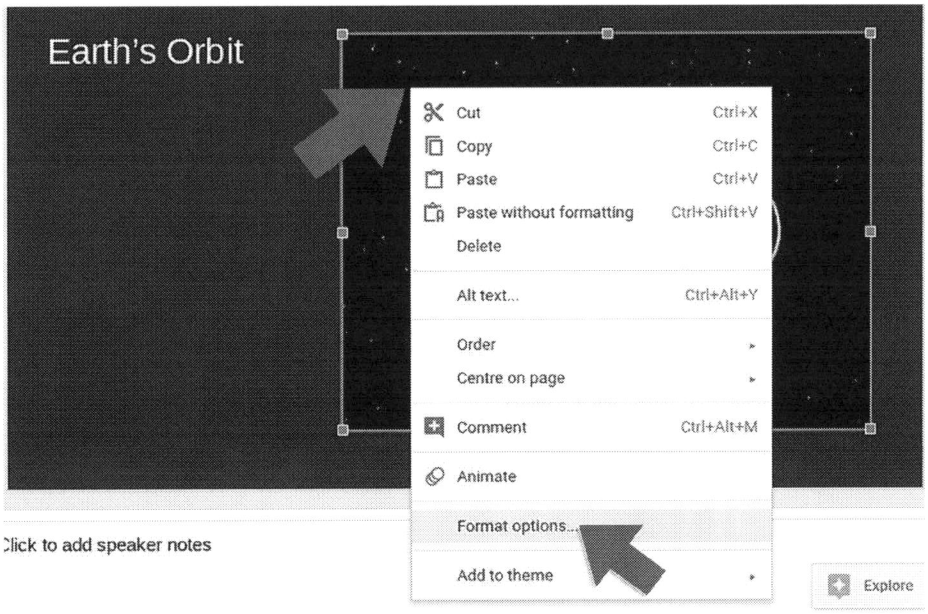

The 'format options' panel will open on the right hand side of the screen. From here hover your mouse over the video progress bar and you'll see a silent preview of the video. Click on the position you want the video to start.

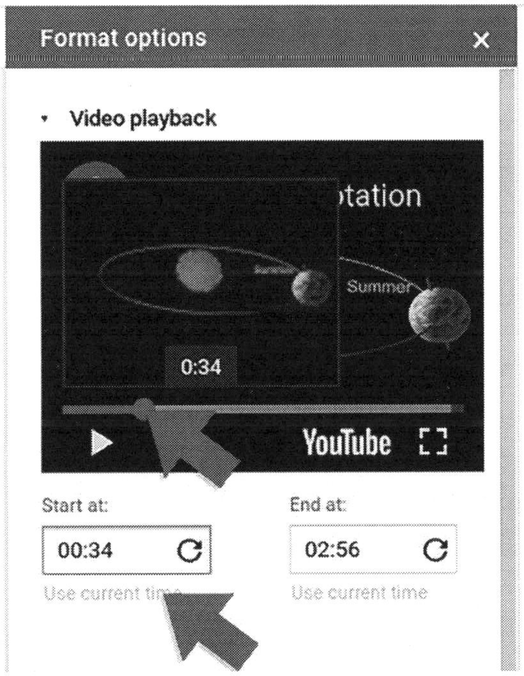

Click 'use current time' to trim the start time to the position in the video. Repeat the procedure for the end times.

Slide Layer Arrangement

In the example below, I've added an image to the title slide.

You'll notice when you add an image, video, or other object, it covers the title or another object. This is because Google Slides constructs slides using layers. So the title "Planet Earth" will be on one layer, and the image will be on another layer.

Now, because the image was inserted after the title, the image layer is on top of the title layer. We want the title layer on top. We need to send the image to the back layer.

To do this, right click on the image or object, then from the popup menu, select 'order'. From the slideout, select 'send to back'.

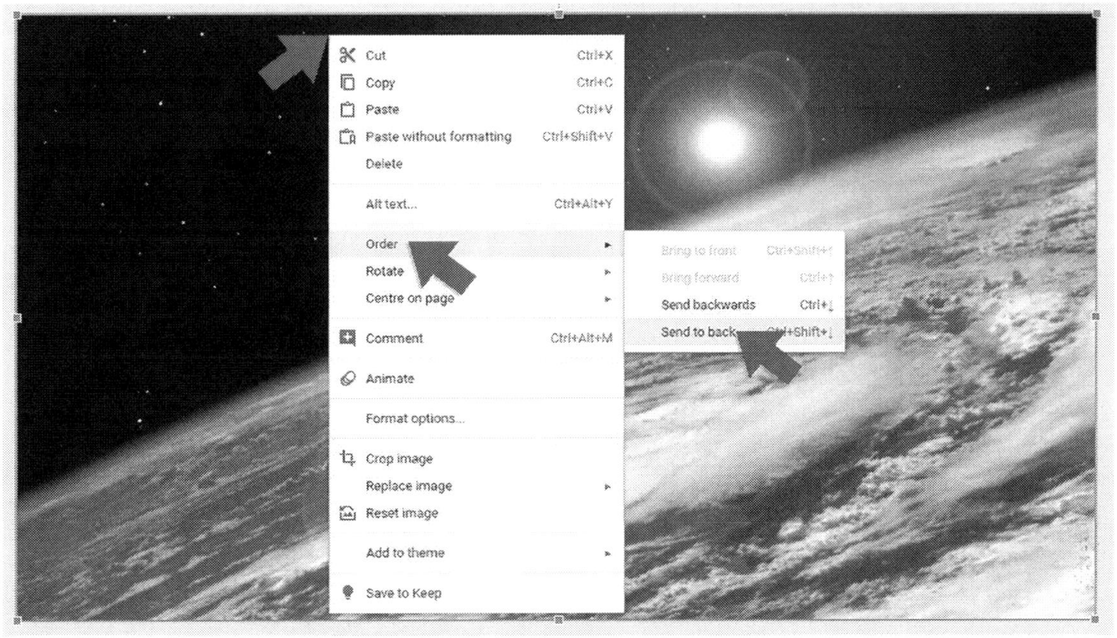

This will put the image in the background. Now you can see the title, and you can drag it into position on the slide.

Add a New Slide

To continue building our presentation we need additional slides to show our information. To add a new slide, click the small down arrow next to the 'New Slide' icon.

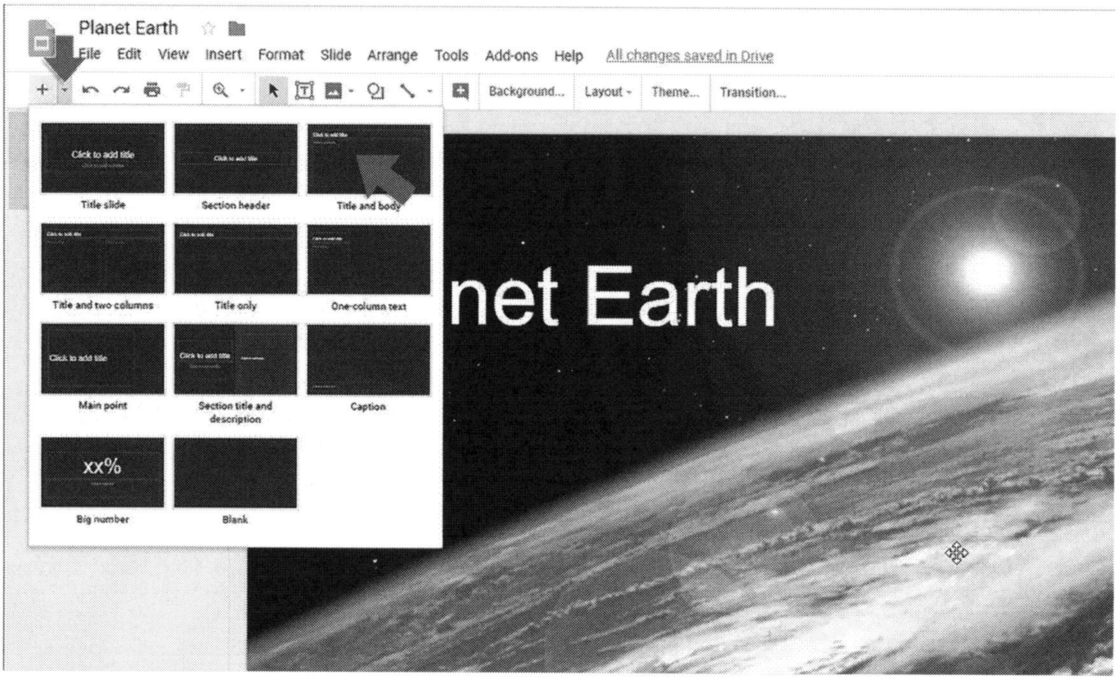

From the drop down menu, select 'title and body' because we want a title on the slide but also we want to add some information in bullet points.

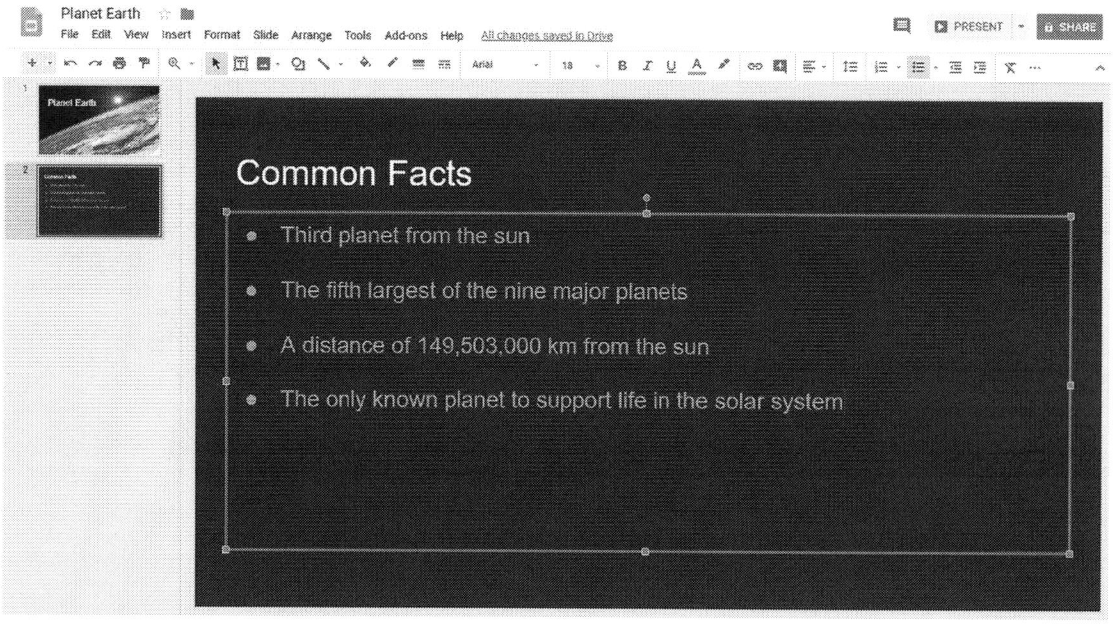

Now enter the data into your new slide.

Change Slide Layout

Select the slide whose layout you want to change. Then go to the 'slide' menu and select 'apply layout'.

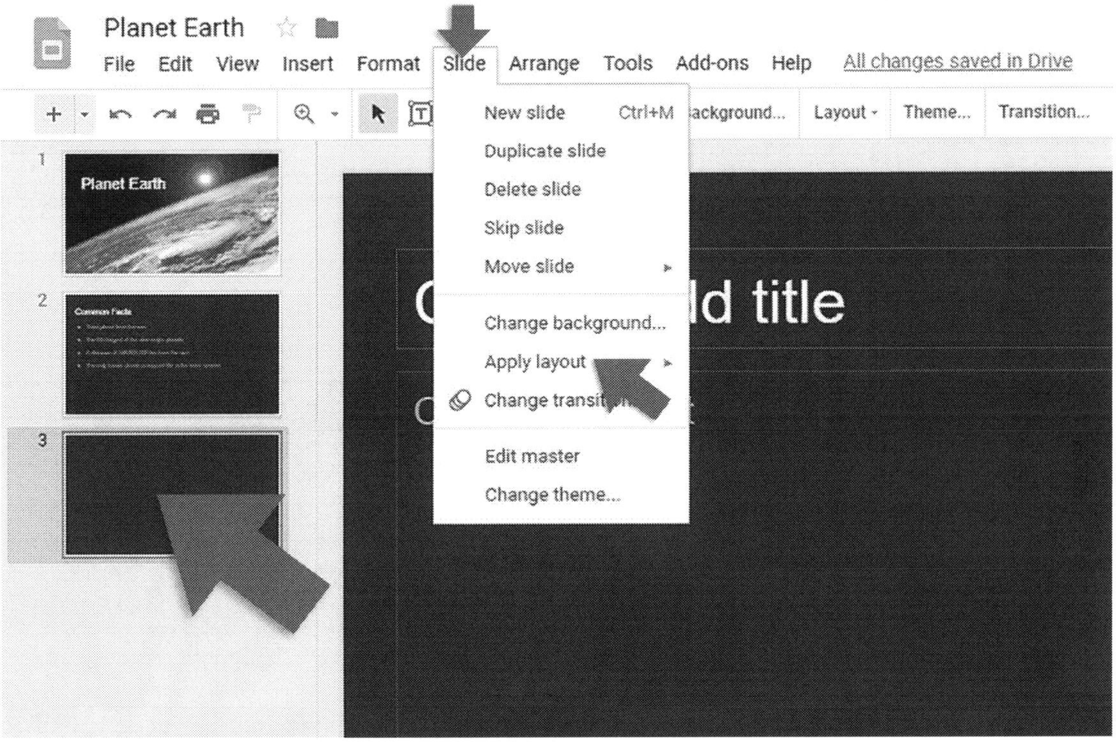

From the slideout menu, select a template from the options.

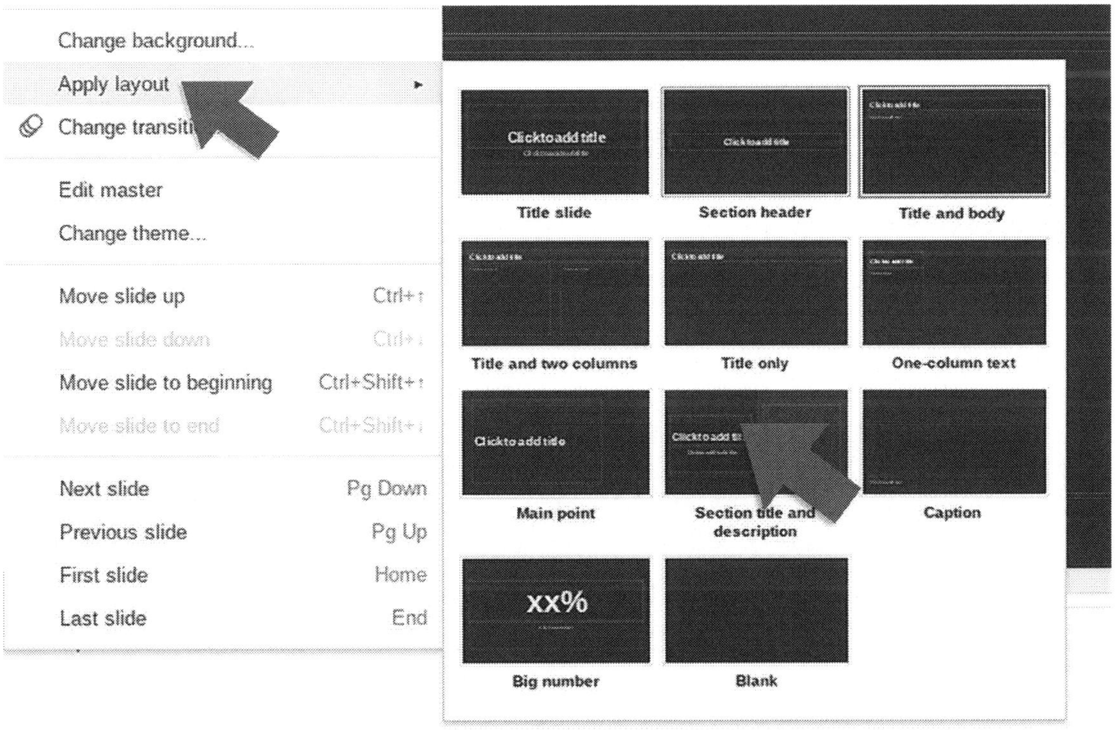

Slide Masters

Slide masters allow you to create layouts and templates that are common to all your slides, so you don't have to make those changes to each slide.

Say you are creating a presentation and want a company logo on the bottom, you can add it to your slide master and the logo will appear on every slide you create.

To edit your slide masters, go to the slide menu and click 'edit master'.

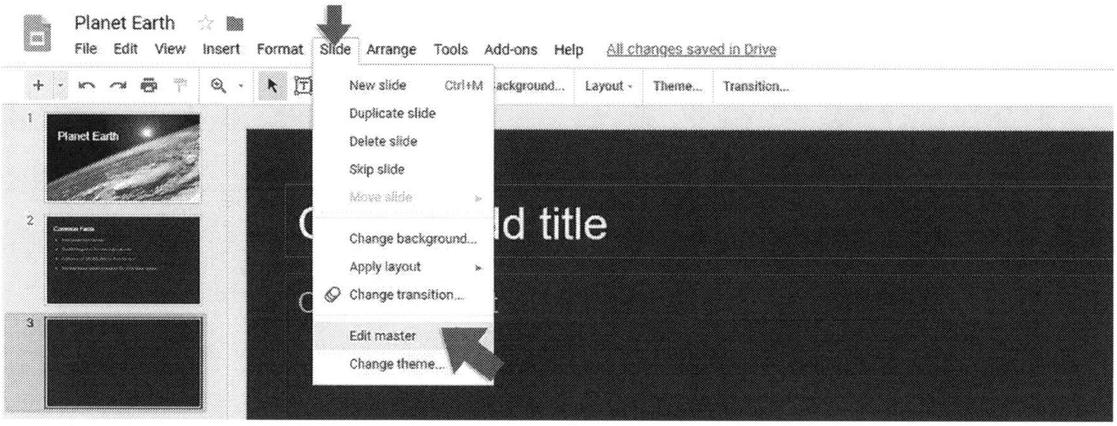

The larger slide listed down the left hand side is your master for all slides. The ones below are masters for individual slide templates such as 'title slides' or 'title and body' slides. These appear in the 'new slide' drop down menu. You can split them up so you can create templates for specific slides.

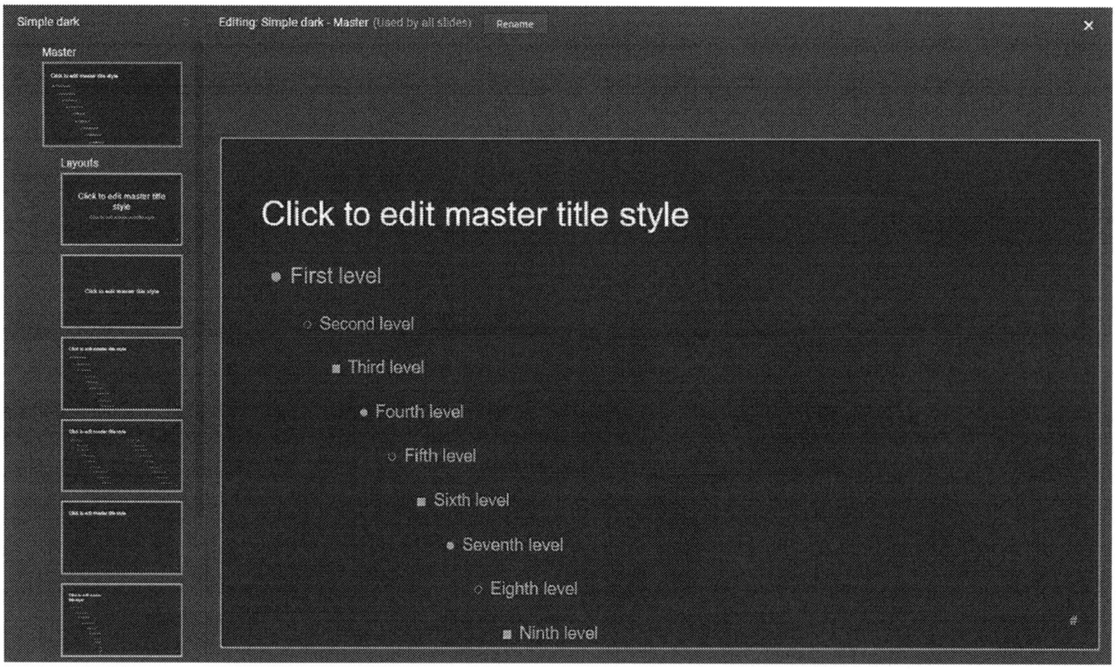

In this simple example, I am going to add the company logo to the bottom right of every slide. To do this, click on the larger master slide in the list on the left hand side.

Open your file explorer and navigate to your Google Drive folder, or the folder where the picture you want is saved. Click and drag your image onto the master slide.

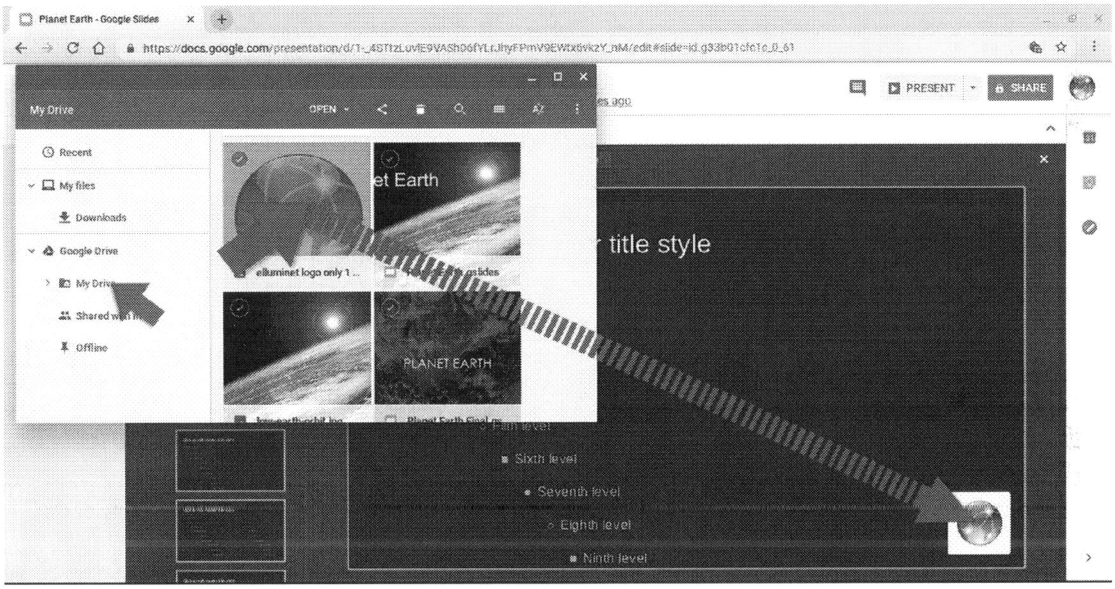

Notice, the logo we just added appears on all the slides.

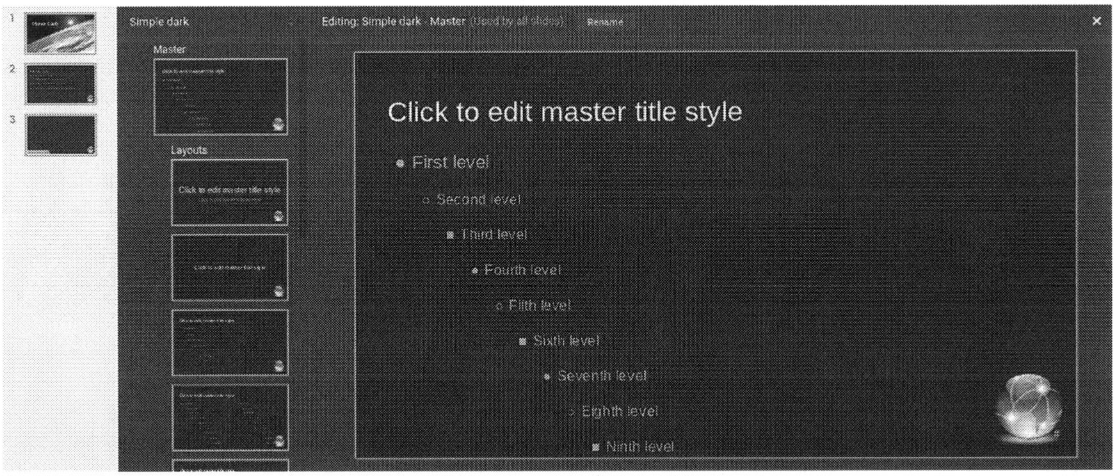

Click the small white x on the top right to close the masters.

Slide Transitions

A slide transition is an animation or effect that is displayed when you move from one slide to the next.

To add transitions to your slides, click the slide you want to add the transition to, then click 'transition'.

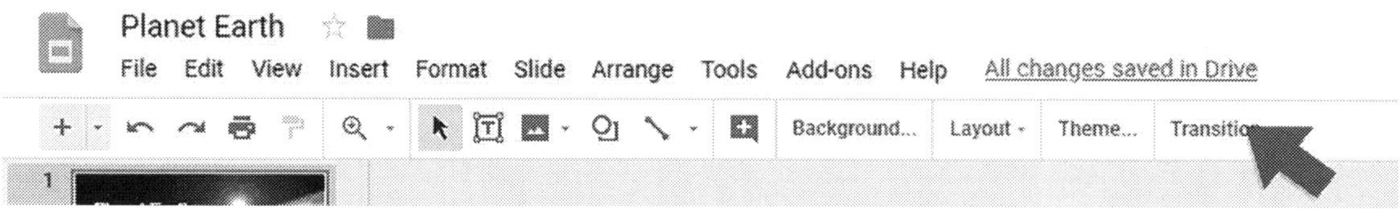

From the animations panel on the right hand side of the screen, you can select from several pre set transitions. If you click on a transition, for example 'fade', this will apply the transition to the selected slide.

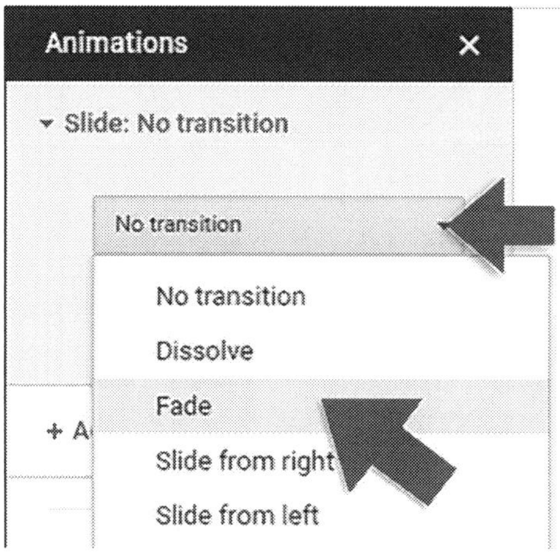

Select how fast you want the slides to transition, using the slider.

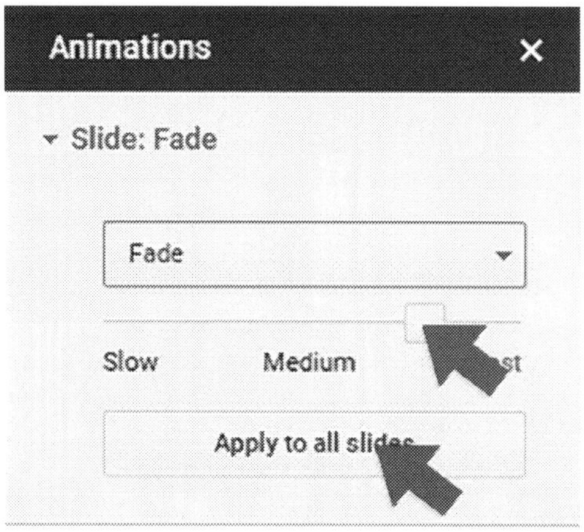

By default, the transition is only applied to the slide you have selected. Click 'apply to all slides' if you want to apply the same transition to all the slides you have added to your presentation

Slide Animations

You can add animations to slides to move text boxes, make bullet points appear, animate shapes and so on. This can help to make your presentation flow so objects and text appear at the right time while you're presenting. Animation effects can also help to emphasise certain points.

Effects

Looking at the slide below, say you wanted each bullet point to appear one at a time, instead of all at once.

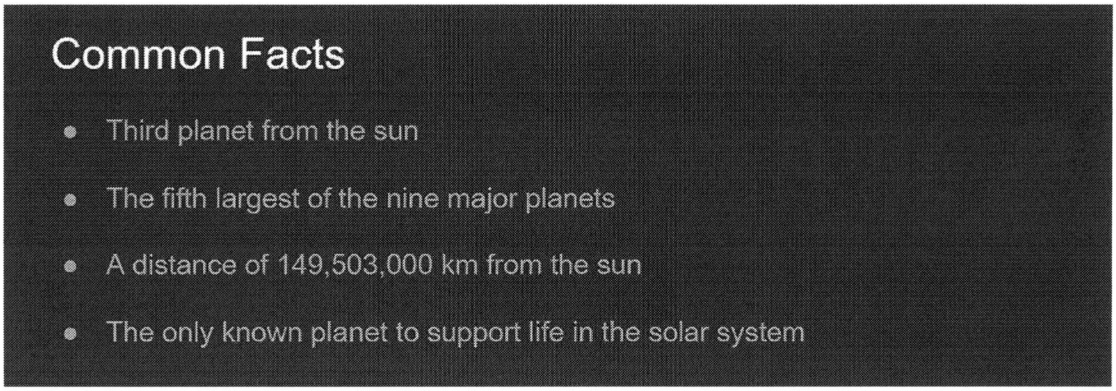

To add an animation effect to the bullet points, click 'transition' on the right hand side of the toolbar.

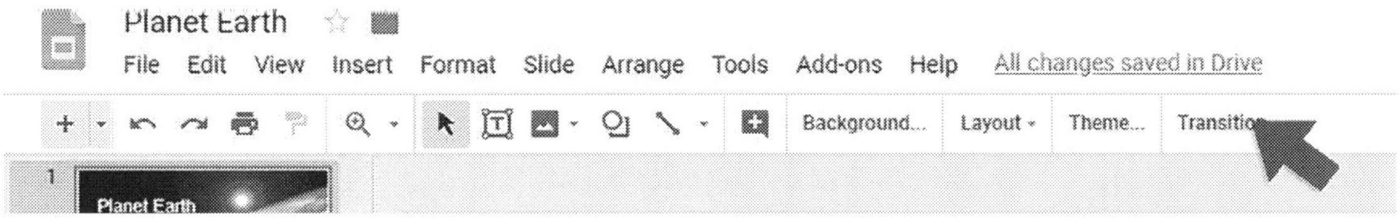

This will open up the 'animations' panel on the right hand side of your screen.

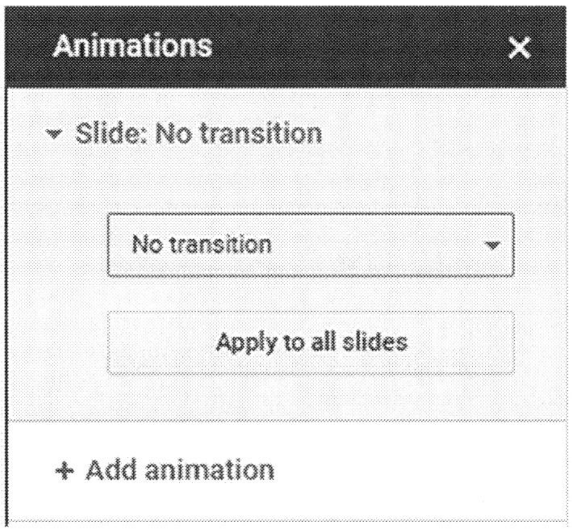

First, select the object you want to add an animation to. In this case the textbox with the bullet points in.

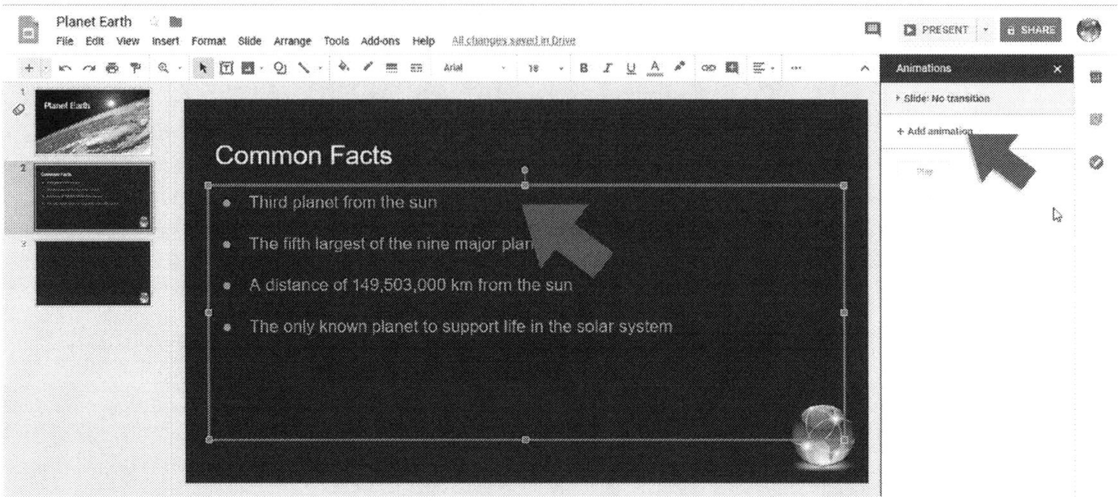

In the first drop down box, select the animation preset you want, eg 'fade in'.

In the second drop down box, select 'on click' - meaning you click the mouse to show the next point.

Select 'by paragraph'. This means a 'paragraph' will appear at a time. A new paragraph is created each time you press return when typing in your slide information into the text box.

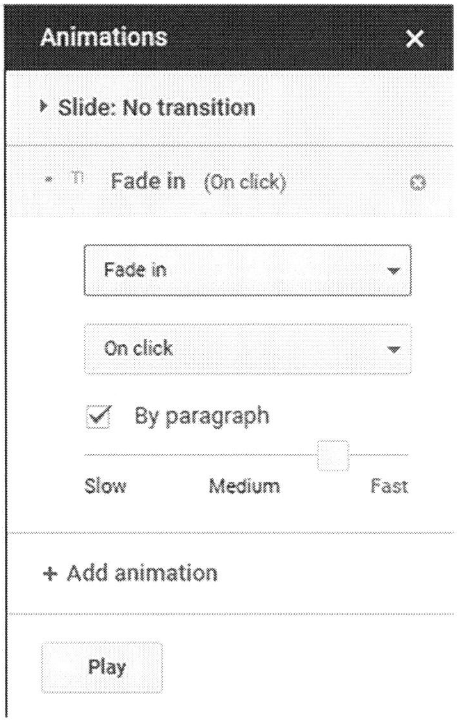

Click 'play' to preview the animation.

Insert a Table

We are going to add a table to a new slide. In this example I have added a new slide with 'title only'.

To add a table to this slide, go to the 'insert' menu and select 'table'. From the slideout, select the number of columns and rows. This table is going to have 2 columns.

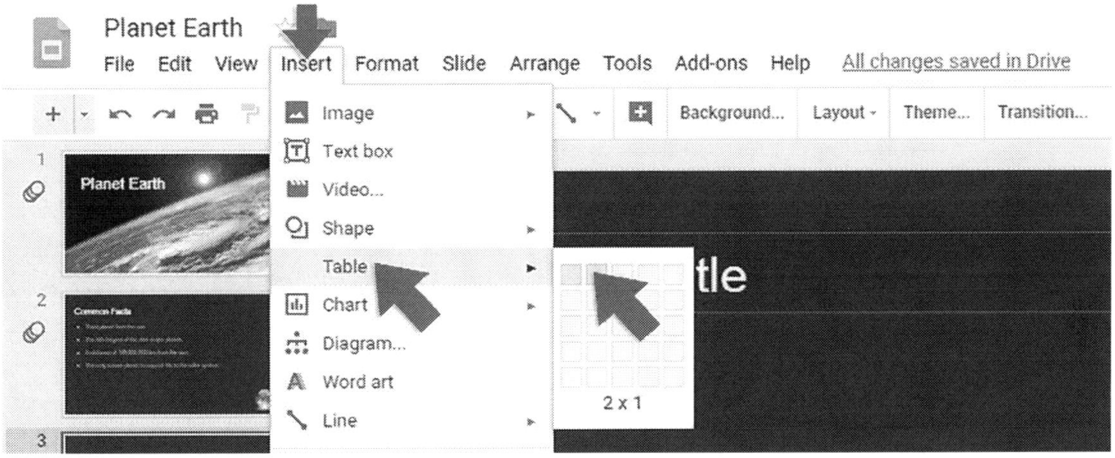

Your table will appear in the centre of the slide. You can type in your data.

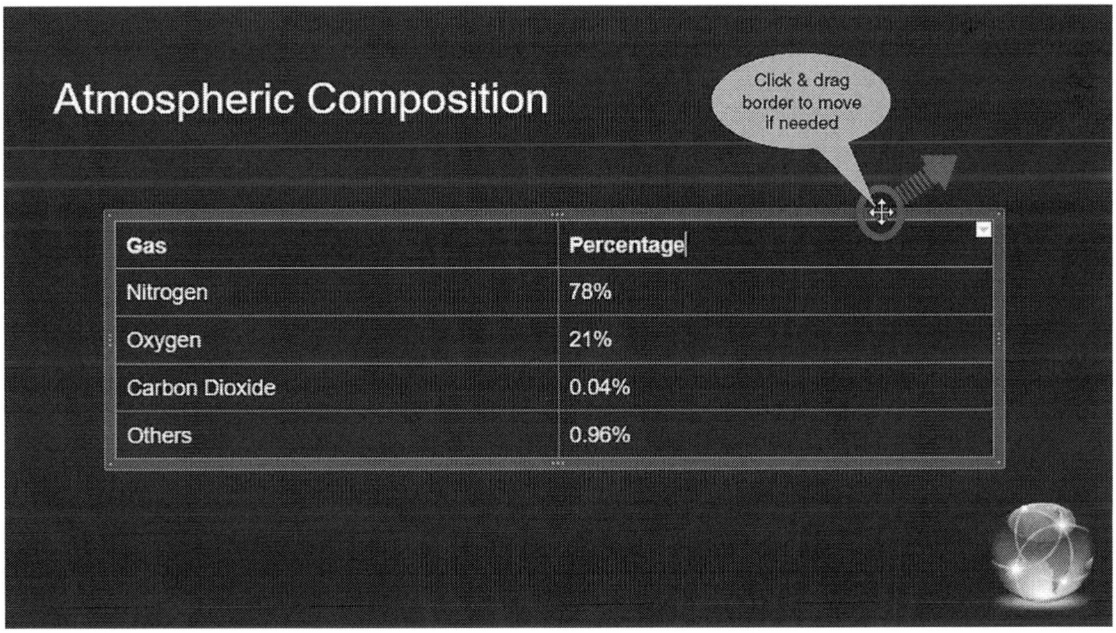

Press the tab key on your keyboard to insert a new row, when you get to the end.

Click & drag the solid double blue border to move the table into position on your slide.

Add a Chart

We are going to add a chart to a new slide. In this example I have added a new slide with 'title only'

Click the 'insert' menu, then select 'chart'. From the slideout, select the type of chart you want. In this example, I am going to use a nice pie chart.

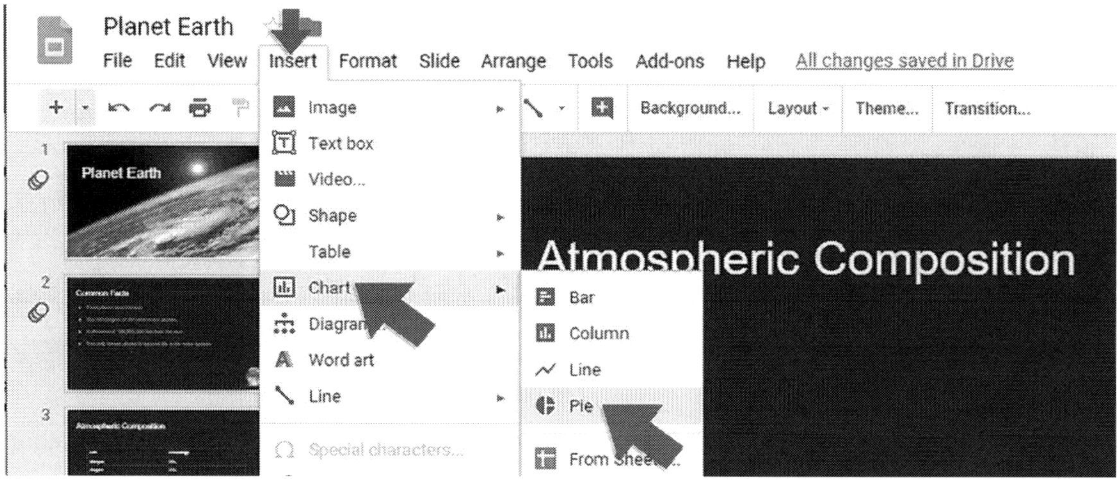

Google Slides will insert a default chart. To enter your own data, click the down arrow on the top right of the chart and select 'open source'.

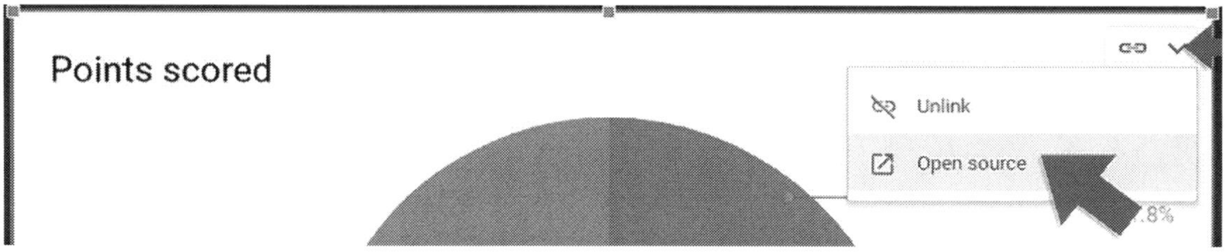

In the spreadsheet that opens, enter your data in the first two columns.

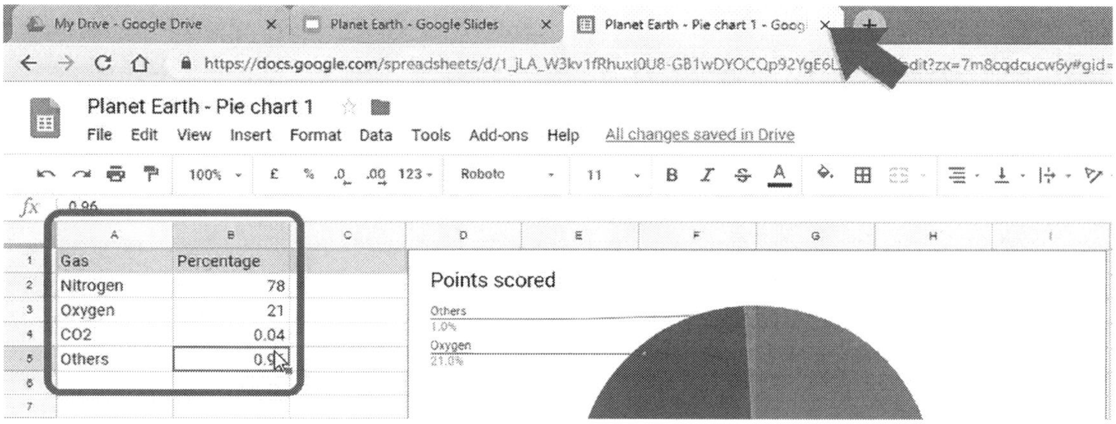

Click the x on the tab at the top of the screen to close and return to Google Slides.

Printing Presentations

To print your slides, click the 'file menu', then select 'print settings and preview.

Click '1 slide with notes' - the second icon along the toolbar at the top, then from the drop down menu, select how many slides you want on each page. For handouts to give to your audience, select 6 slides per page. This will print 6 small slides on each page, leaving them some room to take notes. Click 'print'.

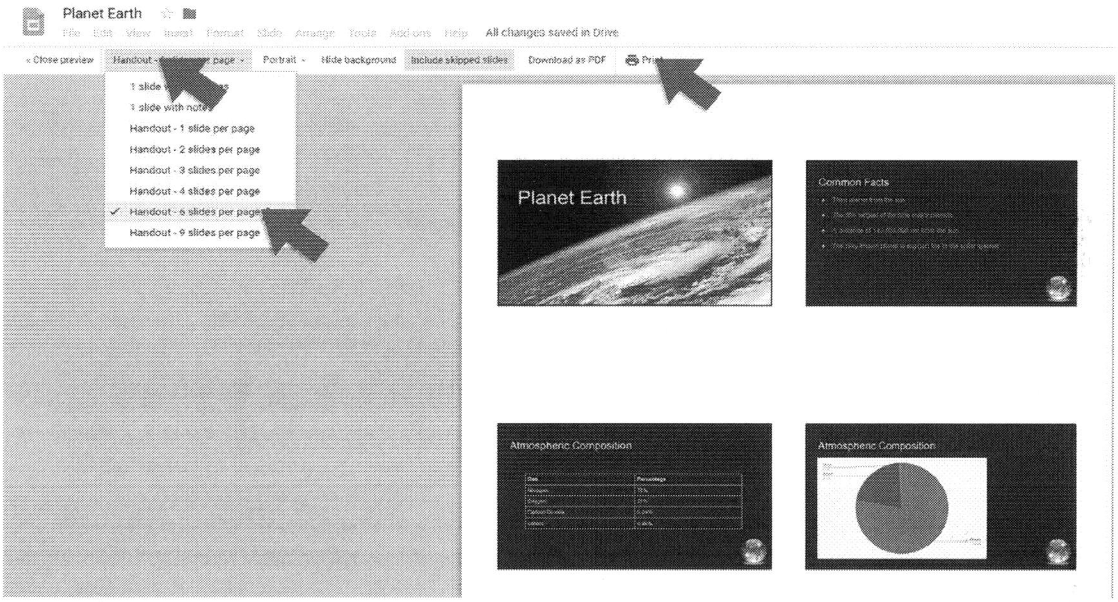

Select the printer you want to print to, and the number of copies you want.

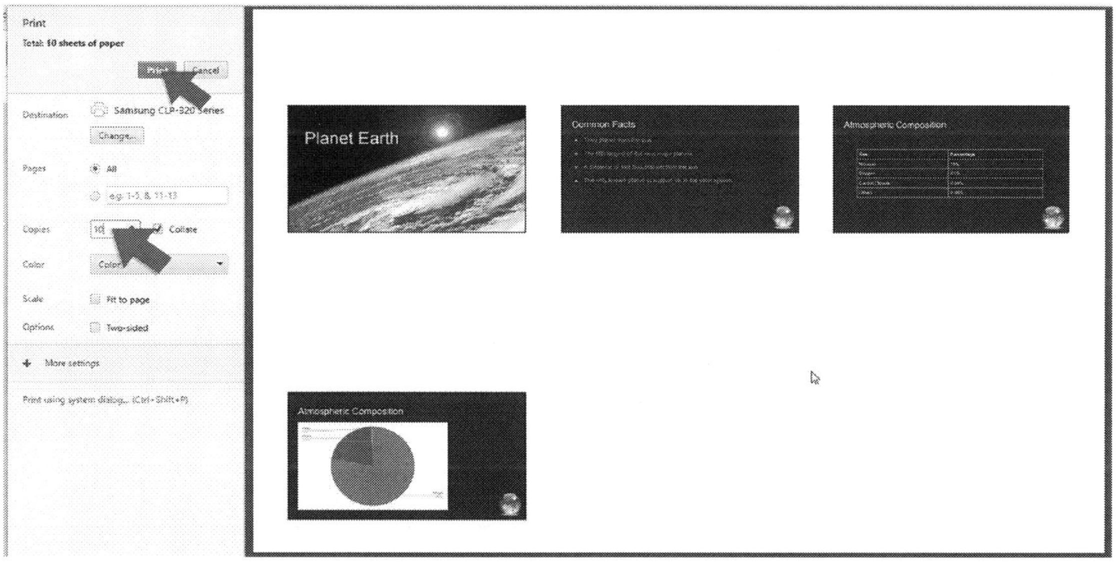

Click 'print' when you're done.

Giving your Presentation

First connect your ChromeBook to your projector or TV. When you do this your ChromeBook will extend its desktop onto the projector or TV. This enables you to have a presenter view on your ChromeBook screen with presenter notes, slide lists and other tools, while the audience see just the presentation.

Open your presentation, then click the small arrow next to 'present' on the toolbar on the right hand side.

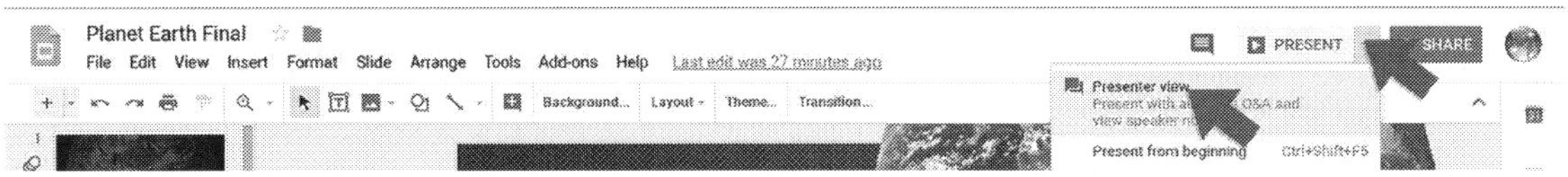

Two windows will pop up, your presenter view, and your presentation view. You may need to drag your presenter view out the way.

Now, move your presentation view onto your projector or TV screen. To do this, click and drag the window tab with your slide, off the right hand side of the ChromeBook screen until it disappears. You'll see it appear on your projector or TV screen.

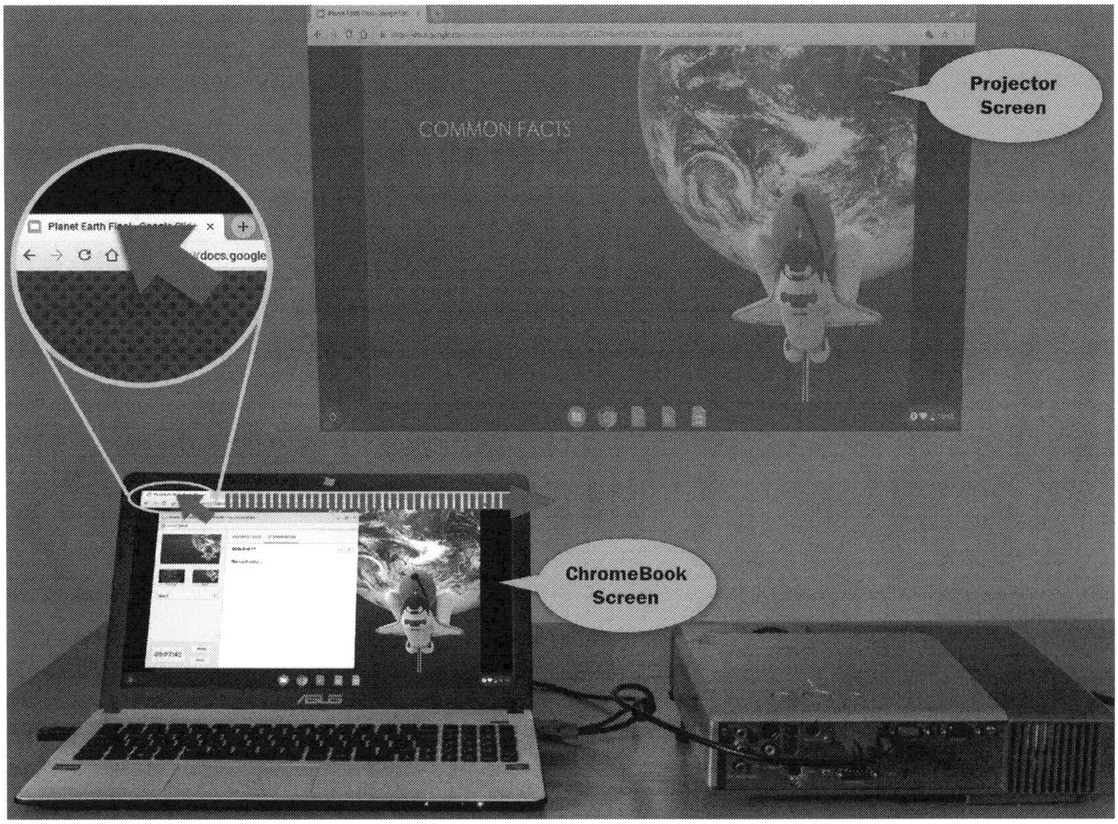

Some ChromeBooks you'll need to drag if off the left hand side of the screen - try this if it doesn't work.

On the projector or TV screen (move your mouse pointer to the right until it appears on the projector/tv screen), click the three dots icon on the top right, then click the 'full screen' icon.

Now, maximise the presenter display on your ChromeBook screen.

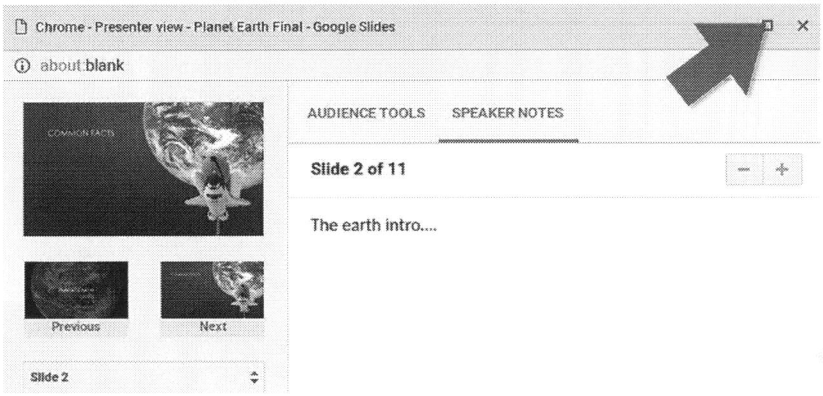

You'll end up with something like this. You'll be able to control your Google Slides presentation using the presenter view on your ChromeBook.

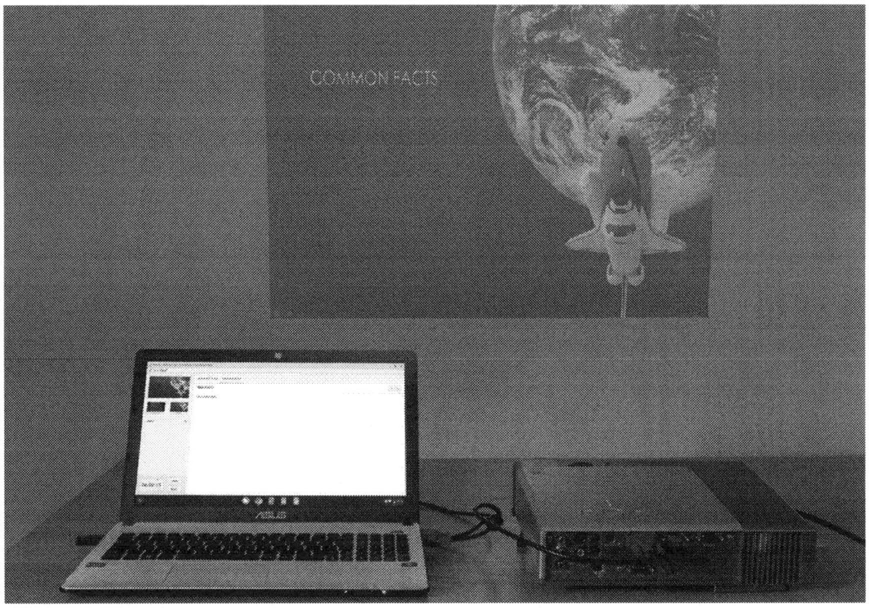

Present with ChromeCast

To be able to cast your presentation to a ChromeCast device, your ChromeBook will need to be on the same Wi-Fi network as your ChromeCast device. The ChromeCast device can be plugged into a TV or a projector.

Open your Google Slides presentation, then click the small down arrow next to the 'present' icon. From the drop down menu, select 'present on another screen'. If it's greyed out, check your wifi settings on your ChromeCast device and ChromeBook.

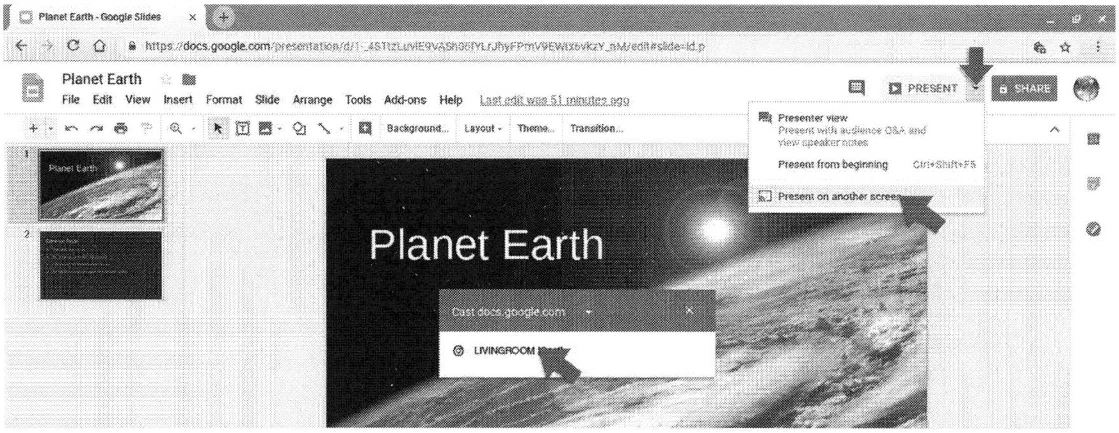

From the popup box that appears, select your ChromeCast device. Your presentation will appear on your TV or projector screen.

Now that your ChromeBook is completely wireless, you can give your presentation.

On your ChromeBook you can use a laser pointer, see your presenter notes, as well as advancing and selecting slides to show. You'll see a control bar popup when you move your mouse pointer to the bottom of the screen.

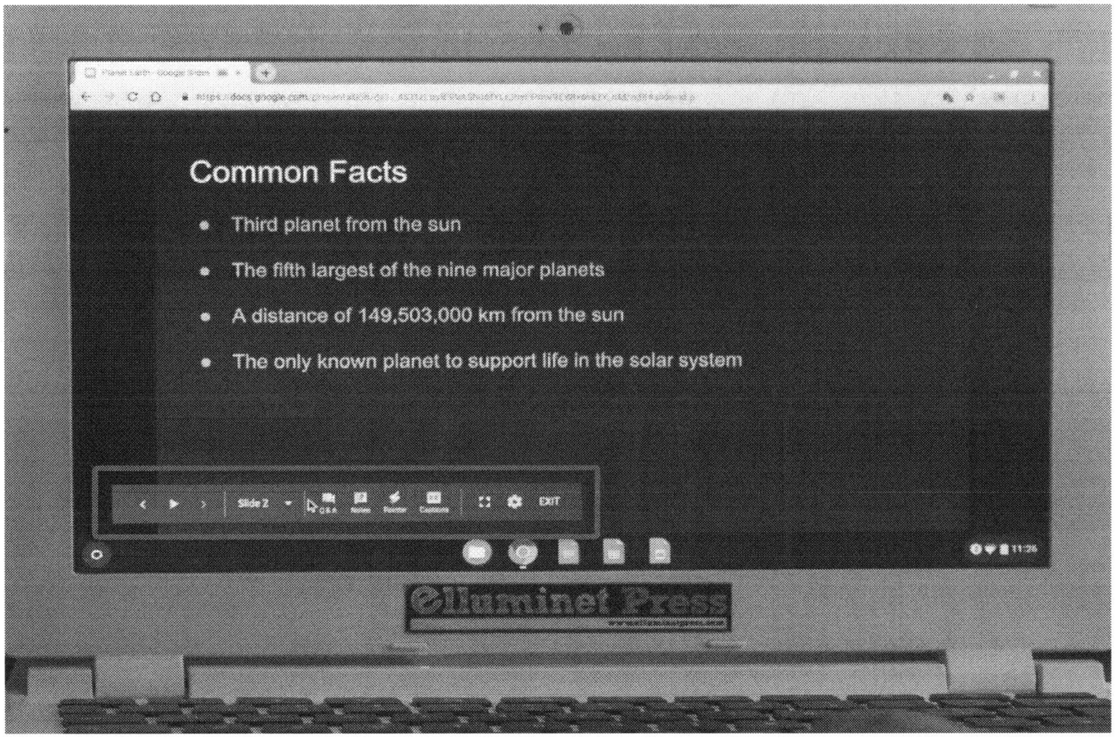

12 Maintenance

ChromeBooks require little maintenance. However, it is crucial to keep your ChromeBook up to date to make sure you have the most recent security updates.

In this section we'll take a look at the powerwash feature which allows you to wipe your ChromeBook should you want to sell it, or start afresh. Note that completely wiping your ChromeBook will erase all data stored locally on your device - so make sure all data you want to keep is saved to Google Drive.

We'll also take a look at the recovery procedure, should your ChromeBook crash or stop responding.

For this section, have a look at the video resources. Open your web browser and navigate to the following website

`videos.tips/chromebook-sys`

Diagnostics

Diagnostics is a somewhat useless app that checks your chromebook for hardware problems such as battery, CPU or memory issues.

To run the diagnostics, click on the clock on the bottom right, then select settings.

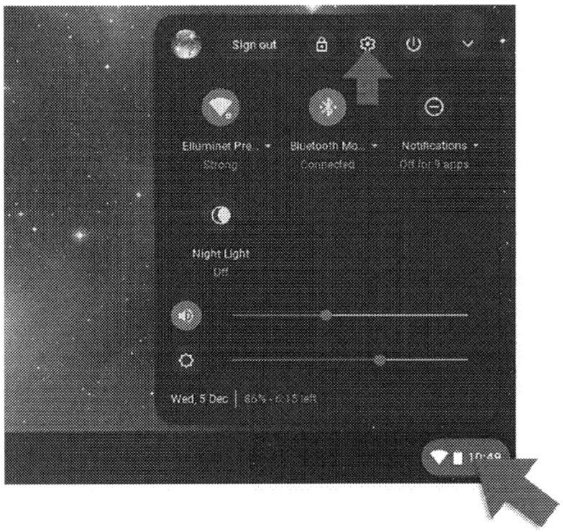

Select 'about chrome OS', then click 'diagnostics'.

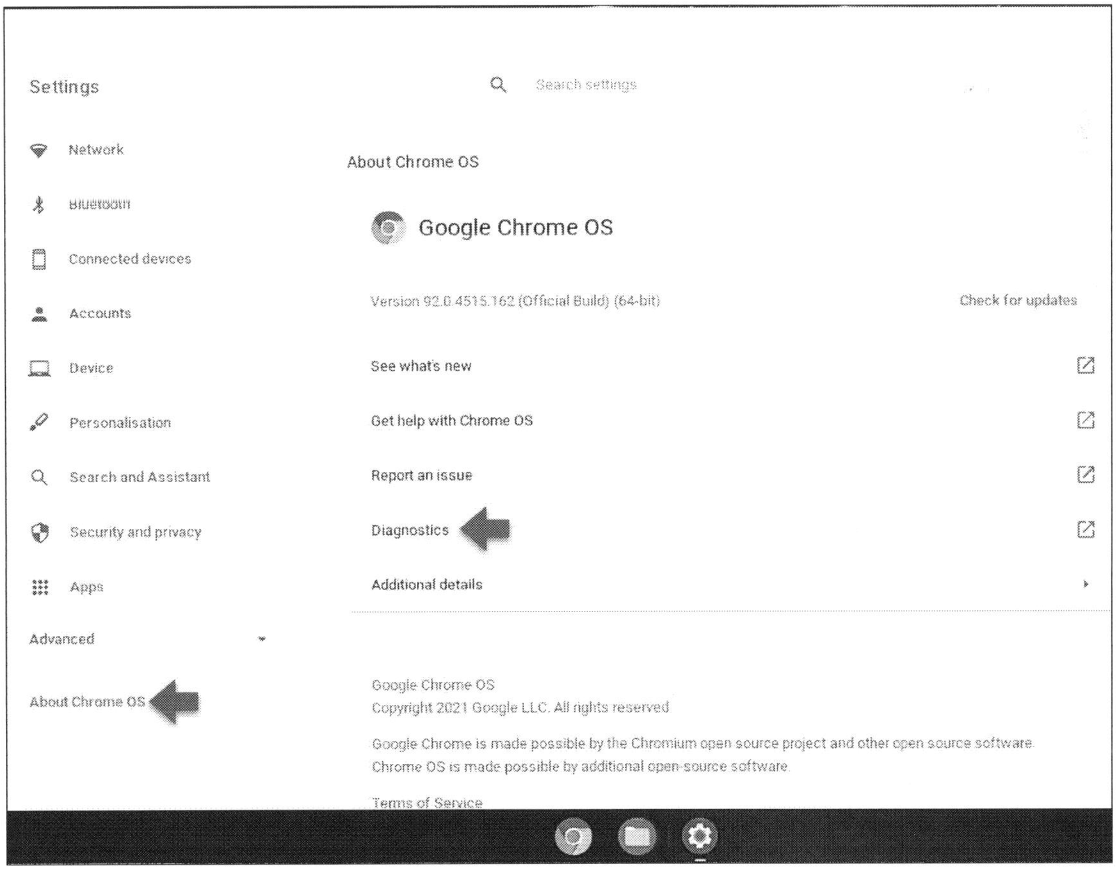

On the diagnostics screen you can run various tests.

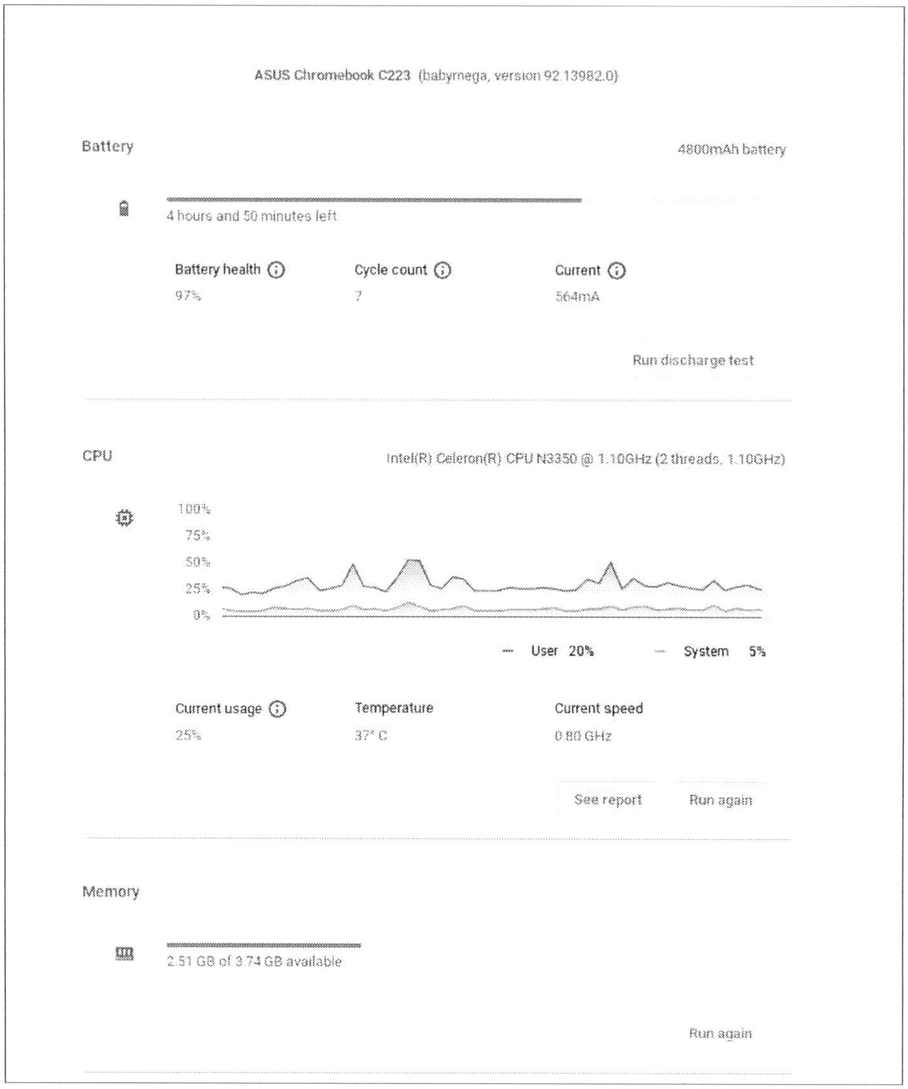

Here, you can run a battery discharge test. This test measures the rate of charge and discharge over a fixed period of time for your Chromebook. If the rate of charge and discharge is very low, there may be a problem with the battery or charging port.

You can run a CPU test. The test will consist of various different test. The stress test mimics high-load situations that are CPU-intensive. The cache test measures cache coherency. The floating point accuracy test repeatedly performs floating point operations against preset values to check for accuracy. The prime search test checks your CPU calculation of complex prime numbers.

The memory test system memory.

To run a particular test just click 'run' on the right hand side next to the test section

Updating Chrome OS

Google release updates to Chrome OS all the time. To make sure you're using the latest release, open your settings then click the hamburger icon on the top left.

From the side panel that opens up, scroll down the list and select 'about chrome OS'.

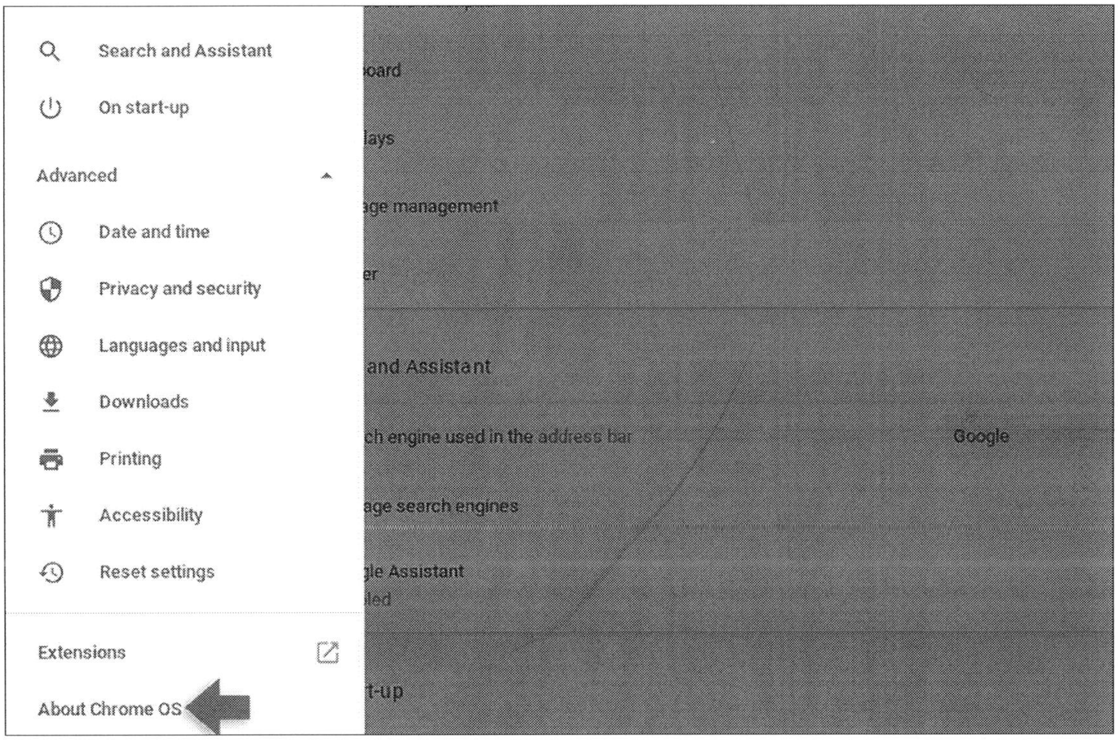

Click 'check for updates'.

Powerwash

If you want to clear your data off your Chromebook, you can use the power wash feature.

Note that this process removes all your data that is stored on your Chromebook. This will not affect anything stored on Google Drive.

To use Powerwash, open settings. Scroll down to the bottom of the 'advanced' settings until you see 'powerwash'. Click 'powerwash'.

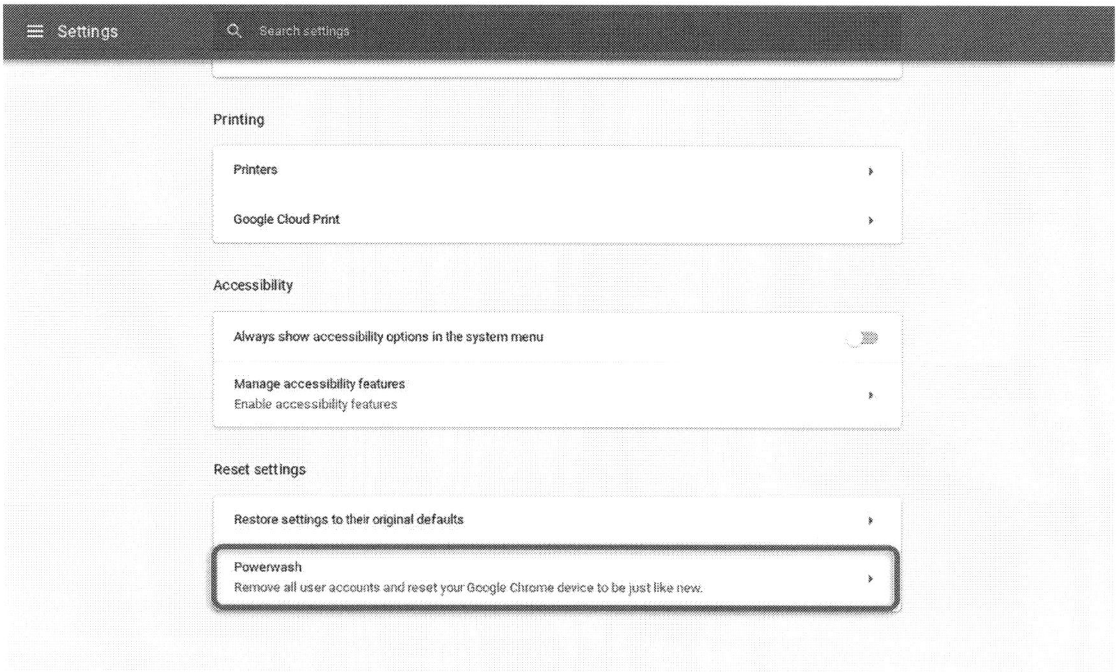

Then click 'restart'.

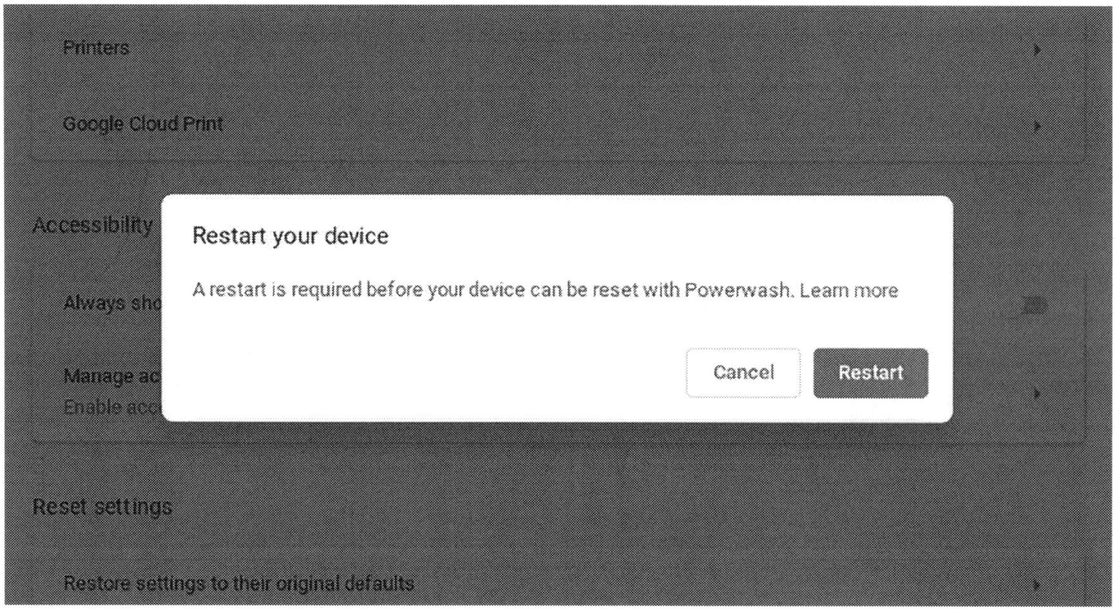

Your Chromebook will restart. Once your Chromebook starts back up, click ‘powerwash’ on the bottom right of the ‘reset’ screen.

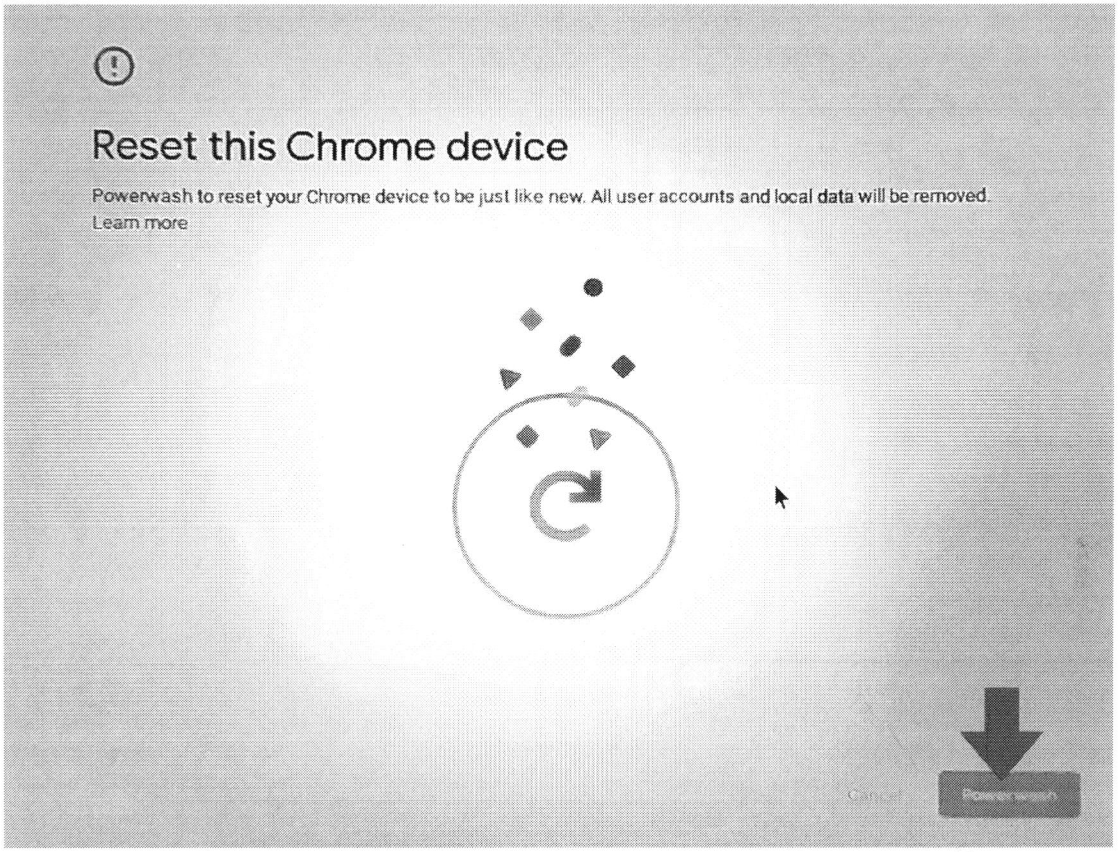

Click ‘continue’ on the confirmation dialog.

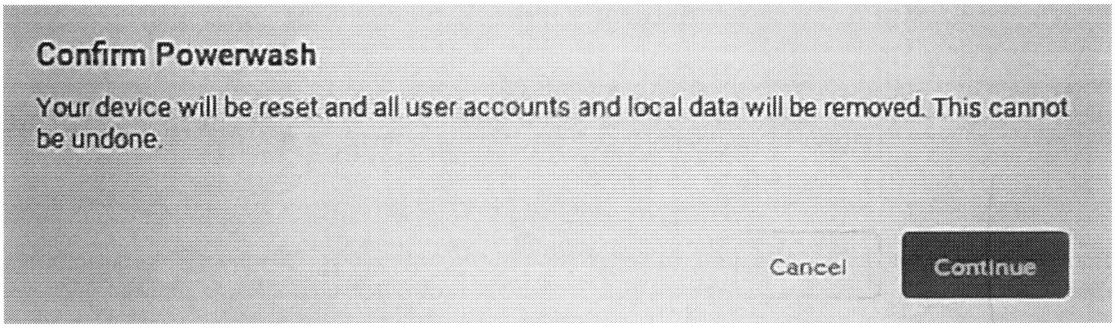

Your Chromebook will reset.

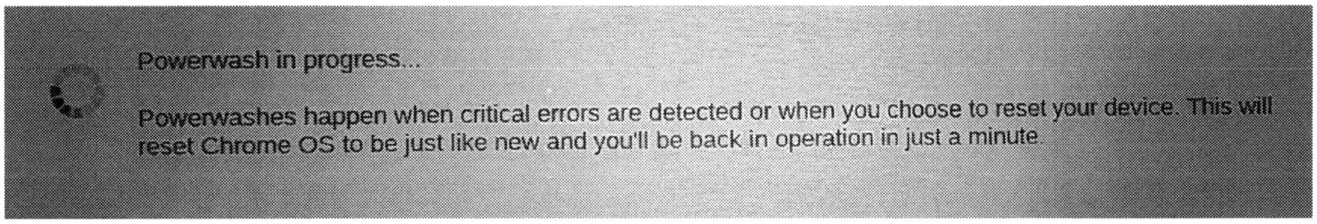

Once power wash has finished, you’ll need to go through the initial setup again. See “Initial Setup” on page 24.

ChromeBook Recovery

First, boot your ChromeBook into recovery mode. Turn it off, then hold down escape, refresh and the power button until you see the recovery screen.

Next, you'll need to download the recovery utility. To to this, go to your PC or Mac, open the Chrome Web Browser and search for:

```
chromebook recovery utility
```

Click the link from the Google search results, as shown below.

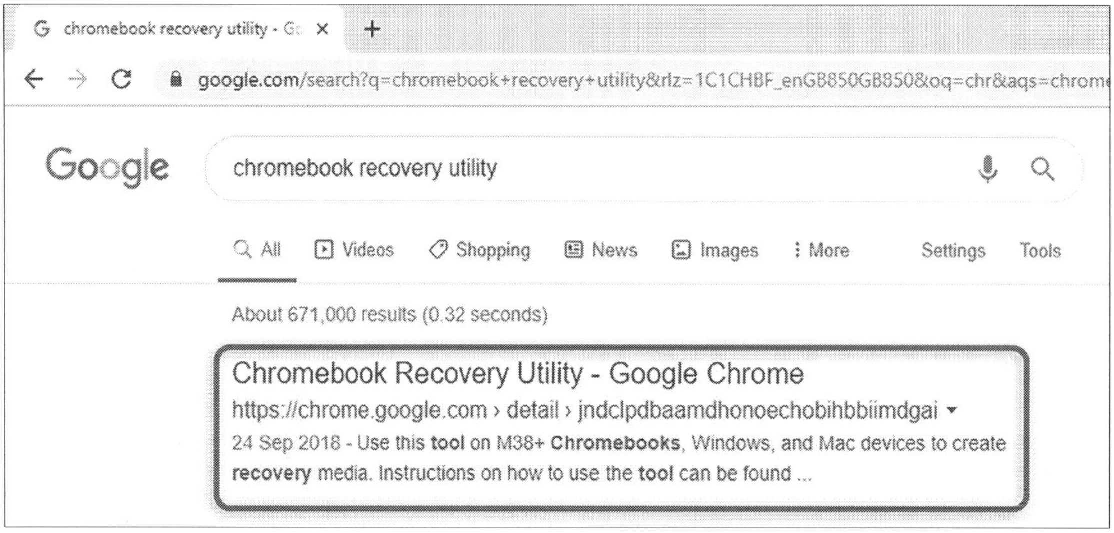

From the recovery utility page, click 'add to chrome', then click 'add app' on the pop up box.

Click 'get started'.

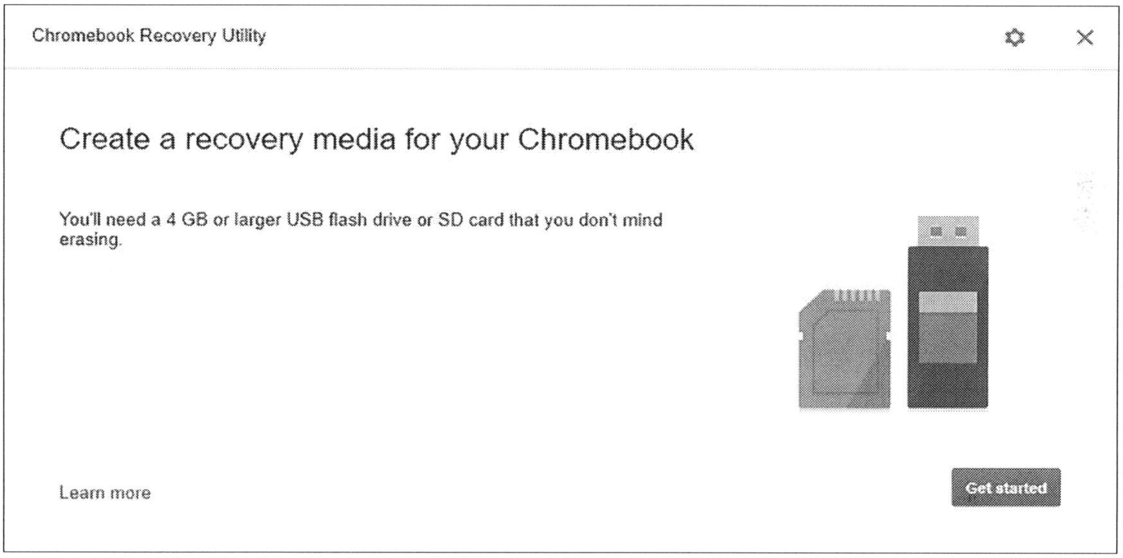

Now, select your ChromeBook model.

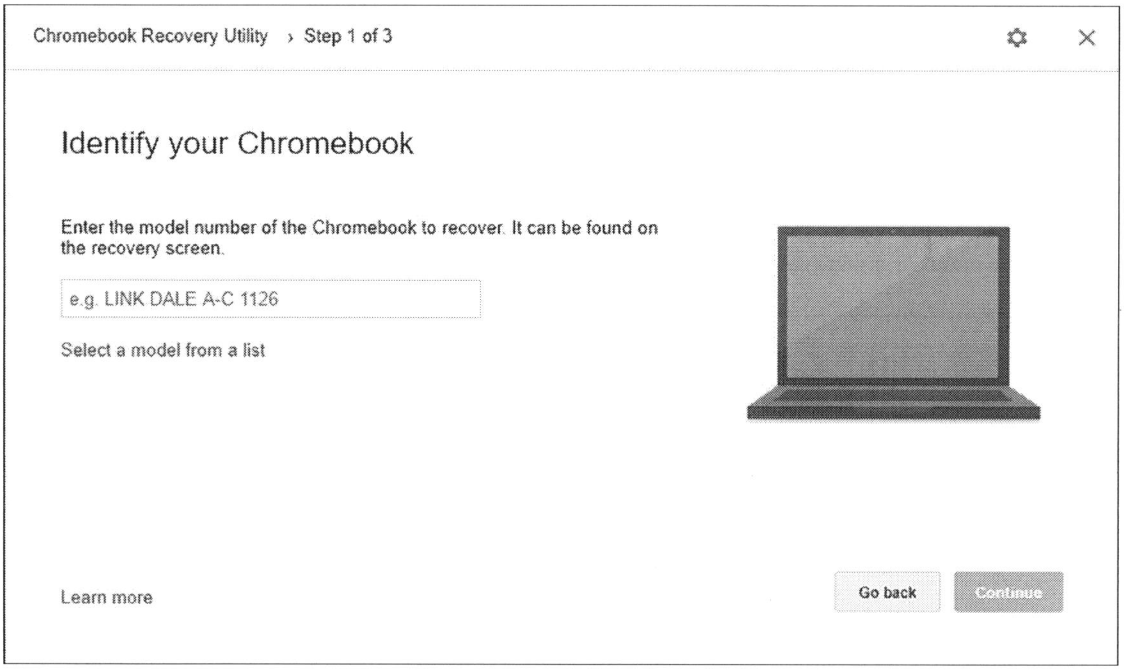

To do this, type the code on the bottom of the recovery screen shown on your ChromeBook, into the text field on the recovery utility. Click 'continue'.

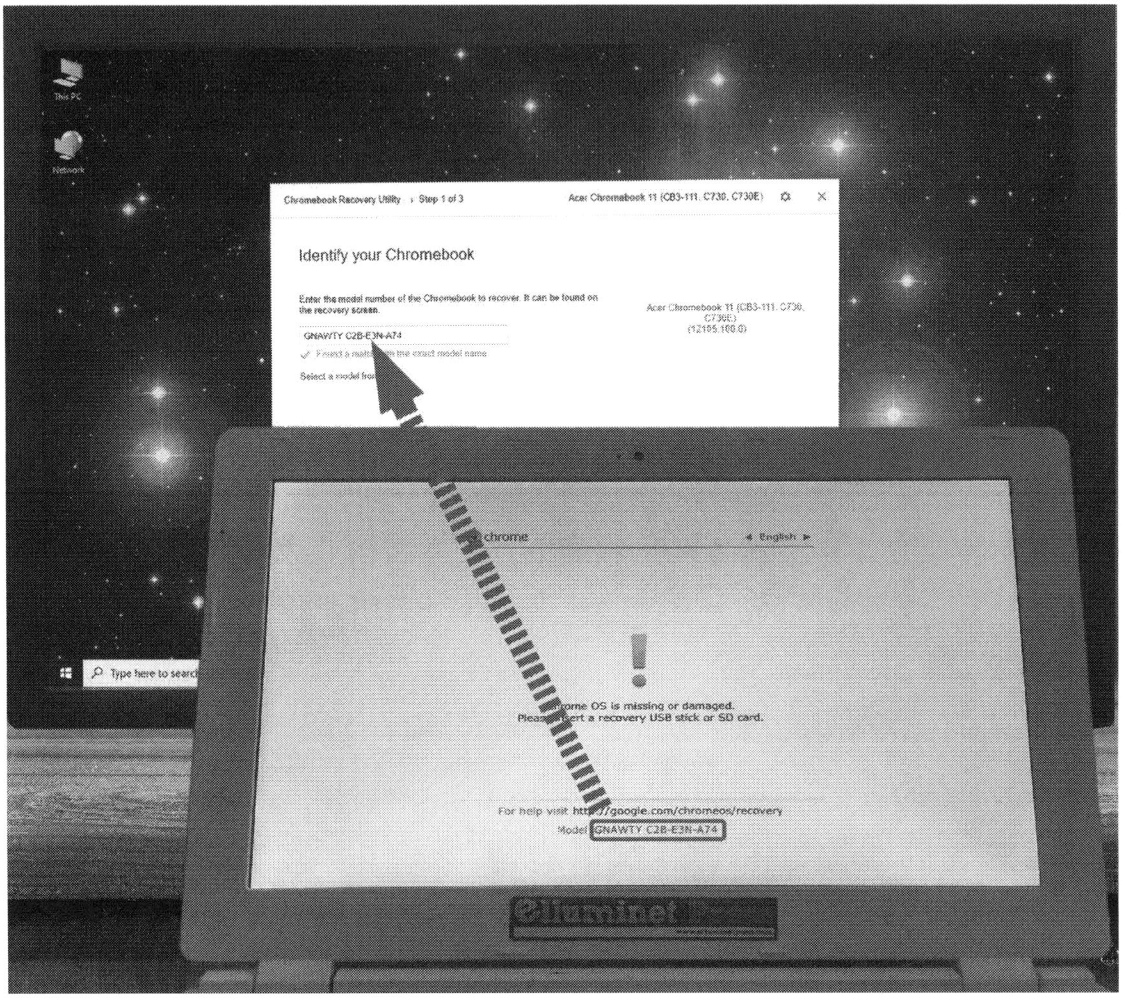

Insert a USB flash drive into a spare USB port on your PC/Mac.

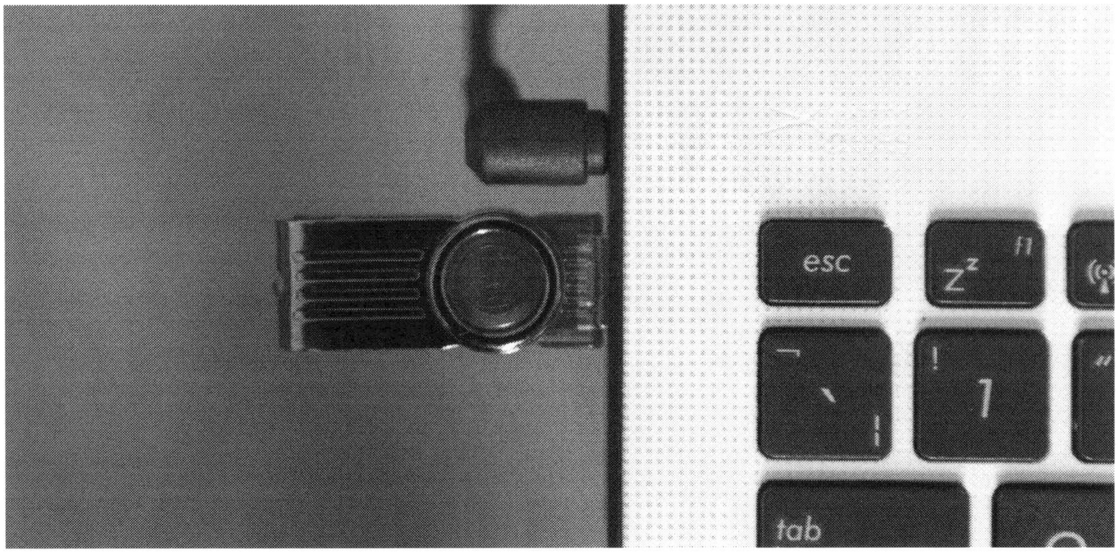

From the drop-down menu, select the USB flash drive you just inserted. *Note that the USB flash drive will be erased.*

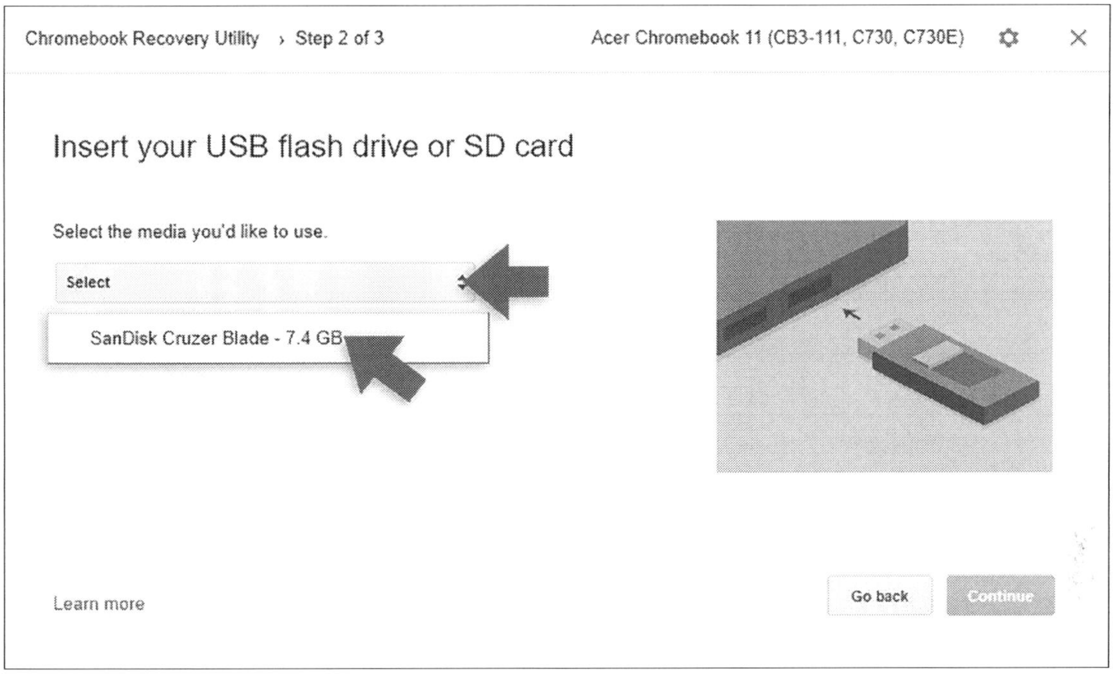

Click 'continue' on the bottom right of the window, then click 'create now' on the next screen. This process will take roughly 15 mins.

Once the process has finished. Remove the USB flash drive, from your PC/Mac, then insert it into a USB port on your ChromeBook

Now you can begin the recovery procedure on your ChromeBook.

Once your ChromeBook detects the USB flash drive, the recovery procedure will automatically begin.

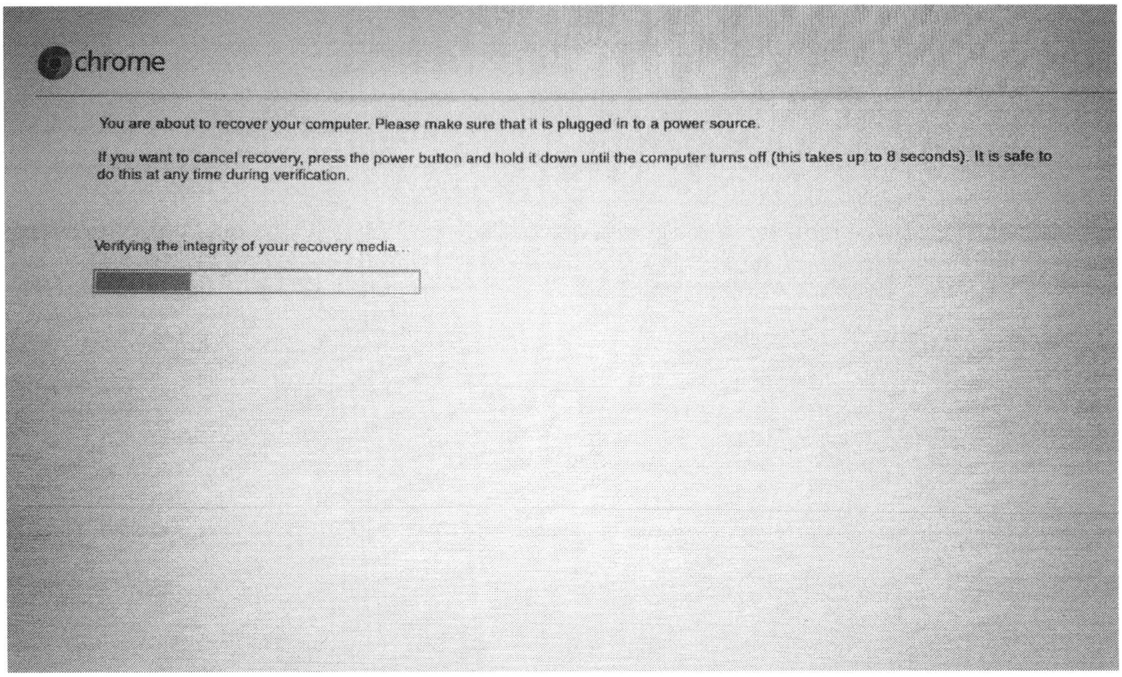

Once the process has finished, remove the USB flash drive, and the system will automatically restart.

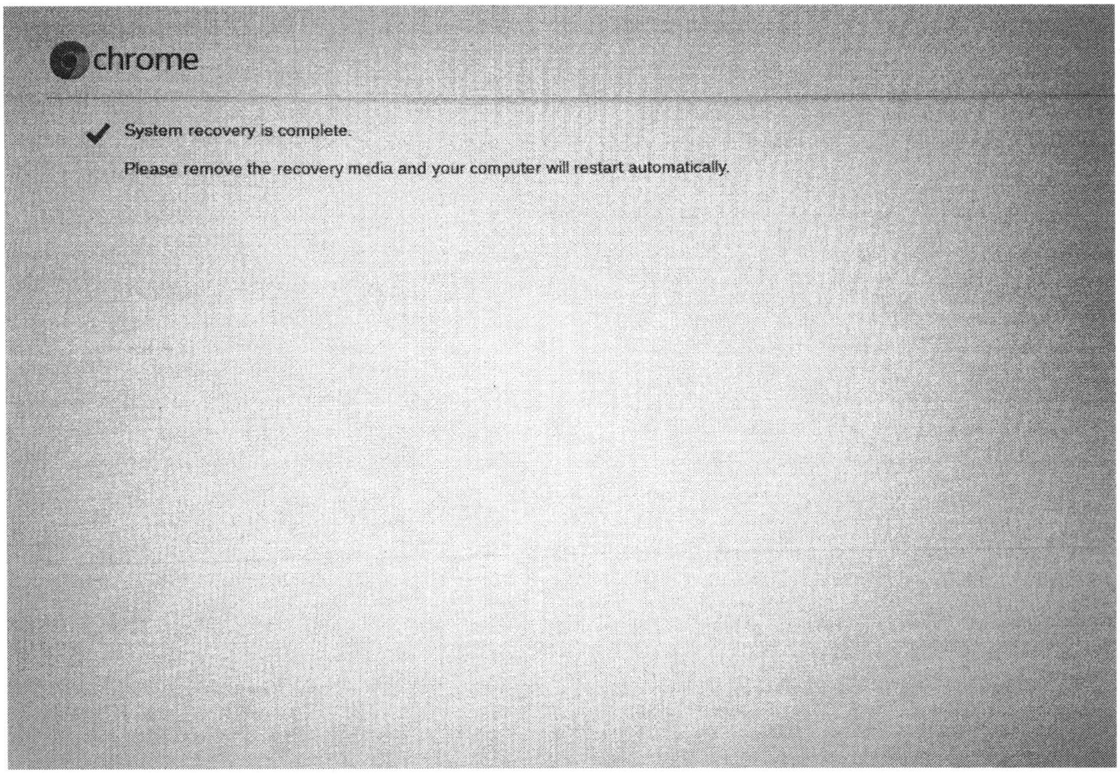

You'll need to go through the initial setup again on page 24.

App Info

The app info screen shows you information about a particular app such as how much space it occupies, permissions, data stored and cache.

To find info in a particular app, right click on the app's icon on the app launcher. Select 'app info' from the popup menu.

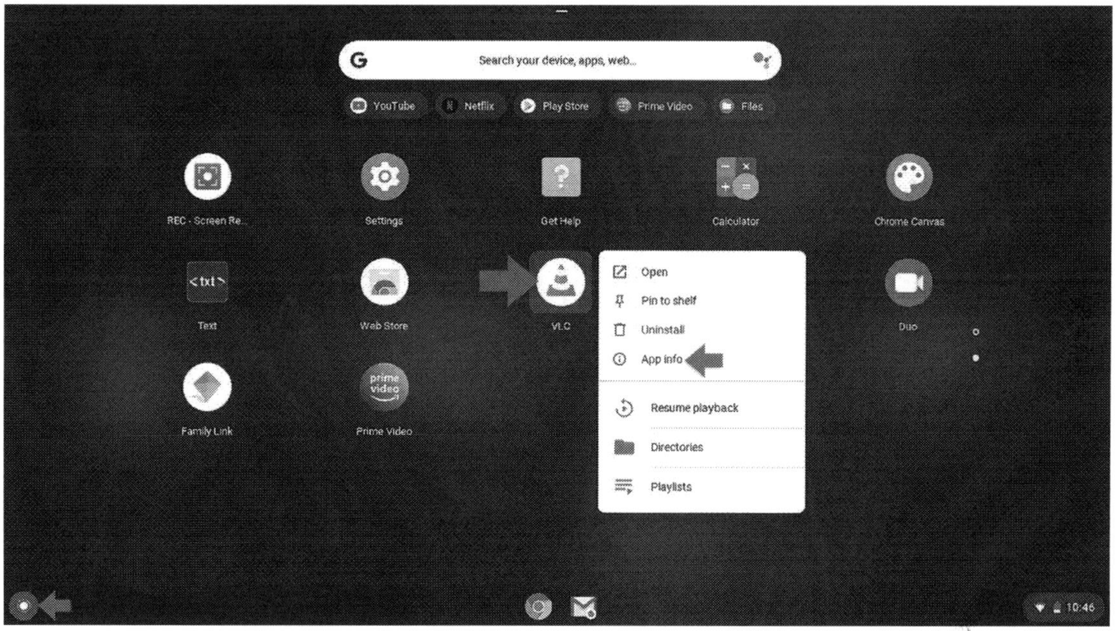

From here, you can set permissions that allow the app to access different hardware, storage or your location.

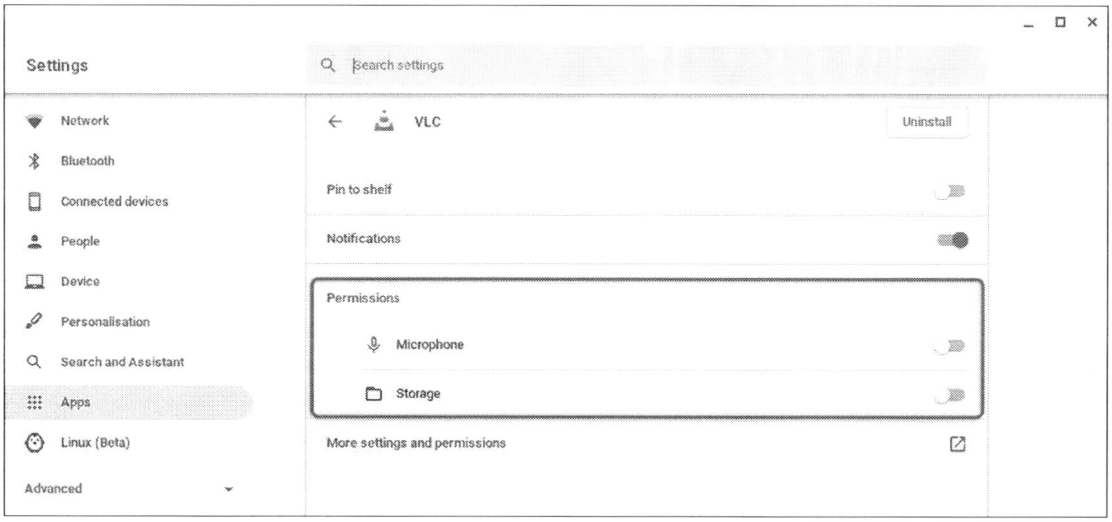

Click the switches on the right to enable or disable the permissions.

Click 'more settings and permissions'.

Here you can uninstall the app, or force it to stop if the app has crashed.

Underneath you can allow or deny notifications, set permissions for this app and see what storage the app is using. Click on these to change them.

If you want to clear the cache or data the app has stored, click 'storage'.

Click 'clear cache' to clear the app's cache. Click 'clear storage' to clear the app's data.

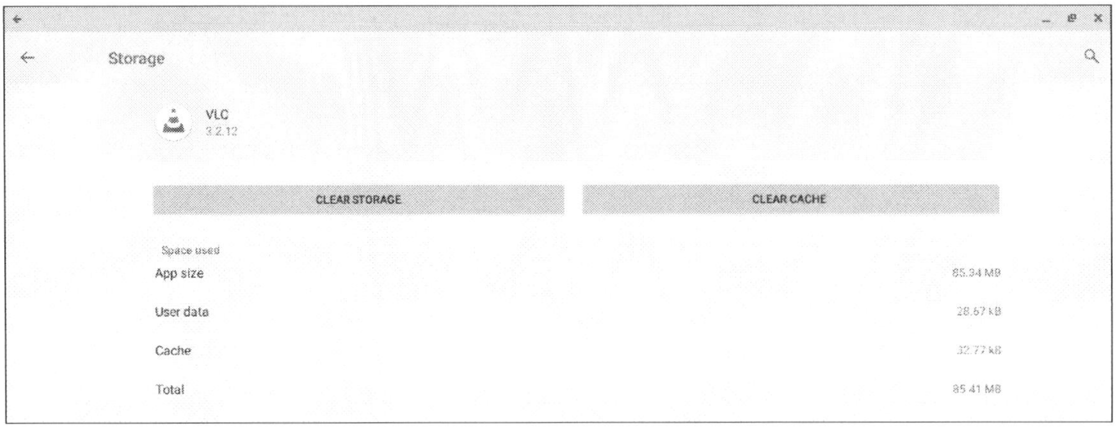

The cache is the temporary storage area used by the app used to speed up your device operates. This is particularly useful when the app downloads data from the internet, this data is stored in the cache so when the data is needed again, it does not need to be downloaded again.

Clearing app storage resets an app to its default state. This will delete any preferences and settings in the app, so use with caution.

VPNs

A VPN is short for virtual private network. A VPN masks your IP address and establishes a secure and encrypted connection between you and the VPN service. This provides greater privacy when using the internet on public Wi-Fi hotspots.

To use a public VPN on your chromebook, you'll need to download an app from a VPN provider using the Google Play Store. There are various ones to choose from and the best VPN services come at a cost. Avoid the free ones. Some good VPNs are `windscribe.com`, `nordvpn.com`, and `expressvpn.com`. *Windscribe is good, as it gives you 10GB free a month.* Open the Play Store and search for the app.

You'll find the app on your app launcher. Once you install and run the app, you'll need to sign up for an account.

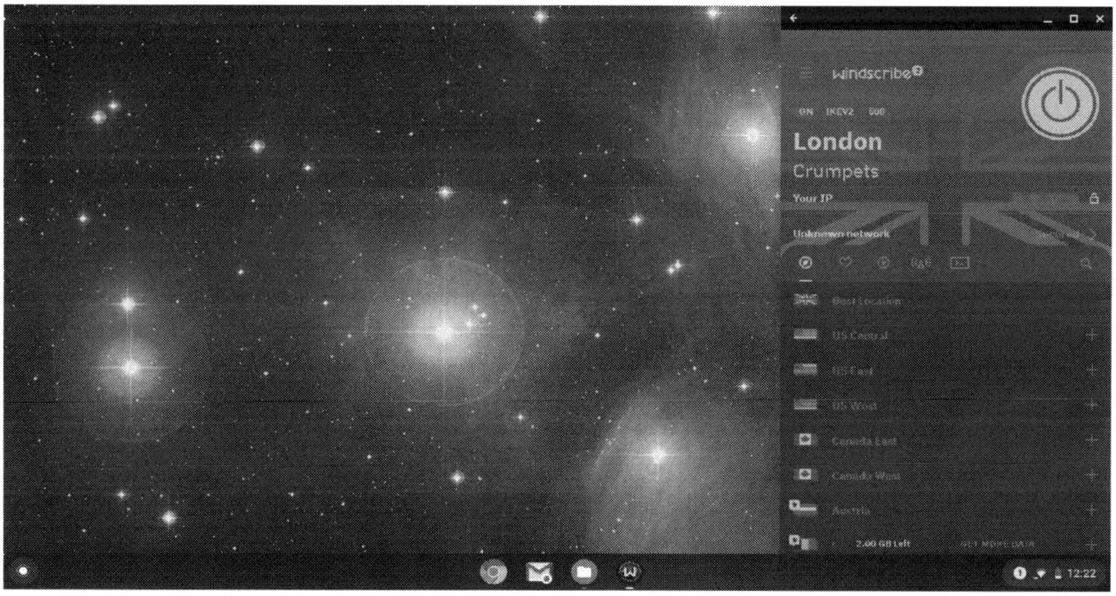

Turn on the VPN.

a Video Resources

To help you understand the procedures and concepts explored in this book, we have developed some video resources and app demos for you to use as you work through the book.

To find the resources, open your web browser and navigate to the following website

`videos.tips/chromebook`

At the beginning of each chapter, you'll find a website that contains the resources for that chapter.

Type the website url into the address bar at the top of your browser.

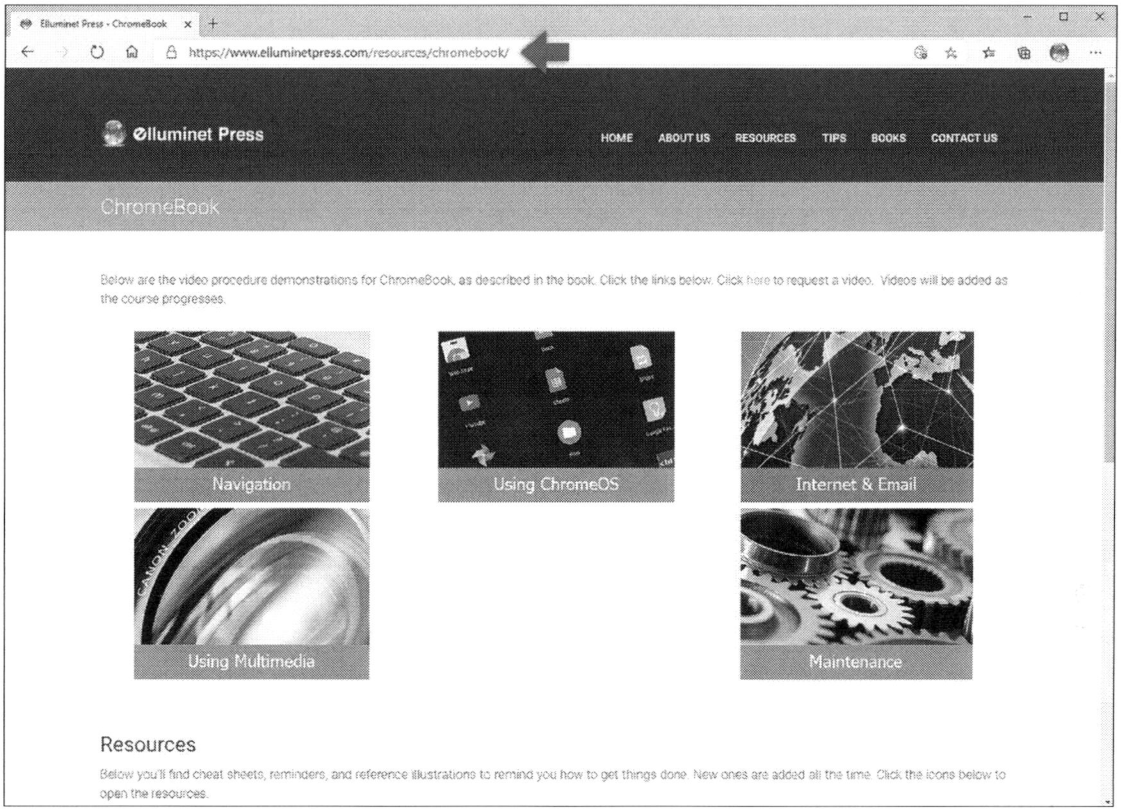

You'll see different categories. Click on these to access the videos.

When you open the link to the video resources, you'll see a thumbnail list at the bottom.

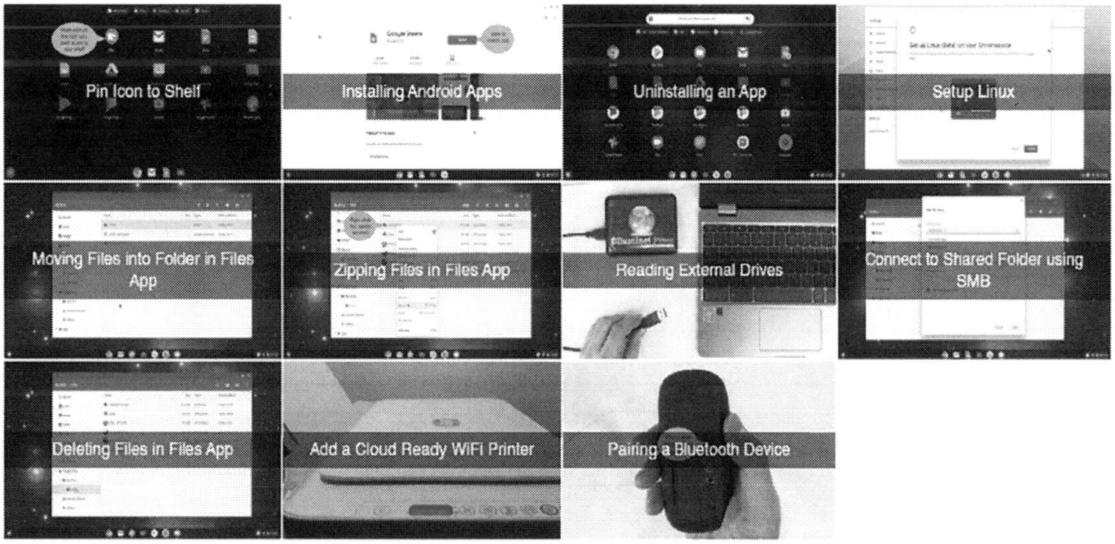

Click on the thumbnail for the particular video you want to watch. Most videos are between 40 and 90 seconds outlining the procedure, others are a bit longer.

When the video is playing, hover your mouse over the video and you'll see some controls...

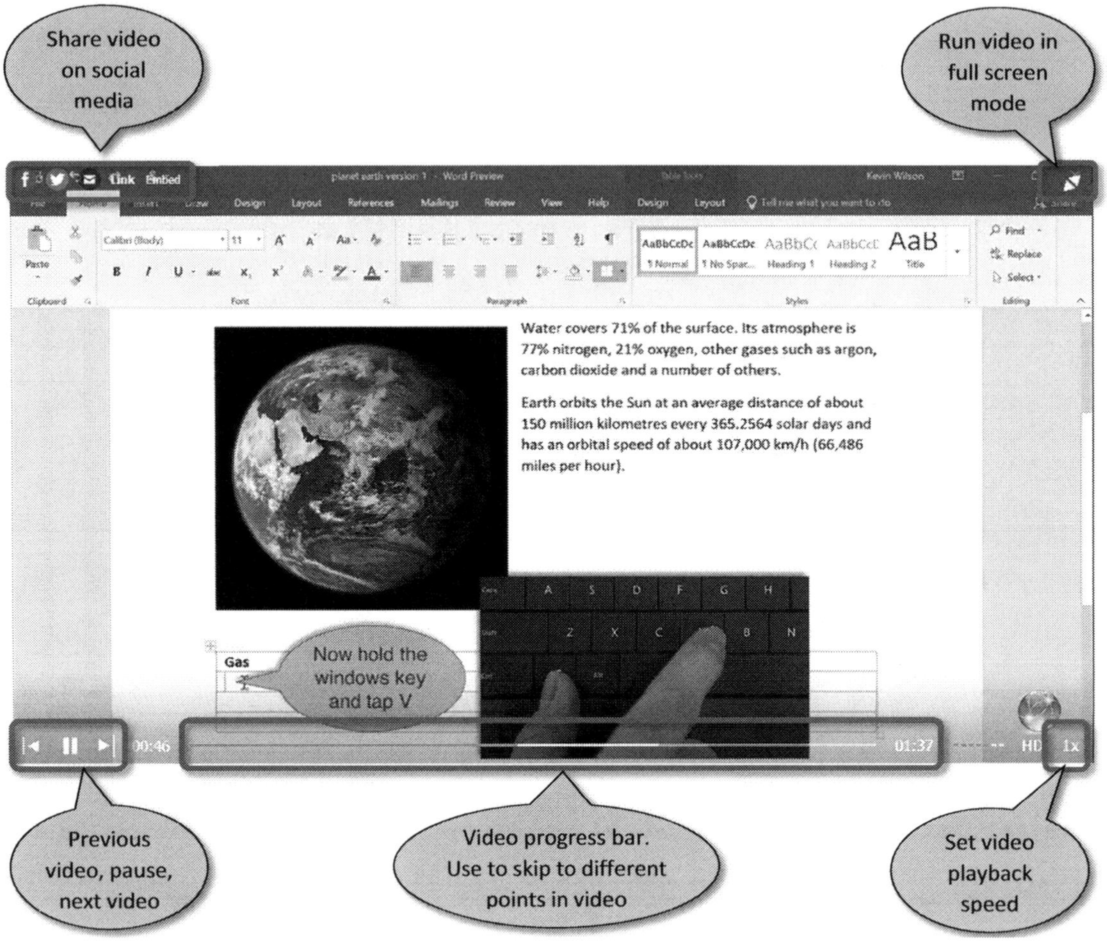

Here, you can share the video on social media, make it full screen. You can also play/pause the video, jump to a particular part of the video using the progress bar and set the playback speed.

You'll also find cheat sheets

Here, you'll find short-cuts, updates and tips.

Keyboard Shortcuts

We've included some common keyboard shortcuts for your to use while you make your way around

Shortcut	Action
Ctrl + Alt + ?	Show all shortcuts
Shift Esc	Show task manager

You'll also find a tips section. Here, we'll keep you up to date with the latest tips and tricks to help you get the most out of Chromebook.

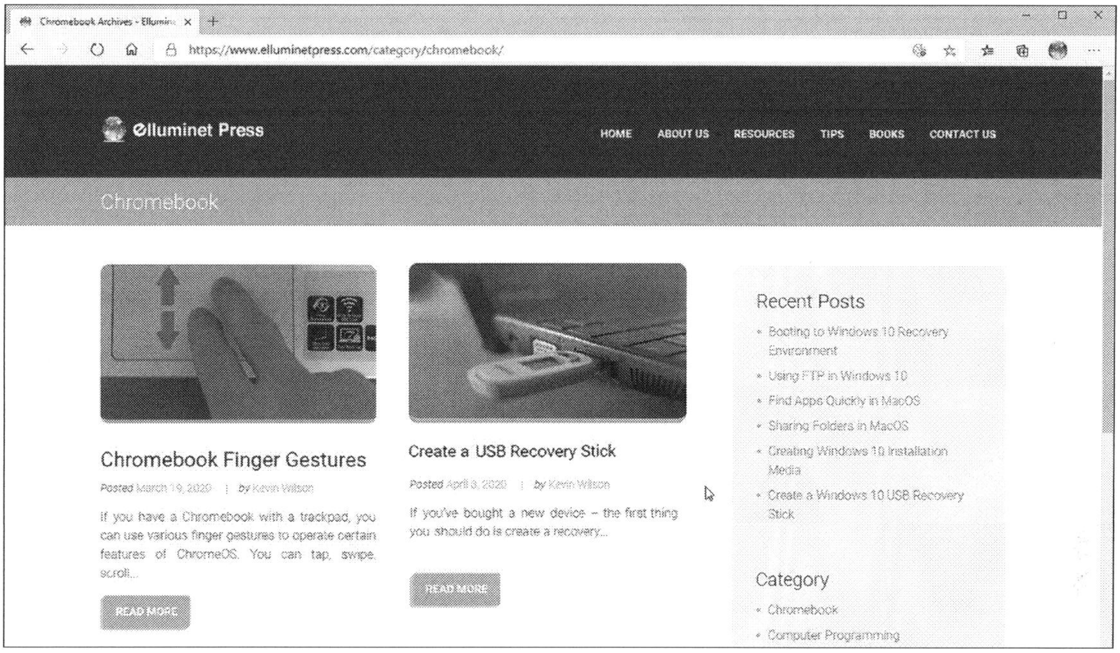

Finally, you'll find a glossary of computing terms.

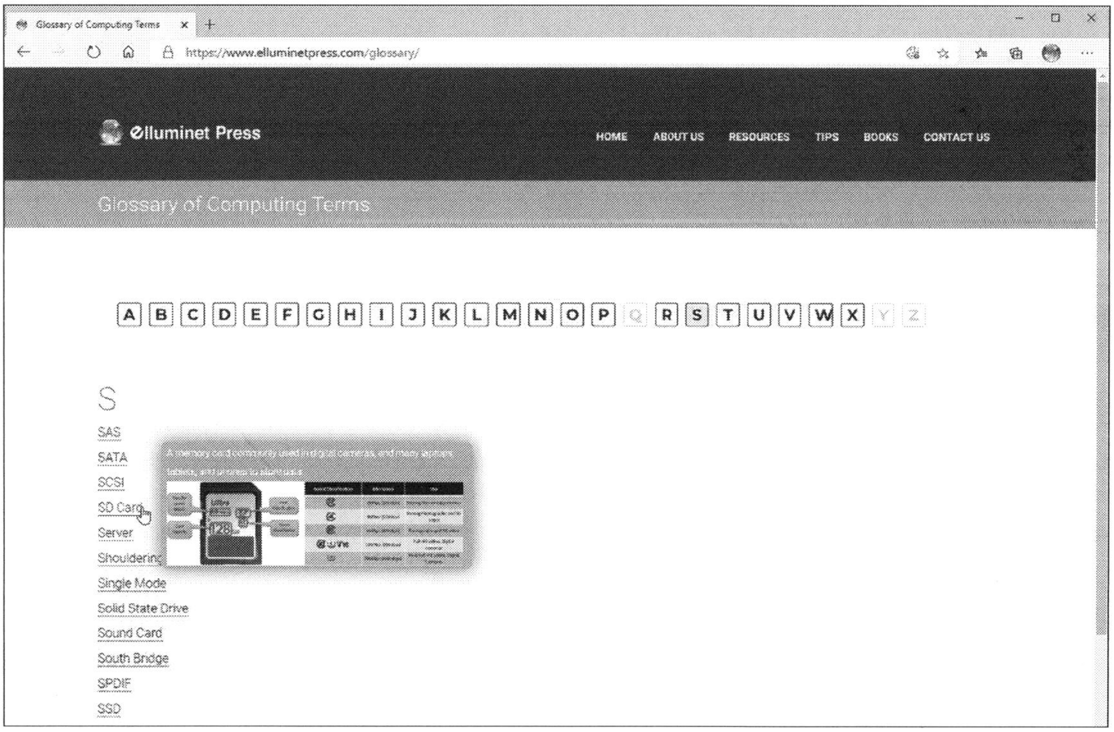

You can find the index here:

`www.elluminetpress.com/glossary`

This is integrated into the resources section.

Index

A

E

F

G

H

P

R

S

T

U

Manufactured by Amazon.ca
Bolton, ON

22105491R00197